VOYAGES AND TRAVELS
TO
INDIA, CEYLON
THE RED SEA
ABYSSINIA AND EGYPT

IN THE YEAR

1802-1806

VOYAGES AND TRAVELS
TO
INDIA, CEYLON
THE RED SEA
ABYSSINIA AND EGYPT

IN THE YEARS
1802-1806

GEORGE VISCOUNT VALENTIA

IN FOUR VOLUMES
VOL. II

INDIA- RED SEA-ABYSSINIA

ISBN : 978-93-5324-451-4 (Set)

ISBN : 978-93-5324-453-8 (HB)

First Published, London,1811

Published, 2020

Published by

Facsimile Publisher
12 Pragati Market
Ashok Vihar, Ph-2
Delhi-110052
E-mail: books@facsimilepublisher.com

Printed at: G. Print Process, Delhi.

Voyages and Travels to India, Ceylon The Red Sea Abyssinia and EGYPT

Author: George Viscount Valentia

VOYAGES AND TRAVELS

TO

INDIA, CEYLON, THE RED SEA, ABYSSINIA, AND EGYPT,

IN THE YEARS

1802, 1803, 1804, 1805, AND 1806.

BY

GEORGE, VISCOUNT VALENTIA.

IN FOUR VOLUMES.

VOL. II.

INDIA.—RED SEA.—ABYSSINIA.

LONDON:

PRINTED FOR F., C., AND J. RIVINGTON,
ST. PAUL'S CHURCH YARD.

1811.

CONTENTS.

VOL. II.

CHAPTER I.

CHAPTER II.

CHAPTER III.

CHAPTER IV.

CHAPTER V.

CHAPTER VI.

CHAPTER VII.

CHAPTER VIII.

CHAPTER IX.

APPENDIX.

CHAPTER I.

Motives for voyage to the Red Sea.—Departure from Mangalore.—Cape Guardafui.—Cape Aden.—Passage through the Straits of Bab-el-mandeb.—Arrival at Mocha.—Reception there.—Departure for the African Coast.—Ras Beiloul.—Island of Rackmah.—Saiel Abaiel.—Amphila.—Howakel.—Miséras.—Island of Valentia.—Arrival at the Island of Dhalac.—Visit to the Dola.—Mr. Salt's Journey to Dhalac-el-kibeer.—Departure for Massowah.—Arrival there.

IT had always appeared to me an extraordinary circumstance, that if the western coast of the Red Sea were really as dangerous as the moderns have uniformly represented it, the ancients should invariably have navigated it in preference to the eastern coast; nor could any suspicions that a western passage existed be removed by the silence of the British officers, after a long continuance of our fleet in that sea. The evils which they had experienced from the want of water, fresh provisions, and fuel, pointed out indeed most strongly the importance of ascertaining, whether these articles were not attainable at Massowah, Dhalac, or the adjacent islands, where in former times, the Egyptian and Roman merchants were induced to fix their residence for the purpose of carrying on the trade with Abyssinia, and the interior of Africa. At Dhalac Mr.

Bruce has asserted, that three hundred and sixty tanks, which had been erected by the munificence of the Ptolemies, were still in a state of preservation to afford, with care, a supply of water, more than sufficient for any fleet which the British could ever have occasion to send into that sea.

The commercial advantages which might attend the opening of a communication with Abyssinia, appeared also worthy of attention; and a more favourable time for making the attempt could never be expected, than immediately after the British naval power had been so fully displayed on the shores of Arabia and Egypt, and when the trade with the interior of Africa had been interrupted in its usual channel through the latter country, first by the conquest of the French, and afterwards by the civil war between the Porte and the Beys, which had caused a perfect separation between the upper and lower provinces.

I confess also that I felt it as a national reflection, that a coast which had afforded a profitable and extensive trade in gold, ivory, and pearls, to the sovereigns of Egypt, should be a perfect blank in our charts, and that while new islands, and even continents were discovered by the abilities of our seamen, we should have become so ignorant of the eastern shore of Africa, as to be unable to ascertain many of the harbours and islands described by an ancient navigator in the Periplus of the Erythrean Sea.

During my stay at Calcutta I had the honour of frequently conversing with the Marquis Wellesley on the subject of the Red Sea, and of stating to him my ideas and feelings; in which I had the happiness of finding that he fully concurred. At length I proposed to his Excellency, that he should order one of the Bombay cruizers to be prepared for a voyage to the Red Sea; and I offered my gratuitous services to endeavour to remove our disgraceful ignorance, by embarking in her, for the purpose of investigating the eastern shore of Africa, and making the necessary inquiries into the present state of Abyssinia, and the neighbouring countries. His Excellency approved of the plan, and it was determined in order to obviate any difficulties which might arise, from the commanding officer differing with me in opinion, with respect to the eligibility of going to particular places, that he should be placed under my orders. The necessary instructions were immediately transmitted to Bombay, and I hastened my departure for Columbo, as it was desirable to reach the Red Sea as early in the year as possible.

When I arrived at Tanjore I received dispatches from Bombay, acquainting me that the Antelope cruizer would be at Mangalore ready to receive me, and convey me to the Red Sea in the beginning of February; at the same time I had letters from Mr. Lumsden, Chief Secretary at Calcutta, inclosing, under a flying seal, the proper orders to Captain Keys, to consider himself as under my command. At Madras I heard that he was actually arrived; yet from my servant's indisposition there, and the previous delay at Columbo, I was unable to reach Mangalore before the 8th of March. This was particularly unfortunate, as it precluded the possibility of my reaching Suez, previously to the change of the monsoon in the Arabian Gulf. It was however some consolation to know that the very heavy gales in that quarter rarely set in before June, by which time I hoped to be safe on land, and that the sailing in unknown seas was probably safer when beating up, than when going briskly before the wind. As far as Mocha, we were certain of having the N. E. monsoon, though probably, on account of the lateness of the season, it would be only light, and we should be much baffled with calms, and for the remainder of the voyage we knew we could take shelter in an harbour, and wait for finer weather, should a gale overtake us. Admiral Rainier, whom I had the good fortune to find at Mangalore, visited me the morning after my arrival, with several of his officers, some of whom had been in the Red Sea; from them I had the pleasure of learning many circumstances, which tended to diminish alarms that might have been excited by the accounts of former travellers; and they confirmed me in my determination of surveying the Abyssinian shore, by the admission of the fact, that, during the whole time our fleets were in the Red Sea, not one vessel had quitted the Arabian coast.

With Captain Keys of the Antelope, I was much pleased, and the concern he expressed at the smallness of his vessel, and the consequent difficulty of accommodating me to his wish, induced me to suppose that I should find him inclined to do every thing in his power to make my voyage comfortable. I determined to go on board the Antelope immediately: I found her to be a brig, quite as large as I expected, about one hundred and fifty tons, mounting twelve eighteen pound carronades, and having on board forty-one Europeans, including officers, sixteen marines, and thirty lascars and servants. For these they had on board six month's rice and salt meat, with forty days water; of course there could be little room left for my baggage. The cabin was of a tolerable size: rather more than one third had been partitioned off for me; the remainder served as a dining-room, in which the Captain and Mr. Salt were obliged to swing their cots at night. For myself, I was perfectly satisfied, but determined to lessen my baggage by sending part of my linen to England from Bombay. Captain Keys accompanied me on board the flag-ship to visit the Admiral, who paid me the honour of a salute: I undertook to convey dispatches for him to England.

On returning to Mr. Ravenshaw's, I instantly began my preparations for departure: these were soon completed, as well as circumstances would permit; and Mr. Salt having arrived we got on board the Antelope by eleven o'clock at night on the 13th of March. By twelve every thing was embarked, and we weighed anchor for the Red Sea, bidding a farewell to India, after a residence of fifteen months. According to the power with which I was invested, I directed the Captain to proceed to Aden.

Our little vessel sailed ill, which was probably owing to the bad condition of her bottom, which was perfectly covered with barnacles, being also deep in the water: she rolled and pitched much, but had one good quality—she obeyed her helm, and wore with facility. The wind was directly against us. The shore that we passed was a bold one; the mountains which I beheld in crossing the table-land, were completely visible. We passed several islands of a rocky nature, and among others one strongly fortified by Tippoo, but for what purpose it would be difficult to conjecture as it affords no protection to shipping.

Till the 26th we had the wind inclining to the west, and consequently made little way. The calms had been frequent, yet the heat had never been unpleasant, and the sea had been as smooth as glass. We were on that day in long. 68° 40′ 15″ and had at length got hold of the N. E. monsoon.

Our latitude was much the same as when we sailed, viz. 12° 1′ 37″. When it is so late in the season, it would be better to sail from Bombay, as the monsoon at that time still keeps close to the shore. As the vessel was lightened by consumption of stock, she sailed better. The delay was the less disagreeable, as it gave me time to prepare charts of the Red Sea from the logs we had procured.

The men caught a dolphin,* a most beautiful fish, generally from two to three feet long. When in the water it appears of a rich dark blue, or green, or golden yellow colour, according to the point of view in which it is beheld. On being caught, it changes rapidly. The body at first is chiefly orange, spotted with the brightest blue: the fins are green, and then blue. The dorsal fin, when the fish is dying, is of a dark green throughout. The ventral fins lie close to the body, where there is a hollow that partly receives them: these are of a bright gold-coloured orange on the outside; on the inside, when alive, bright blue; when nearly dead, a dark green. The anal fin, during life, is blue and light gold colour; at death, lighter, and silvery: the caudal the same. The pupil of the eye dark: the iris yellowish gold colour. It has three rows of small teeth, separated by a grove in the centre. When dying, the blue tint, for a few seconds, sometimes covers the whole fish, and then settles in the blue spots only. Linnæus's description, as far as it goes, is accurate. It follows the ship in company. In its belly was found the flying fish. The Coryphæna hippuris is also called a dolphin by the sailors.

The dolphins on the 31st were about the ship in shoals. The men killed eight. We had one

* Coryphæna equisetalis.

for dinner, and it was as good as an albicore. On the 30th we saw many sharks, one of which, seven feet long, the men caught. The following day the dolphins were still more numerous, and every mess had one.

The wind for the last five days had been extremely light, but we had been favoured by a current to the S. W. which enabled us to make a degree a day. The sea perfectly smooth. On the 1st of April the men killed nine dolphins. Long. 61° 59′, lat. 11° 22′.

The current deserted us on the 2nd, and the breezes became extremely light. We had plenty of dolphins; and several very singular species of sea-blubber floated by. One was a large scarlet mass, about seven feet long and two or three wide, a part of which was got on board; it consisted of a great number of distinct living substances, adhering to each other. Each was about four inches diameter, tubular, and closed at the ends. A circular thread of scarlet spots was twined in circles amidst the gelatinous substance. Another was about two inches long by one in diameter; partly hollow. It had a dark yellow spot and one red, close to each other, at the lower extremity. It was covered with fine prickles externally, which, produced no smart on being touched.

As we approached the land, the breezes became more light; the fish, less afraid of the ship's foul bottom than they would have been of a clean one, were in great abundance. With the bait of a cockroach, my servant caught a small fish of the genus Diodon, but not of the species described by Linnæus, though I think it is the one mentioned in Chambers's Dictionary under the name of Guamajacu atinga, and for which he quotes Piso's Nat. Hist. lib. V. cap. 16. The description perfectly corresponds, but the drawing given has no resemblance. Mr. Salt drew it and I stuffed its skin, which was thick and glutinous. It is covered with prickles, which it has the power of expanding when it blows out its body; the cavity of which is filled with a very large air-bladder, and a liver disproportioned to its size. Its length is about four inches: as we caught several, I conclude this to be its full growth. No injury follows the puncture of one of its prickles, though a juice exudes from the base, of a bright yellow colour, that permanently stains paper and other substances. It puts out two small tentacula from its mouth as it swims, and lives a considerable time out of water. Towards evening the wind began to come round to the southward.

On the 12th at day-light the African coast was in view, bearing N. W. distant about eleven leagues. As we approached it most rapidly, by twelve we were only about three miles from Cape Guardafui. The Cape itself is not very high, but the land behind it is extremely lofty. It consists of rocky beds, one over the other, with gullies apparently formed by the rain. Not a vestige of vegetation was seen. We made it in 51° 10′ E. and 11° 50′ N. There was a considerable cross swell as we rounded the land. Our little vessel was going seven knots, which I did not expect from her. We had during the whole of the last day a strong set to the south, which took us thirty miles. We coasted the land during the whole time. Mount Felix is united to the main land by a low sand; it is conspicuous, and cannot be mistaken. We were opposite to it after it was dark.

On the 13th a very pleasant breeze came on from the north of east. We steered W. and by N.

straight for Aden, and passed the high land behind Cape St. Peter. The coast is very high and barren: it was still in sight at night, though a haze, which extended across the whole sea, concealed the base. The stars near the horizon were hardly visible. Several meteors, called falling stars, shot occasionally across the sky; but no aurora borealis had appeared during the whole voyage. A heavy dew fell all night. The sea was smooth, though we went at the rate of six knots an hour.

We had a very fine breeze during the whole night of the 13th, but no land was visible on the following morning. The sky was clear, and the water smooth. At twelve o'clock we had run one hundred and twenty miles in twenty-four hours.

At eight in the morning of the 15th a part of the African shore was in sight, distant about eleven leagues, which was as high as that on the opposite side. At one, Cape Aden bore right a-head W by N $\frac{1}{4}$ N. distant eleven leagues. We went on till night, when it was so near, that we determined to come to an anchor. We passed the head land, and anchored at nine o'clock on the other side, close as we supposed to the town; but could not be certain, as no one on board had ever been there, and we had no directions respecting making it. The land sheltered us, and we had little motion.

At day light on the 16th we found no town was visible, and thought we had not got far enough; and that it lay beyond another head land, nearly W. accordingly we weighed anchor at six, and steered along shore. Cape Aden is a very lofty rock, on the top of which are several ruined towers. The bay we anchored in, was a fine one, about six miles wide, and as many deep. On proceeding we found our mistake: that in which we anchored was Back Bay, and Aden itself was on the eastern side of the head-land. The bottom of every bay was a sandy beach; beyond that ran a chain of mountains at a distance. I never beheld a more dreary scene; nor one that less accorded with the idea that might be formed of the country from the beautiful description of Milton: no "Sabæan odours" came off to gratify our senses, from the shore, nor did they ever exist there, but in the mind of the poet, as a more wretched country does not exist; for the myrrh and frankincense come from the opposite coast, though the Arabs were, and are still the medium of conveyance to Europe.

It would have been a serious loss of time to have beaten back, and therefore I determined to go on, though much vexed at a mistake, which prevented our having excellent water, instead of that which is to be obtained higher up, and is invariably brackish. Back Bay is the best watering-place, though it is five miles from the town: the only expence is three dollars demanded by the Dola, as I learned from Lieutenant Powell of the Wasp, who was there in 1803. In East Bay it is purchaseable, but at a high price. On the western side is a range of rocks extending out nearly as far south as the hill of Aden itself. The tops of these are singularly broken, and rise into Gothic spires in several parts: two of these have got the names of Ass's Ears. Another bay is west of them, in size and appearance exactly like the former. Its western boundary is a range of rocks, one of which so perfectly resembles a funnel as to deserve that name: it can never be mistaken. The coast is shelving to the south of west. Before sunset the Cape itself was perfectly visible like a gunner's quoin, Cape St. Anthony being on our bow. This is not very high land. We kept at the distance of three or four leagues to avoid a shoal that extends out from it. The breeze continued from the eastward, and freshened as we advanced. At ten the island of Perim was in sight, and soon afterwards we entered the smaller straits which run between it and the land. We kept nearer the island than the main, with from eleven to six fathom water. The breeze was assisted by the tide, and soon brought us under shelter of the promontory. We anchored by twelve in smooth water, in defiance of a very strong breeze.

Before day on the 17th the small boat was hoisted out. My servant and Mr. Hall were sent on shore with their guns and dogs, in hopes of killing us some game. After an early breakfast Mr. Salt and I, attended by Mr. Hurst the midshipman, and four sepoys, went on shore to see the country, and collect shells. We landed on the beach, on which nothing grows but a species of salicornia. A ridge of broken hills, detached from the Cape, rises about a mile from the shore: this we determined to ascend. The way up was craggy, but the heat of the sun was tempered by the strong breeze, and the fatigue was relieved by discovering several curious plants, and some mineral specimens. From the summit we had an excellent view of Cape Bab-el-mandeb and the island of Perim. A bay to the eastward of the Cape extends inwards a considerable way: the land between that and the westernmost, in which the ship lay, is perfectly flat, and a dry salt sand: if the sea were to rise only a very few feet it would cover it. Already part of it is a lake of salt water. Accidents have occurred from mistaking this east bay for the strait; a circumstance that can never happen, if it should be only observed that Perim is perfectly flat, which ought to be kept close on the larboard side; whereas Bab-el-mandeb hill is the loftiest land in the neighbourhood. The hill on which we were, rises suddenly out of a plain of sand; no others are near it.

The shooting party were at the bottom of the hill, from which we soon descended, and joined them. They had seen several antelopes, and had wounded one, but it escaped. They had killed some partridges, and also purchased some milch goats very cheap, and remarkably fine. On reaching the sea shore we found a great many Arab fishermen, with a profusion of mullets, and other fish. These we purchased and sent on board, to procure, in return, a supply of water, none of which was to be obtained on the land. The boys went in amongst the coral rocks, and procured a few shell-fish, that were fine of their kind. It was still early, and as the breeze continued, we determined to walk along the shore to point Bab-el-mandeb. Between us was a small creek communicating with the salt-water lake, now nearly dry, over which we were obliged to pass in the boat. As we advanced, it was less pleasant, from the air being frequently heated by the sand over which it passed, which gave it all the effect of the hot winds of India in scorching the skin, and producing intense drought. Dr. Macgie, who had accompanied us, and Mr. Salt bathed, from which they suffered considerably, but not so much as the two officers of the ship, who, from being more exposed, were soon of a perfectly red colour.

On the beach is the tomb of a Mussulmaun saint, which, though a heap of ruins, is much visited. The extreme point is low, but rocky. We procured from its sides several shells, but none of value. It was now three o'clock, and we were all heartily fatigued. We took to our boat, but the breeze had so freshened that nothing but the shelter of the land prevented its being difficult to get on board. I am convinced that the Straits are not above three miles wide. We all took the precaution of anointing our faces; those who had had their bodies exposed, suffered severely; we, who were more prudent, escaped with losing the skin off our noses. The bay in which we had anchored was most excellently defended by the island and promontory, and is much frequented by vessels that are too late to reach Mocha by day-light. Behind the hill, on which we were, is a wood of stunted mimosas, which seems of considerable extent, but would soon be exhausted, were Perim to be inhabited. We were too far out, and not land-locked, for some mountainous islands were visible through the Straits, composing part of the cluster called the Seven Brothers. The high land of Africa could be seen over the island, reaching up towards the north. This is, according to Bruce, the myrrh and frankincense country.

On the 18th before day, the anchor was up, and we set sail. At sun-rise we could perceive a ship enter the Straits and follow us. We had no doubt that this was the Fox frigate, Captain Vashon, as no other was likely to be in these seas, and Admiral Rainier had informed me that we should meet her here, as, at the request of the Bombay government, he had directed her to proceed to Mocha, to convoy to India the trade from that place. The breeze continued extremely fresh, as we sailed along the Arabian shore: the coast itself is low land, but the chain of mountains was seen, though with difficulty, from the haze, extending N. at about thirty miles from the shore. At ten, Mocha was visible: we were obliged to keep out, to avoid a dangerous shoal, till the great mosque bore E. by S. when we stood right in for the town. We anchored at a distance of about four miles, in little more than four fathoms. The wind was very fresh, and the swell, though broken by the shoal, was considerable. We saluted the town with three guns, which were answered by one. The Fox soon afterwards came in, and anchored about a mile to the N. W.; she could not get more to the S. on account of the wind. A fishing boat came off with fish; it was small and narrow, and the people nearly naked; the sail was cloth, and held by the hand. It went with great velocity, and very close to the wind. The fish was excellent.

Captain Keys wrote to Mr. Pringle, acting Agent to the East India Company, to inform him of my arrival. Mr. Pringle came off, while we were at dinner, to invite me to the Factory. He told me that he had notified my arrival to the Dola, or Governor, and had enquired, in case I visited him, how he would receive me. To this he answered, that he was not well, and would not move from his seat. Mr. Pringle added, that as the meeting him at the door had been insisted on by General Baird, and had been complied with, he could, on no account, advise me to visit him in any other manner. I assured him that I should be entirely guided by him, as my only wish was to act in the manner that would be most conducive to the advantage of the English character; and that I considered him as the best judge on such an occasion.

After dinner, attended by Mr. Pringle, Captain Keys, and Mr. Salt, I quitted the Antelope, and was saluted with seventeen guns. These the Dola chose to take as a compliment to himself, and returned it with one. We were so conveniently anchored, that the S. W. wind was a side one, both for embarking and disembarking. We were soon at the pier, and proceeded immediately to the factory. I took care to let the Dola know, that the seventeen guns were not intended as any compliment to him, or the state, as the Antelope would certainly never again salute the town, till the former guns had been returned: to this I received no answer. This circumstance, trifling in itself, very strongly marks the Arab character.

More than a month having been consumed in the voyage from Mangalore, it was thought advisable to lay in a sufficient supply of water and provisions, before we proceeded to a coast of which we had no positive information. This was not completed till the 8th of May, when the Antelope was reported by Captain Keys to be ready for sea. During my stay at Mocha, I resided at the British Factory, where Mr. Pringle did every thing in his power to make me comfortable. He had filled this situation, since the departure of the British armament, to the satisfaction of the Bombay Government, and was very well acquainted with the Arab character, and the trade of the Red Sea.

I was painfully surprised at learning from Mr. Pringle, that the idea of examining the western side was so disagreeable to Captain Keys, that he had applied to him to allow him a room at the factory, till he could procure a passage back to Bombay, as he was determined, in consequence of ill health, to give up the command to his first officer. Mr. Pringle, at my request, pointed out to him in such strong colours the consequences that would ensue, that he abandoned his intentions; but an impression of anxiety was left on my mind, which by no means diminished the evils necessarily attendant on a voyage of discovery. I, however, determined to execute the business I had undertaken, in defiance of any surmountable obstacle, and therefore began to make every necessary enquiry respecting my intended route.

I discovered that a regular communication existed between Mocha and Massowah, and between this latter place and Suakin; that Massowah was by no means the unsafe place which Mr. Bruce represented it to be in his time; and that pilots could be procured for the whole way. As, however, the upper part of the voyage was to be performed through very narrow straits, and at a time when the N. W. winds were blowing strong down the gulf, I thought it would add greatly to our safety, to hire a country vessel, called a Dow, to go a head, and show the way. This would also enable me to visit many islands which the Antelope might not be able to approach. A dow was therefore hired for four hundred dollars, to go to Dhalac, Massowah, Suakin, and up to the latitude of the river Farat, where we meant to end our observations, and make the best of our way to Cosseir. I hired also an Arab boy of the name of Hyder, as an interpreter till the Antelope returned. He spoke English tolerably well, and bore an excellent character. I intended to have sailed on this day, and I dined on board the Fox, on my way to the Antelope, but a proposal from Captain Vashon made me alter my intention. This was, that if I would stay till the morrow, he would accompany us to Jibbel Teir and Dhalac. The pleasure of his society, and the use of his boats, were inducements too powerful to be resisted; the agreement was therefore made.

It being tolerably calm by six o'clock, I quitted the Fox, where I had slept, and went on board the Antelope. To my very great surprise, I now learned, through the medium of Hyder, that the pilot knew nothing of the passage from Jibbel Teir to Massowah; that the usual way was stretching across to the Abyssinian coast, and working up it to Dhalac. Captain Keys felt himself incapable of conducting the vessel through an unknown and intricate sea, and consequently all idea of Jibbel Teir was abandoned. The only inconvenience was respecting Captain Vashon. As we were under weigh, I could not go on board the Fox with any comfort, owing to the heavy swell. We however ran the brig so close to her, that our main top sail caught in her yard, and was rent. I told him where we were going, and our reasons. He answered he should go the old way by Jibbel Zeighur. We could say no more, and separated. He waited a little for a shore boat, and then made sail to the northward, whilst we stretched right across rather to the south of west. The wind was very fresh, as usual, from the S. E. with a considerable swell. The Abyssinian shore was soon in sight right a-head, which the pilot said was Ras Beiloul. This, according to Niebuhr, is the name of a town and district.

Our pilot seemed a sensible old fellow, and I was happy to find that he was an inhabitant of Dhalac. He expressed great pleasure at meeting Mr. Macgie, the surgeon, whom he had known before. He had been much employed by the English, when at Perim, and had purchased a boat with the money which he had obtained from them. He gave his directions clearly; and when they heaved the log, told them that it was not necessary, as he knew where he was, and there was plenty of water. We did not however choose to trust him. As we got nearer the African coast the wind became more moderate. We now perceived a lower point, stretching from Ras Beiloul, which the pilot said was Ras

Firmah. It is the most easterly point. Nearly south of it, and close to it, is an island, Saiel Beiloul. At three we closed in with the land, and anchored about three miles west of a head-land, which the pilot called Ras Bunder Beiloul. Like a true pilot of Mr. Bruce's description, he gave orders to anchor so suddenly, that it was impossible to obey, and, consequently, we were carried farther from the shore than we meant; however, at a mile and a half from it we had a sand and mud bottom at thirteen fathom. A chain of islands and rocks had continued the whole way to the north of us, the largest of which the pilot called Jibbel Anish, but which must be the Jibbel Azroe of the charts.

The bay we now entered is of very great extent, and excellently defended from the south winds. The water was smooth, though strong gusts came over the hill. The width of the channel, opposite to Mocha, proved to be less than I conjectured from the view of the Abyssinian land when there. I did not lose any time in sending off my servants in the pilot's boat to the shore to look for shells. The people bear a bad character; but probably the accounts of their ferocity are exaggerated. Our pilot offered to go to the village, which he said was beyond the hills. The whole coast had a black, barren appearance, except where it was broken by white sand.

After dinner Mr. Salt and Captain Keys went on shore in the boat, and took with them the lead line. They found, contrary to Mr. Bruce's assertions, "that there was no anchoring ground on the Abyssinian shore, and that you might have your bowsprit over the land without any bottom astern," that the land gradually shallowed to seven fathom within a quarter of a mile of the shore. They found an inner bay perfectly defended, except to the north. A strong gust of wind prevented their entering to sound it. It was about five miles round. Under a stone were lying a net and iron head of an harpoon, but they saw no native. A few mimosas and herbaceous plants were all the vegetation; but as yet I had not been able to discover Mr. Bruce's Absinthium. My servant procured some beautiful specimens of the Neritæ. Many dead shells showed the riches beneath the sea, but, as I had no diver, I could only wish for them. The seamen caught several cat-fish, as they call them.

We got under weigh at six next day, and steered N. N. W. directly across the Bay, which, as it was clear, appeared of a magnificent extent. It could not be less than twelve miles deep, and about thirty from one head-land to a large island, which formed the other extremity. In the bottom, the land had a very singular appearance; large masses being perfectly flat, and others of a conical figure. It blew fresh with a considerable swell. By twelve we were across, and discovered an archipelago of islands and rocks around the island above mentioned, which the pilot called Rackmah. He informed us that there was a river, and very civil people, where every article was to be procured. As this was to me a very interesting assertion, I was greatly pleased by Captain Keys proposing that we should bear up and examine into the truth of it. At half after twelve we did so; and with regular soundings as we approached the land; at length we cast anchor under the lee of the island, in four and a half fathom, with a hard sandy bottom. I asked the pilot if he could persuade the natives to come down to us, and I would make them some presents. He said, no, they would meet us on the beach, but would never come on board. This suspicion could not have originated without cause, and I fear that they, or their neighbours, have experienced ill treatment from European vessels. We saw several groves of trees, which made us hope the pilot had not deceived us.

Mr. Salt wished to go to the village, which was at some miles distance up a bay. He was accompanied by Mr. Hurst, the midshipman, and Hyder as an interpreter. I went in the boat to the island to examine it, and was attended in another boat by a Naig and three sepoys, my servant, and some lascars. We found an excellent landing-place about a mile and a half from the ship. No shells, that were new, met our notice; we therefore ascended the hill, which was composed of a blackish brown stone that looked as if it had been burnt. Vegetation was nearly annihilated. I saw a Salicornia, an unknown shrub, and a species of Indigofera, of which I collected seeds. On descending to the opposite shore, I found the green trees I had observed, to be a species of Rhizophora that covered the beach. Some flamingos were seen, but too distant to be reached with the gun. Two natives, who lived on the island, were brought to us by the report of a shot: they seemed not to be afraid, and were very civil. They understood a little Arabic, and had not the woolly head. My people went to their hut, and procured some turtle. They seemed to be there merely for the purpose of catching them: and they had no boat. Not expecting that I should meet with any inhabitants, I had nothing with me to give them; but being unwilling they should go unrequited, I wrapped my handkerchief round the young boy's head, which was shaved all over, except a tuft above the forehead. We found that a sandy bar extended from the island to the main, and formed one side of the bay; the other islands above mentioned were beyond it, and, at a distance, they looked as if in a line with it. The passage is about two miles across, with shallow water.

After coasting a rocky head-land, which at first we had supposed an island, we proceeded to a third, which was likewise connected by a sandy bar, and formed altogether a most excellent bay for small vessels. We here procured a few good shells, and discovered the tomb of a native chief, around which had been set up a circle of stones. At one end were the bones and shells of several turtles, half burnt. In the middle were several drinking vessels: one was an English China sugar bason. We found a second tomb nearly similar, and were again informed by some of the boatmen, that this belonged to a chief. As these islands have no names among the pilots, I gave it that of Burial Island. I did my best to procure the native names, as it might be of use to future navigators; and wherever I succeeded, I have, as accurately as I could, preserved them. On the northern side were some excellent oysters fastened to the rock: their shells were of a fine purple at the edges, and by no means inelegant. Soon after it was dark, I got to the ship: there was a considerable swell, which rendered it by no means pleasant, and the wind was right against us. The island we first went to is by far the largest in the group, and forms the north-eastern point of the bay. It consists of two hills divided by a low sandy plain; the highest is to the N. W. In no part is it more than two miles and a half wide. Its latitude 13° 50″ N. Long. 42° 10″ E. To the eastward every thing is clear, and it may be approached very close. Mr. Salt had, as we perceived from the ship, gone several miles up the gulf between Burial Island, and another to the northward of it.

As the wind was right against him, we did not expect him to return soon; but our anxiety was removed by perceiving his boat before it was quite dark. He arrived at ten completely fatigued, and without having been much gratified. The river had vanished, though certainly in the rainy season torrents had run to the sea, of which he perceived visible marks. At present there were only two wells about sixty yards from the sea: the water of the nearest was as bad as the Mocha water; that of the farthest was better, and in tolerable quantity. He met with no village, but saw three men, with a numerous troop of camels, and two flocks of sheep: the natives were extremely civil, offered him water, and willingly exchanged a fine sheep for some tobacco, refusing a dollar that was offered. They had driven their animals down to the water, and were returning to their habitations at some distance in the interior, but they objected to the party's going thither. They wore crooked knives, like the Arabs, by their side, and had spears lying at the wells. They knew the old pilot, and shook the whole party by the hand, without expressing the least fear. They had curling black hair, drawn out into points in every direction. There was plenty of the mimosa close to the water side. The swell continued all night, and the heat was most oppressive.

We were under sail by six, our dow preceding us. We continued coasting along the land, which receded considerably to the west. At first we had soundings, but afterwards none with 15 fathom. We kept about twelve miles from land: a great many islands and rocks were seen, none of them so far out as we were. At twelve we were opposite to one which the pilot called Saiel Abaiel. Its long. is 42° 10′ E. lat. 13° 50′ N. It is impossible to sail along a safer coast than this: not a sand-bank appeared, and the rocks were all close to the land. The wind became light from the eastward: during a part of the night it was calm. We cast the lead, and had bottom at 37 fathom, with a current carrying us somewhat to the north. We kept all night nearly the same distance from the land, with regular soundings from 37 to 40 fathom.

On the 13th we had variable winds.—At twelve a pleasant breeze: we were then 14 miles from shore, with 21 fathom water; the country hilly and barren; lat. 14° 26″, long. 41° 38″ 30′. We continued coasting along shore till evening, when we came so near as three miles and a half to a low point that advanced beyond the mountains. It shoaled gradually till we anchored in seven fathom, with a sandy bottom. It was uncommonly sultry in the night: the wind for a short time at south. We discovered that we had anchored off a low cape called Ras Kussa, whence the land runs rapidly to the westward; we make it by computation in lat. 14° 34″ N. long. 41° 23″ E.

We weighed anchor at five with a light breeze directly in our teeth, so that we were obliged to tack off and on. In the morning we saw two dows, which met us. The bank from the headland continued a considerable way out. At eleven o'clock we had 21 fathom 9 miles from shore; but the tack before, when six miles from shore, we had only 6 fathom. The immediate beach was low land, and a great haze hid the mountain from our sight. At twelve we were in long. 41° 13″, lat. 14° 41″. At six we anchored in six and a half fathom, sand, off a low black rocky point, near which the pilot affirmed there was a well of fresh water. He also said that these rocks extended to the depth of 5 fathom. A low island bore by the compass NW $\frac{3}{4}$ W. The night was extremely sultry, and the water smooth. The coast was low, and the haze continued so great that we could only see the tops of the hills beyond it.

We weighed anchor at four, the wind right ahead, but it soon came round. We anchored at twelve in seven fathom, to give the pilot an opportunity of getting some articles he wanted from a village which he said was near us. Further on there is a bay, formed by the main-land, and a chain of islands to the N. and W. They called them Ras Amphila, Bunder Amphila, and the Islands of Amphila.* Mr. Salt and Captain Keys went on shore on the island, which is uninhabited: Mr. Salt brought me back some seeds, one of which was of a very beautiful purple icosandrous plant, with succulent leaves. He found the island to be about a mile broad, by three long, perfectly flat and sandy. It was thickly covered with a low shrub and herbaceous plants, among which was the Portulaca officinalis in abundance. They saw several snakes, which the Abyssinians wanted to catch. The dow's people brought me some shells of the same kind as I had procured at Mocha. The pilot boat did not return all night. We saw a dow round the island, and enter the strait beyond the point. The night was rather cooler.

After we had weighed anchor on the 16th, the pilot arrived, and brought us some sheep. He asserted this to be a place of some trade, which was confirmed by the appearance of several dows. We kept without all the five Amphila islands, which were equally flat and sandy, raised only about ten feet above the water, and without a

* That nearest us they called Kuddo; but I believe they often gave us false names.

single tree on them. The shore stretches out rapidly to the westward, is low, but backed by lofty hills, of fantastical forms. Some high trees grew on the water's edge. As we coasted along, by the assistance of a kind of sea breeze, it was extremely pleasant. At twelve our lat. was 14° 52″, long 40° 58″ 45′. We passed Ras Ratta, which is a very conspicuous piece of land, and of a singular form. We found all the charts of the coast extremely incorrect. At three or four leagues distance, when without every island, it is impossible to have a coast more free from danger. This day we had from about ten to fourteen fathom. Late in the evening we passed two remarkable headlands, which extend considerably from the shore, and which I conceived were islands. Several rocks were between them, and the usual line of the main: The pilot called them Ras Sarbo and Ras Rorah. A lofty island ahead appeared faintly at sun set. The pilot cast anchor off an island which lay in the bay formed by the head-land. It was low, and perfectly flat. The soundings were unequal, from sixteen fathom suddenly shoaling to ten; but as they afterwards continued regular at fourteen till we anchored, I conceived there was some error. The night was immoderately sultry.

On the 17th we did not weigh till six; as there was not a breath of air till the sea breeze set in, which had hitherto invariably been the case about nine. We passed the island looked for by the pilot; he called it Howakel. It is lofty, rugged, and about nine miles in length. Off the north of it are three low sandy islands. The coast here again began to approach them, from which at one time it had apparently been three leagues distant. In the evening we saw four small islands to the eastward, distant five leagues: the pilot called them

Miséras; of which the curious name of the Great and Little Miseries, as laid down in Mr. Apres de Menonville's chart is probably a corruption. We came to anchor about six o'clock between the main and an island, which, from the pilot's considering it as an important mark, we called Pilot's Island. The sky to the N. W. was cloudy, and the sun set behind a dense body of clouds. This the pilot said denoted a S. W. wind; and he was right. It blew rather fresh till ten o'clock, when it came round to the E. of N. and was extremely sultry.

On the 18th we were not under sail till six, when, for the first time, we kept within the islands. As the channel was narrow, and the wind against us, our tacks were but short. The channel is not above a mile wide, but the water is ten fathom and upwards. Pilot's Island is small and woody, has two spits of sand extending parallel to the shore for a considerable distance, one at each end; it is distant from the main three miles, and every danger is visible. The sea breeze changed the northwest monsoon a little in our favour, so that for some time we ran along shore. However, we could not get a sight of Dhalac in the latitude, and nearly in longitude in which Mr. Bruce placed it, viz. lat. 15° 29″, long. 40° 15″ 30′; yet he says it is visible at the distance of nine leagues, which is in itself impossible, as he admits that the land is low. I began to fear that he had invented much in his travels. The soundings were regular the whole day. We passed within several islands, keeping close to the shore, which was flat, with gentle acclivities beyond, covered with wood; and farther off, the lofty mountains of Abyssinia appeared nearly hidden in the haze. At four we came to anchor within a mile and a half of the land. In fishing from the ship, the hooks caught on some dark brown pieces of coral, from the holes of which issued a profusion of living animalculæ: each was nearly brown, about a quarter of an inch long, with a black head. I put a specimen several times in water, and they extended themselves directly: when out of the water they did not retire, but hung close to the sides, one over the other. We also caught a very large specimen of the pearl muscle, with a piece of madrapore growing on it. The night was as sultry as ever. We passed a vessel this day.

On the 19th we sailed at four: the north-west wind still continued sufficiently strong to be pleasant. We had to work between an island that was ahead of us, and the main, in a passage about three miles wide. The channel was nearly as broad, as it was deep water close to the main land. We were not through till eleven, when we bore away along the Abyssinian shore. We passed another vessel this day.

A great deal of trade seems to be carried on at Massowah. The coast also seemed tolerably full of inhabitants. Last night there was a fire on the shore. Our pilot declared he could not reach Dhalac this day: he wished to anchor off an island to the west of us, which forms a bay, where he said large vessels may anchor in safety. The people, he declared to be very good friends of his, and very civil. We entered it in a S. S. W. direction, and anchored off a very picturesque island. The bay fully answered the pilot's description: it is eight or nine miles deep and about seven miles wide. A sand bank, which runs off from the island forms its N.W. defence. Behind that is another bay. The water is deep. We anchored in seventeen fathom, and at only three quarters of a mile from the shore.

As no description of the island has ever been given, and we were, probably, the first Europeans that had visited it, we called it Valentia. Mr. Salt went on shore to take the different bearings, from which we formed a plan of the harbour, &c.; my servant went with Hyder in the dow's boat to procure shells. The men did not choose to assist, so that I got very few, but from these I was convinced that with proper assistance, it was the best spot for the purpose at which I had hitherto touched. Mr. Salt was accompanied by two of the inhabitants to the summit of the hill: they were very civil. The water we got from a tank was good, and we procured a few sheep, which belonged to the Nayib of Massowah. The high hills of Habesh were in full view: and in one part, a ridge appeared between us and them, which terminates a point said to form the bay of Massowah, and is called Ras Gidden. The night was as sultry as usual.

On the 20th we heaved anchor at five. Our pilot seemed to be less acquainted than usual with the islands. We made a direct N.E. course, but tacked incessantly. The distance we ran was about twenty-two miles, when we anchored in another bay, the extremities of the land extending from N.W. by W. to S. by E. It was very deep and a village was situated on the bank at the bottom of it. This, he said, was Dhalac, but it agreed so little with the description I had met with, that I had considerable doubts on the subject. I enquired for Dhalac-el-Kibeer, which he told me was at some distance, but that the port was not safe for vessels of our size; nor would he dare to take us there without permission from the Dola.

A native soon came along side, on a catamaran, formed of four pieces of wood, about ten feet long, and six inches in diameter. On this he floated nearly naked. On recognising our pilot, he came on board, but seemed considerably alarmed. He was a fine muscular figure, with a large black beard, not woolly. He afterwards proved to be the son of the Dola, who commanded the whole island on the part of the Nayib of Massowah. He pressed us to land, which I determined to do. He then begged leave to accompany me. By an unfortunate fatality, I consented to our pilot's being of the party. As from the appearance of the young man, who was perfectly naked, except a cloth wrapped round his waist, I had no very high idea of the Dola's dignity, I consulted the former what present I should take on shore. Money, cloth, rice, tobacco, &c. &c. were mentioned; in short I found any thing would be acceptable. I dressed myself in an Asiatic dress, as did Mr. Salt. Hyder went with us as interpreter. The water on this shore is shallow, and has undermined the madrapore rocks, of which the beach is composed, in such a manner, as to render a landing in most parts impracticable. At length we entered a strait, formed by an island called Nokhara, and the mainland of Dhalac. Here is a very excellent but small landing place.

The pilot and native went on to announce our arrival, while we reclined in the shade of a rock, and caused our people to collect some oysters, that grew in large clusters, suspended from the roof of the caverns, formed by the beating of the sea. At length more natives arrived, who begged us to advance to the village. We were met by a tall native, almost naked, with a cast of the wool in his hair, who, my pilot said was the Dola, and to whom the present was to be given. He accompanied us till I was met by another man, in the Arab dress, with a cap; his beard white as snow, and he had a more respectable appearance than the former. I immediately conceived this to be the Dola, but the old pilot would not admit it. We were conducted into a house, built like all the others in the place, of madrapore, drawn from the sea, squared, and raised about twelve feet from the ground. It was thatched with a species of grass, and had one door, but no window. The bare earth formed the floor, and there was no furniture except five beds, made of wood, with cords drawn across and raised about three feet from the ground. These were covered with matting made of the leaves of the doom-tree.* I seated myself on one, Mr. Salt on another, the rest were occupied by natives and my lascars, who were sitting together in amicable equality.

No one was armed even with a knife. I again urged that I thought the man in the Arab dress ought to have the present, but was over-ruled. The native therefore received a piece of blue Surat cloth and ten dollars, while the other had only a piece of blue cloth. Coffee was immediately ordered, and our conversation commenced. I stated that we wished to procure water and sheep, for which we would willingly pay. They assured us they would supply us: a specimen of the former was produced, and was excellent. I could not state the quantity wanted, but referred them to Captain Keys. They spoke in the highest terms of their master, the Nayib of Massuah, or, as they pronounce it, Massowah. They said, he was a good man, and if I wanted one pilot would give me two. There were plenty on the island, who could pilot me to Suakin, whither I told them I was going. The old man was now recognised as being the Nayib's representative, and Governor of

* A species of palm tree.

all the island, and our young visitor on board as his son. I more particularly engaged him to attend me during my stay, by a promise of a present on my departure. They told me that the place I was on was an island called Nokhara, and the constant residence of the Dola, who had subdolas at every other station; that Dhalac-el-Kibeer had formerly been the principal residence, that now the port was bad, and could not admit our ship, but that we were very well situated where we were.

In defiance of the heat, I determined to visit the wells or tanks, where the water was kept, conceiving they were probably near the village. My young Dola accompanied me. We passed through the narrow passages that separated the houses from each other, without seeing a female, or being importuned by a beggar. There was a small unornamented oblong building on the road side, which I learnt was a mosque; near it were a few tombstones and two doom-trees. We ascended nearly a mile along a small foot-path tracked in the rock, on which nothing grew except a few stunted plants of the mimosa. Here the channel which separates Nokhara from the larger island of Dhalac, became visible, and below us in the valley, the site of the water was distinctly marked by a kind of meadow, and several plantations of doom-trees. It was distant another mile, but as I had advanced so far, I determined to proceed. On my arrival I was much surprized to find that the well was a natural one, formed by a chasm in the rock, which was covered for several feet with good soil, and occasionally produced excellent herbage. It was about seven feet from the water, which presented a clear surface of about ten feet long, by three wide, irregular in its shape, from the rocks protruding sides.

As it never fails in the driest season, and supplies the whole island, the reservoir probably extends under a great part of the plain. Its superincumbent bed prevents the heat from having any effect on it. At the distance of forty or fifty yards they had sunk a well, and at the same depth had found water. The Dola told me, that at Dhalac-el-Kibeer, you could not search three feet deep without obtaining it. On returning to our boat we found the Dola there, who assured us, that water and fresh provisions should be ready in the morning, when I intended to proceed to the opposite island with my tent, and view the port of Dobelew, where Mr. Bruce had anchored.

When I returned on board, I stated my plan to Captain Keys; and observed to him, that as every thing hitherto had appeared so totally different from what we had been led to expect from Mr. Bruce's statement, I conceived it to be of the greatest public advantage to ascertain the real situation and shape of the islands; that for this purpose, I requested the use of one of the boats on the morrow, to attend me till my return, which would probably be in the course of two days. To this I received a positive refusal; with the information, that it was contrary to the regulations of their ship, that any of their boats should be out all night. These regulations were singularly urged by a person, who had kept his boat two nights on shore at Mocha, merely because he preferred sleeping on land; though in consequence he was not on board the Antelope to receive me on my return from the Fox.

I was awakened early the next morning by a violent dispute between Mr. Salt and the pilot, who, although he had the evening before consented to our arrangement, declared that he would not go, nor should his boat go, unless he received ten dollars; a demand which was positively refused. By the interference of Captain Keys he was induced to proceed, but returned under some other pretence; when the Captain ordered the cutter to be prepared. On this he instantly departed, fearing to lose an opportunity of plundering the party. I staid on board: Keys went on shore to the Dola. He found a large collection of skins filled with water, lying on the beach, covered with mats to protect them from the sun. These were sent on board in the boat, which made three trips, and nearly completed our supply. The Dola demanded only a dollar for twenty-seven skins, which is much cheaper than at Mocha, and the water was far better. The goats we procured were excellent, and not inferior to the mutton we before got. I obtained some shells, but none equal to what I expected. Several of the natives came off in the course of the day. At night I received a note from Mr. Salt, informing me that he had reached Dhalac-el-Kibeer, but that the Dola of the place would not permit him to move without an order from the Chief Dola at Nokhara. He requested me to procure this, and send him a piece of Surat blue cloth. All this was complied with, and I endeavoured to compose myself to rest.

Captain Keys went the following morning on shore. At night Mr. Salt returned with a view of Dhalac-el-Kibeer, and made a report of his tour, which led to the following observations. Standing in shore at half a mile from the ship, there were soundings at 3, 2½ and 2 fathom, at two hundred yards from the shore. The ship bore W. by S. ½ S. the extremities of the bay from S. by E. to W. by N. ½ N. They proceeded along shore till the ship bore W. N. W. ½ N. when a sand appeared equidistant from them, about three miles, bearing W. S. W. Close to a plantation of doom-trees, about two miles from the place where they landed, were sixteen wells like those at Nokhara, but the water was not more than two feet below the surface. Here two shepherds were tending, and drawing water for, several camels with their young, a great herd of asses, a few fine goats, and two sheep. As soon as the camels were supplied and driven off, some water was placed in the stone for the birds, which arrived in vast flights, particularly doves. A plantation of date-trees had been lately formed here; which at present did not bear fruit. They hired two asses for a dollar, but they were low and unmanageable.

About four miles and a half from the wells they passed a creek, where they met with a great number of pelicans, plenty of madrapore, and sea-weed, but no shells. On the right was a salt-marsh, which probably, at high spring tides, is connected with one more distant. They rested under the shade of a mimosa, till Hyder, and old Hassan, the boat-man, joined them. The pilot had constantly kept up with them. A native came down from a hill with some milk and water; he was very civil, but objected to their going to the place from which he came; to avoid affronting him, they did not press it. He got ready two asses, and went on with them. The road was rocky and uneven, and in several places the earth had divided, and formed clefts, about three feet across, where widest, and several hundred yards in length. They were of considerable depth; and the splashing of the stones thrown down, proved that there was water at the bottom.

After a fatiguing journey of five miles from their resting place, they got to Dhalac-el-Kibeer by two o'clock. A pleasant breeze had enabled them to bear the heat. At a little distance from the town they were met by several of the inhabitants, and among others by the priest; he differed in appearance from the rest in nothing except his having a string of beads round his neck. Mr. Salt and his companions were conducted to the Serai, had couches prepared for them, obtained milk and water to drink, and soon afterwards coffee. Their visitors were numerous, as the curiosity of the whole place was excited to view the first Europeans that ever had, in their time, visited them. Mr. Maxfield's uniform in particular excited much curiosity. On their expressing a wish to go out with their books and papers, the priest informed them, that without an order from Nokhara he could not allow it, but that he would, if they pleased, send off a messenger instantly, who might be able to return in the course of the night. This was done, and, as I have before observed, the letter to me was faithfully delivered. Upon expressing a wish to be left to themselves, every body retired, and some very good cakes with milk and water were sent them: these, with the articles they had brought with them, afforded a very tolerable meal, after which they again had coffee. In the evening, under pretence of bathing, they visited the harbour, and, in consequence of what the priest had said, made some observations. They slept on couches in the open air, but were very much disturbed by the rats, which, in the course of the night, seized and carried off from under Mr. Salt's bed, a napkin laid in a basket, which contained all their provisions. Before they were up, the messenger arrived with all the articles sent for, and the necessary permission from the Dola at Nokhara. The piece of blue Surat cloth was immediately presented to the priest of the place, and seemed very acceptable. After breakfast, they set off to make their observations.

A little way to the south of the town is the tomb of a most holy Mussulmaun prophet and saint, Abou-el-Heimen. A light is kept constantly burning: to support which, they assured Mr. Salt, it was customary for all travellers to give half a dollar. He would not be the first to break so laudable a custom, and therefore gave the money. Near this place are the ruins of a tank; it was 28 feet long, by 12 broad, and about 18 feet deep. It appeared to have been originally arched at top, and resembled another at some distance; the form of which was a regular oval, flat at the bottom, of great breadth, and 20 feet deep; the sides also arched at top, leaving a circular opening in the centre about three feet diameter, towards which large gutters were formed in the rock to bring in the water. Near the sea were four others: one was much larger, two others smaller than those above described, and circular. The one in ruins was cut out of the solid rock, then lined with stone and chunamed. There was no water in any of them, but a sediment appeared at the bottom; and on stooping down to look into them, the air was found extremely sultry. All these, they heard, were built by the Parsees, of whom nothing is known except from tradition; from the same source, they have an account of 316 tanks, similar to those above mentioned; but they admit that they never saw or heard of any one who had seen more than twelve or fourteen: they added, there were none at Dobelew.

Dhalac-el-Kibeer was formerly the principal port of the island. The town is about half a mile from the sea, with a sloping beach of sand between. The harbour is nearly inclosed by a chain of nine islands that lie off at the distance of about two miles. Beyond these the island of Chumma was visible, bearing from S. W. $\frac{1}{2}$ S. to S. $\frac{1}{2}$ W. while the extremities of the land bore from S. E. to W. S. W. At present there is scarcely water enough for a dow to approach the shore: till near the islands, it is seldom more than three or four feet deep. Only two vessels were there, one belonging to the place, the other to Massowah. The port still exhibits many vestiges of its former consequence. On the northern side are the ruins of two small mosques built of stone, with round cupolas at top, but of a rude workmanship. In the one towards the sea is an Arabic inscription cut on a stone placed in a recess. Around the mosque a great number of monumental stones are placed upright in the ground, at the heads of the persons whom they commemorate: many are well carved, and beautifully adorned with flowers, and other ornaments: some in Cufic, some in Arabic characters. As the stones are in general of a portable size, Mr. Salt was desirous of taking one away; but, as he was assured by the priest that this could not be done without express permission from the Nayib of Massowah, he contented himself with taking a copy of one inscription, which seemed to be held in the highest veneration, although externally it had nothing to recommend it, being indifferently carved, and having a corner broken. The priest informed him that it belonged to the Sheik or Sultaun, (he is called both), who built the tanks. It is immediately opposite to the principal mosque, and by the natives constantly kept moist with oil. Among the ruins were several pieces of brick and glass, some of which were perfectly clear. The women seemed to be kept out of the way, as they never appeared except at a distance, and the men objected to their being approached by strangers. The men had not the curling head of the Negroes. There are no trees near the town except two doom-trees and some Acacias. In spite of the opposition of the old pilot, who assured him that there were Bedowees, &c. in the place, Mr. Salt determined to go up a small ascent, whence he had hopes of seeing the Antelope. He set off alone, but finding that he persevered, several of the natives soon followed. He ascended without the least molestation, and had the good fortune to ascertain the following bearings. The Antelope N. 35 W. the mosque nearest the sea S. ½ W. the other end of the town S. b. E. distant a mile and three quarters; the extremes of Chumma S. ½ W. and S. W. b. S.; a sand S. W. b. W.

Leaving the hills, Mr. Salt proceeded about half a mile north to a creek, which they said is the same that separates Dhalac from Nokhara, and ends here; a small boat may come up it. Dobelew is reckoned two days journey distant; Nokhara one; so that their day's journey is about nine miles. About four o'clock the party set off on its return. When they got to the wells, the baggage, with old Hassan, was not come up. They waited some time, and at length sent the pilot to look for him. It was nearly two hours before he made his appearance, with a pitiful story that he had fallen asleep on the road, during which all the things had been stolen. The pilot soon came back by a different way. This old rascal had made so many attempts to cheat them, though in most he had been frustrated by Hyder, that Mr. Salt had not the least doubt that this was another plan to extort money, by re-obtaining the articles lost; he was the more confirmed in his idea, from the pilot's extreme anxiety to have them intrusted to old Hassan, as being honest, instead of a younger man; who could have kept up with the party. The only important article was Mr. Salt's drawing book; he therefore threatened the severest vengeance if the book, &c. were not produced by morning. They returned to the vessel, and by day light the next morning the old rogue brought every thing, pretending they were obtained with difficulty from a person to whom he had given two dollars, which he desired might be repaid him. This was positively refused, and he only got the four dollars that were originally given for his boat.

I had many observations to make respecting Mr. Bruce's account of these islands, but resolved to defer them till I could fully enter on the subject. In the morning the Dola came off in the boat: he breakfasted with us on coffee and sweetmeats, and seemed much pleased. I gave him a few pounds of coffee. In the course of the day, his son brought several baskets of shells, among which were some very excellent. I learnt nothing more respecting the place, as the boats were employed in bringing water. At night, however, Mr. Hall, the first Lieutenant, was permitted by Captain Keys to go to a reef, whence he procured some very fine sea eggs (Echini); one species had spines a foot long, and sharp as a needle; the other was of a larger kind, and when cleaned, very beautiful. The madrapore was not remarkable. Of coral or coraline I saw no specimen.

I had given notice to the Captain that I wished to proceed to Massowah. The old Dola came on board in his catamaran, (rather an undignified conveyance,) with his son, who requested a passage to Massowah: this was willingly granted. His father sent a letter by Keys to the Nayib, praising, as I heard, our good behaviour while at his island. He received the money due to him, and having expressed a wish to hear one of the great guns, as he called them, fired, he was saluted him with one, as his catamaran left the side of the ship. We weighed anchor between ten and eleven, and with a tolerable breeze bore away for Ras Gidden, which, since we had left Valentia, had never been out of sight. The pilot kept us so much to windward, that at three o'clock we were opposite to Massowah, though distant about three leagues. The wind was very light, and we were not able to get completely into the bay, but anchored without. We were alarmed during this day's sailing by a man calling out that there were shoals right a-head; but they proved only masses of floating fishes spawn, which had so defined an outline, and were so extensive, as to have the complete appearance of shoals. In the night we heard several guns from the shore.

CHAPTER II.

Arrival at Massowah.—Reception there.—Visits to the Nayib. —Preparations for the continuation of the voyage.—Disputes with the Captain of the Antelope, and consequent determination to return to Mocha.—Transactions at Massowah, and price of articles there.—Visit to the island of Valentia.—Return to Mocha.—Desertions from the ship.—Encouragement given by the Arab government to European seamen to become Mussulmauns.—Departure of Mr. Salt for India in the Antelope.—Voyage in the Fox frigate to Aden.—Transactions there.—Return to Mocha.—Transactions there.—Voyage to Bombay.

AT six, on May 24, we were under weigh, but were obliged soon to come to an anchor, as the land-wind was against us, and there was no room to work. Mr. Maxfield had been sent off in the jolly boat to the shore, where we saw a considerable crowd collected close to a mud building, which we presumed to be the castle. On his return he informed us, that the natives had perceived our approach, and had taken us for the Wahabees, in consequence of which the Nayib had come over from Arkeko, and they had been all night under arms. Mr. Maxfield informed them that a great man was on board, going to Suez, who would probably pay the Nayib a visit; that we wished for permission to enter the port, and obtain water and provisions; that we were willing to salute the fort with three, five, or seven guns, whichever the Nayib would return. He was at the head of his troops, and replied, that he should be happy to see the great man; that the island and every thing it afforded was his, and that he would return five guns, but did not wish for more, as it would alarm the Bedowees of the surrounding country, and make them hasten down to protect him. Mr. Maxfield said the natives were extremely civil, and told him, he might stay if he pleased, and send away the boat. This he thought suspicious, for which we laughed at him, and compared him to Mr. Bruce, who thought the man near Crab Island must be a villain from his smiling.

We so strongly suspected our old pilot, that we would not permit him to leave the ship till I had gone on shore and secured a good reception. During the whole voyage he had been threatening the Naqueda, or native master, of the dow, that he would, on his arrival here, complain to the Nayib of his injustice in giving him only fifteen dollars for piloting the ship to Massowah, when he himself received so large a sum as four hundred. When he saw the dow's boat going on shore without him, he thought they might make their story good, and his rage exceeded all bounds: he called to them, on their peril, not to proceed, and, when they went on, continued muttering to himself, and told the Captain he was so angry, that if his head should be cut off, it would not prevent his complaining.

Several Banians came off in a boat, the end of which was covered with green and red silk. They brought an additional invitation to me from the

Nayib. Our salute of five guns was immediately fired, and was answered, first by two guns near the castle. These were loaded with ball, the whizzing of which, though the guns were pointed wide of us, we could plainly hear, and from such bad marksmen was by no means pleasant: the third from the same place missed fire. At length two more were fired from the same place, and, half an hour afterwards, a fifth from the other side of the town, all loaded with ball. I had a letter from Devage, the India Company's broker at Mocha, to one of the Banians, which I delivered. I consulted him on the subject, and then determined to go on shore. I put on a plain Indian dress of muslin, with a shawl round my middle, in which I stuck my tulwah, or Indian sword. Mr. Salt and my servant had also dresses of that country, and Hyder went as interpreter.

We set off in the boat, under a salute from the ship, followed by all the Banians. We landed close to the town. There were three brass cannon there, much injured by time: with these they attempted a salute, but as the first missed fire, and I advanced, I cannot tell with how many they intended to honour me. I landed at a pier, with a small open space, that led to an ancient gateway, on one side of which was a large building. In one of its balconies I perceived several well dressed people. There was a considerable crowd, but they behaved very well. I entered by the gateway, and turning to the left, passed through several ruined rooms, and ascended a slope of rubbish to a large apartment, the end of which was covered with mats, on which was seated a very numerous assemblage of half clad natives. On the left side, in the balcony, was the Nayib, and several well dressed men. Opposite to them were two old fashioned English elbow chairs with high backs.

On entering, I made my salaam to the Nayib, who pointed to the chairs. Mr. Salt and I immediately seated ourselves, my servant and Hyder standing by. The Nayib was in one corner; he was dressed in white muslin with a shawl of scarlet for a turban, precisely similar to the one I wore round my waist. Next him, (as I have since learned,) was his brother, the Sirdar of the forces, in a large Janissary turban of scarlet: the others were his sons and secretary, &c. The crowd followed us in, and were now crouched on their haunches, over the whole surface to the door, completely filling the room, like Milton's devils in Pandæmonium; but in no other respect would the comparison hold, for their countenances were generally pleasing and intelligent, free from the traces of violent passions. I delivered a message to Hyder, expressive of my thanks for the answer the Nayib had returned me in the morning. Hyder interpreted this to the Banian, who went stooping, and in a low voice communicated it to the Nayib. Our whole conversation passed in the same way, and was merely complimentary: as I had been informed it would be wrong to enter on any business at my public audience. He told me that the island was mine, and begged I would make what use I pleased of it; that a house was prepared for me, and that he hoped I would continue in it during my stay. To this I assented. Coffee was brought, after the Arab fashion, in very small china cups, without milk or sugar: these were placed in larger ones of gilt filagree, to prevent the fingers from being burnt. Afterwards a caftan of red silk was thrown over my shoulders. They enquired who Mr. Salt was; and, on being informed he was my Secretary, there was some confusion, and a man went out. I now wished to take my leave, but was desired to stay till my house would be ready. I suspected what afterwards proved to be the case. A man entered, and immediately a caftan of blue cloth with yellow silk facing was thrown over Mr. Salt.

I now made my salaam, and the Nayib rose to attend me. We went down together. The troops in the gateway got up from their couches to make their salaams, which he returned by a wave of the hand. He attended me a considerable distance, but without saying a word. At a sharp turning he departed one way, and directed some of his people to shew me another. At length I reached a small house by the sea-side, nearly opposite to the Antelope. Here, in a stone built room, several couches were prepared, some with carpets and some with blankets thrown over them; it was however comparatively cool, from the thickness of the walls, and the many openings which admitted the sea-breeze. The Banians attended me, and I was soon overpowered by visitors. After obtaining some sherbet, I sent off Mr. Salt to inform the Captain of what had passed, and to invite him on shore. I then told my visitors I wished to go to sleep, and they immediately retired.

The next day I was informed by the Banian that the Nayib intended to visit me in the evening, when I should have an opportunity of delivering my present. About four o'clock he sent for Hyder, and told him to acquaint me that he had no such intentions; that if he came he must have all his people and troops with him, who would all expect presents from him; and added, what have I to give them? He wished that when it was quite dark, I would come alone to his house, when he would give me a private audience. As I was assured that the reason assigned was a real one, I consented to his request, without hesitation.

Accordingly, about eight o'clock, the Banian, and another person, arrived to conduct me. I did not even take Mr. Salt with me. Hyder carried my present concealed, which consisted of a handsome pair of shawls, a gold tissue dress, complete, but not made up, and a piece of kincaub. He received me in an undress, sitting on a bed of the country, out of doors, in one of the yards of his house: the only light was from two small lanthorns, the one suspended, the other on the ground. He made his salaams in return to mine, by placing his hand on his breast, and pointed to a seat placed close to his, at right angles. Perceiving Mr. Salt was not with me, he sent for him, and he soon arrived, accompanied by my landlord.

We had a long conversation, in which I represented that my motive for coming was to ascertain, whether our ships could with safety pass up this coast to Suez, and obtain water and provisions on the way. I pointed out the great advantage that would consequently ensue to his people, and expressed my satisfaction at having hitherto met with so much civility from his subjects, and in having succeeded in ascertaining what I wished. He replied that the island was mine, and that I might do what I pleased. That if our ships came, they should have every thing he could supply them with. That here they were very civil, good people; but, that, on the main, though they belonged to him, he could not equally answer for them. He offered sherbet in a silver cup, which the person who brought it, tasted in my presence.

I now produced my present, prefacing it by saying, that I was not a merchant, but a man of rank in my own country, travelling for amusement, and returning thither after a long absence; that I therefore had no merchandize, nor any thing worthy his acceptance; nevertheless, I wished him to accept a part of what I had, as a mark of my respect and gratitude, for his attentions since my arrival. He received my present, but said, What is this for? Have you not every thing? what do you ask from me? I replied, that through his kindness, I had every thing I wished for, and I hoped he would continue it to me and mine. I mentioned the pilots; he said they had been sent for. I asked permission for my people to look for shells, and to shoot. He begged me to apply to the Banian whenever I wished them to go out, and I should have some of his people to attend: but said there was a contagious disorder on the islands and therefore he wished us not to visit them lest we should bring it back. He assured me the ship should have every supply she wanted. He gave Hyder five dollars, and, after coffee, we took our leave much pleased with his behaviour.

He was rather a small man, of a grave countenance, and about forty years of age. His name was Edris; he had been nine years Nayib, and bore a most excellent character. He was the son of the late Nayib Hannes or Othman, who was the son of Achmed, of whom Mr. Bruce speaks so well, and who was nephew and heir of Hassan the then Nayib, but did not survive him.

The heat was very great; the thermometer at 96°, and less air than usual. I was for a day or two exceedingly unwell.

The Nayib sent frequently to enquire after me. His brother and sons were all here. A great number of the natives visited the ship: by the Captain's orders they had coffee and raisins, with which they were much pleased. My room was as pleasant as could be in this climate. I viewed from my window the island of Valentia, distant about five leagues, Ras Gidden, and the chain of mountains that lines the coast of the Red Sea from this place to the plains of Egypt. Behind these the summit of Taranta peeps out, which gives credit, by its height, to Mr. Bruce's account of the diffi culty he had in ascending it. The island of Shiek Said is pleasingly covered with trees, and seems to be nearly in the middle of this unruffled bason.

When I became a convalescent my visitors were numerous, and my host proved extremely intelligent. I gathered from him the following information. Dhalac is considered as a profitable government for the person who holds it. The Nayib receives from him only sixty dollars in money, and also obtains some camels, goats, and asses. If any thing should throw a large sum into the hands of the Dola, the Nayib would send to him and claim it; but if as in our case, it amounted to no more than thirty or forty dollars, he would let him keep all. The Nayib lives generally at Arkeko, where he has a very good house, and one wife, although the place is not so pleasant as Massowah; but in this he finds his interest, because the greater part of his dominions lie there, and his people have an easy access to him.

On the hills of Jibbel Gidden, and those behind Arkeko, are elephants, the teeth of which are exported: from Habesh they send gee, hides, gold dust, civet, sheep, and slaves. Of the latter the number is lately much lessened: a very satisfactory circumstance, and a proof of the increasing civilization of that country. The Suakin trade in slaves is, they say, proportionably augmenting. In return, they send up British broad-cloth, arms, ammunition, and the different manufactures of India: a little grain is also brought down from Abyssinia. They have, in their own country, plenty of goats and oxen; the sea supplies them with an inexhaustible variety of fish of the finest kinds; so that their living is by no means bad: game also seems in the greatest plenty. Water at Arkeko is not very good, but abundant. On the island of Massowah are about thirty tanks, which are filled in the rainy season: these are kept closed, and are, I believe, private property. They are not sufficient for the supply of the place, and much water is brought every morning by the boats from Arkeko.

The houses are each surrounded by a fence of reeds: the rooms are detached, and built of the same: within, they are lined with mats. The common people are extremely civil, and no one carries any arms, except the immediate family of the Nayib. My Ascar had no weapon except a stick. The natives did not seem jealous of their women, who came down to bathe, and perform their ablutions close to the place where I sat, without any appearance of shame. The slaves of the neighbours had, I believe, been found not over coy by the Europeans on shore. My next door neighbour was the Sirdar of the Ascarri, and I suspected, the intercourse was permitted by him, and that he shared in the profit. I saw only one deformed person, a female dwarf with bandy legs, who bathed before us regularly every day. The men and women are naturally well made, but child birth destroys the figures of the latter.

The Ascarri are completely under the influence

of the Nayib, who pays them out of the duties which ought to be remitted to Constantinople. They still recognise the Sultaun as their master, but it is a mere form. The Nayib pays nothing to the King of Abyssinia, but they are, I understand, on very good terms.

The Banians here are very comfortable: they say they have ever been the same, and some of them were those mentioned by Mr. Bruce. They are allowed wives, if they please, which is not the case at Mocha; and they seem less oppressed. They amount to eighteen in number, and carry on a considerable trade. The Nayib receives ten per cent. ad valorem on all goods exported and imported, and one dollar for each individual who enters the country to trade. The pearl fishery is renewed to a certain degree by the people of Dhalac, but although the best banks belong to the Nayib, he receives no share of the profit.

We were still delayed here, though the dow was ready for sea. The pilot arrived from Dhalac, but went back immediately to procure two more, who he said were absolutely necessary for so large a vessel. If the passage above should prove as clear as that below, this delay will never be necessary hereafter: I had indeed to regret that we did not do more; but Captain Keys threw every difficulty in our way, prevented Mr. Maxfield from making many observations that he wished, and, as we were all convinced, endeavoured even to mislead us by false longitude. Latterly he concealed it entirely, and then he declared his time-keeper was out of order, and that he should take Mr. Bruce's longitude, and begin a new rate. We determined not to follow him, but (as we should anchor every night,) to endeavour to carry on a chain of bearings the whole way to Suakin. Mr. Maxfield had finished a chart of the harbour, and proved Mr. Bruce's to be erroneous. It seems indeed that his was a copy from that of a Portuguese, corrected by a bird's eye view.

I sent to the Nayib for permission for Mr. Salt and my servant to go out on a shooting party on the main-land. To this he willingly assented; and said he would send to Arkeko for mules and people to attend them. The Sirdar procured me some good shells, but begged Hyder would desire me to remember, and take care of him; adding, he wanted dollars. I told Hyder to say I had only sufficient for my expences, as we never travelled with much money, and that I could procure no more till I got to Egypt; but that of what I had, I had given him a part. He, however, seemed to hope for something, as he was very active in procuring shells.

The shooting party returned by ten o'clock, with seven birds of the pheasant kind, with mottled black, or rather brown and white feathers, the neck bare, and yellow underneath, red and bare about the eyes: they also killed a hare, and two small deer, which tasted exactly like the roebuck. Fortunately for the sportsmen, it was cloudy the whole of the morning, who, however, were heartily fatigued and sore in the feet. Thermometer 98°. The Sirdar brought me another collection of shells, which contained only one worth having. I explained what I wished, and he sent the men off again. Hyder privately promised them a present, if they exerted themselves, which should not be mentioned to their master. My servant bore the climate well: he went out on a catamaran like a native, and brought me from the reef a considerable variety of madrapores, some very beautiful.

The most desirable article to the natives is

cutlery. They asked for some pencils and paper, and every kind of nick-knack. They had scarcely seen any of our European conveniences, and were much delighted with them. They learned their names, and pronounced them with great facility. The Nayib's son asked for powder and ball, to kill me an elephant. One of the pilots arrived from Dhalac: he seemed doubtful whether he could take the ship to Suakin, but wished to wait for his brother's opinion, who had been sent for.

The Banian came to me to say, that he was my servant, and would do whatever I pleased; that if I did not choose to let him manage the Captain's business, he would never go near him. I told him, I had no such wish, but desired he would prevent any underhand dealings with the pilots, to induce them to declare the voyage to Suakin impracticable. He assured me that he would. This visit gave me great satisfaction, as it assured me I possessed a sufficient influence with the pilots to induce them to speak the truth. I had been not a little astonished by an observation Captain Keys made to Mr. Macgie, that if we could not go to Suakin, we must return back to Hodeida, there being no passage between the islands above Dhalac. How this could be known to him, except from the accurate Mr. Bruce, I know not; I therefore suspected a plan to prevent our continuing our researches. Indeed, Hyder told me that the Naqueda was constantly desiring the Captain's interpreter to persuade his master that the winds were too strong for the ship to venture among the rocks of Suakin. He naturally wished his voyage should end here, that he might pocket his four hundred dollars, without any farther trouble. I was afraid our old pilot might corrupt the new ones, and therefore requested the Nayib to send him off before their arrival, which he did. I found, however, that I only got rid of half the evil.

The Nayib sent to request I would come to him, to meet Captain Keys and the pilots. I sent in answer, that I would with pleasure obey his commands, but that I did not wish, on this occasion, to meet Captain Keys, as he had nothing to do with my arrangement. They came a second time to request, that if I did not choose to come myself, I would send Mr. Salt. I now entered with them into a full explanation of my situation; that I was at liberty to go wherever I thought proper; that my wish was to go to Suakin; but before I could decide, I must consult the pilots. That I should then inform Captain Keys what my plans were; and it remained for him to settle with the men, with which matter I had no concern. That in consequence our meeting would be useless, or the attendance of any one on my part, when he waited on the Nayib. They were themselves perfectly satisfied (my landlord and the Banian), and immediately went to the Nayib. In a short time they returned with both the pilots, and a very kind message from the Nayib, in the true Asiatic style, "that he only wished to know my will to obey it; and that he had sent the people for me to do what I pleased with them."

I found the brothers equally well behaved, and intelligent. They informed me that the first part of the voyage was open sea, through which they could conduct the ship night and day, if I were not afraid. I asked if, at this time of the year, they could steer a dow day and night; they said, yes. Then I said, we should not be afraid to go on. They continued, "that at a place called Ageeg, the passage became narrow, between rocks and islands, but that the former were all above water; that it was sufficiently deep, and about a mile wide; that there was a place where we could anchor, and that a fair wind of one day would take us to Suakin." I asked, if we should find any difficulty in getting from Ageeg to Suakin, and whether they would carry us to Jidda. They said they would not go themselves, but that they would take us on the outside of a very large island, where we should be in the main sea, and could run ourselves easily to that place without assistance." I was now perfectly satisfied, and told the Nayib's messengers, that I should write to-morrow to the Captain, to inform him of my plans, and require him to make the proper arrangements with the pilots. I begged them again to express to their master how very grateful I felt for his numerous attentions to me, which I should take care to represent to all my countrymen, who might visit the Red Sea.

I sent to require a boat to carry my servant to a reef opposite the town to search for shells, which was complied with. He had not much success. The natives, in the course of the day, brought me some new species. There was a great variety of dead shells thrown on shore of a species, of which I was not able to procure living specimens: they probably came from some of the opposite islands. Money will hardly induce the natives to exert themselves. I found our landlord's name was Abou Yusuff, or Father Joseph, and he well became the title, for he had all the appearance of a jolly, good natured, Benedictine monk.

On the 8th I wrote officially to Captain Keys, informing him of my intention to go to Suakin, but that if the winds should prove too strong, I might probably go only to Ageeg, and then proceed for Jidda. He afterwards saw the Nayib. The pilots and Naqueda of the dow were there.

The Captain required the Naqueda to hire both the pilots, which he refused. He then demanded that he should give back the four hundred dollars. The Naqueda offered one hundred, or said he would hire one pilot. The Captain said that one must then go in his ship, and the dow go ahead without one. This the man positively refused, and said he would not go to Suakin. The Nayib told him, if he did not do what the Captain desired, he would put him in prison; and so the conference ended. I had this from the Banian, who was present, and was sent by the Nayib to communicate it to me. Mr. Salt and my servant caught some very beautiful small fish; they also procured a few shells.

The Captain was again sent for by the Nayib in the evening, who wished him to pay one pilot, and the Naqueda the other, but nothing definitive was settled. I had a most extraordinary answer from the Captain at night, stating, that there had been much delay by taking this passage, that we should not be able to reach Suez, and most probably not even Tor; and notifying to me that the Antelope must leave the Red Sea by the middle of August, in order to save her passage for the season. The pilot informed Hyder, that the Captain's interpreter had been talking with him, and telling him that if he went with us, he would be starved, for there was no rice on board.

I wrote a reply to Captain Keys, stating that I considered his letter as a declaration, that he would not obey the Governor General's orders, and requiring that he would communicate to me his instructions from the Bombay Government, and give me a definitive answer in regard to his intentions of obeying the Governor General, with respect to my future voyage.

About four o'clock my landlord came to me

from the Nayib, to say that the pilots were ready to go to Suakin, as I and the Captain had desired. That the Captain had been with him and refused to give two hundred dollars, (which the pilots asked, and the Nayib desired they might receive,) saying he would give but one hundred and sixty, and that if the Nayib did not make them accept this offer, that he would go back immediately to Bombay. The Nayib desired him to express to me, that the Captain, neither last night nor that day, had behaved civilly to him: that he staid there merely to assist me; that he wished to return to Arkeko, and desired to know my intentions, and when I meant to depart; and added, that he wished to have my commands to go to Arkeko. He also used an Asiatic expression, that the Nayib said "the Captain had two tongues." I expressed my extreme regret that such a circumstance should have occurred. I stated that the Captain was no servant of mine, but of great people of my country in India, who had ordered him to carry me to Suez; that I could therefore only represent to them his misconduct, when I had no doubt he would be punished. That I wished as much as possible to be gone, but that my departure in some degree depended on the Captain; that, however, I would myself with pleasure visit the Nayib, and take my leave of him in the evening, and hoped he would not stay a moment longer there to be insulted.

As soon as he retired, the Banian arrived, who confirmed what had passed at the interview, but knew nothing of the Nayib's message to me. He advised me to give something to the Nayib that night, and promise something more when I went on board the ship. I went about eight o'clock, and had merely a conference of civility. He wished to know whether I should want pilots or not. I told him I was going to write to the Captain, and his answer would decide me, and that I would positively let him know the next day. I found the Nayib, dressed in a dark India muslin, in the same place, with the same attendants, and without any arms. He confirmed all the Banian had said. I made apologies, and pleaded that all the English were not like Captain Keys. He positively refused returning to Arkeko till I departed.

I received an answer from Keys. He expressed his concern that I should suppose it possible he could intend to disobey the Governor General's orders, that he conceived they were issued under the idea that our voyage would be over long before the fifteenth of August, and that, therefore, on that day, he should positively depart on his return to India. However astonished I might be at his thus placing his conjectures in opposition to his Excellency's most positive orders, I had no means of preventing his carrying his resolution into effect; as he, however, professed his resolution to comply with any request of mine till that period, it remained for me to decide what I should do.

To continue my voyage, for the purpose of surveying the coast or visiting Suakin, was totally out of the question, as nine weeks were evidently insufficient for that purpose; I had therefore only to consider, whether, by abandoning all my plans of discovery, I could reach Suez within the time he was pleased to allow me. He had in his letter declared that it was highly improbable, and upon calculation we found it impossible. The average passage of the ships during the Egyptian expedition, was six weeks from Mocha to Cosseir, a fortnight of which took them to Jidda, as the wind is fair to Jibbel Teir. Our pilots told us we should be more than that time in getting there, and we should be obliged to stop to take in water, of which the ship could not carry a quantity more than sufficient for forty days; and also provisions of every kind, of which they did not pretend she had above two months stock on board: of bread she had not one month's. These articles are not to be procured in Egypt. The Antelope's bottom was also in a state that prevented her sailing quick. The Captain was evidently alarmed, and would not carry much sail; I could not therefore calculate on getting to Cosseir in less than eight weeks. If I staid there, I had only a week to write to Mr. Rosette, to receive his answer, to prepare a guard of camels, to pass to Kenne, and thence to secure boats to go down the Nile. This would have taken up at least six weeks; and for my safety it was necessary that the ship should still wait till I could send back intelligence of my safe arrival. Unless, therefore, I meant to deliver myself into the hands of the greatest thieves and robbers in the world, without any protection; my stay at Cosseir was out of the question; to get in a week to Suez from Cosseir was impossible; and indeed in all probability it would have been three weeks. My stay there, to make the necessary preparations, would have been at least a fortnight, and the subsequent delay about a week. Unwilling, therefore, as I, of course, was, to measure back my way, and submit to the confinement of a ship for four months, I was compelled to do so, and I determined to write in the morning to Captain Keys, directing him to go to Mocha, where I could consult with Mr. Pringle; and wait there for Captain Vashon, who would probably give me a passage to Bombay, where he would arrive with the coffee in time for me to take my passage in one of the Chinamen. By these means I should be certain of getting to England in January. The moment I quitted the Antelope she came under Captain Vashon's command.

I therefore wrote fully to Captain Keys pointing out the impracticability of my getting up to Suez, within the period he had prescribed, and the absurdity of my wandering about till that time in a rough sea. I concluded by giving him notice, that in a few days I should return to Mocha. I sent to the Nayib to say I should not want the pilots, and gave them ten dollars, as a compensation for the trouble they had in coming over. The Dola of Dhalac arrived, and paid me a visit: I suspected he brought over presents to the different men, for our landlord got two goats, one of which he gave to Mr. Salt, and the other to the Doctor. The latter had plenty of patients, but in general they were cases of debility from intermittent fevers.

Captain Keys went on board in the morning. I wrote to him, and requested two of the Europeans might assist my servant in collecting shells and madrapores, as I should have no future place to touch at, where they would be found in such variety. This was complied with immediately. In short, the Captain seemed to be in high glee at having escaped the dangers of the voyage; an idea that superseded every other; or else he expected that he should, by his politeness in future, prevent me from exercising that retaliation which was so completely in my power. The Nayib wished to persuade us to pursue our original plan of going to Suakin. The fact was, he would have got at least one hundred dollars out of the two hundred which the pilots were to have received, and he did not like to lose the money.

My servant and the men brought some very fine

specimens of madrapore, and the natives some new shells. At night we heard a most terrible uproar of women, screaming and crying: on enquiry we found that a dow had arrived from Jidda, and brought intelligence of the death of the master of one of the neighbouring houses, whose brother was in the service of the Nayib. On going out, we found the street crowded with people, all crying, as well as the women within the habitation. The tom-toms soon set them a dancing; and this continued to our great annoyance all night, with only occasional intermissions. They told us this would be continued every morning for two years; but as the town has been free from this nuisance since our arrival, and probably several people have died within the last two years, I did not give credit to their assertions.

We learned from the dow that Captain Vashon arrived at Jidda about ten days before she sailed; I hoped, therefore, he would soon get down to Mocha. The Nayib in the evening sent to request some vinegar, and something to smell to for the head-ach. I sent some Chili vinegar, and one of my silver stopper bottles, filled with volatile alkali, which were acceptable.

Early in the morning, all the women in the town were down at the water side in their best clothes, to wash themselves and the widow in the sea, after having assisted her all night in her lamentations. At the end of four months she may marry again. None of them attempted to keep their faces covered. Their dress consisted of two pieces of the striped cloths of Arabia, one worn round their middle, and another over their shoulders. Their hair was plaited, whether woolly or not: the pains taken with these plaits, when the former is the case, conquers nature, and gives a length of several inches to the hair. They wore ornaments of beads, small hoop ear-rings of gold or silver, and sequins. The dress of the men is nearly similar. The higher order wear the Arab dress, or a plain shirt and drawers of the same: the common people, a single wrapper round the middle. They use sandals, as drawn by Niebuhr. My servant and the men went off with the catamaran for the islands. The boys brought a great many shells: some were good.

Nothing particular occurred during five days; we had been chiefly employed in packing the madrapore. The air till the 18th had been much hotter, the wind rather southerly. The clouds hung over the Habesh hills, and rain on the 16th fell so near as Arkeko. It lightened much, and thunder was heard at a distance: dappled clouds covered the horizon every morning. The thermometer was never above 96°, yet the want of the usual breeze made us suffer more than if it had been 100°. The Nayib left Massowah on the 16th, and the next day sent to say he would come back, which I requested he would not. A man who was ill of the small-pox died. No wonder the disease is so fatal, as the natives confine the patients, as soon as they are seized, to a warm room. After the Nayib's departure I had no water nor any thing else sent me, and was consequently obliged to buy, which we considered as a hint that they wished us gone; the seamen were allowed water only from Arkeko, of which they complained bitterly, as having a mixture of the sea water, no more of the water of the place being allowed to be sold, except to me. I this day notified to the Captain my intention of going on board in the morning.

The day was a busy one, and I was pestered with visitors. Mr. Macgie and the sailors went on board at six, and Abou Yusuff watched me very closely lest I also should make my escape. The Banian brought me a piece of Habesh cloth, and Mr. Salt a pair of horns. We were told the Nayib had been at the wars against the Bedowees, and had driven them away, having taken one prisoner, and retaken the cattle they had driven off. He threatened to return before I went. I was very much vexed at discovering that I had lost my thermometer, a thing which could be of no value to any native. My servant was quite as much so on missing a shawl and several shirts of his own. I found living here by no means cheap, though the necessaries of life are not dear. The following is a list of several articles with their prices.

A few rhinoceros horns are to be had at 7½ dollars per frassel.

Gold per Massowah wakea, 11¾ dollars. N. B. The Mocha wakea is to the Massowah as 5 to 6; 10 wakea yield one of silver, as they say.

Civet, 3½ dollars per wakea.

Rhinoceros horns, 7½ dollars per wakea.

Elephants teeth, 22 dollars per frassel.

A good female slave, 60 dollars.

A good male ditto, according to his age, from 40 to 80 dollars.

Rice per bag of 105 lb. 5 dollars.

A rotol of gee, 2 dollars.

Fowls, 12 for a dollar.

Goats, 2 for ditto.

Sheep, 2 for ditto.

Cow, 1 for 5 dollars.

Camels, 4 to 5 dollars.

Horses, 100 dollars.

Mules, 15 to 50 dollars.

Asses, 3 for 4 dollars.

Water, 23 skins for a dollar.

Fire wood, a man's load for 3 dahab or harf (360 beads.)

Sequins do not pass current; dollars and Venetian glass beads are the only money in use; 2760 of the latter make a dollar. The subdivision is into 23 dahabs of 120 beads each.

The whole charge of the Nayib, for water, wood, and fresh provisions during our stay for the use of the ship, was sixty dollars. The people are extremely civil, and seem perfectly happy. The soldiers have each three dollars per month, which proves that that sum is adequate to maintaining a family. Many fruits and vegetables, I have no doubt, would grow here. I saw none of the former, and of the latter only a species of Solanum. From the highest to the lowest they are importunate beggars, and, from my experience I can add, occasionally thieves. The usual price of a house is one dollar per month; yet my landlord was ever asking for something, and seemed hardly satisfied with the ten dollars which I gave him for the twenty-six days I had occupied his house. I saw several Abyssinians, and had much conversation with them respecting their country. The account that they gave me was found afterwards by Mr. Salt to be in many respects inaccurate, and must be uninteresting to the public, as I have given, in another part of my travels, the observations which were made by him and two other gentlemen during a residence of several months with the Ras Welleta Selasse, in the province of Tigré.

At five in the morning I escaped in the Captain's boat from all my beggars, except from Abou Yusuff, and the Banian, who determined to attend me to the ship, which had already quitted the harbour. The land breeze was fresher than usual, and a considerable swell came from the northward, but the Captain continued his course, and it was two hours before we overtook him, when the sun was already extremely powerful. I gave the Banian a shawl, in return for many little presents he had made me, though I knew that he had handsomely profited by purchasing every article I wanted for my table. He had been extremely attentive, and deserved a reward. He had some difference with the Captain before he left the vessel, but I did not enquire into the cause. I sent a sword by him to the Nayib, as a last proof of my regard, with many wishes for his health and prosperity. He and Abou Yusuff at length departed, I believe, well satisfied with the presents made them. We had already stretched out a considerable distance from Massowah. The breeze was pleasant, and after rounding the point of the shoal, we anchored in Antelope bay, within a quarter of a mile of Valentia Island, by four o'clock. The Captain wished Mr. Maxfield to survey it, and I consented to stay two days for that purpose. Mr. Salt and he went out in the evening to measure a base. It was so sultry that I slept on the deck.

The next day Mr. Maxfield was too ill to go out; Mr. Salt went to take some bearings, and I obtained a boat and some sailors to attend my servant in collecting shells. The heat was very great, and my situation extremely unpleasant. As Mr. Maxfield was too unwell to continue the survey of the island, I determined to depart the next day. A great quantity of biscuit was this day condemned and thrown overboard. I heard that the salt provisions were in an equally bad state, and that there was only a small quantity of spirits on board, it was therefore fortunate that we did not continue our voyage; yet the Antelope was reported to me as being ready for sea.

We weighed anchor with a pleasant breeze from the W. N. W. The dow went a-head after clearing Antelope bay she kept farther out from the land. The man at the mast head, about half after nine, called out that there was shoal water a-head: no notice was taken by the officer of the watch, and we passed over the identical shoal, which we had in going up observed and laid down. Fortunately for us there were three fathom and a quarter on it, so we passed in safety. It is only a few hundred yards in extent. Our dow was of much use. We sailed all night; light airs and pleasant. I slept on the deck.

We continued along shore till night, confirming our chart by new bearings. We found it as accurate as we could expect. A light breeze; little sail carried. At night still less.

June 23.—At day-light Jibbel Zeigur was E¼S.; the Abyssinian land hardly visible through the haze. At nine Jibbel Aroe bore from E¾S. to S.E¼E. We passed it before dark, leaving on our right the white rocks, which we had seen from Bunder Baileul. We found that instead of a cluster of small rocks, the Aroes consisted of one large island, with five or six to E. and S. of it of different sizes; the passage was seven miles wide at least, and there was apparently deep water close to the shore and rocks. We then made with a freshening breeze for the Arabian coast, which was visible, but did not reach it till near twelve, when we cast anchor. There was a considerable swell.

June 24.—At six we were again under sail and coasting down; by seven saw the town of Mocha: before twelve came to an anchor, closer in than we were before. The swell was much less than when the wind blew from the south. We were much surprised at the colours not being hoisted on the factory, but a boat coming on board, we learned that

Mr. Pringle was well. I requested the boat to go on shore, which was ordered, and I landed about two o'clock. Mr. Pringle was excessively astonished to see me, believing me dead, from my flag not being hoisted, and there being no salute. I soon explained to him the cause, and took possession of the upper apartments at the factory. We found here an American ship which came from Salem near Boston, for a cargo of coffee.

To my great astonishment I was informed this morning that two English boys belonging to the Antelope, who had been left here in consequence of illness, had deserted to the Dola. I immediately sent my servant to them to enquire the reason, and to try to persuade them to return. Their answer was, that the evening before they had been sent for by Captain Keys, who asked them if they were not quite well; they replied, nearly so. He then said he supposed they were tired of being idle on shore, and would be glad to return to the ship. They said they had not been idle, and that they liked best to be on shore, because they got plenty to eat. "Very well, gentlemen," he replied, "you will be pleased to go on board to-morrow morning, and I will give you a note to Mr. Hall, who shall punish you for this." This, they said, decided them, and in the night they got over the wall. One fell, and was severely hurt. Both had the liver disease, and must inevitably perish in this climate; I therefore consulted with Mr. Pringle, and we determined to do all we could to get them back. Captain Keys sent for my ship servant, and gave him a lecture for presuming to obey me in going to the boys without his permission. He also declared his resolution of visiting the Dola himself. We were sorry for this, but conceived we had no right to interfere: as his threats had driven them away, it was not very likely that any declaration of his would bring them back. They could have no confidence in the promise of a Captain of the Bombay marine, after a transaction that took place during the expedition to Egypt. A man was delivered up by the Arabs to the Captain of the Cruizer, on his pledging his honour that he should not be punished; yet, as soon as he had him in his power, he tied him up, and flogged him in the presence of the very people to whom he had made the engagement. A promise is by the Arabs considered as most sacred, and the laws of hospitality bound them to protect the man; their indignation, therefore, was excited beyond all bounds. The Banian, who attended Captain Keys, informed me that the boys repeated this story, and told him they would never go back.

When I applied to the Dola to let me and Mr. Pringle see them, it was positively refused, though in the morning it had been acceded to; he pretended, that as the Captain had seen them, it was unnecessary that any one else should. As a last resource, I wrote to Mr. Pringle's interpreter, the Hadgi, who was at Sanna, to make the strongest remonstrances to the Vizier, to claim them as my servants, and to represent that the offence was greatly aggravated by their being taken from the factory which was more immediately under the protection of the Imaum. I likewise desired that he would obtain for me a definitive answer, whether they were determined to persevere in their present system of encouraging our sailors to desert, that I might, on my return, be able to represent the case properly to the India Government. The extent of this evil calls loudly for remedy, and nothing can in my mind be easier, as a single ship would oblige them to restore every renegado. Some years ago the French bombarded the town, in consequence of the Dola's not paying a debt of seventy thousand dollars. They first fired on his house, where they killed several persons; and afterwards on a Friday (the sabbath of the Mussulmauns), threw a shell into the great mosque. This brought the Dola to his senses, and the cash was paid. He even grew so polite as to lower the duties from three to two and a half per cent. Our character certainly suffers very considerably in the eyes of the native powers for having so long submitted to the insult.

The system of decoying away seamen in a Mussulmaun port, which is so very serious an inconvenience to all Christian ships, is not done from any religious motive, but from an idea that all Christians understand the working of great guns, and to this office they are all destined. In the time of Niebuhr the pay of a renegado was one dollar and a half per month; it was then raised to two dollars and a half: and within the last ten months has been encreased to four dollars, in consideration of the high price of every article. The Captain of the renegadoes is an Italian, who, thirty years ago, came here in the command of a native vessel from India: he turned Mussulmaun, sold the vessel and cargo, and shared the profits of his villainy with the Dola of that time. He is now the active instrument in inducing others to desert their religion; he watches for them on the pier, and invites them to the Jew's town, where spirits are to be purchased. If intoxication follow, they are carried in that state to the Dola's, whence it is not easy to make a retreat. A shew of liberality is kept up by permitting their friends to see them for the first three days, during which time they are never circumcised, but the most liberal offers are made; and the temptation of free access to the women can seldom be resisted by the sailor. Repentance soon overtakes them from poverty, and the deprivation of their usual comforts.

They are not much troubled on the score of their new religion, though at first they are obliged to learn the necessary prayers, and the forms of prostration and ablution. These are acquired at Moosa, a town about thirty miles up the country. On their return to Mocha no compulsion is used to make them attend the mosque. At present there are only four white renegadoes, though numbers deserted from our fleet during their stay here. It was then thought necessary to conciliate the Yemen Government; and consequently, though threats were used by several officers, whose men deserted, yet nothing was done, and the Arabs were confirmed in their insolence by our forbearance. One man deserted from Captain Vashon during the time he was here. He was immediately demanded from the Dola, who in very haughty terms refused to deliver him up, advising the Lieutenant, who delivered the message, to keep his men on board, if he wished them not to turn Mussulmauns. He was permitted to see the man, who on being asked why he took such a step, turned away without condescending to give any answer. Captain Vashon, though extremely indignant, did not feel himself justified in resorting to violence, and very properly avoided using any threat, which he did not mean to carry into effect. I wish every officer had done the same, and our character would have been more respected in Yemen.

I heard there had been great confusion on board the Antelope since our arrival; yet Captain Keys tranquilly staid on shore: on the 2d, indeed, he went on board to punish two men, one of whom he immediately sent on board an American vessel which came in after our arrival. By what authority he did this it would be difficult to discover, as I can hardly conceive that a power is vested in the officers of the Company's marine to transport his Majesty's subjects. The man came to me, and informed me that he was a deserter from the Lancaster, Sir Roger Curtis. Another of the Company's apprentices escaped, as I learned, on board the American. The Captain of which said, very properly, that he believed he was there, but without his knowledge or consent, and that he wished the Antelope's people would find him. They searched the ship, but without success. She sailed on the 4th of July, and with her two of his Majesty's subjects.

Another of the seamen, also a deserter from a King's ship, fled to the Dola, and became a Mussulmaun. He, and the one who sailed in the American, were the two that were on shore with me at Massowah. Mr. Hall went to see him, but was only abused.

The heat of the weather was more oppressive than I had hitherto experienced; the winds were northerly, and extremely warm, though the thermometer was only 92° and 94°. I could bear no covering at night, and was so completely relaxed, that I was obliged to take a few glasses of wine. The swell in the road is much less than when the southerly winds prevail. The rains fell every day to the northward, and on the mountains of the interior, but not a drop reached Mocha. We obtained grapes, which were tolerable, and some very indifferent figs and peaches.

Since my arrival here my suspicions at Massowah were fully confirmed. The masters of the dow, on being interrogated by Mr. Pringle, declared that Abdulcauder was sent to them by the Captain to advise them not to procure a pilot, to represent that if they did not, I should be obliged to go back to Mocha, and that they would get their four hundred dollars for nothing; on the contrary, if they went on, they would not only have to pay one hundred for a pilot, but would incur the danger and expence of a long voyage with a contrary wind. Abdul cauder admitted that he was sent, and that he did deliver the message. I found also from them, that he declared his objections to the voyage before he left Mocha, saying, all he wanted was to go straight to Suez. The dow's bargain was to hire only one pilot at Massowah; consequently Captain Keys' demand of hiring two, was unjust.

I was again informed that two more boys had run away from the Antelope. They were two of the youngest apprentices, and swam away in the night. This was the more astonishing, as two sentinels were mounted every night. Mr. Pringle represented in the strongest terms to Captain Keys the shameful degree of negligence that must have taken place, to enable those boys to escape; and advised him, at any rate, to punish the sentinels, if he did not choose to go on board and look after his ship himself. He said that he had done all he could by ordering an officer's watch; that he conld not punish the sentinels, as he should then be obliged to put the officer of the watch under an arrest. There was no replying to so military and conclusive an argument. Mr. Hall came on shore early, and, on receiving the Captain's instructions, went to the Dola. He saw one of the boys, and asked him if he had turned Mussulmaun. He said, yes; on which Mr. Hall drew forth a pistol and attempted to shoot him. Fortunately it was not primed. The guards rushed on him and poor

Devagee, who was frightened out of his life, and secured them. The Dola only said, "Carry that madman to Mr. Pringle." Had he wounded the boy, his own death would probably have instantly followed; and even the factory might have been in danger, as we had no intimation of his intention, and the gates were left open.

To our very great delight the Fox frigate came in sight early in the morning, and towards noon was at anchor in the roads. I wrote to Captain Vashon, merely stating that Captain Keys's conduct had been such as to oblige me to abandon my voyage; that I would explain to him the whole if he would send off a boat, and ended, by requesting him to give me a passage to Bombay. The boat immediately arrived, with a very kind note, offering me every accommodation the Fox could afford, and saying he should wait dinner for me. He requested to see Mr. Pringle on business, who therefore accompanied me on board.* I found that he had come down from Jidda, in consequence of the Wahabees successes. They had taken Yambo, and were besieging Medina, which must soon be starved into a surrender. The Sheriffe, much alarmed for Mecca and Jidda, the only two places remaining in his possession, came down to the latter place to see Captain Vashon, to whom he had applied for assistance; and particularly requested, that the Fox would accompany his fleet to retake Yambo. Adversity had lowered his pride, and he was all politeness and attention; yet, during the Egyptian expedition, he had treated Admiral Blanket with the greatest insolence, and no Englishman could land there without being insulted.

Captain Vashon did not conceive it prudent to comply with any of his requests, but said he would with the utmost expedition communicate them to the Government of India. The application had at his desire been made in writing, signed by the Sheriffe and Pacha, who were, I believe, not a little disconcerted by his answer. The delay will, I suspect, be fatal to them. Provisions were already so scarce at Jidda, that the Sheriffe could not supply the Fox; and as the Wahabees were in possession of the whole country, they could only be procured by sea. The Janisaries from Yambo and Cosseir had come down thither, the latter of which places the Mamelukes had seized, who prudently sent away the Turkish soldiers; for if the enemy intended starving them out, this increase of force will only hasten their ruin. Captain Vashon brought down a man to buy rice, but the quantity to be procured at Mocha is but small. I proposed to Captain Vashon to let the Antelope return to India with his dispatches, as she was of no farther use to me; and I thought the sooner she was gone the better, as she was daily losing her men. He approved of my plan, and it was decided that I should resign my nominal command the next day, and that she should be ordered off as soon as our letters were finished.

Captain Vashon came on shore in the morning, to whom I communicated all that had passed. I wrote officially to give up the vessel, and notified the same to Captain Keys, at the same time requiring the assistance of the apprentice Thomas Smith, who had acted as my servant during the voyage. This he complied with; and here ended all my connections with the Antelope. As I had much to represent to the Government at Bombay, which could not be done by letter, and, as I thought it advisable that no misrepresentations should go abroad previously to my arrival there, I requested Captain Vashon would order Captain Keys to give

Mr. Salt a passage, in order to deliver safely my dispatches to Mr. Duncan, and forward those for his Excellency the Governor General. With this he complied.

A singular circumstance occurred that evening. The Italian renegado came to Mr. Pringle, and earnestly requested that he would try to induce the two last boys not to stay at the Dola's, as their situation would be wretched. This he would have never dared to do without the Dola's consent; and it seems an additional proof of the idea I entertained, that religion had nothing to do with their receiving deserters. These boys were too young to be of any use, and he would be glad not to pay them the four dollars each per month for doing nothing. The Dola seemed considerably alarmed that day: during our dinner all the guns on the batteries were shotted. A portion of his fears may be attributed to the Fox's having moved this morning much closer to the northern fort.

One of Captain Vashon's Maltese marines deserted to the Dola. He was perfectly drunk, and refused to return with the officer. Captain Vashon applied to Mr. Pringle, as Resident, for his opinion respecting the effect it might have on the India Company's trade, if he should deem it eligible to support the dignity of the British flag, by recurring to force to obtain the whole of the renegadoes. The reply was indefinite: that he thought after the ships were loaded it would be of little consequence, so far as the coffee trade went, as that only amounted to 1700 and odd bales per annum at an average of the last ten years, and it might be procured elsewhere; but that a very large import of India goods took place annually; and how far that might be injured he could not venture to say. Surely Mr. Pringle might have recollected that the Imaum or his subjects procured the money to pay for the articles, only by the sale of their coffee, and that, consequently, the one trade would follow the other, whether to Loheia, Hodeida, or Aden. Captain Vashon sent on board the Antelope, and took out four men whom the officers pointed out as being suspected by them to have deserted from King's ships. One fellow who has turned Mussulmaun, broke out of the hospital, and, as it is said by himself, a man was killed in the affray. He however sent to me to beg a Bible. I complied, and thought it my duty to write to him, warning him of the criminality of his conduct. I received a long answer, in which he told me he could now be as good a Christian as before, and indeed that he had more time to pay his respects to God Almighty. The two unfortunate boys, that were left here, are recovered from the effects of their change, and removed into the Dola's house, where they are particularly well treated. They are to be put into the cavalry: but when this Dola departs, his successor will probably use them like the rest, and wretched will be their fate. I hope Government will take some steps to assert the dignity of the British flag, and recover to their country those, whose youth may, in some degree, palliate their desertion.

The man above mentioned had been up at Moosa, and came down, without leave, to beg some medicine from me. He had applied to the Dola of the place, who told him, that if he prayed as often as he did, he would not be ill. The man looked wretchedly, and told me he was afraid I was right in saying he should soon repent it. One of the boys who fled from the factory was very ill with the liver complaint, and extremely low spirited, constantly reproaching his companion for having persuaded him to take such a step. They were all to set off in a few days for Sana to be shewn to the Imaum. The change of climate, with bad food, will probably soon end them. Sana is extremely unhealthy to Europeans and natives of the Tehama. It was probably their residence there, and journey through the mountains, that laid the foundation of those diseases that carried Mr. Niebuhr's companions to the grave.

Mr. Salt sailed on the 9th in the Antelope, for Bombay, with a strong breeze from the N. W. He took with him letters for Mr. Duncan, in which I officially forwarded to him charges against Captain Keys. I also sent a detail of all that had passed, together with copies of the correspondence between me and Keys, to Major Shawe, to be laid before his Excellency the Governor General.

Captain Vashon proposed to go down to Aden for a fortnight, and, as I felt myself extremely relaxed, I wished to try the air of the more open sea, and accepted his invitation to accompany him.

On the 15th I went on board the Fox to breakfast. It was however calm, and we did not sail till noon. We passed the straits at seven, and found a most pleasing difference in the climate. It was cool, except when a strong gust of wind came off from the promontory. In the night it became nearly calm.

We were off Cape St. Anthony. A brig was in sight at day light, to which we gave chase. She proved to be an American from Salem, but last from the Isle of France. The calm continued most part of the day, with a heavy swell from the eastward of south. Still the air was cooler than at Mocha, and I felt myself most sensibly relieved.

July 18.—With variable winds we got by four

o'clock to an anchor in Aden roads, distant from Fortified Island about a mile. The swell was much more considerable than I could have expected, as the wind came right over the land. The town of Aden has a most miserable appearance from the sea. It is nearly a heap of ruins, out of which two minarets and two mosques rear their whitewashed heads. The rocky peninsula, on which the town is situated, has all the appearance of the half of a volcano, the crater of which is covered by the sea, and on the edge of which lies the town; the rocks rise to a very considerable height. On the summits are numerous small square forts; and a second ridge towards the bay is covered with the ruins of lines and forts. Fortified Island was also covered with works, so as to resemble the hill forts of India. It must have been impregnable; and a very little trouble would render it so again.

That the trade of Arabia should at present have quitted Aden with its excellent harbour, for Mocha, an open road, liable to very heavy gales of wind, can only be attributed to the sovereign of Mocha having been till lately in possession of the whole of the coffee country; but as his kingdom is torn in pieces by the Wahabees, Aden will probably recover its former importance, and again become the mart of an extensive trade, as it was in the time of the author of Periplus; who most certainly designated it under the name of Eudaimon. It is the only good sea-port in Arabia Felix, and has the great advantage over every harbour, within the straits, that it can be quitted at all seasons, while it is almost impossible to repass Bab-el-Mandeb during the S. W. monsoon. The present heaps of ruins and solitary minarets, give but little idea of the splendour which Marco Polo describes it as possessing in the thirteenth century; any more than the humble Sultaun of a little territory will bear a comparison with the Mussulmaun chieftain who could bring into the field 30,000 horse.

Aden must then have been at its highest state of prosperity, and was, probably, from the commercial convenience it afforded, the capital of Arabia Felix. Its decline seems to have been gradual, for in 1513, Don Alphonso Albuquerque found the fortifications sufficiently strong to twice resist his attack, although trade had in a great degree fled to Mocha and Loheia.

Aden appears to have tranquilly remained under its Arabian masters till this period, when hostilities between the Soldan of Egypt and the Portuguese, having induced the former to bring ships across the desert, and embark them on the Red Sea, a naval war took place between the two powers, and its excellent harbour rendered Aden an object of great importance to each party. In 1516 it was attacked by the fleet of Selim, who had conquered the Soldan of Egypt; but without success: however, in 1539 Soolimaun Basha, when proceeding to attack the Portuguese in India, treacherously seized the sovereign of Aden, and got possession of the place. The fortifications were greatly increased by the Turks, and some of their enormous pieces of cannon were mounted on the walls. It was considered as a place of such importance, that so late as 1610, when Sir Henry Middleton was there, it had a Basha, as Governor, and the walls were still very strong.

As the power of the Turks gradually declined, the Arabians, by degrees, threw off their yoke; and in 1708 Aden was found by the French in the possession of an Arab prince. The fortifications were in ruins, and the baths were the only places which, by their rich marbles, bore any marks of ancient magnificence. These have now totally disappeared, and not a single piece of cannon defends the walls. The Sultaun has a small tract of country belonging to him, which he has hitherto defended from the Wahabees. He is much attached to the English, and offered to hold his country under them; at the same time giving a proof of his sincerity, by admitting the whole army of Colonel Murray within his walls.

Banians from Mocha reside here, to carry on the trade with Berbera, and purchase the myrrh and gum arabic, which is still brought hither by the Samaulies, and pays to the Sultaun a duty of three per cent.

An American was in the harbour, on board of which a son of the Honourable Mr. Goodhues, a senator of the United States, was supercargo. Mr. Pringle had written to him by me; I forwarded the letter, with an invitation to come on board the Fox.

By day-break I went with Captain Vashon on shore, to look out for a place to pitch our tents. We found a tolerable one on the ruins of the houses near one of the rocks. The Sultaun's house is a very wretched one externally; all the others seemed of basket-work and matting. The wind freshened very much as the sun rose, and by eleven it blew so strong that we were obliged to let go another anchor. It was fortunately right off the land, but the hills formed eddies, and caused the gusts to be very violent. Mr. Goodhues came early and staid the whole day. In the evening it lulled, and the tents were pitched on shore.

July 20.—The wind was very hot, but at night I returned on shore to sleep. It was extremely unpleasant from the heat. The Sultaun came in at noon. He always comes down for some time at this season; for what purpose I know not.

On the morning of the 21st I left the shore for the ship. The wind freshened every morning from the W. or S. and blowed all day hot like an oven. At night it lulled, but too late to enable us to go on shore. The nights were cool and pleasant, but there was a considerable swell. At this season, Aden is altogether a most unpleasant place. Grapes and pomegranates are to be had in plenty, but no vegetables. The beef had hitherto been bad, but we were promised some good bullocks, that had been sent for by the Sultaun.

The wind continued as usual; except that on the night of the 22d, so violent a gale commenced all at once, that every body expected our anchors would have been brought home. The heat and dust were insufferable. The swell also was very great during the day. As, therefore, living on shore was impossible, and we had no particular business at this place, it was determined that we should return on the 27th to Mocha. A very great variety of dead shells were thrown upon the beach: but there are no shoals, and we were unable to procure live specimens. I purchased some from the crew of the Fox, which they got at Jidda, and had several given me by Captain Vashon and Lieutenant Flint. The boats were sent out every morning when the weather would permit, but with very little success. At first, for some reason, the natives sent us off bad water; but on strong remonstrances we procured as good as could be wished.

The pier does not extend far enough out, for the boats to reach it at low water: this is extremely inconvenient. The Sultaun procured us excellent bullocks; he was himself the sole dealer in these articles. He was extremely civil, sent Captain Vashon and me a present of a cow, two sheep, and seven goats, and invited us on shore, saying, he had horses, &c. at our service. The limes were excellent, and in profusion. Fire wood is to be obtained. The climate is healthy, and I suspect we were particularly unfortunate in having it so unpleasant. Our tents were blown down and torn to pieces.

July 27.—Yesterday the wind was so violent that no boat put off after the early part of the morning. One that went on shore was nearly swamped in returning. My servant went out on an ass, and procured me another plant of the balsam of Mecca, and some seeds. At seven in the evening it suddenly fell calm, and a light sea breeze sprung up. Last night it began to blow at half past one; but, fortunately, this morning it became moderate, which enabled us to get off our tents, bullocks, fruit and water. Towards evening it again blew so fresh that we left our anchor behind us when we weighed for sea.

July 28.—A ship was in sight early, bearing from the Straits: we gave chace, and neared her considerably, till it fell calm. We suspected her to be a French privateer, and cleared for action. She hoisted American colours, but immediately took them down again. At night she was out of sight.

August 2.—The vessel we chased steered in so strange a way that we did not wish to leave her, and, consequently were considerably delayed. On the 29th she was visible in the morning, but astern. On our firing a gun to leeward, and hoisting our colours, she took no notice, but continued her way. The winds were extremely light from the south, with frequent calms. The moment we passed the straits, the change in the atmosphere was most singular: the heat became so great that the cabin was insupportable: and the prickly heat came out in one night with more violence than I ever before experienced. The chace for these two last days has been ahead, and this morning we perceived she had run to the N. of Mocha roads. We got into an excellent birth off the north fort at six this evening. The heat had been so oppressive that I determined to go on shore, though the gates were shut, and therefore landing at the pier was out of the question. We got as near the beach as possible, to the south of the town. The water is so shallow that the men were obliged to carry me a considerable distance. We got in at a little wicket, which is kept open till eleven. Mr. Pringle had given over expecting me, but my old comfortable quarters had been prepared for my reception.

At length the ship came into harbour, and proved to be an American, last from the Isle of France.

I found that, on our coming in sight, all the boys that had run away from the Antelope had been sent up to Moosa, lest we should persuade them to desert back again. They were in a wretched state, and sorely repented the steps they had taken. They had not the indulgences of other Mussulmauns, but were considered as slaves, and obliged to do as they were ordered for their four dollars a month, a pittance scarcely sufficient to keep them alive; yet were the Dola who converted them to be recalled, even this would be diminished. I received the following reply to my application to the Imaum: "That old customs could not be altered; that no man had ever been given up who had applied to the Dola; that he knew the English were very powerful, and wished to do every where just as they pleased; but that, with the blessing of God, nothing would happen."

By the American that came last, a letter was received from the Banian, who went down to the Isle of France, to obtain the repayment of the money he had advanced for several years as rent of the French factory. He took with him two Arabs, and I strongly suspect that they were sent to make application to the French Government there, for assistance against the English. The above speech of the Imaum seems to confirm it.

I learned that several applications were made at the American's ship for the letter, and that they expressed the greatest alarm lest Devagee should get hold of it. The letter of course could not be procured by us, but the contents were published in part; highly extolling the French power, and stating that they had taken sixteen sail of our China fleet, and brought them into the Isle of France. This could only have been said to encourage his employers. The report was contradicted by all the Americans, to the great displeasure of the Dola.

Another circumstance confirmed my suspicions respecting the application to the Isle of France. The Americans have been supposed by the Arabs to be friends of the French, and have been frequently spoken to as such, asking them if they were not so, and assuring them that the Arabs all were, and wished to see the French back again.

Some very fine specimens of the shells of this shore were procured by Abdullah, a servant of Mr. Pringle, and two boys that went out with him. I employed myself in sorting and packing my shells, and other curiosities, for Europe. Botanising was out of the question, from the intense heat of the climate: rarely is the thermometer under 90° day or night, and generally it was 92° or 94°. The wind was frequently southerly, more especially towards the middle of August, when the sun became vertical; at other times it was calm for hours together.

Mr. Pringle requested me to visit a Seid called Sidi Mahomed Akil, a man of very considerable property, who had the best house in Mocha. He was a Wahabee, and much hated by the Dola. Though occasionally there, he was a native of Morabat, where his wives lived: he had also houses at Jidda, Muscat, and somewhere on the Malabar coast. He had married a relation of the Imaum, but not liking her, sent her back the next morning, with her dowry. As I wished much to see an Arab house, I complied with Mr. Pringle's request to visit the Seid. The house was lighted up; and as he had notice of my visit, every thing was in the best possible order. He met me at the door, and hurried me from one flight of narrow steps to another, till at length we reached two very pleasant wooden rooms on the summit of the house, the sides of which were composed of venetian blinds: they were carpeted, and had English elbow chairs covered with cushions.

We were served with sherbet spiced with nutmegs, and afterwards with coffee, scented with cloves. We abused the Dola most cordially; and as the Seid had just come from Jidda, we afterwards fell on the Sheriffe. He seemed to think, that however the Sheriffe might resist for a time, nothing but a strong external assistance could prevent his being ultimately starved into a surrender. The force of the Turks was estimated at about

1,000; these are superior to any Arabs, and would be quite sufficient to defend him from the Wahabees. The Seid mentioned that he was going to Bombay, and hoped I would there assist him in obtaining some favour he wished from Government. I told him I had no such power; but as I should be at Mr. Duncan's, I would willingly obtain him an opportunity of making his own application.

The conversation became more free than I expected from an Arab. He laughed about the women, and asked me if I wished to become acquainted with all the secrets of the harem. I said, certainly. He then said he would give me a book which would answer that purpose. From what he afterwards said, it must much resemble a work of Peter Aretin, well known in Europe. He however forgot his promise: other things intervened, and I never got the book. The next morning, he sent me a history, and a collection of fables. He had a library of some hundred volumes, chiefly polemical, and among others, a most beautiful Koran in Persian and Arabic characters, written on vellum. The pages that faced each other, had the same sentences in each language; the whole was richly ornamented. He valued it at two hundred and fifty dollars. The rooms below, that I saw, were of a good size, and were filled with many nick-knacks which he had picked up in his different voyages. On my taking leave, we had rose water thrown on our handkerchiefs. He conducted me back to the door. There cannot be a stronger instance of the timidity of this Government, than its permitting such a man to live in the town; he is in avowed correspondence with the Sheriffe of Abou Arish, and, through him, with the Wahabee Chief, Jund. Possibly, however, the Dola may have been making terms for himself. He was only continued in his office because his successor was sent to Beit-el-Tahih, where the Wahabees were making rapid encroachments. He found, however, that he could not resist them, and has returned to Sanna, saying, "that as there were many outgoings and few comings in, it was useless to stay." He may now resume his appointment to the Government of Mocha.

On the 14th of August, the Banian of the Nayib of Massowah arrived on his own affairs. As he was in perfect safety, it was more easy to make him speak freely. He spoke of the Nayib as a most excellent man, but allowed that he was much controlled by his brothers, and those about them, who were very great rascals; and he confirmed what I had before heard, that, immediately after my departure, they had obliged him to give up to them a great proportion of the presents I had made him. The poor Banian gave a melancholy account of his distress after he quitted the vessel to return to Massowah. He had no water with him, and could not drink any which was contaminated by having passed through the hands of Christians.

He informed me that since my departure, the Aboona of Abyssinia had died, and that fifty people had arrived thence, on their way to Egypt, to fetch another; a circumstance extremely agreeable to every body at Massowah, as they were respectable people, and spent a great deal of money. The Nayib receives one hundred ounces of gold; but the Janisaries, not existing, cannot receive forty ounces, as Mr. Bruce asserts, though they possibly did so, in much more ancient times, when the power of the Porte was unbroken. The Ascarri, who may be considered as their successors, receive nothing, as the Banian most solemnly declared.

The Nayib also claims, and receives, all the horses and mules belonging to the messengers. I was much gratified by finding that the Abyssinians had desired the Banian to enquire if there were any English vessel at Mocha that would undertake, for a handsome reward, to convey them to Suez, and bring back the Aboona. It shews a flattering opinion of our national character.

In a conversation at Massowah with my landlord, Abou Yusuff, the assertion of Mr. Bruce, that no one would be permitted to enter Abyssinia by that place, had been confirmed. I asked the Banian his opinion, and was surprised to find that he positively asserted the contrary, and that, to his knowledge, the Nayib would have no objection. I enquired if there would be any danger in the journey. He said not the least; that he would be answerable that the Nayib should place any one in the King's presence at Gondar in perfect safety. I then asked what the Nayib would take to do so, finding horses, mules, guards, &c. from Massowah to Gondar? He said, four hundred dollars; and, on my repeating the question, said, he would himself be responsible for it, and would, if I pleased, give it me under his hand. I had no reason to doubt his assertions, yet I could not help suspecting, that the brothers of the Nayib would attempt to extort presents from any unprotected traveller.

My friend Seid Mahommed Akil got into an unfortunate dispute with Captain Vashon, to whom he had applied to permit two native vessels, bound for Cannanore, to sail without delay. He declared they were both his, and gave a certificate under his hand that they were so. They were accordingly permitted to depart. He next applied for leave to sail in his own dow, which was also complied with, on his pledging himself that he had no specie on board except his own. The very morning of his departure several Banians went to Mr. Pringle, and informed him that all the Surat merchants' agents had sent specie by him, and even brought a list of the bags with their private marks, and to whom they belonged. Of this Mr. Pringle sent instant notice to Captain Vashon.

The dow had actually quitted the harbour, but boats were sent after her, and a shot fired. She took no notice of this, but a second went right over her, and brought her to. People from the ship were sent on board her, but the wind and current rendered it impossible to get her along side of the Fox. The Seid went on board to Captain Vashon, and complained greatly, declaring he had no cash but his own, (the money was in two bags, the outer one with his name, the inner with the true direction). The information received was too positive for Captain Vashon to mind what he said; the dow was therefore ordered along side with him on board her. By the negligence of the warrant officer on board her, the dow got among the others in the harbour, and the Seid escaped to the shore. He immediately applied to the Dola for assistance to protect the vessel, and complained heavily of the British Captain's conduct. The Council met, and sent to request Mr. Pringle would come to them, which he did. The Seid stood out that he had no money but his own; and Mr. Pringle declared he would prove the contrary. He produced the list, and the tables were completely turned. The Dola said the money must be relanded, as it had not paid him the half per cent. duty on the export. Mr. Pringle said he had no idea that Captain Vashon would permit this. The Dola remonstrated and said she had been detained in the port, which was an insult to the Imaum. This Mr. Pringle denied. The Dola said the whole sea from Perim to Camaran belonged to the Imaum. This Mr. Pringle ridiculed in the strongest terms, and warned him that he had better take care what he was about, as it might lead to hostilities between the two countries.

A circumstance which I had omitted to mention in its proper place, led however to a different determination. The Fox, a few days before, had been driven on shore in consequence of her anchor coming home, but fortunately the ground was soft. It lulled immediately afterwards, and the tide was rising; she therefore escaped with the loss of her rudder only, and was in safe anchorage by night. The rudder was found the next day with only the iron work damaged. A forge was erected on shore to repair this, and it was in part completed when the dispute took place. An officer and some Europeans were on shore to superintend it. Captain Vashon fully perceived, the moment the dow got close to the shore, that he could not without open hostilities secure her removal. From the unprotected state of the Europeans on shore, and the incapacity of his ship to go to sea, he was induced to abandon her, and accordingly withdrew all his men by signal. As soon as the Dola learnt this, he became extremely valiant, and ordered twenty soldiers and an officer on board the dow. These received two dollars each from the Seid, and the officer ten. On enquiring what he was to do if the English soldiers resisted, (they very well knew that all had been withdrawn two hours before this time) he was told gravely, he was to fire on them, and use the power put into his hands.

Mr. Pringle then interfered in the name of the Honourable Company, and demanded that the treasure might be landed and examined. This was done: and, of course the bags he had described were found. Captain Vashon had mentioned to Mr. Pringle the certificate respecting the Cananore ships belonging to the Seid, and was assured it was a gross falsity, accordingly he gave the paper to Mr. Pringle to shew the Council, thereby to prove what a rascal the Seid was. On its being produced, his confusion was very great, and he attempted to deny his hand writing, his signature being in English characters; Mr. Pringle, however, proved it, by producing a great many other papers signed by him in the same manner, with his signature in Arabic underneath. He was now completely convicted, and received a severe reprimand from the Bas Kateb and Kadi, the other two members in Council. Since this transaction the Seid declares he will not go to Bombay, and has been proposing to the Americans to take him to the Isle of France. I presume he is now so angry with the English, that he wishes to get assistance against them from that place. The Americans having asked him one thousand rupees for his passage, which he would not pay, I afterwards heard that he determined upon sailing in his own dow for Muscat.

When the Fox was aground, application was made to the Imaum's minister for their boats, which was positively refused; and we were subsequently informed that he expressed his hopes she would not get off, as then he should obtain her guns and powder. This expectation was in consequence of a claim made here, that all wrecks belong to the Imaum. The Forté frigate was, on a similar occasion, given to the Sheriffe of Mecca by Admiral Blanket: this they consider as a precedent. In this, however, he would have been mistaken. She would not have gone to pieces; and a battery with two hundred men would have commanded the town, and secured a safe depot for her stores. She was ready for sea before the 24th, the day fixed by the merchants for the departure of their vessels; nor did she make any more water in the twenty four hours, than before the accident.

On the 23d I went on board, with my servants, and was received by Captain Vashon with the usual salute. For several days past I had been extremely indisposed, which I believe was chiefly owing to drinking some French claret brought by the last American. The heat of the weather too had been very oppressive, and I was rejoiced to try a change of air. Mr. Pringle dined with us, and took his leave.

We did not sail till the 25th. We passed the Straits that night, and were the next day overtaken by a severe squall. Not one ship had put herself under convoy, or received a single order. However, the ship, the brig, and the two dows laden with coffee for Mr. Forbes, sailed at the same time, and Captain Vashon determined to see them safe, at least, beyond Cape Aden, where alone it was probable a French vessel might lie to intercept them. This had been the case once during the last war, when there was no convoy, by which the native merchants lost nine lac of dollars. Had it not been for this, we should have taken advantage of the squall, and got far on our way; as it was, we lay to. We had constantly light breezes to the end of the month, with a current, sometimes to the northward, and sometimes to the southward of E.

On the 1st of September we were carried by a strong southerly current within sight of Mount Felix, and, to our great mortification, instead of having to look out for the land of India, we had not yet got clear of Africa; an extraordinary circumstance for the season.

It was so fresh a monsoon that Captain Vashon did not think it safe to venture into Surat roads, which are totally unprotected; we therefore directed our course for Bombay. By three o'clock on the 12th Malabar Point was in sight, but we were not close in with it until the evening, when an officer came on board us from a Company's cruizer, anchored at the mouth of the harbour, and immediately took us in. It was dusk, but the scenery was still sufficiently visible to be admired. The islands that separate it into several parts are covered with wood to the top; beyond them the main land rises into a chain of mountains of the wildest and most picturesque forms imaginable, to which the Island of Bombay, covered with cocoanut trees, forms a contrast by its flat figure. It was dark when we came to an anchor: no King's ship was there. I immediately sent a note on shore to Mr. Salt, to request that he would notify my arrival to Mr. Duncan, and would come on board in the morning.

CHAPTER III.

Residence at Bombay.—Departure for Poonah.—Harbour of Bombay.—Panwell.—Campaly.—Tillegam.—Arrival at the British Residency near Poonah.—Account of the Dusserah.—Visit to the Paishwa.—Dreadful famine.—Dinner at the Paishwa's country house.—Dinner given by the Dewan of the Empire.—Paishwa's character.—Political observations on the Mahratta Empire.

MR. SALT came on board, accompanied by Major Green the Town Major of Bombay, bearing the Governor's invitation to me to reside at his house during my stay. I left the Fox soon afterwards under the usual salute, and on landing received a similar compliment from the fort. Mr. Duncan's palanquin conveyed me to the Government-house, where I was met by himself, and most kindly congratulated on my arrival. After breakfast he expressed his extreme regret at the misconduct of Captain Keys, who, he informed me, had been under an arrest since his arrival. He also kindly assured me that, whatever were my future plans, I should have his best assistance, and that if I should determine to go to Suez or Bussorah, he trusted he could find me a better vessel than the Antelope, and a better commander than Captain Keys.

The kindness that I invariably experienced from Mr. Duncan, and the information of which I found him possessed, made me almost rejoice that I had been obliged to return from the Red Sea. The anxiety which I had experienced during my voyage was fully compensated by the discovery, that the western shore was navigable, and that it could supply provisions. I lost no time in communicating to the Marquis Wellesley the result of my voyage, and urgently represented the eligibility of a small vessel's being dispatched to Massowah, to continue the survey from that island to Cosseir. I at the same time stated to his Excellency my intention of returning to Europe by the Persian Gulf, and requested he would have the goodness to send me letters of recommendation to the Pacha of Bagdad. I expected that this Chief would afford me every assistance in crossing the Desert, as he was anxiously looking for assistance from India to resist the incursions of the Wahabees, and had actually an Embassador in Bengal, who had been received with every attention, having all his expences paid, and the crazy vessel in which he had arrived, repaired by the public. I therefore preferred throwing myself on his protection, to again braving the adverse winds of the Red Sea. As the answer could not be received from Calcutta in less than six weeks, I thought the interval would be very satisfactorily filled up, by paying a visit to Poonah; I therefore wrote to Col. Close, the British Resident with the Paishwa, to enquire whether he conceived it would be politically advisable; and if he did, to request that he would state to his highness my wish to pay my respects to him. I was obligingly favoured with an immediate answer, expressing the satisfaction it would give him to receive me at the Residency, and informing me that the Paishwa was much pleased at the idea of my visit, which he wished should take place at the approaching festival of the Dusserah, which would commence on the 13th of October; a wish with which I most readily complied.

On the 6th of October every preparation, as I understood, had been made for my departure by the orders of the Governor: tents had been sent on to the different stations at which I should stop; forty bearers had been procured for our three palanquins, and the Governor's gold sticks had been ordered to attend me. Captain Young, who was stationed at the first post in the Mahratta country, as Commissary of stores for the army in the field, had orders to provide every thing, and attend me himself to Poonah. Above the gauts Colonel Close had undertaken to form arrangements for my conveyance.

The river, on which Panwell is situated, is in the dry season only an inlet of the sea, and navigable to that place at high water; we were therefore obliged to consult the tide. It turned at eight, and we set off with it, under a salute of fifteen guns from the fort. The Governor's Aides-decamp, and Major Green, attended me to the water side. The balloon boat, from its drawing less water, was preferred to the yacht; it had a cabin, and held us very well. The harbour improved in beauty as we advanced. The islands are, in general, covered with wood; but Butcher's Island is clear, except at the northern side, where several buildings are erected close to an old Mahratta fort. Among the lofty hills, which formed a back ground to the scene, Funnel Hill was most conspicuous from the singularity of its shape: the summit has all the appearance of a vast pillar, elevated in the centre of a flat, on the top of a rock. The whole range of hills is singular in its appearance, and continually afforded subjects for Mr. Salt's pencil. We passed between the islands of Salsette and Elephanta, where the bay begins to contract in its dimensions. The sea breeze here overtook us. The entrance to the river Pan is defended by a small fort, which was built by the English, and formed into a depot during the old Mahratta war: it is now nearly in ruins. The river was full; the trees being actually half covered by the water. The paddy fields presented a cheering prospect by their healthy state, and even the mountains were covered with verdure, except where their smooth surface was broken by rocky pinnacles rising to a great height. The clouds floated around them, and occasionally, in part concealed them from our view, which greatly improved the scene. High cultivation and picturesque scenery have no where in India been so perfectly united.

The tide had just turned as we reached the landing-place near the village of Panwell. I was extremely shocked at discovering the vultures and Paria dogs disputing over the body of a poor wretch, whom the recent famine had hurried to a better world. Captain Young employed twelve men to bury the bodies, at an expence of forty-five rupees per month. They have sometimes performed this office to thirty in a day; during the rainy monsoon, the average was twenty-five. The want of rain had caused a scarcity, which had been heightened into a famine by the devastations of the Mahratta war. Holcar and Scindiah laid waste whole provinces, and through a vast extent of country left neither tree nor habitation. The British power has hitherto protected the Guzerat, Cokan, and the neighbouring poor of Bombay. It has even gone farther, and has daily fed twelve thousand people from the stores of rice procured from Bengal.

They were now reaping the first crops, but poverty still rendered numbers the victims of famine. Captain Young was hardly settled, and his habitation was new; it is situated on a rock, which in the rains, is an island. His business was to forward all the stores for our garrison at Poonah, which would otherwise have been almost starving. These proceedings have been fortunate for the poor, as nearly five thousand people have been employed, who have had provisions from the stores; one hundred and fifty people have also been charitably fed every day at the kitchen on rice; yet the deaths for six months were estimated by Captain Young at four thousand. Rice being procurable here, the poor wretches exerted themselves to crawl down, and perished even in sight of the house.

The Aumildar of the district came to wait on me with presents of fruit. He was a handsome Brahmin, but was very troublesome, and wished to tax even the Bombay people, that were here on public service. In consequence of a reprimand, he was obliged to desist. I therefore paid him little attention. The village seems populous, and is prettily situated on the banks of the river, in a plain surrounded by lofty mountains, one of which much resembles the table-land of the Cape. The priest of the tomb of Kurrun Ali Khan also waited on me. It is a neat building, with a dome, and two small pinnacles, that peep out from a grove of mango trees. Kurrun, he informed me, was a native of Lucknow, who lived here for six years. There are twenty-five readers of the Koran attached to the tomb.

I was much mortified to find that the tents had not been carried on, and that the superintendant of our stores was not even arrived. The bullocks could not carry the tents, and we were obliged to apply to the Aumildar for cooleys. These were not obtained till night, so that all removal was impracticable. We found Lieutenant Smith at this place, a complete invalid; and as Dr. Murray, who attended me in a medical capacity, thought that the journey up the Gauts might render him essential service, I persuaded him to join our party. Dr. Murray's and Captain Young's palanquins and bearers had not made their appearance.

October 7.—Our Italian superintendant arrived early this morning, and by ten we got his baggage, as well as our tents, safe on the way. The widow of the famous Nana Furnese sent me some breakfast, with her salaams. She is a young girl of sixteen, and is said to be pretty; he married her when an infant; she resided here with her uncle. Our Mussulmaun priest sent us some excellent rice pancakes; as he had also the credit of being a good curry maker, we persuaded him to go on with us. Before breakfast we walked through the village to visit a pagoda. It was dedicated to Mahadeo, and had nothing to recommend it, the pillars being wood, except a good tank in front of it. The building was filled with poor, who live there, and beg in the town. Some children among them were living skeletons, with scarcely a muscle to be seen. As we returned we were shocked by one of Captain Young's charnel-men dragging a dead body in a state of putrefaction. The Mussulmaun tomb has also a tank covered with the red and white nymphæa in high beauty. We dined early in order to get off in time; when it came to the point, our Mussulmaun friend would not go, and the Italian was left behind, as his horse was not arrived. The part of the village that we now passed through, is extensive, and we were happy in not beholding so many wretched objects as on the other side. The paddy fields, as we proceeded, had in many places interrupted the road, and rendered it difficult to pass. We winded among the hills, and at half-after seven, reached our tents, close to the village of Choke or Chouke, a distance of thirteen miles. We had only one large tent, so that some of us slept within, and the others, in their palanquins, under the outer fly. In consequence of the tents not being sent forward a day before, we were obliged to wait there till after breakfast: and indeed with difficulty we procured men sufficient to carry them on.

The Aumil of the district came and brought fruit, fowls, and kids, which we accepted. It was the middle of the day when we set off: we passed through a country like that of yesterday: the crops very fine, and nearly ripe. The hills preserve their strata perfectly horizontal. We passed several miserable wretches hardly alive, and an occasional stench too often informed us of the vicinity of dead bodies. We reached Campaly, a stage of twelve miles, by day-light: it is close to the foot of the pass, surrounded by hills covered with jungle, and has a very fine tank, and a neat pagoda. Several small streams were descending from the table-land, and a rivulet ran through the village. All ideas of pleasure were however banished by the sight of several wretches who were too weak to raise themselves up, to receive the charity that was offered them. Close to the choultry were bodies in every state of decay; some with their cloaths on, that could not have been dead above a day or two; others with only a small portion of flesh left on their bones, by the vultures and jackals. The vale was so small, that the tents could not be pitched at a sufficient distance from the effluvia, to prevent its occasionally reaching us.

October 9.—We set off at half past five. For a great part of the Gaut we were obliged to walk, though it was by far easier than the Bessely Gaut, nor was it half its length. The village of Candalla being just at the top, we had sent our breakfast to it. There is a very large tank, and below it a plain, which exhibited a more horrid spectacle than Campaly: above one hundred dead bodies lay upon it, on which the vultures and Paria dogs were feeding: famine was in every face, several houses were uninhabited, and the last victims had never been removed from the places where they perished. We assembled all the poor that were alive, and gave them several pice each. The harvest is now so near that it may be hoped not many more will perish. We had but little appetite for breakfast, and hastened from this scene of horror. The country was fine and well cultivated. Our bearers were in high spirits; the air was cool, and we reached a spot near the celebrated caves of Carli by half after eleven, a distance of fifteen miles, where Colonel Close had pitched his tents for our reception, which were excellent, and provided with every proper convenience. The Killadar* of the Esapoor fort came to pay his compliments; he had a guard of native soldiers, and told me his garrison consisted of two thousand. A messenger bearing excellent butter,

* Military Governor.

and a profusion of fruit, arrived from Colonel Close, who sent to say, that we need not reach Poonah till the 12th. For the first time we had the good fortune to be at a distance from any village, and its melancholy accompaniments; a mango tope formed a screen to the south, and a pellucid tank was in our front. A very heavy thunder storm discomposed us a little, as the rain beat partially through the tent. The crashes of thunder were the most tremendous I ever heard, and were so close as to give reasonable ground of alarm. The Esapoor Killadar came again in the evening with fowls, sheep, &c. It rained in the night.

The want of cooleys obliged us to stay breakfast where we were, and make our own people assist in carrying the baggage. It was as cool as in England during summer, and consequently the men got on well. The whole way was through a valley covered with pieces of agate, onyx, and cornelian. The hills were green to the top, and the paddy fields frequent. We halted two miles from Tillegam, the Rajah of which place sent his servant, who spoke English, to congratulate me on my arrival. Our stage was twelve miles.

The cooleys came, but too late for us to set off before breakfast. The road lay through a level country, without cultivation or trees, except near the village. The Rajah of Tillegam had sent his head man early in the morning, to invite me to visit him as I passed through. I excused myself, as I had not yet seen the Paishwa. The truth was, I did not know the proper etiquette, and wished to consult Colonel Close. I however expressed a hope that I should be able to see him on my return. I passed to the right of Tillegam, between it and a fine tank. I saw no very wretched objects. I reached the tents a little beyond Chinchoor, a distance of twelve miles, by half after twelve, having passed through a populous town, and forded a river. Captain Frissel arrived from Colonel Close to attend me to Poonah.

At day-light I entered my palanquin: the gentlemen rode, except Mr. Salt and Lieutenant Smith. The country had been devastated by Holcar, and the village of Ound, situated on the bank of the river Moota, was nearly in ruins. On the opposite shore I was met by Lieutenant Colonel Close, the Resident at Poonah, and the officers of the British detachment at that place. The Colonel had elephants, camels, and a very well dressed suwarry. We alighted and mutually paid our compliments, afterwards forming one party. A little to the westward of the village of Gunnais Coondah, so called from an adjacent temple dedicated to Gunnais, the deputation from the Durbar of his Highness the Paishwa was waiting to receive me, close to a small pagoda which commanded a view of Poonah, distant two miles. The chiefs were on elephants in covered houdahs. A large body of horse was drawn up: the officers made their salaams, as I passed along the line. At a little distance I halted, and the Colonel went on. A carpet was spread on the plain: the deputation alighted, and after a few minutes, I advanced. We met on the carpet. Each person was presented separately to me by the Colonel, and embraced; we then seated ourselves without chairs or cushions. The chief person was Abbah Poorundery, the Jaghirdar of Sapoor, a handsome young man, with an expressive countenance, and pleasing manners. He wore several ornaments of pearls and jewels. He was accompanied by Anund Row, the Paishwa's Minister for the British affairs; Kistnagie Rowannie, the assistant Dewan of the state; and Seedogie Row Nepawnkur, who commanded a body of horse, along with General Wellesley, during the late campaign in the Decan. There were also several Maunkarries, officers whose duty it is to attend the Paishwa on all visits of ceremony: these were seated behind. Anund Row delivered the congratulatory compliments of his Highness on my arrival near his capital. He expressed his satisfaction that it had taken place at so propitious a season as the Dusserah, and hoped it was an omen of the continuance of friendship between the two nations. Colonel Close replied in my name, with the general Asiatic expressions of regard for his Highness, and my conviction that the friendship would be lasting. As they were considered to be my guests, I presented to the Chiefs pawn and attar with my own hand. Colonel Close's Dewan gave pawn only to the Maunkarries. We all then arose, and having made our salaams, departed; they towards the town, we to Colonel Close's residence at some little distance from it.

After the hurry of a march, and the inconvenience of a tent, I found myself most pleasantly situated under Colonel Close's hospitable roof. His gardens are on the banks of the Moota, where it joins the Moola, and forms the Mootamoola river. This runs into the Beema, which again falls into the Kistna. It is singular that by these means a person, when not forty miles distant from the western shore of the Peninsula, might proceed by water to the Eastern Sea. It is a charming spot, adorned with cypress and fruit trees. At the point a very handsome bungelow is erected, where breakfast and dinner are served; at one end is a billiard table for the idlers. The Colonel keeps a very excellent table; beef, however, out of respect to the prejudices of the natives, is never used. Holcar, when here, had so little control over his Patan troops, that the sacred animal was frequently slaughtered. Sir Charles Mallet, when he first came as Resident to Poonah, was obliged to live in a wretched house in the town, which had been provided for him: finding this extremely unpleasant, he pitched his tents during the summer on the banks of the river, but on the commencement of the rains was forced to return to town. He remonstrated very much, and at length obtained permission to erect a temporary house in this garden. One night it was burnt down, and Sir Charles being then enabled to complain with effect, was allowed to build the bungelow, which now is used as the Resident's office. Still not a fence was permitted; and even the present Resident had great difficulty in obtaining permission to erect a gateway and several additional buildings. The large bungelow on the banks of the river was built for a festival, at which his Highness assisted, in commemoration of the conclusion of the Mahratta war. On the opposite bank the natives burn the dead bodies, and afterwards commit the remains to the stream.

October 13th was the day of the celebrated Hindoo festival of the Dusserah. The Paishwa was to attend, and perform a principal part. As I had not been presented to him, it was contrary to etiquette that I should fall in his way; I was therefore obliged to observe the festival at a small distance. As soon as his Highness quitted the palace, Colonel Close and I mounted our elephant, and attended by the horse guard and suwarry, proceeded across the river to the British lines, where all the troops were drawn out in line, with the artillery on the left. We retired behind them, by way of being incognito. His Highness passed obliquely along the line to a spot where a branch of a tree had been stuck in the ground. Here he descended from his elephant, and performed the proper ceremonies, which we could not observe. On their being concluded a royal salute was fired. His Highness then mounted, and passed in front of the line from right to left, being received with presented arms. The regimental colours were lowered, but not the King's; and as he passed the artillery, another royal salute was fired. He was mounted in a howdah of looking glass, and had but a little suwarry. The only interesting part of the sight was the British troops, now for the first time assisting at this holy ceremony at the capital of the Hindoo empire. Formerly Holcar, Scindiah, and the other chiefs, used to attend, and their prodigious bodies of horse covered the surrounding plains. Whole fields were then devastated, the Paishwa himself setting the example; but now his attendants only gathered a few heads of grain. After celebrating together this festival, they were accustomed to set out on their predatory excursions into the neighbouring countries; but these excursions are now probably terminated for ever. It was considered a fortunate day to begin a war, after a celebration of the victory obtained by Ram over the giant Rawan.

As I could see but little, I applied for information, through Colonel Close, to the most intelligent Brahmins, who gave me the following account. "When Ram was on his way to attack the giant Rawan, who had carried off his wife Seeta, he arrived at a place called Kiskinda, which was governed by an ape or monkey named Walee. Walee had seized the wife of his brother Soogreoo, and expelled him from the town. Soogreoo, attended by four other monkeys, viz. Hunoomân, Nul, Neel, and Jamoowunt, took up their abode on a mountain six coss from Kiskinda. Ram happened to pass over the same mountain. As soon as he was seen by Soogreoo at a distance, the latter sent Hunoomân to ascertain who he was. Hunoomân explained to Ram the case of Soogreoo, and prevailed on him to espouse his cause; and he then introduced them to each other. In a short time Ram destroyed Walee, restored the wife of Soogreoo, and gave him the government of Kiskinda. Ram, attended by Hunoomân, on whose back indeed he rode, moved from Kiskinda to attack Rawan on the 10th of the moon Aswin, which is celebrated as the Veejya Dasmee, or the 10th of victory, generally called the Dusserah. The first night Ram halted under the shade of a tree called Gokurnee,* which derives its name from the resemblance of its blossom in shape to a cow's ear; go, in Shanscrit, signifying cow, and kuru, ear. Ram then performed his devotions under the tree, which was itself one of the objects of them. When the devotions were finished, the monkeys by whom he was attended brought him leaves of the Gokurnee, as the only offerings then in their power to make. In a short time, however, all the leaves of the tree were expended. They then brought the leaves of another tree, that was at hand, called Aptah; and, when they were all expended, the leaves of a third tree, called Shummee, were brought. Ram then ordained, that, if he should be successful in his expedition against Rawan, devotion should for ever be paid to those trees on the Veejya

* This was brought me at Chinchoor; I think it is a Cassia. The shummee was also brought: it is a Mimosa.

Dusmee, that is, to one at a time; to the Gokurnee, if procurable; if not, to the Aptah, or last, to the Shummee. After the monkeys had made their offerings to Ram they interchanged the leaves among themselves."

This is the history of the origin of the festival, as given to me by a learned Brahmin, who consulted his friends on the subject. The Aptah was the tree used here: I saw the leaves; it is a species of Bauhinia. When a tree is not in a convenient situation, a branch of it is procured, as was now the case. The ceremony is described in the Shanscrit books, that treat on the ceremonies of the Hindoos to be observed each month throughout the year. The same Brahmin gave me the following account. "The devotion paid to the tree on the Dusserah, may be performed by every Hindoo of every cast, without the assistance of a Brahmin; neither is it necessary that any part of the person's clothes should be taken off. First, he throws a little water over the tree or branch. He then throws on a few grains of rice. He next rubs on a little powdered sandal wood mixed in water. He then ornaments it with flowers. A little sugar, or any sweetmeat, and some betel nut, prepared in the usual manner, are then laid before the tree as offerings, and some is given to a poor Brahmin, who also takes the money laid before the tree. This concludes the ceremony, which is celebrated throughout the Hindoo governments. At Poonah, however, an addition is made, which is not ordered by any of their books. The Paishwa receives a number of leaves from the bough, which he gives to his followers, and which they interchange, in imitation of the monkeys. His Highness afterwards holds a durbar, where nazurs of from two to five gold mohurs are presented, and in return he gives each a leaf.

He also sends Khelauts and leaves to the Rajah of Sattarah, and Scindiah. The Brahmin could not say that there was any motive for, or effect assigned to, the exchange of leaves. I should suppose it was a kind of compact that they would assist each other in their approaching warfare. It took place in the evening, and it was nearly dark when we got home.

His Highness had fixed the following day to receive my visit of ceremony. The fortunate hour was about four o'clock; when, having received intelligence that the deputation from the durbar was on the opposite side of the river, we set off. I was attended by the Colonel and suite, my own suite, and our suwarries. A salute announced my departure. The Paishwa's minister for British affairs, and the assistant Dewan of the state after paying their compliments, put themselves at the head of the procession, to show me the way to the palace. They were attended by a large body of horse, and some soldiers; an escort of British infantry waited also on the opposite shore, and joined my suwarry. On entering the place before the palace we found his Highness's cavalry and guard of infantry drawn out, with his elephants and suwarry: they were by no means splendid. As we passed under the Nobit Kanah the kettle drums beat. Within the walls the servants were all at their posts, and the crowd considerable. In the windows were numbers of the higher orders. We quitted our palanquins at the foot of the stairs, which we mounted, attended only by our Chubdars and Ausubadars. A small anti-room led to the durbar. At the door I waited a few seconds, till I saw that the Dewan of the state, Sadasheo Maunkesor, was sufficiently near; when, having quitted my slippers, I stepped on the white cloth with which the whole room was covered, Colonel Close supporting my left arm. I embraced the Dewan, and presented the officers of my suite. At that moment the Paishwa entered the room, and stepped on his guddy or throne. I hastened towards him, supported as before, by the Colonel, with the Dewan on my right. His Highness continued standing, and slightly embraced with his right hand, I doing the same. His brother was on his right, to whom I was next presented, and who also embraced me. I then returned and presented to the Paishwa the gentlemen of my suite, who were also embraced. We then sat down. The Dewan was next his Highness on the left, but rather behind: I was close to him; next to me was the Colonel, and then the other European gentlemen. We had no chairs or cushions, and were not permitted to put out our feet, as showing the sole of the foot is considered as disrespectful. His Highness had no slippers on.

The etiquette of the court is silence: and when any thing is said, it is in a low whisper. I spoke to the Colonel, who translated it to the Dewan, who stretching himself out towards his Highness on his knees with his hands closed and raised up, in a low voice reported what I had said. The answer was returned by the same conveyance. By the direction of Colonel Close I first enquired after his Highness's health, and was answered that he was well, and hoped I arrived in good health at Poonah. I then asked after the health of his brother. The message was carried across the room, in front of the guddy, by Anund Row. The answer was complimentary. His Highness now expressed a wish, through the Dewan, that we might retire into a more private place, that the conversation might be more free. This originated solely from himself, and was as unexpected, as it was flattering. Indeed, the whole of his Highness's conduct had evinced a wish to pay me every attention. The deputations sent to meet me were the highest honours he could bestow.

I immediately arose and followed him into a very neat small room, attended by Colonel Close, the Dewan of the state, the sub-Dewan, and the minister for British affairs. His Highness seated himself on a small turkey carpet in the corner of the room. He placed me next him on his left, and the rest formed a part of a circle in face of him. He now began a very interesting conversation, in which he considerably relaxed from his etiquette, smiled, and frequently spoke immediately from himself to me and Colonel Close. With all the disadvantages of interpretation, I could frequently perceive that he gave a very elegant turn to the expressions he used. Among many other compliments, he expressed a wish to give me a fête at his country-house, to which I with pleasure assented. This had been previously arranged, and was to take place after he had honoured me with a visit. On political subjects he spoke fully, and clearly, and seemed much better informed than I had reason to expect. After about an hour we returned to the Durbar. I was so extremely tired with my position, that it was with some difficulty I could rise, and for a few minutes was obliged to rest against the wall. No conversation passed after he was seated on the guddy. Pawn was placed before him in a large gold plate; on the top was a gold box, containing a parcel of the same; attar, rose water, and spices were in the same line. Anund Row, the minister for British affairs, gave rose water, pawn and attar with spices to all the party, except the Colonel and me. He began at the lowest, contrary to the etiquette of the other Asiatic courts that I have visited. The Dewan gave pawn, rose water, attar, and spices to the Colonel; to me he gave attar and rose water. We then arose, and his Highness presented me with the gold box, filled with pawn from his own hand. As I was to visit him at his country-house, the giving of presents was deferred till that time. We made our salaams and retired, the Dewans attending us to the door. We then returned as we came; but the sun being set, there was no salute.

His Highness and his brother were in plain white muslin dresses, without a single jewel. The Dewan of the empire had some handsome flat diamonds in his turban, a necklace of emeralds, and large pearls, and ear-rings of gold, suspending the finest pearls I ever beheld. They were perfectly round and clear, and were as large as the pupil of the human eye. The palace is a tolerable handsome building, and was very clean. The Durbar room is large; it is supported by wooden pillars handsomely carved. His guddy was of white muslin, richly embroidered in gold and coloured silk. His attendants stood round without the pillars, except a few with silver sticks. Holkar did not much injure the palace, but he carried away every thing moveable; a small armoury and the elephant-houdahs did not escape. The town is indifferent; several houses are large, and built with square blocks of granite, to about fourteen feet from the ground; the upper part is a frame work of timber, with slight walls merely to keep out the wet and air. The lime, bricks, and tiles are so bad in this country, that the rain washes away any building that does not depend on timber for support. A great plenty of this useful article is brought from the gauts and the westward; it is not much dearer than at Madras. Holcar's stay did not improve the town. He pulled down several large houses in search of treasure, and they say found a great deal. We forded the river both going and returning; the foundations of a granite bridge rise above the water; but they were laid in misfortune, and superstition will not permit their superstructure to be completed. A bridge of boats had been laid across by General Wellesley, but it has not been kept up.

The spectacle of dead bodies on the banks of the river, in every state of putrefaction, was truly distressing. During the famine, many were murdered for the rice they had just received from British charity, which, I am proud to say, extended to this place, whither a very handsome subscription, amounting to 40,000 rupees, was sent, which had been collected at Bombay under the patronage of Lady Mackintosh. Colonel Close had the distribution of it: he had previously fed fifteen hundred people daily with boiled rice; but the sight of the food rendered them nearly frantic; confusion ensued, and numbers lost their share, particularly the more helpless. The Colonel therefore determined that this contribution should be distributed in money, each person to receive sufficient to purchase one good meal in the four and twenty hours. Eight pice were adequate to this; children had a smaller sum, who, with the women, had the preference. About five thousand daily were relieved, and it sustained them till the new crops were gathered in, so that their lives were actually saved to society. The money operated less on their feelings, than the food: the confusion was consequently less. It was regularly the business of an officer, with a guard of sepoys, to superintend the distribution. The sending up rice from the coast was considered as ineligible, from the expence of conveyance. Indian wheat and juwarry had already been got in; rice was expected to be so in about a fortnight. The officer commanding the garrison was particularly careful in protecting the fields around the town; the English name was therefore very popular among the lower orders. The guard of one hundred seapoys was not more than sufficient for these purposes. Several Brahmins, who were no objects of charity, mixed with the beggars and tried to obtain a share: when detected, they were instantly punished with four dozen lashes, in defiance of the holiness of their character; nor has this been since objected to. His Highness feeds a great number of his own cast, but his charity has not extended further.

It is impossible to teach a native Prince the duty of protecting his subjects. During the scarcity, the number of lives saved by the Residency were many, not only by food, but by attendance and wine, when necessary. The poor wretches, during the rains, perished by hundreds, even in sight of the house. General relief was impossible. Not only would they have sold their children, but they would have been grateful to any one who would have accepted them. Now the evil is over. Leasing is allowed in India, which at this moment feeds many. Any person may earn sufficient to maintain him by going to the fields and working, or even bringing in a bundle of grass. The camp sustains many hands. In no country are the means of life procurable with greater facility than in the Mahratta states; it is a garden, which would produce crop after crop as fast as they could be sown. Tanks might every where be formed, so as to render a supply of water certain at all seasons.

I had intended, on the 16th, to receive the Vakeels of the native powers, who might be at Poonah; but the Vakeel of Scindiah being on the eve of his departure, obtained permission to pay his compliments this day. His name is Juswunt Rao Goreporah; his family is very respectable; one of his relations, Morari Row, held Gooty from the Poonah Government, and was one of its Generals: he is mentioned by Orme. From the respectability of the family, the British on the conquest of Mysore, gave to them the little district of Sondoor, a beautiful valley, situated between Chittledroog and Neydroog, and completely surrounded by the British territory. Juswunt Rao Goreporah himself was high in Scindiah's confidence, and was the Vakeel appointed by him to negotiate the latet reaty of peace with General Wellesley. His other Vakeel, Naroo Hurry, also waited upon me: the former alone spoke. The conversation was merely complimentary; but they expressed great anxiety for the arrival of General Wellesley. They received pawn and attar on their departure.

The other Vakeels paid me a visit next morning. Among them was the Vakeel of Imrut Rao, the adopted brother of the Paishwa. Ragonaut Rao had no hopes of children at the time he adopted him; but afterwards, the present Paishwa and his brother were born. The disappointment of Imrut Rao's hopes has prevented his being on good terms with his Highness; they are now, however, apparently reconciled, through the mediation of Colonel Close. Imrut Rao is on his way to Benares, to perform his ablutions. He is the first of his family that ever did so, and he is, I learn, highly gratified by the circumstance.

A nephew of Colonel Close arrived from Hydrabad, three hundred and seventy miles, which he had rode in twelve days. He describes the Nizam's country as being as much devastated by famine as this. Several villages had not a living creature in them, and the dead bodies were lying at the doors, and in the houses. He had been himself nearly starved, having procured only native grain since he left Hydrabad, with now and then some milk. This must be owing to the want of rain, for Holcar and Scindiah caused no devastations in that country. Mr. Salt has taken a few views: one very beautiful is from the gardens, taking in the junction of the rivers, and the pagodas built on the opposite side, a very favourite spot among the Hindoos. Mahadeo is the deity chiefly worshipped. The pagoda is beyond dedicated to his wife, Parbuttee, who, with her son Gunnais, share in the adoration. This pagoda has a pretty effect, as it crowns the top of a sugar loaf-hill, and behind it is the flat mountain on which is situated the fort of Saoghur. Holcar never took this place, nor could his offers tempt the fidelity of the Killadar. It seems strong, but does not cover the whole surface of the hill, so that on one side it is accessible. On the whole I think Poonah well situated, and when it has a little enjoyed the blessings of tranquillity, will be a handsome capital.

His Highness having fixed a day to return my visit, Colonel Close had a very large tent pitched in front of the house; two others were joined to it without their sides, so as to form one large apartment: the guddy was sent forward, and placed in the centre, as at his own Durbar. On his coming in sight, Colonel Close mounted an elephant, and advanced to meet him. At the door of the tent I awaited his approach. He came close up, but did not dismount till the Dewan of the state, the Sub-dewan, and the Dewan for British affairs had paid their compliments, and had presented to me the different Sirdars and Maunkarries who attended him. They made their salaams, and passed by into the tent. His Highness then descended from his elephant, with his brother, who rode behind him. I made my compliments, and leaving a space on my right hand for him to walk in, moved into the tent. We all seated ourselves as at the Durbar. A few compliments passed, while the nautch girls were singing and dancing. As his Highness was considered as master of the house, the pawn and attar were placed on the ground before him, and he ordered it to be given to the Sirdars, and other attendants. I then requested his Highness to permit me to attire him, and his brothers; which being acceded to, the trays were brought forward, and laid before them. I got up, and crossing the musnud, began with his brother. The jewels were first placed in his head dress, consisting of a serpaish,* jigger,* and toorrah.† I then put the mala‡ round his neck: a person stood behind who fastened the strings. The same ceremonies were then gone through with his Highness, but in addition he had bracelets of diamonds. A telescope, and bonbon box, ornamented with a beautiful picture of the goddess Gunja, were also given to his Highness.

* Ornaments for the head of diamonds and coloured precious stones.

† Mahratta ornament of several strings of pearls fastened together and suspended on one side of the turban.

‡ A necklace of pearl with a jewel of coloured precious stones suspended from the centre.

His brother had a bon-bon box, with Indra painted on it. The figures were appropriate to their character. I then gave them pawn and attar, as he did to me, except that the attar was poured into my hands, and I gently rubbed it down both his shoulders. This was done at his particular request, and is the highest possible compliment. His Highness was in such excellent humour, that although it was a public visit of ceremony, he frequently addressed himself with smiles to me and the Colonel.

The ministers did not receive attar, as it was my wish they should stay till the rest were gone. There is a great jealousy between these officers and the Maunkarries, so that to have made them any presents in the company of the latter, would have been an insult to their dignity. We mentioned to the Dewan that a horse and elephant were at the gate, as presents to his Highness. These are always given on state occasions, but without being habited, as up the country. It was nearly dark before the Paishwa departed. The nautch-girls had sung some very interesting Mahratta, or, as they called them, Deckany songs, which we now made them repeat, as a relaxation from the fatigue of a state visit. I afterwards learned that on this day there was a great religious festival, at which his Highness ought to have assisted, and that he was fined several hundred rupees for his absence. This provided a handsome feast for the Brahmins. Parbuttee pagoda was illuminated all over at night.

The presents were provided by the India Company. His Highness's were worth about twelve thousand rupees. The others altogether nearly eight.

At a little after four we set off with the usual suwarry to pay a visit to the Paishwa at his country-house, the Hora Baug. The road for a considerable distance was covered by his Highness's suwarry, chiefly horsemen, so that it was rather difficult to get to the gate; fortunately I had a party of sepoys from the lines, who joined on the opposite bank of the river, and made way for me. It is prettily situated on the bank of a very large tank, perfectly irregular in its shape. In the centre is a small island with a pagoda. The opposite bank rises gradually into a sugar loaf hill, the summit of which is capped by the white buildings of the pagoda dedicated to Parbuttee. The house itself is insignificant, and has never been finished. The garden is fine, and is ornamented with several noble mango trees, and a great number of cocoanut trees, which I had seen no where else above the Gauts, and which several people told me would not grow there. The guddy was placed in a verandah, opening to a bason of water, with fountains, and covered by a trellis of vines. We had the pleasure to announce to his Highness the surrender of Chandore to the united army of the British and the Paishwa, under Colonel Wallace, who was rapidly conquering the hill forts of Holcar, that extend towards the Guzerat, in hopes of preventing his making an incursion into that fertile province or into the territories of the Paishwa, to maintain his predatory bands. His Highness was in great spirits, and observed, that his father always wished for the friendship of the English, but that it remained for him first to reap the blessings of it. He had said in a former conversation, that he would mention another circumstance on a future occasion; it turned out to be a request, that I would procure him an Arab mare. The Colonel of course assured him that I would do my best; but unfortunately I knew it was impossible, as the Arabs never will part with their mares.

We soon had notice to move up stairs; the Paishwa passing through a back door, while we mounted, by a narrow stair case, to a platform with two verandahs, one at each end. In the farther a white cloth was spread, on which were plantain leaves equal in number to the English gentlemen present. On each was a Brahmin's dinner, consisting of rice, plain and sweet, pastry thin as paper, and rolled up, pastrycakes, bread, and pease pudding. Along one side was a range of sweetmeats, laid in a row, having the appearance of paints on a pallet; on the other were seven different kinds of curried vegetables. On one side of the leaf were rice milk, gee, and some other liquids, in small pans of plantain leaf, which were all excellent of their kinds. We had taken the precaution to bring spoons, knives, and forks, which we used actively out of respect to our host, who soon joined the party by seating himself on the guddy, a little on the outside of the verandah. Of course, he could not contaminate himself by eating in our presence.

On giving notice that we had finished, he retired, and we soon followed. After seating ourselves below, the betel was laid at his feet and served round. My servant had placed himself at the bottom of the line, by a hint from Captain Frissel, and was consequently served first. They proceeded upwards till they reached me, where they stopped. The presents were then brought in, again beginning with my servant. These were better than had ever been given on a former occasion, the shawls being new, and good ones for this part of India. A horse and elephant were at the door: the former was a fine animal, and in good condition: a most unusual circumstance at Poonah.

After this was concluded, a sword was given into his hands, and by him presented to me: it was handsomely mounted in green and gold, and had a very fine blade: it was not part of the present of ceremony, and I therefore valued it the more. I assured him I would hand it down to my son, and my son's son; and kept it by me, instead of delivering it to my servants, as I had done the trays. The nautch-girls were the same as on the Paishwa's visit to me. A few compliments passed at taking leave, and he paid the usual one of requesting to hear of my welfare. The Dewan attended to the end of the carpet, and then took his leave. We returned through the town, which is much larger than I expected, and the bazar much finer. There are several large houses three stories high; the pagodas are insignificant.

A deputation arrived from the Dewan of the empire, requesting I would honour him with my company to a party at the Paishwa's garden. This was merely a matter of form, as I had previously consented, his Highness having expressed a wish that it should be so, as a proper close to the attentions I had received at Poonah. The party set off at the usual hour. We were received at the entrance by the Dewan, who walked by my side to a carpet divided in two by a single pillow, and spread where his Highness's guddy had been yesterday placed. He sat on the right hand of it, I on the left; my party next me, in a line down the room; his, on the opposite side. We soon adjourned up stairs, where a dinner, as before, was laid out. The Dewan sat close to us, and conversed the whole time. I praised some of the sweet things, and requested he would send me some for my journey, which he took as a compliment, and immediately promised to do. I begged him for the last time most anxiously to preserve, by his endeavours, the alliance between the two states, and to represent to his Highness that this was the last wish I had to express. He replied, that the Mahrattas now depended upon the English for protection. I requested Colonel Close to enforce, in the strongest terms, my denial of this: that the dependence was mutual, and only that of one friend on another. Though he had made the remark, he seemed pleased at the denial, and assured me nothing should be wanting on his part, but that he was only what his master pleased; on which I concluded with my personal wishes for his continuance in office.

Colonel Close had been so kind as to permit the Assistant Resident, Captain Frissel, to attend me to Bombay, and meant to go himself as far as Chinchoor. The following was the day fixed for our journey. I had procured several old figures of Hindoo deities, and some of considerable merit; my people had picked up a large collection of agates, which are here in profusion. Many of my people were ill of fevers and colds, a very common complaint among the inhabitants of the Cokan, when they ascend the Gauts. It is also the case with Europeans, a circumstance that I cannot avoid considering as extraordinary, though the same took place in the Tehama of Arabia.

The empire of the Mahrattas, which had once been sufficiently powerful to contest the possession of India with the Mussulmauns, though weakened by the total overthrow they experienced at Panipüt, was yet in a very flourishing state; and was prevented only by its internal dissensions from carrying its victorious arms through the greater part of the Peninsula. The treaty of Bassein, however, has, in fact, annihilated this empire, and has, in its stead, established the relatively independent states of the Berar Rajah, the Paishwa, Scindiah, Guikwar, and, if he should not be conquered in the present war, Holcar. An incalculable degree of security has been by these means acquired for the British provinces, which, after the conquests of Tippoo, had only to fear an union of the Hindoo Princes of India.

In the preparatory steps to the attainment of the important objects of an union between the Paishwa and the British, the greatest difficulty was the wavering and uncertain character of his Highness, who wanted sufficient firmness to adopt those decisive measures, of which he could not avoid perceiving the necessity, surrounded as he was by open and concealed enemies, and only nominally in possession of his legal power. Lord Wellesley gave way to his timidity, indulged him in his caprices and delays, and, at length, most perfectly acquired his confidence. In my private conference with his Highness, which I have before mentioned, he expressed his great satisfaction at the arrangements that had taken place; he spoke in the warmest manner of the comfort and security he enjoyed since his alliance with the English, and seemed extremely anxious to impress me with the idea that the friendship of our nation had been sought by his father previously to his time, and consequently was not a new measure. He spoke of the benefits as mutual; and declared his conviction, that, as it was both their interests, he had no doubt the two nations would continue united. He expressed great anxiety for the arrival of General Wellesley, when, he said, every thing would go on well, and the disturbers of the tranquillity of India would soon be annihilated. He then turned the conversation to myself; declared that he considered my arrival at so propitious a season as a very good omen, and rejoiced that my stay in his Capital, and the manner in which we associated together, would prove to the public the real friendship between the two countries. He particularly wished that I would, in England, make known that these were his feelings. In reply, I in general assured him of the regard which the English nation had for him and his family, and my conviction that the empires united were invincible. I told him that I would certainly make known his favourable sentiments towards my countrymen on my return; that, however, it would be unnecessary, as Lord Wellesley undoubtedly had already done so. I then declared the high character his Excellency bore among his countrymen, and the confidence we had in his talents and integrity. If, however, any troublesome people should in England pretend, that Lord Wellesley's friendship had induced him to give too favourable an account of the Paishwa's sentiments, I should, with the greatest satisfaction, step forward to contradict them. I afterwards expressed my gratitude for the honours he conferred on me, which I considered as a proof of his friendship for my country.

Colonel Close was highly gratified with the result of the conference, and assured me he had no doubt of the Paishwa's being sincere in what he had said. He had never seen him so evidently pleased, or heard him more unequivocally declare his sentiments. His heart is excellent, which is proved by the intimacy that subsists between him and his brother Chimnajee; they live in the same house, and seem to have only one purse and one opinion; yet this brother might be viewed with some jealousy, as having been himself installed Paishwa during the troubles which followed the death of Mahdoo Rao Narain. His Highness is like the majority of his countrymen, superstitious to a high degree: he however relaxes from the strictness of his moral obligations in one respect, having had three wives and several mistresses. His brother's conduct is more strict, and is, in every respect, so steady, that when seated at the Durbar he moves neither hand nor foot, and seems a candidate for the office of Swamie.

His Highness at the festival of Gunnais has a large party of ladies to dance before the deity, on which occasion he is accused of dressing himself out to the greatest advantage. Although this is according to precedent, yet his brother thought it might appear not sufficiently dignified in his present situation, and he accordingly sent a private friend to Colonel Close, who began by stating the Prince's high satisfaction at the British conduct, and the conviction of their extreme anxiety for his brother's prosperity. He then mentioned the dancing, and his fears concerning it, asking if Colonel Close could not give a hint to his Highness on the subject, which, coming from him, might have great weight. Colonel Close in reply observed, that he saw no possible means by which he could with delicacy interfere in a business, which related solely to their religious policy, but that if he would point out any means that occurred to him, the Colonel would try to use them. The Prince then sent to say, that if no means occurred to the superior understanding of Colonel Close, there were no hopes that he should discover any; and here the matter ended.

A perfect degree of cordiality subsists between the Mahratta durbar and the British Resident, yet frequently it is almost impossible to transact business from the interference of their superstitions. The waiting for a fortunate day may put off the most important concerns; and if a member of the minister's family dies, he is shut up for a month, and all business is at a stand. Formerly these difficulties were purposely brought forward, but even now we cannot quite get rid of them.

Our influence has hitherto been used to conciliate the minds of all. The brother of the widow of Nana Furnese had been put in prison during some former disturbances: we obtained his release. Imrut Row, his Highness's brother by adoption, was also essentially served by us. A friendship will probably never exist between them, but in the arrangements at a peace with Holcar, he may have a provision, and be kept on terms with his brother, without the power of doing him mischief. Imrut Row's absence, on a pilgrimage to Benares, will give time for the Paishwa's resentment to wear out, and his religious prejudices will be gratified by the benefits to be derived therefrom by the whole family.

Imrut Row was certainly the chief cause of the Paishwa's misfortunes, having invited Holcar down to Poonah, and corresponded with him the whole time. This was ungrateful and unjustifiable, his Highness having ever been an affectionate brother to him. It seems to have been their plan to place a son of his on the throne, in whose name the father would have governed. If they had seized the Paishwa, he would have been kept a prisoner. Imrut Row has thoroughly repented of his misconduct, abandoned all his evil connections, and thrown himself upon the protection of the English. His allowance is at present from them, and their interest is employed in his favour, with his justly irritated brother. His son is with him, and is a very fine boy. Nana Furnese's family were implicated in the conspiracy, but we induced his Highness to pardon them. He did it a little unwillingly, and has not restored their property.

When two Frenchmen landed on this coast, and made their way for Poonah, his Highness was on a religious journey to the source of the Kistna. On their overtaking him, he never admitted them to his presence, but sent them prisoners to Poonah. Colonel Close was not here, but, as soon as he heard of it, sent to desire they might be given up as our enemies. The Colonel was very much alarmed lest they should escape from the town, where they were slightly guarded, or be liberated by any of his Highness's enemies, when it would have been difficult, nay almost impossible, to prove that he had not connived at it. The Paishwa immediately gave them up, but put in a plea, that as we wished to imprison our enemies, we should not wish to liberate his; and this seems to have been his only motive for not sending them immediately to the Resident. I understand, they were much surprised to find his Highness so attached to the English. Bonaparte had probably calculated on a very different reception. They were intelligent men, who certainly had before been in the country, and their escape might, in many ways, have been disadvantageous.

The Paishwa is extremely exact in the performance of all the duties of his religion. This is supposed to be increased by some anxiety about the present state of his father's soul. Suspicions respecting the death of Sewai Mahdoo Rao Narain, who died by a fall from the terrace of the palace, were entertained by many. Some thought Ragonaut Rao had been instrumental to his fall, but Colonel Close believes him to have been innocent. He conceives that the Paishwa threw himself down in a fit of spleen, in consequence of a severe lecture he received from Nana, who treated him as a child. This happened when the Dewan discovered, that he had been carrying on a correspondence with the present Paishwa and his brother, the object of which was to liberate themselves from the severe tutorage of the old gentleman. They were all young men, and what they did was very natural, but the event proved fatal. The death of Narain Rao bears still heavier on Ragonaut Rao; though he was killed in an insurrection of his guards, yet it was generally supposed they were instigated by his uncle, who would have instantly reaped the profit of the crime by becoming Paishwa, had not the Brahmins declared, that one of his wives was with child, and that that child would be a son. It turned out so; and though on the boy's death, Ragonaut Rao had the power of the state for some time in his hands, yet for the want of a few forms he was never actually Paishwa. His son Chimnagee is reckoned as the sixth, and the present as the seventh, as will appear from the pedigree of the family, which will be given in the Appendix. His Highness's filial piety in endeavouring to liberate his father's soul from the stain of these crimes, by his own works of supererogation, is worthy of praise, however we may pity the ignorance that gives rise to an expectation of success.

The satisfaction expressed by his Highness at the result of his alliance with the British, and which every part of his conduct has shown to be unfeigned, will be easily accounted for by an examination of his situation prior to its taking place, and a comparison of it with his present ameliorated condition. Although the Paishwa was recognised as the representative of the sovereign, by the great feudatories of the Mahratta states, Scindiah, Holcar, and Guikwar, and by the Rajah of Berar, yet the control which he could exercise over princes, who each independently possessed revenues and forces equal to his own, must at all times have been trifling; but latterly Scindiah had, in fact, reduced him to a state of subjection, and merely used his name as a cloak to his ambitious plan of uniting in himself the whole power of the Mahratta empire. In this attempt he met with resistance from Holcar, who was defeated by him, but whom he imprudently permitted to retire unmolested to Chandore, where having rapidly increased his forces, he attacked the troops of Scindiah and the Paishwa forty miles from Poonah, in turn defeated them completely, and got possession of the capital.

The Paishwa took this occasion to escape, though he was so hurried as to be obliged to leave his family behind him. Thus driven from his rights and territories by the successive attacks of these feudatory chiefs, it was natural that he should seek for assistance against them, where alone it could be procured. He accepted therefore the offer of offensive and defensive alliance made to him by the British Government in India, and ultimately concluded with them the treaty of Bassein on the 31st of December 1802. The most active preparations were immediately commenced for the re-establishment of his Highness in his just rights. Major General Wellesley proceeded at the head of an army from the southward, and obliged the troops of Holcar to evacuate Poonah, having saved that place from being plundered by a rapid march of sixty miles in thirty-two hours. His Highness made his public entry into his capital on the 13th of May 1803, since which period he has, by the assistance of his allies, gradually got possession of his territories, the prosperity of which has been greatly increased by the uninterrupted state of tranquillity which has followed the successes of the British arms.

In another respect, his Highness has been essentially benefited by his connection with the British Government; I mean in the improvement of his finances, by the arrangements which have been adopted according to the plan recommended by Colonel Close. Formerly every Sirdar retained, with impunity, whatever part of the revenue he pleased, and in many of the provinces no part of it found its way to the treasury of the Paishwa. This was the case in Bundelcund, which was estimated at sixty lac of rupees per annum, and in the districts ceded by Tippoo, which were estimated at forty-one lac. The former has been given up to the British by a treaty, subsequent to that of Bassein, and now nets forty-four lac, of which thirty six are retained for the payment of the subsidiary force, and his Highness receives the other eight. The latter was originally ceded to the British, and, though given up on receiving Bundelcund, the system of collection had been so far improved, that his Highness now obtains from it above twenty-one lac. The provinces nearer to the seat of government were of course more productive; but even these were liable to all the peculations which naturally existed under a weak government, and were too frequently devastated by the hostile presence of the contending chieftains, or by the more amicable but not much less dreadful, annual assemblage of undisciplined cavalry of the Dusserah. These evils are put an end to by the British victories; and it seems probable that the territories above the Gauts will be rendered secure from any future hostile incursions, by Colonel Wallace's conquest of the hill forts that belong to Holcar, and which command the passes between the two countries. The presence of a subsidiary force ready to enforce obedience, has also operated in causing the payments to be regularly made.

His Highness's gross revenue may be fairly estimated as follows:

		Rupees.
In Guzerat - -	Ahmood - -	2,00,000
	Jumbooseer -	5,00,000
	Duboy - - -	1,25,000
	Cokan - - -	9,00,000
	Sevendroog, &c.	2,00,000
Above the Gauts, N. and W. of Poonah	Juneer - - -	10,00,000
	Sungumnere -	10,00,000
	Ahmednuggur	4,00,000
Added by the treaty of Seringapatam, 1792 - - - -	Savanore - -	8,72,838
	Bankapore -	7,51,278
	Darwar - -	4,15,608
	Bundelcund -	8,00,000
		R. 71,64,724

Were the above revenue realised, it would be more than sufficient for the maintenance of the Paishwa, as chief of the Mahratta empire; but this is far from being the case, though it is impossible to know exactly what portion of it reaches his treasury. The actual expence of collection is very great; the hill forts are numerous, and the garrisons large, which must be regularly paid; provisions are sent in kind for the use of his family; and what is a still greater expence, he is obliged to connive at many abuses to conciliate the chief natives who are about his person. Yet there is no doubt that he receives double the sum he ever did before: and it is probable, that by following the suggestions of the able and upright officer who manages the British affairs at his court, he will shortly be in affluence, and have a full treasury, to which he may recur in cases of emergency. At present, should only a lac or two of rupees be wanting, he must borrow it, or procure it by harsher means. This is entirely owing to mismanagement, for were the above provinces under the British Government, they would yield twice the sum at which they are estimated, without any additional burthen to the inhabitants.

Nothing can have been more prudent and conciliatory, than the conduct of the British since the connection between the two powers. No object has been pressed hastily or warmly, and every opportunity has been seized to oblige his Highness. By the treaty of Bassein he had been induced, at the particular request of the Company, to accommodate them by a grant of a small slip of seacoast in Guzerat, valued at ten lac per annum; yet on a representation being made that the district of Olpar had formerly been in the possession of a Sirdar, to whom he was particularly attached, it was immediately exchanged with his Highness for a district of equal value in Bundelcund, although Olpar was particularly desirable on account of its vicinity to Surat. It would be an object of the greatest importance to the British Government, to obtain a cession of the tract of land below the Gauts from Damaun to Carwar, as it would complete the security of the sea coast from the Gulf of Cambay to the Indus; but unfortunately the greater part of this, was a grant of the Mogul to Bajee Rao, the first Paishwa, as a jaghire, and being therefore considered by them as a private property of the family, they are extremely unwilling to alienate it. This reason was candidly admitted, and the subject dropt. Any alarm which might have been excited in the Paishwa's mind, (a mind timid from a deficient education, having been brought up by Brahmins in complete seclusion, where he was taught nothing but their religious ceremonies, of which he is a perfect master,) by the idea that the British wished to grasp at every thing, and merely to employ him as an instrument of their ambition, has been done away by the free gift of the strong fort of Ahmednuggur and the district around it, which was conquered by Major General Wellesley, and to which he had no claim; and still more strongly since, by their having engaged in a war with Holcar, on terms so beneficial to him, and so triflingly advantageous to themselves, even if complete success should attend their arms.

The friendship which the Paishwa evidently feels for the British, must in a great degree, be attributed to the able conduct of Colonel Close, the Resident, but still more so to the confidence he places in the military and civil talents of General Wellesley, to whose active exertions he owes his re-establishment at Poonah, an event that might never have taken place, had the service been entrusted to a less able officer. Rapidity of movement was in this, as in every other Indian war, of the first importance, and to render this practicable, a regular supply of provisions was absolutely necessary. Of this branch of the military art, General Wellesley has shown himself a perfect master; and has added to it a decision in council, and a spirit in action, which have rarely appeared in India. The provinces which his arms have conquered, have been conciliated by the protection he has invariably afforded them from all military oppression; and a personal confidence has been excited by the suavity of his manners, and an invariable attention to their religious prejudices. Uniform success attended him in the Mahratta war; but since the disturbances excited by Holcar, he has not commanded, and events have been less prosperous. It is natural therefore that the Paishwa should wish anxiously for his return, with a firm conviction that the tide of victory will again attend him.

Holcar, who is an active and able man, had very wisely employed the time, while his rival Scindiah was engaged in a destructive war, to occupy all the estates of his family, to replenish his coffers and recruit his forces. Had he been satisfied with this, he might have tranquilly retained the possession, although an illegitimate son of the late Holcar, and consequently not the representative of the family; but, instead of this, he made the most unreasonable demands of property beyond Delhi, which, he said, had been held prior to the battle of Paniput; and, on being refused, commenced actual hostilities by levying contributions on the Jeypoor Rajah, an ally of the British. Colonel Monson entered his country, and took

Rampoora; but unfortunately despising his enemy too much, had his supplies of provisions cut off, and was obliged to make a retreat, in which he was pursued by Holcar, and lost a great number of men, and all his ammunition and cannon. It is probably in some respects fortunate, that Holcar has been thus drawn to the northward, where he can make no impression against General Lake's army, as he might otherwise have plundered the plains of Guzerat, and done incalculable mischief to the Guikwar, an evil that is now prevented by the success of Colonel Wallace.

The original Mahratta system of warfare had been greatly changed by Scindiah: instead of vast bodies of cavalry, which by forced marches would attack an unsuspecting province, and retire with their booty before a sufficient force could be assembled to resist them, he attempted to establish an army of infantry, disciplined after the European system, and commanded by European officers. As these increased in numbers, he diminished the other, but fortunately was seduced by his vanity into a war with the British, before his plans had been matured. Warned by his fate, Holcar has, in a great degree, depended on his cavalry, of which he has eighteen thousand, independent of twelve thousand Pindanis, or undisciplined free booters, while his infantry does not amount to above ten thousand men. Such a force can make little resistance to the army opposed to him, when under General Wellesley, whose appearance will give confidence to all. This is one great advantage in employing an officer, in whom the Supreme Government can place unlimited confidence. Much may be done at the moment of victory, which would be impracticable were an application necessary to the seat of Government; more-particularly in a war with a Mahratta power, whose whole system of policy is delay. Had not General Wellesley been authorised to treat after the battle of Assaye, without referring to Calcutta, the enemy would have had time to recover their panic, recruit their forces, and prepare for another war.

CHAPTER IV.

Departure from Poonah.—Arrival at Chinchoor.—Visit to a supposed Incarnation of Gunputty.—History of the Founder of his Family.—Visit to the Rajah of Tillegam.—Account of the excavated Pagodas at Carli.—Visit to the Hill Fort of Low Ghur.—Return to and Observations on Bombay. Fortifications—Town—Dock-yards.—Marine.—Trade.—Insalubrity of Climate.—Country Residences in the vicinity.—Manner of living.—Establishment of the Bombay Literary Society.—Evils attendant on the cheapness of spirits.—Character of the Persees.—Embassies to Persia.—Visit to the Pagodas at Salsette and Elephanta.

AT sunrise, on the 22nd October, I departed from the hospitable mansion of Col. Close, where I had spent ten most pleasant days. Soon afterwards the village of Ound was pointed out to me, as a remarkable instance of the manner in which the possessions of the different Chieftains of the Mahratta empire were separated from each other. This little district, though surrounded on every side by the territories of the Paishwa, is the property of Scindiah, while, at the other extremity of the empire, Culpee belongs to his Highness. In the same manner

Waufgorn, though only twenty-four miles north of Poonah, gave birth to the family of Holcar, to whom also belongs Kooch, on the banks of the Jumna. This intermixture of estates was formerly considered beneficial, as preventing a separation of interests; but now that the union of these independent Princes is at an end, it has been proposed to exchange such detached possessions, and consolidate the territories of each.

My palanquin bearers were very lazy, so that I did not reach the encampment at Chinchoor till nine o'clock. I found there Colonel Chalmers and my other friends, who had kindly attended me thus far, that we might together visit the extraordinary personage, described by Captain Edward Moore, in the seventh volume of the Asiatic Researches, and who is believed, by a large proportion of the Mahratta nation, to be an incarnation of their favourite deity Gunputty. Immediately on my arrival I sent a messenger to Chintau-mun-Deo, who is the present reigning Deity, with the usual compliments, notifying my intention of paying him a visit in the evening, and requesting that he would, in the mean time, send some learned Brahmins, who could give me an account of his family. A most gracious answer was returned; and with the most learned of his Brahmins, came one of his own relations.

Colonel Close undertook most kindly to make every inquiry that I wished, and by his assistance, and that of Captain Frissell, I collected the following history of the Deo's ancestors.

Mooraba Gosseyn was a native of Beder, and a Mahratta or country Brahmin. In his youth he would attend to no business, but used to run up and down the country collecting flowers, and offering them to the deities. His father, finding he could make nothing of him, turned him out of doors. In passing Moraishwer, near Baramutty, he was struck with the deity Gunputty, and determined to pay him regular devotion. He however went on to Chinchoor, which had then but two houses, and no name: pleased with the spot, he took up his residence there. In the morning he regularly performed the ablutions in the river, and then set off for Moraishwer, distant twenty-five coss, where he performed his devotions to Gunputty, and at night returned to Chinchoor. The Pingli family of Mahratta Brahmins were at that time in great power at Moraishwer, and performed the Pooja. On the first grand festival of Gunnais Chout, Mooraba, having prepared his necessary offerings and flowers, conceived great hopes of his being able to perform the ceremony, which he thought would be particularly meritorious. The Pingli Brahmins being in possession of the civil power, performed the ceremonies with great splendour. Mooraba, being poor, could not approach for the crowd of richer suppliants. At this he was severely mortified, but at length retired to the foot of a Naipte tree, which still exists there, performed his Pooja, and left his offerings. In the evening he, as usual, returned to Chinchoor. In the course of the night the offerings were transposed, Mooraba's being placed before the Deity, while the Pingli's were found at the foot of the tree. The Poojanie Brahmins, astonished and alarmed, inquired to whom the accepted offerings belonged, and learned that a Cokan Brahmin had been there the day before, had performed his devotion at the foot of the tree, and had since disappeared.

On Mooraba's appearance the following day, the event was instantly communicated to the Pingli, who ordered him to be brought before them. On their interrogating him respecting the whole business, he simply related what had passed. They then demanded where he lived; he replied "below the Gauts, but the place has no name: you may come along, and see where it is, if you please." Believing this to be impossible from the distance, unless he were a sorcerer, they immediately ordered him to be driven across the river, and forbad his return under pain of punishment.

Mooraba was now completely heart-broken. He laid himself down at the foot of a Mimosa, and humbling himself before the Deity, deprecated his wrath; and declared his willingness to give up his life to him, which he conceived necessary, as he could not eat till he had performed his devotions, and he was now completely debarred from the possibility of doing so. On looking up he perceived a Brahmin standing before him, who was, in reality, Gunputty. He inquired the cause of his grief, and after hearing his whole story, comforted him, offered him utensils and provisions, and added that he would himself conduct him to the Deity. To this arrangement Mooraba objected, stating, that if the sacrifice were made of things not procured by himself, he should have no merit. Mooraba therefore requested that the Brahmin would advance him the money necessary to purchase the offerings, and would, as a security, keep his lota, or small vessel in which he was accustomed to dress his provisions. To this the Brahmin replied, that without his lota he could not mix up the offering; that therefore he should first procure the articles, and, after the ceremony was over, and the lota washed, it might be given as a pledge. To this proposal Mooraba assented, and, attended by the Brahmin, went into the town, no where meeting with any obstruction. After the devotions were over, they returned to the foot of the tree, and eat together. Mooraba then went down to the river to wash his lota, that he might give it to the Brahmin, but on his return he could no where see him. Mooraba now feared the shopman might have been cheated, and therefore returned to him for the purpose of lodging his lota in pledge; but, finding that the Brahmin had paid for every thing, returned to Chinchoor with his lota.

That night Gunputty appeared in a dream to the Pingli Brahmins, and other magistrates, and told them he was extremely offended at their ill usage of the poor Brahmin, who had shown so much devotion to him by his daily pilgrimages, and so much zeal by his offerings, and that therefore he was determined to be served by him, and to quit them. Mooraba arrived, as usual, in the morning at the foot of the tree, but dared not to approach any farther without his friendly Brahmin. As soon as his arrival was notified to the Pingli, they set out to visit him, attended by the magistrates and other Brahmins. Poor Mooraba, extremely alarmed after the ill usage he had already received, retreated as they advanced. They however at length induced him to stop, by assurances that they only came to pay their respects to him. They then told him the dream they had had, and requested he would stay at Moraishwer. This he positively refused. They then demanded where he lived. He said they might send a man with him who would see. This they did, but the man could only keep up with him for ten coss. He then lost him, and returned to the Pingli. Mooraba himself returned in the morning to his devotions. The Pingli again sent a person with him, who again returned, having got only ten coss, as before.

This continued for some time; at length Gunputty appeared in a dream to Mooraba, still preserving the form of the friendly Brahmin, and told him that he had too much trouble to go every day to Moraishwer to perform his devotions; that, the next morning he, Gunputty, would visit him at his own habitation, and take up his abode with him. The morning ablutions of Mooraba were performed up to his middle in the river: he, as usual, dipped his hands, joined together, and his head at the same time, under the water; when he raised them up again, he was equally surprised and delighted, to discover in his hands the image of Gunputty, as worshipped at Moraishwer. On recognising this, he took it home, smeared it with red paint, prepared a shrine for it, and ever afterwards performed his pooja to it, without thinking it necessary to visit Moraishwer. The fame of the Deity's taking up his residence at Chinchoor brought thither a great number of Brahmins, and one of great respectability offered his daughter to Mooraba. They were married, and after a certain time the God appeared in a dream to Mooraba, and told him his wife was with child, that he would have one son only, and that that son would be himself, "woh humara avatar howega." He therefore directed him to call his name "Chintau-mun-Deo," which was one of the titles of Gunputty.

The event of course fulfilled the prophecy of the Deity, and Chintau-mun-Deo received the adorations of the surrounding country. He, in his turn, had a son, who was called Narain Deo, and from that time they have taken this name, and that of Chintau-mun-Deo alternately; the seventh in descent being the present Deo, and who goes by the latter name. Major Moore calls him Bawa, and his father Gabajee, but these are only familiar appellatives, like Baba, Appa, Nana, so common among the Mahrattas, and so puzzling to strangers. Each Deity at his death has been burnt, and invariably a small image of Gunputty has miraculously arisen from the ashes, which is placed in a tomb and worshipped.

I asked my informers whether Chintau-mun-Deo, who was himself an avatar, performed pooja to his other self as taken out of the water; they replied, certainly, for that the statue was greatest, nor was his power diminished by the avatar. I then wished to know how it was clear that the descendants of Chintau-mun-Deo were avatars. They replied that when Gunputty first took up his residence with Mooraba Gosseyn, he was asked by him how long he would stay with him, and was assured it should be for twenty-one generations. As Captain Moore had stated that it was only for seven generations, I repeated my inquiries, but they were positive it was for twenty-one. I suggested the possibility of a failure of the male line, which they would by no means admit, declaring that Gunputty had made the promise, and he would take care to fulfil it. I think however they have not acted with their usual prudence, for the present Deo has no son, and his wife is still a child: were any accident to happen to him before she is old enough to have children, I think the Brahmins, ingenious as they are, would have some difficulty in carrying on the imposture.

Captain Moore mentions the constant miracle of the Deo's expences being so much greater than his income: this might easily be accounted for by the secret contributions of other Brahmins, who are essentially interested in the imposture, or by the supposition of a secret treasure having fallen into their hands, by no means a singular circumstance in a country, where perpetual danger induces every body to bury a large part of their property, without intrusting the secret to any one. Of this some conjecture may be drawn from an event, that has lately taken place at Bisnagur. A man has appeared there, who declares that he is sent by heaven to rebuild that ancient city: he has actually laid out the plan of the new town in a regular manner, with gardens to each house, and goes on building rapidly. Whenever he wants money, he goes to the top of a hill, where he declares he receives it from heaven, but probably he has discovered some secret treasure, from which he draws such ample resources.

The Deo resides on the opposite side of the river, in a very excellent house for the country, part of which was built by old Nana Furnese, and part by Hurry Punt. We went over in a boat, and landed at the place where the former Deos were buried: they were burnt, and their ashes deposited in small stone pagodas. In each is the Gunputty that appeared on the occasion; they are of different sizes, without any merit. The temple of the first deity is the largest, and is of stone without ornaments; the walls very thick, with strong doors, and bolts on the inside. Our Brahmin friends accompanied us, and pointed out every object. We did not enter the little buildings, but approached close to the doors. When we reached the habitation of the Deo, we were seated in the verandah described by Captain Moore; the small door was open, which communicated with the room where the Deo was seated, on a small elevation; but as the room was dark, he was hardly discernible. I presented a nazur, as did the Colonel. The money was given into the hands of a Brahmin, who laid it at his feet. He looked at it attentively, and then motioned to have it taken away.

After a compliment, the people enquired if there were not a medical gentleman with us. On being informed that there was, the Brahmin said, the Deo wanted his assistance. A window had been opened, which gave us a full view of him; he was a heavy looking man, with very weak eyes; it was to relieve these that he now applied for assistance. Mr. Murray said he wished to examine them. The Deo accordingly moved forward on his seat, close to the light, and Mr. Murray was admitted into the sanctum sanctorum. His Godship was too anxious about his eyes to recollect his dignity; he explained his case himself, and answered pertinently to all questions. A film had grown completely over both eyes, so that little assistance could be afforded without constant attendance, and that it was impossible to give. He would not permit Mr. Murray to touch his eyes, as he said he had then performed his ablutions for the day. In the morning there would have been no such objection, as he could have been purified; but now he was only waiting for our departure to have a large party of Brahmins dine with him, and there was no time for purification. Almonds were brought to him, of which he took a handful, and emptied them into mine, which I held underneath to receive them. I entered the inner apartment, as did the other gentlemen in their turns. He took care that no one touched him. He also gave me a pan full of rice, which he said was of a very fine sort, and particularly holy.

We now took leave, and Mr. Murray told him he would send him something for his eyes. He said, if I had any enquiries to make, he would answer them. I merely asked if I should reach my home in safety. The reply of course was, that every thing prosperous would attend me. The

Brahmins returned with us, but before their departure took occasion to observe, that they worshiped him, but he worshipped Gunputty. This brahminical imposture has been of great use to the country during Holcar's invasion. It was never plundered, which was probably owing to the Chief's superstition; but the Brahmins attribute it to a miracle. They told us several stories: as that, when some Patans attempted to approach the town, they saw a guard of supernatural horse drawn up to protect it; and that another party that came even to the tope in which we were encamped, close to the river, and directly opposite the holy burial place, were seized with such violent pains in their bowels, that they were obliged to retire in dismay. On our return we were pestered with several beggars.

At day light we took leave of our hospitable friends, and with ease reached Tillegam to breakfast. I was met, about a mile from the town, by the Rajah's cousin, who attended me to the tents, where he and the minister paid their compliments, and delivered an invitation from the Rajah to visit him: which I promised, as I found, by enquiries at Poonah, that he was a respectable man, a Mahratta, holding under that government, on the tenure of military service only. He was formerly powerful, but at present, like many others, is much reduced. As his territories lie between Poonah, where the British subsidiary force is generally stationed, and the presidency of Bombay, it is advisable to be on good terms with him. One anecdote does him great credit: he fed nearly the whole of his village during the late famine.

Four o'clock was the time settled for our visit, as he wished us to take a repast with him, and had sent for our table, knives, forks, and spoons: the

Ministers came to attend us. The town was larger than I supposed, and seemed thriving; his own residence bore the marks of ancient splendor. He received us in a small verandah on the ground floor, covered with a piece of velvet carpeting. Several decently dressed people were around him. He was rather a young man, with a good-natured open countenance. To our enquiries after his health, he answered in English, that he was very well. His English interpreter then said, he was there to teach him that language. Mr. Frissel found that he also spoke Persian tolerably: a very remarkable proof in a Mahratta of a desire to acquire information. We adjourned to the repast up stairs, where we found some good meat curries, and a bottle of brandy, a liquor I did not expect in a Rajah's house, but to which he has the character of being considerably attached.

On returning down stairs, it was whispered to Mr. Frissel that there were more gentlemen present than he expected, and that therefore he had not prepared presents for all of them. It was settled that a distinction would be indecorous, and that he should offer them only to me. They consisted of a dress, a part of which he wished to put on, but Mr. Frissel told him it could not be permitted: he tied a small serpaish round my hat. The minister inundated me with plain water instead of rose water, which was not very agreeable. I had however the pleasure of afterwards seeing all the rest of the party undergo the same punishment. Pawn and attar were served round, and we took our leave. We had a party of Bazeegurs or Nats, who are described by Captain Richardson in the seventh volume of the Asiatic Researches, to amuse us at our tents. The women tumbled very actively, and were remarkably robust figures. Their small tents were pitched without the town, and were in size like those of our gypsies. Captain Richardson has, in the work above quoted, pointed out other circumstances of resemblance, that certainly justify, in a very great degree, his conjecture of their having a common origin. The similarity of language is almost a conclusive argument.

In order to visit the Caves of Carli to more advantage, we had the tents pitched at the foot of the hill, which contains these interesting antiquities. It is nearly opposite to the fort of Low Ghur, distant about four miles, directly across the vale. The chain of hills here runs nearly east and west, but this protrudes from them at right angles. The chief cave fronts due west. There are also a few in a bluff point at the southern extremity, the entrances to which are visible from the bottom. The whole road was covered with small agates, of which I collected a few. It was a long stage, and I did not reach the ground till eleven. The Killadar of Esapoor paid me a visit, and informed me that he had received orders to show me the fort of Low Ghur. In the evening, Hurry Punt Bow, deputy to Cundeh Row Rastieh, Ser Soobah of the Cokan, who was on his road to the country below the Gauts, came also to wait on me, and brought presents of fruit, &c. Cundeh Row, being supreme head of Low Ghur, Esapoor, and most other forts in the country, had sent Hurry Punt to represent him, and receive my visit. He was a fine old man, with a white beard, and smiling countenance. I gave him notice of my intention to be there on the 26th, to breakfast, and desired guides to be sent.

Breakfast was sent up to the caves, and we went there before the sun became hot. The ascent was steep, but rendered easy by steps which had been cut in the rock. The whole brow of the hill was covered with jungle, which concealed the caves till we came to an open space of about one hundred feet, which had been levelled by the cutting away of the sloping hill, till a perpendicular surface of about fifty feet had been found in the solid rock. Here a line of caverns had been excavated, the principal of which struck me with the greatest astonishment from its size, and the peculiarity of its form. It consisted of a vestibule of an oblong square shape, divided from the temple itself, which was arched, and supported by pillars. The accompanying view will give a better idea than words can, of its internal appearance. The length of the whole is one hundred and twenty six feet, the breadth forty six feet. No figures of any deities are to be found within the pagoda, but the walls of the vestibule are covered with carvings in alto-relievo of elephants, of human figures of both sexes, and of Boodh, who is represented in some places as sitting cross legged, with his hands in the posture common among the Cingalese; in others he is erect, but in all he is attended by figures in the act of adoration; and in one place two figures standing on the lotus are fanning him with chouries, while two others are suspending a rich crown over his head. I think it therefore beyond dispute, that the whole was dedicated to Boodh. The detail of the different ornaments and figures, with drawings of them, I sent to the Bombay Literary Society, in whose works they will appear; it is therefore unnecessary to repeat them here. The inscriptions are numerous in different parts, and are all in the same unknown character which is found at the Seven Pagodas, and is described in the fifth volume of the Asiatic Researches. We copied all that we could discover, and chalked over the letters for the benefit of any traveller that might come after us. There may be others concealed under the coat of chunam which still covers a great part of the wall; where it is broken off, the marks of the chissel are perfectly visible.

The ribs on the roof, which are seen in the drawing, are of wood, and are very difficult to be accounted for. They cannot be supposed to be of an equal age with the excavation, yet who would have been at the expence of replacing them? The followers of Boodh no longer worship here; the country is in possession of their great enemies, the Brahmins, and the pagoda itself is considered as haunted by evil spirits, in defiance of the vicinity of the holy goddess Bowannie; so much so, that the native draftsman who drew the cave at Ellora for Sir Charles Mallet, could not be induced to accompany us by any persuasion of Colonel Close, declaring that if he did, the evil spirit would injure him.

Without the vestibule stands a pillar twenty four feet high, and eight feet in diameter, on which is a single line in the unknown characters. On the capital are four lions, much resembling the Chinese. Opposite to it was another pillar, but it was removed about forty years ago, to make room for the insignificant temple of Bowannie, which now occupies its place. A view of the whole front, which was too large to be introduced in this work, is given by Mr. Salt in his Indian Views.

The Paishwa has settled a revenue on Bowannie's pagoda, and there is a regular establishment of Brahmins to attend her, while the splendid abode of Boodh is completely neglected.

A line of caves extends from about one hundred and fifty yards to the north of the great one. These are all flat-roofed, of a square form, and appear to have been destined for the attendants on the pagoda. In the last is a figure of Boodh, and in another is an inscription. They evidently were never finished.

A veil at present is suspended over the relative antiquity of the Boodhists and the Brahmins, which may possibly be hereafter removed; but these hopes are lessened by the recollection, that all the learning that has yet been found in India, has been in the possession of the Brahmins, who seem to have completely triumphed over their dangerous rivals, the Boodhists, who profanely gave precedence to the Royal Cast, above the holy race of the Priesthood.

Lieutenant Ambrose joined us. I was sorry to find that he had lain the preceding night under a mango tree, in the tope where we had encamped in going up, without any thing to cover him. He was a lively, pleasing young man, who had been in the navy during the Egyptian expedition, and afforded us great assistance in copying the inscriptions. Before night I was happy to find, that we were possessed of every inscription and necessary admeasurement. Mr. Salt's work was more extensive; he therefore determined not to accompany us to Low Ghur, but again to visit the caves on the morrow, and join us at the mango tope, whither we meant to remove our encampment. To the Brahmins who attended the small pagoda, dedicated to Bowannie, and to others who lived in the great cave, we gave some rupees, as they had been civil and useful.

Very early on the next day all the party, except Messrs. Salt and Smith, set off for Low Ghur. The road across the valley was good, but when we began to ascend, the palanquins were of little use. We saw a line of caves facing due west on our left under the hill, on the summit of which is the fort of Esapoor. My servant visited them by my orders, to examine if there were any thing worthy of inspection. He reported that there was a small arched temple, similar in plan to that at Carli, but that the pillars were plain, and there was not any inscription or figure of Boodh, and that smaller flat caves were on each side, but uninteresting; we did not therefore take the trouble of climbing to them. Hurry Punt had taken great pains to render our ascent easy. The bushes were cut away on both sides, and in many parts, the road had been levelled. The mount we ascended was part of Esapoor; we left the fort rather to the left, and as we came close to it, we were hailed from it. The walls were covered with men, and on the reply that it was the Lord Sahib, they sounded the trumpets, and gave a cheer.

At the top we were met by the acting Killadar of Esapoor, who conducted us to the village at the bottom of the rock, on which Low Ghur is built. Here we left the palanquins, which had only been of use the last half mile. We mounted by a very steep path that led in a zig-zag direction to the top. There are five gates with parapets and loop holes for musquetry: these were far from adding to the strength of the place, as in many parts they afford lodgements for a storming party. At every gateway was a guard. In the open space before the hall of audience, Hurry Punt was ready to receive me. He conducted me to the durbar, where a guddy was placed with one pillow. He sat down on the left of it; I seated myself in state upon it: my party on my right hand; his, beyond him on the left. After a few compliments, we adjourned to a breakfast prepared for us in a verandah, near at hand, and afterwards, in defiance of the heat, walked round the fort.

On the north side is a range of decayed cannon which were always useless, as the height of the perpendicular rock is too great on every side, to be stormed. Towards the west, a very extraordinary ledge extends several hundred yards in length, by about twenty wide. A wall is built along, on each side, to prevent accidents: at small distances are houses, inhabited by the guard, which we found drawn out to receive us. Though this ledge is lower than the main body of the fort, yet it is of sufficient height to prevent any attack, the rock being perfectly bare, and perpendicular. The whole in shape considerably resembles a tadpole, the fort representing the body, and this ledge the tail. From the summit the view was very extensive: the sea beyond Bombay appeared to the west; inland a chain of hills was visible in every direction, whose tops frequently rose into fortified summits, with rocky sides, as perpendicular as Low Ghur, The most extraordinary circumstance was the regularity of the strata, and the equal height of the rocky sides: were the line continued from one hill to another, it would touch the corresponding parts of similar strata. The summits were mostly green, and capable of cultivation. Low Ghur has numerous tanks, and several small streams from the springs above were falling down the rocks. Esapoor is higher, and only a musquet-shot from Low Ghur. Were the former, however, in the hands of an enemy, it could do but little harm, as this place is very extensive, and is protected from shot by rocks in almost every direction. Lieutenant Ambrose had been here before, when it was surrendered to the British arms. He told us that the quantity of ammunition and stores of all kinds was prodigious.

Dondoe Punt was the person who had been intrusted with the custody of the fort by Nana Furnese, and refused, after his death, to give it up. Here Nana had deposited all his treasures, the plunder of the treasury at Poonah, and the savings of his administration. Here also resided his widow. Dondoe at first demanded the restoration of Nana's adherents to their offices under the state, which of course, the Paishwa could never consent to, they having all been rebellious, both under Nana, and afterwards under Imrut Row. At length he gave up this point, and only required permission for himself and the widow to retire with their private property. He always denied that there was any of Nana's there, but the Paishwa thought otherwise, and conceived that when he had concluded the treaty with the English, they would take it for him by force. General Wellesley negociated for him, and on Dondoe's promising to behave as a faithful subject of the Paishwa, he was permitted to hold the fort. When, however, his Highness went, as he annually does, to bathe in the Kistna, the garrison of another fort, held by the same man, fired on him, and would not permit him to pass to a pagoda. This the General took up, and threatened to storm Low Ghur. At length terms were agreed upon: Dondoe gave up the place, retired with his personal poperty to Tanna, and the widow to Panwell. Their personal safety was guaranteed by the British, and 12,000 rupees, per ann. were secured to the widow. She has also one of Nana's houses to retire to at Poonah, whenever she pleases.

The garrison seems numerous, but as the followers of Hurry Punt and the Killadar of Esapoor were there, I cannot guess the amount: to have asked, would have been useless. The buildings are miserable. The old gentleman, when I took my leave, presented a handsome pair of shawls, a piece of kincaub, and a piece of cloth. We examined the gateways as we came down, and I am quite convinced that the whole of the artificial works much lessen the natural strength of the place. Each high side of the way forms a sheltering place, secure against all attacks from the top, whether of musquetry, or their more usual weapons, large stones rolled down from above. The gateways and parapets have the same effect. Had the whole been scalped off, and only a strong work at the top, I believe no earthly power could have taken it. It is considered as the strongest fort in the Paishwa's possession, and an order from him was necessary to see it. The magazines are cut in the rock, but are now nearly empty; however, as the state grows richer, they will probably be replenished.

We set off next morning for the top of the Gaut. Candalla had presented too melancholy a spectacle for us to wish to stay there again; we therefore went on to the point, about a mile beyond. The scene was magnificent. The small plain which served for our encampment was on the extremity of a tongue of the table land. On one side the sea was visible; on the other Low Ghur, and the other hills: close to us, between these objects, was a woody glen, with impassable rocky sides, the depth of the whole gaut, at one extremity of which a cascade fell two or three hundred feet. In the rainy season it must be tremendous. Mr. Salt took a view of it as it was, but the scale reduced the stream to insignificance. Captain Young is Commissary for the supplying of the British subsidiary force with rice; and by contracting on moderate terms, and to be paid only for what he actually delivered, put an end to one of the most enormous abuses that existed. We here met several of his bullocks loaded with rice, which he stopped, and humanely gave two seer to each person who came to us from the village. It is an almost incredible circumstance, but which strongly marks the patient forbearance, the resignation of the Hindoo, that during the whole of the late dreadful famine, grain has passed up to Poonah through villages, where the inhabitants were perishing themselves, and, what is still more dreadful, seeing their nearest relatives perishing for want, without a single tumult having taken place, or a single convoy having been intercepted!

As we walked down the Gauts, the change in the climate was very evident. The heat was most oppressive, with not a breath of air. We encamped at Colapore, which we had left on the right as we went up, where we found in the Choultry an old woman dead, a lad nearly so, and a young woman much reduced. We first gave some congee to the boy, which his stomach bore, and afterwards some rice. The old woman was buried, and the young one went off gaily with a sufficient sum to keep her till provisions should be again in plenty. We had fowls and eggs from the Patale of the village. Our people were all better, though some were still obliged to be carried.

The next morning before day-light I was in my palanquin. By eight I reached Panwell. I received the compliment of sweet cakes from Nana's widow, and learned that her brother Purseram Punt had arrived four days before from Poonah to assist in receiving me. He had been confined by the Paishwa, together with the other connections of the Nana, till the British interest obtained his release, when he became a constant visitor to the Residency. He is a modest, well-behaved young man, and in great favour with the Colonel. When presented to me, I expressed a wish to see his sister on my return, and asked whether it was against the Mahratta custom, that no purdah should be between us? He allowed that, by their own principles, there would be no impropriety in my seeing her, but that they had adopted from the Mussulmauns, since they had been so powerful in India, the custom of keeping their women concealed. He, however, promised to do his best for me, if I would visit her on my return to Panwell; to which I consented. He did not appear in the morning, nor Dondoe Punt, the late Governor of Low Ghur, who had come down on a visit to the widow, probably also to assist in receiving the visit. As I suspected that their absence was meant as a mark of dignity, in stealing the compliment of the first visit, Mr. Frissel sent to them to say, that he expected they would come here. The answer was, they were coming immediately, which they did.

Dondoe is a laughing old man, and talks a great deal. He soon began with Mr. Frissel about his own merits in giving up the fort to us, and his claims to compensation. To this but little was replied. We asked him respecting some steps down into the rock at the narrow end of the fort. He said it was intended by one of the Sattera Rajahs, who visited the fort, to have made another outlet at that end, but it had never been completed. He allowed he had only three months provisions when he capitulated. The garrison, in his time, varied from one to three thousand men, according to circumstances. He had lived there thirty years without ever descending, and complained that the climate below did not agree with him, but supposed he should soon get accustomed to it. He said that several hundred horses, which he had brought down with him, had all perished. Captain Young said in English, it was a great blessing to Panwell, where most of them were kept, for his followers had plundered the whole country to maintain them. We did not after this observation, express much pity for his loss. Four o'clock was the hour fixed for visiting the lady. He said he heard I meant to visit Salsette, and he should be happy to entertain me. If I did not go to Tannah, where he lived, he would meet me at the caves: to which proposal I assented.

At four the whole party set off with my suwarry. The little widow's house is not large, and most of the people in it are Brahmins. We were introduced into a small court, and seated on carpets covered with a white cloth, in a verandah, at the end of which was a door with a purdah of rushes, through which it would have been easy to distinguish any object, had not the room beyond been darkened. As I took no notice of the widow not being visible, the attendants began the subject by repeating the observations her brother had made at Poonah about the Mussulmaun women. It was evident they meant me to see her, from their having fixed up a linen curtain to conceal her from the people in the court of the house, I therefore wished to hasten them on, and replied, that it was very well, they might do as they pleased, and that I was satisfied. They knew I was not, and wished me to go nearer the purdah, which I refused. The brother then began to observe that, as I was going to England, he hoped, now that I knew his sister, I would be a friend to her there. I told him that I knew nothing of his sister; I only knew a purdah that was hung before her, and to that only I could be a friend. He laughed, and went again to speak to his sister. I and Mr. Frissel approached close to the purdah, and he spoke directly to her, and she replied.

After innumerable difficulties we were gratified with a sight of her: she was really a very pretty girl, fair, round faced, with beautiful eyes, and apparently about seventeen years of age. By the customs of India she can never marry. She is considered as the representative of the family of Nana, and as such is much looked up to by all his numerous dependants. She wishes to adopt a son, who would in that case succeed to the claims of the old man. These were too many, and too important, for the Paishwa to wish to see them revived; she will consequently never obtain her wish. She made several requests to us: first, that she might obtain some of her personal jewels, which the Paishwa had in his possession: and secondly, a garden-house near Poonah, which belonged to Nana. These requests Mr. Frissel assured her Colonel Close would employ his interest to procure for her. She will probably succeed. After some more conversation I received a dress, and Purseram Punt tied a serpaish on my hat. It was with difficulty I saved my coat from having the attar rubbed down the sleeves, but I begged to wave the honour, and, with Mr. Frissel's assistance, succeeded.

The tide served at ten on the following day, when we embarked in the balloon, and reached Bombay about four. Bombay, as a place of consequence, owes its origin entirely to the Portuguese; for in 1530, when it was ceded to them, it was merely a dependance on the chief residing at

Tannah, in the island of Salsette. Its favourable position at the entrance of the finest harbour on the western shore of India, soon excited the attention of its new masters, and a fort was erected by them to defend the anchorage. Nevertheless, the vicinity to Goa, the capital of all the eastern possessions of the Portuguese, prevented it from becoming a place of any great importance during the time it continued in their hands; but, on being ceded to the English in 1662, as part of the portion of Queen Catherine of Portugal, it rapidly rose into consequence, and ultimately became the great naval arsenal of that nation, and an independent Presidency, though certainly only the third in rank.

The fortifications of Bombay have been improved as it has increased in trade and importance: and lately a very considerable addition was made to their strength by including Dungaree Hill within the fort. This place previously commanded the town; it is however doubtful whether it would not have been more advisable to level the hill, as the lines of defence were before too extensive, requiring a garrison of several thousand men to defend them, while there were rarely as many hundreds in the place. Towards the sea Bombay is extremely strong, and battery above battery completely commands the harbour: to the land side it by no means offers the same resistance; but this is of little consequence, as, at present, were an enemy once landed, and capable of making regular approaches, the town must surrender. The houses, which are lofty and combustible, approach so close to the walls, that were they once in flames, it would be impossible for any troops to stand on the ramparts. A bombardment would lay the whole town in ashes in a few hours, and even the magazines themselves would probably share the same fate.

If Bombay and the valuable arsenals and naval stores which it contains, are to be rendered secure against an enemy, a large proportion of the town ought to be destroyed, and the fortifications brought nearer to the dock-yard, and within a much narrower compass. Accident has rendered this a much easier and cheaper work than it formerly would have been; for a most dreadful fire has reduced one third of the town to ashes, in the very division which would, were the above plan adopted, be thrown without the walls. It was with the utmost difficulty that the rest of the town was saved from destruction by the exertions of the Governor and the military. The old Government-house, which is within the old fort, was frequently on fire by the flakes that were carried towards it: had they been unable to extinguish it, the magazine must have shared the same fate, from its being close to it, and the unfortunate town would have been carried to all the points of the compass by the explosion of several thousand barrels of gun-powder.

To complete the plan of reducing the size of the fort, many houses must still be purchased, and pulled down; and the destroying of the old fortifications, and the erection of new, would carry the expence to a great height. It is hardly reasonable to expect that this should be defrayed by the East India Company, who can only be considered as tenants under a short lease; but that it should be done by some arrangement with the Supreme Government at home, cannot for a moment be doubted, when it is considered, that our most implacable enemy has all his attention turned towards our Indian possessions, and that in no place are we so vulnerable as at Bombay, from the smallness of the surrounding territory, and the distance from which all supplies must be drawn. If any hostile spirit does remain in the breasts of the Mahratta chieftains, and of which I fear there can be no doubt, Bombay affords to the French the only means of communication; and a brilliant success in an attack on that place would give spirits to every secret enemy, and induce them at once to throw off the mask. Of the ultimate result I should still have no fear; but the mischief of such a war would be incalculable, and the expence would be far greater than the alteration of the fort of Bombay, which the Governor seems to have some hopes will take place, for he has, for the present, refused permission to the inhabitants to rebuild their houses, which were consumed by the fire.

Many other alterations seem necessary to render Bombay as secure from surprise as it is from an open attack. The public landing place is, at present, in the dock-yard, and free access is allowed to this important spot during the whole of the day. At night centinels prohibit the approach; but the guard in the harbour is hardly sufficient to prevent boats from reaching it, without exciting suspicion; and so large is the bay, that an enemy might enter it at night, without being discovered by the solitary guard-ship, which is frequently its only protection. The expence that would attend the necessary precautions against this danger would be trifling, and cannot therefore be an impediment; but there seems to be a want of active zeal in those to whom the superintendence of the dock-yard is committed, that leaves it thus open to inspection, and possibly to injury.

It is in the light of a marine arsenal that Bombay appears of the greatest importance, and its value has been hitherto little diminished by the conquest of Trincomalée, which, at present, affords only a scanty and precarious supply of fresh provisions for a fleet. Here are established docks for the repair of the King's ships, as well as of the vessels belonging to the East India Company's marine, an establishment that seems, at present, of little use, and of which the expence is incalculable. Most of the situations in it seem to have sunk into sinecure employments, and its very existence must have been doubted by its former enemiés, the Pirates. If the East India Company are really in embarrassed circumstances, it appears to me that in no part of their establishment can they more easily œconomise than in the marine of Bombay; even if they do not think it advisable to abolish it at once. Were a new system adopted, and a reform carried into the higher and lower orders, I believe the marine might become a respectable and useful establishment. As far as the exertions of an individual can go to the completion of this, I have no doubt that success will attend on Captain Money, the present Superintendent of the marine; but it will require the power and the perseverance of a Hercules to cleanse this Augean stable.

Some of the present arrangements of the marine seem to have been ingeniously formed for the sole purpose of acting contrary to the system of the King's navy. Instead of an officer who is appointed to a vessel, continuing for a length of time in her, till he is acquainted with the characters of those under him, it is a very unusual circumstance for an officer to command the same vessel for two successive voyages; and if, by accident, he should do so, it is probable that he may lose every officer under him. I have known a Lieutenant appointed to three different vessels in four days; and the Panther cruizer had three different commanders in one week. This system of perpetual change, annihilates that pride which a Captain in the King's navy feels in the neatness and good condition of his ship, and leaves to the Bombay marine commander, no motive for exerting himself to bring his vessel to the highest possible state of improvement. It has indeed no one advantage, and can only enable the Superintendent to provide whenever he pleases for a new favourite, and to keep in implicit obedience to his caprice the officers, who must be conscious that if they offend him, they can instantly be removed to the most disagreeable situations.

If the East India Company determine to make their marine a respectable body, this evil must be rectified as well as many others; they must increase the number of their officers, which, at present, bears so little proportion to the size and number of their vessels, that the Mornington of twenty-four guns, and the Ternate of sixteen, when they sailed from the Persian Gulf, had each only one Midshipman. They must enforce the proper regulations in their vessels, and make the officers amenable to a strict judicature; and, above all things, they must avoid exercising that most mischievous of all privileges, the reinstating such officers as have been dismissed by a court of inquiry. They must also arrange with his Majesty's Government the real situation of their marine officers, who, at present, claim, under their directions, a relative rank with the officers of the King's navy which is not recognised by them, owing to which, disputes often occur, and more serious consequences have frequently been expected to follow. The respectable officers of the marine would rejoice in every reformation, and would be fully repaid by the benefit which would accrue to the service, for any losses that they themselves might sustain. That there are some men of high honour and unimpeached bravery in the marine, I can vouch from my own knowledge, and I cannot have the least doubt that there exist many others, whom it was not my good fortune to meet during my short stay at Bombay.

The establishment of the dock-yard is almost entirely composed of Persees, a people of whom I shall have much to say hereafter. It has been attempted to appoint an European master-builder, but the new comer has seldom long survived his arrival, and the only builders are now Persees. They are certainly fully equal to the business; but the absolute monopoly they possess has given rise to many abuses. The person who contracts to supply the timber, and the person who examines it on its receipt, are both Persees; consequently the articles are frequently of inferior quality. The master-builder has only people of his own persuasion under him; no complaint therefore is ever made of neglect of work on the one part, or of overcharges on the other. A still greater evil arises from the local circumstances of the dock-yard, which is a perfect thoroughfare, nay more, a fashionable lounging place for all the idlers of the town. The consequence is, that instead of working the whole day, many of the artificers only make their appearance to answer to their name at the hour of calling the roll, and if they please, depart immediately afterwards, without any possibility of their being convicted of the neglect of work; for the dock-yard is open to the town, and they may pass and repass as often as they choose. The frauds which must arise from the same cause are incalculable, and call aloud for reform; than which nothing could be more easy, by the shutting up of the yard from all but the workmen and officers, and the introduction of the regulations of his Majesty's docks at Portsmouth, Plymouth, and Chatham. The Bombay Government have, to a certain degree, felt themselves obliged to submit to these abuses, from the dread of the Persees giving up the ship-building business, of which they are the only possessors. I cannot believe that such would be the result of an attempt to reform abuses, though it might take place if they conceived their monopoly was in danger, as they are a rich and independent people. With caution, every necessary arrangement might be formed, and the workmen be retained in a situation, for which, by their talents and experience, they are now so well adapted.

The Presidency of Bombay has sunk into political insignificance since the supreme authority of Calcutta has undertaken all the arrangements with the Mahratta empire and its other neighbours; but in the late war, and indeed at this moment, it has a load thrown on it which it finds very difficult to bear; the supplying of the armies on this side India with provisions and money: in consequence of which, the outgoings per month are above fifteen lac of rupees, independent of the civil establishment; although its whole revenue, including the ceded districts in Guzerat, does not amount to above forty lac. The deficiency is provided for by bills on Bengal, and it shows a very favourable state of trade at Bombay, that so large a sum is procurable at no very high premium.

The trade of Bombay is at present, however, very inferior to what it was in former times, which is chiefly owing to the indulgences given to the Arabs, particularly to the Imaum of Muscat, whose flag being recognised as neutral, his vessels sail to and from the Isle of France, carrying there provisions, and taking back prize goods, which they purchase at half their prime cost. The navigation-act with respect to them seems to be totally suspended in India: they enter their vessels at Bombay as English, and navigate from one part of the Peninsula to the other without having an European in the ship, or one rupee of the property in them belonging to a British subject. They have frequently a French protection also: so that they enjoy every privilege, and are French or English, as it suits their convenience. No wonder that their navy is rapidly increasing, while the English builders can hardly find sufficient employment to keep their gangs together.

Bombay has been said to receive its name from the Portuguese words bon bain, or good bay; but this, I believe, is a mistake, as it was the original name of the island before the Portuguese possessed it, and was probably called after a Goddess Bomba, who is, as I am informed by Mr. Duncan, at present worshipped there. The town within the walls was commenced by the Portuguese, and even those that have been since built, are of a similar construction, with wooden pillars supporting wooden verandahs. The consequence is that Bombay bears no external resemblance to either of the other Presidencies. The Government-house is a handsome building, with several good apartments, but it has the great inconvenience of the largest apartment on both floors being a passage room to the others. Mr. Duncan, from system, avoids all parade; and even admitting that the general principle were right, which, I have before observed, I believe not to be the case, it is here certainly carried to too great an extreme, for a more ragged, dirty set of beings than the Government peons I never beheld.

The view from the fort is extremely beautiful towards the bay, whose smooth expanse is here and there broken by the islands that are, many of them, covered with wood, while the lofty and whimsically shaped hills of the table land, form a striking back ground to the landscape. The sea is on three sides of it, and on the fourth an esplanade, at the extremity of which is the black town, embosomed in a grove of cocoa-nut trees. The situation ought to be healthy, but unfortunately experience proves that it is not so.

The fever is at present making most alarming ravages, and the liver complaint is more frequent and more fatal here, than in any part of India. Mr. Duncan and Dr. Scott assure me, that this season is more than usually unhealthy; but they both admit the general insalubrity of the place, and particularly, that exposure to the land breeze, which sets in every evening, is generally followed by a fever, and frequently by a loss of the use of the limbs. This breeze is chillingly cold at present, and its deleterious effects may probably be attributed not only to this, but to the noxious vapours that it brings with it from passing over the rank vegetation which springs up in the marshy boundaries of the bay immediately after the rains are over. The Island of Salsette is still more unhealthy than Bombay, the jungle being closer, and the valleys more closed in. The young cadets that came out this year were sent to the new establishment at Varsova, when the fever immediately attacked them. They were instantly removed to Bombay, but many fell victims to the violence of the disease. Moderate living, cautiously avoiding opposite extremes, is found most conducive to health. Here, as in other parts of India, gentlemen are to be met with, who have enjoyed their health in defiance of intemperance, or with great abstemiousness, and both recommend their own example; yet, in my mind, both are exceptions to a general rule: hundreds certainly perish from intemperance; and the abstemious life of the native by no means shelters him from fevers, and their result with him is more frequently fatal, from the impossibility of lowering his temperament when attacked.

The rage for country houses prevails at Bombay as generally as at Madras, and the same inconveniences attend it; for as all business is carried on in the fort, every person is obliged to come in the morning, and return at night. The Governor is almost singular in living constantly in town, having lent his country house at Perelle to Sir James Mackintosh. This place was the property of the Jesuits, and is the handsomest in the island. The apartments and verandahs are extremely handsome, and the former chapel on the ground floor is now a magnificent and lofty dining room. It has, however, the inconvenience of not being open to the sea breeze, and appears to be far from healthy, for Sir James and Lady Mackintosh, with a great proportion of their family, had been attacked by an intermittent fever. The generality of the country houses are comfortable and elegant; and if they have not the splendid Grecian porticos of Calcutta and Madras, they are probably better adapted to the climate, and have most unquestionably the advantage of charming views; for even the Island of Bombay itself is broken by several beautiful hills either covered with cocoa-nut tree groves, or villas of the inhabitants.

It cannot be expected that the third Presidency in point of rank, should vie with the others in splendor or expence. The society is less numerous, and the salaries are smaller ; economy is consequently more attended to by a kind of tacit compact ; the style of living is however frequently elegant, and always comfortable and abundant. I confess, that having so lately quitted my native country, I preferred it to the splendid profusion of Calcutta. The necessaries of life are here dearer than in the other parts of India ; the wages of servants are consequently much higher. Rice, the chief food of the lower orders, is imported from Bengal even in favourable years ; at present the famine has raised it to an alarming price. Grateful, however, must the inhabitants be to Providence, for having, at such an eventful period, placed them under the British protection, and relieved them from those sufferings, which afflict the nations around them. The subscriptions, which were entered into to extend this benefit beyond the limits of their territory, do honour to the gentlemen of the settlement. Hospitals were opened for the gradual administering of relief to such as were too much exhausted to feed themselves, and hircarrahs were placed on the confines to bring in those whose strength had failed them before they could reach the fostering aid, that was held out to them by the hands of British benevolence. The preservation of several hundreds of thousands on the Malabar coast may be attributed to the overflowing supplies which Bengal was able to pour out for their support, in consequence of the fifty years tranquillity which she has enjoyed under her present masters. India, under one supreme controul, can never expect to feel the effects of famine; for a season which causes a scarcity in one part, generally produces an increase of produce in another; and the devastations of hostile armies will be at an end, which can alone counteract this beneficent arrangement of Providence. For the sake of the population of sixty millions, as well as for our own sake, we may therefore wish that the British influence in India may remain unshaken by external force, or internal dissatisfaction.

A Society has been established at Bombay on a plan somewhat similar to the Bengal Asiatic Society, but it intends to limit itself to the present state of manners among the inhabitants, rather than to launch into ancient mythology, or the history of the country. Much I think may be expected from the active superintendence of Sir James Mackintosh, whose talents would throw a lustre on any society, and whose discourse on the first day of their meeting would have been heard with satisfaction by the father of Asiatic literature, Sir William Jones himself. Sir James is ably supported by Mr. Duncan, who is, I believe, as learned as any European in the wild fancies of the Hindoo mythology, and was the writer of those papers, on the singular Hindoo customs at Benares, and the two fakeers that resided there, which were communicated by Sir John Shore to the Asiatic Society, but without stating from whom he had received the intelligence. To these are added the names of many other gentlemen, whose long residence in India, and known acquirements, may fairly justify an expectation in the public, that without rivalling their prototype at Calcutta, they may communicate much interesting information respecting that part of India which has come under their immediate observation.

One of the greatest evils in India is the cheapness of spirituous liquors, which leads to a dreadful mortality among the European soldiers, particularly on their first arrival. The quantity allowed by Government is too great, if not totally useless. In the field, it is a gallon for every twenty men, or two drams each: at other times only half the quantity. This might probably do no harm, were it not that the soldier is able, at his own expence, to procure as much as he pleases, in addition, from the camp followers, who are licensed by Government, and pay a duty on all they sell. This plan has been adopted in preference to allowing the profits to be received by the commanding officers, which had led to the greatest abuses. To deprive the soldier of an injurious quantity of spirits is impossible in a country, where an execrable kind is sold at a low rate in every village; it has been therefore considered as more advantageous, to secure him a supply of a less deleterious kind. Could the quantity allowed by the Government be reduced one half, a diminution would no doubt take place in the deaths; and every exertion ought unquestionably to be made, to preserve the lives of persons, so valuable to their country, as the soldiers employed in India.

The greater proportion of the inhabitants of Bombay are Persees, descendants of the ancient Persians, who fled from the persecution of Shah Abbas, who in the sixteenth century destroyed the temples which had till then remained in the mountain Albend, and drove the worshippers of fire to seek an asylum in other countries. Bombay they have almost entirely made their own, for hardly a house or a foot of land in the island belongs to any other. They form a body of people totally dissimilar to any in India, and seem to have perfectly domesticated themselves in their new abode, where they receive a protection, for which they are very grateful. I asked a very respectable Persee why they built such splendid habitations, and purchased land at a price that yielded only four per cent, when they could so easily make eight or twelve. His answer, I believe, conveyed the real sentiments of his nation. "This is our native country, where we are also to die: we have now no other home to look to, and therefore like to have some certain property for our children to inherit: you English are only here for a short time, and therefore wish to make as much of your money as possible, that you may return to your country, where I suppose you act, as we do here." They are a very rich, active, and loyal body of men, greatly increasing the prosperity of the settlement by their residence in it. There is not an European house of trade in which one of them has not a share, and generally indeed it is the Persee that produces the largest part of the capital. Their influence is consequently very great, and the kind of brotherly connection that subsists among them, enables them to act with the force of an united family. The conduct of the Government towards them has been indulgent and wise. They openly avow their obligations, and express their conviction, that they could in no other part of the East obtain the same advantages. I consider them as a most valuable body of subjects, and am convinced that, unless from mismanagement, they will ever continue so, and form an important barrier against the more powerful casts of India.

From the length of time which Bombay has been under the control of Europeans, the Persees, since their residence there, have adopted little of the Asiatic manners. They indeed wear the dress, which they informed me had been adopted on their arrival, but they eat and drink like the English. Ardiseer Dady, one of their richest members, gave me a most magnificent entertainment. The table for the Europeans was chiefly covered with English cookery, but they sent me from their own, several dishes, which were very highly seasoned, and good. The wines were excellent ; but when I adjourned to their table, I was not a little astonished to find liqueurs placed opposite each Persee, which they drank in glasses as freely as wine, and which, though they sat late, seemed to have no effect upon them. Their houses are furnished with a profusion of English looking-glasses, prints, and paintings. They always light them up remarkably well ; but on this occasion the whole gardens were illuminated with torches and lamps, which had a most brilliant effect. The band playing in the verandah, and the crowd of differently dressed people, had the semblance of an English masquerade. Coffee and tea, pawn and attar, lavender water, and other perfumes, completed the melange of this Anglo-Asiatic entertainment, from which we departed about midnight.

To the credit of the Persee humanity, they provide for all their poor : and to the credit of their private morals, there is not a single prostitute, or mistress to a gentleman, of their cast, in the settlement. They are generous and splendid in the higher orders; and in the lower, active and intelligent, far surpassing as servants the Mussulmauns or Hindoos. They mostly speak English with propriety. In their persons they are a handsome race, fairer than the natives, though not possessing the clear skin of the Europeans. In their manners they are uniformly conciliatory and mild. I confess that I infinitely prefer them to any race of people in the East, subject to the British control. They have numerous temples to Fire, but their priests seem to have no authority in temporal concerns, nor much spiritual control. Their religion is tolerant, and, as far as it throws no impediment in the way of the public service, must be considered politically a good one. Sir William Jones petulantly attacked the authenticity of their sacred code, the Zend Avesta, as translated by Monsieur Anquetil de Perron; but he himself, before his death, was convinced of his error. Sir James Mackintosh is studying the language, and will probably favour the world with some additional information on the subject; but from the accounts that I have received, I have no doubt of the authenticity of the original, or of the fidelity of Monsieur Anquetil de Perron's translation.

The beauty of the esplanade, every morning and evening, is greatly heightened by the votaries of the Sun, who crowd there in their white flowing garments, and coloured turbans, to hail his rising, or pay respect, by their humble prostration, to his parting rays. On this occasion the females do not appear, but they still go to the wells for water, as did the wives of the ancient patriarchs. Many of those in a higher line of life, retire from the city to their country residences early in the evening, in which case they assemble in their one-horse chaises at a beautiful spot called the Breach, where a former Governor built a noble causeway at an expence of 10,000 rupees, thereby saving a considerable tract of country from the gradual incroachments of the sea, which had nearly made its way across the island. It is a work of great merit, and has stood firm against all the violence of the S. W. monsoon. The India Company were however offended at the expence, and the poor Governor lost his place. The tract that was recovered has hitherto been marshy and useless, but some gentlemen have undertaken to drain it, and, apparently, are likely to succeed.

The strict attention that is paid in Bengal to the conduct of the Cadets on their arrival, unfortunately does not exist at Bombay, and the consequence of the neglect is melancholy. On their landing they too often are obliged to live at the tavern, not having any fixed place of abode, where they not only run in debt, frequently to the blasting of their future prospects, but by the facility of access to wine and women, sow the seeds of those complaints, which afterwards carry them prematurely to the grave. Varsovah had been chosen as a residence for the Cadets, but in 1804 the fever broke out there, and they were obliged to be removed to Mehum, but not before numbers had perished from the unhealthiness of the climate, and, it is said, from the want of proper regulation in the establishment, the young men having been permitted to bathe when they pleased, and expose themselves to the effect of the night air.

It was at one of the country houses in the vicinity of Bombay, that the unfortunate accident of the death of Hadjee Khaleb Khan took place in July 1802. He had arrived only a few days before as Ambassador from the Persian Court to the Government of India, when a dispute arose between some of his Excellency's followers and the sepoys who guarded the house, in consequence of one of the former's insisting on entering a part of the garden, which the Ambassador had ordered to be kept private. The centinel, in obedience to his orders, refused to permit him, when the Persian, who was drunk, at length drew his sword, and, being joined by his countrymen, a regular battle ensued. The Ambassador, who had retired to his couch after having himself too freely indulged in the pleasures of the table, arose on hearing the tumult, and rushed out to separate the combatants. In the confusion he was not known, and a chance shot in a moment put an end to his life. Several of his followers also perished, but they deserved their fate; for they had irritated the sepoys by the most insulting language, and the severest ridicule of their religious prejudices. The Ambassador's nephew, though severely wounded, recovered, and received the kindest attentions from the officers of the Bombay Government, who were fully exculpated in his mind, from any blame respecting the untimely fate of his uncle.

The Marquis Wellesley learned, soon after his arrival in India, that attempts were making by Tippoo to form a close alliance with Zemaun Shah, Sultaun of Cabul, and to induce him to attack the British in the North, at the time when he should occupy their attention by hostilities in the Peninsula. To render the projects of Tippoo abortive, his Lordship sent a respectable native, Mindi Alli Khan, to the Court of Ispahan, to open a communication with the present sovereign, who was at that time engaged in hostilities with Zemaun Shah. He was directed to urge the King to approach the frontiers of Korasan, as soon as his enemy should move towards the Indies; and, if he should find a favourable reception, Mindi Alli Khan was to announce the Governor General's intention of sending a public embassy to arrange a commercial treaty, and cement a close alliance between the two countries. The King of Persia was fully aware of the importance of the British alliance, and complied with the request made to him. Zemaun Shah, who had advanced as far as Lahore, immediately returned back, and his brother, taking advantage of his unpopularity, deposed him, and, with the barbarity so common in Asia, put out his eyes. India having been thus relieved from immediate alarm, Major Malcolm was, in 1799, sent to the Court of Ispahan, where he completely conciliated the sovereign and his ministers, and induced them to refuse to receive a person deputed with the most conciliatory propositions from Bonaparté in Egypt. Commercial arrangements were also entered into, and every required security was granted to the British for more freely carrying on their trade.

The unfortunate fate of the Ambassador, who was sent to repay the compliment of Major Malcolm's mission, has been before observed; but there was no reason to suppose that it would have any effect in diminishing the friendship between Persia and India; since the Governor General immediately sent off an explanation of the transaction by a Mr. Loveit, who was directed to carry the letter to Persia. Unfortunately for the East India Company, he became alarmed at Busheir, and delivered the letter to Mr. Manesty, who immediately raised himself into an Ambassador, and departed for Ispahan, determined to rival Major Malcolm in importance. He had already drawn for a lac and forty thousand rupees, which would not pay half his expences. Lord Wellesley, at first, ordered the bill to be refused payment, but on considering that it might affect our credit in Persia, he altered his intention, but directed that Mr. Manesty should be made responsible for the amount.

The King of Persia, engaged as he was in a

difficult, and rather disastrous war with Russia, rejoiced to hear that another embassy had arrived from India, and hastened to meet it at Balk, where he received the Ambassador with the highest honours. It was immediately urged by the King, that we should afford him assistance against his enemy; and he was not a little mortified to find that the affair of Hadjee Khaleb Khan's death, about which he was perfectly indifferent, was the only subject on which the new ambassador could speak. Had a simple messenger, like Mr. Loveit, carried the letter, this inconvenience would have been prevented, and the Company would have saved three lac of rupees, that is, if they should please to allow Mr. Manesty his expences, a point which will be referred to them by Lord Wellesley.

With prudent management, I think a close connection might be cemented between the two countries, as the trade between them would be beneficial to both; and the only difficulty, the impracticability of our assisting one ally against another, might be obviated by a friendly mediation at St. Petersburgh. At present our respectability is not great in the Persian Gulf, where we have submitted to have our merchant vessels plundered, and our cruizers insulted, by the piratical states on its shores. Of these the most powerful are the Johesserm Arabs, whose coast extends from Cape Mussendom to Bahrein. Their chief ports are Rosselkeim, about forty leagues S. S. W. of the Cape, and Egmaum, about twenty-four miles further on. Through the systematic forbearance of the Bombay Government they have risen to a great maritime power, and possess at least thirty-five dows of different sizes, carrying from fifty to three hundred men each. They have few guns, but, being brave and fierce, chiefly attack by boarding, with their crooked daggers stabbing every one who resists. They have taken two large vessels belonging to Mr. Manesty, and had even the impudence to attack the Mornington frigate; but were beaten off. The Honourable Company's cruizers have positive orders to treat these pirates with civility, never to attack them, but only to act on the defensive: the consequence is, that they only look at the stronger vessels, but take every one that has not the power of resistance.

Independently of the real loss, which the native merchants suffer from the value of the captured cargoes, this mean submission ought to be ended, from the conviction of the degradation we suffer in the eye of Persia, by permitting it. A dignified independence, a visible power of supporting the honour of our flag, of protecting our friends, and punishing our enemies, are necessary for the acquirement of the confidence of an Eastern sovereign. Persia herself neither is, nor can be, a great naval power. Were we to protect her coast from the depredations of these pirates, who even extend their devastations to the villages on the sea shore, she would be gratefully attached to us, and would be bound by the strong tie of interest to protect the northern frontier of our dominion, by being prepared to enter the territories of the Abdalli, should he leave them unguarded to attack us. To ascertain the real value of a close connection with Persia is impossible; but some idea may be entertained of it, by a reference to the splendour with which the barren island of Ormus shone forth under the Portuguese, when they monopolized the trade of the Gulf, and secured it from the attack of pirates by a marine, as pre-eminent in those days, as ours is now in every part of the globe, except in the Eastern seas.

I had been so highly gratified by the pagoda at Carli, that I determined to visit others in the Island of Salsette, which, according to the accounts I had received, were formed on a similar plan. Accordingly I set off early on the morning of the 22nd of November, accompanied by Mr. Salt, and some of the Governor's family. We breakfasted at a small village of Ambola, where we were received by the Portuguese Curé, and afterwards we turned out of our way to examine an extensive excavation, which Monsieur Anquetil du Perron has described in his introduction to the translation of the Zend Avesta, and has given a plan of it, under the name of Djegueseri.. All the apartments were square, and the roof was flat, throughout; in the centre was a smaller building with a lingam; the whole was therefore probably dedicated to Mahadeo. Several groups of figures in basso relievo, adorned the walls. They were much decayed, and the whole had a very unpleasant appearance. The floor, being lower than the surrounding country, was extremely damp, and the light, admitted at the three entrances, was nothing better than darkness visible. They run north and south, passing through a small hill that, in parts, is covered with jungle. There was no appearance of attendant Brahmins, but the lingam had been newly ornamented.

We went on to dinner to Mont Pesier, where our tents were pitched for us. Here are the ruins of a very handsome church and monastery, which, I understand, formerly belonged to the Jesuits: Monsieur Anquetil du Perron says, to the Franciscans; but I am inclined to consider my information correct, from there being the remains of an observatory on a small hill in the neighbourhood, which was more probably the work of the intelligent followers of Ignatius Loyola, than of the lazy monks of St. Francis. The church was originally lined with pannel-work of wood, disposed in compartments, and richly ornamented with carving. In the centre of each was the head of a saint, tolerably executed, surrounded by wreaths of flowers, and other fanciful sculpture, in a very excellent taste. The whole is in ruins, the roof having fallen in. The author, whom I have before mentioned, attributes this to the devastations of the Mahrattas, who, he says, carried away the wood work to Tannah; but this appears improbable. Timber is not scarce: and if they had carried away the more solid work, they would hardly have left behind them the parts that were richly ornamented. Under the church a small pagoda has been formed out of the rock; it is square, and flat roofed, with a few deities, and other figures, in basso-relievo. These the good priests had covered up with a smooth coat of plaister, and had converted the whole into a chapel. At present the original proprietors have been uncovered, and have again become objects of adoration to the ignorant native.

Early on the morning of the 23d we departed for the Caves of Kenneri, which are the most important in the island, and are formed out of a high knowl, in the middle of the range of hills which divides the island nearly into two equal parts. I soon found that, limited as I was for time, it would be impossible to investigate the whole of the caves, I therefore gave my chief attention to the great cavern, which resembles the one at Carli, in being oblong, and having a coved roof, though it is inferior to it in size, in elegance of design, and in beauty of execution. It has the same singular building at the upper end, and the vestibule is equally adorned with figures. Its peculiar ornaments are two gigantic figures of Boodh, nearly twenty feet high, each filling one side of the vestibule. They are exactly alike, and are in perfect preservation, in consequence of their having been christened and painted red by the Portuguese, who left them as an appendage to a Christian church, for such this temple of Boodh became under their transforming hands. I have given a view of the front of the temple, and an etching of the gigantic figure of the presiding deity, whose image, in all the usual attitudes, embellishes several other parts of the vestibule; and one in particular is ornamented with the conical cap worn by the Chinese Fo. The entrance, on which there are several inscriptions in the unknown character, faces the west. It is worthy observation, that these two circumstances, and the coved roof, seem to be peculiar to the temples dedicated to Boodh; at least it is so in the two I have seen, and in the one at Ellora described by Sir Charles Mallet in the Asiatic Researches. In one of the large square caves which adjoin that above described, are many figures, and one that is very remarkable, as it shows Vishnou himself in the act of fanning Boodh with the chourie: a superior deity may, however, be supposed to reside in the circular temples, for within them is no image, unless the circular building called by the natives the Dhagope, can be considered as a prodigious lingam. I ought to add, that in the cave of Ellora there does appear a statue annexed to the Dhagope, which, from the manner of holding the finger of one hand between the finger and thumb of the other, is probably designed for Boodh.

The innumerable caves, which have been formed in every part of the hill, are square, and flat roofed. I cannot but consider them as meant for the habitations of the attendant Brahmins. A very curious tradition is mentioned by Monsieur Anquetil du Perron, as having been recorded by a Jesuit in a history of the Indies, printed in Portugal; it is, that the whole of these caves were the work of a Gentoo king, some thousand years ago, to secure his only son from the attempts of another nation to gain him over to their religion. This must probably refer to some disputes between the Brahmins and the Boodhists, and might, if it could be traced, throw some light on the relative antiquity of the two religions. The most perplexing circumstance, that the character used by the latter is now no longer understood, while that of the former is in constant use, makes it difficult to believe that the Brahmins are justified in their claim to superior antiquity. It is a subject, however, on which I cannot presume to give an opinion.

It is not only the numerous caves, that give an idea of what the population of this barren rock must once have been, but the tanks, the terraces, and the flights of steps which lead from one part to another; yet now not a human footstep is to be heard, except when the curiosity of a traveller leads him to pay a hasty visit to the ruined habitation of those, whose very name has passed away, and whose cultivated fields are become an almost impassable jungle, the haunt of tigers, and the seat of pestilence and desolation. After copying the inscriptions and taking views of the most interesting objects, we with difficulty made our way through the jungle to an open space, on the verge of the cultivated tracts, where our tents were pitched out of the way of fever and tigers.

We reached Tannah, the capital of the Island of Salsette, to breakfast, and were hospitably received by Mr. Spencer the Resident. A small fort commands the passage between the island and the Mahratta country, but is otherwise of little use. Confined as the settlement of Bombay formerly was, the acquisition of Salsette was an incalculable advantage, from the certainty which is afforded of a constant supply of fresh provision for the town and fleet. Little however has hitherto been done to increase its produce, and the greater part remains an useless jungle, instead of being converted into fields of rice, and plantations of sugar; even wood itself is only procured at a very high price, chiefly for want of arrangement. If no better use is to be made of the island, it might certainly supply this article at half the price that is now paid for it. Dr. Scott has set a good example of enterprize, by establishing a very valuable sugar plantation. On the 25th we returned to Bombay in the Government boat.

I was afterwards tempted by the verdant appearance of the Island of Elephanta, which rears its woody head nearly in the centre of the bay, as much as by the report of its celebrated cave, to pay it a visit. The accurate Niebuhr has given so good an account of it, that a description is unnecessary. I have only to observe, that I do not think either his drawing, or the etching in the Asiatic Researches, have given the character of the triune deity. Brahmah's countenance admirably expresses the undisturbed composure of the creator of the world; Vishnou's, on the left, has every feature of benevolence, while the lotus which he holds in his hand seems to be expanding under the genial ray of his eye. Seva's, on the contrary, has a ghastly and dire scowl, that well accords with the objects that he holds before him, two of the most venomous of serpents, the covra copel. I was much surprised at the ingenuity of the conception. and the merit of the execution, of these figures. How superior must they have appeared when in a state of perfection!

It was pleasing to me to find, that the great cave of Elephanta, which opens to the north, and has a flat roof, had no inscription in the unknown character, nor any figure of Boodh. Of the numerous deities of the Hindoo mythology, many have been honoured with a place; but the most curious figure, and which has been noted by every traveller, is that of a female amazon, which, from having four arms, most probably represents some super-human personage. Did the romance of the Amazons reach Greece from India, or were there ever such personages in the Eastern world, are interesting questions, but at present incapable of solution. There is no appearance of any great violence having been used to injure the figures. Had cannon been employed by the Portuguese for that purpose, the marks of the balls would have been visible, and the destruction would have been among the figures. As it is, the pillars are more rapidly decaying than any other part. The water is permitted during the rains to lodge in the cave, and the stone, being a soft one, moulders perceptibly away in the vicinity of the open air. The scene, from the little level space in front, is extremely beautiful, and a cool breeze tempers the heat in the most sultry day of summer. The beauty of the place has however been considerably diminished by a wall, which has been erected across the front, to prevent cattle from getting in, and, as I hear, to prevent curious visitors also from treacherously carrying off the legs, heads, and arms of these helpless deities.

CHAPTER V.

Departure from Bombay.—Arrival at Mocha.—Visit to the Dola, and Bas Kateb.—Preparations for continuing the Voyage.—Departure from Mocha.—Aroe Islands.—Sir H. Popham's Chart of the Red Sea.—Howakel.—Arrival at Dhalac.—Mr. Maxfield's Report of his Voyage.—Reasons for supposing Howakel Bay to be Opsian Bay of the Periplus.—Mr. Salt's Report of his Visit to Dhalac-el-Kibeer, Girbeshid, and Dobelew.—Captain Court's Survey of Dhalac.—Observations on Mr. Bruce's Account.—Arrival at Massowah.—Commercial arrangements.—Dispute with the Dola of Arkeko.—Departure from Massowah.

MR. DUNCAN had most obligingly ordered one of the Company's vessels, the Mornington, to be prepared to convey me to Bussorah, whither I had determined to proceed, when all my plans were changed by the arrival of dispatches from the Governor General, recommending a continuation of the survey of the Red Sea, and at the same time delicately hinting, that I might possibly be induced to make an attempt to complete what I had so well begun. On receiving from Mr. Duncan assurances that every arrangement should be made for the immediate departure of the vessel, and that I should be permitted to select the officers, I determined to comply with his Excellency's intimation. The Panther cruizer, being a smaller vessel than the Mornington, was considered as more suitable to the service of surveying, and was therefore ordered to be got ready. Lieutenant Charles Court was appointed to command her, in consequence of the very high character which he bore, as a seaman, and a man of science.

Lieutenant Maxfield, who had been second Lieutenant of the Antelope, received the appointment of the Assaye, a small French schooner, which had been taken by a King's ship, and had been purchased by the Bombay Government, on the recommendation of the Marine board, as being a capital sailer. She was intended to accompany us as a tender in the more difficult navigation which we had reason to expect above Massowah.

Mr. Macgie was, at my particular request, nominated as Surgeon, although not in the East India Company's service, in consequence of the experience I had in my former voyage had of his abilities, and his great attention to the health of the men.

Two time-keepers, and the instruments requisite for nautical observations and land surveying, were provided by the Bombay Government; and Mr. Duncan completed his kind attentions to my comfort by directing Captain Court to keep a table for me at the expence of the East India Company.

Captain Rudland of the Bombay army having expressed a wish to join our party, instead of returning to England by sea, I rejoiced in obtaining for him the necessary permission from the Governor, and the Commander in Chief, as an additional European gentleman would be a great satisfaction in crossing the desert from Suez to Cairo. Nothing could be more favourable than the season, as the monsoon was N. E. to the straits of Bab-el-mandeb, and S. E. from the Red Sea to Suez; we were therefore impatient to depart, and the 1st of December was fixed for that purpose. It was however not till the 3d, that Captain Court received his final orders, which were in every respect to obey the instructions that he should receive from me. I parted with Mr. Duncan, whose amiable and benevolent character must conciliate the esteem of all who know him, with great, and I flatter myself, with mutual, regret. He paid a last attention to me by sending his Aid-de-camp and the Town Major to attend me to the sea shore, and saluting me on my departure.

We set sail at four in the morning of Dec. 4th, with a very pleasant breeze, and before night the land was completely out of sight. The Panther had been considered as a bad sailer, and we were led to suppose that the Assaye would constantly keep ahead; we however found the contrary, with a fair wind. The Panther sailed tolerably well, and we were obliged to shorten sail for the Assaye.

On the sixth I experienced the deleterious effect of a land breeze in Bombay harbour. I had unfortunately forgotten on the night of the third, that I was still within its reach, and the port-hole of my cabin had been left open: in consequence of which a severe attack of fever came on, but without a cold fit: and, as I was at sea, which is generally prescribed as a certain cure, I hoped not to suffer long.

I had no return of my fever on the 14th. On the

15th we saw the Arab shore. It was the high land of Kisseen, distant about eighteen miles. As there was now no danger of the Assaye's not making her passage, I determined to make the best of our way to Mocha: accordingly Mr. Maxfield was sent for, and directed to stop at Aden, and enquire if Mr. Pringle was there, a circumstance by no means impossible; and if he was, to bring him up with him. We made sail in the evening.

We coasted along with pleasant land and sea breezes; passed Aden early in the morning of the 18th; through the Straits of Bab-el-mandeb, with a stiff gale from the S.E. during the same night; and at seven anchored considerably to the northward of the north fort of Mocha. It blew so heavy a gale that we were not able to make the roads. The Panther was extremely crank, and totally unable to make any way when close to the wind. This defect was in some measure compensated by our discovering that though the swell was very great, she rode well at anchor. Besides, she was very comfortable, drew little water, and went well before a wind. She had however a very considerable heel to starboard, that was much against us, and for which we could not account. It will hardly be believed, that in a vessel reported ready for sea, there was not a single buoy; yet such was the fact, and we were daily in the habit of discovering similar deficiencies. Two fishermen, who, in consequence of their supplying the British squadron in the Red Sea, had been named Admiral Blanket, and Lord Bombay, came off in one of the native boats, by whom I sent a short note to Mr. Pringle, and received an answer, saying he would be with me as soon as the weather would permit. We were a little alarmed on getting into sight of the roads to perceive three large ships there. They hoisted American colours as we approached, and we soon found that they were of that nation, two from Salem, and one from Baltimore.

We made an attempt on the 20th, with the tide in our favour, to reach the roads, but without success; and had the misfortune, in heaving our anchor, to injure the capstern. On examination it appeared, that though newly put together, for the Panther had lately been in dock, it had been made of old wood, partly consumed by the dry rot. However vexatious the delay might be, it was impossible to proceed till this injury should be repaired. We had also here to procure money for the expences of the ship, and for my own private expenditure, by drawing bills on Bombay, which had been recommended to us as more advantageous than bringing cash from that place. Captain Court also required an interpreter, and I wished to get a servant who spoke English and Arabic; a communication with the shore became therefore absolutely necessary; but as I could not venture during the violence of the gale, in our small boat, I wrote to Mr. Pringle, stating all our wants, and requesting, if possible, he would come off in an American long boat, which would be a much better sea-boat than ours.

I received in the course of the next day letters in abundance from Mr. Pringle, but he did not come off, though he certainly might have done so in the American boats, which went several times to their ships. Surprised at this neglect, I accepted Mr. Salt's offer to go on shore in a native boat, and return in the morning either with or without Mr. Pringle. I also desired him to wait on the Dola, and request, in my name, permission for a servant and interpreter to accompany me up the Red Sea.

Early in the morning Mr. Salt returned, and with him Mr. Pringle, in an American cutter. Mr. Salt had, according to my request, seen the Dola, who had behaved with the utmost politeness, not only permitting the servant I applied for to accompany me, but also giving me leave to hire any one I pleased for an interpreter. He at the same time assured Mr. Salt, that he was extremely concerned he was not properly acquainted with my rank when I was last at Mocha, in consequence of which he did not pay me the requisite attention, but that now, if I chose to land, his horses and people should meet me; and, if I visited him, I should be saluted with four guns on my arrival, and on my leaving him. I was not a little astonished at this ridiculous change in his behaviour, being certain that he was perfectly informed of every particular respecting me, before I landed from the Antelope; however, I determined to go on shore, and treat him with equal politeness. It was usually calmer in the morning, but we had delayed till it blew very fresh. We attempted to make the shore opposite, but found rocks at some distance, and were obliged to beat four miles to windward, which took us up several hours. It was extremely unpleasant, the boat making more water on one tack, than we could bale: but on the other we were able to get her dry. She sailed well, or it would have been impossible for us to reach the shore.

After much difficulty and some danger we landed, and found horses waiting for us. Captain Crowninshield and the other Americans who were on shore met us without the town, as did Devage, and many others; at the gate the Dola's horses and tom-toms were waiting, which preceded me with their incessant din to his house. I was permitted to ride to the steps of the door, a very unusual condescension at the present day, though formerly it was allowed to all Europeans who visited the Dola. It was the fast of Ramadan, when the Arabs eat nothing from the rising of the sun to the setting; to make which as easy as possible, they turn night into day, carousing during the whole of the former, and dedicating the latter to sleep. The Dola was not awake, so that he could not receive me, and I was kept waiting a few minutes; however to compensate this neglect he rose up to pay his compliments to each of the gentlemen of my party, who were successively presented to him. The usual compliments passed. Rose water was presented, and our chins perfumed with frankincense. To a bearded Arab this must be a pleasant ceremony; but to us I always thought it had a ridiculous appearance, and smiled when my friends underwent the operation. The Americans were very sensible and intelligent men, particularly Captain Crowninshield, who belonged to the very respectable house of that name, and Captain Bancroft, who was originally educated for the bar, but obliged by ill health to give it up. Abdallah, whom I wished to take with me as my servant, agreed to go, and immediately began to procure us the necessaries wanted. We urged Devage to get us a dow without delay, and immediately procured from him the money we required.

We hired a dow for three hundred dollars to go the voyage to above Suakin. I paid the Dola an evening visit, Mr. Pringle having previously sent him presents, in my name, to the amount of five hundred dollars, and to the Bas Kateb two hundred. Nothing particular passed, except his saying that he begged I would consider Mocha as my house, and that the gates should be open for me at any hour. He expressed a wish to have some private conversation with me before my departure, I said, I would wait on him the evening before I embarked. Mr. Criddle, our youngest Midshipman, was with us; the Dola wanted to know if he was my son, whence arose a conversation respecting our sons. He showed me his, and told me he had one more, an infant. He then asked after mine. His manners were bad and his whole appearance mean. The apartment was small, and the staircases, as usual in Arab houses, narrow and inconvenient, with numerous doors at the landing places; probably meant as a defence against a sudden attack.

The Americans kindly lent us their boats and carpenters to repair our capstern. The wind rendered all communication with the vessel extremely difficult. We spent a very pleasant Christmas day at the factory, being fourteen in number, a large party of white faces for so distant a part of the globe.

Our dow met with an accident in being launched, in consequence of which we were still delayed. We therefore determined to send off Mr. Maxfield in the Assaye direct to Massowah, with letters for the Nayib, informing him of my intention to visit him, and requesting that two pilots might be procured to conduct the ship to Suakin, assuring him that the two hundred dollars should be paid for them, being the price he had previously demanded. Mr. Maxfield had instructions to meet us at Dhalac, where we intended to water. I wrote at the same time to the Banian, to desire he would expedite the procuring of the pilots.

Mr. Maxfield sailed on the 27th; but there was so much sea that he parted his cable, and left his anchor behind him, nor were we able to recover it. We lived very pleasantly at the factory: all the officers that could be spared coming on shore. The Americans exerted themselves to please and serve us. The weather was very pleasant, and the nights perfectly cool.

We were fortunate in procuring a pilot, who bore a most excellent character, and had been for thirty years sailing between Mocha and Suakin. He was brother to the Naqueda of the dow. He asked one hundred and fifty dollars for the trip, and I gave them to him, lest there should be any delay at Massowah. It rendered us completely independent of the Nayib. On the evening of the 30th I visited the Dola, to request the gates might be opened for me at four o'clock in the morning, that I might be gone before the wind freshened. He said it could not be, and began to argue about it. I was very angry, and told him, that if he had not offered it, I should never have made the application. He wanted me to go out at the sally port, which I positively refused, and desired that the servants might be turned out of the room that we might speak in private. This was done; and Mr. Pringle pointedly reprobated his caprice about the gates. He then said they should be open.

We had now a very singular political conversation of about two hours. It began by his observing that old customs should be preserved. This I denied, and said they ought to change with the times: that in India we had become masters by the will of God, and that many customs existed before that period, which must now be laid aside. He replied, "I know very well that is the case in India; but what do you English mean to do with Yemen?" I replied, laughing, "nothing, but to get as much coffee from it as we can." He said, he believed we were all Wahabees. I told him I knew but one Wahabee, and that was Sidi Mohammed Akil. He laughed, and asked how I knew him to be one. I replied, he told me so.

He now asked Mr. Pringle's permission to say something to me, which being of course granted, he began a regular complaint against that gentleman; "that without his knowledge he had written to the Sheriffe of Abou Arish, who was making war against the Imaum, and taking his country from him." The fact certainly was so; but it was merely commercial, respecting coffee to be purchased at Loheia. This I represented; but he seemed by no means satisfied. I assured him in the most solemn manner, that I knew it was the determination of the Bombay Government not to assist the Wahabees against the Imaum of Sana; and that had such been their intention, they would have sent a direct intimation, and not through the medium of Mr. Pringle, who was only a civil servant employed for the purposes of trade. He could not, for some time, be convinced. He said, "Why was not the letter shewn?" And asked me explicitly, if the carrying on such a correspondence was not criminal. I replied, that if Mr. Pringle wrote to any enemy of the Imaum, in a way that could be injurious to that Prince, while living under his protection, he would certainly act criminally, and deserve to be punished; but if it was merely about coffee, he must not blame Mr. Pringle, but that Providence which had placed the coffee country under the control of the Sheriffe; that where the articles were to be had, there the merchant would go. He said it had never been so, and that the Imaum would not permit coffee to be exported from Loheia. I asked how he would hinder it. He laughed, and said, "well, if you are determined, you must send ships to Loheia, but the Imaum will not like it."

He enquired where the Assaye was gone, and where I was going. I told him, to Massowah, as he might know by the pilots I had hired. He was evidently uneasy, and under an impression that I had some hostile intentions. I again repeated all I had said; and added, that had I received any instructions from India inimical to him, I should have proceeded directly to Loheia, and not visited him and drank coffee with him. He at length declared he was satisfied, and that I had removed a heavy load from his mind. When I arose up to take my leave, I requested to put his hand into Mr. Pringle's, to which he consented; and I left them professedly friends. He conducted me the whole length of the room quite to the door, a compliment he never before paid to any one.

The whole conversation gave me a much better opinion of his understanding than I had before. He certainly had reason for his alarms; and the manner in which he pushed forward the enquiry was decorous, yet able. The Wahabees were assembling a very large force at Loheia and Hodeida. They had collected the revenue of Beit-il-Fakih and the surrounding country, and sent to Mocha to say they would be there as soon as Ramadan is over. They have many friends in the town, and I see nothing that can resist them. To add to the Dola's alarms, I arrived in a vessel, which, instead of anchoring in the roads near the fort, kept aloof to the north; and instead of landing, I only sent off letters to the Resident. To his fears, therefore, I attribute his civility; and in this idea I am confirmed by Nathaniel Pierce, one of the men, who, from fear of Captain Keys, ran away from the Antelope, and turned Mussulmaun: this man, through my servant, applied to me, stating the wretched situation he was in, declaring his sincere repentance, and beseeching me to permit him to attend me, even as a slave, to Europe. I consented to receive him, and he came off in the boat last night. He tells me that the Dola has been alarmed ever since my departure, suspecting that I was gone to the Wahabees, and would return with them. He frequently asked Pierce if I was as great a man as Sir Home Popham, and whether he thought I should come back. Pierce assured him I should not; yet here I was, at the moment the Wahabees were expected.

I confess I felt very great pleasure in depriving the Dola of this man at so critical a moment. All the old renegadoes had gone off with a party of fifty Turks belonging to dows, who marched them down to the pier in the middle of the day, and the Dola's askaris dared not attempt to prevent them. They became Wahabees, and are now at Loheia, ready to march against Mocha, every foot of which they are perfectly acquainted with. They know the proper place for the attack, and even sent word to Pierce not to be near the middle fort, as they should enter there. This may be done with the utmost facility, as the ports are only a few feet from the ground. The Dola is so much alarmed that, on about one hundred Wahabees coming to one of the gates, and offering to inlist with him, he gave them a dollar each, and sent them away; afraid to take them, and yet afraid to refuse. It is singular, that the very act of procuring converts, on which the Dola so much prided himself, should now conduce to his ruin. His violation of the law of nations recoiled on his own head. One of the two boys, who escaped from the factory, was dead; the other was to be married this Ede. The little boys were very ill. I sent them some medicine which they took secretly; the bigotry of the Mussulmauns will not allow them to do it openly. Some laudanum I gave Pierce was taken from him: they said it was sheitan, and that prayers were better. All the remaining renegadoes meant to try to get off in the three American ships: when we went on shore they were at Moosa, so that our people did not see them.

Early in the morning of January 2, our little dow was along side, and we received from the shore our last stock of vegetables. At eight we weighed anchor and steered for the Aroe Islands, so called in the charts, but probably a corruption of Jibbel Arish, the name of the largest island. We had a very stiff breeze, and a strong current to the northward. The swell lessened as we approached the African shore. This was the case during our last voyage, and it was satisfactory to find it the same at this season. Our vessel was so crank that we were obliged to carry only close-reefed topsails on the cap. We passed between the white rocks, which the pilot called the Children of Arish, and the islands, as on our return from Massowah, and were extremely surprised to find how incorrectly they were laid down in Sir Home Popham's chart of the Red Sea; the Great Aroe having been left out, while the others were none of them in their true position. Captain Court expressed his surprise, that Mr. Maxfield had been able to lay the places down so accurately in his chart, from the little assistance he received. We went close to Rackmah, and upon the credit of Mr. Maxfield's chart, sailed all night. It blew very fresh, and there was a considerable following sea. The Panther was so light, that we could not make her go less than seven knots with a double reefed fore-topsail close to the cap. We kept rather without the line of the Antelope's course, and had deeper water, with sometimes no soundings.

Ras Kussar was in sight next morning, and the weather more moderate, with a smooth sea. We found that our dow had left us in the night, having probably run in shore for shelter. We coasted along, going as near the shore as possible. Captain Court was indefatigable in taking bearings. We did not think it safe to pass betwen Pilot's Island and the African shore in the dark, and therefore in the evening came to an anchor in ten fathom, under shelter of a small island called Adjuice, a little to the north of Howakil. There were several fishing boats, and some dows, which ran away on our approach. Our pilot seemed well acquainted with the coast, and was on the whole a much more intelligent man than the one we had in the Antelope. He expressed great astonishment during the day at our knowing the names of the capes and islands.

In the morning one of the dows came along side. They were only fishing, and belonged to the eastern coast of Arabia. They said that the island, though inhabited, had no water; but that there was some on the main land behind Howakil. The former part of this account was certainly true at this time, as they begged some water from us, which we willingly gave them; but it is impossible to suppose that this can be always the case, or the inhabitants would remove to the main land. Don Juan de Castro, who anchored here in 1540, with the Portuguese fleet under Don Stefano de Gama, says that there was water on the great island, called from its figure Whale Island, by which he undoubtedly meant Howakil. They describe the Bay as not deep, nor fit for large vessels, having an entrance for dows at the southern extremity. As I considered this as probably the Opsian Bay of the Periplus, I had given Mr. Maxfield directions to examine it in the Assaye.

We sailed at day-break. Our pilot took us without Pilot's Island, through a new and good channel, but no soundings. We had baffling winds as we approached Dhalac, and did not get to an anchor till dark. We were nearly in the old spot. Our friend the Dola came off on his catamaran, and was rejoiced to see us. We told him we came for water. He said we should have it, and every thing else we wished for. He received a present of tobacco and rice: the people all wanted some of the latter. There has been no rain since I was here, and the island is nearly burnt up. Many of their cattle and goats have died in consequence. It was determined that Captain Court should go on shore to settle every thing to-morrow. During the night we had a fresh gale from south.

Captain Court, Mr. Salt, and Captain Rudland went on shore on the 5th, and arranged every thing with the Dola for surveying the island: he himself consented for forty dollars to accompany them. They had a camel for their baggage, and asses for themselves, two Europeans as servants, and Mr. Criddle, the youngest midshipman, as assistant observer. They took with them a week's provisions; on the 6th they went on shore and departed. The Dola left a request that our people would not wander about the island, nor fire off guns in the interior, as it would alarm the inhabitants: this I faithfully promised to prevent.

The situation of the ship made it absolutely necessary to examine the state of the hold. We found that she had not sufficient ballast by several tons; that all the fire-wood had been placed under the ground tier of water-barrels, thereby raising the centre of gravity above a foot; and that the casks which were sent on board as new, had leaked out nearly the whole of their contents, being made of old worm-eaten ship timber; another instance of the neglect in every department of the marine at Bombay. Would any one believe that these vessels were received into store as new, and issued again as such! Every thing was removed, and new stowed. The water was put at the bottom, and we took in six hundred and eighty-seven skins full. The Assaye received two hundred and eighteen. The water on the island near Nokhara was exhausted the second day; the rest was procured from the wells on Dhalac, near the doom-trees, where Mr. Salt formerly landed. When they shall have been more accustomed to water ships, it will be done more expeditiously. After the 6th the wind from the S. changed to light variable airs, with a land and sea breeze. When it blew freshest there was no swell, nor can there be, as on every side, at thirty miles, this anchorage is land-locked. The ground is mud and sand, without coral.

On the 6th Mr. Maxfield was in sight, and late at night anchored close to us. On the 7th he came on board with a letter from the Nayib of Massowah, couched in the most friendly terms. He sent one pilot, and had hired another, who was to be ready on my reaching that place. He sent a man to procure me every thing I wished for at Dhalac, whom I dispatched immediately to Captain Court.

Mr. Maxfield informed me, that on leaving Mocha roads he had not been able to weather the Aroe Islands, but had been carried to the northward by the strength of the current, where he had found a free passage, which is laid down in the charts. Agreeably to the instructions he had received, he steered for Howakil, and came to an anchor among the Sarbo Zeghir Islands, forming a very safe bay, which he named Assaye Bay. He attempted to enter the harbour behind Howakil, but was driven back by a very strong current, which he could not stem with his sweeps, as the wind was adverse. The only passage that appeared practicable was extremely narrow, and had two shoals extending from the points of entrance. The natives' account, that it is passable only for dows, seems therefore to be true; and Howakil Bay can be an object of curiosity only to ascertain whether the Opsian stone is found in it; for I think the description of the Periplus so exactly accords with what we have seen, that there can be no doubt of its being the Opsian Bay.

The vast accumulation of sand, that existed in the time of the Egyptian traveller, is now become a cluster of low sandy islands, nearly level with the sea, which are designated in the chart as the Arenah Islands; and the bay itself most admirably answers the description of βαθύτατοσ; for it is the deepest on the whole western coast of the Red Sea, except Foul Bay in lat. 23°, which cannot, from its position, be the one described. The distance from Aduli to the Opsian Bay, as stated in the Periplus, is eight hundred stadia, or, according to Dr. Vincent, eighty miles, which it ought to be, if the stadium used was the Roman, of ten to a mile; but I confess I am inclined to suppose that it was the Egyptian, of fifteen to a mile, which will make the distance a little more than fifty-three miles. This is, in fact, the real distance from the Arenah islands to the sea shore near Massowah;

at twenty stadia, or about a mile and a half, from which, stood the town of Aduli. It is highly improbable, in stating the distance between this town and the bay, that the author should have meant to carry his admeasurement to the cape at the farther extremity, instead of the one at the entrance; yet Dr. Vincent has been obliged to measure the distance to Cape Sarbo in order to make it seventy-five miles, which is still short of the eight hundred stadia mentioned in the Periplus. This difficulty, as well as many others that still encumber the work, may be removed, by supposing that the Egyptian stadium was the one meant by the author; and nothing seems to me more rational than the idea, that an Egyptian merchant sailing from Egypt would use the stadium of that country. It is, however, with the greatest hesitation that I venture to differ from Dr. Vincent, whose perfect knowledge and laborious investigation of ancient geography, entitle him to the highest deference in every point connected with it.

During Mr. Maxfield's stay at Massowah, the Nayib had given a very strong proof of his friendly regard: two of the lascars belonging to the Assaye ran away from the vessel, but were caught by some Arabs, belonging to a dow, before they could reach the shore, and carried before the Nayib, who immediately sent them to Mr. Maxfield, with a request that they might not be punished, which was promised and faithfully performed. The evils that attend the trading with Mocha from the Arab spirit of proselyting, will not therefore be extended to Massowah. On the 8th, another complimentary letter arrived from the Nayib, with a present of sheep, vegetables, limes, and water.

I dispatched the dow with her people to Valentia Island to look for shells, and employed my servant and another European in the same pursuit. They procured a few fine specimens of Cypræa, but the others that they brought were of little value.

I sent Alli Nohri on shore to procure sheep: he brought off twenty goats, for which he said they demanded fourteen dollars; and if I did not like them at that price, I must send them back. Astonished at conduct so different from what I had before experienced, I instantly did so, being convinced that it was a contrivance of this rascally Arab, who wanted to purchase every thing here, as he did at Mocha, and have cent. per cent. profit. I was convinced of his knavery by another incident. The dow brought a heifer to sell, and asked four dollars: we objected, and they would have taken three; but Alli Nohri prevented them by saying in Arabic, it was cheap at four: this they afterwards owned to my servant and Pierce.

January 14.—Captain Court, Mr. Salt, and the party, all returned, having surveyed the southern and eastern parts of the island. Mr. Salt made the following report of their proceedings during their absence.

" We left Nokhara at seven in the morning, and crossed the creek to Dhalac; but not finding the asses ready, walked to the wells on the sea shore, marked by the doom-trees, and whence latterly the water was procured for the ship. The distance was about one mile and three quarters. The country was dried up, as not a drop of rain had fallen since our last visit to the island, yet the wells were as full as ever, the water being within two feet of the surface, and good. Near the wells were some bulbs, apparently Frittilaria, of which specimens were sent on board, and also a small knotty root of a species of grass of an aromatic flavour, which is eaten by the natives. We were obliged to wait till twelve, when Captain Court took the meridian altitude, and also a set of bearings. This is a more convenient place for a vessel to water at than Nokhara, as the water is near the shore, and it is well marked by the doom trees. At the wells was a small flock of sheep, ten or twelve in number. The date trees seemed not to have thriven since we were here, yet the soil is far better than at Mocha: a flight of small birds, not unlike averdavats, came and settled among their branches; and two vultures, of different species, that had fled, like ourselves, for shelter from the wind and sun, remained stationary under their shade. The number of goats that we this day met with is worthy of observation, considering that there was scarcely a blade of grass to be seen; but the mimosa, that braves the most burning heat, seems to afford sufficient nourishment to these as well as to the camels that roam at large about the island. The asses at length arrived, and were more steady than usual; but the ride was unpleasant from the heat of the sun, and the force of the wind.

" After passing by the salt marsh, we stopped a few minutes, and endeavoured to procure milk or water, at a place where I had formerly obtained both, but in vain. We went up to the building where I had before been requested not to go, and found that it was only a shelter for their kids. On our arrival at Dhalac-el-Kibeer, we experienced a most welcome reception from the inhabitants. My friend the priest, who was acting as Dola when I was here with Mr. Maxfield, now presented to me the real Dola, a venerable old man, who had then been confined by indisposition. I was glad to see that they had not forgotten me, and that they expressed pleasure at our arrival.

Captain Court made an observation, and after the sun had set we took a short walk, and then laid ourselves down, well satisfied, on the humble couches prepared for us. Thermometer at Dhalac 80° in the morning, 87° at noon.

" January 8.—After breakfast we set out with all our implements of surveying, and, while the two Europeans were measuring a base from Sheik Abou-el-Heimen's tomb, made a circuit to the southward to examine the tanks. We found twelve all nearly of the same construction, though some were much larger than others, and one was uncovered and square. Captain Court thought the largest would hold one hundred and fifty tons. They were cut out of the solid rock, and chunamed, but not lined with stone. Thence we went round to the eminence, which Captain Court had fixed upon for the other extreme of his base, at about a mile from the mausoleum. While he was engaged in taking bearings, I rode off to the point whence I had before seen the Antelope, but wandered about for a considerable time in vain, then mounted a tree, but with as little success; at length I got upon the top of a large upright stone, that stands, like a land-mark, in the middle of the plain, when I was gladdened with a sight of the Panther, which I kept steadily in view, retreating until I came into the line of the measured base, at about one mile from the stone. Captain Court took bearings from this spot, and a meridian altitude, with an artificial horizon. We afterwards returned by the north mosque, and, on our way, examined three more of the cisterns, all similar to those we had seen in the morning.

" We had fixed with the Dola to depart at noon, but it was already past that hour, and we had not nearly finished our observations; so we dined at two; at half past three Captain Court took sights, and at four went down to the mausoleum, to take a set of bearings from its summit, while in the mean time I examined the inside, in the centre of which was the tomb, covered by two pieces of coloured Indian chintz spread on a wooden frame. We extended our walk, by going round to the southern mosque, in which is a rough inscription. The architecture is tolerably regular, and the arch of the dome well formed. We then looked into five more cisterns, one of which differed from all the others, in having the roof supported by five pillars, though it was not so large as some we had seen in the morning. Its dimensions, which were taken by a man we let down by the log-line, were as follows; its longest diameter twenty-four feet, its shortest twenty-two; the pillars six feet in circumference, and six feet distant from each other, but at unequal distances from the wall, some two feet, some four feet; they were somewhat thicker at top, but had no regular capitals. The depth of the tank was thirteen feet, and the whole was covered with chunam. The birds seen this day were white-breasted crows, vultures, kites, pelicans, small birds of the sparrow kind, water-wagtails, the abou hannes of Bruce, and which are called so by the natives here, ring-doves, and a bird of an iron brown colour, about the size of a pigeon. Thermometer as yesterday.

"January 9.—We departed early in the morning from Dhalac-el-Kibeer, having procured asses for all our people, and camels for the baggage. On parting we gave a piece of blue cloth to the Sheik-el-Belled, a dollar to Abouel--Heimen's tomb, and another to my friend the Sheik of the mosque, and distributed some tobacco to the people who had assisted us in onr excursions. As there was scarcely a breath of air, the heat was intolerably oppressive. The road lay at first south-easterly, over a stony plain, on which not a blade of grass was discernible. After marching about three miles, a large bird, that was passing to the left, induced us to stop until the musquets were brought up; it was of a brown colour, and appeared not unlike a cassowary; the people said it was good to eat; on firing at it, it ran away, expanding its wings, but did not attempt to fly. Soon after we had recommenced our march, the road began to incline about N. E. by E. over a low sandy plain, about half a mile wide, and nearly four miles in extent, with ridges of rock on either side, that gave it somewhat the appearance of a river's bed. The rocks on the left rise into a remarkable cliff, not less, I imagine, than thirty feet above the plain; the strata lie horizontally, and are so regular that when near us, they resembled the walls of an ancient castle.

"At a little before twelve we turned off the plain, and ascended the rocky ground to the right; when our guides pointed out to us the village of Gerbeschid, about a mile in front, which was easily distinguished, (as are all other villages or towns on the island,) by the doom-trees rising above the Mimosas, with which this part of the island more particularly abounds. We reached it soon after twelve, and took possession of a tenement, in every respect like what we had at Nokhara and Dhalac. From the last place Gerbeschid is by the road about nine miles distant. It is a most wretched assemblage of about twenty huts, and is distant three miles from the sea. It is difficult to conceive how its inhabitants manage to preserve their existence, as the drought has killed great part of their goats, on which they depend chiefly for their support, a considerable quantity of cheese being annually exported from this place to Loheia. The putrid carcases of the dead goats still lie around the town in every direction, and send forth most pestilential effluvia. The few that survive are too ill fed to give milk, and too lean to afford substantial nourishment if killed, so that these poor people are obliged to live almost entirely upon fish, of which there is also but a scanty supply; their water, which is drawn from wells, is indeed tolerably good, but very muddy. During the most favourable seasons, this place produces few even of the necessaries of life; the additional deprivation is therefore more severely felt than it would be, probably, in most parts of the globe.

"Captain Court took observations for the latitude, and a lunar observation for the longitude; and after dinner walked towards the sea in an easterly direction. Hence the land is seen at a very considerable distance to the south, forming a creek or bay, which Captain Court afterwards ascertained to be a part of the main land of Dhalac. I learned from the Sheik-el-Belled that there were forty or fifty men living here, about eighty women, and only about ten children in the whole place; which I have reason to believe true, from the very few we saw, both then, and on our return. He added the following particulars; that they had lost between two and three hundred goats and kids; that they have but eight wells, and no tanks of any description; that from Ras Shoke to Ras Antalou is four days journey; that their principal employment is making mats, and that some of their people are engaged in the sea-faring line at Loheia. Thermometer at day light 80°, at night 90°.

"January 10.—We rose at day light, and in the

course of an hour had all ready for departure, but were detained, much against our inclinations, by the loss of a bunch of keys, for which we ransacked the house and baggage in vain; it was past seven, when finding, probably, that we were determined not to go without them, a boy belonging to the village brought them to us, pretending that he had found them on the road. The track this day led over a plain, quite level, but not so stony as on the west side of the island. The wind was blowing light from the N. W. The direction of our march lay to the N. E. on our setting out; the sea was three miles distant on our right, and two miles out lay the island of Irwee, its extremes bearing from S. E. to east. Off its northern extremity are two trees on the edge of the water, which appeared, at the distance we were, like rocks. We continued a direct course for about two miles and a half, when we saw the high trees about Dobelew, bearing from us due north; we could likewise just distinguish to our right on the horizon the island of Dalcoos. We soon after passed on our left a miserable kind of edifice, which they called Sheik Othman's tomb. The country here made some slight approach towards vegetation. I observed a few trees of a different species of mimosa from what we had hitherto seen, as also a parasitical plant entwining round its branches. We arrived at Dobelew at nine, and computed it to be four miles and a half from Gerbeschid. It appeared to be full as large as Dhalac-el-Kibeer, had a white tomb at the east and west ends, and two smaller ones on the north.

"They conducted us at first to a wretched hovel, from which they had just driven their goats; but, on our expressing dissatisfaction, they found us another somewhat more decent, and, to compensate for their rudeness, turned a family out of the next habitation, and gave it to us for a cook-room. This was, however, after having been severely reprimanded by the Nayib's servant, who had evidently received very strict orders to provide for our accommodation; he had throughout been of the greatest use to us, and had uniformly paid attention to all our wishes. There was no milk to be procured here, but we got a kid, with some little trouble, and three fowls.

"The weather was so cloudy, that the sun was not visible at twelve; but Captain Court afterwards took a double altitude, to ascertain the latitude. In the evening he went and measured a base from the north-western mosque to a goat-shed half a mile distant, and at the latter station took a set of bearings, having in sight the islands of Irwee, Dalçoos, and Saiel Sezan, and to the west, the village of Saied-el-Ait. We used our utmost endeavours to procure a boat to go over to Irwee, but in vain. We were informed that there is only a small village on the island, visited by a few fishermen on catamarans; that its coast is low, with here and there a tree upon it; and that the water between it and the nearest point of the coast to Dobelew, is shallow, and full of shoals. We now proposed to the Dola going up to Ras Antalou; but he assured us, that the only practicable means of doing so, would be to go by water from Nokhara, since, on the road from this place, there were neither asses nor camels to be procured, nor people to afford us accommodations of any kind. It was determined, therefore, that we should walk in the morning to a rocky eminence, called Jissoom, which is the highest land in the neighbourhood of Dobelew. Abdallah and the two seamen went down to the sea side in the morning to look for shells; but the few that they were able to procure were of little value. I urged the Seid to send out some of the fishermen on the same pursuit, and promised to pay them handsomely; but the inhabitants of this village seemed to be as idle as they were poor, and in consequence nothing could be done.

"January 11.—We set out on our proposed expedition at half past six, marching in a direct line for Jissoom, which bore from us N. 35° E. We had advanced about three miles, when we came to a creek of salt water that crossed our road at right angles, which we passed over, the water being shallow. As we proceeded a herd of deer galloped by us on our right, at no great distance. Having reached Jissoom, Captain Court fixed his theodolite, and took the bearings of all the islands, and principal objects around us, as follows, Dobelew from S. 31° W. to S. 27° West. Irwee from S. 37°, $\frac{3}{4}$ E. to S. 3° W. Saiel Arabie S. 64° E. Dalcoos from S. 86° E to N. 86$\frac{1}{2}$ E. Saiel Sezan from N. 59° E. to N. 52° E. a distant island from N. 55° to N. 45° E. Dalhedeia N. 21°$\frac{1}{2}$ E. Delgammon or Derghiman, of which there are two, Kibeer and Zeguir from N. 19° E. to N. 30° W. Saiel-el-Ait, the village we had before seen, S. 79° W. We found that the creek we had passed completely insulates Jissoom hill, and the low land around it, forming nearly a circular island about two miles in circumference. On the point of Dhalac bearing N. 38° W. is a village called Ebáru. All around us there appeared to be shoal water as far as the eye could reach.

"Here we measured the distance back to the northern mosque, and arrived at half past ten. The weather cloudy, and thermometer only 82° at noon day. Captain Court took a meridian altitude, and at four p. m. he went out, and, proceeding from the northern mosque, measured a base to the water's edge, in a line with the northern point of Irwee. He found the space between Ras-el-Shoel and Irwee, which forms what Bruce calls the harbour of Dobelew, filled up with sandy shoals, and small islets, excepting close to Irwee, where there appears to be a channel sufficiently deep for boats of small burthen. Hence the south end of Irwee makes in one, and seems almost connected, with the main land of Dhalac. Seied-el-Arabie and Seied-el-Sezan were both in sight, but, from some particular effect in the atmosphere, they were not able to distinguish Dalcoos. As far as this chain of islands extends outwards, Captain Court is satisfied that the water is shoally, and that no vessel would be safe in attempting a passage within them, except small craft; and it is only a few days ago that two dows were lost on the outside of Irwee, driven in by stress of weather. During Captain Court's absence I endeavoured to get as much information as possible concerning the place, and, for this purpose, one of the elder inhabitants, who had spent his life in pilotting vessels to and fro, was brought to me by the Nayib's man. He confirmed to me the names of all the islands we had seen in the morning, which agree most perfectly with what Bruce has called them. He recognized every island, excepting two, mentioned by Bruce, as I named them from the book. Abdel Gaffar's tomb, however, they assured me was on the island of Noorah, off Ras Antalou, where is a small village, and not on Dahalottum, as asserted by Bruce. They say, there are two islands of el-Surat, the largest of which had once wells and inhabitants, but the latter have removed, and the former have been all filled up.

" January 12.—About two o'clock in the morning a heavy shower of rain fell, which obliged us to remove our cots, on which we had hitherto slept in the open air, into the house for shelter; but the covering of these habitations is so little adapted for keeping out the inclemency of the rainy season, that we could not find even one "snug corner." Captain Court went out at dawn of day, and took a set of bearings from the top of the northern mosque. The water, which we this morning procured, was filled with so thick a sediment, that we were obliged to give up our tea. The well itself we found, on measuring it, to be seven fathom deep, and with only three feet water. This is, I think, the most inhospitable place we have visited. The men were by no means obliging, and seemed to be jealous, or the women were extremely shy, for they evidently kept out of our way as much as possible. The character of the people is probably, in no small degree, affected by their intercourse with Arabia. The shell of a turtle was lying in the yard, about two feet and a half diameter; they speak of them as being very common; by a small piece of the shell which remained, it appeared to be of that species which yields the true tortoise shell. The stench of dead goats was as unpleasant to us here, as at Gerbeschid. There are more doom trees than at the other villages, besides many other species of tree.

"At half past nine we quitted this miserable place. Captain Court took an exact account of our bearings, and found Gerbeschid to be, as we computed, only four miles and a half from Dobelew. We saw a covey of partridges on the road, and got to our journey's end by half past ten. Immediately on our arrival at Gerbeschid, we looked out for an eminence, from which we might see some one of the points which Captain Court had taken, and thus connect the line of bearings: but, after mounting walls and houses in vain, we almost despaired of success, the situation of this village being extremely low, and no rising ground in the neighbourhood. At last we resorted to the old expedient of ascending to the top of the mosque, an indignity which we found might be always compensated by the gift of a dollar, and here, after piling a triple story of couches, one upon the other, which were procured from the owner of the adjacent house, we gained, most fortunately, a good bearing of a goat-shed, whence Captain Court had taken his last bearings. Hence we likewise saw the cliff, and the high land of the Abyssinian coast, somewhere near Hurtoo. The day was unluckily too cloudy to get any solar observation, which made it the more important that we should get a point of bearing between Gerbeschid and Dhalac-el-Kibeer; we therefore determined to wait until morning, and proceed at daylight, when we expected to attain our object, by mounting the cliff. I learned to day, that there were at this time seventeen trankies, from near Muscat, looking out among the islands for pearls, tortoise-shell, wood, or indeed whatever they could pick up; many of these we saw lying off the coast in different directions. Thermometer 82°$\frac{1}{4}$.

"January 13.—Left Gerbeschid at half past seven, and reached the cliff in about half an hour, having more spirited asses than usual. We computed the distance to be two miles and an half. Leaving our animals at the bottom, we ascended to the highest point, on which stand the two trees, which were set from Gerbeschid. This cliff is nearly perpendicular, except in one or two places, where loose fragments of rock, that have fallen, form stepping-places, which render the ascent easy. In some parts of the rock are deep chasms, that appeared almost the work of art. The view from the top fully answered our expectations, and discovered to us, somewhat unexpectedly, a sight of the Panther, an object most particularly interesting to our purposes; it appeared over the point of Dhalac, nearest to Nokhara, on the opposite side of a large salt-water lake, which was distant about three quarters of a mile, and which apparently is deep enough for the largest vessels. We could also just distinguish one of the mausoleums at Nokhara, distant between six and seven miles. We had at the same time in sight Cape Sarbo, and the island of Howakil, the high peak behind Hurtoo, and the village of Gerbeschid.

" As the surest way of ascertaining the sites of these objects, Captain Court measured a base of eight hundred paces, and took bearings at each end. The land descends, in a sloping line, hence to the lake, round which is a sandy beach. On coming down we observed a few deer, which were very wild, and speedily bounded over the rocks out of sight. The valley, formed by the cliffs, which we passed through a second time to day, seems by far the richest part of the island; it is well sheltered, the soil is good, and there was, even still, a little verdure covering the greater part of it. I also observed three species of shrubs, different from what I had before noted. It is probable that even the small quantity of rain which had fallen, occasioned, in a great degree, the more luxuriant appearance of this valley, or it might be the difference of our feelings, at the times that we passed through it. Two or three species of birds, the plumage of one of which was very beautiful, were seen flying from bush to bush. We arrived at

Dhalac-el-Kibeer at half past one. Thermometer 84°. 5′.

"January 14.—At day-light I went with Abdallah and the two Europeans to the northern mosque, for the purpose of getting possession of some of the monumental stones, mentioned in my former account. The best finished inscriptions were engraved on stones, which were too heavy to carry away. I therefore made choice of two of the most perfect, carved in different characters, that were portable, and wrapping them up very carefully, proceeded back to our lodgings, not quite satisfied, I own, with the propriety of what I was about. Our proceedings having been observed, by the time we reached the house a crowd had assembled, among which were several principal inhabitants. I immediately perceived that they were acquainted with what we had been doing, and that they wished to examine the contents of our bags, which we evaded, and got our plunder safe into the yard. The crowd now began to increase, and I heard them debating the matter rather warmly on the outside. Soon afterwards they came into the yard, in a body, with Seied Yusuff and the Nayib's messenger at their head; there were also, among the foremost, the Sheik-el-Belled and the Sheik of the mosque. Abdallah being called, they began a most lamentable complaint against our proceedings, said these stones were sacred to the dead, and that the Nayib had positively forbidden that any of them should be removed. The Nayib's man, however, who was spokesman, said nothing as from himself, but premised every sentence with, "thus do they infer." The Seied Yusuff also (having been previously bribed) kept a becoming silence; so I cut the matter short by telling them, that they might rest assured that I should do nothing except what the Nayib approved; and that I should not think of arguing with them upon the subject, (whom it did not at all concern,) but would settle the matter with their superior, when we arrived at Massowah. This, I told them, was my determination, and forbad Abdallah to interpret another word on the subject. The only fear now was, that we should not get any animal to carry them away. As soon therefore as tranquillity was a little restored, we took an opportunity of making rather a larger present than we had intended, to the two Sheiks, and distributed the remainder of our tobacco among the lower order. This completely removed their scruples, and they immediately assisted, most cordially, in repacking the sacred spoils, and in fastening them on the back of a camel. It was eleven o'clock before we got away: we saw many deer on the road, and, by accident, caught a doe big with young, that had been previously wounded. She was large, of a light-dun colour, white on the belly and rump, with small black horns, which were circled with rings. Captain Court stopped at the wells to take the meridian altitude, and, at half past one, we were welcomed on board the Panther by all our friends."

This second tour of Mr. Salt through Dhalac, has completely proved that the account of it, as given by Mr. Bruce, is in a great degree erroneous; and leaves it extremely probable, that he never landed on the Island. "The three hundred and seventy cisterns, all hewn out of the solid rock," have, after the most minute investigation, been reduced to less than twenty ; and of these not one is to be found at Dobelew, where he asserts, as an eye-witness, "that they are neglected, and open to every sort of animal, and half full of the filth that they leave there after drinking and washing in them." If the plan of the island of Dhalac, the harbour of Dobelew, and the surrounding islands, as laid down by that excellent hydrographer Captain Court, and now given to the public in my chart, be compared with the description of Mr. Bruce, hardly one point of resemblance will be found between the two; and I trust there will be no doubt in the public mind to which the credit ought to be given.

The round harbour of Dobelew, with its narrow entrance, is no where discoverable, and the town itself, instead of being, as Bruce states, three miles S. W. of the harbour, is, in fact, on a parallel with the northern extremity of Irwee, which forms the harbour, and is an island; a circumstance which ought to have been known to him had he actually been on the spot. It is not however with Captain Court only that Mr. Bruce differs; his bearings, as given by himself, are irreconcileable, and, after several attempts, it was found impossible to lay down the islands between Jibbel Teir and Dhalac from his account, which is much to be regretted, as it is improbable that any other traveller will venture through the shoals on the eastern side of the island, when a passage so much safer is afforded on the western.

The account given by Mr. Bruce of the animals drinking out of the cisterns, and washing in them, is evidently untrue, from the construction of them, as described by Mr. Salt, they being arched over, with a hole in the centre.

The impudence ascribed by Mr. Bruce to the women of Dobelew makes me still more doubtful of his having been at that place; since it is hardly probable that they would have totally changed their habits in a period of thirty years, during which time it is evident that their poverty had not diminished.

The errors in Mr. Bruce's account of Dhalac-el-Kibeer, its harbour, and the numerous tanks on the island, might have been excused, had he stated the circumstances less positively, and given them only as he received them by the report of the inhabitants. In Mr. Salt's first visit to Dhalac-el-Kibeer, he heard from several, that there was a tradition among them of three hundred and sixteen tanks: and this tradition was probably mentioned to Mr. Bruce, and, if given by him as such, would have been justifiable. The same observation will hold good respecting the harbour, which, from his journal, it is evident he could not have seen, and to which he only transfers the information that was given him respecting Nokhara. I can by no means extend the same indulgence to his account of the islands, and their relative bearings. When a person attempts to give geographical information to the public, it is necessary that this information should be accurate; and that he should not advance, as certain, a single circumstance, of which he has not positively informed himself. That Mr. Bruce, on the contrary, has erred in many points, and falsified in others, must be clear by a comparison of his own bearings with each other, and of the whole with the chart of Captain Court. I feel him to be the less justifiable on this occasion, as he had it in his power to give a true account of the island, and its dependencies; for his having been at anchor somewhere near Dobelew is proved by his knowledge of the names of the numerous islands in its vicinity, and by his having stated its latitude as

15° 42′ 22″, which is within two miles of its true position, 15° 44′.

I dispatched Mr. Maxfield at night with a message to the Nayib, saying that we should be at Massowah the next day. We took a cordial leave of the Dola, and, in consideration of his good conduct during the survey, gave him several presents, and left a letter, certifying how well he had behaved. The Nayib's man demanded the money for the water in his master's name, and the forty dollars were delivered to him. There had been one thousand skins put on board the boats; we paid for the whole, though some had burst. The water was not quite so good as on our last visit, which was owing to the drought. It was, however, as good as the best at Mocha.

By four o'clock next morning it began to blow very fresh from the south. It was full moon, and the tide rose by the lead line near nine feet. We attempted to get up our anchor, but it came home, and we were obliged to let go another, which brought us up. It moderated towards evening; and the wind coming round to the eastward, we got under weigh, and in five hours, were within soundings. After four hours sail we fired a gun, and burnt a blue light as a signal to Mr. Maxfield, and in half an hour a second, which was answered. We stood on till we were met by him in a boat. He brought us safe into harbour, about eleven, to the great astonishment of our pilots. The sea was perfectly smooth as we approached the main land.

Our anchor dragged in the night, and a strong breeze from the N. drove us close to the shoal on the N. E. extremity of Massowah. We had all our anchors out, and the weight of them alone saved us, as the ground was too hard for them to lay hold of. It grew more moderate at noon, and before night, the vessel was warped into a place of safety. By agreement we saluted the fort with three guns, which were returned. The Banian came on board, and I gave him a commission from Mr. Pringle to act as broker of the India Company at Massowah. He informed me the Nayib would be happy to see me, and would receive me at his durbar, but did not wish to return the visit on board the Panther, which, of course, I did not press. There was some mention of the political situation of Massowah, which I did not perfectly understand. Captain Court declined leaving the ship, our party therefore on shore consisted of Mr. Salt, Captain Rudland, and myself. We were received precisely as on my former visit. I had a similar kelaut; Mr. Salt one that was old, and tarnished. I went to Abou Yusuff's house, where several of the natives paid me visits, whom I treated with coffee and sweetmeats. I was assured of every supply that I wanted.

Determining on the following evening to visit the Nayib, I ordered two barrels of gunpowder to be brought on shore, one of which I sent to him, as a present in the name of the Bombay Government, the other in my own; at the same time the Banian presented my salaams, and requested that he would permit some of our party to shoot on the morrow, attended by some of his people. The answer I received was, that when he saw me, we would talk over that and other circumstances. Surprised at this equivocal answer, I called the Banian aside, and desired to know what was the meaning of it. He at last told me, that it was to see what present I meant to make him, before he gave his orders. I expressed myself extremely displeased, and told him to inform the Nayib, that I did not consider myself as bound to give him any thing; that I was willing to pay for every thing I had, and wished, out of friendship to him, to induce English ships to come here for provision and water, by which he would reap a very considerable advantage; that even had a present been necessary, the gunpowder in the morning was more than sufficient, as I knew they valued it at five hundred dollars. I desired him to mention this to the Nayib, and add, that as I did not understand the Arabic language, the business had better be settled through the medium of himself, and my Arab servant Abdallah, and that therefore I would decline visiting him in the evening.

The answer was long, turning much on the attentions I had received from the Nayib, on his wishes to serve me, on his wanting money, as his brothers were importunate to get a portion of what they believed he received, and urging, as a conclusive argument, Captain Keys having given two hundred dollars. This put me into a worse humour. I told the Banian that Captain Keys had in this, as in other things, behaved extremely ill; that it was an act his Government highly disapproved of, and which therefore I could never follow. He said the Nayib knew two hundred dollars would be no object, and that if I requested the Captain to give it, he would comply in a moment. I told him it was out of the question; that I was determined not to give a dollar, nor would the Captain; that some presents I had prepared, which I thought would be acceptable to the Nayib, but that I neither would deliver them, or visit him, till all idea of a present of money was abandoned. He took

Abdallah with him, and brought back an answer in the evening, that the Nayib considered me as one of his best friends; that he ever wished to oblige me; that the horses should be ready for the shooting party; but he hoped I would fill his belly. I laughed, and desired to know what would do this. The answer was, two hundred dollars. I asked if this was insisted on; he said, no, I was to do just as I pleased. On this I dismissed him. Alli Nohri was sent on shore in the course of the day to return to Mocha, as I did not consider it safe to take him with us, after his misconduct at Dhalac. Captain Rudland, Mr. Salt, and Mr. Maxfield, slept at the old residence of Captain Keys; Mr. Macgie, and all our servants, staid with me at Abou Yusuff's. Captain Court, from the difference of conduct in the Nayib, thought it advisable to send six marines on shore as a guard. The air was cool and pleasant the whole night.

Captain Rudland, Mr. Salt, Mr. Macgie, my servant, and Pierce, were out by break of day on a shooting excursion: the Nayib's son went with them: Captain Court came on shore to breakfast with me. Soon afterwards the Nayib's servant, who attended Mr. Salt at Dhalac, came with the Banian, and represented, that Alli Nohri had been saying, that I had given him two hundred dollars for the tomb stones mentioned in Mr. Salt's account, and as much to the Dola of Dhalac; that the Nayib was very angry with them, and he begged I would take all the blame on myself. I told him I not only would, but that I considered myself as at liberty to keep them on the sole condition of the Nayib giving his permission; and that if he wished it, I would restore them. This I desired the Banian to tell the Nayib. He also informed me, that Alli Nohri had declared I came to build a fort, and conquer the island, and that other ships were coming.

I felt heartily vexed at having let this fellow go on shore, who had probably excited suspicion and alarm in the breasts of the natives, which it would be almost impossible for me to eradicate, and which would disappoint my well founded hopes, that every thing would go on in the usual amicable way, and that a permanent commercial arrangement would be formed with the Government of Massowah. I told the Banian I was astonished at the Nayib's giving any credit to such a rascal; and that after my former visit, he ought to have known me better, than to suppose me capable of meditating any thing hostile to him. On the Banian's return, he declared the Nayib did not believe a word that Alli Nohri said, and was perfectly convinced of my friendship; that, however, the stones were not his property, but belonged to the Sultaun of Rome; and consequently he could not give them to me. I replied, I knew too well his connection with Rome, not to laugh at this reason, but he should have them; at the same time I took it very ill, as I could not forget that he offered them to me when I was last here.

Soon afterwards a respectable man made his appearance, and was introduced to me as Vizier of the Nayib. When last here I had heard nothing of such a personage, and now suspected he was an instrument to procure money through another channel. He said he had been to the Nayib, and represented, that it would be a discredit to him, if, after I had bought these stones, I should be obliged to give them up: and that on his advice the Nayib had consented to let me keep them, and I might give him what I pleased. I said I would not, on any pretence, give a single dollar. He replied, the Nayib did not wish it; that he gave up all claims to it, and hoped we were now as good friends as ever. I assured him we were, and that I would visit him on the morrow; in the mean time, as he had acted like a friend, I begged his acceptance of a shawl. I now spoke about trade. He said the Nayib would arrange the duties, and no anchorage should be demanded for any English ship. It was settled that he should come in the evening.

The eldest son of the Nayib, after he returned from the chace, wished to go on board the ship; I therefore went with him. Captain Court showed him the whole, and gave him a few pounds of powder and some balls. I also presented him with a rich piece of kincaub, sufficient for a dress. He was highly pleased, and sent us some fowls in the evening. He was about eighteen years old. His manners were gentle, his figure tall and well proportioned, and his countenance expressive of good nature. His younger brother was to go on board at some other time. He had asked for some powder and ball, saying, that, when last here, I had given him nothing. I told him he should have a shawl, as well as the powder and ball; we were consequently excellent friends. He begged me not to say any thing about it to his brother. I employed myself in cleaning and packing sea shells, which I procured from the children of the town, who collected them in every direction. My European servants and the people belonging to the dow were active in the same pursuit, but, except Cypræa, few of any value are to be had in the harbour. Our sportsmen had great success, and brought home a variety of fine game.

We enjoyed some pheasants and a chevreuil, for

dinner, with some French claret purchased from the Americans. Our Dhalac friend, the Nayib's servant, drank several glasses of Madeira, and was perfectly intoxicated. Abou Yusuff would not taste it: he said the other was a soldier, and that all soldiers were allowed wine, but that he was a Sheik, and could not. We laughed most immoderately at his claim to this title, which he had never before mentioned; and declared he was Sheik Sheitan or Sheik Affrit; a joke which, though coming from Christians, he bore with the greatest good humour. Soon afterwards the Vizier came in, when we instantly cleared the table, took coffee with him, and entered on the subject of the duties. I have given in the Appendix a list of the articles on which the Nayib demands a duty, and the sum demanded, which is in general moderate, though graduated by no regular principle of trade.

Abou Yusuff told me at night that he was in great want of a pair of shawls to give to a friend. I told him I was very happy to hear it, as I was precisely in the same predicament. He and others had advised Pierce not to stir out at night, as Alli Nohri had been trying to excite the people to use him ill for having again turned Christian. We thought it a wise precaution, and he kept close. This day a dow arrived from Jidda belonging to Mocha.

Very early in the morning the Nayib's two sons, attended by the Banian, came to me to request, in their father's name, that I would go on board the ship; representing that the Dola of Arkeko, Emir Moosa, who, though a younger brother of the Nayib, was more powerful from his influence with the soldiers, had come over to Massowah to make the Nayib demand money from us for anchorage; that the Nayib was determined not to do it, and that therefore it might probably end in fighting; that if I was safely out of the way, he might do his worst; but that till then, the Nayib would be miserable, lest any thing should happen to me. I assured them I had not the least fear; that I was fully able to defend myself, if their uncle attacked me, which I hardly conceived he would dare to do; and that if the Nayib wished it, I would guard him also. An answer was returned strongly expressive of anxiety for my safety, and begging as a favour that I would go on board; adding, that every thing I wished should be done for me. On consideration I determined to comply; at the same time stating that it was merely to oblige him, and not out of any fear of the Dola of Arkeko, whose power I heartily despised.

In the course of the day we frequently heard that the Nayib and Dola were disputing violently. As the interference of a subject, however powerful, was fatal to all idea of trade, I determined to bring the business to an issue one way or other; I therefore sent Abdallah to the Dola, with my salaams, adding that I had been given to understand he came over to Massowah with purposes hostile to me; that I had left the shore not out of fear of him, but to oblige the Nayib; that if he had any thing to say to me, he might come on board the ship, or I would send a person to converse with him on shore. Abdallah soon came back with an answer, that he came here for money, and demanded a thousand dollars for the anchorage of the two vessels; that he desired I would send him an answer by the Banian, whether I would pay it or not; for if I did not, he would get it from him. I learned from Abdallah, that on his saying this, there had been a considerable altercation, the Nayib declaring that the Banian had no obligation to pay, and that he had never made nor would ever make, such a demand from us. The Dola continued, that he would not come on board the ship, nor did he want to see any body from me. The Nayib had called Abdallah on one side, and desired him to say to me, that he wished the English ships of war would take in what they wanted at Dhalac, where he could take care they should have every thing, and not come here, as it made disputes between him and his brother.

I learned from the Banian, that by an agreement with these turbulent relations he paid them half of the duties on merchandize; that when our vessels arrived, the Dola had supposed the Nayib made much money, and demanded a share; nor would he believe, at first, that we gave no money; that the Askari at Arkeko gained nothing by us, and were therefore equally vexed, and determined to try the experiment whether they could not bully us out of payment for anchorage. The Banian added, that though the Dola had but seventeen armed men with him, he had completely intimidated the Nayib, and had possession of all his power.

I considered the demand of the Dola, that I should pay anchorage, after I had but the evening before settled with the Sovereign of the country that no English ships should ever pay any, as a gross insult, much heightened by the manner in which it was made; I therefore determined to take it up in a strong way. I asked the Banian if he was afraid to deliver any answer I might wish to send: he said, no; and I then directed him to assure the Nayib of my esteem and regard, and my wish to do every thing to serve and oblige him; that his brother had treated me with insolence in making a demand, which he only could have a right to make, and that therefore I was determined to resent it. I sent word to the Dola, that the English ships of war never paid anchorage here or any where else; that at any rate he had no right to demand it; and that if he did not immediately send a man to make an excuse for his insolence, I would sail in the morning for his town of Arkeko, and burn it down to the ground.

The Banian took this threat and brought back for answer, that he would send to Arkeko, to report that the English never paid anchorage, and would inform us in the morning what was their determination. I sent again to say, I would not wait till morning; that I would have an immediate answer, or would be at Arkeko myself in the morning to settle the business. Soon after the Naqueda of the Dow, Unus Barilla, came on board laughing, and said there had been a violent quarrel between the Nayib and Dola; that the Askari of Massowah had taken part with the former, declaring the English were very good, and ought not to have any demands made on them. It had nearly ended in blows; but at length the whole town being in an uproar, and the very boys taking up stones to pelt the Dola's soldiers, they had retired to their boats on the opposite side of the town, and slipt off unperceived by us.

The Banian soon afterwards arrived, and confirmed the fact. He brought a message from the Dola, that he did not require any money for the anchorage, nor had he the least wish to offend the English. The Nayib sent to say, he had gone to Arkeko to settle every thing; that he would return the next day, and come on board the Panther; till when he begged I would not move. The transaction had now taken the turn I wished; they had tried the experiment of threats, to establish a dangerous precedent, and had failed. I therefore agreed to wait till morning. I was much pleased by a visit from the Nayib's youngest son, which shewed great confidence in us at such a moment. After having been served with sweetmeats and coffee, I gave him a piece of kincaub, and several little articles which he admired. He then asked for some soap, which was of course given to him, and a box to keep his things in. Captain Court also presented him with some powder, which is always a most acceptable gift. Abou Yusuff and his brother both came on board in the evening.

The Banian came off in the morning of January 20, and informed me he had received a letter from the Nayib, declaring that he and the Dola solemnly agreed no anchorage should ever be demanded from English ships; that the English had ever behaved well; that Massowah was theirs to come to whenever they pleased; and that they begged every thing might be friendly between us. The Nayib would come to Massowah when I pleased, and would come on board and settle the duties. I had much conversation with the Banian respecting the political situation of this country, and the probability of danger to any vessel that might come loaded to it. He assured me from himself, that they would certainly be satisfied with the duties, and would do her no injury. He informed me that the Dola was not dependent on his brother, but shared the power with him, though the latter was first in rank; that they divided the duties between them; and that the real cause of the late disputes was a suspicion on the part of the Dola, that the Nayib had concealed the cash he had received from us. Dhalac and other places are the Nayib's private property, in which his brother does not share. The third brother is Sirdar of the Askari. They are first paid out of the duties: the amount is one thousand five hundred dollars per month, and when there is a deficiency the Dola first is obliged to make it good, and then the Nayib; and about this there are frequent hostilities.

The Nayib used to receive his khelaut from Jidda, and still nominally owns the Sultaun of Rome as sovereign. He is therefore certainly the sovereign of the country, though controlled by the influence of his brother. Something of this kind seems to have been the case in Bruce's time. Achmet, whom he mentions as the Nayib's nephew and heir, certainly exercised a power in some parts of the country, while his uncle had it in others, and the duties seem to have been shared between them. At the death of Edris, Emir Moosa, his brother, will, by the laws of the country, be Nayib, but the sons of the former will then succeed, in preference to those of the latter. This custom, which I am told prevails in the other tribes, must frequently give rise to revolutions. The number of soldiers is very inconvenient, as the duties often do not amount to the sum of one thousend five hundred dollars, required for their monthly pay: they are, however, so connected by marriage with the Nayib and his family that it is impossible to reduce them. The Nayib calls them all brothers. The Sirdarship of them is always in the family. The two last years the trade, they say, has decreased, yet we had a constant succession of dows coming in, and going out, during the whole time we were here. I assured the Banian that I wished to see the Nayib, and that I was as much his friend as ever. He brought me a present from himself of Abyssinian cloth, and honey; the latter was put up with the wax, was very white, and remarkably good.

The Vizier came off between three and four, to say that he had written for the Nayib, and to procure me a letter from the Dola, declaring that he would make no claims for anchorage of English ships, and that he wished to be at friendship with them. I made, of course, the same professions in reply, and gave him coffee and sweetmeats, as we did to all our guests. He then requested we would give him two pieces of plank: as they were small, he requested a third, which was complied with, and the old gentleman left us well pleased. We tried the whole day, but without success, to procure fowls; they are chiefly at Arkeko, and as the Banian will not buy them, there is a difficulty in finding others to do it. The Banian came again in the evening, about eight, to say the Nayib was come, and wished me to go and see him: this I most peremptorily refused. He then requested that Abdallah might go, to which I consented, and sent by him to the Nayib eight china dishes, which I heard would be acceptable. After settling our accounts, he gave me another piece of Habesh cloth, and I gave him a shawl. I wrote a letter to Mr. Pringle, stating my ideas respecting the trade of Massowah, and requesting he would never employ Alli Nohri. Abdallah, on his return, brought a letter to me from the Nayib, and another for the Dola of Suakin. My servant and Pierce were out a great part of the day, so also were the dow-boys; they procured a few good Cypræa, but no others.

At four next morning, we began to unmoor: at half after six the Nayib's elder son, his brother the Sirdar, the Vizier, Abou Yusuff, and the Banian came on board, as they said, to express the Nayib's anxious desire that I should go away in friendship with him. A question was added, which betrayed their real motive, which was, whether I meant to give any thing else to the Nayib. At first I determined to do so, knowing that he really was tormented for money; but I afterwards considered that it would be better, to express some feeling of disapprobation at my difference of treatment on this my second visit. I therefore called the son and Vizier into the cabin, and assured them that I parted a sincere friend, but that I must feel mortified at being obliged to leave the shore, and could not therefore send a present as a proof of satisfaction; that I would only send an ivory box of castor, an article here of great value, as a mark of friendship. I gave one, also, to each person of the party. The land breeze and our boats soon cleared us of the harbour, and delivered us from our visitors. The young Hammed (the Nayib's son) seemed to part with regret. Captain Rudland gave him a pair of pistols. His brother got some powder by a private hand.

On maturely considering all that had passed I was inclined to consider these circumstances as increasing instead of lessening, the security of Massowah for British ships. They are convinced we will not be imposed upon, and yet are willing to pay well for every thing. The Banian assured me the Dola is now of the Nayib's opinion, that it is better to secure a moderate profit, than to lose all by preventing ships from coming there. It is possible that the Nayib had in reality no objection to his brother's trying the experiment of bullying us out of the thousand dollars, while he should still profess to be our friend, and become a mediator in case of hostility. I learned that the threat of going to Arkeko terrified them beyond measure; so that whatever they meant, the result has been equally good. I warned them that a King's ship came every year to Mocha, and that, if an unprotected vessel should be injured, she would make them repent it. The Ascari of Arkeko were gaining nothing by us, and therefore cared nothing for us; but there was hardly a family at Massowah who did not derive advantage from our stay, either by collecting shells, bringing fish, &c. for the ship, by labour, or by the presents of the gentlemen. They therefore took our part: and I am convinced that they would never willingly permit an Englishman to be injured.

The two little Abyssinians whom Captain Keys had purchased at Massowah, and taken to Bombay, had been repurchased by the Government, and sent back by the Panther, to be returned to their native country, if the Nayib should desire it, as a proof that the British would not violate the laws while in his dominions. On communicating these circumstances to the Nayib, he replied, that this could be settled at our first interview. Affairs took another turn, and the boys were left in our hands; at their own wish they were now entered on the ship's books, and instead of the slavish names of Sidi and Pompey, assumed the more Christian designations of George Habesh, and Harry Gondar. Christians they were born, but of the doctrines of Christianity, or indeed those of any other religion, they had no idea; I therefore placed them under Pierce, to teach them to read and say their prayers.

CHAPTER VI.

Observations on the Periplûs.—Massowah Bay the Bay of Aduli.—Valentia Island, Orine.—Monsieur Gosselin's Theory erroneous.— Asseez, Ptolemais Theron. —Berenice in Foul Bay.—Departure from Massowah.—Arrival at Port Mornington and Wellesley's Islands.—Ras Asseez.—Bother'em Bay.—Arrival at Suakin.—Transactions with the Natives.—Departure from Suakin.

THE true position of Myos Hormus, at the upper end of the Red Sea, being very doubtful, it seems to me that it would be a more clear method of ascertaining the places mentioned by the author of the Periplûs, to measure his distances from Aduli, which, I think, has been fixed near Massowah, by Dr. Vincent, in a most incontrovertible manner.

I most fully agree with this able and learned elucidator of the Periplûs, that the ancient positions are much more accurately to be ascertained by existing circumstances, than by the astronomical observations, which were originally made with very imperfect instruments, and have come down to us with numerous errors and imperfections; and it is for this reason, that I consider the position of Aduli as ascertained; for not a circumstance is mentioned in the Periplûs, as belonging to it, which cannot be discovered in the Bay of Massowah. The Island of Diodôrus, which was separated from the main-land by so narrow a channel as to be fordable at low water, is easily referred to Toualout; while the Orine, to which the merchants retired, on their being plundered in their former residence by the Barbarians, is now satisfactorily asscertained to be Valentia Island, whose numerous hills well intitle it to its ancient name, whose distance of seventeen miles from the coast of Aduli accords with the two hundred stadia mentioned in the Periplûs, and whose embosomed situation in Annesley Bay, explains the hitherto incomprehensible description of the Periplûs, that the continent was adjacent to it on both sides; and the assertion of Cosmas, that it was but two miles distant from the main land; an assertion that Dr. Vincent could not reconcile with the two hundred stadia of the Periplûs. The islands called Alalaiou, many in number, small and sandy, still remain a memorial of the accuracy of the original describer, and may be found in Captain Court's chart, surrounding the island of Dhalac. Were any additional evidence necessary to prove that Aduli was situated in the Bay of Massowah, a very strong presumptive argument might be drawn from the fact, that the great export trade of Abyssinia in ivory and rhinoceros' horns, and the imports in European and Indian articles, still continue to find their way through the same passes of the mountains to Massowah, and that the elephants still are, occasionally, but rarely, seen in the neighbourhood of Ras Gedam.

Since my return to England I have been very much astonished by the singular theory which Monsieur Gosselin has advanced, in his Recherches sur la Géographie des Anciens, and by which he

8

has carried the Bay of Aduli to Assab, where the whole coast is covered with low, sandy islands, and reefs of coral, without a single point of resemblance to the description of the Periplûs. M. Gosselin might have been aware that, as it was a journey of only eight days from Aduli to Axum, the latter place could never have been at Assab, a distance of above three hundred miles; neither was it probable that the Romans would have passed so excellent an harbour as Massowah, where a ready communication existed with their chief mart at Axum, by a journey of little more than one hundred miles, and proceed three hundred miles farther, by sea, to a bad harbour, whence their land journey would also be extended to treble the distance.

The strange assertion of Monsieur Gosselin, that the author of the Periplûs reckoned only eight hundred stadia, from Aduli to the straits of Bab-el-Mandeb, has been properly taken notice of by Dr. Vincent. It is indeed difficult to conjecture what could have given rise to the mistake; a mistake, however, which became necessary, when his argument had carried Aduli to Assab, which is within fifty miles of the Straits.

Dr. Vincent conceives that it was the difference of one hundred and twenty-one miles between the distances of seven thousand stadia or seven hundred miles, as given in the Periplûs, and the real distance of five hundred and seventy-nine miles from Berenice to Aduli, that induced Monsieur Gosselin to carry the latter to Assab; and he himself seems to feel a difficulty in reconciling them. It however appears to me, that this may be done by admitting that an Egyptian merchant used Egyptian stadia, and that he calculated the distances from the difference of latitude alone, without bringing to account the longitude, which was run down at the same time, as I think will appear by the following calculations.

From Aduli to Ptolemais Theron is 3000 stadia ;

From Ptolemais Theron to Berenice 4000 stadia ; which, at the Egyptian stadium of fifteen to a mile, will make the distance from Aduli to Ptolemais Theron two hundred miles ; from Ptolemais Theron to Berenice two hundred and sixty-six miles.

If therefore Aduli be in	15° 36′,
Ptolemais Theron will be	18° 56′,
And Berenice -	23° 22′.

The position of Berenice has been laid down from local circumstances with as much certainty as that of Aduli. It is described by Strabo as situated in the bottom of a bay, which, on account of its numerous shoals and rocks, had been designated ἀκάθαρτος, immundus, and, as being at the extremity of the Thebais or Upper Egypt. The latter observation limits our conjectures to within 23° 30′ and 24°, and the former fixes us in the bottom of a bay which has preserved its name, and among modern navigators is called Foul Bay.

According to D'Anville this is in	23° 15′,
——————— Gosselin - -	23° 28′,
——————— an English chart	23° 19′.

Though the distances in the Periplûs deserve a greater degree of credit than usual from their being given in words at full length, instead of figures, yet I cannot receive them without some degree of caution, from their being evidently given in round numbers, without any fractional parts, and from a knowledge of the difficulty of measuring distances at sea, without a nicer degree of observation than was probably employed by Egyptian merchants, or is now used by those of our own nation.

I should therefore consider the relative distances between Aduli, Berenice, and Ptolemais Theron, as a more certain guide to the discovery of the latter. The whole distance is five hundred and seventy-nine miles, three sevenths of which, or two hundred forty-six miles, if measured from Aduli on the chart, will exactly reach a peninsula in latitude 18° 24′, of which I shall hereafter have occasion to speak, and where the more valuable data of local circumstances seem to point out the Ptolemais Theron of the Periplûs.

I am well aware that it is impossible to reconcile this conclusion with the positive assertion of the ancients, that Ptolemais Theron was in the same parallel as Meroe; but I have before observed, that little credit can be given to the accuracy of their admeasurements; and I feel less alarm in differing from them, and in my placing Ptolemais Theron where I have done, from having the sanction of D'Anville, who has, in defiance of all difficulties, conjectured that it lay between 18° and 18° 30′ N.

We kept about ten miles distant from the shore, which, as we sailed along with a land breeze from the N. W. and afterwards with the sea breeze N. E. by E. appeared low, sandy, and without trees, but was backed by lofty mountains covered with clouds, the soundings gradually deepening from eleven to thirty-five fathom, the bottom mud the whole way. The course of the shore was nearly N. then N. by W. To the eastward was a chain of low islands, with doom-trees on them, distant about five or six miles, leaving a noble and clear channel of fifteen miles. On two of these the pilot informed us that water and goats could be procured. The sea was as smooth as glass. The pilot said we might go on all night, and run in as close as six fathom with safety; as however, it was our wish to examine the whole coast, we determined to anchor, and about seven steered W. right in for the coast. We were astonished, when in twenty-two fathom, with the white appearance of breakers; when the Captain immediately let go the anchor. The pilots declared that it was only fish, and so it proved; for soon afterwards, they approached and passed under the vessel. It is singular, that the same circumstance should have been observed by Don Juan de Castro, and should have had the same effect, of inducing him to let go his anchor. He does not account for it, because it happened in the night, but he mentions, that it cast flames like fire; which confirms the conjecture, that the brilliant appearance of the sea is owing to fish-spawn and animalcula. Don Juan passed this spot on the 20th of February, one month later than I did, but the spawning may probably continue for that period. It was nearly calm the whole night, so that we lost but little by anchoring.

January 22.—We were under sail as soon as Captain Court had taken a set of bearings. The breezes were light, and there was a tide against us. The coast was low, with the lofty mountains at a distance; between them and the sea were occasionally hillocks, some of which might have been thought hills, had it not been for their more lofty neighbours. The coast still kept a northerly direction with very little westing; in sixty miles N. only seventeen west. The soundings as usual, and the chain of islands to the eastward, low, with a few trees, that often had the appearance of ships under sail. We had anchored in seven fathom, with a good bottom. About half a mile nearer was a chain of madrapore rocks, with four fathom and a half on them, as Mr. Hardy reported, who was sent with our boat to examine it. A little to the southward was a small port, called by the pilot Mirsa Mombarrick: two dows were in it; a small island is at the entrance. Our pilots say there is no village, but that the natives come down from a little way inland, and that there are water and provisions. A calm, as usual, at night.

In the morning I perceived that immediately on the beach, the whole way we could see, was a strip of bright verdure, though beyond it, all was as barren as usual. The boat was out early to examine the reef. We weighed at seven, but it soon fell calm, and obliged us again to come to an anchor. The boat was sent again to survey the beach beyond the reef. The officers reported it was hard sand, and it shoaled to two fathom water within half a mile of the shore, when the rocks again began. They were followed by a great number of sharks, some very large. They brought a branch of the tree, which proved to be Mr. Bruce's Rack; it had fruit on it, which Mr. Salt drew. The breeze sprang up about eleven; but our boat was not back till twelve, when we weighed. We again anchored at night, after having made twenty-seven miles, with a strong sea breeze. There was some swell from the N. E. probably owing to the sea being open to the main channel, where the monsoon prevails in all its force. At least there were now no islands in sight to the eastward from the mast head. The coast had changed its appearance; the smaller range of hills are near to the shore. The soundings were this day irregular, but there was always plenty of water.

January 24.—The sea breeze sprang up earlier, and we were under sail by nine. Our friend Unus Barilla brought us some very fine fish. Inland we could distinguish large groves of trees, and others to the north, on the sea shore. These the pilot said are doom-trees, and that there are also great quantities of the common mimosa. He described the country as inhabited by Bedowee, and as being a part of the sovereign of Sennaar's dominions. Lions, panthers, and elephants are in great numbers; this may therefore be considered as a part of the great forest, from which Ptolemy Philadelphus procured the latter animals, and for the convenience of hunting in which, he established the port of Ptolemais Theron. We were at twelve o'clock in latitude 17° 12′, where Mr. Bruce has placed a deep bay, near which, on the projecting point of a head-land, Dr. Vincent conjectures Ptolemais Theron was built. I watched the coast as we passed along, and can positively assert that it was, as usual, low, and free from headlands, without a single projection that could justify Mr. Bruce's chart, or give weight to the consequent conjecture of Dr. Vincent. Towards evening the coast began to run off more to the west, and the soundings were very irregular, from nineteen to thirty-six fathom in a cast, with a bottom, sometimes of mud, and sometimes of coral rock. The swell was greater, and from the S. E. in the same direction as the monsoon on the opposite shore. We anchored about eight in thirteen fathom, mud, but rocky near us. Lest we should drive, we let go our best bower anchor.

It rained a short time the next morning,

when we were within two miles of the shore, which began to have a bolder appearance. The hillocks were near the shore; beyond them a number of detached conical mountains; and in the back ground the same lofty range that had been constantly visible. On one of the hillocks was a small white Mussulmaun tomb; another was visible seven miles north, close to the sea. Our pilot said they were Turkish, but that at present no inhabitants were there. He called it Mundalow. I did not wish to examine it, as the buildings were evidently modern. On the tops of some of the other hillocks were protuberances, which were either watch-towers in ruins, or rocks; which at our distance it was impossible to distinguish. At ten a remarkable range of hills was in sight, making four pointed tops. At eleven it was clearly seen, N. 55° W. over a low point of land, covered with trees. At half after eleven another tomb was visible on the shore, the skirting of trees having ended. Near the land were several reefs. At twelve the wood again began. The hills abovementioned ended in a very conspicuous point, off which was a detached sugar-loaf hill, and no high land visible to the northward. The northernmost extremity of the land, the pilots say, is a Ras; but as they have changed the name several times, I shall not record it. We had during the day a brisk monsoon at S. S. E. which carried us at the rate of seven knots an hour, with a heavy following swell. By five we came to an anchor in eight fathom, mud and sand, in a very fine bay, among a cluster of low islands. We had excellent soundings the whole way in, after we had passed the low point of land abovementioned, which is called Aveed, and off which ran a reef about three miles, in a N. E. direction. It forms the south-eastern point of a bay that seems full of shoals, the N. W. side of which is formed by the islands among which we anchored. Here the Assaye led the way; and as we approached the shore, Mr. Maxfield hailed, and told us that his pilots said there was no passage with safety. Our pilots denied this, and went on. There are several passages leading to land-locked bays, from the bay we are in. Many dows were on the outside, when we came in sight, which fled immediately into one of the inner bays, whither I believe our pilot meant to conduct us, had not the point been too far to windward.

Very early in the morning many of the dows got out, and passed close by us, having, I suppose, recovered from their fright. Our cutter went off with Abdallah and the pilot to make our compliments to the Dola, and invite him on board; he had also directions to purchase for us fowls, eggs, and any other articles of provision, and to learn what he could respecting the place. He did not return till twelve, when the Dola came with him, a Bedowee; the Sub-dola, a decent well-dressed Arab; and the Sheik, a respectable old Bedowee, with the curls of his hair incrusted with fat, who brought me a present of three fowls. Their coming at once on board, without any scruple or fear, gave me a favourable impression of their own upright intentions, and showed a strong degree of confidence in us, and a liberal judgment of our motives for visiting this unfrequented shore. No European ship has been here since the time of the Portuguese. We gave them coffee to drink, a present of tobacco, and a frassel of raw coffee. Captain Court obtained from them the names of the hills in sight, and of some of the islands. There are several of these, each under a separate Sheik, but all under a Dola, who is sent from Suakin, not from Massowah, as we were there given to understand. Badour is the name of the village where the Dola resides; it is a miserable little place, one small mosque being the only stone building; the rest are grass huts. It is on a small island, close to the water. There is no trade, except an export of ghee, and some tortoise shells. The dows now come this way from Suakin, Jidda, and Massowah, from fear of the Wahabee. We saw a large drove of cattle on the shore, and learned that there were plenty, as there must be when ghee becomes an article of exportation; but these unfortunately belonged to a Sheik who was absent, and were therefore not to be procured. Our civil Sheik, who visited us, had his cattle at some short distance; we were consequently obliged to wait till next day. Sheep are also in abundance, and poultry: the prices demanded were, however, high; for a bullock they asked seven dollars, but came down to five; fowls were only eight for a dollar; sheep were more reasonable, a fine fat one being procurable for a dollar. We got some eggs in return for a little tobacco. I should, however, observe, that the Dola said money was little known here, and that Surat cloth would be much more valuable. Unfortunately they chose none but white, and we, on the credit of Mr. Bruce, had laid in blue. We asked what quantity of white cloth would procure a bullock. He said two pieces, which are each worth only a dollar. Had we therefore been in possession of this article, we should have purchased every thing reasonably. There is not a fisherman on the island, and they say, there are no fish near it; a singular fact, which seems corroborated by the bad success of our people, who have hitherto caught only one.

Captain Court lost no time in sending Mr. Maxfield with the Assaye into the harbour, directing him to begin the survey of it, and, for the sake of expedition, allowed Mr. Crawford to accompany him.

On the 28th and 29th Captain Court and Mr. Maxfield were actively employed in completing the survey of the harbour, and surrounding land, while Mr. Salt made an accurate drawing of the hills; which, after having from Massowah kept at a distance from the coast, here approach the sea, and rising one above the other, as they retire inland, form a mass of a most irregular out-line. The islands which form the north-eastern side of the harbour, and the peninsula which protects it on the north-western side, are chiefly of madrapore rocks. The head land, formed by the peninsula and islands, is by the natives called Ras Akeek; but they use the word generally, without applying it to any particular spot. It is the Ras Ahehaz of D'Anville. The only entrance for large vessels is at the northern extremity of the harbour, though dows enter at the southern. The passage is rather narrow, but the whole navy of Europe might lie within as in a bason, protected from every wind, in from five to seven fathom, with a bottom free from every danger. The town, which is situated on a larger island within the harbour than any of those that protect it from the sea, is a still more wretched place than Dhalac-el-Kibeer. Water is to be had, which, though not very good, is equal to that at Mocha; and our eyes convinced us that fresh provision might have been obtained, had we possessed the articles necessary for barter.

The harbour itself I immediately determined to name after the Governor-General of India, through whose assistance alone I had been able to pursue my plan of ascertaining the real situation of this unknown part of the coast; I therefore named it Port Mornington, and the islands, which form its barrier against the waves to the north-eastward, Wellesley's Islands. The bay in which we anchored we called Panther Bay.

When it is considered that Port Mornington lies on a most dangerous coast, off which are numerous shoals, low islands, and rocks that render the navigation dangerous, the discovery of it must be allowed to be of great importance. As high as 17° north it appears from the Portuguese, and Sir Home Popham's chart, that the range of coral rocks and sand banks, which run to the eastward of Dhalac, are not at an end; but beyond that degree the sea appears open till 19° north, where the shoals again commence. Port Mornington is therefore accessible without danger at any season of the year, and will afford to any ships not only a secure asylum, but a supply of water and fresh provisions. I cannot help expressing my astonishment, that, during the continuance of our fleet in this sea, no attempt was made to examine a coast which offered no impediment, and where the Victor's track had plainly demonstrated that a safe passage existed among the islands.

The neglect with which all ancient authors have passed over this, though the best harbour in the Red Sea, is so extraordinary that I know not how to account for it. It is certainly very near the place where the Astaboras is said by Strabo, to mingle a small proportion of its waters with the sea, but from the most accurate inquiries we could trace no vestige of any such circumstance; nor is it probable, that a stream could make its way through the lofty chain of mountains which binds the western shore of the Red Sea. I think that Wellesley's Islands are the six Latomian islands of Strabo, and possibly the harbour itself may be the Sabaiticon Stoma of the same author, since in his description they immediately follow Ptolemais Theron.

On our first arrival we were assured, that no trade was carried on here; but this appeared to be so contradictory to the fact of a great number of dows resorting to it, that we determined to be more particular in our inquiries. We soon perceived that the boats belonging to the dows left their vessels early every morning, went to the main land, and returned at night; but we could discover nothing large that they either took with them, or brought back. At length an old Naqueda paid Mr. Maxfield a visit, and produced a certificate from Admiral Blanket, that he had been employed by him. This led to a more intimate acquaintance, and a more free conversation, but on the subject of trade it was difficult to get any answer from him. On being asked what so many dows did there, he said they were all Wahabee. On Captain Court's objecting to this, and saying, that they would then have molested him; he only replied, "God is great!" On being pressed, he owned that there was a trade carried on with the Bedowee, and that it was intirely by barter. I know tortoise-shell is obtained here, and I should suspect that gold is the chief article received in return for India goods. Mr. Maxfield wished to go to the main land, but the Naqueda advised him on no account to do so without a guard, as there were several wandering tribes of Arabs in the vicinity. I wished to stay long enough to conciliate them, and a open communication; but this was impossible ; and I therefore did not permit Mr. Maxfield to hazard the inconveniences that might attend such an expedition.

Our people liberated Port Mornington from the opprobrium of having no fish in it, for, with a net, they caught an abundance. I was less fortunate in my conchological pursuits, not having procured a single shell during my stay. The Assaye came out of the harbour early in the morning, Jan. 29th, and soon after twelve we were under weigh, with a moderate breeze. Immediately on clearing the peninsula we saw three small islands, but the main land retired and formed a deep bay. Our course lay W. N. W. the coast here running off much more westward than usual.

About four o'clock we came up with a headland, which ran a long way into the sea, and which the pilot called Ras Asseez. It at first appeared as an island, from the lowness of the spit of sand which united it to the continent. As I had been induced by D'Anville's arguments to suppose that Ptolemais Theron lay somewhere near the latitude we now were in, I inquired of the pilot whether he had ever been on shore there, and he assured me he had, but that there were no inhabitants, though the Parsees once possessed the place, and that there was one large tank still remaining. He also said, that though it was not an island, yet that it was cut off from the main land by a ditch, which, at high water, was sometimes nearly full. These circumstances so strongly convinced me that this was Ptolemais Theron, that I should have stopped and landed, had not the vessel, during the time we were conversing, past it for some way. Captain Court was however particularly careful in taking its bearings, that its shape might be correctly laid down.

Asseez is in 18° 24′ N. lat. and in 38° 18′, long. east of Greenwich, and therefore its position agrees with that I have attributed to Ptolemais Theron, in the beginning of this Chapter. I consider, however, the circumstances I have mentioned as forming a much stronger proof of its actually being that place; and I can venture to assert, that no other place exists on the whole coast that will answer the description given us by the ancients, which in many respects is more minute than usual. The peninsula of Port Mornington could alone create a doubt, as it is in nearly the same latitude, and at a distance of only seventeen miles; but this peninsula is much more uniformly elevated above the sea, and has even rocks, which would have been a work of infinite labour to cut through, and could not have been done privately, as we are informed by Strabo the works of Eumedes were executed at Ptolemais Theron. It is also ascertained from the Periplûs, that the settlement of Ptolemy was not a port, and was only approachable by boats, a circumstance that is still the case at Asseez, but which is contrary to fact at Port Mornington. It seems probable to me that Ptolemy would fix his station for hunting elephants, not at the farthest extremity of the Shumeta or Nubian forest, where elephants were procurable, but at the place nearest his own dominions, within the limits of the forest; and this would certainly be at Asseez, which gave him an opportunity of hastily, and privately, securing his settlement from any hostile assaults of the people, among whom he was settling himself without their consent. This might indeed induce him to prefer Asseez to Port Mornington; but that he should pass so fine a harbour to go down still further on the coast to a more inconvenient position, seems to be improbable. Port Mornington may have afforded protection to his vessels, though the military station was at Asseez: and it is not impossible, that the latter place may have afforded facilities of embarking the elephants, which the former did not.

Our pilots mentioned as a fact that Cushtan, the district most abounding in elephants, was directly behind Asseez, which if true, (and as they could not possibly conjecture what answers I wished them to make to my questions, I think there is no reason to doubt it) affords a very sufficient argument why Ptolemy fixed his hunting station there in preference to any other place. I have only to add, that he could not do it much higher up, as elephants are never seen at Suakin. Asseez is, undoubtedly, the long point of sand which is mentioned by Don Juan de Castro, and is laid down by him in 18° 30′, a trifling error in latitude. It is a singular circumstance, that Pliny states Ptolemais Theron as being five days sail from Aduli, and we were exactly that period in reaching Port Mornington, and might have easily gone on to Asseez. The ancients probably anchored every night as we did. We anchored as soon as it was dark in ten fathom, mud.

January 30.—As soon as Captain Court had taken his observations we set sail. By ten Ras Howie was in sight. Here a very fine bay opened between it and the main. The Ras is a low spit of sand, partly above water; beyond was a chain of islands. The wind was from the north of east, and without tacking we could not weather it. Our pilots much wished us to anchor, and wait for a fair wind, as, they said, there was no anchoring ground after we left this, till we reached Suakin, which we could not do in one day, unless we sailed early in the morning. We, however, remonstrated, and asked if we could not go within the chain of sands and islands. They both said they could not venture to take the ship, as, in one part, there was not above two fathom and a half of water. We then persuaded them to let us tack, and weather the point. This was agreed to; and by twelve we tacked back, being sufficiently to windward. Here we crossed the Assaye. Mr. Maxfield hailed us to say, that his pilot assured him the passage was very safe, having fine anchorage the whole way, and three fathom and a half in the deepest part; that on the outside of the island there was no anchorage, but deep water: that it was impossible to reach Suakin by night; and that even a whole day would hardly be sufficient. On this Captain Court replied, that in consideration of the anchorage he would try the passage; and directed Mr. Maxfield to go ahead, and sound.

Mr. Maxfield had received signals for the purpose of communicating to us every occurrence, such as what water he found, any approaching, or any actual danger: we sailed accordingly for nearly two hours in a most noble passage, which gradually narrowed and shoaled. Mr. Maxfield made no signal, and we went on till we were in four fathom, when we made a signal to him to inform us in what water he was; but before he could answer we were in three fathom, with islands close to us on each side. No signal appeared from the Assaye, but we perceived that, on a sudden, all her sails were lowered in evident confusion. We were ourselves in but two and a half fathom, and therefore, as soon as we had cleared one of the islands, let go our anchor. The ship instantly swung round against a rock, with only one and a half fathom, and there struck. At this moment our dow, which had been crowding all sail behind us, came up, and Unus leaped overboard and came to us. He then dived, and ascertained the situation of the vessel's bottom, and of the anchor. Our boat sounded around, and we found that we were in a cul-de-sac, with rocks in every direction, even that in which we entered. To add to our alarm, it was apparently high water, and how much the tide might fall we knew not. The only thing in our favour was the perfect smoothness of this salt water lake, which no wind could possibly ruffle. The Captain was active and collected. He instantly began to lighten the vessel by pumping out the salt water which was in the casks; Unus brought his dow along side to take in our guns; our yards and top masts were lowered, and an anchor was carried astern to warp us out. At the earnest request of Captain Court, I and the other gentlemen removed to the Assaye, that he might be more at liberty. My European and other servants staid on board, and assisted the ship's company.

To our good fortune, the tide did not fall quite a foot; the wind was light; the ship was therefore perfectly manageable, and wore round as she was towed. She with great difficulty cleared another rock; but by four, I had the satisfaction to be hailed, and told that she was safe in a quarter less two fathom, being more than she now drew. By night she was warped further out, and safely anchored in two and a half fathom. I returned at seven to the Panther. Mr. Maxfield had our boats to bring him close to us. Our crew, the Captain assured me, had acted wonderfully well, much better than he could have expected; but of Unus Barilla he spoke in the highest terms of praise. He had rendered every personal service, with a cordiality and friendship that surprised him. He had, without scruple, received the loaded cannon on board his dow, and had come to cook his provisions in ours. He had headed the workmen, had cheered them with singing, and had put up a prayer of thanksgiving when we were in safety. He, in consequence, obtained handsome presents from me, Captain Court, and Captain Rudland. To him in a great measure the safety of the vessel was owing, although probably she might have been saved by sending the guns to the island. This, however, would have been a work of time as well as difficulty, for the water round the island was shallow.

Very early in the morning we began our warping, and brought the vessel free of all danger. We then sent off Mr. Maxfield to examine a passage, which all the pilots declared to be the true one, but which Mr. Maxfield's pilot had quitted for the cul-de-sac, where we had so nearly been lost. Mr. Salt visited the island near which we grounded: he procured a species of Orobanche, with a very large yellow bloom, a Stapelia, a Commelina, and a syngenesious plant that eat well as a salad. Several grasses also grew there. It was singular to find such a variety of plants on a little spot of arid sand. A curious nest, three or four feet in diameter, composed of sticks and madrapore, was found on the ground; it belongs to a very large species of bird that was seen by my servant on another island. Four large eggs were brought me of a fine blue colour.

Mr. Maxfield on his return informed us, that the passage for a very considerable distance was good, with from seven to ten fathom; we therefore determined to try it. The wind continued to the N.

of E. which made tacking necessary; we, however, got into the true channel before night, and anchored in good ground. The mountains were visible in the evening, which here again come near to the shore. The hills above Suakin were pointed out to us by the pilots.

We were under weigh about seven; the wind was fresh from the N. E. so that we could only just lie our course; the sea was perfectly smooth, and it rained a little. The channel was extremely narrow, in some parts not more than a cable's length from shoal to shoal. Mr. Maxfield kept ahead, making signals of eight and ten fathom. About five miles from our anchoring ground we bore up round a point of sand. Unus Barilla had gone on, and sagaciously anchored his dow at the entrance of the narrows, where there is said to be only three fathom: we could not however reach him for the wind; and the pilots determined to keep on for another passage ahead, Mr. Maxfield still leading. He soon came to an anchor, as we did instantly, and when he bore up for us, we learned, that though he was in ten fathom, he found the passage so narrow that he did not like to enter it. It was fortunate he came up to us, for though his anchor had been down not more than a quarter of an hour, yet it was nearly worn through by the rocks, while we were in strong clay. We now determined to send the boats to examine the passage to windward: Mr. Hardy went in the cutter, Mr. Maxfield in the dow. When they returned, their reports were rather favourable; but as they penetrated only about five miles to windward, and the pilots were positive they could not take the vessel through, with the wind that now blew, and as they said it might continue these twenty days, we were for some time uncertain how to act. We were unwilling to return to Ras Howie, and beat round the outside of the shoals, as we should leave it undecided whether a passage existed within them or not ; yet to stay here was impracticable, as we were pressed for time, and had only twenty days water on board. At length Mr. Hardy proposed that he should go off with the dow and cutter, and ascertain the passage the whole way to Suakin. This was approved, and we beat up to the windward extremity of the land-locked harbour, in which we were lying, and which, had it proper and safe entrances, would be one of the finest in the world, being in size about six miles every way, with generally ten fathom and a good bottom. The passage is, however, unfortunately so complicated, and the sand islands are so alike, that no ship could venture through it without a pilot. We passed right over one shoal not many yards wide, on which there was only three fathom, and another of the same size, which had five. The sea was as smooth as glass, and the weather fine with us ; but it rained hard over the lofty mountains of Africa, which, according to Mr. Bruce and D'Anville are of porphyry. I do not know what authority either had for the assertion.

Mr. Hardy returned, and reported that he had found no passage through which the Panther could possibly be taken. He had been at Suakin, and had seen the Turkish Dola, from whom he brought as presents to me two bullocks, ten sheep, ten fowls, and a basket of vegetables, which were most acceptable, as our live stock was reduced to a few fowls. A Dola of the Bedowee also resides there, who was considerably alarmed at the report of an English ship's coming, under an idea that she meant to attack the island. He therefore proposed to seize the boat and crew. This indeed would have been a more difficult matter than he supposed, as the seven sailors with Mr. Hardy had musquets and plenty of ball cartridge. The Turkish Dola, however, prevented any thing unpleasant. He assured the Bedowee that he knew the English well, that he had frequently seen their ships at Jidda, and that they never did any harm to any one. They, however, were still uneasy, and said, the English never came before, why should they do so now? At length they swore Unus on the Koran, that all the people in the Panther were good people, and meant no harm to Suakin. This he did willingly, and instantly all was friendship. Mr. Hardy stated our situation, and the Dola sent us two pilots to bring us clear of the dangers. He sent a very civil message to me, that he would prepare a house for me on shore, and would fire every gun he had in compliment to me, as he knew that the English and the Sultaun of Rome were always friends. They confirmed the circumstance of Jidda being besieged, which accounts for their civility. My servant went to look for shells; he procured a few, and one most beautiful fish.

During the night two of the Lascars ran away with the jolly boat; they took with them the sails and rudder of the cutter, which, to prevent pursuit, they also cut adrift. Most fortunately it was not far off, and was soon secured by Mr. Maxfield's small boat. The fellows were out of sight from the mast head. We sent Unus direct to Suakin to represent the circumstance, and offer a reward for the boat, which is a serious loss. Our new pilots were most respectable men, and as Mr. Hardy declared that they were perfectly acquainted with every shoal they passed, we had sufficient confidence in them to return by a new route. An island and a shoal formed in one place a very narrow passage, which we had to work through right in the wind's eye, but fortunately we cleared it. The rest of the passage was broad enough for the ship to work tolerably well. It was far preferable to the one by which we entered. The pilots expressed their astonishment at any body's having been able to bring a vessel like the Panther into such a place, where a large dow could hardly enter with safety. In the time of the Egyptian trade, this port seems to have been as little known as Port Mornington: it may, however, be the Euangelion Limen of Ptolemy; but without some better authority than his tables, it would be absurd to speak positively on the subject. Don Juan de Castro passed through the bay, and by the narrow passage, which Mr. Hardy examined in going in the cutter to Suakin. His Marate and Shaback may be sought for in vain, among the windings and mazes of this singular harbour, which presents on the charts such a mass of confusion, that at my request Captain Court called it Bother'em Bay. The weather was fine, the wind light, and the sea as smooth as glass: we had eight, nine, and ten fathom till we got into the channel by which we had entered, at about three o'clock, and soon afterwards we came to an anchor.

February 7. We weighed anchor about six, with a favourable wind to quit the straits, but directly contrary when we had to bear up for Suakin. We continued to tack till three o'clock, when we came to an anchor about four miles E. by N. of Ras Howie, in eleven fathoms, mud and sand: we did this from the goodness of the bottom, lest we should be obliged to let go in a worse, for the wind was fresh, with a considerable degree of swell. We had overfalls during the day, but never less than five fathom. It rained in the evening.

The next day it blew so fresh, with rain, that we could not attempt to stir, the wind being right in our teeth. Mr. Maxfield's cable parted; we sent our cutter to heave the anchor by the buoy, but the rope was so rotten that it immediately broke. He let go two small anchors, but they would not hold; we were therefore obliged to give him a hawser, and let him hang to our stern. It moderated in the afternoon, after several heavy showers, when the swell went gradually down, till at night it was perfectly calm.

We weighed at daylight in hopes of a fair wind. It freshened gradually till one, when we were nearly opposite two islands, which the pilot named something so like Hurroo Riot, that I could not help being amused with the resemblance. These islands, they said, were half way from our anchoring ground, yet we had not made above nine miles, and we understood Suakin was a good day's run. There is here good anchorage, and they wanted us to stop; but as there was a favourable breeze, we represented to them the probability of our reaching Suakin, to which they acceded. The clouds hung over the high hills, and perfectly concealed them from our view during the greater part of the day; the pilots therefore were very anxious to come to an anchor about four o'clock, with which we complied, as the water was gradually deepening. We had a good bottom in twenty-four fathom; the Assaye was fastened to us.

At seven we weighed anchor, and made sail with a light air from the southward. We passed between some islands, and found good soundings, but with overfalls at very short distances; the water as smooth as glass. We were, in fact, sailing in a channel, formed by a reef and a chain of sand banks ; there were also shoals between us and the shore. We were not a little surprised to find excellent anchoring ground within six miles of Suakin, when the water became too deep. We went too quick to get soundings till off the entrance of the passage, which is not sixty fathom wide, but leads to a wider reach, where the pilots insisted on our casting anchor, though at above a mile distance from the town. As they confessed that they had received orders to do it from the Dola, we submitted, and let go an anchor in sixteen fathom, the deepest part of the land-locked bason being nineteen fathom, perfectly free from rock. A small fort was building on a little island to the northward. We sent Abdallah in the evening with compliments to the two Dolas.

In the night a strong gale came on from the north-westward, and overset our anchor into the deepest water. It however, struck there, and held us at a few yards distance from the S. easternmost shoal, in not a very pleasant situation. Captain Court and I were both on deck, and I was just returning to my cot when we saw a boat coming down the harbour. It nearly ran foul of us ; on being hailed, Abdallah answered, and we found that he had brought us off a bullock as a present from the Dola, and numerous compliments. It blew very fresh all night, and the sea beat very heavy on the outside of the reef and shoal. In the morning the haze was so great, we could hardly distinguish the town ; the mountains were perfectly covered.

Two boats came to us at breakfast ; one with the pilots ; the other contained the son of the Bedowee Dola, who brought a present of sheep and vegetables. This visit gave me great pleasure, as it proved a total change of opinion in our favour, and showed a great confidence in our hospitality, as his father had been the person who proposed detaining Mr. Hardy and the boat's crew. He was a good-looking young man, and handsomely dressed. He assured us of every assistance from his father, who was, he said, the chief of the most considerable tribe of Bedowee in the vicinity. He informed me, that the letter I brought from the Nayib of Massowah was for himself. It was immediately delivered. He read, or pretended to read it, and said it was very well. He sat down to breakfast, and used his spoon properly: he tasted the tea, and liked it very much. Abdallah returned with him to the shore, but came back soon. He brought me word the Turkish Dola was very angry with the young Dola for having visited me first, who had pleaded, that he only came to get the Nayib's letter, which he had learned I had for him, from a dow of the Nayib's, that had quitted Massowah since I did. The Turkish Dola sent me word not to receive presents from any body; that he was master here, and would supply the ship with every thing she wanted.

I had sent a message by the young Dola, that I intended to go on shore the next morning to visit the Chiefs, but the Turkish Dola now sent word by Abdallah, that he desired I would not; that the people would all be wanting to give me presents, and to obtain others in return; seeking under that pretence to sell their articles at a higher price than they would otherwise bring; but that he would himself pay me a visit in the evening. I suspected the fact was, that he wished to secure all the presents himself. At night another message came off, that the Bedowee Dola had insisted on coming with him, and that therefore he would not come; but if I chose to pay him a visit on shore, he should be happy to see me. I sent word I certainly would. We gave a salute to the town of three guns in the morning, which was returned. I, Mr. Salt, and Captain Rudland went on the little island. We found no shells. A Salicornia, a Statice, and a species of grass, were the only plants. A few fishermen were at the fort. We procured some fine mullets for a handful of tobacco. The wind was very unpleasant all day, but our anchor held fast. We got several boat-loads of stone from the vicinity of the fort, which we distributed in the hold as additional ballast.

The Bedowee Dola's son, Emir Mohammed, came off early in the morning to attend me on shore, and brought us two bullocks as a present from his uncle, who, (and not his father, as I before understood,) is Emir of the Chief Bedowee tribe in the neighbourhood. Captain Rudland, Mr. Salt, and myself, wore Asiatic dresses; Captain Court was in his uniform. We departed soon after breakfast, under a salute of seventeen guns. On landing, one gun was fired, which shook the mortar from the gateway under which we were passing. Two Janisaries in decent red dresses conducted us to a little plain room, at the upper end of which was placed a common couch of the country, covered with a carpet and two cushions; on the right of this were three chairs, a fourth was soon brought. Opposite was a low stone bench covered with carpet; behind us was the same, both extending the whole length of the building. A reverend Arab of sixty, tall, and thin, was presented to us by Emir Mohammed, as his father. The usual compliments passed. After being seated a little time, the Turkish Dola entered, and making a general salaam, seated himself. We paid our compliments through Abdallah, and returned thanks for the pilots he had sent us, and the provisions. He said he was happy to assist the English, who were ever friends of the Sultaun of Rome. Coffee was brought, and nothing interesting passed, till I asked if he had any late news from Misr. He said, yes, very late. That all was now quiet there; that the Turks had got possession of the whole country, having an army of 60,000 men. That the English had entered the Port of Iscandaria with sixty vessels of different descriptions, and had landed soldiers there. He added, that the Beys were quiet, and that there were five Turkish Pachas there. On asking about Jidda, he assured me that 10,000 Turks had liberated Mecca from the Wahabee, and were on their march to Jidda. Yambo also was under a Turkish Pacha. I made many inquiries, if possible, to detect him in an error, but he answered so correctly as to induce us to believe the account, so far as related to a British force being at Alexandria, and Egypt's being quiet; two most important objects to us, as securing our safe passage through Egypt, and a speedy departure from Alexandria for Europe. It much increased our impatience to reach Cosseir.

After sitting an hour, sherbet, made with honey, was handed about. Afterwards a khelaut was put over my shoulders, which, to my great surprise, was of the most holy colour, green. Such a gift would never have been permitted in Turkey a few years ago. Even the wearing a bit of that colour would have been dangerous to a Christian. It was handsomely lined with ermine. I asked Emir Mahommed where these skins were procured: he said they were not of this country, but that the dresses were sent from Constantinople to be given on public occasions, and that the Dola brought them from Jidda. Captain Court, who sat next me, had a yellow khelaut, lined also with ermine, but old and discoloured. I was surprised at their being so good. The Dola was a dignified man, with good manners. He wore a scarlet cloth dress, lined with blue silk ; his attendant officers were in similar dresses; and this uniformity gave an appearance of respectability to the little divan we were seated in. Around the room were hung sabres, matchlocks, European guns, and blunderbusses. Before our departure, he promised to come on board the Panther the next day. His servants escorted us to the water side, and kept off the crowd.

The town is nearly in ruins: two minars give it a handsome appearance at a distance, and the buildings, being white-washed, and on an elevation, look much better than they really are. It covers the whole of a small island, as it did in the days of De Castro, but the extensive trade, which, according to his account, had rendered it superior to every city he had seen, except Lisbon, has nearly vanished, and instead of numerous ships, unloading their cargoes on every side of the island, into the houses of merchants, I could only perceive a few miserable dows anchored along side of a few wretched houses. The port however still retains all its advantages, and vessels larger than the Panther might anchor close to the island, where there is seven fathom. D'Anville's chart is accurate as to the outline, but he has erred greatly with respect to the depth of water, which is from fifteen to nineteen fathoms the whole way to the town. He has likewise been mistaken in the relative size of the two islands, which is nearly equal, and in its latitude, which, after the Portuguese, he has stated as 19° 20′ N. instead of 19° 4′ 8″.

I believe D'Anville is correct in his supposition, that this was the Soter Limen of Diodôrus, the Theon Soter of Ptolemy, but I think it ill deserves the description he has given of it, as the safest asylum for navigators on this coast. The reefs and shoals that lie off it, in every direction, render an approach to it extremely dangerous, and the narrowness of the mouth makes it almost impracticable to enter it with any, but a leading wind. It is difficult to account for a narrow passage between two lines of coral rock having continued for so long a period free for vessels, without having been filled up, either by a sea constantly breaking on its mouth, after having passed over sand banks, or by the clouds of sand which at one season of the year are borne towards it from the desert. Since the Turks have ceased to have a fleet in the Red Sea, and have sunk into political insignificance in Arabia, Suakin has been kept from total ruin only by the caravans, which still come annually from the interior of Africa, by Sennaar, to that place, in their way to Mecca. The town itself is all that belongs to the Sublime Porte, and their Dola, or Aga, dares not put his foot on the main land, which belongs to a powerful tribe of Bedowee, who take their name from the town, and call themselves Suakini. To them, as I have before observed, belongs the country around Port Mornington, and their influence must extend to Macowar, as Emir Mohammed has offered to send a man with us to that place, who, he says, will procure us provisions the whole way, but he at the same time warns us on no account to land ourselves. As we returned to the ship it blew fresh, but as the passage was marked out by buoys, fixed on the sand heads, we met with no accident; what a convenience it would be at Mocha, if the same precaution had been taken by the Government!

February 13.—The weather was much more moderate and cool. The Dola paid us an early visit, and was in high good humour, talking much of his friendship for the English, and claiming an acquaintance with Captain Court, whom, he said, he had seen at Jidda. This, though a mistake, was acquiesced in from prudential motives. I enquired how long he had been at Suakin. He replied, two years; that the appointment was annual, but that frequently the same person was allowed to stay ten years in office—I presume, if he contrives to bribe the Pacha at Jidda, in whose hands is the appointment. I learned from him, that the caravan will set off to-morrow for Sennaar, and will be about twenty-five days on the journey. He said all was quiet there, that the King was dead, and no one had succeeded, but that the Vizier managed every thing. As he had several people with him, I again asked, if there was any river on any part of this coast. They all positively assured me that there was not, though there was plenty of fresh water at several places. I also enquired respecting ruins on the coast; particularly if any pillars existed: they equally denied knowledge of either; and the Bedowee declared, that if there were any they could not be ignorant of them. The Turkish Dola drank coffee; the old Bedowee eat some sweetmeats, but only just tasted the coffee.

Some of the followers had sat down on one of the couches. The Turk asked why I permitted it; I replied that I could not presume to give any orders to his people, when he was by. He however did not order them to remove, nor do I think they would have obeyed: but he said laughing, " they are like the animals I send you on board, goats and sheep, ignorant and stupid, they know no better." He requested permission to have his hookah, which was granted. He declined sherbet, and after a visit of several hours said he wished to have his present, and take his leave. Abdallah put on him a shawl of gold tissue, which is worn as a scarf over the right shoulder, and under the left arm. I also presented him with a turban of the same materials. The Bedowee Dola had a scarf of an inferior quality. He took his leave in much good humour, and was saluted with three guns, as he was on his arrival. We had brought off several loads of stone from the island to use as ballast, but the Dola objected to this, saying he wanted it to finish the fort, as he wished to make the place strong against the Wahabee; the fact was he wanted to be paid for them. We applied to the young Dola, Emir Mohammed, who said he would send us one thousand stones.

My servant killed a beautiful flamingo: the under feathers of the wing, black; the rest gradually shading from a fine scarlet to a pure white. It was four feet from the tip of the beak to the extremity of the toe, and about the same from wing's end to wing's end. Abdallah procured us from the town a good vegetable, a Chenopodium, that tasted exactly like spinach. This, the Hibiscus esculentus, and green pumpkins, were all that were procurable.

The people themselves seemed civil and good natured; none of them were armed: they wear a piece of white cloth wrapped round their middle, and thrown over the shoulder. In general their figures are very fine, and the expression of their countenances good. They are of a dark copper colour, their hair is somewhat woolly drawn out into points, and dressed with fat, occasionally powdered with red; a piece of wood is stuck through it, nearly horizontally, which they frequently use to disturb any animalcula that bite too hard. It is in shape like a porcupine's quill, and of course polished by the grease. They also use it to separate the hair into ringlets and turn it round the finger. Many had the long hair behind separated by a narrow shaved passage, from the front curly division, which was formed into an oval. They certainly are on the whole a well looking race of people. Their skins are perfectly clear from eruptions of any sort, but are much marked where actual cautery has been applied as a remedy for local disease. We saw great numbers during our stay, as every day strangers came off in the water-boat to view the ship. I have given an etching of a man, who was above six feet high, and had a most singular expression of countenance. The likeness is admirably preserved. It is impossible not to be struck by the resemblance between them and the South Sea islanders, as drawn in Captain Cook's voyages. Their teeth, which are beautifully white and regular, they constantly clean with a piece of the rack-wood. They wear nothing on the head, which is sufficiently protected from the sun by the mass of wool and grease that covers it.

We got fifteen barrels of water a day, good, and tolerably clear. They have both wells and tanks. Fish in abundance and cheap; the mullets are particularly fine. Mr. Maxfield's pilot made his escape on shore. We had detained him lest he should breed any more mischief. I recollected that I had two letters given me by Devagé when I was coming hither in the Antelope. I looked them out, and sent them to the people, who immediately came off, and proved to be very respectable men; merchants of course. I learned from them that nothing was brought from the interior of Africa to this place, except slaves, horses, gold, and ivory: in which articles, however, a very considerable trade is carried on.

Abdallah, who had been sent on shore for provisions, returned with the water-boat. He brought me word, that there had been vehement disputes on shore; that Emir Mohammed told him, he had learned we gave five hundred dollars to the Nayib of Massowah, and that the Bedowee Emirs wanted to come off, with presents, and ask for the same sum. That both Unus and he had inquired whether this was in his letter, and defied him to produce it. He said, no, it was not, but he had been told so; no doubt by Mr. Maxfield's rascally pilot. They declared it was an absolute falshood; that the English never gave presents of that sort, that they only came here for provisions, and would pay for what they got, but would receive no presents or make returns. The two Dolas and the Emir took our part, and the whole business was amicably adjusted. Three sheep were sent off, but Abdallah told me the Emir said they would be one dollar and a half each. This was evidently an imposition, though they were worth double the price of those we obtained at Massowah. One of the merchants to whom I had letters, was on board; I spoke to him, and he admitted the price was too high, for that a dollar was sufficient for the best, three-fourths for a middling one, and half a dollar for a small one. I said that, at that rate, I would buy for the crew; but if the other price was charged, I should not want half the quantity, as I should only buy for myself. He said, he was a friend of Emir Mohammed, and would speak to him. A brother of Emir Mohammed was on board, to consult Mr. Macgie, who also promised to do the same. Abdallah brought a message from the Emir, that his brother was that day to be married, and requested that when the town guns were fired, we would fire three, which was promised. He also requested a few pounds of sugar-candy, and two candles: the former we sent, the latter we could not spare. Abdallah went on shore. The boys went a shell-hunting on the reefs, and procured some very good ones. The wind varied much in the course of the day. It was once E. The weather was moderate and pleasant.

February 15.—The water-boat and Abdallah came off as usual. He brought two large sheep for a dollar each, and some vegetables, but not sufficient for the ship's company. On enquiring respecting grain, we learned that none was to be had here, except juwarry, and for a hundred weight of that they asked three dollars, no very pleasant intelligence, as we were short of rice, and other articles; the cock-roaches having eaten much and wasted more. The weather, as usual; wind from the N. E. and N. W. We took on board more stones, having received the requisite permission, on paying seven dollars. I had a letter from the Dola, saying that the pilots who brought us in had in the first instance been promised thirty-five dollars. We had paid them twenty, with which they departed extremely well satisfied; this therefore was too barefaced an imposition to succeed. We laughed at the demand, and refused to pay it.

February 16.—The water came off at eight, and

Abdallah brought two large sheep, with a request from the Dola, that we would give him some tobacco. We sent him ten pounds. Unus came off for his letter, and to take his leave, his bargain extending only to this place. We gave him from the Company thirty dollars for his exertions in saving the Panther when aground, with which he was the more delighted, as he had no expectations beyond the presents we had given him that night. We asked if he would hire himself to accompany us as far as Jibbel Macowar, to which place we meant to have pilots; their knowledge of the coast extending no further, as they there strike off for Jidda. He said he had no objection, but that he must consult his crew, who were only hired to Suakin. Many of the men of the water-boat had been very pressing every day for drams. This morning they again made their representations to me, through Abdallah. I told them, that I had been informed Mussulmauns did not drink any thing of that sort, and consequently had not provided myself with a sufficient stock; but that in future, now I had found out my mistake, I would take care to have plenty. This excited a laugh against the petitioners, and their friends continued to ridicule them till they left the vessel. I should recommend to every person, who means to touch on this coast, to have spirits to spare: all soldiers drink publicly, and many others in private. I need not observe, that, to those who like it, no present is so acceptable. Common white cloth is another useful article for barter. Our tobacco has been of the greatest service, our sweetmeats have also been acceptable to all visitors. We sent Abdallah on shore to procure fowls, even at only four for a dollar, our stock of them being completely exhausted. It is a bad precedent, but they really seem to be scarce. At each place we were told there were plenty at the next, but, on our arrival, we only experienced disappointment. The air was pleasant and cool.

February 18.—It rained hard till ten, when the young Dola came off with several of his friends, and his sick brother, who was rather better. We had a long conversation about Jibbel Macowar, which by Bruce is placed in 24° N. and by others in 21° and a half. They talk of its being as far from hence as Massowah. We cannot ascertain precisely where it is, which we are anxious to do, that we may know what price to pay the pilot. The Emirs offered to hire us one on shore, but we thought it more advisable to have him sent to us, that we might make the bargain ourselves.

The young Dola informed me, that he had frequently been with the caravan to Sennaar, since his father had thought him old enough to have the care of it. I asked him, if the Vizier continued to collect the revenue from the inhabitants of the southern country, as they passed up into the sands; he said he knew of no such thing. I made every possible inquiry, but in vain, he still persevering in his assertion, that no such thing ever took place. I made Abdallah translate to him Bruce's history of the Zimb or Tsaltsalya, but he positively asserted that he had never heard of the animal. As he was extremely free in his communications on every other subject, and had no motive for concealment on this, I cannot attribute to him a wanton and deliberate falshood, merely because Mr. Bruce has asserted the contrary, on whose veracity, I confess, I have lost all dependence. These declarations of Emir Mohammed are confirmed by the testimony of Mr. Brown, who assures me, that, when travelling in Africa, he made the same inquiries of people who had visited Sennaar, and with the same success. I can declare from my own knowledge, that there is no foundation for his assertion that the same migration takes place from Cape Gardafui to the Straits, any more than there is for the idea, that the chain of mountains, which runs parallel to the Red Sea, divides the seasons equally, and that it is fair on one side, while the torrents of rain pour down on the other. This is certainly the case in the peninsula of India, from which, probably, Mr. Bruce caught the idea. His own travels gave him no opportunity of ascertaining the fact.

The young Dola requested a letter from me to show at Mocha, which he frequently visits in the way of trade. He also hoped we would give him a present, when we settled accounts, for the trouble he had taken. He again drank tea, and praised it.

After his departure the Steward informed the first Lieutenant that there was not a single day's rice on board, although, when we sailed from Bombay on the 1st of December, it was understood that we had a sufficiency for five months. Upon examining the accounts, we found there ought to be one hundred and thirty-three maund, supposing every man had had his full allowance since our departure, which had not been the case. It was too large a quantity to have been consumed or wasted; we therefore must have owed the inconvenience to a fraud. The hurry in which the Panther was sent to sea rendered it impossible for Captain Court to look to the stores. We immediately sent to the town to buy all the juwarry that could be got.

We now thought it advisable to examine our other stores, and the result was a discovery that we had only a sufficient quantity of flour left for one week, the cock-roaches having devoured the rest. Fortunately our crew had been served with biscuit for a period ending the 1st of March. This deficiency fell on the white men, and was really alarming. The Captain called them all aft, and stated the discovery: he told them that any grain that could be purchased here, should be bought at any price; that at Cosseir they should have wheat; but that they must make their present allowance of biscuit last till the 15th of March, by which time he had every reason to hope he should reach that place. To the Lascars he promised juwarry, and fresh meat. The whole were in perfect good humour, and assured him they were satisfied.

We have every reason to rejoice that we made Suakin the day we did: ever since, the wind had been so steady to the northward, that we could not have quitted Bother'em Bay, and our distress there for water and provisions would have been great indeed. It was also fortunate that the northerly winds had blown only at a period when, by our having a complete stock of water to take in, they caused no delay. Their continuance however excited an unpleasant suspicion in my mind, that the monsoon had changed; which Mr. Macgie increased by the information, that he once sailed on the 1st of March from Jidda, and was six weeks in reaching Suez. The delay, however, was in getting through the Straits of Jubal. The natives consoled me by saying, that this is always a rainy month with them.

The cutter's crew, with my servant and Pierce, went to collect shells, and brought a good many, some new, but chiefly Cypræa; handsome, but common. In the evening of Feb. 20th, the Emir, the old pilot, and Unus came off. The Emir agreed to let us have a boat of his; and the old pilot said, if we would pay him the fifteen dollars, he was ready to engage. Before we would promise this, we demanded what he asked for pilotage: he said one hundred and sixty dollars; adding, that he received thirty or forty for a dow. We were amused by the argument, though provoked by the impudence of the demand. The Emir told him he was a fool, and I observed it was so totally out of the question, that I would say nothing more. At length he wished to know what I would give; observing that it was a very large vessel, and a very dangerous passage. I replied, that he seemed to have forgotten his telling me that the way was good to Macowar, and that the size of the vessel was nothing to him, as we did not want him to be answerable for it. That I considered it as worth one-third as much as the pilotage from Mocha; and that I would therefore give fifty dollars, and no more; that on the same principle I would give one hundred for a dow. If they did not choose to take that, I would sail without either. The argument lasted a long time: the Emir wished me to give sixty, which I refused, and they went away without any thing being settled; but Unus said apart, that he would settle every thing.

The next day Captain Court took bearings for a plan of Suakin harbour.

As I had several letters to write, I requested the other gentlemen to pay their visit to the Dola without me. They set off soon after breakfast. On their return, I found that, after visiting Emir Mohammed, they had gone to pay their compliments to the Turkish Dola. He was at first in a very ill humour. The pilot had positively refused to go with us for less than sixty-five dollars; they therefore applied to the Dola to know if he could assist us. He now broke forth, and represented, that we could not expect to hire another pilot, when we had not paid the last all his wages. The Captain repeated to him our reasons; but he positively declared, he had himself hired them for thirty-five dollars. Captain Court assured him, that had the men claimed five hundred on his word, we would have paid them, and that the money should be sent to him on the morrow.

Emir Mohammed came on board in the evening with the merchants; all our accounts were settled, which were not very exorbitant. For his own boat he would charge nothing, only the men's hire who came in her. The water was twenty-five skins for a dollar; the bullocks six and seven dollars each; the sheep a dollar each, and sometimes a little less. All the vegetables were only two dollars. Captain Court and I gave, each of us, letters of recommendation to him, and to Unus. I also wrote to Mr. Pringle in favour of the latter.

Captain Court and I, on mature consideration, determined to submit to their demands, and pay the hundred dollars for the dow, and sixty-five for the pilot; since, if we did not, it would be out of our power to examine the coast as far as Macowar, which I was extremely anxious to do, both from personal inclination, and a sense of duty. The dangerous state of the Assaye also made a boat desirable; besides that we were unacquainted with the passage among the shoals into the open sea. We therefore notified our change of sentiment to the Dola, who promised that every thing should be ready by to-morrow evening. We were impatient to be gone, as the weather was very fine, and the wind in the middle of the day came round to the east.

February 22.—The pilot and Emir Mohammed came off in the morning with two nephews of the Turkish Dola. They would not drink coffee, which is not permitted till they are fifteen, but they took sweetmeats. I gave the Emir fifty dollars, a turban, and cummurbund, for his exertions. We sent the old Dola a little oil of cinnamon, and fifty pounds of powder. The old pilot agreed to go, and received his money. Unus took his leave with sorrow. He begged a flag, and wanted other articles, which, being unreasonable, were refused. The Emir obtained from us a half-hour sand-glass. On his departure we saluted him with two guns. A dow arrived yesterday from Jidda. I was happy to hear from the Turkish Dola, that she brought a confirmation of the Egyptian news, and that there was a Pacha waiting to pass from Suez to Jidda with a large army. The weather was very mild, and at twelve the wind came round to the eastward, and gave us hopes of a favourable change.

February 23.—The dow came off early in the morning. From the narrowness of the harbour we were obliged to warp, and made but little way; our crew not being sufficient, and our boats scarcely strong enough to sustain the weight of a large cable. It blew fresher than yesterday, from the N. and N. E.

In the night the wind gradually increased to a gale, and we were nearly driven on the southern shoal, by our anchor's falling into the deepest part of the channel: there, however, it held fast. When more moderate, we warped farther, but dragged back, the wind being fresh, and right into the mouth of the harbour. We kept quiet the whole of the afternoon.

February 25.—It blew fresh and adverse in the night, and till the sun rose, when the swell and wind went down. We again began to warp out, but our anchor fell into deep water, and we were within ten feet of the southern shoal. We found, to our cost, that in northerly winds this harbour is a prison. It is too narrow to work in, and too deep to warp out of, with facility. When the winds are from the south, there is a regular land breeze every morning, which obviates all difficulties. The old pilot says, that southerly winds blow here eight months out of the twelve, but never for any length of time without intermission. From all I can learn from different people, who have been in the Red Sea, I believe that there is no season in which the winds blow from one point without changing for a few days; and, in the middle part of the gulf, they may almost be called variable, at least as much so as in the British Channel, where, for nine months in the year, the wind blows from the westward. We for five weeks had N. E. winds, yet the monsoons of this sea are said to be N. W. and S. E. After a hard day's labour we regained the spot from which we were driven. It was fortunate for us that we procured at Mocha some native hawsers made of grass, with which we cleared the harbour, by fastening them to the beacons raised at the points of the shoals by the pilots of the place. These hawsers are much lighter than the European, and a less boat will consequently carry them out. If Suakin was in the hands of an European power, rings might easily be fixed in these rocks, and the warping out would be no longer difficult. As it is in the hands of the Turks, more has been done than could be expected. On getting out we found anchorage at twenty-five fathom, when in entering we could find no bottom, from the rapidity with which we moved. This is of great importance, as the passage into the harbour is so extremely narrow.

CHAPTER VII.

Departure from Suakin.—Lent Bay.—Sheik Baroud.—Daroor.—Danger of the Panther among the rocks.—Loss of anchors—Recovery of them.—Salaka.—Mousetrap Bay.—Gale of wind.—Obliged to return to Mocha.—Observations on Macowar, probably the Berenice Pancrysos of the Ancients.—Observations on Mr. Bruce's supposed Voyage from Cosseir to Macowar.—Conjectures respecting Myos Hormos.—Arrival at Massowah.—Visit to the Island of Valentia.—Return to Mocha.

IT was moderate in the morning, February 26th, with a fine land breeze, when all the dows left the harbour. Unus passed us, making his salaams, with his English colours flying. By nine we were under weigh, accompanied by Mr. Maxfield, the dow, and a smaller boat. The sea breeze did not set in favourably, but held to the N. of N. E.; we, of course, made but little way. The channel was very narrow, and our tacks short. About twelve it freshened considerably, and continued to do so till four, when it was due north. The pilot pointed out an anchoring ground, for which we stood: but he changed his mind, and pushed on for another, which we soon found it impossible to reach; and indeed his account of it was not very pleasant: he said it was near the shore, and in forty fathom. It blew very fresh, and the sky promised a gale. Captain Court therefore returned to the first. We had only our stay-sail and mizen set, yet were going five knots an hour. As we neared the shore there were no soundings, till the man in the chains called out four fathom rocks. Exceedingly alarmed, we instantly tried to let go the stream anchor with the chain, but it would not run; we then let go the bower, which went. The next heave was ten fathom, mud, and then fourteen, in which we let go the stream anchor. We now found ourselves in a perfect bason formed by a circle of rocks, over a part of which we had passed. The pilot knew what he was about; but being rather alarmed, and anxious, he had omitted giving us notice that we should pass such a shallow spot. The entrance is narrow, as not half a cable's length to larboard we found a quarter less one. Mr. Maxfield kept to starboard under bare poles, but came in very fast. He had nothing to fear where we had passed. It blew a gale all night; and we had reason to be thankful that we had safely entered this bason. We were sufficiently protected from the swell, and had excellent holding ground, a fine blue clay; yet never did we run a greater risk than in entering. Not knowing the place, we were obliged to trust to a pilot with whom we could have no communication, except through an interpreter. He was alarmed; the ship was going at the rate of five knots an hour, and the evening was dark; yet, with all this, we were to pass a strait where a mistake of half a cable would have carried us to destruction.

It blew too fresh in the morning to heave our

anchors. Perceiving that the shore next to us was formed of a parcel of islands covered with trees, a party was sent off to cut some wood. Mr. Salt and my servant went in the boat; they returned at nine. Mr. Salt could find no plants; and he reported that these islands, at low water, are connected with the main land, and that they are only a kind of sunderbunds, composed of the rack tree, with a reef of rocks towards the sea protecting the whole line. My servant shot one of the very large grey birds, that we have often mistaken for natives; it stands nearly six feet upright. By the meridian altitude we made the day before but seven miles. Though the Panther sailed better for the ballast we took in, yet, from her great height above the water, she made hardly any way against a foul wind. Had the monsoon set in from the northward, I know not what we should have done. On the next day was to be a new moon, from which we had considerable hopes, as the day had been moderate, and the sky clear.

It blew however too fresh to stir with safety, as we found by experience; for in trying to get under weigh, our anchor dragged, and we were obliged to let go another. We therefore continued in statù quô, hoping that the change of the moon would yet bring a change of weather.

It blew a gale in the night from the N. N. W., so as to oblige us to let go a third anchor, by which we rode safely. It lulled towards morning, and we attempted to get under weigh, though there was a considerable swell. In doing this we drifted to within a quarter of a cable's length of the rock, that has but a quarter less one on it. In the course of the morning we contrived to get an anchor down farther from it. It blew very fresh;

but the sky was clear. A fishing boat from Suakin brought us fish. The fishermen promised to follow us as far as possible; our custom was too valuable to be given up easily.

It blew very fresh again in the night: the Assaye dragged, and then parted her anchor. Mr. Maxfield let go his last when only in three fathom, rock, at which time there was a very heavy swell from the northward. His situation being dangerous, he fired signal guns of distress. We immediately sent off our cutter with a hawser, and fortunately his vessel rode safe till it was fastened; we then warped her astern of us. It was extremely alarming for us also, since, if the wind had come round two points to the westward, we should in all probability have been driven on the dangerous rock that was so near us. We had three anchors down, and a fourth ready to let go: fortunately the wind continued in the same point. It was cold all day, and the motion was considerable. Mr. Maxfield came on board to report, that his ship made much more water, and that the whole of her was, he believed, rotten. The pilot also added his share of comfort, by positively asserting that the N. W. monsoon had set in, and that we should have no change of wind. This would have been bad news, as we should have been obliged to go to Jidda to obtain a supply of provisions, and abandon the survey of the coast to Macowar, which I find Bruce positively asserts is in 24° N. and that he was there.

March 3.—It was more moderate during the night, and towards morning quite calm. We took advantage of it to get up two of our anchors, putting down one at a sufficient distance to secure us from the rock, before mentioned. At twelve the wind was from the eastward, but too light for us to venture out at so late an hour. The Captain and Mr. Hardy went to examine the Assaye, and found her quite as bad as reported, her timbers being perfectly rotten. They thought that she might be trusted in fine weather, but were satisfied that whenever we met with a change of the monsoon, she must be abandoned. Yet but four months since she was purchased by the East India Company's marine officers at Bombay, after having been, as they said, regularly inspected, and reported fit for service.

March 4.—The breeze came off from the land, and we got safe out by seven from our unpleasant station, which we called Lent Bay, having passed the reef in two fathom and a half; soon afterwards we had no soundings. At twelve, we found no bottom with eighty fathom. The shore was as usual protected by a reef of rocks, and was composed of small islands covered with the rack-tree. There was another reef to the eastward, leaving a channel about three miles wide. In the evening we had soundings of twenty-seven fathom, mud. We cast anchor, as we supposed, in a similar bottom, but, on sounding, found fourteen fathom, rocks. If a vessel carried very little sail, she might find out a good anchorage; but the ground is so unequal that, when moving fast, there is no certainty that the next throw of the lead may not differ several fathom in depth, and more essentially in the quality of the bottom. The night was moderate.

Our stream anchor was entangled among the rocks, and we were obliged to leave it there, after having used every exertion, but in vain, to raise it. The breeze was fine, but hung too much to the northward; the channel was from $2\frac{1}{2}$ to $3\frac{1}{2}$ miles wide. A whole fleet of dows was in sight,

given by D'Anville of about ten miles; he has made an equal error here, by placing his Dradate in 19° 45″. Though he certainly took his information from De Castro, he corrected the latitude five miles, but he has not done it sufficiently. The narrow passage in which we were sailing, and which, the pilot said, reaches to Macowar, would be impassable for any vessels, if it were not for the numerous small harbours, into which a vessel can run in bad weather. As the sea is perfectly smooth, in consequence of the reef to the eastward keeping off the swell, vessels with oars could always make their way against the strongest monsoon, when the force of the wind in the open channel would be irresistible. If the ancient navigators kept along the shore, which seems probable from the list of promontories, and other land marks, given in Ptolemy's tables, it is singular that no notice has been taken by Strabo, the author of the Periplûs, or by Pliny, of the many harbours which are laid down by D'Anville between Myos Hormos and Ptolemais Theron. There is no ancient name which can with any degree of probability be affixed to Mirza Sheik Baroud.

We set sail by day-light March 7th, with the land breeze, which soon afterwards freshened considerably, and at length set in with a considerable swell from the N. N. E. As the land lay nearly in this direction, we made but little way, having to tack every twenty minutes, and generally missing stays. The pilot told us there was no anchoring, except in rocks, till we reached another harbour, distant twenty miles. At twelve the wind continued steady, and convinced us we could not reach it; we therefore turned about, and got safely into our old birth at Sheik Baroud. We instantly sent Abdallah to the dow to learn if any Bedowee were in the vicinity, and to offer the Naqueda ten dollars as a present, if he would procure us a sufficient supply of sheep or goats, over and above any profit he might make in the purchase; he brought us word that none were to be had here, but if we would send a person with money to Torateit, where our dow, and several others, were at anchor, we might the next day have goats and sheep in return. He undertook to go with our messenger, but we preferred trusting him with the money, having his dow as a security; and accordingly sent him forty dollars. Two men who had seen us at Suakin brought off some rock cod as a present, for which we gave them two dollars, to their great satisfaction. They promised to procure us a supply of fish.

Mr. Maxfield's vessel has made much more water by the exertion of beating to windward. I got some fine shells, and our men caught some rock cod and several sharks.

We did not attempt to move on the 8th. The Captain and the other gentlemen went in the cutter up the bay, which extends considerably inwards, with deep water. The dow man brought us two bullocks, for which he declared he had paid twenty dollars, and seven sheep for eight dollars; the other twelve he wished to keep, as a security for the present; but said, that if we would send him more money, he would procure more provisions. This we did, but desired him not to send it away, as we must have it back if we sailed in the morning.

It blew from the west of north, and we got underweigh by day-light, as did the dow. We sent the cutter on board, and got back our dollars. The wind gradually came round to the N. E. so that we lay well up shore, and by four o'clock anchored in an open bay, behind which was a harbour called Daroor. We were in ten fathom, mud and clay, but had the reefs very close to us on both sides. The Assaye was at our stern.

In the night it blew fresh, but moderating towards morning, we attempted to get under weigh. After getting up one anchor, the other dragged, and obliged us to let go the first again. It came on to blow very fresh from the northward, veering in the middle of the day to the N. E. The swell was great, and we were as much exposed to it as if we had been in the open sea. Captain Court, the other gentlemen, Abdallah, my servant, and the pilot, went up the harbour, and landed on the shore: they spoke to several natives, who were very civil. They gave them tobacco, and to oblige them, cut some buttons off their coats, which were greatly prized. The Bedowee wished them to go up to a village at some distance; but this was not thought prudent. The pilot asked them to get us some sheep. One man said he would try, and bring them to the beach if he succeeded. They saw some bullocks and a great number of camels. My servant killed three flamingoes. We roasted one, and found the breast very good. The harbour is of considerable extent, when the narrow entrance is once passed. This is very short, and lies nearly E. and W., so that the land breeze in the morning will always carry a ship out. It is perfectly land-locked, and has from two to four fathom water, with a mud bottom. Had we been aware of its excellence, we should have run in at first, and not lain tumbling on the outside; but unfortunately the sun was right in our faces, and made it difficult, when we arrived, to distinguish the reefs. This, by its relative latitude with Suakin, should be the Dorho of D'Anville; but the latitude is, as usual, erroneous, being 19° 50′; only five miles more than the latitude he gives to Dradate. Its longitude is 37° 33′. The hills are still extremely high, and line the coast regularly at the distance of a few miles; the intermediate space is flat sand, with a few trees. The beach itself is frequently a sunderbund of rack trees. Some islands in the harbour are completely covered with it. Plenty of dry wood might be picked up along the beach.

The night was nearly calm; and in the morning a light breeze from the land made us hasten to get under weigh. It however took from four to six to raise one anchor. On trying to get up the other, the wind headed us, and the anchor dragged. We again let it go, but the weather being extremely fine, we soon after again set to work. Unfortunately one anchor caught hold of the other, and we got close to the southern reef; so close that we could distinguish the beautiful coral of the rocks that threatened us with destruction. The anchors prevented the ship from wearing round into a channel which opened to the southward, and exposed us to the most imminent danger, as there was not a foot between the vessel's bottom and the rocks, which were there so steep, that had she struck, she would probably have gone over. Captain Court instantly cut both cables, and by the blessing of God the ship wore clear of danger, though without an inch to spare. Had a squall then come off, such as we had experienced just before, the ship and every thing in her must have been lost; and though our lives might have been saved, we should have been left on an inhospitable shore, with no assistance but from the Assaye, who had not three days provisions for us on board.

When recovered from our alarm, we found reason sufficient to make us uneasy, as we had only our sheet anchor left. We therefore determined to return into Daroor, and endeavour with the Assaye to recover our two bower anchors: fortunately a buoy was left to one, and a considerable quantity of cable to the other. The wind freshened very considerably, and the Panther was as crank as ever; we therefore determined not to trust to our sheet anchor in a heavy swell, but to run into the harbour. This we did, and found it as smooth as glass. We let go in two fathom, mud, but dropped into three. It blew a gale from the E. of north, so that the mountains were, as usual on such occasions, concealed from our view by clouds of sand. Mr. Maxfield had cast anchor on the outside to be ready to assist in getting up the anchors. Mr. Hardy went off to him with cables, &c. but after ascertaining their position, found it blew too fresh to do any thing, and returned.

We perceived a native on the shore, and sent off for him. He proved to be one of our dow's crew, who informed us, that Emir Mohammed had been up to Torateit, and conceiving that the monsoon (Shamaul) had set in, and would prevent the dow's coming on, had sent him by land to procure here what provisions we might want. This conduct of Emir Mohammed gave me great pleasure; it was attentive and friendly, and argued well for a future connexion between the natives of the African coast, and the English, if cultivated by those who follow us, and not violated by caprice or tyranny, as has too often been the case. We have done the best we could to leave behind us a good impression of the British character, and, so far as we can judge, have succeeded. I sent the Suakin man on shore, with instructions to persuade, if possible, one of the chief natives to pay us a visit. Mr. Hurst, in the boat of the Assaye, was driven on the reef as he was returning to the vessel, from having fastened a warp to the buoy of our anchor. Fortunately he landed safe with his men. We sent a boat with people to their assistance, who brought them clear of the surf. Mr. Hardy, with the cutter and crew, went to pass the night with the Assaye, to assist her in case of accident, as Mr. Maxfield had imprudently anchored her close to the reef. They got down an anchor for her farther to windward. It blew a perfect gale from the W. of N. in the night.

March 12.—It blew too fresh for Mr. Hardy to do any thing with the anchors; he therefore returned on board. We got the Assaye's boat on board, and repaired her. Two natives appeared on the beach; we sent a boat, and one came off. He brought a basket of broiled fish to sell. We requested him to procure some raw, which he said he would do. He was the same man that our gentlemen had seen when they went on shore. He said he had brought down two sheep yesterday, but as nobody came from the ship, he had taken them back. He expressed no fear or surprize; he told us there was water, but that they had no vessels to bring it in We gave him a dollar for his fish, and he went off to get more. Captain Rudland and my servant went on the northern shoal in pursuit of a large flight of birds, which were gone before they could land. They walked a considerable way, and saw several natives spearing fish, who retired as they approached. Captain Court went on shore to take the meridian altitude. He made the latitude 19° 48′ 30″. N. The refraction was so great, that it is almost impossible to take a true observation.

The Emir Mohammed's man came on board in the afternoon, with the Sheik of the village, who rode to the water's edge on a very fine camel. A man came down with four sheep to sell, but it was impossible to purchase them, as he even refused two dollars each. The Sheik brought me one as a present. He was a decent looking man, and was armed with a sword. I gave him two dollars and some tobacco, with which he was well satisfied, though they seem to have little knowledge of the value of money It was extremely vexatious that Mr. Bruce's assertion of blue cloth being preferred by the Bedowee, should have prevented our bringing any white, which would have insured us a ready supply of all we wished. The fisherman came with some very fine mullet. We gave him a dollar, which he asked; he then wanted more: we offered half a dollar, which he objected to, and at length would not have the dollar. The Sheik scolded, but he took it patiently, and insisted on more, saying, "what would you do if I did not bring you fish? you would starve!" We assured him he was under a mistake, though a very natural one for a native of a country, where fish constitutes their chief food, and where it is caught in profusion, and with facility. They have no grain of any kind: milk, and goats, and sheep, are their other provisions. The Sheik promised to assist our native in procuring sheep: the fellow wanted more money, but we objected to giving it till he had procured us something in return. It was rather calmer in the evening, and Mr. Hardy went again on board the Assaye with the boat's crew.

Early in the morning the cutter and Assaye set to work with one of the anchors, it being very moderate. One of the Europeans dived in five fathom, and fastened a hawser to the junk of the cable. It was got up with great ease, and the Assaye brought it into the bay, when we had again the pleasure of fastening it to our bows. We saw the fisherman on shore. Pierce went off, and found him at breakfast on broiled fish, with his wife and family. He said he would go and catch us some, as soon as that was over. He sent a sting ray, another species, and four of the ray saw fish. Abdallah caught three new species of fish, the day being very calm. In the evening the Assaye went out again, and returned with our other anchor, which had fallen from among the rocks into the sand, and was got up with the same ease as the first; and before night we had the satisfaction to be in a safe station, with our lost anchors at our bows, and in every respect ready for sea. The man brought us some fish, for which we gave him two dollars. He begged to choose two shining ones, an evident proof of his ignorance of their value as money. Our man came from the village with two sheep, for which he had given four dollars. He restored the rest, saying that he could procure no more for money, as the natives did not want it; but that with white cloth, we might have procured plenty. I made him take a piece of Lucknow chintz as a present to the Sheik, and desired him to request he would assist us in the purchase of some cattle. The weather was much warmer.

The next was so fine a morning that we began at four to weigh our sheet anchor, but it stuck so fast that we were not off till seven, leaving our man and money behind. The weather was pleasant, but we were still confined by reefs to the E. and obliged to make short tacks. We were alarmed near one of them by finding ourselves within twenty yards of a sunken rock, with which our pilot was unacquainted. We hove to, and sent an officer in the cutter to sound, who reported that there was only three and four feet of water on it. It was not above twice the size of the boat, and no bottom close to it. We accurately ascertained its position, as it is the most dangerous spot we have discovered in the Red Sea. The shore runs N. and even a little easterly. As the wind was from N. by W. to N. E.: we did not make much way. We passed a small anchorage among the reefs close to the shore, which the pilot called Aroos, and another which he called Fadja. This is a good harbour, by his account, and lies in 20° 3′ N. It is evidently the Fusha of D'Anville, though with the usual error of latitude, as he has placed it in 20° 15′. The wind towards evening was more favourable, and we ran on in hopes to reach a good harbour called Howie-terie. This is not mentioned by D'Anville, nor by the Portuguese, from whom he copies; which is owing to their having gone on to Arekea, a mile further north, which Don Juan de Castro describes as the most defensible harbour he had entered, and as being above two miles long and one wide. Nothing can be more accurate than their description of the coast, as rising into hills and tumuli, with the mountains behind. These elevations are of most singular forms, and rise out of the level Tehama in an abrupt manner. During the former part of the day the country was a little wooded, but afterwards it had a most barren appearance. At sun-set the pilot could distinguish none of his marks by which to enter the harbour; we were therefore obliged to make the best choice among evils, and work all night, as there was no possibility of anchoring. By his watch Captain Court regulated the tacks, and we were assisted by a fine moon, and by the calmness of the night. We stood off and on, till twelve, when we lay to, lest we should reach a part of the channel where the pilot said there were sunken rocks. Providentially it was moderate all night, and we met with no accident. In a channel unknown to us, only three miles wide, of which by night the pilot was equally ignorant, with rocks and shoals around us, as far as we could see, our situation was certainly alarming. We all felt it so, and Captain Court never quitted the deck till we lay to, and then only for short intervals. All the crew were kept on deck the whole night.

We had, as usual, the morning breeze from the land, but towards nine it fell calm. We were among the shoals and rocks, of which the pilot was last night afraid. We passed by a sunken one as bad as that of yesterday: on others, there was sufficient water, and close to them sixteen fathom, hard sand; the next cast, no bottom, seventy fathom. At twelve we were in latitude 20° 11′ 23″; we could see Howie-terie, and by our bearings ascertained that it was in 20° 10′ 38″. Arekea was also in sight, which is erroneously stated by D'Anville to be in 20° 32′, though its real latitude is 20° 11′; a greater mistake than he has yet made, and for which he cannot blame the original Portuguese authors, who have not given its latitude, but only mentioned its distance from Suakin. Beyond was a lofty mountain which we named Tridactylos, from having at first mistaken it for the Pentadactylos of Pliny: hitherto, however, only three peaks had appeared. It continued calm till two, when a light breeze sprung up from the southward of east. We experienced during the calm, a current against us, of about a mile an hour; the breeze gradually freshened, and came round to the southward. The passage continued narrow, and very dangerous, from the numerous shoals. We had once soundings in ten fathom, mud, with the shoals so narrow and close, that we clewed up to let go our anchor; but the pilot persuaded us to go on for the anchorage of Salaka, which we reached by five, after passing a bar of rocks in 2½ fathom, with less on either side. When in, we had ten fathom mud, but not sufficient room to swing with safety. The anchorage was open to the southward, but protected by a spit of low sand on the other sides. It was far more dangerous than Lent Bay; but we had no remedy. It blew fresh, with a little rain in the evening from the south.

In the night it blew a gale from the south for a short time, and obliged us to let go our sheet anchor. Towards morning the wind came round to the west of south, and we hove up two anchors; but before we could get out, the wind came round to the S. E. and prevented our moving It was so truly vexatious to see four dows sail by us about eleven, with a fair wind, while we were fast in a pound, that in a splenetic fit I gave it the name of Mousetrap Bay. Salaka lies in lat. 20° 28′, which differs from D'Anville about the same number of miles as usual. In the evening the wind came round off shore. I got some dead specimens of very fine shells.

It was moderate all night. We swung round with our stern over the rocks in three fathom, and not a hundred yards from us had a quarter less one. It was cloudy and hazy. The old pilot, as well as ourselves, expected from the appearance that we should have a fresh wind; but our situation was so dangerous, from not being able to give the ship a sufficient scope of cable, that Captain

Court determined to try to beat to Macowar, which appeared from the mast head to be a fine harbour, distant about ten miles. We had not cleared the rocks half an hour before the gale began to freshen, and by eight blew so hard, as to put an end to all hopes of our reaching Macowar. The shoals were so numerous around us, that we were in danger every tack, and once were obliged to wear ship to save us from a reef that was but a few yards ahead. To return to Salaka was impossible, and would have been madness had it not been so, as we could expect nothing there but to be driven on the rocks. Captain Court was therefore under the necessity of trying to make Howie-terie, which the pilot said was an excellent port. We had double-reefed topsails close to the cap, yet went six knots, with a very heavy swell. Our old pilot very ably conducted us through a labyrinth of shoals, and by nine we were in a safe channel.

It was a most mortifying circumstance to be driven back, so near the completion of our labours; for at Macowar the open sea commences, and we should have had only the usual difficulties of navigation to contend with. Providence had singularly interfered in confining us at Salaka while the wind was fair. Had we been less impatient, and rested at Arekea, we should the preceding day have run the whole way with ease. However, I was resigned and satisfied. We had been deterred by no dangers, or inconveniencies however great from prosecuting the voyage: we had been for some time without bread; we had not two days flour or rice, and could procure no live stock except sheep, which will not live long on ship board with the provisions we could give them. Our seamen had nothing but juwarry and salt meat, and of the former scarcely sufficient for sixteen days; the spirits were very likely to be out before a fresh supply could be obtained; and, owing to the leaking of our casks, there was not more than three weeks' water on board. The delay of being driven back eighteen miles, with almost a certainty of the Shemaul's continuing to blow against us for some days, made it necessary to consider what place we should look to for supplies. Captain Court suggested that the water and juwarry could be replaced at Suakin, and that we could then go out into the main channel at Howie; but, on considering the deficit of other articles for the crew; that no rice, flour, poultry, or vegetables, could be procured for ourselves: articles, which the shattered state of my own health rendered not luxuries, but necessaries; considering also that the ship was deficient in ballast; and though better from having put her guns in the hold, yet still crank; I determined to return to Mocha, where every thing could be had that she required, and then try to beat up to Cosseir. I was also inclined to this decision, by the dangers we had experienced in Suakin harbour, and the probability, that now the northerly winds were certainly set in, we might be detained there on wretched food, as long as we should be by the additional voyage to Mocha. I therefore gave the necessary directions to Captain Court. Our dow had come into Salaka the night before: by her we learned that the boy we left at Sheik Baroud had gone on to Macowar. We knew that he would be disappointed, but he had ten dollars to console himself. Our dow did not attempt to move. It blew a very fresh gale, and we reached Sheik Baroud before dark.

It was a very great mortification to me to be thus obliged to abandon my voyage of discovery, at the moment when our difficulties were so nearly ended; for had we once got out into the open sea, we should have been able to run over to Jidda, where supplies could be procured: for this, the Shemaul would have been a fair wind. Every important object had, however, been attained respecting the passage within the shoals, from Suakin to Macowar, a passage which no vessel will probably again attempt, till an extensive trade shall have taken place in the Red Sea, when, probably, the advantages it holds forth of smooth water and occasional land and sea breezes, may cause it to be navigated by small vessels in the adverse monsoon. I think that a vessel with oars would, at such seasons, find it infinitely preferable to the open sea, as was the case with the fleet of Don Stephano de Gama, to the account of whose voyage by Don Juan de Castro I have so frequently had occasion to refer. Had there been any doubt of there being a free communication from this passage to the open sea near to Salaka, after the account of the Portuguese navigators, it would be removed by the track of Captain Court in the Panther cruizer in the year 1795, who approached sufficiently near to the island of Macowar to ascertain its position, and to perceive that the sea was free in its vicinity; thus confirming the assertions which had been made to us by our friends at Massowah and Suakin. During our unfortunate confinement in Mouse-trap Bay, frequent visits were paid to the mast head, and numerous bearings were taken of the rocky Island of Macowar, and its adjacent harbour. All these so perfectly agreed with the observations made by Captain Court on his former voyage, that I cannot but consider their identity, and consequently their actual position, as sufficiently established. If, hereafter, navigators should use this passage, which among the moderns was first navigated by the Portuguese, and next by myself, they will receive important assistance from the chart of my amiable and able friend Captain Charles Court, to whose indefatigable exertions during a voyage of considerable danger, and perpetual anxiety, in taking bearings, and making every useful nautical observation, the public is indebted for the accurate chart of the Western Coast of the Red Sea, which I have the pleasure of laying before them. As a tribute of that esteem which I entertained for his private character, and professional abilities, I have called the narrow passage between the shoals from Suakin to Macowar, Court's Passage.

It would have given me particular satisfaction to have examined the port of Macowar, on account of the advantages, which it has over any of those in Court's Passage, from its being accessible to vessels without their entering the shoals. It was invariably represented by the pilots as being an excellent harbour; and that it is one, is confirmed by Don Juan de Castro, who speaks of it under the name of Salaka, for Mouse-trap Bay could never be meant by a port which received the Portuguese fleet. Water is undoubtedly to be procured there, though, in very dry seasons, it is not very good, and fresh provisions are in abundance. An amicable intercourse with the Bedowee might be established through Emir Mohammed, and the Suakini tribe, by which means, not only supplies might be obtained for any ship without the risk of entering the dangerous harbour of Jidda, but probably a very considerable trade might be carried on direct with the neighbouring Arab tribes, who are at present supplied with the coarse Indian cloths, which compose their dress, at a very high price, through Suakin, or Jidda.

Macowar becomes a place of much more importance, if Monsieur D'Anville is right in his conjecture of its being near the Alaki of Abulfeda, and the Ollaki of Edresi, described by these authors as a mountain rich in mines of gold and silver. * The conjecture seems more than probable from the evidence adduced by D'Anville of the concurrence of the bearings and distance between Assuan and Salaka, and Assuan and Ollaki, and of the agreement between the position of Salaka, and the mountains which, in the time of the Ptolemies, yielded such great abundance of the precious metals. The similarity of the name must also be considered as no trifling support to his conjecture, since the modern Arabian names are so frequently only corruptions of the classical names given by their authors. If D'Anville is right in his conjecture, and even an unsupported conjecture ought to be received with the greatest deference from such authority, he has also satisfactorily ascertained the position of the Berenice Pancrysos of the Egyptians as being the present Macowar or Salaka of the Arabs. I can in some degree confirm the conjecture of D'Anville by the evidence of the pilots, at a time when they fully expected we should reach Macowar, and should therefore be able to detect any falsity they might advance, that at a little distance from the village in the harbour, were some ruins, and large tanks, that bespoke ancient magnificence. I can also assert that the mountains which, from Port Mornington, have kept at a considerable distance from the shore, here again approach it, a circumstance which confirms the description of the Arabian au-

* In my edition of Edresi, by Hartman, I find the name written Alalaki.

thors, and the statement of Diodorus, that the mines were situated on the confines of Egypt, and near to Arabia and Ethiopia, consequently on the shore of the Arabian Gulf.

To the question, why are these valuable mines no longer worked? it would be difficult to give any positive answer. We find by the account of Diodorus, that it was only by the most violent exertions that the Ptolemies were able to work them; and that so dreadful was the slavery of those, whom force alone had driven to the employment, that death was considered as preferable to such a life. He also represents the veins of gold as running in an irregular manner between the strata of rock. It is probable, therefore, that the difficulty of procuring it increased; and that the heavy hand of power being removed, no people were found who would voluntarily undertake so dreadfully laborious an employment. These mines may however be again worked in some future period, since the science of modern times has so much improved and facilitated the operations of mining; but whether this is a "consummation devoutly to be wished," for the sake of the inhabitants, is, I think, a matter of considerable uncertainty.

Although I was not so fortunate as to reach Macowar, yet I was sufficiently near it to convince myself, that the accounts I had received at Massowah and Suakin of its actual position, were perfectly true, and that Mr. Bruce's adventures at, and near it, were complete romances. I confess that I always had some doubts in my mind respecting his voyage from Cosseir, from the absurdity of the account he gives of his taking a prodigious mat sail, distended by the wind, then blowing a gale, in his arms, and yet having one hand at liberty to cut it in pieces with a knife. Nor could I more easily credit his finding at Jibbel Zumrud or Sibergeit, the pits still remaining, "five in number, none of them four feet in diameter, from which the ancients were said to have drawn the emeralds." That five wells should now exist, which have not been worked since the days of the Romans' holding Egypt, a period of thirteen centuries, in a country where the sand is driven about by incessant gales; that he should find a man who had twice before visited these unworked mines situated in a desert country; and, above all, that he should there have found, "nozzles, and some fragments of lamps," still lying on the brink of these wells, which would have been covered with sand by one single Shamaul, or north wester, are circumstances of such extreme improbability, that nothing but the highest character for veracity could induce me to believe the person who narrated them.

Had these been all the objections, Mr. Bruce's friends might have pleaded that there was no positive proof against him. He has however convicted himself, by pretending to give us latitudes. He declares that, by his own observations, Jibbel Zumrud is in lat. 25° 3′ N. when, in fact, it is a place as well known as any part of the Red Sea, and is in 23° 48′. It might be supposed that this is an error of the press, were it not that he has placed the island in the same latitude in his extraordinary chart, of which I shall have to speak hereafter; and also that the account of his voyage renders a lower latitude impossible. He says, that he sailed from Cosseir with a light air on the 14th of March, and, about twelve on the 15th, was three miles from Jibbel Zumrud. For these twenty-seven hours it is impossible, with a light air, to allow him more than a degree of latitude, which, with the addition of the longitude, would amount to seventy miles.

Besides, on his return, with a strong gale, Jibbel Zumrud was on his lee bow at day light, and he arrived before sun-set at Cosseir, having run the same distance in eleven hours, which occupied twenty-seven hours with a light air: consequently the distance could not be more than seventy miles. D'Anville seems to have led him into the mistake, who places, not the Island of Emeralds, but Maaden-el-Zumrud, or the emerald mines, in 24° 45'.

Mr. Bruce departed from Jibbel Zumrud on the 16th at three in the afternoon, and on the 17th at twelve he was, as he says, four miles north of an island called Macowar, which he found to be in latitude 24° 2' N. The asserted position of this island cannot be owing to any error of the press, not only for the same reason, of his having given the run of a degree in the twenty-one hours, but also from his stating that it lies off the celebrated Ras-el-Anf, or Cape of the Nose, where he rightly observes, that "the land, after running in a direction nearly N. W. and S. E. turns round in the shape of a large promontory, and changes its direction to N. E. and S. W". It is evident that there is an island in the position he has given to Macowar, which is by mistake called Emerald Island in Sir Home Popham's chart, but is in fact the Kornaka of Don Juan de Castro, while the real Jibbel Zumrud is placed in its proper position, but is called St. John's island. Mr. Bruce says, that Macowar is the place, "to which the coasting vessels from Massowah and Suakin, which are bound to Jidda during the strength of the summer monsoon, stand close in shore down the coast of Abyssinia." He adds, "that arrived at this island, they set their prow towards the opposite shore, and cross the channel in one night to the coast of Arabia, being nearly before the wind;" and he finishes the paragraph by the modest assertion, that " the track of this extraordinary navigation is marked on the map, and is so well verified, that no ship-master need doubt it." Not one word of this narrative can be made to agree with the islands actually in the vicinity of Ras-el-Anf; nor could any thing be more absurd than to suppose, that the dows would beat against a contrary monsoon as high as 24° 2′ N.; when they would have a fair wind for the port they were bound to, Jidda, when in lat. 20° 38′ N. That the entire description of the island, and the plan of starting from it for Jidda, is perfectly true, when referred to the real Macowar, I can, from my own information, and the evidence of the pilots, most positively assert; and the declarations of the natives are strongly corroborated by their total ignorance of the western coast above Macowar. No pilot could be found at Massowah, or Suakin, who would undertake to carry the Panther into Foul Bay, where I was particularly anxious to go, and look for Berenice, though they all knew the way as far as lat. 20° 38′.

I think it clear from the above observations, that Mr. Bruce has represented himself, in the first place, as visiting an island called Jibbel Zumrud, in lat. 25° 3′ N. though in fact, that island lies in 23° 48′, and afterwards as reaching another island, Macowar, in 24° 2′ N. which, in fact, lies in 20° 38′.

I think it appears equally clear that it was impossible for him to have made a voyage from Cosseir to the real Macowar, a distance of nearly four hundred miles, in the period he allows himself, from the 14th of March to the 17th, and consequently that he never did see that place, although his description of it, and also his assertion that the Arabs there quit the coast of Africa to strike off for Jidda, are both accurate.

I think it impossible to account for these errors in any other way than by considering the whole voyage as an episodical fiction compiled from the accounts of other navigators, and the information he might pick up at Jidda respecting the course of the Arab navigation; an idea which I strongly entertained on the spot, and which has been confirmed, since my return, by the observation first made by an ingenious but anonymous writer in the Monthly Magazine, that of twenty charts or drawings taken by Mr. Bruce's assistant, Luigi Balugani, in the Red Sea, not one relates to the pretended voyage from Cosseir to Jibbel Zumrud. I am surprised that the same writer did not take notice of the equally remarkable circumstance, that not a single observation of latitude is to be found in Mr. Bruce's list, as taken either at Jibbel Zumrud, or Macowar, or even the island which he named after himself, though he has asserted in his voyage, that he ascertained the position of these places by the meridian altitude, and has actually given observations made at Cosseir, both before his departure, and immediately after his return to that place.

The only celebrated port of antiquity, that remains to be ascertained on the western shore of the Red Sea, is Myos Hormos, which is mentioned by the Periplûs, as being one thousand eight hundred stadia, from Berenice. These, if considered as Egyptian stadia, will make one hundred and twenty miles.

Berenice is nearly in latitude 23° 23′ N. If therefore we calculate, as in the former case, by latitude alone, Myos Hormos must be in 25° 23′ N. which brings us to that part of the coast where Don Juan de Castro has laid down two ports, close to each other, which he calls Gualibo, and Tuna; but if we measure the distance on the chart, we shall find that, owing to the promontory of Ras-el-Anf extending so far to the east, the one hundred and twenty miles will only bring us to about latitude 25° N. I have before had occasion to observe that less dependance can be placed on the distances, as given in round numbers in the Periplûs, than on local circumstances mentioned in that work, or in the works of others, on the same subject. De Castro is the only modern, who has visited and described the coast from Foul Bay to Cosseir, and we must therefore refer to him, to see if there is any place, within a few miles of the latitude, that probably belongs to Myos Hormos, which will answer to the description given by the ancients of that place. It is stated by the author of the Periplûs, as being λιμὴν, a port, and not an open road, and as being on the extreme border of Egypt. Strabo calls it "λιμένα μέγαν," a large port, with a winding entrance, and having three islands lying off it. Diodôrus speaks of a port, which he calls Aphrodites, but which seems to be the same as Myos Hormos, from the description of its being a port with a winding entrance, and as being placed at the foot of a mountain of red rock, which shone so as to hurt the eyes; a circumstance which, by Agatharchides, is attributed to Myos Hormos, who positively declares, that they are the same port, though differently named at different times.

Such are the accounts we have received of the ancient port of Myos Hormos; and it is a coincidence of circumstances that could hardly have been expected to be noted by a traveller who did not direct his attention particularly to a comparison of what was before his eyes, with the description of former navigators, that Don Juan De Castro describes a port called Shakara as encompassed by a very red hill, and near to it another "very capacious and noted harbour, called Shawna, where, according to the report of the Moors and inhabitants, there stood formerly a famous city of the gentiles." The latter place is laid down by De la Rochette in 24° 53′, and the former in 25° 8′, either of which would sufficiently agree with the distance from Berenice as given in the Periplûs. As the red hill is represented as being a very large one, it might be supposed to reach sufficiently near to Shawna to have been described by the ancients, as a mark of that port, where are probably existing the remains of ancient magnificence which have have given rise to the Moorish account. But if this difficulty were removed, the circumstance of the three islands is still remaining to cause a doubt of Shawna being Myos Hormos. I can only observe, that at present there is no proof that three small islands do not exist, opposite to their harbours, and that we know of no other that will answer the description given. Strabo and Diodôrus both observe, that two of these islands were covered with olive trees, and the third was frequented by sea birds. This description is so positive that I cannot admit the supposition, that there might be other islands which were over-looked; yet this would be the case were Myos Hormos placed opposite to the Jaffateen Islands. A still stronger objection to this conjecture is that the coast there is perfectly open, and cannot therefore be considered as a port with a winding entrance. There is indeed a harbour formed by the cluster of the Jaffateen Islands, but the word ὑπέρκεινται of Diodôrus, and πρόκεισθαι of Strabo, evidently prove, that these islands lay off the harbour, and were not a component part of it.

As the coast from Ras-el-Anf to Cosseir is perfectly free from hidden dangers, it is to be hoped that some future navigator will find leisure to examine the numerous harbours which, according to Don Juan de Castro, lie within that space. If an ancient town actually exists, water must no doubt be found near it; and it is probable that there is a passage through the mountains, from the name of one of the ports, Sharm-el-Kiman, which is translated "the opening of the mountain." If so, how valuable would a port be, to which vessels could resort, for such supplies as the Bedowee can afford, instead of being obliged to lie in a miserable roadstead at Cosseir, unprotected from the S. E. monsoon, and even where water itself is unattainable, except of a brackish quality!

I submit the preceding observations, on the ancient geography of the Red Sea, to the public, with some diffidence, because the view I have been induced to take of the subject, chiefly from observations made on the spot, differs, on some points, from the judgment formed by Dr. Vincent, after a mature consideration of the information handed down to us by ancient authors; but as in the position of the Opsian Bay, I have been already flattered by the sanction of this candid and learned annotator on the Periplûs, I feel perfectly convinced that I am affording the highest gratification to his mind, in endeavouring, by local observations, to elucidate the work he has investigated with so much acuteness, although my conclusions may, on some points, differ from his.

We were clear of Mirza Sheik Baroud early in the morning of March 18th. The wind was more moderate, but a great swell followed us. At twelve we were off Suakin, and sent our old pilot on shore in the cutter. We gave him ten dollars, and three pieces of Surat cloth, being satisfied of his merit, and of his having served us faithfully. Now that we knew the dangers of the navigation, his demand of sixty-five dollars did not appear so unreasonable. Before dark we got a sight of Hurroo Riot Island, which ends the narrow passage between the shoals. We took a new departure from it, and sailed on all night.

March 19.—At daylight we were off Akeek. The wind was more moderate, with a land breeze in the morning, and a sea breeze after twelve o'clock.

March 20.—A continuation of moderate breezes and pleasant weather during the whole day.

March 21.—We lay to after nine o'clock last night, as we were by our reckoning ten miles from Massowah; but a current carried us beyond it. The morning was fine, but at eight it began to rain, with a strong gale from the N. W. It cleared up about ten, and we got into Massowah harbour. I sent Abdallah on shore to make my salaams to the Nayib, and to bring off the Banian. The Nayib returned civil messages, and the Banian came on board. In the course of the day we procured some fowls, but no goats, sheep, or bullocks were to be had without delay, as, the rains having failed, the scarcity was great, and the remaining stock had been sent up the country; the tanks were completely exhausted, and the inhabitants were obliged to drink the Arkeko water, which is brackish.

The Nayib sent at night a present of Habesh cotton cloth, and honey, with a message that his daughter was going to be married, who was also my daughter, as he and I were one. This was a broad hint for a present, which I could not evade; I therefore sent the bride a piece of gold tissue, and some Lucknow chintz. The native pilots so positively assured us that the N. W. monsoon had set in, and our own experience gave such weight to their report, that we were induced to abandon our intention of trying to reach Suez during the present season, and adopted in its stead a determination to open a communication with the Court of Abyssinia, and if possible, to send some of our party up into the country. The Banian had frequently mentioned to me that the Ras Welleta Selassé was anxious to hear from me; I therefore delivered him a message for that chief, expressive of my wishes, which I requested him to put on paper, and send up by a special messenger to Tigré, for which I agreed to pay him fourteen dollars, he covenanting that the man should be back at Massowah with the answer in fifteen days. He now spoke less cautiously of the political situation of Massowah, and acknowledged that it lies at the mercy of the King of Abyssinia, and could offer no resistance were he to choose to attack it, as his most forcible instrument would be starvation, by cutting off the supplies from the upper country. In fact, Massowah is only of importance from being the port of Abyssinia, and were the trade to be turned into any other channel, it would sink into insignificance. I found that my friend the Nayib had, after my departure, made Currumchund pay sixty dollars for the cattle and sheep, which he had sent me as presents during my stay: he, of course, was repaid the whole, as it was not dearer than they would have cost had they been supposed to be purchased instead of given. We were told that there were accounts in the neighbourhood, of our boat having been broken on the shore, between this place and Akeek, but that the Lascars had escaped. We could not learn the truth of this. The natives sold us fish for empty bottles. My servant went a shooting on the point which covers the north side of the harbour, and in a few hours killed six antelopes, and three hares. The night was sultry.

The Banian came again in the morning to take his leave. We sailed for Mocha at seven, but the wind was so fresh from the E. that we could not weather the N. extreme of Valentia shoal; we therefore kept to the W. of it, in a very fine bay, about five miles wide from the Island to Ras Gedam. The soundings the whole way were from thirty to forty fathom, mud. Captain Court gave it the name of Annesley Bay. At half after eight we anchored close to the western side of the island in twelve fathom. An officer in the boat went out to sound, and discovered close to us a reef of rocks, which run off from the shore; fortunately the wind kept to the E. and we were safe till morning. The Assaye had gone up the bay, close to the main land, and was not in sight.

At five we weighed to get into safer anchorage. We found soundings and good bottom as we went S. along shore. We tried to pass through the channel, made by the S. extremity of the island and the main land, intending to anchor off the village, as the Antelope had done. The passage is free from all hidden danger, and sufficiently wide: two rocks are in the centre, but rise considerably above water. The wind was so fresh from the N. E. that we could make no way, and therefore came to an anchor under shelter of the S. W. point of the island. Soon afterwards Mr. Maxfield joined us. He reported that he had been nearly to the extremity of the western part of Annesley Bay; that the water gradually shoaled to four fathom, mud, when he had come to an anchor. It is certainly a noble bay from its size, from the goodness of its bottom, and from its being perfectly protected from every wind that blows in this sea. It is not surprising that the ancients preferred anchoring in it to the narrow harbour of Massowah, where the ground is hard. Though the channel between the island and the main land is sufficiently deep to prevent its being forded, yet it is so narrow, that a communication is kept up with the greatest ease. The trade that comes down from Abyssinia might easily be brought to the bottom of the bay at the southern extremity of Gedam, instead of passing along the side of that mountain. The distance would be less, as Dixan, the first town of Abyssinia, lies nearly due south of Massowah, and the facilities of embarkation would be equally good. I have no doubt that the trading inhabitants of Orine brought all their goods by this road after they had removed from Massowah or Toualout; and independently of the security from the attacks of the barbarians, they might be very probably induced to remove their station by the facilities which Annesley Bay afforded them, in embarking their elephants' and rhinoceros' teeth.

At ten o'clock all the passengers, with Mr. Macgie and the boys sent to collect shells, landed on Valentia Island, to walk to the village, while the two vessels beat round to the anchorage. Captain Rudland, and my servant took their guns, and soon parted from the botanisers. We had tolerable success, as the herbaceous plants were many of them, in seed. The only trees were of the genus Mimosa, except one which I had never before seen. The southern part of the island is a cluster of small hills sprinkled with trees and herbs. We were obliged frequently to ascend by narrow winding paths, made by the natives. The rock is visible in every part, and is dissimilar from that of the other islands near, not having any marine productions in its composition. Water seems plentiful, from the verdure of the little valleys stretching between the hills to the sea shore, forming a remarkable contrast to the burnt appearance of the neighbouring country. In one place the shooters actually found a spring. Two years have now passed without a fall of rain, consequently it may be safely asserted that water is always to be procured here. The goats were numerous on all the hills. The most lofty of these overhangs the village, and its base forms a rocky protuberance within high-water mark. We named it Mount Norris, out of respect to my father, as being the highest place in the island. It was fortunately low water, and we were able to pass round it. The village then came in view, consisting of about forty round and square basket-work huts. The hills here became less, and the plain much larger, being a mile in length, with a grove of Mimosas at the end: beyond this, my servant had shot several very fine wild geese. The Dola and inhabitants of the village gave us a very civil reception, the former appropriating a great part of his house to our use, having couches in it covered with mats, as at Dhalac. The day had fortunately been over cast, and there was a pleasant breeze; yet a walk of four miles, continually ascending and descending, had completely fatigued me, and worn out the shoes of the whole party. We had seen a large heap of the saw-fish's saws in one of the vales; these we sent for, and purchased for a dollar. They kill the fish for the fins, which is a large article of export to India: it finds a market in China with those of the shark, where they are used, like the birds nests, to give a glutinous richness to the soups.

I now applied for sheep and bullocks for the Panther, but was extremely disconcerted by the discovery that German crowns alone were current here, and we had only Spanish dollars. However, the Dola very kindly took my word, that I would pay for them as soon as the ship anchored. There were no sheep, but the goats were excellent, though dear; one large, or two small, for a dollar. A drove of cattle was brought for me to choose out of: they were by far the finest and fattest I had seen in the Red Sea; for one I paid ten, for the other six dollars. As it would not have been safe to send the largest on board alive, I wished to have him killed. The owner hesitated a little, and desired to be first paid; but the Dola passed his word for me, and he was led to the slaughter. This was performed in a most unbutcherlike manner, with an old sword. They were several minutes in cutting through his neck till they reached the arteries.

As the Panther was at two o'clock too far off to give us any hopes of dining on board, we applied to our friendly Dola, who readily undertook to give us the best the island would afford. A fine young kid was killed, and delivered to his wife, who performed the office of cook, in an inner room, where we were not permitted to enter: a goose was also delivered over to her. In about two hours the whole was served up in very clean bowls of wood, and instead of a table cloth we had new mats. The good lady had also made us some excellent cakes with juwarry and ghee; pepper and salt were laid beside them. The only desiderata were knives and forks: of the former they had but one, which had killed the kid, and now was employed to cut it in pieces. It was excellently roasted; and I do not know that I ever enjoyed a dinner more. It was nearly dark before the Panther anchored. I procured the German crowns, paid all my debts, gave my good landlady, and every one who had assisted us, presents, and returned on board after it was dark. We procured here some ghee, which the officers assured me was better than any to be had at Massowah or Mocha. It gives me great pleasure to be able to speak so favourably of a little island, to which I must now naturally be attached. If ever a trade is carried on with Habesh, it will again rise into importance. Supplies could constantly be procured from the main land, where we saw with our glasses numerous droves of cattle, and flocks of sheep. The abundance of water renders it preferable to Massowah, and its vicinity to that place makes it better than Dhalac, while the bays are superior in anchorage to either.

It was nearly dark when we got sight of the Aroes, or Anish Islands on March 26th. The rocks, between which and the high land is the channel, were not visible, yet, as it blew fresh, Captain Court took the bearings, and determined to stand on. We went under our topsails, Captain Court himself keeping a look out. The risk was considerable from the sunken rock, and breakers of Anish; however, we providentially passed safe between them at eleven o'clock, when Captain Court declared he would not again venture it on any consideration. We lay to part of the night, that we might not pass Mocha, the wind being still fresh from the north.

At daylight we stood on, having had a current against us in the night. The airs were become light, and there was every symptom of a change of wind. At two we were nearly in the Roads, when it began to blow very fresh from the south. The guns had been got up, and loaded, to salute, when the first squall took us; one gun got loose and ran out, so that the port could not be shut. The ship was so crank that we were obliged instantly to take in most of our sails ; we, however, fortunately reached a tolerable birth. We set off in the cutter as soon as possible, and got safe ashore at some distance above the north fort. We were met by Mr. Pringle, Mr. Bancroft, and a new party of Americans, arrived since our departure, who all resided at the British factory, were I once again took up my residence. It blew very fresh all night, and made us rejoice that we had ventured through the Aroes, as otherwise we should have been driven back to Rackmah.

CHAPTER VIII.

Description of Mocha.—Construction of the houses.—Fortifications.—Garrison.—Cavalry and Infantry exercise.—Jews town.—Arabian women.—Appearance of the Arabs and their food.—Government of Mocha.—Police.—Character of the Arabs resident in towns and Bedowee Arabs.—Arabian horses.—Climate of Mocha.—Mr. Salt's Tour to Moosa—Observations on the formation of the Tehama.—Measures pursued in sinking a well at Mocha.—Foundation of Mocha.—Establishment of European Factories.—Account of the trade in Coffee, Gum Arabic, Myrrh, Frankincense, Gold, Ivory, and India Goods.—The Fair of Berbera.—Possibility of penetrating into Africa.—Government of Yemen.—Account of the Imaum and Family.—Account of Sana.—Polygamy.—Rise and present state of the Wahabee power.

THE appearance of Mocha from the sea is tolerably handsome, as all the buildings are whitewashed, and the three minarets of the mosques rise to a considerable height. The uniform line of the flat-roofed houses is also broken by several tombs, which are called Kobas, after a celebrated mosque at that place, which was consecrated by Mohammed himself, and was similar to them in its construction, being a square edifice covered with a circular dome. On landing at a pier, which has been constructed for the convenience of trade, the effect is improved, by the battlements of the walls, and a lofty tower on which cannon are mounted, which advances before the town, and is meant to protect the sea gate. The moment however that the traveller passes the gates, these pleasing ideas are put to flight by the filth that abounds in every street, and more particularly in the open spaces, which are left within the walls, by the gradual decay of the deserted habitations which once filled them. The principal building in the town is the residence of the Dola, which is large and lofty, having one front to the sea, and another to a square, where, on a Friday, he and his chief officers amuse themselves in throwing the jerid in the manner described by Niebuhr. Another side of the square, which is the only regular place in the town, is filled up by the official residence of the Bas Kateb, or Secretary of State; and an extensive serai built by the Turkish Pacha during the time Mocha was tributary to the Grand Seignior. These buildings externally have no pretensions to architectural elegance, yet are by no means ugly objects, from their turretted tops, and fantastic ornaments in white stucco. The windows are in general small, stuck into the wall in an irregular manner, closed with lattices, and sometimes opening into a wooden, carved-work balcony. In the upper apartments there is generally a range of circular windows above the others, filled by thin strata of a transparent stone, which is found in veins in a mountain near Sana. None of these can be opened, and only a few of the lower ones, in consequence of which a thorough air is rare in their houses; yet the people of rank do not seem oppressed by the heat, which is frequently almost insupportable to an European. The floors, as well as the roofs of the larger houses, are made of chunam, which is sustained by beams, with pieces of plank, or thin sticks of wood, laid across, and close to each other. As they never use a level, the floors are extremely uneven ; but this is a trifling inconvenience to people who never use chairs or tables, but are always reclining on couches, supported on every side by cushions. The internal construction of their houses is uniformly bad. The passages are long and narrow, and the staircases so steep that it is frequently difficult to mount them. At the Dola's, numerous doors are well secured on the landing places, to prevent any sudden hostile attack. Little lime is used in any of their buildings ; a constant care is therefore necessary to prevent the introduction of moisture; but with caution they last for many years. If however a house is neglected, it speedily becomes a heap of rubbish; the walls returning to their original state of mud, from which they had been formed into bricks by the heat of the sun alone. The wooden materials very soon vanish in a country, where firing is extremely scarce, so that even the ruins of cities, which were celebrated for their magnificence in former times, may now be sought for in vain.

The best houses are all facing the sea, and chiefly to the north of the sea gate. The British factory is a large and lofty building, but has most of the inconveniencies of an Arab house. It is however far superior to the French or Danish factories, which are rapidly falling to decay. The lower order of Arabs live in huts, composed of wicker-work, covered on the inside with mats, and sometimes on the outside with a little clay. The roofs are uniformly thatched. A small yard is fenced off in front of each house; but this is too small to admit a circulation of air. It is singular that these habitations should be crowded close together, while a large part of the space within the walls is left unoccupied.

The town of Mocha is surrounded by a wall, which towards the sea is not above sixteen feet high, though on the land side it may, in some places be thirty. In every part it is too thin to resist a cannon ball, and the batteries along shore are unable to bear the shock of firing the cannon that are upon them. Two forts are erected, for the protection of the harbour, on two points of land which project considerably into the sea, at about a mile and a half from each other. An English man of war would level either to the ground with a single broadside. There are two other batteries within the town, but they are in a still more defenceless state. The guns on all these places are useless, except to return a salute. The Arabs, when they purchased them from infidels, considered them as Sheitan, or belonging to the devil, and therefore immediately set to work to make them holy. To effect this, they with the most perfect ignorance enlarge the touch-hole, till nearly the whole of the gunpowder explodes by it, which is also the way by which it very frequently enters. As, however, they have never had occasion to use these guns hostilely, they are not aware of the mischief they have done. The walls on the land side are a sufficient defence against the Wahabee, who always storm a town by means of their cavalry, and the numerous round towers have a very imposing effect on people who are totally ignorant of the use of artillery. Although under constant alarm from the Wahabee, they have neglected to repair the fortifications, and seem to consider the many small doors, nearly on the level of the ground, as affording no facility of entrance to an enemy. Near the sea gate a part of the wall has actually fallen down, and has been repaired with a few boards and matting. The town runs, for about half a mile, in nearly a straight line facing the sea, but afterwards the walls take a circular direction inland. The space thus included is in part not built upon, and, I should suppose, does not contain a population of above five thousand souls.

The garrison, in general, consists of about eighty horse, and two hundred matchlock-men, who receive a regular pay of two dollars and a half per month, for which they provide their own arms, and powder and ball for exercise; but when they quit Mocha, they are supplied with every thing, and have four dollars in advance. There is not a vestige of discipline among them, but they are by no means bad marks-men, though they are a long time in taking aim. When on guard at the different gates, they recline on couches, with their matchlocks lying neglected by their sides; while the right hand is occupied, either in sustaining the pipe, or a cup of coffee. Their matchlocks are good, and richly ornamented with silver. This, and their crooked dagger or jambea, are their chief pride; and it requires the most rigid economy for several years, to enable a young Arab to provide himself with them. The troops attend the Dola every Friday to the great mosque, and afterwards exercise in the front of his house. I was present several times to see the infantry fire three vollies, which they do with ball cartridge, or at least ought to do, though I suspect economy induces them frequently to leave out the ball. Before they fire, they throw themselves into loose disorder; a plan which the Dola strongly justified to Mr. Pringle, when he waited on him to announce the late glorious victories of the British in the east. On that occasion he fairly told him, that he was very much surprised our soldiers ever gained a victory. disciplined as they were, "Why," said he, "your men are all drawn up in a row, so that any man may be distinguished by a person who has an enmity to him, and be shot immediately; whereas my men, by standing in disorder, and continually changing place, cannot be known." The ball that they use is small, and ill formed, so that, at the respectful distance they keep from each other, a wound is seldom received. As the chief Mussulmaun inhabitants attend the Dola on the Friday, as well as the soldiers, the procession is handsome, several gay streamers being carried by the horsemen, and before the Dola the green and red flags of the Imaum; on the former of which is figured, in white, the double-bladed sword of Mohammed, which has a much greater resemblance to the figure of an European, with his head, feet, and hands cut off. The Arab dress looks well on horseback, and is composed of the richest satins and kincaubs of India. The flowing scarf, and the turban with the ends hanging low on the back, add greatly to the elegance of the dress.

Without the walls of the town are two extensive villages embosomed in groves of date trees; the one is occupied by the Samaulies, the other by the Jews, who here carry on an extensive but disgraceful trade, in a spirit which is extracted from the date tree; although fiery and unwholesome, it is drunk by the Mussulmauns in private. A more profitable trade is carried on by their females with the seamen; a certain degree of mystery is pretended to, but in reality the fact is known and connived at by the Dola, not only for the sake of the profits which he receives, but as being an additional inducement to the Europeans to desert and become Mussulmauns. Ostensibly any connection between a Christian and an Arab woman is severely reprobated, and, if detected, the female suffers a ludicrous punishment; her head is shaved and blackened, she is led round the town on a jackass, exposed to the insults of the populace, and at length, is driven from the place. At night, however, a dollar or two will induce one of the Dola's soldiers to conduct a Christian to these females, who exist in abundance at Mocha for the use of the Mussulmauns, and he will stay quietly at the door to protect them from intrusion. These villages are not more cleanly than the town; and the gully, in which the river of Moosa has occasionally reached the sea, is filled with an accumulation of filth which, in a more moist country, would certainly breed a pestilence, through here it has no ill effect.

The Arabs are in general a healthy race of people, fevers being very unusual, though severe colds are common during the cooler months. Ulcers are so prevalent, that it is rare to see a person without a mark from them on the legs: this is chiefly owing to their bad treatment; they only apply a piece of wax to the wound, which is never changed till it falls off; cleanliness is indeed no quality of an Arab, either in his person or habitation. The part of his dress, which is concealed, is rarely changed till it is worn out; and it was a work of the greatest difficulty to force the servants to keep even the British factory, free from accumulations of nuisances in every part. The form is gone through, every morning, of sweeping a path across the square from the Dola's house to his stables;

yet, at the same time, a dunghill is formed under his windows by the filth thrown out from his Zenana, so extremely offensive, as often to induce the Europeans to take a circuit to avoid it.

The Arabs, when very young, have an expressive, but mild countenance, and a pleasing eye. As they become men, the change is very disadvantageous: their figures are not good, and the beard is generally scanty; but, in advanced age, their appearance is truly venerable. The fine dark eye is then admirably contrasted by the long white beard, and the loose drapery prevents the meagre figure from being observed. The few women, who were visible, had rather pretty countenances, but in contrast to the males, their legs were of an astonishing thickness.

The food of the Arabians of inferior rank is a coarse grain raised in the country, juwarry, ghee, dates, and, on the sea coast, fish, which is procurable, in any quantity, with very little trouble. The higher orders occasionally had some mutton or beef, boiled to rags, and on festivals, a little pilau. The cawa, made from the husk of the coffee berry, is drank by most of them several times a day, and the pipe is rarely out of the hands of the men. At the factory a very excellent table was kept by Mr. Pringle. The beef and mutton, which are procured from the coast of Berbera, and particularly from Zeila, where the Imaum has a garrison, are excellent. Poultry is in great abundance, and cheap. Sweet potatoes, chilies, onions, and water melons, are cultivated in the small gardens without the town, wherever water is procurable from wells.

Mocha, as well as the other towns belonging to the Imaum, is governed by a Dola. Formerly an

Arab of high rank was appointed to this office, but now that the authority of the sovereign is greatly weakened, it has been considered as more prudent to give the situation to a slave, who can always be removed, and from whom it is more safe to take the profits of his government. The Sheriffe of Abou Arish is an instance of the danger of appointing an Arab of the Prophet's family, who are, in fact, an hereditary nobility, that still consider themselves as intitled to all power among the Mussulmauns. He was appointed to Loheia by the present Imaum, and no sooner reached his government than he prepared to rebel, and with very little difficulty resisted all attempts to drive him out. He has now become a Wahabee, and perfectly secured his independence. The second officer in the town is the Bas Kateb, or Secretary of State. This office is always held by an Arab, who is considered as a licensed spy over the Dola. The third is the Cadi, or Judge; and these three compose the Divan, where all public business is conducted, and where the Dola has only a vote.

The Government of Mocha is the best in the gift of the Imaum; not from the salary, which is trifling, but from the large sums which he is able to squeezê from the Banians, and foreign merchants. The present Dola was a slave of the Vizier, but in consideration of his good conduct, he has received a title from the Imaum, and, with it, his freedom. He is avaricious and tyrannical; but he has realised a considerable revenue for the Imaum, as well as secured a great treasure for himself. He invented a new method of extorting money from the Banians, by confining them in a room, and fumigating them with sulphur, till they complied with his demands. Mr. Pringle has frequently been obliged to complain at Sana of the obstructions he has put in the way of commerce, and probably he will soon be recalled, and obliged to disgorge his plunder. The Arabs have a whimsical apologue on the subject. They say, that when a Dola is appointed, he weighs nothing; that on going out of the gates of Sana he weighs a frasel; that on arriving at his government he weighs two; and goes on growing heavier and heavier, during his stay; but that he dwindles and dwindles as he returns, till the gates of Sana reduce him to his primitive leanness.

The present Cadi is a most respectable character, and I am assured that he would consider it as an insult were a fee to be offered him. The consequence is, that Mocha is in general a peaceable town, and, during my whole residence there, no act of violence took place. The police is strict at night; and if any person should be found out of his house after the Dola has retired to rest, a period that is marked by the drums beating before his door, he would be conducted to prison. Opposite to the British factory is a collection of thatched huts, which answer this purpose, where a prisoner lives as comfortably as he can do in any part of the town. At present a large number of people are confined there, who quarrelled with the Vizier at Sana about religion, broke his windows, and committed several other outrages. They were originally confined in the island of Zeila, but the Dola there, finding that the violent heat of the climate injured their health, humanely sent them back to Mocha, where they still remain, without a hope of release. They are fanatics, and regularly chant their evening prayers in a plaintive, and by no means unpleasing manner.

The Arabs, in general, seem to care very little about their religion. Friday is no otherwise distinguished, than by the flag of the Imaum being hoisted on the forts, and the troops being paraded in the square, whilst the lower order carry on their usual occupations. Money will at any time, induce an Arab to wave his prejudices, of which a curious instance occurred during my first residence at the British factory. Captain Keys had given a pig to Mr. Pringle, which the Lascars of the Antelope refused to bring on shore. Some fishermen were however easily procured, who, for the usual fee of a dollar, brought it safe to the factory. Admiral Blanket, the chief of the fishermen, attended it himself, in a state of perfect intoxication; but this was probably done to diminish his scruples in touching so unclean an animal.

A longer residence among the Arabs settled in towns, has only increased the dislike and contempt, with which I behold them. They have all the vices of civilized society, without having quitted those of a savage state. Scarcely possessed of a single good quality, they believe themselves superior to every other nation; and, though inveterate cowards, they are cruel and revengeful. Superstitious followers of Mohammed, they do not obey one moral precept of the Koran; and though they perform the prescribed ablutions with strict regularity, yet I never heard of a vice, natural or unnatural, which they do not practise and avow; and, though they pray at regulated times to the Deity, yet they also address their prayers to more saints, than are to be found in the Romish calendar. Hyprocrisy and deceit are so natural to them, that they prefer telling a lie, to speaking the truth, even when not urged to do so by any motive of interest. To this they are trained from their youth, and it forms a principal part of their education. As a government, they are extortioners and tyrants; as traders, they are fraudulent and corrupt; as individuals, they are sunk into the lowest state of ignorance and debauchery; and, in short, require to be civilized than the inhabitants more of the South Seas.

The difference between this character of the Arabs, and that given by Mr. Niebuhr, may at first sight appear extraordinary; but the difference is more in appearance than reality, as it is evident that he takes his opinion from the reception he had met with among the wandering tribes. He seems, however, to have imbibed a partiality for the nation in general, which the conduct of the Dola of Mocha, in particular, by no means justified; and he has attributed virtues to them, which I cannot admit them to possess. Whatever his reception might have been among the tented tribes in Yemen, it was neither hospitable nor generous. Many, even in that country, are charitable, but it is an outward duty of religion; and never extends beyond their own sect. I am perfectly ready to concur with him in his character of the wandering tribes, who I believe, are less civilized, and have fewer vices. The virtue of hospitality, so necessary in the barren deserts which they occupy, is completely theirs; and their bravery, and strict sense of honour, elevate them far above their countrymen, who reside in cities. I should feel happy in supposing that this was owing to their blood being less contaminated by the mixture of slaves from every nation, a degradation from which they are preserved by their poverty; a poverty, however, that is invaluable, as it secures their freedom.

The Arabs have essentially altered their conduct towards Christians, who may now walk about the streets of their towns without being liable to insult. The different events which have taken place in India, and have so conspicuously elevated the Cross above the Crescent, have struck a panic to the heart of the Mussulmaun throughout the East. It cannot be supposed that he has beheld the change without repining; but it has forced upon his mind a conviction of the superior power of the Christian, whom he hates as he ever did; but now fears instead of despising. The English have been the chief instruments in producing this change, and are therefore less popular in Arabia than their rivals, the French. Arabia was for a long time too remote from the scene of action to form any idea of the British power; the veil was removed by the expedition to Egypt, when they were supported by the firmaun of the Grand Seignior, ordering them to destroy any of the ports in the Red Sea that did not afford them protection; and when it was evident that they had the power to put the order into execution. Still, the neglect, or timid caution of our officers, in submitting to the insult of having their seamen stolen from them, and circumcised, in defiance of their remonstrances, prevented the Arabs from feeling our real power; and this was heightened into contempt, by the not resenting the affronts which were heaped on Sir Home Popham, who endeavoured to make his way to Sana as an Ambassador, but was obliged to return, as I have been informed by Mr. Pringle, in no very pleasant manner: though attended, when he set out, by a guard of one hundred marines, which he ought either not to have taken, or to have employed in protecting him from insult. The defeated soldiers of Scindiah at length returned in hundreds, and, after great difficulty, convinced the Dola, and the inhabitants of Mocha, that the English actually could, and would fight: a fact which Mr. Pringle had found it impossible to make them credit.

A calm and moderate firmness would, I have no doubt, easily procure, for Christians in Arabia, every immunity and privilege which, as strangers, they could require. A single ship of war could at any time stop, not only the whole trade of Mocha, but also the necessary supplies of provisions from Berbera. This would force a compliance with the reasonable demand, that the deserters should be given up; and this, once accomplished the idea of impunity would be done away, and not a seaman would ever afterwards place any confidence in their threats. A disgraceful prohibition also ought to be removed; a Christian is not permitted to go out at the Mecca gate, although the Jews and Banians are. This is the more singular, as the two latter are considered by Mussulmauns as inferior in character to the former, the Jews not believing in Christ, nor the Banians in Moses or Christ, who are both revered by the followers of Mohammed.

The British factory, though one of the best houses in the town, has many inconveniencies, independently of its construction, the chief of which is its vicinity to the Dola's stables, where the asses keep up an incessant braying, particularly if any noise in the night excite their attention. The horses are, in the day time, brought out into the streets, where they are fastened by their hind legs with chains to the ground, and by the head to the wall, so that it requires some precaution to pass between them, and still more to enter the gates of the factory, from the crowd of children belonging to the stable-keepers, who demand, rather than petition for, charity. The horses of Arabia are celebrated for their superior qualities, and certainly I saw some at Mocha of uncommon beauty, particularly about the head and neck. The Imaum is the only horse-dealer in his dominions, and these were his property, being sent down to Mocha for sale. The price rarely exceeds one thousand dollars. The Arab system of riding totally destroys a horse in a very short time. He is taught only to walk, canter, or gallop, as at the menage; and when at full speed is made to stop short by means of a strong bit, which ruins his mouth in a year or two, while the force employed throws him on his haunches, and very frequently founders him at an early age. The asses are of two species; the one has a stripe of black down the shoulders, and cross bands of black on the legs; the other is like the Spanish, and as fine a breed; the mules are consequently very handsome.

The climate of Mocha is more sultry than any I have yet experienced, in consequence of its vicinity to the arid sands of Africa, over which the S. E. wind blows for so long a continuance, as not to be cooled in its short passage over the sea below the straits of Bab-el-mandeb. This monsoon continues above eight months in the year with such force, as frequently to render all communication between the vessels in the road, and the shore, impossible. For the three or four months that the opposite monsoon from the N. W. blows, the heat is much greater, and the airs are light. These winds extend only to Jibbel Teir; from which place to above Jidda, they may be considered as variable for the whole year, though the prevailing one is generally from the same point in which the monsoon blows in the lower part of the Gulf. Above Cosseir an extraordinary change takes place, for, thence to Suez the wind blows for rather more than eight months from the N. W. At

Mocha, during the prevalence of the S. E. wind, a thick haze covers the opposite coast, but the moment the north-wester commences, the opposite mountains and islands gradually appear. The high land of Assab is visible from Mocha, as given in the drawing, although its distance was ascertained to be seventy miles, by a set of cross bearings taken from the island of Perim. This proves that there is a great degree of refraction in the atmosphere, of which indeed we had still more positive proof, by the appearance of several other headlands at the same time, and which we knew were much too low to be seen directly at the distance they actually were: a very singular phenomenon also occurred, which has been taken notice of by the ancients—the sun set like a pillar of fire, having totally lost its usual round form, a splendid testimony in favour of Agatharchides, who says, the sun rose like a pillar of fire.

The country, in the vicinity of Mocha, is more dreary than can well be conceived: to the foot of the mountains it is an arid sand, covered with a saline efflorescence, and producing in abundance the common Mimosa, and a species of Salicornia, whose embrowned leaves, and burnt appearance, gives little idea of vegetation. Near the town the date trees are in profusion; but their stunted growth shows the difference between the soil of Arabia, and the fertile plains of India: even where a brackish well has given an opportunity of raising a few vegetables, the scene is still cheerless, from the fence of dried reeds, which is alone visible. Mr. Salt, by the permission of the Dola, paid a visit to Moosa, and intended to have gone on to Beit-el-Fakih, but was recalled in consequence of the disputes running high respecting the renegadoes. He describes the country, even there, as uninteresting, though the mountains were fine, and there were fields of grain, and other appearances of cultivation. This is owing to the river, which rises in the hills, and at one season is full of water, though it, in general, loses itself in the Tehama, without reaching the sea. Once, indeed, it found its way to Mocha, where it carried away a considerable part of the Jews' town, which is built in its usually unfrequented bed. Had Mocha not existed, and had a vessel by accident approached the coast at that time, the mariners might justly have reported, that a river of fresh water there emptied itself into the sea. Future navigators would have positively contradicted them; and they would have been accused as liars, without having merited the title. I think it probable that the accounts of the river Charles above Jidda, and the river Frat opposite to it, have originated in a similar circumstance. By the influence of money Mr. Salt experienced a civil reception: he drew the town, of which I have given an engraving; and also the Dola's son, who did the honours of the place, his father being absent.

The singular appearance of the flat Tehama of barren sand, extending from the mountains to the sea, has given rise to the supposition, that it has been formed by gradual incroachments on that element; a supposition which is greatly confirmed by the strata that Mr. Pringle passed through in sinking a well, within the walls of the factory, and which are as follows:

1.	Rubbish of buildings, - - the level of high water.	8 feet,
2.	Clay - - - -	2 ditto.
3.	Sea mud and wreck, -	1 ditto.
4.	Broken madrapore and shells	6 ditto.
5.	Sea sand and shells, -	11 ditto.

In this measure he still persists, though the water oozes in so fast, that he has been obliged to sink a frame of wood, to keep it out. In the third measure the water was mephitic, and extremely offensive. As the depth increases it becomes less brackish, and at present one hundred pounds of water yields about one pound of salt. It is evident therefore that, at Mocha, the Tehama, to the depth of twenty-eight feet, is composed of marine productions, except indeed the clay, the position of which seems to me most extraordinary. The harbour of Mocha, formed by the two forts, and the spits of land on which they are built, is still gradually filling up. Dows cannot now lie in it; and the sea, which once washed the walls, is now at some little distance. A longer period has shown this gradual incroachment still more in the ancient harbour of Okelis, close to the straits of Bab-el-mandeb, where the Egyptian fleet could once lie, but where there is at present little more than a foot of water.

The celebrated ancient mart of Moosa was probably at Mocha, from the appropriate description handed down to us of its excellent anchorage on a sandy bottom. But if so, it ceased to exist for many generations, till the accidental residence of a hermit, and the discovery of the coffee, again brought it into notice. The history of the accidental landing of the crew of a ship, bound from India to Jidda, of the visit paid by the Captain to Sheik Shadelei, and the consequent sale of his cargo to the Arabs, who were followers of the Sheik, was narrated to me by the Hadje Abdallah, and confirmed by the Bas Kateb, to whom I applied for information. Mocha, according to these learned natives, was not in existence four hundred years ago; from which period we know nothing of it, till the discoveries and conquests of the Portuguese in India opened the Red Sea to the navies of Europe. The first entered it in 1513, under Don Alphonso Albuquerque, with an intention of uniting themselves with the Abyssinians against their common enemy the Mussulmauns, but returned without having reaped any advantage. In 1538, Soolimaun Basha, commanding the fleet of the Soldan of Egypt, stopped at Mocha, on his return from his disgraceful expedition against Diu.. It is only mentioned in his voyage as a castle, and was therefore probably a place of little importance, and had a Turk for its governor. In 1609, when the Red Sea was first visited by the English under Alexander Sharpey, Mocha had greatly risen in importance. and had become the great mart for the trade between India and Egypt. The Turkish governor was, at that time. a man of prudence and liberality, so that the English traded without any injury ; but his successor, in the following year, had very different ideas, as Sir Henry Middleton experienced to his cost, who was betrayed, and kept a prisoner for some time. These circumstances were too inimical to trade to admit of its continuance, and there was only a Dutch factory at Mocha, when. Monsieur de la Marveille visited it in 1708, and established a factory for his countrymen. Between that period and 1738 the English must have arrived, as, according to Niebuhr, they were there when the French bombarded the town, and obliged the Dola to pay his debts, and reduce the duties from three to two and a half per cent. Mocha was probably then at its highest state of prosperity, when the English, the French, and the Dutch carried on a regular trade with it, and by means of the navigation round the Cape of Good of Hope the expence of the freight of coffee was much lessened, and the consumption of it in Europe began proportionably to increase.

Coffee is the only article of trade produced in Arabia, and formerly the whole of this was carried from Loheia, by dows, to Jidda, and thence, either by the caravan of pilgrims to Constantinople, or, in large Turkish vessels by sea to Suez, and across Egypt to Alexandria; whence it found its way to every part of Europe. As early however as the beginning of the last century, the large European vessels began to carry the coffee round the Cape of Good Hope; which so much reduced the duties in Egypt, that the Porte sent an embassy to Sana to complain of this new system of trade, and to request that no coffee might be exported except through Egypt. The average quantity, that annually went up to Jidda, was about sixteen thousand bales till the year 1803, when a single American ship appeared, and by the great profit of her voyage, induced so many others to follow her example, that the quantity sent to Egypt was reduced nearly one half. Previously to this event, the Porte seems to have had little cause of complaint against the European merchants, as will appear from the following account of the quantity of coffee exported by them during the eight years prior to 1803.

	Bales.	
In 1795,	2154;	2100 for the India Company.
1796,	2000	for the India Company.
1797,	130	for a private merchant.
1798,	72	for a private merchant.
1799,	1866	for a private merchant.
1800,	6441;	1000 for the India Company.*
1801,	1340;	716 for the India Company.
1802,	——	

* The French were in Egypt.

The Company have, according to the above statement, which was given me by their broker, taken in the eight years not quite six thousand bales of coffee, a circumstance that seems, at first sight, unaccountable, as the Americans not having then made their way to Mocha, the market remained free from competition, and coffee was at its usual price of from thirty-six to forty dollars the bale of 305lbs. net. At present a competition having arisen, by the Company's broker and the Americans bidding against each other, the price has been raised to fifty dollars; but, at that price, above eight thousand bales have been exported direct for America, and two thousand bales for Bombay, for the use of the Company

The actual expence at which this has been brought to market, will appear in the calculations No. I. and II. That the subject of the coffee trade might be brought into one view, I have added in No. III. a calculation of the expence of bringing coffee direct from Mocha, by sea, to England; in No. IV. of bringing it, in dows, by the way of Egypt, to Alexandria; and in No. V. of bringing it the same way in a vessel, hired at Bombay for the purpose.

No. I.

Calculation of the Cost and Expences of 2,000 Bales of Mocha Coffee brought to England by the way of Bombay, as at present practised by the Honourable the East India Company.

			Dollars.
2,000 bales of 305lbs. each, at 50 dollars per bale			100,000
Commission to the purchaser, 5 per ct. }		Dollars.	
Duty - - - 3 per ct. }	12 per ct.	12,000	
Cleaning, shipping, &c. 4 per ct. }			
Freight from Mocha to Bombay - -		22,477	
Insurance on 141,500 ds. at 5*l.* per cent.		7,075	
Interest on 141,500 ds. for 4 months, at 9 per ct.		4,245	
Cooley and boat hire, 1 per cent. on the amount insured - - - - -		1,415	
Damage and waste, estimated at $2\frac{1}{2}$ per cent on ditto - - - - - -		$3,537\frac{1}{2}$	
Cooley and boat hire on board the vessel at Bombay, 1 per cent. - - -		1,415	$52,164\frac{1}{2}$
Cost on board, and ready for sea at Bombay -			$152,164\frac{1}{2}$

	£		£	s.	d.
At 5*s.* per dollar, the local value of the dollar			£38,041	2	6
Freight on 2,000 bales from Bombay to England, reckoning on 382 tons for cwt. 5,730 gross weight, at 15*l.* per ton - - -	5,730				
Insurance on 42,500*l.* at 10 per cent.	4,250				
Interest on 42,500*l.* for 1 year, at 9 per ct.	3,825				
Loss in weight, estimated at 7*s.* 2*d.* per cent, on sum insured - -	3,187	10			
Landing charges, at 1 per cent. on ditto	425		17,417	10	
Cost to the Company, when warehoused -			£55,458	12	6
Or 10*l.* 3*s.* 8*d.* per cwt.					

The above would be the cost to the East India Company, were they to purchase the coffee themselves at Mocha; but as they frequently prefer to enter into a contract for the delivery at Bombay, they in fact, must pay a profit to the contracting merchant.

No. II.

Calculation of the Cost and Expences of 2,000 Bales of Mocha Coffee from Mocha to America, according to the present practice of carrying on that Trade by the Americans.

			Dollars.
2,000 bales of 305 lbs. each, at 50 dollars per bale			100,000
Commission to the supercargo,	5 per ct.		
† Duty - -	3 per ct.	12 per ct.	12,000
† Packing, shipping, &c.	4 per ct.		
Insurance on 110,000 ds. at 10 per cent. -			11,000
Freight - - - - -			19,000
Interest on 100,000 ds. for 1 year, at 6 per cent.			6,000
Supercargoes expences on shore - - say			400
† Loss in weight, damage, &c. 10 per cent on the sum insured - - - - -			11,000
† Landing expences, &c. 1 per cent - -			1,100
Duty in America 4 per cent on the value, which is estimated at 93 ds. per bale, and makes 186,000 ds.			7,440
At 4*s.* 6*d.* per dollar			167,940
			£37,786 10
Or 6*l.* 18*s.* 9*d.* per cwt.			

The above estimate was given me by a very respectable American captain, excepting the articles marked †, which, however, must fall upon the American traders, and every other exporter of coffee from Arabia.

No. III.

Calculation of the Cost and Expences of 2,000 Bales of Mocha Coffee brought to England direct from Mocha, by Sea.

			Dollars.
2,000 bales of 305 lbs. each, at 50 dollars per bale			100,000
Commission of purchase, 5 per ct. Duty - - 3 per ct. Cleaning, shipping, &c. 4 per ct.	12 per cent. -		12,000
Cost on board at Mocha, at 4*s.* 6*d.* per dollar -			112,000
		£	£25,200
Freight on 382 tons, at 15*l.* per ton -		5,730	
Insurance on 28,000*l.* at 10 per cent -		2,800	
Policy duty on 28,000*l.* at ¼ per cent. -		70	
Interest on 25,200*l.* for 9 months, at 5 per ct.		945	
Loss in weight, 10 per cent on sum insured		2,800	
Landing and charges, 1 per cent. on ditto		280	12,625
Cost when warehoused in England - - -			£37,825
Or 6*l.* 18*s.* 10*d.* per cwt.			
The above quantity being 5446 cwt. 1 q. 20 lbs. if sold at the present price of 380s. per cwt. would produce the sum of - -			£103,482 2 10

I suppose this article imported for re-exportation, and not subject to any duty at our own Custom-house.

No. IV.

Calculation of the Cost and Expences of 2,000 Bales of Mocha Coffee conveyed by the Red Sea, and across the Isthmus to Alexandria.

			Dollars.
2,000 bales of 305 lbs. each, at 50 dollars per bale			100,000
Commission to the purchaser,	5 per ct.	16 per cent.	16,000
Duty to Egypt - -	7 per ct.		
Cleaning, shipping, &c. -	4 per ct.		
Freight by a dow to Jidda on 1,564 bales of 390 lbs. each being equivalent to 2,000 bales of 305 lbs. each, at 2½ ds. per bale - - -			3,910
Duty to the sheriffe, 3 dollars per bale - -			4,692
Transhipment at Jidda for Suez, 1 per cent. -			1,000
Freight by a dow from Jidda to Suez, at 2 ds. per bale			3,128

	Paras.		Patacs.	Paras.	Dollars.
Landing at Suez, and porterage at - -	10	per bale	173	70	
Factorage at Suez -	45	ditto	782	—	
Camel hire from Suez to Cairo - - -	270	ditto	4,692	—	
Fee of the leader of the caravan - -	21	ditto	364	84	
Weigher's fee and housing at Cairo - -	3	ditto	52	12	
Duty at Cairo - -	2,475	ditto	43,010	—	
Factorage at Cairo -	30	ditto	521	30	
Porterage and weighing on departure - -	10	ditto	173	70	
Canvas wrappers, and packing - - -	120	ditto	2,085	30	
Carriage to Boulac, and Janissary - . -	40	ditto	695	10	
Custom-house dues -	120	ditto	2,085	30	
Boat hire to Rosetta -	60	ditto	1,042	60	
Landing and re-shipping for Alexandria -	20	ditto	347	50	
Factorage at Rosetta -	30	ditto	521	30	
Boat hire to Alexandria	15	ditto	260	60	
Landing and housing at Alexandria - -	10	ditto	173	70	
90 paras per patac, at 160 per dollar			56,981	66	32,052
			Dollars		160,782

No. V.

Calculation of the Cost and Expences of 2,000 Bales of Mocha Coffee conveyed from Mocha, in a Vessel hired for the Purpose, to Suez, and thence to Alexandria.

		Dollars.
2,000 bales of 305 lbs. each, at 50 dollars per bale		100,000
Commission to the purchaser, 5 per ct. Duty to Egypt - - 7 per ct. Cleaning, shipping, &c. - 4 per ct.	16 per cent.	16,000
Freight of a vessel from Mocha to Suez and back, for 5 months, at 2,000 dollars per month - -		10,000
Insurance on 125,000 dollars, at 7 per cent. to and fro		8,750
Expences to Alexandria, as per calculation No. IV.		7,857
Duty at Cairo 3 per cent. on the value there, 120 dollars per bale - - - -		7,200
Interest on 100,000 dollars, for 5 months, at 9 per ct.		3,750
At 4*s*. 6*d*. each	Dollars	153,557
		£34,550 6 6

In the estimate No. IV. no allowance is made for the risks by land or sea, or the wastage of 10 per cent. by the drying of coffee. The Arab merchants cover this by the price, which, when 50 dollars per bale at Mocha, is at Suez 90 dollars, at Cairo 120, and at Alexandria 137.

Although three per cent. be the duty levied by the Imaum on all coffee exported beyond the Straits, yet he demands seven per cent. on all that is sent up the Red Sea, even by Europeans.

From the foregoing calculations we learn the following very important facts. That the Mocha coffee which the East India Company brings into the English market for sale, costs £10. 3*s.* 8*d.* per cwt.; that the Americans do actually take it to America, where it costs them only £6. 18*s.* 9*d.* per cwt.; and that they are therefore enabled greatly to undersell the East India Company in the markets of the Mediterranean, where the actual consumption is: but that it may be brought direct to England, in British vessels, and only cost £6. 18*s.* 10*d.* per cwt.; which being only one penny per cwt. more than it costs in America, it is evident, that it might be re-sold by the British in the Mediterranean, at a less price than it can be by the Americans, and consequently that the trade might be completely recovered out of their hands, were it not for the insuperable impediment of the Red Sea being within the charter of the East India Company.

It may also be considered as worthy of remark, that, with respect to the produce of Arabia, the discovery of the passage round the Cape of Good Hope seems to have been of little use: since the articles, according to the present system of trade, as carried on by the East India Company, can be delivered equally cheap at Alexandria by the old route.

Independently of coffee, the export trade of Mocha is very considerable in Gum Arabic, Myrrh, and Frankincense; which is imported from the opposite coast of Africa, but chiefly from Berbera, without the Straits, where a great fair is annually held, which begins in October, and continues till April. The first caravan is always the largest. It brings down about fifteen thousand bahar of gum arabic, each 320 lbs.: also all the myrrh that is consumed, about two thousand bahar. The former produces on the spot about fifteen dollars, the latter twenty-two dollars per bahar. The Frankincense is chiefly cultivated near to Cape Gardafui, and is exported from a harbour of the Samaulies, called Bunder Cassim, near to Jibbel Feel, called by the English Cape Felix, and is usually sold at about twelve dollars per bahar. A small quantity of these articles, at present, finds its way to Bombay, and thence to Europe, while the larger proportion goes up to the Red Sea to Egypt, and some is consumed in Arábia and Persia.

The Samaulies, who inhabit the coast from the Straits to Cape Gardafui, have a kind of navigation act, by which they exclude the Arab vessels from their ports, and bring the produce of their country either to Aden, or Mocha, in their own dows. Aden is so much better situated for trade with Berbera, in consequence of both monsoons being favourable for passing and repassing, that the greater part of the myrrh and gum arabic is carried to that place, where the Banians of Mocha have each a partner established, to conduct their business. By these means a monopoly is established, and the trade is loaded by them with the most enormous profits, though they profess to clear only fifty per cent. As the Samaulies claim only half a dollar freight per bahar, the expence of bringing these articles to market will be shown by the following calculations.

GUM ARABIC.

	£	s.	d.
15,000 bahars of 320 lbs. each, at 16 dollars per bahar, are 240,000 ds. at 4*s.* 6*d.* each	£54,000	0	0
Expences of unpacking, repacking, sorting, and delivery, at 4 per cent. - - -	2,160	0	0
Agency 5 per cent. - - - - -	2,700	0	0
Duties to the Sultaun of Aden, 3 per cent. -	1,620	0	0
Cost on board at Aden	£60,480	0	0
Freight on 3,000 tons, at 15*l.* per ton. -	45,000	0	0
Insurance on 67,200*l.* at 10*l.* per cent.	6,720	0	0
Policy duty on ditto, at ¼ per cent. -	168	0	0
Interest of money on actual disbursements at Aden 9 months on the sum of 60,480*l.* at the rate of 5 per cent. - -	2,268	0	0
Duty on 42,857 cwt. at 4*s.* 2*d.* per cwt. 27½ per cent. and 8*s.* 3*d.* per cent. - -	12,127	18	6
Landing charges, housing, &c. &c. 1 per cent.	604	16	0
Cost in the warehouse at London	£127,368	14	6

	£	s.	d.	
Said 15,000 bahars or 42,857 cwt. if sold here at the low price of 10*l.* per cwt. would produce -	£428,570	0	0	
Or - - -	28	11	5	per bahar.
Whereas the cost is only about	8	9	9	per bahar.
Which leaves a profit of -	£20	1	8	per bahar.

In the above estimate I have taken the price of gum arabic, as it was in the beginning of September 1808, when the continental markets were shut. It has frequently been sold in London at 30*l.* per cwt.

GUM MYRRH.

	£	s.	d.
2,000 bahars of 320 lbs. each at 22 dollars per bahar 44,000 dollars at 4*s.* 6*d.* - -	£9,900	0	0
Expences of unpacking, repacking, sorting, and delivery on board, 4 per cent. - -	396	0	0
Agency 5 per cent, - - -	495	0	0
Duties to the Sultaun of Aden, 3 per cent. -	297	0	0
Cost on board at Aden	£11,088	0	0
Freight on 400 tons measurement, each bahar measuring 8 cubic feet, at 15*l.* per ton -	6,000	0	0
Insurance on 12,320*l.* at 10 per cent. -	1,232	0	0
Policy duty on 12,400 at $\frac{1}{4}$ per cent. -	31	0	0
Interest on 11,088*l.* cost on board for 9 months, at 5 per cent. - - -	415	16	0
Duty on 640,000 lbs. at 8*d.* per lb. 27$\frac{1}{2}$ per ct. and 8*s.* 3*d.* per cent. - -	28,977	15	6
Landing charges, housing, &c. 1 per cent. -	110	17	6
Cost in the warehouse at London	£47,855	9	0

Said 2,000 bahars, or 5,714 cwt. sold at 25*l.* per cwt. would produce £142,850, or £71 8 6 per bahar.
Whereas the cost is only - - 23 18 6 per bahar.

Which leaves an apparent profit of - £47 10 0 per bahar.

Myrrh is frequently sold at 40*l.* per cwt., and I was informed by a most respectable broker that the 2,000 bahars would find a market at that price if there were no competition ; which would be impossible, as the above quantity is all that is produced. I have taken the price of September 1808.

FRANKINCENSE.

	£	s.	d.
10 bahars of 320 lbs. each at 12 dollars per bahar are 120 dollars, at 4*s.* 6*d.* each - -	£27	0	0
Expences of unpacking, repacking, sorting, and delivery on board to 4 per cent. - -	1	1	7
Agency 5 per cent. - - - - -	1	7	0
Duties to the Sultaun of Aden 3 per cent. -	0	16	2
Cost on board at Aden	£30	4	9
Freight on 2 tons at 15*l.* per ton - -	30	0	0
Insurance on 35*l.* at 10*l.* per cent. - -	3	10	0
Policy duty - - - -	0	5	0
Interest on 30*l.* for nine months, at 5 per cent. -	1	2	6
Duty on 28 cwt. 2 qrs. 8 lb. at 6*s.* 2*d.* per cwt. 27½ per cent. and 8*s.* 3*d.* per cent. - .	11	19	3
Charges of landing, housing, &c. 1 per cent.	0	6	0
	£77	7	6

	£	s.	d.	
Said 10 bahars or 28 cwt. 2 qrs. 8 lb. sold at 5*l.* cwt. would produce 142*l.* 17*s.* or	£14	5	8	per bahar.
Whereas the cost is only about -	7	14	9	per bahar.
Which leaves an apparent profit of	£6	10	11	per bahar.

The quantity of incense to be procured being unlimited, I have only made the estimate per 10 bahars. A great quantity is consumed in Catholic countries.

The prices, at which the gum arabic, myrrh, and frankincense are stated to be purchased, were the actual prices at Berbera in 1805; but the competition raised at Mocha by the arrival of the Americans affected these articles in as great a degree, as it did the coffee, and raised the price to a ruinous height. I have not however any hesitation in asserting, that the British may, with the utmost facility, secure the trade to themselves: but if Arabia should in future be as much neglected as it has hitherto been, the trade will again fall into the hands of the Americans, who will undersell us in every market in Europe, and justly laugh at our remissness and folly.

From the fair of Berbera, Arabia draws her supplies of ghee, and a great number of slaves, camels, horses, mules, and asses; but the profit on these articles is much less than on the sale of India goods, which is the return made to the inhabitants of Africa, for the whole produce of the country thus brought to Berbera. Many chiefs of the interior, and particularly the sovereign of Hanim, who lives twenty days journey west of Berbera, send down caravans of their own, to purchase, with gold and ivory, the manufactures of India. It is much to be regretted, that the sale is at present clogged by the unreasonable profits of the Banians, which of course, greatly diminish the consumption. Were a regular trade carried on at Aden, whose sovereign would rejoice at the adoption of any plan likely to increase his small revenue, and were the profit reduced to about forty or fifty per cent. the consumption would probably increase ten fold, for, at present, the Africans have no limits to their purchases of these articles, except the amount of their sales of ivory, gold, &c. The profits of the Banians would indeed be diminished, but the honest manufacturer would be a gainer in an equal proportion.

It is a well known fact, that even in India, the muslins of British manufacture find a considerable market; and a few pieces of a checked pattern, which I had in Arabia, were universally admired. It is probable, therefore, that, if these were sent out to Aden, they would find a ready sale; as would, I have no doubt, our printed and quilled callicoes. The different articles of hard-ware, which are much wanted by every uncivilized nation, at present, only reach the eastern coast of Africa by the way of Bombay and Mocha, though the estimates, that I have before made, respecting the return of Arabian articles to Europe, show equally, that British manufactures could be carried to Mocha, at a little more than half the price they at present obtain.

The Samaulies, through whose territories the whole produce of the interior of Africa must consequently reach Arabia, have been represented by Mr. Bruce, and many others, as a savage race, with whom it would be dangerous to have connection. I think that this is an unjust accusation, and sufficiently disproved by the extent of their inland trade, their great fairs, and their large exports in their own vessels. A great number of them live close to Mocha, and are a peaceable inoffensive race. Some Indian vessels were wrecked on the coast between Mount Felix and Zeila; the chief immediately seized all the property, but he not only saved the lives of the crews, but maintained them till they were sent to Mocha. This might have led to a closer intercourse, had it not been for the misconduct of the commander of a small vessel, who during the Egyptian expedition, stopped at the same place, and tried to force the chief to bring water on board, without being paid for it. On receiving a civil refusal to this unreasonable request, he sent his people on shore to storm the town. The inhabitants laid an ambush, and cut them all off. The chief immediately wrote a letter to Mr. Pringle, which I saw; in it he professed his good will towards the English, and cited his conduct towards the wrecked mariners as a proof of his not wishing to injure that nation, but stated, that it was out of his power to oblige his people to comply with the unreasonable request of the Captain, and that the destruction of the assailants was only owing to their own misconduct. I fear that this is not a solitary instance, and that on every side of Africa, the natives have occasionally had reason to consider a stranger and an enemy as the same thing.

In their persons the Samaulies are neither Negroes nor Arabs. They have woolly hair, drawn out into points, in every direction, but their noses are not flat. They are finely limbed, with a very dark skin, and beautifully white teeth. The expression of their countenance is neither fierce nor unpleasing. I consulted several of the respectable merchants of Aden and Mocha, respecting the possibility of penetrating into the interior of Africa, by the caravans, which return from Berbera, and they uniformly agreed that, by securing the friendship of one of the Samauli chiefs, and learning the language, an European might, in his own character, make the journey in safety. It would certainly however be more wise that he should pass for a Mussulmaun, but not for an Arab, a nation whom they detest. I think it probable that a trade is carried on westward from Hanim, by which a communication exists with the nations in the vicinity of the mountains of Komri. If so, a traveller might at length reach the sources of the Nile, by departing from Berbera, which is the position nearest to them, that is accessible to Europeans.

The riches of Yemen may be considered as solely owing to its coffee, for it is from the sale of that article, that its merchants receive the dollars in Egypt, with which they purchase the manufactures and spices of India. In former times the balance of bullion, which was remitted to this latter country; amounted to twelve lac of dollars per annum. This year it will not be above two lac, a falling off, which is chiefly owing to the increase of the Muscat merchant vessels, which, under the protection of the neutral flag, carry rice to the isle of France, and bring thence prize goods, which they purchase at half their original cost; by these means, not only injuring the regular trade of Surat and Bombay, but greatly encouraging the privateering of the Isle of France, whose inhabitants would otherwise have no means of disposing of the property they capture. It is even believed, that frequently the Muscat flag is only a cover, and the goods thus exported to Arabia, are bonâ fide, French property. Arabia itself consumes only a small proportion of its imports, the residue, after paying a duty of three per cent. on the import, and seven on the export, is sent, by dows, to Massowah, Jidda, and Aden, for the fair of Berbera. On the returns of gold, and ivory, a very considerable profit is also made by the Banians, who nearly monopolise the whole trade.

The number of these Gentoo merchants, at present resident at Mocha, is about two hundred and fifty; there are also about thirty at Beit-el-Fakih, and fifty at Zebeid. Most of them come from Jeygat, a piratical state at the entrance of the Gulf of Cutch; they come young, and stay till they have made a sufficient property to live comfortably at home. They never bring their wives with them, from a dread of their being insulted by the Arabs: Nothing but the great profits attending their trade, could induce a person of any property to live so wretched a life; yet Devagé, the Company's broker, is considered as sufficiently rich to command three or four lacs of dollars at a moment's notice. The Arabs are perfectly aware of their riches, and frequently extort money from them, particularly when about to return to India. Devagé's brother, who, was, before his departure, the head of the house, escaped on board an English vessel, without having undergone the last squeeze which the Dola intended to give him. Devagé, to avoid punishment, was obliged to prove, that he had been carried on board against his will. The Gentoos live according to their own laws, and show a great obedience to the chief Banian, who acts for them in all public concerns. In private life they are inoffensive and timid; and even their religious prejudice, which prevents their destroying any thing that has life in it, is amiable. As traders, however, it is impossible to speak well of them, for no tie of honesty binds them. One merchant boasted to Mr. Pringle that, in a sale of silk, he had made ten frassels turn out twelve and a half. This, however, was after that gentleman had detected their frauds, and had procured proper weights for the use of the factory.

A very large kind of dow, which is called a Trankey, is employed in the trade between India and Mocha. These vessels have the privilege of not paying any duty to the Imaum, while a ship that lands any part of her cargo, is obliged to pay five hundred dollars, and a brig three hundred. This prevents the vessels that come for coffee, from bringing any articles for sale, as a whole cargo would not be sold under some months, and the profits upon a few pieces of muslin or cloth, would not equal the five hundred dollars. It is however "an old custom, and cannot be changed."

Yemen has probably reached its greatest prosperity, and may indeed be considered as on the decline. The coffee country is gradually falling into the hands of the Sheriffe of Abou Arish, who has become a follower of Abdul Waheb, and has opened the port of Loheia for the exportation of coffee. The Sultaun of Aden also procures a small quantity, and will probably increase his territories at the expence of the Imaum. His port is so far superior to any other in Arabia, that I cannot but believe it will soon become the mart for all that is exported, except to Suez. The rise of Mocha has been owing to accidental circumstances, which now no longer operate, and its trade will probably remove to Loheia and Aden. As the dynasty of the present Imaum may be thus at an end, I have been induced to bring down the history of his family from the time of Mr. Niebuhr, to whose accuracy on this and on every other occasion, I am bound to pay the tribute of approbation.

According to Mr. Niebuhr, in the year 1763, the eleventh Imaum, El Mahadi Abbas, reigned in Sana. His eldest son Abdallah died before him; according therefore to the usual Mussulmaun custom, he was succeeded by his second son Ali, the present Imaum, who assumed the title of Elmansôor, on his accession in the year 1774. El Mahadi Abbas left, beside Ali, the following issue. 3d, Khassem. 4th, Mohammed. 5th, Achmed. 6th,

Yusuff. 7th, Ismael. 8th, Hassan. 9th, Hossein. 10th, Abdulrachman. 11th, Jachia. 12th, Ibrahim. 13th, Soolimaun. 14th, Saduc. 15th, Salauddien. 16th, Saleb. 17th, Yacoub. 18th, Sherifuddien. 19th, Shumsuddien. 20th, Abdulkerim. The present Imaum has only nine sons. 1st, Achmed, 2d, Hassan. 3d, Abdallah. 4th, Mohammed. 5th, Jachia. 6th, Ismael. 7th, Khassem. 8th, Abbas. 9th, Saiid. Achmed has three sons, Khassem, Ibrahim, and Abdallah; while his brother Abdallah has already fifteen. It is supposed that at the death of the Imaum the succession will be disputed by Achmed and Abdallah; the former, though the eldest, is the son of an Abyssinian slave; he is rich, but avaricious, is the favourite of his father, and has great power as commandant of the military force at Sana. The latter is the son of an Arab wife, is in his manner open, in his character liberal, and consequently a great favorite of the soldiers.

The Imaum is, at least, seventy-eight years old, and fast approaching to dotage; he will not hear of any danger, and endeavours still to amuse himself in his sooty harem of four hundred Abyssinian slaves. The Vizier attaches himself to the party of Abdallah, though, before the Imaum, he treats them with equal respect. As the powers of the old man decay, their hostilities become more open, and the Hadje Abdallah informed me, that, during his residence at Sana, they actually drew their jambeas on each other, in their father's presence, but were separated by the Vizier. If, while disputing about the succession, they do not exert themselves to raise a force sufficient to resist the Wahabee, they will have no kingdom to succeed to. The whole disposable force of Yemen did not then exceed six hundred horse, and three thousand foot; not a tenth part of the force that their enterprising enemy could bring against them.

Although Sir Home Popham failed in his attempt to reach Sana, Mr. Pringle, the present acting Resident, has twice visited that capital, without meeting with any insults or difficulties. He informed me that Sana is in latitude 15° 20′ N. and longitude 46° 45′ east of Greenwich, and described the town as handsomely built, and surrounded by gardens. The palace is a residence not unworthy of a prince, and a considerable degree of dignity and splendour is kept up. On his first visit he carried presents to the amount of thirty thousand rupees, in shawls, satins, muslins, and other rich articles for the harem. These were extremely acceptable to the Imaum, and Mr. Pringle's reception was consequently most gracious. On his second visit he unfortunately changed his plan, and took handsome sabres and pistols, which were by no means suited to the present taste of the Imaum. He was however very polite, and even assured Mr. Pringle, that he would issue orders that the French should receive no supplies in any of his ports. Had they actually appeared, I believe that he neither possessed the power, nor the inclination to refuse them.

The difference of climate between the Tehama and the hills of Yemen is so great, as, generally, to produce illness in those who change from one to the other. The air at Sana is cool, and, in the nights, even cold. Grain grows in abundance, and a profusion of fruit adds greatly to the luxuries of the table. A portion of these find their way to Mocha, where I have tasted apples, peaches, apricots, plums, and a variety of grapes. Of the latter, a small kind was particularly admired, which was called kismis, and had no stones.

It has been argued by Mr. Bruce and others, that polygamy is necessary in the East, in consequence of two females being born to one male. I inquired of the Hadje Abdallah if this were true, according to his experience; and he assured me that it was. I confess, however, that I received the information from the Mussulmauns with some doubt, as it is evidently used by them as an argument in support of their law, which gives them the privilege of having more than one wife. Dr. Russell, who, from his long residence at Aleppo, had better opportunities of investigating the truth, not only expresses a strong doubt on the subject, but also gives, in a note, the report of a Maronite priest, who was employed in 1740, to number that nation in Aleppo; by which it appears that there were one thousand five hundred and thirty-three females and one thousand five hundred males; a disproportion that cannot serve as the ground for an argument in favour of polygamy. Mr. Niebuhr also gives several lists, made by the Christian missionaries, of the children annually baptised by them in India; and here the males and females were nearly equal to each other, but rather in favour of the males; and though in the list of those baptised in Persia there are only one hundred and nineteen to one hundred and fifty-one females, yet this difference is far from conclusive, even if it were not supposed to be owing to some accidental circumstance: a conjecture that may by no means appear improbable, when it is observed, how greatly this list differs from the others, taken in equally hot climates, and where polygamy is as common as in Arabia. Were the fact, as asserted by the Mussulmauns, to be proved, I should still doubt whether polygamy was not the cause, instead of the effect, of the birth of the supernumerary females.

It is now above forty years since a new sect started up in Arabia, which has rapidly increased, and is likely to cause a greater change in the political situation of that country, than any event since the time of Mohammed. Abdul Waheb, a private individual, born, according to Niebuhr, in El Aiàne, a town of the district of Darale, in the province of Nedjed-el-Ared, has given his name to his followers, who are from him called Wahabee. This extraordinary man, for many years, studied the sciences in Arabia; and after travelling through Persia, and residing for some time at Basra, returned to his native country and proclaimed himself the reformer of the Mussulmaun religion. The province of Nedjed was at this time divided into a multitude of smaller tribes, each governed by its own Sheik. To these, Abdul Waheb pointed out the abuses which had crept into the Mussulmaun religion, particularly the worshipping of saints, and the use of spirituous liquors and other exhilarating articles. He reprobated the doctrine of the two sects of the Sunnis, with respect to the denying that the Koran was either created, or existing from all eternity, but admitting that it was inspired by God, as a guide for the conduct of mankind. However, as the greater part of the Sheiks were Sunnis, he conciliated them by acknowledging the authority of the sayings of Mohammed. My good friend the Hadje Abdallah, who was avowedly a Wahabee, and was in Mecca at the time it was taken by Suud, gave me their profession of faith, which is as follows.

"There is only one God. He is God; and Mohammed is his Prophet. Act according to the Korân, and the sayings of Mohammed. It is unnecessary for you to pray for the blessing of God on the prophet, oftner than once in you life. You are not to invoke the Prophet to intercede with God in your behalf, for his intercession will be of no avail. At the day of judgment it will avail you. Do not call on the Prophet; call on God alone."

These doctrines rapidly spread among the different tribes, whose power was nearly equal, and tended gradually to the recognition of a supremely controlling power in the person of the Reformer; which completely destroyed the former balance of power, and gave to Abdul Waheb a preponderating influence in the north-east part of Arabia. The Sheiks, who did not acknowledge either his spiritual or temporal power, at length united against him, and, under the command of the Sheik of Lachsa, who was alarmed for his own safety, attacked him in his native city. Abdul Waheb defended himself successfully on this occasion; and on another, when his enemies marched against him with four thousand men. He from this time gradually extended his territories, and his faith. Sheik Mekrami of Nedjeran was one of his most powerful followers, and, according to the conjecture of Mr. Niebuhr, contributed greatly to his prosperity; a circumstance that was confirmed by Hadje Abdallah, who met the Sheik twenty-seven years ago at Mecca, and had much conversation with him.

Abdul Waheb was too able a man to leave neglected any means of increasing the activity of his followers; obeying, therefore, the example of Mohammed, and fully aware of the influence which self-interest has over the human mind, he added to the inducements of religious zeal, the temptation of plunder, by declaring, that all the property belonging to those who were uncoverted, was unholy, and to be confiscated for the use of their conquerors.

Numbers, therefore, to save their property, professed themselves Wahabee before he marched against them, and immediately began to attack their neighbours, in order to oblige them to change their religion, and give up their property. By these means Abdul Waheb secured to himself the supreme power over the whole province of Nedjed, while, by his most powerful servant, Sheik Mekrami, he carried his hostilities into Yemen. On his death he was peaceably succeeded in his spiritual and temporal power by his son Abduluziz.

I have not been able to learn the date of Abduluziz's accession, but he reigned till May 1803, when he was assassinated, while at prayers in a mosque at Darail, his capital, by an Arab, whose daughter he had forcibly carried away from her home many years before. The Arab had immediately sold all his property, and with a patient perseverance followed the footsteps of his oppressor, whom, at length, though his spiritual and temporal sovereign, he sacrificed to his private revenge.

During the reign of Abduluziz, the religion of his father was extended over the greater part of the peninsula of Arabia, either by the arms of his son Suud, or by his followers. Many Arab tribes of the Great Desert also recognized him as their religious head; and even in temporal concerns, indirectly admitted his authority, by remitting him a proportion of their plunder, for charitable purposes, when they took possession of the celebrated burying-place of Hossien at Arbela, and, according to their invariable practice, destroyed his magnificent tomb, so highly venerated by the Persians, and by the other followers of Ali.

The Sheriffe of Abou Arish had, as I have formerly mentioned, been appointed by the Imaum of Sana, Dola of Loheia, where he soon became independent. The different Sheiks, who held many of the districts of Yemen, under a kind of feudal tenure, which admitted the right of the soil to be in the Imaum, but who hardly paid him any thing for it, were encouraged by the success of the Sheriffe of Abou Arish, and threw off even the appearance of obedience. The Imaum was too weak to conquer them; but they had a more powerful opponent in the Wahabee, who soon reduced the Sheriffe of Abou Arish to obedience, and to the necessity of adopting their religion, plundered him of his whole property, and then told him to go and indemnify himself in Yemen. He followed their advice, or rather orders; and, recognizing Suud as his sovereign, carried devastation in his name, to the gates of Mocha. Beit-el-Fakih, and the greater proportion of the coffee country, are his, and Hodeida alone prevents him from securing the Tehama from Loheia to the straits of Bab-el-mandeb. Although this place remains to the Imaum, as a possession, it is useless; since the Dola was obliged to burn the town, to prevent the houses from being occupied in the attack on the forts. In the latter his soldiers remained perfectly safe, as the Wahabee had no cannon; but he will probably soon be obliged to embark, and fly to Mocha in search of food, when Mocha itself must expect to be attacked.

Mecca and Medina have been so long recognized as the two principal cities of Arabia, that the Wahabee who aspired to the sovereignty of the whole country, were particularly anxious to secure them. Galib, the present Sheriffe, is a monster of iniquity, having scrupled no means to accumulate treasure, and having poisoned two Pachas, and a young prince of the Maladives, who came in a vessel of his own to Jidda, on his way to Mecca. He was of course unpopular, and his subjects by no means inclined to defend him. Even his brother-in-law, Mozeifé, had so little confidence in him, that, on being sent on a mission to Daraie, he quitted his own party, and became a Wahabee. Abduluziz, conceiving this a good opportunity to attack the holy cities, early in January 1803, intrusted Mozeifé with the command of twelve thousand men, who fought several battles with his brother-in-law, and constantly defeated him. In February of the same year he laid siege to Tayif.

Galib, who had here his finest palaces and most flourishing gardens, hastened to its relief, and defended it for several days, till his nephew Abdullah secretly retired in the night to Mecca, when, conscious of the detestation in which he was held by his subjects, and dreading lest they should place Abdullah in his stead, he abandoned Tayif, having set his palaces on fire. Mozeifé immediately entered, and his followers commenced their usual devastation. Eight hundred males were put to the sword, but the harems were respected. Many houses were burned, and the whole were plundered; but the treasure of the Sheriffe had been conveyed to Mecca with his wives and followers. All the holy tombs were destroyed, and among them that of Abdullah Ebn Abbas, the uncle of the Prophet, an edifice celebrated throughout Arabia for its pre-eminent beauty and sanctity. The grave itself, and the stone which covered it, were not disturbed. Mozeifé, as a reward for his treachery, was appointed Governor. Abduluziz had no intention that Mecca, Medina, and their sea ports of Jidda and Yambo, should be held by any descendant of the Prophet as a viceroy under him; he therefore sent his eldest son Suud to command the victorious army at Tayif, which marched so unexpectedly against Mecca, on the 26th of April 1803, that the Sheriffe, panic struck, determined to retire, with all his treasures, to Jidda. He effected this in the night, leaving his brother to make the best terms he could with the enemy. On the following day Mecca, for the first time since Mohammed entered it in 629, was obliged to submit to a hostile invader, who, however, strictly conformed to the terms of capitulation, and neither plundered nor injured the inhabitants. The religious prejudices of the Wahabee were greatly offended by above eighty splendid tombs, which covered the remains of the descendants of Mohammed, and formed the great ornament of Mecca. These were levelled with the ground, as was also the monument of the venerable and respected wife of the prophet, Kadija. The coffee houses next felt the desolating zeal of the reformers. The hookahs were piled in a heap, and burned; and the use of tobacco and coffee prohibited under severe penalties. The holy places were plundered of their valuable articles, but the Caaba remained uninjured. The Wahabee have asserted, that the veneration paid to the black stone was idolatrous; and disapproved of the ceremonies practised by the pilgrims at the stone of Abraham, which is placed near the well of Zemzem, and is supposed to have on it the mark of the Patriarch's foot, formed while he stood there to build the Caaba. Into this mark the water is poured from the well, for the pilgrims to drink. Suud seems to have justly estimated the benefits which Mecca enjoyed from the annual influx of pilgrims; he therefore acted with moderation, and confirmed the Cadi whom the Grand Seignior had appointed. He also wrote to him the following letter.

"Suud to Selim.

"I entered Mecca on the 4th day of Moharem, in the 1218th year of the Hejira. I kept peace towards the inhabitants. I destroyed all the tombs which they idolatrously worshipped. I abolished the levying of all customs above two and a half per cent. I confirmed the Cadi, whom you had appointed to govern in the place agreeably to the commands of Mohammed. I desire that, in the ensuing years, you will give orders to the Pachas of Shaum, Syria, Misr, and Egypt, not to come accompanied by the Mahamel,* trumpets, and drums, into Mecca and Medina. For why? religion is not profited by these things. Peace be between us, and may the blessing of God be unto you! Dated on the 10th day of Moharem." This answers to our 3d of May.

On the 11th of May Suud marched against Jidda; but the delay at Mecca had given time to the Sheriffe to prepare for his reception, by bringing on shore all the cannon from the vessels in the harbour, and planting them on the walls. An attempt was made by the Wahabee to storm the town, but it failed; Suud, however, contrived to cut off all supplies, even of water; in consequence of which numbers perished by thirst, in the nine days that the blockade continued; and at length the Sheriffe was forced by the inhabitants to offer a sum of money to Suud, on condition of his abandoning the siege. The arrangements were actually made for the payment of a lac and thirty thousand dollars, when the intelligence arrived of the death of Abduluziz, which induced Suud to return instantly to Daraie, lest any rival should dispute the succession. Jidda was thus saved, and even Mecca fell

* The richly ornamented covering for the Caaba.

again under the controul of the Sheriffe; but Tayif, the most lovely spot in Arabia, a spot so unlike the surrounding country, that the Arabs believe it to have been a part of Syria, detached and dropped during the general deluge, still remained in the hands of Mozeifé.

In 1804 Medina, with its treasure, which had accumulated for ages by the donations of the faithful, became a prey to the Wahabee: and the tomb of the Prophet shared the fate of those of his descendants. Jidda was again attacked, but without success, as the Sheriffe had received supplies from Egypt. Yambo fell, but was retaken on the sea side. The Pacha of Syria forced his way through the undisciplined troops of Suud, and the usual ceremonies were performed by the Faithful at the holy Caaba; probably for the last time; for the numerous hordes of the Wahabee now cover the Desert with their flying squadrons, and render a passage too dangerous to be attempted.

The Johassen Arabs, who acknowledge the religious supremacy of Suud, have occasionally entered the Red Sea, and, should they obey his call, and appear with their powerful naval force before Jidda, resistance would be unavailing, and the descendants of the Prophet would cease to reign in Arabia. The Imaum of Muscat has perished in battle, and his son is said to be under the control of a Wahabee guardian. Yemen has no natural means of resisting the vast power of her opponent, and must sink under the imbecility of her government. In the vast peninsula of Arabia, the little state of Aden alone offers any rational means of resistance to the power of the Wahabee, by the wisdom of her sovereign, and the bravery of his little army. Gratitude calls upon the British to prevent his ruin; for to them he has ever been an attached and useful ally. During the expedition to the Red Sea, his port was open to them; and, on General Murray's quitting Perim, the British troops were, with an unbounded confidence, admitted within his walls. On the appearance of the Johassen fleet in his harbour, in 1804, while a large Surat vessel was lying there, he sent his soldiers on board to protect her from the pirates, and obliged them to put to sea, without receiving any supplies, though they offered him the half of the plunder they had already made, if he would permit them to remain. These repeated acts of friendship now call for a return, which it is perfectly in the British power to afford.

The Wahabee, conscious of their want of arms and ammunition, and fully convinced of the benefit they would receive from a trade being opened between India and their ports, have made repeated offers to the Bombay Government, of granting immunities and exclusive privileges to the British merchants, if they would establish a factory at Loheia; they would therefore willingly comply with any request in favour of the Sultaun of Aden as an ally of the British, and would, with little regret, give up an attack on a power, whom they have hitherto found capable of resisting them.

No answer has yet been given to the applications of the Wahabee; and the Bombay Government behold, without concern, a revolution, which is again connecting the disunited Arabs under one supreme master. It is a circumstance well worthy of remark, that this has, for the first time since the death of Ali, occurred at a moment, when the surrounding kingdoms of Asia and Africa are sunk into the same state of imbecility and distraction, to which they were reduced under the Romans, when the dissolute and lukewarm Christians were obliged to yield to the ardent and zealous followers of Mohammed.

Low as the power of the Turkish empire is now fallen, I do not expect that the Wahabee will completely prevail against it, unless, by a communication with Europeans, they obtain supplies of arms and ammunition, and, with them, learn a proportion of European discipline. I consider Arabia, however, as lost for ever to the Sultaun; and, consequently, that he has ceased to be the head of the Mussulmaun religion. The order of Mohammed, that his followers should, once in their lives, visit Mecca, can no longer be performed. The sacred city has heard the dim of hostile arms, and is in possession of a Prince who denies to Mohammed that veneration which he has received for twelve hundred years. His descendants will soon cease to reign; and although the Korân may be revered for a longer period throughout a portion of Asia, the mighty fabric of Islamism must be considered as having passed away, from the moment that Suud entered Mecca on the 27th of April, 1803.

CHAPTER IX.

Proceedings at Mocha during my absence.—Massacre of the officers of the Alert by the Arab crew.—Survey and condemnation of the Assaye.—Disputes with the Dola.—Captain Court's survey of the Straits of Bab-el-mandeb and the neighbouring islands.—Incorrectness of Sir Home Popham's chart.—Observations on the Factory.—Preparations for the visit to Abyssinia.—Departure of Mr. Salt, Captain Rudland, Mr. Carter and their attendants for Abyssinia.—Arrival of Captain Barton from Suez.—Conduct of the Americans.—Incursions of the Wahabee.—Alarm at Mocha.—Conduct of the Dola.—Arrival of two vessels under Seid Mohammed Akil from the Isle of France.—Departure from Mocha.—Visit to Ait.—Arrival at Massowah.—Return of Mr. Salt with the Baharnegash.

ON my return to Mocha, it was with very great pain I discovered that an unfortunate attachment to spirituous liquors, brought on originally by the solitude of the Factory, had so greatly gained on Mr. Pringle, that, instead of conducting himself with the prudence and discretion, which had heretofore conciliated the natives, and given respectability to the British character, he had, during my absence, thrown every thing into confusion, and was on the worst of terms with Devagé and the Dola.

Soon after my departure, a letter was received by Mr. Pringle from the Nakib, or native chief, of Macullah, informing him, that he had detained in his harbour a vessel which had entered under Arab colours, but which he had discovered to be English; that the Arab part of the crew had risen on the officers, had murdered them all, and had piratically changed the destination of the vessel. The Nakib concluded with professions of esteem for the English nation, and desired Mr. Pringle to send some person to Macullah, to receive and take charge of the property. Captain Benzoni, a respectable Italian, who had been in the service of Seid Mohammed Akil, but was discharged by him because, as Captain, he would not take a false oath that a ship, which the Seid had intentionally run on shore to cheat the underwriters at Bombay, was lost by stress of weather, was then at Mocha, and was immediately sent down to Macullah, with a letter to the Nakib.

Mr. Pringle, nevertheless, made a bargain with an American captain, to carry him there in his way home, and followed Benzoni, who had in the mean time prepared the ship for sea, which proved to be the Alert, from Bengal, loaded with rice and piece goods. The Nakib had immediately given Captain Benzoni possession of the ship, and had assured him that he would account for the rice, which he had landed and consumed. Mr. Pringle, however, on his arrival, was seized with a groundless panic, and ran away in the night, without concluding any arrangement with the Nakib. He next proceeded to Aden, with the Arab colours hoisted below the English, to the great mortification of the Sultaun, whom he abused and threatened. The Alert had very little water, her casks were therefore landed for a supply; but in the night Mr. Pringle again moved off, leaving them behind. On reaching Mocha, he remonstrated with the Dola for his former ill conduct, and threatened to fire on the town. Fortunately he did not carry his folly so far, and he was brought to his senses by discovering, that he had neither water nor provisions on board. He was obliged to hoist signals of distress, when the Dola permitted him to receive supplies, and at length to return to the Factory.

Immediately on my arrival, the Dola, and the Banian of the Sultaun of Aden, waited on me, to complain of the conduct of Mr. Pringle, and I felt it my duty to assure them, that nothing could be more contrary to the orders of the India Government, than the whole of his proceedings. He was indeed perfectly convinced of this himself, and, as his many amiable qualities had now recovered their former influence, a reconciliation was established without difficulty: poor Devagé was deeply incensed; nor could I do more than induce him to come to the Factory on business while I was there; Mr. Pringle having, in one of his fits, struck him on the cheek with the sole of his slipper, the deepest insult that can be offered to an Asiatic, among whom it is considered as a mark of disrespect to show even the sole of the foot.

The Assaye was surveyed by the officers and the carpenters of the American ships; who reported, that the whole of her iron-works were totally decayed, her timbers deficient in number, and together with her bows and upper works, very bad, her bottom worm eaten, and rotten, and not a bolt to be discovered in her; they therefore declared it was impossible for her to go again to sea. It is really astonishing how Mr. Sutherland, and the committee of survey, could have reported her fit for the service of the marine, since she could not have been in a much worse state than when she entered the Red Sea. I reported the circumstances to Lord Wellesley, Mr. Duncan, and Captain Money, the new superintendent of marine; and as Mr. Maxfield was now thrown out of his command, and his crew were to be returned to Bombay, I suggested to Mr. Pringle the eligibility of their being turned over, marines and all, to the Alert, and that the Assaye should be broken up. This was agreed to; and on the 2d of April, Mr. Maxfield entered on his new command, and began to prepare for sea. On the 8th arrived the Company's cruizer Princess Augusta, Captain Bennett, having on board my friend Captain Sparks, as commissioner to Macullah, for the recovery of the Alert, dispatched by the Government of Bombay, who had learned the fate of this ship, by the means of a Banian at Muscat. The owners had turned her over to the underwriters, who had appointed Messrs. Forbes their agents at Bombay, by whose authority a Captain Loan was deputed to take the command. Mr. Maxfield was of course superseded, but, with Captain Court's permission, returned to Bombay with my dispatches for the Government there, and for his excellency the Governor General. He also took rough drafts of our discoveries, which Captain Court had paid me the highly flattering compliment of dedicating to me. Mr. Hurst being an acting Lieutenant, I thought it would be pleasanter for him to return, than to do duty with us as a midshipman; I therefore exchanged him for an officer of the Augusta of the name of Denton, who was reported by Mr. Criddle to be a friend of his, and of whom Captain Court spoke favourably. He turned out a fine, manly lad, who had been educated at Eton.

Captain Sparks declined settling the accounts of the Alert, with which he was by no means satisfied, the expence of bringing her up, and preparing her for sea, amounting to five thousand dollars. As he was also not quite convinced, that Mr. Pringle was right in leaving Macullah in the way he did, without settling with the Nakib, he thought it his duty to return to that place. Mr. Pringle determined to accompany him in the Augusta, he having engaged Captain Bennett to return to Mocha, and convoy the trade to Bombay in August. The underwriters had sent about ten thousand rupees in presents for the Nakib; but as it was evident he had so large a sum in his hands, Captain Sparks disposed of the articles here. I purchased two telescopes, and some pieces of muslin. I again wrote fully to the Governor General respecting Arabia, and the Red Sea, and took the liberty of suggesting that Mr. Maxfield should be sent back in a small vessel, to survey the outside of the shoals from Jibbel Tier to Macowar, and the coast thence to Cosseir.

The arrival of so many English had driven the Americans from the Factory; we had to regret the absence of Captain Bancroft, but certainly it was not decorous that so large a party should live at the expence of the East India Company, as they had hitherto done, even during Mr. Pringle's absence at Macullah.

Though the Dola and I were on most friendly terms, it was not possible for him to leave off his old tricks of seducing our seamen. Lynch, a Mulatto, who was formerly Captain Vashion's cook, but who, having ran away from him, was now a seaman of the Princess Augusta, and Gardner, a marine boy, were reported this morning as being in the Dola's house. I was on the Pier when I heard of it, and returned to the Factory by the Square, Gardner scrambled over a wall, and came running towards me, followed by several of the Dola's people. He conjured me to protect him, declaring that he had no intention to turn Mussulmaun; that the night before he had been drinking in the Jews' town, and that he knew not how he had been carried to the Dola's; that on awaking he had requested to be liberated, but without success, and that Lynch had endeavoured to persuade him to stay. The Dola's servants were unwilling to use force to carry him back, while I was present; I therefore got him safe into the Factory. The Dola was a little ashamed, and pretended he knew nothing of the business. The ships sailed this day, leaving me to act as Resident at Mocha.

Messrs. Forbes having again obtained a contract from the Bombay Government, to supply them with two thousand bales of Mocha coffee, had sent one of their confidential servants, Mohammed Ali, to superintend the purchase. The Wahabee having in a great degree cut off the supply from Mocha, Mr. Pringle determined to comply with the request of the Dola of Hodeida to send there and purchase. On Mohammed Ali's attempting to embark, he was put in irons by the Emir Bahar. I instantly sent to the Dola to demand his release as a British subject, and to ask by what right he prevented any of our nation from going where they pleased. He immediately liberated the man, who he said had been arrested by mistake; but added, that he had positive orders from the Imaum, not to permit any one to go to Hodeida;

that, as he was but a servant, and must act as he was ordered, he hoped I would not be angry with him. I believe he spoke truth, and consequently felt no resentment against him; but as I considered the Imaum's orders as a violation of the neutral privileges of the British flag, I thought it my duty to send off a dow to Aden, where she would certainly overtake the Alert, communicating the whole business to the Governor General of India and Mr. Duncan. It would seem, from the conduct of the Imaum, that he considered Hodeida as lost to him; or determined, in spite of all difficulties, to keep up the old custom of not permitting any coffee to be exported through the Straits, except from Mocha.

The Americans by no means felt themselves bound by the orders of the Dola. There were no less than eleven vessels of this nation in the harbour; for, as each captain kept his destination a profound secret, they were not aware of the intentions of each other. The arrival of so many vessels raised the price to fifty dollars per bale, and only about one hundred and fifty bales a week were procurable, chiefly from Oudien, in consequence of the conquests of the Wahabee in the neighbourhood of Beit-el-Fakih. The Americans have a private agreement, by which each ship purchases in rotation, according to the time of her arrival. A captain, whose turn would not arrive these ten months, sailed to the northward, evidently to Hodeida, or Loheia. The adventurers of the present season must have found themselves in a very different situation from their predecessors; for, independently of paying nearly double the price for their coffee, as they had only money enough to lay in half a cargo, the expences of freight would be double also. Many had suffered even more severely, having been obliged to quit without any coffee, and to seek for a cargo elsewhere.

I do not know whether it be of much consequence, as Yemen is changing masters, that the Americans are spoiling the road of Mocha by throwing over their ballast. The evil has already become great, for there is now no clear spot, under four fathom, and at a great distance from the shore. In another season not a ship will be able to anchor in safety. Mr. Pringle spoke to the Dola about it; but he did not seem to consider it as of any consequence.

The southerly gales moderated on the 25th of April, and gave us an opportunity of getting fresh ballast on board the Panther, preparatory to her going to the Straits of Bab-el-mandeb, which I wished to examine during the present leisure time.

Captain Court returned from his cruize, having completed his survey, and discovered more errors in Sir Home Popham's chart, than even the leaving out of Jibbel Anish had given reason to expect. These will appear most plainly by a comparison between the two charts; but to those who may have no such opportunity, I will only observe, that the actual distance between the Island of Perim, and the nearest part of Africa, is ten miles and a half, instead of sixteen, as laid down by Sir Home Popham; that the distance between the two shores in latitude 13° is only thirty-five miles, instead of fifty-two; and that there exists a shoal in that latitude, which narrows the channel to fifteen miles, and which is entirely omitted by Sir Home Popham. This latter error is as unaccountable, as it is dangerous; for the shoal lies in the direct course between the Straits and Mocha, and was actually discovered, during the expedition in the Red Sea, by the Antelope cruizer, upon which she was nearly lost.

I took advantage of Mr. Pringle's absence to regulate the Factory, and introduce a reformation among the Arab servants, who are the worst in the world; stealing every thing which lies in their way. Not half the articles issued for daily use at the Factory were actually employed. The meat sent away from the table vanished in a moment, so that our European servants could rarely get any. Sugar, flour, fruit, were fair plunder; even wine and pork were not safe from these harpies. They came in a morning just before breakfast, and, so soon as they had secured the remains, they disappeared, and returned again when dinner was ready. They waited at table, indeed, but it was only till the meat was removed, and the cloth taken away, when they divided the spoils. This, however, I remedied, by having the dishes placed on a side table till we had quite finished. Much dissatisfaction was at first expressed; but I carried the business through triumphantly by the assistance of the Dola, who directed that any servant, on my complaint, should be put in prison. Indeed, on every occasion, where the orders of his master left him at liberty, I uniformly found him extremely obliging.

The British Factory has a pleasant view from the upper windows, but the ruins of a house in front keep off the breeze from the lower apartments. The Dola's stables are also a great evil, from the excuse which it gives to his followers, to be lurking about the door, and endeavouring to seduce the seamen who come on shore, to go and drink at the Jew's town, which so frequently leads to desertion. The danger of fire is great, from the vicinity of these buildings, which consist of wood and mats. If once they should be in flames, it would be impossible to save the Factory and its contents, which, at some seasons, are valuable. The building itself must also be replaced by the Company, as it is obliged at present to do all repairs, paying only five hundred dollars, instead of a thousand, when the landlord took these on himself.

If the stables were removed, and the ground on which they stand, together with that of the ruined house, converted into a garden, the comfort and respectability of the Factory would be greatly increased, and the danger of seducing the seamen diminished. But Arabia seems too much neglected; her trade is considered as of little value, if not as an incumbrance; and her rapidly rising political consequence is overlooked. The guard of sepoys, which formerly protected the gates of the Factory, is removed, and the Resident is obliged to employ Arabs in his establishment, who are the licensed spies of the Dola. Though the consequence of Arabia, in a commercial and political view, may at length force itself on the British Government, it is improbable that Mocha will continue to be the residence of its Factor, since Aden and Loheia offer infinitely greater advantages. I hope, however, that wherever her Factory be established, it will be placed on a footing worthy of the British name.

I received a letter from Currum Chund, saying that he had forwarded my message to the Ras Welleta Selassé, who had sent the accompanying answer. This was in Arabic, expressing his wish that I would come up myself, or send some one to him; but it seemed doubtful whether he had not confounded me with Mr. Pringle the Resident at

Mocha, as the address would suit either, or rather neither, of us. As, however, I considered it an object of the greatest importance, as well as interest, to obtain some positive information of the state of a country, which during a century had been visited only by Mr. Bruce, I determined to send Mr. Salt, with such presents as I could procure at Mocha. Captain Rudland and Mr. Carter having expressed a wish to accompany Mr. Salt, I consented most willingly; and every thing was hurry and preparation for their departure, as the season was so far advanced, and it was necessary they should be back by the end of October to take advantage of the monsoon, which is for so short a time favourable in the upper part of the Red Sea.

On consulting Captain Court and the rest of our party, it was decided that they should go up to Massowah in the Panther, to protect them from the impertinence of the Dola of Arkeko, and to give them more importance in the eyes of the natives; and that Captain Court might afterwards examine the north of Dhalac. Andrew, a renegado boy, who had formerly attempted to escape to the Fox frigate, was, nevertheless, permitted by the Dola to attend Mr. Salt as his servant. He spoke good English, Hindostané, and tolerable Arabic. An Arab, by name Hamed Chamie, was hired to act as interpreter, a very respectable man, born at Mecca, and for some time in the service of Mr. Pringle. When he applied to the Dola for leave, he sent Devagé to me to ask who would be answerable for the Arab, if the natives put him in prison. I assured him he should have the same protection from the Panther that Mr. Salt and the other gentlemen had. With this he was perfectly satisfied. A dow was sent off with letters for the

Ras and Currum Chund, announcing my intentions.

The Augusta having returned with Mr. Pringle, I learned by a letter from Captain Sparks, that as the S. W. monsoon was set in, it was unsafe to carry the ship to Macullah, which was open to that point, though admirably protected from the opposite; that they proceeded thither in their boats from Broom bay, where they anchored. The Nakib was extremely civil. He restored fifty bales of broad cloth, and other articles, to the amount of half a lac, and debited himself six thousand dollars for rice. He declared, that he had received from the ship no other goods. This was probably false, as a large quantity of blue, scarlet, and green cloth, had found its way to Mocha, where it sold for three dollars the gudge. He made a demand of five thousand five hundred dollars for the expences of Ascari and men on board. Had Mr. Pringle staid and settled with him, it is probable a much greater proportion of the goods would have been recovered, as they were not then sold. Captain Sparks considered the Nakib's conduct as altogether meritorious for an Arab. He had given the first intelligence of the ship's being there; had professed the greatest regard for the English nation; and had tried to secure the murderers. He had willingly given the ship to Benzoni, when he arrived at Macullah alone, and unsupported: he had not stolen so much as he might have done, and possibly not even so much as we suspected; for those about him might have plundered unknown to him. Captain Sparks, therefore, made him a present of the five hundred dollars balance, and they parted excellent friends on the 27th, when the Alert set sail for Bombay, and the Augusta for Mocha. The length of her voyage was owing to light airs, and strong adverse currents. At one time Captain Bennett feared he should be obliged to bear away for Bombay, which he wished to avoid, as the Augusta is a grab, and ill adapted for the heavy sea that breaks on the Malabar coast in the S. W. monsoon. Yet the Company's Marine Board have had three built; the Queen, Princess Royal, and Princess Augusta, though so perfectly conscious of their defects, that they are regularly laid up at Massagong during the rainy monsoon.

The waste of wine had been so great in the Factory, and on board the Alert, during our absence, that there was every reason to fear we should soon be totally destitute of every liquor, except indifferent spirits. By reducing ourselves to a short allowance, we hoped to have some till August, when possibly our wants might be relieved from Bombay, whither we had written to state our situation on board the Panther, and to request, if possible, a supply of necessaries for the ship, such as biscuit and spirits; the latter were procurable here only from Mr. Pringle, at a monstrous price, and the former at a still greater. Our boat was also nearly worn out, and several naval stores were wanting. Mr. Pringle wrote to one of the tradesmen to send a large assortment of things for the Factory, almost sufficient to load a vessel. However, in the mean time, we tried what we could procure from the Americans. One captain admitted he had ten pipes of Madeira on board, but said it was meant for his owner's private use, and that therefore he could not venture to sell it but at a very high price, a price that would justify his violation of orders. At length he wrote to say, that on his return it would be worth at Boston six or eight dollars per gallon, but that he would let us have a cask at one thousand dollars. The impudence of this assertion in the first part of the letter, could only be equalled by the folly of sending, at the same time, a Boston newspaper, in which were the current prices of every article at that port. I there found that London Particular Madeira was between three and four dollars per gallon, after the duty was paid. It was mentioned as plentiful, and a dull sale. Now this wine certainly was not London Particular, for I knew that ten pipes of that quality were not sent to all America in the course of the year. But even if they had, the profit was most enormous; nearly three hundred pounds for what cost forty three pounds. Convinced that it was a mean attempt to take advantage of our situation, to which we had been reduced by entertaining his countrymen, I positively refused to have any thing to do with it.

A few days afterwards a Portuguese ship arrived direct from Lisbon. I made application to them, and offered the enormous price of five hundred dollars for a pipe of port. The captain very liberally answered that he had no wine for sale, but that he would give us all he could possibly spare, taking an order on Bombay for a similar quantity. What a contrast to the American!!! I respect a merchant; I consider him as one of the great props of our nation: but when every idea of honour and liberality is absorbed in the pursuit of profit, he becomes one of the most despicable of animals; and if his country should adopt his principles, it must inevitably sink into insignificance. Of this, Holland has been an awful example; and if America does not take care, her decline will follow with still greater rapidity.

On the 18th a brig arrived from Suez, bringing

dispatches for India, from Major Misset, the British Consul General in Egypt. In his letter to Mr. Pringle, he mentioned that two French fleets had made their escape from the ports of France, and it was feared their destination might be India. He also forwarded dispatches that had arrived from Malta. However ill adapted for the sea the Augusta might be, it was thought necessary, as she was here, to send her off immediately: she sailed at four this morning. By her I wrote to my friends in England, and to Government. The Dola had received a letter from the Imaum, approving of his having stopped Mr. Forbes's servant; it now, therefore, became an act of the Government. I laid every thing before Lord Wellesley, and hoped that he would permit me to redress the evil.

By Captain Barton, who commanded the brig, I learned that the troubles in Egypt had induced Major Misset to remove to Rosetta, but that his agent was at Cairo. He assured me that the passing to that place from Suez was as safe as it ever was. The report of there being a British army at Alexandria was false, but had originated from Lord Nelson's appearing off that place. This was a great relief to my mind, and made me look forward with pleasure to my travels in Egypt.

On the 20th Mr. Salt, and the rest of the Abyssinian party, went on board, provided with presents for the King, and Ras, and with such conveniencies for their journey as the circumstances of our situation would allow.

The dow that we had sent to Massowah, and which was to have continued there, to attend Captain Court in his survey, returned with letters from the Nayib to Mr. Pringle and Devagé, and also with letters from Currum Chund to me and Mr. Pringle. In the former, beside repetitions and extraneous matter, he observed, that he did not yet wish me to send my people; that he had not given his consent to their going: and, without his permission, who could enter Habesh? For "was not he the gates of it?" That he must consult his brothers and soldiers, and would send the result by Currum Chund, who would be here next month. Currum Chund wrote and advised me to wait till his arrival, when my messengers might return with him; that in the mean time, he would arrange every thing with the Nayib; but that if I sent them now, the Nayib would want five or six hundred dollars for permission.

The Panther had sailed, but the wind was contrary. I sent off a cutter early, but by neglect the boat was not ready till it was too late. The American boat tried to overtake them, but in vain. The loss of the dow would have been a serious inconvenience to Captain Court, and it was advisable he should know my sentiments on this new occurrence; I therefore sent Unus after him with letters, who would probably overtake him before he reached Massowah, and would stay with him. I stated, that it was evidently a trick, of the Dola of Arkeko, to get money from the messengers, under the idea that they would arrive there in a dow unprotected; that I thought, when they saw the Panther, every thing would be well; but that, if not, I recommended their urging to the Nayib, that if he were the gates of Habesh, I was the gates of Massowah; and that if he shut the one against me, I could shut the other, by not letting a single dow enter the place. I left it to their discretion how they should act; but said I would give no present till my messengers returned. I felt perfectly easy, knowing that Captain Court would act in unison with Mr. Salt, in any transactions which might occur. We had this morning an alarm of the Wahabee, but it proved to be only some plundering Bedowee who had wounded a man at a village close to the town. The Dola immediately set off with his horse and infantry, but the robbers had fled.

July 5.—Was celebrated by the Americans as the anniversary of their Independence. On this occasion they obtained the Dola's permission to hoist their colours on their house. Mr. Pringle asked the Dola if an American factory were established here, and whether the Imaum had entered into any treaty with that nation. He said no; that the Imaum knew nothing about it; that he had permitted it for one day only. That, as a nation, they knew not America; but that the merchants here had promised to bring, next year, the proper presents from their Government to the Imaum and Dola, and to establish an American Factory and Resident. That the Imaum wished to encourage all traders coming to his port. He asked Mr. Pringle if he wished it not to be done. He said that he could have no objection to it, or to the Americans trading here; he only wished to know if they had a Factory, that he might communicate it to his Government. I was much amused by a few merchants making promises for their Government, which they must know would never be performed. Mr. Jefferson and his party are not so fond of trade, or Massachusetts, as to put the nation to the expence of one hundred thousand dollars to serve them.

The alarms respecting an attack of Mocha by the Sheriffe of Abou Arish gained ground. The Banian at Loheia had written to Devagé to give him notice of it, and to advise him to be on his guard. The Sheriffe was said to have at least fifteen thousand soldiers. We had then at Mocha about four hundred and fifty, as some arrived with an escort of coffee from Oudien on the 7th, and were detained. A few more came in on the 10th, wretched looking animals, and rather injurious than serviceable, as provisions were extremely scarce. If the Wahabee had surrounded the town, in a week there would have been an absolute famine among the common people. Fruit had been very scarce, and of grapes we had had no supply during the last fortnight. The weather had been extremely sultry; calm in the day time; the thermometer 90° to 95°; at night occasionally a strong breeze from the north. One night we had a wind as hot as at Lucknow, which drove us all from the upper apartments to the rooms that could be shut up. It lasted about an hour. Hadje Abdallah told us it was the true Simoom, which blows all day at Mecca during the summer months.

On the 15th in the evening the Wahabee carried off seventy camels, loaded with coffee and goods, between this place and Moosa. The garrison was immediately ordered out, but returned the next morning, bringing in with them only one lame camel. The party they went after being too powerful for them to attack, they contrived to go a wrong road. Two Ascari were put in prison for cowardice.

The Dola's new soldiers quarrelled with him, and marched off. There had been no provision of grain in the bazar for some days, and the people were in the utmost distress. The American Captain Elkins, who was in Mocha last year, arrived on the 10th. He found the markets strangely altered for the worse, and knew not what to do. He brought some pumps for Mr. Pringle, which the Dola refused to let pass; a black renegado having informed him, that they were instruments used by the English for drowning a country. He said such things were never seen there before, and he must write to the Imaum on the subject.

The weather for the last three weeks had been very pleasant, the nights being perfectly cool. The wind had been chiefly west, which comes from Habesh, where the tropical rains are in all their force, and had then to pass over the sea. If it change to the east for half an hour, the heat becomes very great. It is nearly as bad from the south, there not being a sufficiency of sea to cool it after passing the burning deserts of Africa. On the 24th we had a heavy squall in the night, when our friends the Portuguese lost an anchor.

The Dola sent above half the garrison a few days before to Moosa, to bring in juwarry. They brought thirty camels' load, which vanished in a moment. He charged three dollars and a half escort money for each camel. This is one way of living on the distress of the country. The poor people have nothing but dates and fish, and not plenty of these.

The Portuguese ship Rosalia sailed on the 26th. Captain de Costa supplied us with five quarter-casks of Port, and took an order on Bombay for the same quantity. He also gave me some oil and some sweetmeats from Rio de Janeiro. I wrote by him to my friends in Europe, to the Governor General, and to Mr. Duncan, to whom I particularly recommended all the officers. We sent by her eight hundred bales of coffee for Mr. Forbes, and took dollars to the amount of fifty thousand on an advantageous exchange to them; so that they would be no losers by their touching here.

The Americans buy their coffee without cleaning, and some of the worst quality; what we take is good. Six ships were there at that time, and Captain Elkins assured me six more were on their passage. He made last year two hundred per cent.

The Naqueda of a dow from Massowah said that seventeen days ago the Panther was there; that at first the Dola made objections to the gentlemen going into Habesh, but that every thing was settled. They had agreed to pay what was customary, and he had made himself responsible for their safety. The soldiers, he added, were all ready to escort them. From this account I hoped they were on their way. It accorded too well with what we knew to be fact, to be all an invention.

July 31.—The Dola sent to prison every dealer in grain, till they should pay him two dollars each for the active exertions of himself and soldiers, in keeping off the Wahabee!!!

On the 28th it rained so heavily as to penetrate the upper apartments, and drive us below. The Dola's stables, which were thatched, sunk under it. The lightning was vivid, and the thunder loud; a dow was struck, and some damage done near the town. It had, for three days, being extremely close in the morning, till about eleven, when the sea breeze set in. After the rain the thermometer was at 80°.

On the 30th, another American, Captain Lee, arrived. He sailed before Captain Elkins, and therefore brought no news, but was so kind as to share with us his Madeira. He thought there were fourteen more ships coming here!

The Emir Bahar, who had offended every one as well as myself, had been turned out of office. The soldiers were again gone to Moosa to bring in a cargo of provisions.

The Dola had notified to Captain Lee that the Imaum had appointed a brother of Seid Mahommed Akil, agent to the Americans, and a Banian, to transact their business, having prohibited the others from selling to them under a penalty of five thousand dollars. This was partly done to annoy Mr. Pringle, but still more to benefit himself, by the large presents he exacts from the Seids. Captain Elkins had brought this on the Americans, by his requesting that some one, besides Devagé, might be permitted to buy for them. He thought they should, by having an option of brokers, get it cheaper than from Mr. Pringle, who let them have it at thirty-five dollars, instead of which it was now up at fifty-two; and they were more exposed to suffer from a monopoly than ever. The price was not likely to fall, and the trade was exposed to ruin. The Dola sent to tell me what had been done: I answered, that I was very happy to hear it, as I disliked the Imaum, for his conduct to the English, and that this act would punish him, by ruining his trade. He replied, that he hoped I was mistaken; but if not, it was no fault of his, as he had positive orders from Sana on the subject. I desired Captain Benzoni to ask him, in confidence, respecting Mr. Pringle's pumps. He declared, he thought them very dangerous things; that all the brass on the inside could be meant for no good. Captain Benzoni explained to him their real use; but he said he had written to Sana, and hoped; if the Imaum bought them, that Captain Benzoni would go and put them up.

Our Suakin friend, Emir Mohammed, arrived on the 5th with letters from Captain Court and Mr. Salt, which were on the whole satisfactory. He also brought a letter from the

Nayib. Captain Court had been extremely civil to him, and had saluted him on his coming on board; with which he was highly pleased. They were in great distress at Massowah for provisions. The Emir dined with us on the 5th, and brought eight of his friends, who were very little at their ease. He said he had dined with us before, and was quite comfortable; so it seemed, for he devoured a prodigious quantity. He had brought slaves and gold. Since we saw him he had been at Senaar. He told me that country was in great confusion; that there had been four different sovereigns within three years: when deposed they are put to death, as Bruce describes, by one of their relations. He said, he could not be responsible for the safety of an European, who should go with him, as none have ever travelled that way, and the people are wild. I determined to pay him every attention, to conciliate the friendship of his powerful tribe.

The Panther was in sight on the 15th to the southward, but the wind being fresh from the north, and the current very strong in the same direction, she made but little way on that day, she was obliged to come to an anchor, just as she reached the sand heads. Captain Court sent on shore letters from Mr. Salt, dated from Dixan, which gave me the pleasing intelligence of his having reached in safety that frontier of Habesh.

Captain Court landed on the 16th.* On the 17th another American ship arrived, commanded by Captain Rowe, whom I had seen before. He fortunately brought some flour for Mr. Pringle, which he turned over to the Panther. Knowing how very anxious Mr. Salt must be to hear of us,

* For an account of his voyage, vide Appendix.

and wishing to write to the Ras respecting his safe return, I spoke to Unus Barilla on the subject, who offered to convey a letter from a town by Amphila, where he had a wife, without its going through any part of the Nayib's territories. It was an important object to find another way to Habesh; I therefore agreed with him, and he was to set off that evening.

Seid Mahommed Akil arrived, with two very fine vessels, from the Isle of France on the 24th: one is the Pigeon, an English prize; the other a country ship, the Peggy, which he purchased on the Malabar coast. The Seid is a descendant of Hossein-ebn-Ali, by Fatima, the daughter of Mohammed, and carries on trade. He hoists a green flag with a red border. I could not comprehend him. He had a quantity of arms and ammunition on board. His captains were French, and it was said, that he had brought assurances from the Isle, that a French resident would arrive in October. Last year he was a violent Wahabee, but this year he declared himself merely a merchant, and of no party whatsoever. He has either sold, or given to the Dola twelve short six pounders, and some shot, for a new fort which he has erected to the north of the town, and to which he means to retire in case of a siege. I suspected the ship and all that it contained to be French property, and that the Arab flag was only a cover.

I was excessively hurt by the intelligence that an American boy, who had entered in the Panther from another ship, and of whom Captain Court had a very high opinion, had run to the Dola's house. He had by an accident broken his arm, in consequence of which he had remained on shore during the last trip, and been treated with the greatest kindness. His conduct therefore was unaccountable. Captain Court applied immediately to have permission to see him, which was granted, but in the Dola's presence. On first addressing the boy, the Dola interrupted Captain Court, by observing, that he had no business to say any thing, but to put the simple question, whether or no the boy were inclined to turn Mussulmaun. This Captain Court resented in high terms, and persevered in pointing out to him the madness of which he was guilty. The old Italian renegado attempted to answer his arguments; but was instantly silenced by Captain Court in the most peremptory terms. The lad, without hesitation, consented to return to us, on which they tried to hustle him out of the room; but the Captain declared he should go with him, and immediately quitted the house.

August 28.—We had another dispute with the Dola. A Lascar had left the ship, but was met by the Serang, who, with an officer, Mr. Denton, was conveying him to the boat, when at the gate he claimed protection from the guard, which was immediately granted, and he was rescued from the officer. I immediately sent to the Dola, representing that this Indian subject of ours was already a Mussulmaun, and that consequently the usual plea of conversion could not justify his keeping him from us. He sent in reply, "that he would protect every body, who wished for his protection, and that I might send word of it to the Government of India." I answered, "that I would do so;" for, that I considered his answer as insolent, and such as no servant of the Imaum ought to have dared to send to the Governor of India. I could only attribute the alteration in the Dola's language, to the confidence inspired by the information brought by the Seid from the Isle of France.

September 1.—Devagé's dow sailed for India: by her I wrote an account of the Dola's conduct. In a conversation with the Bas Kateb, he justified the measure of taking our men, and said, that if the Governor of India wrote to them about it, they should only answer, "it was their custom, and they would do it."

Unus's dow returned; he wrote by his son a joint letter to me, Captain Court, and Mr. Pringle, representing that he had sent off my dispatches, and that the man had promised to be back by the 5th of the next moon. He, however, added, that he had promised to pay him fifty dollars, and could not return till we sent it him. This was certainly an impudent attempt of our friend Unus, as I had before paid him for the whole. I therefore told his son I would not give a penny more, with which he appeared perfectly satisfied, and no more claims were urged.

We were again alarmed by the incursions of the Wahabee, who were certainly in great force. The road to Moosa was unsafe; and why this place was not attacked, I could not conceive.

We had so many delays in passing provisions at the gate for the use of the ship, that Captain Court applied to the Bas Kateb. He declared he knew nothing of it; assured us he would speak to the Dola and Emir Bahar, admitting it was positively contrary to the Imaum's engagement, by which all provisions and stores were to pass free to the Factory and British ships. He hoped it would not happen again. The Dola was angry about the boy's leaving him, and took this method of showing his resentment.

Gardner, whom I have before mentioned, and

another white man, nearly fifty years of age, ran away to the Dola's. Captain Court sent to the Dola, but he was invisible, and could receive no message. On the 6th the Hadje obtained an audience, and was told by the Dola, that he had found these men so determined to become Mussulmauns, that he made them so yesterday. This is with them illegal, as three days are allowed; and it is necessary that a proper examination should take place, to prove their firm determination, and, that they should be instructed in the principles of the religion they wish to embrace. Here, however, the fear of Captain Court's inducing them to return, outweighed the Dola's sense of duty, and he violated his own laws to secure two proselytes.

Captain Court sailed on the 10th to survey a part of the opposite coast. Captain Lee and another American also sailed for Bengal, since the price of coffee here rendered any hope of profit out of the question; the cessation of the English purchases having lowered the markets only to ninety-eight Mocha dollars. The Americans get between two and three hundred bales per week. The whole quantity sold at Mocha between August twelvemonth and last August, was twelve thousand bales. I wrote to Lord Wellesley by Captain Lee, stating all that had passed with the Dola.

On the 10th all the guns were fired to celebrate the raising of the siege of Sana. We never heard here that it had been attacked. It was not the Wahabee that were beaten, but some Bedowee tribes, who inhabit the hills, and are a brave and hardy race, that have had claims on the Imaum since the time they assisted in liberating the country from the Turkish yoke. Their loss, by the

Dola's account, amounted to twenty killed; the Imaum's loss was not mentioned. Most people believed it all a fiction to raise money; as the Dola generally, on those occasions, levies contributions for the expence the Imaum has been at in protecting his subjects.

The weather for some days had considerably changed. It was frequently calm, with easterly winds; we had in the morning a southerly light air, which gradually moved to the west by the middle of the day, to the north in the evening, and round by the E. to S. in the course of the night. These light airs and calms on the 12th, saved the town of Mocha. As I was in bed that night, I was alarmed by a fire which consumed thirty or forty thatched houses, close to the American Factory. If the wind had blown from the south or west, the whole town would have been consumed; but as it was a perfect calm, our fears were over in a few hours. Some Samaulies exerted themselves in extinguishing the fire, in order to save their vessels, which were lying dry on the other side of the wall. The flames were stopped by the stone houses, as these people drove out the window frames, and kept pouring water on the walls. The Arabs did nothing but look on, with the Dola at their head.

On the 16th another American vessel sailed with half a cargo, having no more money. Burns, a seaman, who had run away from an American, and turned Mussulmaun, applied to my servant to get him off. I consented, and Captain Barton was so good as to send his boat, and take him at night on board the brig. Thus the Dola loses his converts as fast as he gets them; for, of nearly one hundred within these five years, there are now only five remaining. Early in the morning we had a slight shock of an earthquake; it was single, and seemed to proceed from the east to the west.

On the 18th Seid Akil sailed to the northward; for what purpose I could not conjecture. I heard he had been proposing to some of the Samaulies to assist him in getting possession of some place opposite to build a town; but this was probably only a pretext to conceal his real intentions. He must have had some secret plans, for it could never answer to keep a vessel of eight hundred tons, like the Peggy, in the Red Sea, a whole season, for the purposes of trade; particularly as she had nothing on board but ammunition and arms. The Wahabee dows infest Camaran, and are continually cruizing off Jidda.

On the evening of the 19th, I was taxed by an Arab, who spoke English, with an intention of taking Mocha: it was done in a laughing way, and I replied in the same manner, that it was not worth having; and that I would not have it if they would give it to me. This, however, confirmed what I had before heard, that the people in general attributed to me intentions hostile to the place.

Another fire broke out about eleven in a stone house, and partly consumed it. The wind was fresh, and had the flames caught one house of thatch, the whole bazar must have been destroyed, as it was close to it, and built of the most combustible materials. Immediately after dinner we were nearly smothered by a sand storm from the east. It was not so terrible as the great north-wester at Lucknow, but no object could be distinguished at a distance of twenty yards. It blew very fresh; a few drops of rain fell towards the end; which sensibly cooled the air. Devagé said it was the most violent he had experienced in eleven years, during which he had resided here.

Captain Court arrived this day, having finished his intended survey. He found Antelope shoal very different from what it was laid down. Assab is no cape, but a very lofty mountain, nearly forty miles inland. A very strong southerly current ran through the larger Straits of Bab-el-mandeb.

Captain Barton sailed for Jidda with a cargo. I wrote to my friends in England, and inclosed my letters to Major Missett, to whom I also sent copies of Lord Wellesley's dispatches to Mr. Jones at Bagdad, and of the Governor of Bombay's letter to Mr. Lock, who was appointed to succeed Major Missett, but died before his arrival. I requested his assistance to reach Cairo from Suez, and recommunicated the wants of the Panther. The wind was from the south, so that the monsoon might be considered as set in. The heat was greatly diminished.

September 25.—The Dola sent me a present of two baskets of grapes. This attention, after the late disputes, I attributed to a report in circulation, that the Capitan Pacha had arrived with a strong force in Egypt, and he possibly suspected that my return and stay here, had some connection with this event. There was another fire in the middle of this day. Captain Court with his boat's crew, and the Americans with theirs, saved the town by their exertions. A large number of thatched huts were consumed, and the tower by the wicket gate was once on fire, but was extinguished: a considerable quantity of gunpowder was said to be in the building. The Dola was not there, and seemed to care little about an evil, by which he does not suffer, but on the contrary rather gains, for he has a quantity of poles belonging to him, which he in consequence sells at an advanced price.

From the 24th to the 28th, the winds were again northerly, but on the 28th they returned to the south. The nights had been calm and sultry; on the same day we had another fire, which only consumed three houses, and at night a man was sent to prison, said to have been caught in the attempt to set fire to the Samaulie town. The steward of the Panther, who had been degraded on account of the deficiency of rice, ran away to the Dola's, as did the black cook of the officers, and two American seamen.

Mr. Denton, in looking for some of the boat's crew in the Jews' town, met with Gardner and some others of the renegadoes, drinking. Gardner abused him very much, and threatened others of the officers. We immediately sent to the Dola, who, in the presence of the Hadje, told the Captain of the fort, commanding the renegadoes, that if the smallest complaint were again made, he would not only put the offender in prison, but flog him severely. The American captains were refused all access to the Dola respecting their deserters, and were absolutely thrust down the stairs by his attendants. I learned from Hodeida, that the American ship was still there, that she had been in danger from the piratical dows, and that the Dola sent troops on board to protect her.

I had notice from a renegado that one of the boys ashore who assisted in packing shells, meant to run away. We sent him on board with some boxes, where we designed that he should be kept. He had no idea that we were acquainted with his intentions. During my tedious confinement, I had amused myself in employing a great number of Arabs in collecting shells for me on the beach.

I paid them generally a few komassis for their trouble, and a day rarely passed without their bringing me a new species. Mr. Macgie and I had packed them with infinite labour, and I now began to send them on board.

The custom-house officers wished to unpack all the boxes, to which I positively objected: they could hardly be persuaded that six large boxes were filled with articles they thought of no value. They at length took a few shells out of some of the boxes to show the Dola.

We had a slight shock of an earthquake on the 2d, in the morning; it lasted about a minute, with a tremulous motion.

Mr. Macgie heard to day from Captain Barton; he had been driven back to Hodeida when beyond Jibbel Tier, by strong north-westers. The American ship was still there, but had only procured fifty bales of three hundred and seventy pounds in the last two months, and for those she paid sixty-four German crowns. She had but three hundred and fifty bales, and lost her season. The place has suffered severely from the Wahabee, but sill belongs to the Imaum. Nothing but brackish water was to be had there.

In a conversation with Seid Akil's brother, he told me that the Dola was not very well pleased with an old Portuguese who had deserted to him—He said he was of no use, and cost four dollars a month. The Seid declared that it was contrary to their books to make Mussulmauns in this way. They could never be so in reality. I replied, that the Dola was very good to pay them four dollars a month till they had learned the language, when the good ones came back to the Europeans, and the others ran away to the Wahabee or Turks, to fight against him

The conduct of the Arabs towards me was totally changed within this fortnight; not an Arab of any consequence met me without making his salaam.

October 10.—The nights for some time had been extremely sultry, and the wind light and variable. On the festival of Sheik Abdurrab, who, by his corpse, has sanctified the island on which the southern fort is built, the colours were hoisted on all the forts, and soon afterwards, to the astonishment of all the inhabitants of the Factory, the Americans also hoisted their colours. This compliment to a Mussulmaun saint was novel in a Christian power; but it was carried still farther; for on the Dola's departing to offer up his prayers at the Sheik's tomb, every ship saluted; some with two, some with three, and some with five guns: some twice, some three times. I was too much disgusted to speak to them myself on the occasion, but on their being laughed at by some of our officers, they replied, that they did not know what the colours were hoisted for; it was the Dola's doing; and was not he master of the roads? I should not have cared for their degradation, had I not been afraid that the natives might confound these Americans with Europeans and Christians, in consequence of which we might have shared in the contempt they appeared so anxious to acquire.

On the 11th, at night, Fowler, whom I have before mentioned as having ran away from Captain Keys, went on board the Panther, as my servant. He was anxious to escape from the wretched life of a renegado, and applied to me to take him. As he understood Arabic, he promised to be as useful as Abdallah was the last voyage. They were equally deserters from the Company's service.

There were many circumstances in his case which rendered him an object of compassion, and his conduct in Arabia was good. He was to have gone up to Sana in a few days to be presented to the Imaum. More pains had been taken with his education than were ever before bestowed upon any one. The Dola had declared that he would not lose him for a thousand dollars; it was therefore, I must confess, a particular gratification to me, to find that he was punished for his inhospitality.

Unus Barilla returned on the 11th, without the letters from Mr. Salt. This was owing to a mistake in writing to him to be here the 15th of the moon, instead of the 15th of the month. He brought an unpleasant report of the Ras's being engaged in repelling an attack of the Galla, and Mr. Salt's being still at Adowah. His account was so confused, that I did not give it much credit.

On the 15th, we agreed with Unus to accompany us up the Red Sea for one hundred and fifty dollars per month. He begged us not to apply to the Cadi for a regular agreement, as the Dola made him pay one dollar for every ten he received from us. We hired six Samaulies to act as Lascars on board the Panther, in preference to Arabs. The wind was to-day south the first time for many days. So late a northerly monsoon had not been known in the memory of man; generally in the middle of September it changes decidedly to the south.

On the 21st we had another fire close to the Factory, which alarmed us so much that the next day we were pulling down all our mat buildings on the roof. They were become the less necessary, as the southerly wind had continued since the 16th, and made a difference of seven degrees in the thermometer; in the morning it was at 84°. The nights were very cold.

We prepared for our departure on the 1st of November. We had grown wise by our late trip, and Captain Court had at my request laid in white Surat cloth to barter for live stock, and some better articles to give to the Sheiks or other chiefs, who might oblige us. We had also taken in snuff, which was before much enquired after.

The officers of the Sheriffe's ship paid us a visit. The Naqueda is a Seid, and offered us every assistance on our arrival at Jidda. They said, they would come on board the moment we arrived there. As they might have it in their power to serve us greatly, I gave the Seid a telescope. I was happy to learn by them that the Capitan Pacha was at Alexandria, where he would stay some time. He recalled the old Pacha of Cairo, and gave that office to the chief of the Arnauts, who cut off three Beys and two hundred and fifty Mamelukes. He told us the roads between Cairo and Suez were perfectly safe. I heard all the renegadoes here meant to go with him.

We received positive information from the Banians, that Seid Mohammed Akil and his Frenchmen had paid a visit to the Sheriffe at Loheia, and presented him with four thousand dollars worth of presents, in the name of the French nation; at the same time requesting permission to establish a Factory on the Island of Camaran. This island produces wood, water, and salt. Its situation is good for watching all vessels that go up or down the Red Sea, but would be of no use in a commercial view. The French seemed to intend attacking Egypt by the assistance of the Wahabee. Mr. Pringle proposed going up there when we sailed, and joining us at Massowah, to communicate the result of his inquiries. At my request he also intended sending an express to India with the news. There can be no doubt that the guns left here by the Seid were a present from the French to the Imaum.

The Dola hearing that I wanted to buy a spear and shield of the cavalry, sent me his as a present; together with one of their battle-axes. They were all handsomely ornamented with silver. I sent to say, I would either pay him a formal visit the evening of my departure, if he would keep the gates open for me to go out afterwards, or I would pay him a visit without ceremony this evening. He preferred the latter; and we all went accordly. The people at his doors said, he expected only me and Mr. Pringle; but we all got up at last. He was, I believe, disappointed in not being able to talk on business. He enquired respecting the distance to England, how far I went by land, and how we travelled in Europe. The conversation then turned on Yemen. He informed me, that beyond Sana iron ore was found in sufficient abundance to supply all the upper country. It is smelted with wood, and is very soft, white, and tenacious. It is used for the rings of hookah snakes; and has the quality of not being corroded by smoke. There is also lead ore, but it is brittle, and of no use. He wished to present me with a piece of silver cloth manufactured at Sana, which I accepted.

He was chewing the buds of a plant which the Arabs call Kaad. It is not unpleasant, rather bitter, and aromatic. He informed me that it is brought in weekly, from the hills, to the amount of two hundred dollars. The Imaum has a large duty on it. On parting, he expressed the usual anxiety for my welfare.

We had been delayed, that Mr. Pringle might accompany us to Ait, the place where Unus's tribe live, and where we expected Mr. Salt's letters. Mr. Pringle was to go thence to Loheia, and join us again at Massowah. Mr. Pringle being ready, I went on board on the 3d. It blew fresh, though we waited till dark, as it usually lulled in the evening. We were attended to the pier by an innumerable crowd of beggars. Captain Court and I gave a scramble of komassis, and to our friends a few half and quarter dollars. Seid Daud, the Sheriffe's captain, came to wish us a good voyage, but could not reach us for the crowd. At midnight the breeze freshened to a gale, but Unus and Mr. Pringle came astern in their dows.

November 4.—At four we weighed anchor in a stiff gale and heavy sea. At eight we were up with Jibbel Anish, when the weather and sea both moderated. We sailed along very pleasantly till dark, when we anchored. Mr. Pringle came in at the same time, but went on shore, close to Ait.

November 5.—The night was very pleasant and moderate. Mr. Pringle and Unus came on board in the morning. No letters from Mr. Salt, nor any intelligence; we therefore determined to make the best of our way to Massowah. Mr. Pringle had a very rough passage; he came between the Abail Islands, and the main, in a passage not wide enough for any thing except dows. His Naqueda told him, that on the northern Abail was found a stone, which he describes as being like green glass. He promised me to visit it, and procure some, as the description suits the Opsian stone, which is probably found in many of the sandy islands of this part of the coast. Mr. Salt found some on Dhalac. At any rate I cannot suppose this the bay named by the ancients after that stone, for it is a fine one, with good anchorage, and by no means filled with sand, as the other is represented to be, neither will it agree with the distances in the Periplûs. Ait is a wretched village of huts. The high hills behind it were once, we were told, part of Habesh. We weighed at one, and with a strong breeze rounded the northern Codalie rock, which forms the boundary of the bay on that side, as the southern does on the other. We then had a free wind and an excellent coast, along which we sailed all night in perfect security.

November 6.—At day light we were in sight of Saboo and Moora, which Unus, who kept well up with us, called Habou-beer; at twelve we were opposite Howakil, with a pleasant breeze; we passed Antelope point at sun-set, and immediately bore up for Massowah, in a direction that would clear the shoals at the extremity of Valentia. At nine we were alarmed by getting into a quarter less three, when nearly four miles N. of it; we immediately stood to the eastward, and cleared the shoal, which seems to be detached. We anchored close to Massowah harbour.

November 7.—At day-light we tried to makethe harbour, but the land wind did not permit us to enter till twelve. Unus had been on shore, and immediately came off to us with the unexpected, but highly pleasing intelligence, that Mr. Salt, and our other friends, were on the road near Arkeko, and would be with us this day. As he accompanied the intelligence with a demand of buxys, we suspected his veracity, and desired him to tell Currum Chund we wanted him on board. A man of the Nayib's came off to deliver his master's compliments, from whom we learned that the Nayib did not wish Currum Chund to come to us. I sent Unus again to insist on it, and Fowler went with him. The Nayib now said he might come, but Currum Chund himself refused, saying that he had made nothing by the English; that he was out of pocket by Mr. Salt, and by the horse and mule he had given Mr. Pringle; and, in short, that he did not choose to come. I immediately suspected that he was afraid of our resentment, now that Mr. Salt was so near, and would explain his real conduct, which I always suspected to be bad, in the Habesh business. The Nayib sent many professions of regard, but begged we would not land, as the Ascari were very angry with us. Soon afterward Mr. Salt arrived, attended by Captain Rudland, Mr. Carter, and the Baharnegash of Dixan. He had also with him a servant of the Ras. They all came on board, when we saluted Mr. Salt with eleven guns; this the Baharnegash mistook for our firing on the town, and conjured us to stop. It was with some difficulty we explained to him, through the double interpretation of Andrew, and a Massowah boy, who spoke Tigré, what the cause really was. I received him as he deserved, for his attentions to our friends, with every mark of respect. He drank wine and ate sweetmeats. We sent Hamed Chamie on shore to provide every thing for him, and pay his expences while he staid. We ourselves examined with the greatest eagerness the drawings Mr. Salt had made in the country, and were never tired of asking him questions.

Till the morning of November 14, we were engaged in preparing dispatches for India, and in arranging for Mr. Carter's and our Arab servants return to Mocha. For this purpose we hired a dow to Hodeida, whence they were to proceed by land. I wrote to his Excellency the Marquis Wellesley, and Mr. Duncan, giving a short account of Mr. Salt's expedition. The Ras

Welleta Selassé had sent a letter for his Excellency, which I also forwarded.

The Sabbath of Habesh commences at sun-set. On the Saturday evening the Baharnegash was on board, and as soon as the sun went down, asked leave to say his prayers. He turned to the east, and in a kind of chant addressed himself to the Deity, and a very long list of saints. His people occasionally joined him. He then prostrated himself three times, calling on God. He performed the whole in a very decorous manner.

The Nayib's conduct was such as greatly to displease me. He pleaded that he himself wished to do every thing that was kind and proper, but that his Ascari were very angry with us; and he begged I would not then land; but that when the ship returned, every thing should be settled to our satisfaction. A fellow struck two of the boys who rowed the boat ashore with Hamed Chamie. The Nayib sent for them, and begged they would not tell me, in consequence of which, I did not hear of it till some days afterwards, when I was assured the man was in prison; I could therefore take no notice of it. Our old friend the Dola of Dhalac paid us a visit on board. We made him several presents. He was ever steady to us; nor could the Nayib dissuade him from supplying the Panther with every thing she wanted during her last voyage. When on board during the gale of wind off Daguera, he owned to Captain Court, that he had received instructions not to do so. The Nayib thought he could drive away the Panther by depriving her of water and fresh provisions. This is the only act of the Nayib that proved any disinclination in himself towards us, for at Dhalac he is absolute master. Some excuse may be made for him, vexed and tormented as he always was by his brothers and the Ascari, whenever the vessel appeared. The Baharnegash used all his influence to induce me not to quarrel with the Nayib. He went on his knees to me, and embraced my feet, nor would he rise till I had promised I would not fire on the town. I told him I felt it was a gross insult to refuse me permission to land; that the conduct of the Ascari was so reprehensible to Mr. Salt, whom they had attempted to rob, that they ought at least to be punished, and the more so, as we had ever acted towards the whole tribe in the most friendly manner. He said it was very true; that the Nayib himself was a very good man, but the people about him were great rascals, and ruled him in every thing. As I cared but little about the landing, compassion induced me not to drive things to an extremity, which might have ended in bloodshed; but I am convinced that no friendship can exist between them and us, till they are taught by dear bought experience, that it is humanity, and not fear, which prevents our resenting their insults.

Currum Chund's conduct has been such as to preclude the possibility of employing him; I therefore had recourse to a Mussulmaun merchant, Hadje Hassan Ben Mohammed Anja. This man was recommended to Mr. Salt by Pacha Abdallah, who is frequently mentioned by him in his tour to Antalou, as an active friend, and greatly in the Ras's confidence. From him I learned, that, independently of their anger, at Mr. Salt's having escaped so well from them, the Ascari were really alarmed by an idea that I was going on to Jidda to procure for myself the sovereignty of Massowah, from the expected Turkish Pacha, and that the English would garrison the island. He said that the Nayib had never received his investiture as Aga of the Ascari, which rendered these people more insolent, as he had no legal authority over them. I pity the poor man; but he is still to blame individually in the transactions respecting Mr. Salt.

The Baharnegash visited us every day. We worked the guns for him, and made the Sepoys go through their exercise. He was much astonished, and delighted, and said that twelve such men would enable the Ras to beat the Galla. I represented to him that the arms were procurable from the English in abundance, if the trade could be opened. He would not eat with us, but drank spirits or wine, and was much pleased with sweetmeats. He was astonished at the number of pieces of china on the table at breakfast and dinner, and always counted them. He was in high spirits, and seemed greatly pleased with the presents we made him, which consisted of a fine piece of kincaub, one hundred dollars in money, a razor, some china, sweetmeats, coffee, snuff, and a number of other little articles. He told us that he had always supposed all the articles brought to Massowah were made in Arabia, but he now found they came first from us. The Ras had sent me his own knife, spear, and shield, and a very fine piece of Habesh cloth; in return I presented him with my silver chourie, an article of great use in Habesh, a bottle of lavender water, of which I heard he was very fond, and a pair of razors.

Nathaniel Pierce, who had accompanied Mr. Salt, was induced by the Ras to stay in the country. Should any connexion take place between Habesh and India, his being there, and understanding the language, will be advantageous. Mr. Salt had left him every thing he could spare, and we sent him several other articles which he had mentioned in his letters. I also procured from Captain Court two of the ship's muskets, some powder, flints, and ball. He had a gun, so that he was the best armed man in Habesh. I wrote to Mr. Pringle to procure me six more, in consequence of the Ras's promise to give him a district when he had six matchlocks. He is a clever fellow, and will, I have no doubt, do well. He had several female protectors, and they have as much power in Habesh as elsewhere. He draws a little, which pleased the priests, for whom he manufactured saints in abundance. I sent him some money, and secured him more, should he wish to leave the country. I intrusted every thing to Hadje Hassan to be sent to Pacha Abdallah, as the safest conveyance. The Baharnegash declared to me in the most solemn manner, that he would protect Pierce with his life. I also sent Pacha Abdallah a handsome present of kincaub, requesting his friendship for this poor fellow: from the same motive I gave another to Hadje Hassan himself, who, in an equally solemn manner, promised to be his friend. I have great hopes of this man's ultimately increasing our knowledge of the interior of Africa. He meant to return by Senaar; he might then be induced to join the katla to Tombuctoo, for which he is well qualified by his knowledge of Arabic, and by his having conformed to the religion of Mohammed, and knowing their prayers perfectly.

The Ras had given Mr. Salt three mules, and he had purchased five more; so that I had now eight to dispose of. Formerly the Baharnegash had given Mr. Salt three; I now therefore gave him his choice of the same number. I sent two to Pierce; one I gave to Guebra Selassé, the Ras's man, another to Hamed Chamie, and the eighth I sent to the Dola of Mocha, to put him in good humour with my people.

On the landing-place opposite to Massowah we discovered a rude fluted column of black granite, with a capital, of which I have given an etching. It was unlike any other I had ever seen, and gave me hopes that, by it, we might discover the ruins of Aduli, from which it was probably brought. We were informed by some of the Shiho Bedowee, who bring milk every morning to the town, that there were quarries of a similar stone in the lower hills, lying due west from Massowah, but we could obtain no positive intelligence of any other columns. They spoke, indeed, of some ruins between us and the hills; but situated as we then were with the Nayib, it was impossible to make any researches at a distance from the vessel.

We were not able to procure a sufficiency of sheep, or water, from the Nayib, which he excused by the want of rain: we were consequently obliged to go to Dohoole; however I sent the Nayib a frassel of coffee, merely as a proof that we parted friends.

The Baharnegash went yesterday. I sent letters by him to the Ras and Pacha Abdallah, and to Pierce.

I have given in the following chapters Mr. Salt's narrative of his expedition, which he delivered to me on his return.

CHAPTER X.

Mr. Salt's narrative.—*Arrival at Massowah from Mocha.—Negotiations with the Nayib.—Difficulties experienced in procuring Mules, Camels, &c. for our Journey.—Preparations for the Journey.—Passage from Massowah to Arkeko.—Transactions there.*

"JUNE 28.—We arrived in the harbour of Massowah this day at noon, having been exactly a week in sailing up the coast from Mocha. During our passage we experienced a regular succession of land and sea breezes. As soon as we had dropped anchor, Captain Court sent his boat on shore for Churrum Chund, the Banian. He declined coming, and returned for answer, that the Nayib, without whose permission it was impossible for him to communicate with us, was at Arkeko; that he was much alarmed at our coming in the 'great ship;' especially as he had written to delay our expedition, in consequence of the country being in a state of confusion; but that he would acquaint the Nayib with our arrival, and would himself come on board as soon as had received permission.

"June 29.—Captain Court again sent his boat early in the morning for the Banian, who still excused himself on the plea of the Nayib's absence; it was therefore determined to send on shore Hamed Chamie, our Arab interpreter, who also spoke the language of Hindostan. He soon came back, bringing us an account that the Banian was greatly alarmed at our speedy return in the Panther, a ship of force. All would have been well, he added, if we had come over quietly in a dow; but that now the Sirdar of the troops was again bringing in his claim of five hundred dollars for the anchorage of the vessel. He moreover assured Hamed Chamie that he had forwarded Lord Valentia's letter to Ras Welleta Selassé. This latter assertion, however, was not quite correct, as we knew, from private information, that it was still remaining at Arkeko in the hands of the Ascari. In the afternoon the Banian himself came on board; but was able to communicate to us little more than a confirmation of what we had heard before. All our present difficulties have arisen from the Sirdar of the Ascari, now in Massowah; we however declined having any communication with him, being determined to transact business only with the Nayib in person.

"June 30.—The Nayib came over in the morning from Arkeko to Massowah, and immediately sent Hamed Chamie to us, with his salaams, and an excuse for not having come sooner; fixing twelve o'clock for our public visit. Accordingly, I, and Captain Rudland went on shore with Captain Court, under a salute of eleven guns, with which the latter was kind enough to honour us for the purpose of giving importance to our mission. On landing, we were saluted with all the guns, both great and small, that they could muster on the island; and then proceeded to the divan, or hall of audience, attended by a havildar's guard of the Bombay marines. The ceremonies were precisely as heretofore, except that our sepoys were marched up and ranged along the lower end of the hall. The divan was crowded; the Nayib, the Sirdar, and the Dola of Arkeko being present. After the usual compliments, coffee was handed to all, not omitting even the sepoys. I and Captain Court then received caftans of blue cloth lined with satin, after which we departed, in the same order as we came, to the house of Abou Yusuff, Secretary to the Nayib, which had been prepared for us by Currum Chund.

"On going off to the ship the former compliment of eleven guns was repeated. After dinner we returned, and took up our abode on shore. The Nayib declared to Hamed Chamie that he had sent Lord Valentia's letter to the Ras.

"July 1.—The Nayib sent us a message in the morning desiring that the boat, which they observed conveying our baggage on shore, should land it at the wharf, in order that it might be examined at the Custom-house, instead of bringing it round immediately to our own house. Captain Court remonstrated with them on the inconvenience of this plan, as the packages contained merely articles that were necessary to us on shore, and which would not be carried out of the house; if, therefore, they meant us to stay on friendly terms, he should persist in bringing the baggage by the most convenient way; but, that if they wished it, it should be opened at our own house for the inspection of any person whom the Nayib should think proper to depute for that purpose. This proposal gave satisfaction, and accordingly two men were sent down, but they appeared to be soon tired of their office, and went away again in the course of an hour.

"The Nayib's brother and the Vizier came to

us before breakfast, demanding, and that in no very delicate terms, the extravagant sum of one thousand dollars, half for the ship's anchorage, and half for permitting us to pass through the country on our intended visit to Ras Welleta Selassé; and this I believe, exclusively of the expences of our three or four days journey through the country. We stopped the conversation abruptly, by saying that we never discussed matters of business before a multitude of people, (for the room was full of strangers) and desired them to choose some more convenient opportunity, as we were then going to breakfast. They promised to do so, and departed. At eleven o'clock, instead of the return of the above chiefs, as had been agreed upon, the Banian came, accompanied by one of the Nayib's secretaries. They informed us that Hamed Chamie had already stated our willingness to pay what was proper; and in consequence, the Nayib had resolved to reduce his demand to three hundred dollars, and to be paid down to the Ascari, and that the expences of our journey should be a subsequent consideration; that he hoped every thing would be speedily adjusted to our mutual satisfaction; but if not, as we had come friends into the country, so he hoped we should depart. As they added that the Nayib wished to talk over the business personally, we declined returning an answer until we should see him; at the same time giving them fully to understand, that no such demand would be complied with, and that, as the indispensable condition of our paying any thing, was the being supplied with convenient means for passing through the Nayib's territory, we should make but one agreement, which must comprehend a supply of mules, asses, a guard, and provisions for the journey. The evening was accordingly appointed for our private visit to the Nayib. After waiting till past seven o'clock, Currum Chund at last came, and endeavoured to put off our visit, stating, that nothing could be done without first settling with the Ascari. We paid little attention to him, and sent Hamed Chamie to the Nayib to enquire, whether he meant to see us according to his appointment, as we should enter into no farther negotiation until he should grant us a personal interview.

"From the situation of affairs, I perceived it was impossible to avoid paying exorbitantly for permission to pass through the country; we therefore came to a determination not to exceed five hundred dollars; and we were induced to comply so far, merely from our extreme reluctance to return without having made every possible effort towards the accomplishment of our mission.

"Hamed Chamie returned with a message, that the Nayib was ready to see us. We found him in his cadjân-house, where Lord Valentia had had his first private audience. He was in a loose undress, sitting at the further end of the room, surrounded by all his principal people, in a similar dishabille: one small lamp hung from the centre of the room, shedding around so faint a light, that we were at a loss to recognize even the Nayib, till he was pointed out by one of the attendants.

"Having made our usual salaams, we were seated immediately opposite to him, and then (Hamed Chamie standing between us as interpreter, and Andrew, a servant, whom we had hired at Mocha, and who spoke Arabic, Hindostanee, and English, on my right hand) the following dialogue took place.

"Salt.—We have now arrived in your territory for the third time; you have received us with the greatest honours; such, indeed, as we have always experienced from your friendship. For these we return you our thanks.

"Nayib.—It has always been my wish to treat you well. You came here as friends; we have always continued as such; and I hope that we shall settle every thing amicably.

"Salt.—It is for that purpose we have waited on you, and I will now explain the reason of our coming. Your friend, Lord Valentia, has received letters from Ras Welleta Selassé, desiring that some persons should be sent to him, in order to open an intercourse of friendship with Abyssinia. We are, in consequence, proceeding to the Ras, having been selected by Lord Valentia for that purpose: we therefore request permission to pass through your country, and such assistance as may be necessary for the prosecution of our journey.

"Nayib.—I have no objection to your passing through my country, but you must satisfy my Ascari. Give them five hundred dollars, and I will supply you with every thing requisite, for which we will settle afterwards.

"Salt.—Why do you demand five hundred dollars for your Ascari? You well know the vessel in which we have arrived is not a trader, but a ship of war, that never pays one single komeassm* to the greatest Sultaun on earth. Even in this sea they go to Suez, to Jidda, and to Mocha, and nothing is ever demanded. It must be fully understood that not a komeassm will ever be paid on this account.

"Nayib.—I know the ship is no trader, and when you were here before this was understood; nothing more shall be said on this head.

"Salt.—What, then, are these five hundred dol-

* The smallest money of Yemen.

lars for? We do not know your Ascari, and can have nothing to say to them: you are surely the Prince of this country, and it is with you only that we can treat. We are willing to give, for your assistance, even more than would be given in any other country, only let us know your demand.

"Nayib.—What assistance do you require?

"Hamed Chamie then entered into an explanation of the number of mules, asses, camels, and attendants of which we should stand in need. Notice being now given that the hour of prayer was at hand, the Nayib and all his people went out, and prostrated themselves on a carpet in front of the house; after which the priest recited passages from the Koran. The moral effects, however, of this religious service were not very apparent: though the highest sum hitherto demanded had never exceeded eight hundred dollars, a message was now brought from the Nayib that he expected a thousand.

"I answered, that the idea of a thousand dollars was ridiculous, and that we would give no such sum, demanding where the Nayib was, and whether he did not intend to return? On this Hamed Chamie called out, not very delicately, I thought, "Nayib Edris, Nayib Edris!" on which the Nayib came in, and resumed his seat, when I thus addressed him.

"You have now made a demand of a thousand dollars; for what? for permitting us to march only three or four day's journey through your country. If you were in our country, you would be received with honour, without having any thing to pay for such permission; even in Arabia no such tribute is ever imposed.

"Nayib.—Three or four day's journey! why it

it is twelve. Moreover, I intend sending my people to insure your safety to the presence of the Ras.

"Salt.—This we do not want; when we arrive at Dixan we shall be met by the Ras's people; besides, what guard is necessary? We shall be safe even should we walk thither, as you well know that both Massowah and Arkeko will be answerable for our return. In one word, if you will provide us with every convenience to pass through your country, we will agree to give you five hundred dollars, which sum nothing shall induce us to exceed. If this offer be not accepted, there are other places through which we can communicate with the Ras, and all the fault of our not reaching him must rest with you. We expected that you would have acted as our friend, instead of which you place every obstacle in our way. We have been here three times; have we not always shown ourselves your friends? This conduct of yours, however, if persisted in, may bring upon you a very different treatment from what you have hitherto experienced from the English.

"This address seemed not a little to alarm our interpreter, for while translating it, he turned round and called upon Andrew to say whether each word, as he again repeated it aloud in Arabic, were not precisely what we had ordered him to deliver; to which Andrew made his repeated affirmations, "just so." The Nayib's countenance shewed that he felt the force of our remonstrance; he was silent for a short time, then turning to his people, he spoke in the language of the country for upwards of five minutes: his manner was persuasive, his action apparently just, and upon the whole he seemed no inconsiderable orator. Afterwards, turning to us, he said, that upon consideration of his friendship for Lord Valentia, and on consultation with his people, he would reduce his demand to seven hundred dollars, which being paid, every thing should be arranged to our satisfaction. We again assured him that we should not in the least vary from our original proposal. After some words between Currum Chund, Hamed Chamie, and the Nayib, he offered to accept of six hundred dollars, positively declaring that we should not pass through his country for less; that the camels, mules, asses, &c. were to be fetched from a distance; that his people were ravenous, and that he had a thousand mouths to fill. To this proposal Hamed Chamie and the Banian intreated us to accede, adding, that they themselves would rather pay the additional hundred dollars, than press the subject any farther This however, we declined, and again ordered them to repeat to the Nayib that we had but "one word;" that we had offered as much, nay more than we were authorised to do by Lord Valentia, and perceiving that the matter was not likely to be adjusted, we would, for the present, take our leave, hoping that, by the morrow, he would be convinced, not only of the fairness, but even of the liberality of our offer. To this the Nayib replied, "These are not the words Lord Valentia would use, but your own." This insinuation brought on a warm remonstrance on my part, which happily produced an apology from the Nayib, and a declaration that he would accept our terms. "God be praised," cried Hamed Chamie, raising his voice, that every one present might hear, "it is settled; five hundred dollars is the sum agreed upon."

After our public business was arranged, Captain Court mentioned; that, understanding rice was exceedingly scarce in the Nayib's dominions, he would on the morrow send him as much as he could spare out of what he had provided for his own people. This offer was received with much thankfulness by the Nayib and all his attendants, except the Banian, who would have prevented Hamed Chamie from mentioning it, doubtless from its not agreeing exactly with his immediate interest. The Nayib was displeased with the Banian's interference, and rebuked him sharply. We now arose, and departed, rejoiced at having brought this troublesome business to a conclusion.

"July 2.—A messenger from the Nayib came early in the morning for the money; we returned for answer, that it was usual with us to pay one half on making a bargain, and the other half on its being fulfilled; that, however, we had no objection to send him three hundred dollars, and that the remainder should be paid on the day of our departure from Arkeko. This gave no great satisfaction; the Nayib said that his soldiers would not leave Massowah till they saw the money: was I afraid of trusting him? I asked the Banian, who brought the message, if he were willing to be security for the Nayib, which he refused. "What have I to do with it?" said he, "I am your servant, and not the Nayib's."

"Previously to coming to a final determination on this matter, we sent to the Nayib to enquire how soon all things would be in readiness for our journey, and were told that it might be fifteen days, or more, as the mules were far up in the country. This assertion, so much at variance with our wish of losing as little time as possible, still further embroiled the discussion. At length, after spending the whole day in altercation, we submitted two propositions to the choice of the Nayib; either, that we would pay three hundred dollars immediately, and the remaining two hundred when every thing was ready; or, which was by far the most agreeable to us, that the whole five hundred dollars should be paid down, on condition of our receiving a written receipt for the money, and an agreement that all the preparations should be completed in ten days, at the end of which time, if there were any farther delay, we should consider him as having forfeited his word, and should employ such means as he well knew were in our power, to enforce the fulfilment of the contract.

"The Nayib at length acceded to this latter proposal, after an ineffectual attempt to evade giving a written agreement.

"July 3.—The money was paid in the morning; and the written agreement made out by Hamed Chamie in Arabic, was signed and sealed by the Nayib; in return, on his requisition, I gave him a counter-receipt.

"July 4.—Some difficulty arose about the bags of rice which Captain Court offered to present to the Nayib. His people did not appear satisfied with the quantity, and therefore hesitated about accepting it; so insatiable are their desires, and so little delicacy have they in making them known. Captain Court repeated to them, that the rice now landed was all that he could at present spare, but that if, by the Nayib's expediting the party to Abyssinia, his stay here should be shortened, he would double the quantity. It will scarcely be believed that, notwithstanding this refusal to accept the generous offer of Captain Court, the people were at that time almost starving for want of grain. On account of a partial failure of the annual rains, not a drop of fresh water was left on the island, and that which came from Arkeko was every day becoming more and more brackish. The boys and girls gather the root of a kind of sea weed to eat; it is by no means unpleasant to the taste, and constitutes a great part of their food.

"About six o'clock this evening an unpleasant circumstance occurred to Captains Court and Rudland. As they were walking through the town, an insolent fellow, lately arrived from Jidda, either from a religious frenzy, or some unknown cause, began to abuse them in a violent manner, as they passed the walled inclosure round his house; and taking up a large stone, was in the act of throwing it at them, when some of the inhabitants, who were near, laid hold of his arms, and prevented the assault, calling out at the same time, that the Nayib was at hand. This proved to be actually the case; for the circumstances having happened close to his residence, he himself, on hearing the noise, immediately came out, and with great kindness took our friends by the hand, and led them into his house. They sent directly for our interpreter, and one of the Nayib's sons came in great haste for me. On my arrival, Captain Court represented to the Nayib, in very strong terms, what had happened, and desired the offender might be brought forward.

"The Nayib said, that what had passed, had passed; he hoped it would be overlooked, as he could not answer for our safety when we went out, unless we were accompanied by some of his own people.

"After assuring him that a repetition of the offence should be punished as it merited, Captain Court informed the Nayib, that, from personal regard to him, he would pass over what had happened, trusting that his present forbearance would not encourage a repetition of the insult.

"While we were at the Nayib's, Unus Barilla, hearing that there was some disturbance in which we were concerned, armed all his men, eleven in number, and drew them up in front of the Nayib's house, where he kept them on watch till the whole affair was settled: an instance of attachment to our interest, both in himself and his Samaulies, highly creditable to their fidelity.

"July 5.—Hamed Chamie waited on us at breakfast time, with the agreeable intelligence of the dispatch of a letter, which I had sent over to Arkeko to be forwarded to the Ras, requesting him to send people to meet us on our arrival at Dixan. For the conveyance of this letter Currum Chund demanded no less a sum than thirty dollars; but exorbitant as it was for the conveyance of a single letter, for so short a distance, I thought it best at the time to submit to the imposition, as it was a point of the greatest importance to acquaint the Ras with the success of our negotiation with the Nayib; particularly as, from several circumstances, we doubted whether Lord Valentia's letter to the Ras, announcing our intended visit, had been forwarded.

"July 6.—The weather since our arrival at Massowah has been intensely hot; the thermometer varying for the most part from 96° to 99° during the day; but we have been relieved by frequent breezes from the south. Nothing particular has occurred, and we have been reducing our baggage as much as possible preparatory to our journey. In other respects affairs are going on so well that we expect to set off by the thirteenth or fourteenth instant.

"July 7.—An attendant of the Nayib came to us in the afternoon, bringing with him a man just arrived from Dowarba. His mode of salutation differed from that made use of at Massowah. He first kissed the back of his hand, and then made a slight inclination of the head. We offered him coffee, which he refused: he called himself a Christian, and said that he was 'all one with us.' We were beginning to question him concerning the news in the upper country, when he was sent for in a great hurry by the Nayib.

"Abou Yusuff came to us in the evening: he told me that he had written a second letter, by order of the Nayib, to hasten the mules; he had also sent two men, of the tribe of Shiho, to attend us. These people are very wild, and inhabit the mountains through which our road lies. He particularly mentioned the mountains of Gidam, Taranta, and Assooba, as frequented by them. He recommended us not to let the ship go away till our arrival at Dixan was announced; and to permit Hamed, the Nayib's son, to go over to Arkeko with us, as the people of this latter place are not to be depended upon; even the Nayib himself cannot trust them; but that if we had his son with us, they would not dare to molest the party. I told him that his thoughts were mine; that I would follow his advice, and that Captain Court had already determined to stay till our letters from Dixan should be received.

"July 8.—The Christian from Dowarba came to us again in the evening, accompanied by an attendant of the Nayib. He appeared to be a simple uneducated creature, from whom we could not expect to obtain any important information; and it was not improbable that he had been selected on this very account, out of four who had arrived, as the Nayib's people were evidently shy of letting us know the object of their mission. From repeated questions, however, we learned, that they had brought from Welleta Sulimaun, Governor of Dowarba,* an answer to a demand which the Nayib had made of some long forgotten tribute. The purport of the answer was, that the Governor was the Nayib's friend, and would prevent, so far as lay in his power, any of the neighbouring tribes from making plundering incursions into the territory of his ally, and that he would continue in all amity; but not a word was said about the money. The Abyssinian Christian took coffee in the evening, on its being handed to him by ourselves, to the surprise, as it seemed, of the Mussulmauns. On his leaving us, I made him a present of a piece of Surat cloth, with which he was much pleased.

"July 9. We were under the necessity of troubling the Nayib at an early hour in the morning, in consequence of a melancholy occurrence, which took place yesterday evening; namely, the death of Woodward, one of the marine boys belonging to the Panther. He neglected to take off his wet clothes, after having been in the water on the evening of the second instant, and was attacked the following morning with a locked jaw, and other violent symptoms, which baffled the effects of opium, and of every other medicine that it was in our power to administer. At Captain Court's desire his death was reported to the Nayib accompanied by a request, that a spot might be pointed out for his interment; which, with great civility, was immediately granted. Another boy was seized in a similar way, whom we were fortunate enough to recover by large doses of opium.

"July 10.—The Nayib left Massowah in the

* The Banian and Amed Yusuff informed us that the mission to the Nayib was from Ras Aylo, the Chief of Serawé, eight days journey beyond Dowarba. Ras Aylo, we understand, is a dependent upon Ras Welleta Selassé.

morning for Arkeko, where he meant to continue for some days. Before his departure he introduced an officer of the Ascari, with whom we might communicate, should occasion require; he also promised to dispatch a messenger on the arrival of the mules from Hamazin.

"July 11.—About 2 P.M. a dow belonging to Emir Mohammed arrived in the harbour of Massowah, from Suakin, having on board three Arabian horses, intended, we understood, as a present for the Imaum of Sana, or the Dola of Mocha. Emir Mohammed himself was expected in the course of a day or two.

"July 12.—The Nayib came over in the morning from Arkeko, to settle the duties of the kafila* and dows lately arrived. I sent to remind him of the near approach of the time which had been fixed for having the mules ready; stating, that from a reliance on his word, I had hitherto avoided troubling him on the subject, and hoped that all would be prepared by the morrow. He returned in answer, that he had already sent twice for the mules, that they were nearly at hand, and, by the blessing of God, all would be ready in three or four days. This manifest evasion and violation of his written engagement brought on much altercation, which was carried on during the whole day by messengers charged alternately with our complaints, and the Nayib's excuses. The particulars it is needless to detail; the result of the whole was, that the Nayib promised to give me a personal interview the next day.

"July 13.—At the appointed hour of our visit, twelve o'clock, we were informed that the Nayib was asleep; the interview was therefore postponed

* Or caravan.

till the evening. At six o'clock we waited on the Nayib, and found him in the mosque, whence he proceeded with us to the Cadjân house, accompanied by two or three attendants. I opened the conference by saying, that, as I was about to dispatch a letter to Lord Valentia, it would be necessary to state to his Lordship the reason of our still continuing at Massowah, after the day had elapsed on which by agreement, we were to have proceeded on our journey to Abyssinia. The Nayib replied, that it would be most agreeable to him to send us off the next morning, but that the mules and asses were not come down so soon as he had expected; he trusted, however, that they would arrive in three or four days; after which there would be no further delay. I answered, that I well knew that the mules might, without difficulty, have been brought to Arkeko from the most distant part of his territory, by the time appointed; I was both surprised and hurt at the delay; that every day was now of importance to us; and that the non-fulfilment of his deliberate and written engagement had placed me in a very disagreeable situation; more especially as I had received private information that the mules were actually at this very time at Arkeko. To these remonstrances he answered as before, that he was as anxious for our departure as ourselves; and that there was no foundation for the report which we had heard.

"I again urged the impossibility of delaying, day after day, without any thing being settled; that the vessel in which I came could not stay much longer, and that as I had determined to proceed, if all things were not ready in three days, I should set out on foot, with such assistance of asses and camels for our baggage, as he might choose to supply; if, however, we were constrained to begin our journey thus unprovided with the stipulated conveniences, I should consider him as no longer acting the part of a friend. The Nayib said that if such were our determination, we certainly might have all his asses and camels, and one mule which he kept for his own riding; and that he would send us on the road where we should meet the other mules coming down. We then ended the conference, by repeating our fixed determination to act as we had informed him.

"July 14.—I went on board the Panther in the morning to make preparations for our departure. The day was extremely hot, the thermometer being at 96° a few minutes after sun-rise, in the shade of a house with stone walls. In the course of the day, three of the Christians, who came down with the kafila, paid their respects to us. They seemed much pleased at the idea of our visiting their country, and answered with great willingness all our inquiries, in spite of Abou Yusuff, who was greatly displeased at their coming, and spoke to them with much harshness. They told us that all was well on the road, and that the Tacazza was passable at all times and seasons, on rafts kept for that purpose. Each of the men had a blue fillet of silk round his neck, a badge of Christianity mentioned by Bruce; they were stout, robust people, with short and almost woolly hair.

"July 15.—We were engaged all the morning in packing and securing our baggage. In the evening some Mussulmauns from Gondar paid us a visit, one of whom spoke Arabic, and appeared to be a man of much information. Among other particulars we learned from him, that the present Ras of Abyssinia is a son of Kefla Yasous, that

Axum is one day's journey from Adowa, and has many curious ruins, some of which are in good preservation. The lake Dembea, he told us, is about the same distance from Gondar, as Arkeko is from Massowah. The head of the Nile gushes out generally from one spring, but when there is much rain it forces its way through many. It is only five days journey from Gondar, and is perfectly easy of access, as all the country belongs to the king.

" July 16.—We went on board the Panther in the morning, and brought on shore such fire arms, ammunition, &c. as Captain Court could spare: on leaving the ship we were highly gratified at being cheered by the ship's company, a pleasing testimony of its good wishes. In the mean time I sent Hamed Chamie to the Nayib, to inform him that the day fixed upon for our departure having arrived, we were all in readiness, that we wished to know if the mules were at Arkeko, otherwise the ship would proceed thither to-morrow, and that we should go on to Dixan, with the asses and camels only, as before stated: to this he answered that there would be no necessity for the ship's going, that he himself would conduct us in the course of the day, and begged that we would get all things ready for our departure: he added, that it would be necessary to prepare provisions for our guard; beside which, if we gave them five dollars each, they would, he thought, be satisfied.

" To this I replied, he might rest assured, that I would never give his Ascari a single dollar more, nor would I provide them with provisions on the road.

" Captain Court at the same time told the Nayib, that he had but one word to say on the occasion; if we were not at Arkeko by the day after he had once taken us in charge, he should go down thither with his ship. The Nayib now took up another ground; he said the road was extremely bad, that the Simooms were raging; and that a great many people were dying daily from these causes; if we therefore persisted, he must detain Emir Hamed as a witness to Lord Valentia, if any accident occurred: that the mules would be ready in three or four days, and that if that were not the case, he would then collect his Ascari, and conduct us himself. We replied, that he knew our minds, and we had no more to say. In the evening we again demanded at what time he proposed to be ready, and after much difficulty extorted an answer from him, that he would go with us the next morning.

" July 17.—I sent a message this morning to know the hour he meant to accompany us to Arkeko: after waiting about three hours, Hamed Chamie, Emir Hamed, and Currum Chund came to bring us the Nayib's answer, which was, that he was busy at the custom-house, and could not fix upon any hour; he also added, that if we chose to go without waiting for the mules, we must pay extra for all the asses and camels he might procure for us, as they belonged to other people at Arkeko. Provoked at these repeated attempts at extortion, I informed them that, having been already acquainted with Captain Court's determination and my own, they might now do as they pleased; they had experienced the good effects of the friendship of the English, and if they were wise, would not brave their enmity. They returned almost immediately with a message from the Nayib, that he would be ready to accompany us at day-break the next morning; in consequence of which Captain Court at my request deferred sailing. In the evening Captain Court went on board; the Banian's boat was loaded with our baggage, and the guard stationed over it for the night.

"July 18.—At day-break the Nayib's boat passed us, under way for Arkeko, upon which we immediately put the few remaining packages into our own boat, and then finding it so full that we were unable to accommodate ourselves, we sent Pearce and two seapoys on with it, and waited till Captain Court came on shore, we then returned with him to the ship, breakfasted, and set off immediately afterwards in Unus's dow, attended by a naig and seven sepoys under charge of Lieutenant Crawford, whom Captain Court had been kind enough to send with us, for the protection of our baggage and persons, which, from all that we knew of the character of the inhabitants of Arkeko, appeared to be by no means a superfluous precaution.

"The sea breeze sprung up and carried us over very pleasantly to the landing-place at Arkeko; on our way we passed over a shoal not known before, Ras Gidam and Valentia being both in one, and Sheik Seid and Massowah open. There is plenty of water for ships of any size till within a quarter of a mile of the shore.

"It was eleven o'clock when we landed, and the intense heat of the sun reflected by the burning sand made our walk up to the house prepared for us, which was half a mile distant, the most oppressive that I ever experienced; we were all much exhausted by it on our arrival, but were soon refreshed by the attention of the Nayib, who was waiting to receive us. Our people were engaged till two o'clock, in getting up the baggage, which was effected without any loss or accident.

"As soon as the boat was ready to return, I sent Hamed Chamie to the Nayib, wishing to know when we were to leave Arkeko, as I was desirous of conveying the intelligence to Captain Court; he replied, that nothing could be done on the morrow, it being their Sabbath; that it would take up the whole of the next day to arrange the baggage, and that on the following morning we should commence our journey. By remonstrating with him, however, on this unnecessary delay, I prevailed so far that the day after the Sabbath was fixed on for our departure. We procured for our day's supply a quantity of water and a sheep; the water was well tasted, but of a whitish colour, and deposited much sediment. In the evening we received two sheep from the Nayib, and in return presented the servant who brought them with a dollar.

"Some of our party wishing to walk at sunset, I requested the Nayib would send one of his people to attend them. He said the women and children would be alarmed, and that the boys would be very troublesome; he therefore begged that we would not go beyond the walls of the enclosure. As we were retiring to rest, the Nayib placed an Ascari as a guard at the door of our house, and desired us on no account to go out during the night, as wild beasts were abroad, and evil minded persons, who would molest us. We slept within our enclosure in the open air, only using the precaution of having our fire arms near at hand. Pearce and one of the sepoys sleeping on the outside of the gate, but with their heads on the threshold, were awakened about eleven o'clock by the Nayib himself, who insisted on their coming in and bolting the door. As a proof that this was not an unnecessary precaution, it may be mentioned, that the Nayib's sentinel, who was stationed at the door, sent in his cap and shoes, lest they should be taken from him in the night. We heard the cries of hyænas, and other wild beasts, prowling about, which, from the noise they made, must have been very numerous; nevertheless, we passed the night without molestation.

"July 19.—Early this morning the Nayib came with some of his people to look at our baggage; and in the afternoon the packages were sorted by the camel drivers, and an account taken. There seemed to be much dispute among the parties as to the number of animals required. Much difficulty was made about the tent, and I was at length obliged to determine on leaving the fly behind. At mid-day the thermometer was 110°.

"We were, as usual, pestered in the evening with a number of messages concerning provisions for the Ascari and camel drivers. I told them we had very little for ourselves, and that I should therefore not take upon myself the care of providing for them. As we were retiring to rest, the same disturbance again occurred about the door of our house being closed and bolted; but the night being intensely hot (and our party much increased by the arrival of Captain Court with his boat's crew, making altogether twenty-six in number, and crowded into a space of not more than forty feet square) we determined to protest against it, and at length prevailed on the Nayib to give up the point; but, as what had passed in our conference with him was not particularly pleasant, we thought it prudent to be on the alert during the remainder of the night.

"July 20.—The circumstances already mentioned caused us to pass a most unpleasant night; we could neither sleep nor rest, so closely were we pent up, and so oppressive was the state of the air.

"Early at day-break some of the camels arrived, and the Nayib came for the purpose of finally settling every thing. On a repetition of a demand for provisions for the people who were to accompany us, we gave him the same answer as before; but added, that wishing to make it easy to the camel drivers, we would give each of them a small sum of money, to furnish them with provisions as far as Dixan.

"At eight o'clock all the camels were loaded, aad proceeded on their way, guarded by Pearce, and Mr. Carter, who volunteered upon the occasion. For myself, I thought it not prudent to brave the mid-day sun at the commencement of a journey, which would doubtless prove sufficiently fatiguing. There were also a few matters yet remaining to be arranged; in consequence of which Captain Rudland and the rest of the party still continued with me at Arkeko.

"Captain Court, completely weary of the place and of the Nayib, returned very early in the morning to the ship, leaving however with us Lieutenant Crawford and the guard. We felt great regret at parting from this valuable friend, whose kind assistance in farthering every object of our mission had been such as to claim our warmest gratitude. With respect to his private stock, there was nothing which he would not have given us; and so far as lay in his power he furnished us, in his public capacity, with those articles which it was impossible for us to procure at Mocha or elsewhere in the Red Sea. Indeed from all our friends on board the Panther we received every kind attention and assistance.

CHAPTER XI.

MR. SALT'S NARRATIVE CONTINUED.—*Departure from Arkeko to Dixan.—Numbers and description of our party.—Illerbehey.—Shillikee.—Wéah.—Hazorta Encampments.—Meet with mules sent down from Dixan.—Hamhammo.—Sadoon.—Tubbo.—Illilah.—Foot of Taranta.—Passage over that Mountain.—Arrival at Dixan.—Proceedings at Dixan.*

"JULY 20.—Our party, on quitting Arkeko, consisted of the following persons. Myself; Captain Rudland; Mr. Carter; Hamed Chamie, an interpreter from Mocha and born at Mecca; Andrew, another interpreter, likewise from Mocha, who spoke English well; Pierce, an English servant, who spoke a little Arabic; two Arabian servants, Seid and Ageeb; a boy from Massowah, who spoke the language of the country and Arabic: and an old man who carried our pedometer: total in number ten. We were accompanied also by an old Mussulmaun Sheik, and his little boy, going up into the country on a trading expedition, both of whom continued with us the whole of our journey, and proved very attentive and useful. Our guard consisted of about twenty-five of the Nayib's Ascari; besides whom we had a guide belonging to the Shiho tribe, and about ten camel-drivers, natives of the country.

"The baggage with its escort had already left Arkeko (as mentioned in the preceding Chapter), and the rest of the party were preparing to follow, when I found that no animals had been provided, except a mule for myself. This was not the time to enter into a long discussion with the Nayib on the subject, I therefore hired an ass for Captain Rudland, four camels for our servants, and four more to carry the tent poles, for which I agreed to pay eight dollars. At four P. M. one camel only arrived, and many excuses were made to detain us. After enquiring into the full extent of the Nayib's demands, the charge of twelve dollars was made out by the Dola and the Nayib's son, for which I gave a draft on Currum Chund. The Nayib now, without assigning any reason whatever, declared he would have twenty-two dollars; provoked at this new and unexpected instance of knavery, I replied in Arabic, before his son and the Dola, that if he said so he told an untruth, for that I would not, on any account, pay a single dollar more. In the midst of the wrangling which this occasioned, the ship most fortunately moved towards Arkeko.* Upon the Nayib's demanding the reason of this, I replied, "Captain Court is coming to see that I am safe, and though, if he finds that all is well, he will immediately go away, yet, he will return in ten days for intelligence which I have agreed to send him from Dixan." The Nayib's son replied in a haughty tone, "Let him come;" but his coming was not equally pleasing to the Dola and the inhabitants of the place; for the former immediately went out

* This, as we found on our return, was merely accidental, the ship having been driven from her anchor by a partial Simoom. It was one of the many lucky coincidences, that occurred in the course of our expedition.

in great alarm, taking the Nayib's son with him, and made so forcible a representation of his fears, that in a few minutes, without more words, every thing was prepared, and we set off.

"After I had mounted the mule, and had proceeded a few yards, Captain Rudland and his ass were completely hustled by the members of the divan, one of whom had actually employed a boy to steal his fowling piece; he only escaped by urging forward his beast, and pouring forth in Arabic all the abuse that he could muster on the occasion. Of Arkeko I have little to say; it is an assemblage of miserable huts, among which are two stone houses with walled yards, belonging to the Nayib: before that in which we resided was a verandah covered with mats.

"We passed out to the southward through gardens, which are cultivated with a degree of care unusual in this country. Immediately beyond lies a burying-ground, and to the right a village, where most of the Ascari reside. In passing along the plain, which is upwards of a mile in breadth, reckoning from the sea to the nearest rising ground, I had an opportunity of observing that the bottom of the bay forms a considerable bight. About a mile and a half from Arkeko are six wells, near twenty feet deep, and above fifteen in diameter. It is from these that the town receives its scanty supply of fresh water. By the evening the wells are so nearly drained, that the water, as it rises in the middle of each, is taken up with a flat vessel like a skimming-dish; it is then put into skins, and brought up a broken ascent by men, women, and children in a state of perfect nudity. The name of these wells is Illerbehey, Bruce's first stage. Having watered the mules and camels, we proceeded on our way, in the course of which, we saw several red deer exceedingly tame, and some small wolves, that bore a near resemblance to the large paria dog of India. We passed another village, beyond which two large flocks of goats were feeding; and observed that all the villages, and gardens, were carefully fenced round with large branches of the thorny Acacia. By the time that we had quitted the plain, it became too dark to make any observations, except such as were forced upon us by the ruggedness of the road. We arrived at length at the rising ground, called by Bruce, Shillokeeb, but pronounced by the natives Shillikee, where we slept undisturbed in the midst of our camels and baggage. There is no water at this place.

"July 21.—As soon as the moon arose, which was about half past two, we commenced our morning's march. The air was pleasantly cool, and the road, which was good, winded among the gullies of the mountains, at times crossing the dry beds of the torrents. There was at this time little variety of vegetation, almost every thing being burnt up: the Acacia, which grows to the height of about forty feet, nearly covered the face of the country; round the trunks of this tree were twined the stems of various climbing plants, which were completely leafless.

"We were much gratified, after being wearied with the sun-burnt foliage of the Acacia, with the sight of green trees at a distance, indicating the presence of fresh water. We accordingly soon found ourselves on the bank of a torrent called Weah, much discoloured by the dirt and rotten wood brought down by it from the hills whence it rises. By the side of this stream we hung up the walls of our tent on the branches of a tree, resembling the cedar in its general growth, except that the boughs droop like those of the weeping willow. The quill of a porcupine was brought me by one of our attendants. Here also we first saw the dung of elephants, though the natives deny that these animals ever frequent this place. Hitherto we have journeyed in nearly a south course, varying a little to the west, and are, I conjecture, about eighteen miles from Arkeko.

"Our Ascari now conceiving that we had advanced so far into the country as to be entirely at their mercy, began to display their insatiable rapacity and insolence. The camel master and drivers also made common cause with them, so that, had they not been deterred by the superiority of our fire-arms, I am persuaded that even our lives would scarcely have been safe. They made demands of tobacco, rice, coffee, and liquor, on the plea that the Nayib had given them nothing but a little juwarry. These we resisted; but, at length promised to buy them some goats and juwarry, if we met with any, and to give them a small quantity of tobacco; but to satisfy such villains was impossible. We quitted Weah at three P. M. and passing the torrent, which was shallow, and running in an easterly direction, proceeded over the plain to the south a little westerly. Captain Rudland made an excursion with his gun, and saw many deer of different kinds, hares, partridges, and guinea-fowl; he was attended by a famous Shangalla hunter, armed with his spear and shield, the latter of which was of a circular form, two feet and a half in diameter, and made of the skin of the rhinoceros. He was a very handsome young fellow, straight-limbed, and appeared to be a truly brave man, for he was well behaved, and despised the wrangling of the Ascari.

"We saw a few people of the Shiho tribe on the

hill, and some wolves: after passing a second stream as muddy as the former, we encamped for the night. The name of this station is Markela; it was at that time occupied by a tribe of the Hazorta, which had come down with its flocks into the low country for water. The Sheik of the tribe called himself a Dancallé. Their encampment was nearly circular, and about a hundred yards in diameter, well fenced with thorns and brushwood: within was a circle of rude huts composed of sticks and mats, and placed at equal distances from each other; while the vacant space in the centre formed a secure resting place during the night for their goats and sheep, of which they had an ample stock.

"After we had settled our encampment, the Ascari came round me, headed by their chief, and in a very insolent tone repeated their former demands, declaring that unless these were complied with, they would instantly leave us, take the cattle, and return. I told them, that they might themselves depart as soon as they pleased; but that I would certainly shoot the first person whom I should see meddling with the camels. I now sounded the man in charge of the camels, and found him more tractable than the Ascari, which convinced me that the whole was an attempt to alarm us. In consequence of what had passed, I ordered all our fire arms to be loaded, and a two hours watch was kept during the night, by myself, Captain Rudland, Mr. Carter, and Pearce.

"The villagers about this time brought in their goats and sheep, consisting in the whole of at least five hundred. I purchased three for two dollars, and distributed them among our guard and drivers; we ourselves supped heartily on rice and salt-fish, having eaten nothing but a little biscuit in the course of the day. The water has hitherto been very muddy, though not ill-tasted. Our computed distance from Arkeko is twenty-four miles.

"July 22.—Our attendants made no preparation for commencing our journey at the time appointed; we found, on inquiry, that the delay was occasioned by the non-arrival of the long promised mules of the Nayib, which were to have joined us at this place. Very intelligible hints were also thrown out by the Ascari, that none of them would move until their former demands were satisfied. From this disagreeable state of suspense we were happily relieved soon after, by the arrival of an Abyssinian Christian with ten mules in his charge, from Dixan. He was sent, by the express command of the Ras, to convey us and our baggage, with all possible speed, to his presence at Antalow, and the strictest orders had been issued to ensure our personal safety during the remainder of the journey. On receiving this welcome intelligence, I called the chief of the Ascari to me, and acquainting him with what had happened, gave him and his followers full liberty to quit us as soon as they pleased. This they none of them chose to do; but finding that all hopes of obtaining any thing by force were now at an end, they promised better behaviour for the future; upon which we consented to their continuing with us.

"By this time it was ten o'clock, and the intense heat of the day induced us to defer our journey for a few hours; we therefore hired, for a little coffee, the hut belonging to the Sheik of the tribe near which we had encamped: it was just large enough to hold our two beds,* which we covered with mats, and thus obtained a comfortable

* Two small beds taken from our sea cots, which Captain Rudland and myself had found very serviceable to us.

retreat from the rays of the sun. The old Sheik and his wife paid us many begging visits in the course of the day, with which we could readily have dispensed, as the lady was neither young nor handsome, and possessed a most invincible volubility of tongue. Before our departure she came in to examine all her valuables, and gave us a vociferous scolding for having drank some water without leave.

"This tribe seem to fare tolerably well; they have milk and butter, and a fruit called Gersa, which when boiled greatly resembles the common pea; they also kill two goats for their daily consumption. The Nayib's two servants, with his mule, quitted us at this place, and at three P. M. the rest of the party set out, mounted on the mules from Dixan, which with our thirteen camels made a very respectable appearance. The road seemed perfectly secure, and well frequented, as we saw, almost every hour, small kafilas of twenty or thirty people passing with merchandize to Arkeko.

"After winding about among the acacias, for three miles or more, we turned into the dry bed of a torrent, where at first we suffered much from the heat. Our servants having neglected the most necessary precaution of filling the skins with water, we were in the course of our march incommoded with thirst, the heat being intense. I was for a time relieved by the kindness of a poor fellow coming down from the hills, who gave me a portion of a small quantity that he carried in a cruise upon his back. As we proceeded, the valley became contracted to a rocky gully not more than one hundred yards wide, bounded on each side, and overshadowed by steep and lofty hills.

"We passed a small burying place on our left;

and soon after, the two ridges of mountains apparently closed, having at their foot a little rising ground called Hamhamou, a few yards distant from the bed of the torrent, where we halted for the night. We had just unloaded our camels, and were congratulating ourselves on having arrived at the end of a harrassing day's journey, during which we had taken no refreshment, except breakfast, when our guide told us that a storm was at hand. We accordingly collected our baggage in haste, covered it over with the walls of the tent, and were in the act of pitching the tent itself, when the rain came on with great violence, accompanied by loud thunder and vivid lightning. We all huddled together in the tent for shelter, but could not boast much of the protection which it afforded. To add to our trouble, it had no sooner grown dark, (the storm being now at its height), than an alarm was given by the Ascari, who were on the outside, that the natives were coming upon us. We instantly seized such fire-arms as were at hand, and rushed out to receive the enemy, into so drenching a rain as would presently have rendered our fire-arms entirely useless. Fortunately, however, it proved to be a false alarm, excited, I have no doubt, by our Ascari, who, if we had not shewn ourselves ready to repel aggression, would in all probability have taken the opportunity of at least plundering us.

"About an hour after this disturbance, we heard the torrent come rushing down, while the thunder still continued roaring in tremendous peals among the mountains. The air was now become so cold as to render both a cloth coat and camoline* very acceptable, although the thermometer, when we

* An Arab cloak.

first arrived at this station, was as high as eighty-four degrees.

"The storm continued for four hours, during which some of our party, exhausted by fatigue, fell asleep, and the rest of us soon after, notwithstanding our uncomfortable situation, followed their example.

"July 23.—It was curious to observe, in the morning, how completely our tent was filled, there being not only ourselves and servants, but the Ascari, camel-drivers, and three asses, that had crept in during the night for shelter.

"The hills that here seem to close, run nearly in a south direction; they are composed of large strata of burnt brown stone, with here and there layers of white spar; they are thinly covered with stunted Acacias and brushwood, and rise so steep as completely to shut out all distant hills. The rising ground on which we are encamped, is at present only a heap of bare gravel and loose stones, covering a rocky base, out of the crevices of which shoot forth a few green bushes. Bruce passed a night on the same spot; and it was his fortune, as well as ours, to encounter here a terrible storm, which, as usual, he describes with some exaggeration; although he was here on the 17th of November, a very different season.

"From this place there is a winding path of a mile or more, leading up the mountain on the eastern bank of the torrent, to some springs and natural cisterns in the rock, from which the tribes on the hills supply themselves with excellent water of a crystalline clearness. While we were at breakfast, a few miserable naked wretches, who live somewhere in the neighbourhood, came to us begging; we willingly made them partakers of our meal.

"Before we recommenced our journey, Guebra

Michael, our Abyssinian guide, came to us, and recommended, as provisions were beginning to fall short, to dismiss the Nayib's Ascari. I was not sorry for the opportunity, and therefore ordered them immediately to depart, with which, as they now found all their consequence was gone, they reluctantly complied, on receiving two dollars each as a bribe.

"We quitted Hamhamou about ten A. M. the water having nearly subsided, and occupying only a small part of the bed of the torrent along which, as before, we took our way. As we advanced, the gully gradually became narrower, and our guides urged us to make all possible expedition, fearing that more water might come down from the mountains. This actually took place about noon, though there had been no appearance of rain; but fortunately it was not in such quantity as materially to impede our progress. Indeed our mules were so well trained, that it was no small obstacle which could disconcert them; and it was continual matter, both for surprise and satisfaction, to see with what care they passed over the rocks and loose stones that incumbered the road, as we repeatedly crossed and re-crossed the stream.

"We passed by a cave inhabited by a family of the natives; in it was a woman grinding corn, and some children playing about her. The general face of the country began to improve, the vegetation was fresher, and we observed a considerable variety of plants; some of them seemed to belong to the liliaceous tribe, and made a very beautiful appearance. Captain Rudland killed a curious bird, of which I have a drawing.

"At half past four we arrived at Sadoon, distant, from Hamhamou, according to our computation, about ten miles. This station is a small green plat, shaded by the same kind of trees as those which we saw at Weah; it is within a few yards of the stream, and is entirely surrounded by woody mountains. As there seemed to be a probability of rain, we pitched our tent, and stowed within it all our baggage for the night. From the time that the Ascari had left us, the nightly watch, which had been kept before by ourselves, was entrusted to Pearce, Hamed Chamie, and the Abyssinian Christian, and muskets fired at stated intervals. The thermometer at day break was 77°, and at noon 86°.

" July 24.—Our expectations of rain were happily disappointed, for the night proved very fine, though cold. In the morning we observed that the stream had deposited the mud by which it was discoloured the evening before, and was now running quite clear: we saw in it a number of small fish resembling gudgeons.

" Between six and seven o'clock we recommenced our journey along the stony border of the stream, sometimes turning off into groves of trees, beneath the shade of which the ground was covered with green turf. Captain Rudland shot a small deer of the same kind as those we met with at Massowah, and a large bird of the grouse kind. After passing a small burying-ground, named Willo, we arrived at a thick grove, not unlike the mango topes of India: the trees of which it was composed also reminded us of the mango trees, from the form of their leaves and manner of bearing their fruit; this latter, however, was not a pulpy berry, but a hard nut inclosed within a thin husk. The natives all declared that it was poisonous; but Mr. Carter eat three or four of the kernels without experiencing any inconvenience.

" Soon after, we arrived at Tubbo, a very

picturesque station, abounding in groves of various shady trees, and surrounded by abrupt cliffs and precipices. Bruce has well described this place; but though there were a great variety of birds around, their notes did not appear to me to be different from what we had often before heard. The mountains hereabouts are inhabited by the Hazorta, Welleihah, and above fifty other tribes, according to the concurrent reports of the people of Dixan and Arkeko; whence it may be inferred that almost each hill has its distinct tribe. The Hazorta are at present, and have been for many years, on friendly terms with the Nayib of Massowah; but a tribe to the eastward, called Hartoo, is at open war with him. A man of the former came down to us unarmed, accompanied by his little boy; they were both of them black, and very thinly clad, and were very grateful on being presented with a small piece of tobacco.

"We saw here two large trees of the sycamore fig, being about nineteen feet in girth at their bases; out of the sides of the larger boughs were growing great bunches of figs, which however, were for the most part devoured by the black ants before they were ripe: a species of Asclepias also grows here in great abundance, as indeed it does all the way from Arkeko; of its wood the inhabitants make handles for their knives and swords. We remained at Tubbo, enjoying the grateful coolness of its shade, till half-past five, and then it was not without difficulty that I prevailed on our people to go another stage. Our road still continued along the bed of the torrent; but besides the trees already mentioned, the tamarind now began to make its appearance: we also saw several monkeys on the hills; they were chiefly of three species; one was the kind common at Mocha; another was distinguished by its large size, and white hair on the head and beard; the third was much smaller than the others, and had a white beard, and white rings on the tail. We also saw the rock rabbit, which appeared to be like the Ashkoko of Bruce. In less than an hour we arrived at Illilah (Lila of Bruce), where we took up our quarters for the night under a tree, without taking the trouble to pitch the tent, there being no appearance of rain. We slept unmolested by wild beasts, and undisturbed by noise of any kind, but found the air very cold towards morning, especially during the strong gusts of wind which came down at intervals from the hills. Our computed distance from Sadoon was eight miles. The thermometer at 5 A. M. was 77°.

" July 25.—We resumed our journey at an early hour, notwithstanding the appearance of the sky foretold heavy rain. The road, which had been very perceptibly ascending all the way from Arkeko, now rose more rapidly; much elephants dung lay scattered about, and the branches of most of the fig-trees were lopped off nearly to the top, to give an opportunity to the cattle of browzing on the leaves and tender shoots, the grass being entirely burnt up: on the sides of the hills we perceived a few huts, and several of the inhabitants.

" After a march of nearly two hours we reached a place called Assubah, where there was a burying ground. We saw here a few men attending a large herd of cattle, of whom we purchased, for four dollars, a cow to serve as provision for our people during the ascent of Taranta. In about a quarter of an hour more we reached our station at the foot of that mountain. We had now proceeded with our camels as far as the unevenness of the ground would permit, it was therefore necessary to seek for some other method of getting our baggage conveyed to Dixan. For this purpose we opened a negociation for the use of some bullocks, with some of the Hazorta tribe, who inhabit the mountains; but not being able to agree on terms, we procured only one of these animals, and finally concluded a bargain with some men and boys, for the conveyance of our packages on their shoulders. During this transaction a man of some consequence among them, called Sheik Ummar, had been making a demand of tobacco, coffee, &c. for allowing us to pass the mountain; this claim not being mentioned to me immediately by those to whom the chief had stated it, he thought himself neglected, rose up in a violent passion, and seizing his spear and shield, rushed down the hill with his attendants, muttering threats as he went. Being unwilling needlessly to hazard the serious consequences which this affair might produce, I sent after him, and in an amicable conference explained the mistake, and gratified him with the trifling presents required. In the evening the Hazorta chiefs all returned, accompanied by an old man of great authority among them. This venerable patriarch, who was said to have around him three hundred relations, placed himself on a rising ground, and having raised his garment on the end of a spear, and demanded silence, made a speech to the following effect.

" Be it known to all, that these people who are passing are great men, friends of the Nayib of Massowah, friends of the Sultaun of Habesh, friends of the Ras Welleta Selassé, and friends of the Baharnegash Yasous; we have received and eaten of their meat, drank of their coffee, and partaken of their tobacco, and are therefore their friends;

let no man dare to molest them." On this there was a general buzz of approbation, and all was quiet and settled. We were however again disturbed by the Nayib's people in the evening, who made fresh demands upon us, backed with threats; to these, however, we paid no farther regard than arming ourselves as usual for the night, which we passed without molestation. The thermometer in the evening was 76°.

"July 26.—The Hazorta chief being this morning in a very friendly humour, I availed myself of the circumstance to make some enquiries concerning the tribe to which he belonged. He told me that they married four wives; that he himself had that number, and nine children, five girls, and four boys; that the population of the tribe amounted to about five thousand; that they possessed many cattle, but seldom killed them, unless they were likely to die from disease or accidents, these animals forming the chief medium of barter for grain with the Abyssinians. On enquiring why they did not raise corn themselves, he replied, that they were ignorant of the art of doing so, otherwise they would willingly supply their own wants, without having recourse to others. He further informed me, that they never stripped the branches from the trees, except for the purpose of feeding their cattle when the grass was burnt up or consumed. Hence it appears not improbable that these people might, by gentle means, be brought to a much higher state of civilization than that in which they are at present; with regard to their population, if their number be only half so many as the chief represented them, they must be considered as a very powerful tribe; and being a brave, though rude people, and in possession of a very strong country, through which lies the only practicable passage into Abyssinia from this quarter, they might assume and maintain an importance much superior to what they actually possess.

"At half past eleven, after about five hours continued wrangling with our people, during which we were several times on the point of proceeding to blows, we at length prevailed on them to fetch the mules, and we began to ascend the mountain; Sheik Umma, from whom I had obtained the preceding information, taking his leave with many expressions of friendship and humility. The first part of the road was smooth and easy; but, as we advanced, it became steeper and more incommoded with loose stones and masses of rock, over which however our excellent mules carried us with great facility, and in perfect safety. Such of the Nayib's people as we had still retained with us to serve as guides, knowing that when we should have crossed the mountain, they could no longer with safety continue their insolence and rapacity, resolved to throw every obstruction in the way of our farther progress; accordingly they began by deserting us; we fortunately however met with a young Sheik descending the mountain, who, for a small recompence, agreed to be our guide, upon which we continued our journey. In about a quarter of an hour afterwards we were overtaken by the Nayib's guide, who had already given us so much trouble: he now insisted on our halting, giving us to understand that there was neither water, provisions, nor resting-place to be found above, and therefore that we must take up our station where we were, and proceed over the mountain the next day. Having said this, he immediately seized Captain Rudland's mule very roughly, and on my passing him he came forwards to lay hold of mine; this however I prevented by drawing my hanger, and threatening him to cut him down if he offered the least molestation. On this he desisted, and seated himself on a stone by the road side in a violent rage. But we had not yet entirely got rid of him, for by the time that we had advanced half a mile farther, he again overtook us, having by some means or other got Captain Rudland's sword from the Sheik, who had been entrusted by that gentleman to carry it up the hill. He now began to abuse Mr. Carter, who had resisted the attempts made to stop the mule on which he rode, and was on the point of drawing the sword, when Mr. Carter took a pistol from his girdle and presented it at him; at the same moment Captain Rudland jumped from his mule and wrested the sword from him. Having thus failed in all his attempts to detain us another day, and being probably intimidated by the result of the last, he gave up the point in despair, and we experienced no farther trouble.

"The whole of this mountain was thickly set with kolquall, which grows nearly to the height of forty feet: towards the top the berry-bearing cedar of Bruce, (called by our guide Cereder) began to make its appearance, and became more abundant in proportion as we ascended; the summit of the mountain being covered with a thick copse of this tree. In the most rugged path of the road we dismounted, to ease our mules, and walked for about half a mile; we then remounted, and gained the top without any further difficulty. As soon as we arrived we found, on looking at our watches, that it was only half past two; so that, notwithstanding all our delays, we had been occupied only three hours in overcoming the exaggerated perils and toils of the passage of Taranta. We now directed our course into a beautiful little green valley shaded by cedars, and adorned by a pool of water; the sight of which was particularly grateful to us, as we had been repeatedly told that there was none on the top; near it was grazing a large herd of cattle. Wandering about the valley we discovered a great profusion of mushrooms, of which, notwithstanding they were considered by the natives as poisonous, we collected a large quantity: part we stewed for immediate use, and the remainder we bottled, and found them both wholesome and highly grateful, in the total want of vegetables which we afterwards experienced. Soon afterwards, Captain Rudland shot an owl of a very large species, and Mr. Carter and myself collected a number of flowers, several of which had bulbous roots; among the shrubs were the sweet briar, and several others highly aromatic. We were soon overtaken by the men and boys, who had charge of our baggage; one of our heaviest boxes, containing ammunition and dollars of considerable weight, was, to our surprize, brought up by a boy about thirteen years of age; and one of the walls of our large tent, together with the two poles, were conveyed by one man from the bottom to the top of the pass in about four hours. It is not easy to reconcile these facts, with Bruce's representation of the extraordinary difficulties with which he had to contend during two days in going over the same distance, unless the re-establishment of peace between the Nayib, and the tribe of Hazorta, had been attended by a surprizing improvement of the road, which is not probable, as by Bruce's own account the trade, if we may judge by the number of slaves, was then fully equal to what it is at present. Besides, we did not meet with a single hyæna or troglodytical cave; and luckily " had not our hands and knees cut by frequent falls, or our faces torn by thorny bushes;" which last, indeed, appears scarcely possible in so open and frequented a path. The only part of our baggage that did not reach us till late at night, was the fly of the tent, and my bed, which were carried on the back of an ox; in consequence of which, the evening being very cold, we arranged our baggage in a half circle, made a good fire in the centre, and slept on the walls of the tent, having previously regaled ourselves with salt-fish, rice, and stewed mushrooms. The thermometer in the evening was 64°.

" July 27.—A shower fell in the course of the night, and when we awoke, the sky was so lowering, that, though our guide declared it was only the common morning mist, we thought it prudent to pitch our tent, under which we obtained shelter from a smart shower of rain which fell soon after. The tops of Taranta, surrounding the little valley in which we slept, had hitherto been obscured by fleeting clouds; at seven they began to clear away, upon which we dispatched the baggage forward, and about eight o'clock set out ourselves. We had not however ascended the first rising ground before heavy rain came on, and continued, with very short intermission, during the whole of the day. Thence the descent became very rapid, and the road lay through gullies, down which the waters were beginning to run with great force; but none of these obstacles seemed to delay our mules; they descended almost like goats from rock to rock, and not one of the whole number made a single false step in the course of the day. Notwithstanding our cloth coats and camolines, we were all wet to the skin, and, on account of the difficulties of the road, were not able long to keep together; so that, while Captain Rudland and myself were proceeding on the direct road, Mr. Carter and Pearce were wandering wherever the mules chose to carry them, and, as it aftewards appeared, they had actually arrived within half a mile of Dixan, when they turned, and made a circuit of about five miles.

"Captain Rudland and myself took shelter in a village about three miles from Dixan, under a hut divided into many compartments, and inhabited by several families. They paid us every attention that their miserable means would allow; and an old woman, who spoke a little Arabic, brought us some water which was much discoloured; among the group we observed two handsome young women, who had fine teeth, and silver rings in their ears. House-sparrows were seen to fly from under the roofs of the huts; and the cattle were lodged in the same apartment as the women and children. The mode of building here is by raising walls of the required height, adjoining, and at right angles, to a steep slope on the side of a hill, and then laying on a roof of sods, pitched so as to correspond with the general descent of the hill, which gives the appearance of caves to these habitations. We much regretted having nothing with us to give these poor people but an empty wine bottle; with this, however, they were well satisfied.

"Our companions soon after joined us, and about two in the afternoon, after the most unpleasant day we had yet experienced, we reached Dixan, completely wet, and without any of our baggage, which was all scattered upon the road in proportion to the strength or willingness of those who carried it. We were received by the Baharnegash Yasous, and the head men of the town, who were waiting at the house prepared for us.

"Soon after our arrival, the Baharnegash sent us some large flat barley cakes, some honey, and hydromel; and upon this, with a little of our Dhalac cheese, we were glad to make our dinner.

"July 28.—The thermometer in the morning at day break on Taranta was 59°; in the course of the day it varied from 61° to 66°. We passed a most miserable night, the air being extremely cold, (thermometer 59°) and the few cloaths we had with us completely wet; for my own part, I sat till nearly morning with my feet in the embers of a small fire which occupied the centre of our cave. I call it so, because being constructed on the same plan as the habitation before described, it is evidently copied from natural or artificial excavations. It may be said, in favour of this mode of building, that there is hardly any other better suited to the hilly nature of the country, or which, with so little labour, will afford an equally secure protection to the inhabitants and their cattle from the inconveniences of the weather, and the wild beasts that are continually prowling about during the night. We all found ourselves unwell in the morning, in consequence of the fatigue of yesterday; nor did the gloominess of the weather, for the rain still continued, contribute to raise our spirits. At about ten o'clock, Hamed Chamie, and the rest of our servants, arrived in as wretched a condition as ourselves; they had however been better accommodated during the night, at a village where they had procured a sheep, and were well treated by the inhabitants. Our boxes were brought in one by one, most of them drenched with water; but, fortunately, the cloth and presents designed for the Ras, and my smaller box of valuables, escaped undamaged. Towards evening the greater part of our baggage arrived, and an additional demand of five dollars was made by Guebra Michael: this Hamed Chamie resisted. The Baharnegash at first expressed his displeasure at this new charge; however, he afterwards came to me and stated, that his nephew had promised the money as a gratuity to the bearers, some of whom he had pressed into the service on the road. To this Guebra Michael gave his hand as a pledge; on which I ordered the money to be paid to him. It rained the whole day; the thermometer varied from 61° to 63°.

"July 29.—We were kept awake during the greater part of the last night by the barking of dogs, which were alarmed at the near approach of hyænas and other wild beasts.

"I had a conversation this morning with the Baharnegash respecting our conveyance hence to Adowa. He said that his orders were to pay us every possible attention; and added, that my letters had been forwarded to the Ras; but as he was unacquainted with their contents, he should be glad of some information respecting the object of my coming. I replied, that the English was a very powerful nation, which had complete command of the sea; and that an English nobleman, then at Mocha, had sent me for the purpose of promoting an intercourse of friendship with Abyssinia; which, if properly encouraged, could not fail of proving most beneficial to the whole country. I was induced thus far to explain myself, not only from the generally friendly manner in which he had behaved towards us, but also to secure his good offices in furtherance of our views. He expressed his entire satisfaction with my communication, and proceeded to inform me, that it was necessary to write immediately to Basha Abdallah, Secretary to Nebred Araur, Governor of Adowa, stating what animals we should want for our own riding, and for carrying our baggage, which, on my requisition, would be immediately sent down; that he himself had only three mules, but that they were all at our service. I told him, whatever had been arranged by the Ras, would meet with my hearty concurrence, and begged that he would hasten the messenger; and also urge to Basha Abdallah the necessity of sending the mules as speedily as possible, since I was obliged soon to return to Massowah. Accordingly I wrote a letter, which he promised to dispatch immediately, requesting to be furnished with twenty-five mules; to which I was led to expect an answer in six days. For the carriage of the letter I paid two dollars. I found the Baharnegash himself was under orders to attend me up to the Ras, which he professed he should do with pleasure. I was informed that, after we had ascended the mountain of Taranta, the natives, headed by that rascal the Nayib's guide, had assembled for the purpose of detaining our baggage, but our friend Guebra Michael, by his very strenuous exertions, succeeded in getting it up in safety. This, joined to the very insolent manner in which our guide had endeavoured to stop us on the ascent, as already mentioned, gave us good reason to suppose that some serious mischief was meditated, which our promptitude in crossing the mountain enabled us to avoid.

" The day being tolerably clear, we collected some plants, dried all our things, and made ourselves in other respects as comfortable as our situation would admit.

"July 30.—I was engaged all the morning in writing letters, copying my journal, and preparing a packet for Lord Valentia, containing an account of occurrences up to our arrival at Dixan, which was dispatched in the afternoon, and, as I afterwards learned, arrived safely. Towards evening Captain Rudland walked out with his gun, in hopes of meeting with game or hyænas; he however met with no success, having seen only two large spotted deer, which were exceedingly shy: during his absence I employed myself in taking a sketch of the mountains of Tigré. The day was clear and fine, though with much thunder and lightning in the evening. The thermometer was 66°. We were none of us well, which I attributed to change of food and climate.

"July 31.—A letter, of which the following is a translation, was received by the Baharnegash from the Ras's Secretary at Adowa, whom the natives style Bashaw Abdallah. After the usual compliments, 'Expecting that by this time the English are arrived at Dixan, I shall send my man Negada Moosa for them with horses and mules. I desire that you will pay them all the attention in your power, and will dispatch a messenger as soon as possible to acquaint Ras Welleta Selassé, with their safe arrival. The Ras commands that all care may be taken of them; that you will provide them with houses, with meat, and with drink of the very best, as your head must answer for it. In short, take as much care of them as you would of Ras Welleta Selassé, and so soon as they arrive, send me instant intelligence thereof.'

"In consequence of the receipt of this letter, I thought proper to make remonstrances about the high price that we were charged for provisions.

The Baharnegash told me that he would very willingly give whatever he had of his own, but that the articles which we wanted, were such as they themselves did not consume; and, owing to a late scarcity, which had been felt very severely so far as this place, they were extremely difficult to procure; it was not therefore in his power to afford us any relief in this particular; a representation which, from the poverty of the place, I had afterwards reason to consider true.

"The day was tolerably fine: about eleven in the forenoon, however, there fell a smart shower, during which an alarm was given of an hyæna being seen near our cave, by Mr. Carter and Pearce. Captain Rudland went out with his gun in pursuit of it, but was unsuccessful. I was myself too unwell to stir out, and was therefore engaged in drawing. More rain fell in the evening.

"August 1.—This morning the messenger who was dispatched with my letter to the Ras from Massowah, arrived hither on his way back from Antalow. He reported, that on the receipt of the letter the Ras issued immediate orders to a chief at Adowa to have in readiness the same number of animals as we had engaged from the Nayib; and to send them to meet us at this place as soon as he received intelligence of our arrival. The Nayib's charge to me for the conveyance of this letter, was, as I before mentioned, thirty dollars, of which the bearer declared that he was paid only two. Frequent showers fell during the day. The thermometer in our cave was 70°.

August 2.—I walked out in the morning with Captain Rudland; collected a few plants, and killed a bird called by the natives Warré, of which I took a sketch. Our people were engaged in repacking the baggage preparatory to our departure. The day was fine without rain. The thermometer in our cave was 75°.

"The Baharnegash, attended by his brother and Guebra Michael, paid us a visit at a late hour in the evening, and after some conversation on common occurrences, began mentioning the names of several, supposed English, gentlemen, who had formerly passed this place; these we imagined to have been Bruce and his attendants: they soon concluded their discourse by saying that our countrymen had made the inhabitants of the place a present of one hundred dollars, and therefore they hoped that I would do the same. Upon my evading this, and referring the Baharnegash to the Ras, he went so far as to assert that he had a rightful claim to the money, and being an independent chief, would demand it in the Ras's presence. I replied, that to my certain knowledge no English gentlemen had ever given any such sum; that one only had ever passed through this town before, and that he had given only forty dollars to the late Baharnegash, for which sum he had received in return a fine black horse: that we had already been at a very considerable expence, and as we were going up by desire of the Ras, and looked for no advantage ourselves from the journey, I should certainly not give him any thing at present, but should on my arrival at Antalow report the affair to the Ras, and guide myself entirely by his determination.

"After this had been explained, the brother began to raise his voice and interfere; but I stopped him at once, by telling him that I would not suffer him to meddle with the affair; on which he rose from his seat in a violent passion and left the house, followed, to our great satisfaction, by the Baharnegash and his nephew, who seemed happy thus to get rid of a demand which they found themselves too weak to support.

"In a few minutes Hamed Chamie returned with a message from the Baharnegash, saying, that his people were very hungry, and that it was on this account only that he had asked for money; he hoped, notwithstanding, that we should continue good friends, and that he was ready to accompany us as soon as the mules arrived; he also begged that what had passed might not be mentioned to the Ras.

"August 3.—I took a walk, as usual, after breakfast, and collected a few specimens of plants. The day was fine, and without rain. In the course of our walk we saw a large bird much resembling the Abba Gumba of Bruce; but a shower coming on at the moment, prevented our sportsmen from pursuing it. When the rain was over, Captain Rudland went out again, and killed a large bird called by the natives Derhomai (or water fowl, from Derho, a bird, and mai, water), of which I made a drawing. This bird inhabits low marshy grounds, and feeds on worms. We had it cooked, and found the flesh tender and well flavoured.

"At a late hour in the evening the brother of the Baharnegash waited upon Hamed Chamie, repeating his demands for money in the name of the town's people, declaring that it was their right, and that they were determined to be paid. Hamed Chamie said, that an answer had already been given by me to the Baharnegash; and he very properly got up, called for him, and brought him to me, complaining of the behaviour of the people. The Baharnegash, after desiring Hamed Chamie to pay no attention to them, said, that as our food and lodging had been provided by himself, no other person could possibly have any demand upon us.

" August 5.—Nothing particular occurred this day. The weather was bright and mild, like a May day in England.

" August 6.—So much rain, accompanied by thunder and lightning, fell this day, that we were scarcely able to stir out of doors. I amused myself with drawing, and Captain Rudland in collecting information from the inhabitants.

" The Baharnegash was very urgent to have a picture for the church: accordingly I set Pearce to work, who painted one of the Virgin Mary and the infant Christ, in most flaming colours, which gave great satisfaction. The thermometer in our hut at noon was 64°.

" August 7.—A letter was received from Basha Abdallah at Adowa, stating, that the mules were not to leave that place till to-morrow, and would therefore probably not arrive here before Sunday. This delay was attributed to the necessity of sending to the Ras at Antalow, for an order to have more mules purchased, as the people at Adowa refused to send their mules for our accommodation.

" A kafila came in from Massowah, by which the Baharnegash received a letter from Currum Chund; but no anwer arrived to either of our letters sent to Massowah. Reports were in circulation that Captain Court had been firing on Massowah, as the natives described an iron kettle which burst over the town.

" We heard that the dead bodies of three men had been found, washed down by the torrent, on this side of Taranta.

" Our sportsmen, having seen a dead horse and an ass lying in the skirts of the town, were out for two hours in the evening in pursuit of the hyænas, which they supposed would be attracted by the carcases. They discovered a great number of these animals growling and fighting over their food, and making at times a hideous roaring; they must be possessed of great strength, as a single one was observed dragging along the entire carcase of the horse; in size they varied considerably, but Captain Rudland and Pearce both agreed that one of them, which they wounded, was quite as large as a small ass. Some dogs of the village were gnawing the carcase, but they retired, snarling, to a small distance, on the approach of the hyænas, who in their turn did not seem to have any inclination to attack the dogs. Intermixed with the hyænas, and feeding on the carcase very amicably at the same time with them, were smaller animals, supposed to be jackalls. The morning was cold and foggy, but the weather cleared up about breakfast time, and continued tolerably fine for the remainder of the day.

"Intelligence arrived that a kafila, on its way hither from Massowah, had suffered severely by the sudden rise of the torrent at Elleilah, one man, ten camels, and a great part of the baggage were washed away.

"August 8.—I walked out in the morning, and collected some plants. In the evening we all sallied forth on an alarm of an hyæna. We saw two, one of which Captain Rudland was lucky enough to shoot; the ball passed through the right shoulder and lodged in the neck, on which the animal immediately fell. Pearce ran up to it, and threw large stones upon its head, and Mr. Carter thrust his sword down its throat, which soon dispatched it.

"On hearing the shot, the people of the village all came out, many of them armed with spears;

but we could not prevail on any of them to assist in carrying our game home, as all the Abyssinians hold the hyæna in utter abhorrence. Our servants, however, brought him in great triumph, and hung him up to one of the posts before our door, that I might take a drawing of him in the morning.

"August 9.—My first care in the morning was to examine the hyæna that we had shot the preceding night: it was a male, of the spotted species (canis crocuta), and is called by the natives Zubbee; its prevailing colour is a dirty light brown inclining to yellow, with black spots: the extremity of the tail is covered with long and coarse black hair, like that of a horse's tail; on the back is a ridge of long hair, of which that part between the loins and head inclines forwards, while the rest points towards the tail, shortening by degrees, so that it lies quite smooth on the rump. The length of this animal from the nose to the insertion of the tail was four feet three inches; its height, from the top of the shoulder to the sole of the fore foot, was two feet four inches and a half; and from the crown of the rump to the sole of the hind foot was two feet one inch and a half. We afterwards saw several considerably larger, and of a darker colour.

"When the inhabitants came out to us last night, on hearing the report of Captain Rudland's gun, they were accompanied by several of their dogs, which, as soon as they perceived the hyæna stretched out and roaring on the ground, fell upon him, and seized him with great fury; but as I have already mentioned, these two animals, in ordinary circumstances, though mutually inimical, seldom venture on a contest. We have more than once observed their passing and repassing, each snarling, but neither venturing to begin an attack; and, one evening, both were seen feeding on the same carcase. The hyæna, however, always retires from the presence of man; and the dogs, by barking, give notice to their master of its approach.

"While we were touching and skinning the hyæna, the inhabitants looked on with evident signs of horror and disgust; the Baharnegash, however, begged the liver of the animal, which forms one of the ingredients of an ink in which charms are written, that are worn round the arms as amulets from all evil. The man who was sent for the liver seemed as much afraid of it as of a snake, and carried it away with great caution on the end of a long stick.

"After we had skinned the hyæna, we left him on the grass about one hundred yards from our hut, where he remained untouched by the dogs or vultures during the whole day; but as soon as it became dusk, the carcase was dragged off and devoured by other hyænas.

"Having finished these observations, we took a walk of about three or four miles, but met with little worthy of observation. We killed a lizard of a light blue colour, of which I made a drawing, and took a camelion alive. On our return we were overtaken with very heavy rain, hail, thunder, and lightning.

"I was engaged during the afternoon in making drawings of some plants that we had collected in our walk.

"News arrived that Captain Court had been under the necessity of landing fifteen men from the Panther at Massowah, and of threatening the Nayib, before he could get possession of the packet which we dispatched hence: to this no answer has as yet been received.

"August 10.—I wrote a letter this morning to the Ras, informing him of our delay at Dixan, and that, as we had received no intelligence with respect to the time when the mules from Adowa would probably arrive, we should within in three days proceed with such conveyances as we might be able to procure at this place.

"Five dollars were required by the Baharnegash for the carriage of this letter to Antalow; with which demand, having no alternative, I was obliged to comply.

"We rode a short distance out of town, but the weather compelled us very soon to return; on our way back we passed over the highest part of the irregular hill on which Dixan is built; and which Bruce has not very accurately described, when he compares it to a sugar loaf, as may be seen in one of my larger views.

"On our return, we found that a fresh demand had been made on Hamed Chamie for some pepper for the messenger about to depart with our letter to Antalow; but this, being too valuable an article to part with, we absolutely refused. The letter, in consequence, was returned by the Baharnegash with the five dollars to Hamed Chamie; I immediately sent for the Baharnegash, and represented to him my surprise at what had passed: assuring him that I should leave Dixan in three days, and, if the letter should not arrive at Antalow before me, the blame would fall upon him. I afterwards thought it expedient to inclose the letter to Bashaw Abdallah, as the communication from Adowa to Antalow appeared more open than from this place. The Baharnegash attempted, but in vain, to prevent the letter being sent, by telling us he had information that the mules would be here to-morrow.

"In the evening there arrived a man from the village of Dagozie, two days journey hence, with intelligence that the mules from Adowa were near at hand. He brought also a lean cow from his uncle, who is Kantiba, or chief of the village above mentioned, as a present; in return for which I gave him two pieces of cloth. This, however, did not satisfy him; for, when we had retired to rest, he came to inform me, that, as he was about to set off for Hamazen, if I had any thing to give him, he begged to receive it immediately. After enquiring what were his demands, I learned that he had the modesty to expect a gift of an equal value with the mule he rode upon, which he estimated at the trifling sum of forty dollars; upon this I referred him to Hamed Chamie, as was invariably my custom on such occasions, and he soon got rid of him, by recommending him to take his cow back again, for which he thought he had already been most amply paid.

"August 11.—In the course of this morning two men arrived, bringing intelligence from Negada Moosa, that the mules would be here on the morrow; but we had so many similar accounts, that I told the Baharnegash I should pay no farther attention to verbal messengers, and, as these people might have come merely for the purpose of getting the usual recompence of a piece of cloth, I did not choose to comply with the custom any longer.

"Heavy rain attended by thunder came on at noon, and the remainder of the day was so dark and dismal, that in our hut we could not see to do any thing without a candle. Our whole party was unwell with violent colds. We killed a vulture, which upon examination, we pronounced "to be a bird of passage," since we could not discover any of that powder which, Bruce says, the hill birds of this country are provided with, and which, it is to be observed, all the birds that we have hitherto killed have been without.

"August 12.—We passed the morning in anxious expectation of the arrival of the mules, and in preparing our fire-arms, &c. for the journey. About twelve o'clock intelligence was brought us of their approach, and soon after, the Baharnegash introduced Hadjee Hamed, and Negada Moosa; they brought each of them a letter from the Ras, in Arabic, mentioning the former as a man in his confidence, to whom we were to make known all our wishes, and the latter as appointed to take charge of our persons and baggage. They seemed to be men of more respectability than any we had hitherto met with since we left Mocha, and their retinue and attendants were numerous, and decently clad. They brought us information that the Ras and his family were well; that he was himself exceedingly anxious to see us, and had given orders to bring us up, without delay, by the nearest road, to his presence; that all things were prepared for us by his special orders in the villages through which we had to pass; and that if any man should dare to molest us, his head must answer for it. They likewise mentioned, that when we arrived within two days march of Antalow, an additional retinue would meet us. Hadjee Hamed, immediately on his coming into our hut, recognized me, and I soon recollected that we had met at the village of Badoor, on one of the islands of Port Mornington, and that he then informed me he was on his way from the Sheriffe of Mecca to Ras Welleta Selassé. After having taken coffee, they retired with Hamed Chamie, and I gave an order for the purchase of five sheep for the better accommodation of the party.

"Dixan was now extremely full of strangers, for besides our attendants from the Ras, there were kafilas hourly coming in both from Massowah and Adowa. The day was cloudy with a little thunder.

"August 13.—Hadjee Hamed and Negada Moosa sent Hamed Chamie early in the morning to deliver me the mules sent by the Ras; I therefore went to the door of our hut, and all the mules, in number twenty-one, were brought before me; sixteen of them were of a large and coarse breed, for the conveyance of baggage, and five of a lighter, for our riding. This ceremony being over, the Baharnegash informed me, that he would provide me with three more, a sufficient number to accommodate all our people. I gave orders to have every thing prepared for setting out by daylight on the morrow, having consented to remain here this day at the request of our new attendants, who were anxious for a little rest, and with whom I felt desirous to commence our journey on as good terms as possible. They afterwards brought me flour and other necessaries, and informed us that every thing in future, would be provided for us, free of expence, by the Ras's commands.

"In the evening the Baharnegash visited us with his brother, who had been a very troublesome fellow; and as we knew that he could not come for any good purpose, we evaded all communication, on the plea of our interpreter being out of the way. The cause of their visit, as we afterwards learned, was this: the Baharnegash had promised us three mules, but being himself in possession of only two, he expected to obtain the third from his brother. This man, however, positively refused to accommodate him, saying, that as we had made him no present we should have nothing belonging to him. The Baharnegash used the most urgent entreaties; but all in vain. The only terms on which he would agree were, that his brother should give him an equal share of what he might receive from us. The Baharnegash told him that he was going on with us to Antalow, and that it might be very long before he should receive any thing; he was nevertheless willing, to give him half, so anxious was he to keep his word with us. His brother, however, demanding immediate payment, the Baharnegash was under the necessity of sending to a neighbouring village to purchase a mule, which was brought in the evening.

"The houses of Dixan are flat-roofed, and without windows, and, instead of chimneys, have two pots of earthenware rising out of the roof, but so narrow as to give vent only to a small portion of the smoke: the houses are built round a hill commanding an extensive prospect of the mountains of Tigré, and country around, which consists almost entirely of rocky mountains, on many of which are to be observed villages constructed much in the same style as at Dixan.

"The only public building in this place is the chapel, which we visited. It is a place of a mean appearance, with a conical thatched roof, and mud walls. On entering the door of the inclosure (A) the boys who conducted us kissed the door posts: and we, in conformity to their customs, pulled off our shoes and hats, on entering the door of the building itself (B). • The inner building was shut. The aisle that surrounded it (c c) was strewn with rushes; and on the walls were painted rude figures in glaring colours of St. George and St. Haimonout on horseback, with spears, and various other strange figures in as many strange postures. The priests bear large keys in their hands, like that which the painters place in the hand of St. Peter. The natives all appear fond of crosses. The Baharnegash was highly pleased with one given to him by Captain Rudland. Most of the Christians here have a cross marked upon their breast, or their right arm, or forehead, which with a blue silk string round their necks, they seem to think indispensable badges of their religion. They kiss every thing that has the least claim to sanctity or respect, a strong instance of which was the Baharnegash's kissing the letter which I delivered to him for the Ras's Secretary, Bashaw Abdalla.

"The people whom I have hitherto seen, with few exceptions, are idle, ignorant, and dirty; they are of a very dark complexion, few having a claim to the appellation of copper-coloured given them by Bruce. It is usual for them to say prayers over every thing they eat, drink, receive, or give away, concluding the ceremony with blowing upon it, in the same way as a conjuror does on his balls.

"In these prayers they always turn the face to the east, as they turn the heads of the animals which they kill to the west. They refuse to taste of any thing killed by Mahomedans, whom they hold in great contempt.

"Boys marry at fourteen years of age, girls at ten, eleven, and twelve; both are circumcised on the eighth day after their birth; this operation is performed by women.

"The number of wives possessed by each man

varies from one to ten, according to their property, or as they are able to support them, as each woman must be furnished with a separate place of residence.

" Most of the laborious occupations, both abroad and at home, devolve upon the women; such as grinding the corn, bringing in wood and water, which is brought from a valley about a mile from the town, cultivating the ground, and picking herbs for the consumption of the day. They carry their children on their backs, and wear tanned hides round their waists; their necks and arms are ornamented with beads, and white shells; and the women of the higher class allow the nails on the left hand to grow to a great length, wearing cases of leather on their fingers several inches long, to preserve them.

" Slaves are very dear at this place, if we are to be guided by the report of the inhabitants; but the price of these animals, like that of every other put up to the highest bidder, is greatly regulated by their outward appearance. If nature has been favourable, and given them fine features, with a tolerably fair skin, they sell for a great deal more than those of a darker colour.

" The proportion of land capable of cultivation, as far as we had an opportunity of observing, is scanty, consisting of a few spots on the sides of the hills, and the drier parts of the valleys.

" The present seems to be the season of spring in this country; some of the inhabitants are now ploughing their fields with wooden ploughs. These are rudely shaped out of the root or branch of a tree, and sometimes the shares are formed of iron. After twice ploughing the land, the clods are broken with rude hooked instruments by the women, who at the same time pick out the weeds; the grain is then strewn upon the ground, and they seem to make choice of the worst samples for seed. There are a great number of goats belonging to this place, but they are now mostly dry, in consequence of which milk is not to be obtained without great difficulty; the whole that we have been able to procure has not exceeded a pint per day. A small goat costs half a dollar. The sheep are most of them black, but some of them have white faces: the skins of all are valuable commodities, as they make excellent coverings; and no man moves a hundred yards from his house without having one hung over his shoulders.

"We have as yet observed but few cows, and those miserably poor. There is plenty of barley and juwarry, but we have not hitherto seen any wheat.

"White cloths are preferred at Dixan before any other colour. Tobacco, black pepper, looking-glasses, snuff, spirits, and large beads, are good articles for barter: green beads are at present in fashion, and therefore fetch a better price than any others.

"The musical instrument that we heard at Massowah, and which I imagine to be Bruce's lyre, is in use here; it was played upon by one of the young priests. Their singing is, if possible, ruder than their music, and both together are intolerable.

"Bruce says that they allow no figures in relief; the few that we have yet seen are two faces at the head of the couch on which I sleep.

"The duties arising from the merchandize that passes through Dixan are collected by the person, at whose house the travelling merchant chooses to put up. Travellers are housed and fed during their stay, for which the landlord is recompenced either in goods or money. The rate at which they pay on these occasions is said to be so very exorbitant, that I could give no credit to the report.

"The Baharnegash seems to preside over Dixan and six or seven adjoining villages; these appear to have agreed among themselves to continue in peace with, and faithful to, each other. If at any time an offence be committed, the whole body assembles, and the affair is discussed; but punishment is seldom inflicted, because the offender has an easy mode of evading it, by joining another hill tribe. It has been repeated to us by many of them, that they pay no tribute to the Ras; and they asserted more than once that they were entirely independent of the Tigré government. This, however, from several circumstances that occurred, we did not believe to be strictly the case; they may not pay him any revenue, but it is evident that they stand in awe of his authority.

"The Baharnegash carries on the affairs of his government entirely by verbal messages. Judging from the little attention that the Geesh characters in Bruce's book excited when we shewed them to him, I do not believe that he is himself capable either of writing or reading.

"There are no schools for the education of youth, in any language, that I could find out, at Dixan: we met with only a few persons who could read the church Bible, which I apprehend is the sole book in their possession; and those who have obtained even this degree of knowledge are considered as priests; at least in their own opinion. Of this order, upon trial, not one in twenty could write the characters which they read; indeed we found but one man in Dixan who attempted to write the native tongue: from this person we begged the different characters of the Geesh alphabet; but his obvious ignorance in this respect, gave us evident proof of his inability. Upon enquiry, we found that this person was not a resident at Dixan, but travelled about the country in the character of a physician as well as priest, and had for some time past been exercising his skill in the former profession.

"The present Baharnegash is a tall elderly man, with a mild countenance; the top of his head bald, and his hair bushy round his ears. His dress, like the rest of his people, consisted of a single garment wrapped round his body, and his only ensign of office was a peeled staff about six feet long, which was also borne by his relations, and those in authority under him. He performs the duties both of chief priest and governor, and recites prayers to his people both morning and evening, on which account he incurs some ridicule at court. The form of prayer commences with chanting three times over Jehu Arozoo (praise be to Jesus), in which he is joined by the whole assembly. This is followed by Binta Mariam Arozoo; then Haimanot Johannim, Georgis. Welleta Selassé, &c. which are all in like manner three times chanted by the congregation. To this succeeds the invocation, with which it began, Jehu Arozoo; the chief then recites several prayers, to which the congregation answer, Amen. The service ends with the whole congregation prostrating themselves three times, with their faces to the ground, calling out on the name of God—Tabbait—Tabbait—Tabbait. After this prostration the Baharnegash generally continues praying by himself for a short time, and immediately after issues orders for the day, which chiefly relate to the care of the cattle, and similar employments.

APPENDIX.

APPENDIX.

I.

PEDIGREE OF THE PAISHWA, referred to in p. 127.

- WISSOJEE PUNT of Sewurdhun.
  - WISSHONAUT, 1st Dessaie of Sewurdhun.
    - BALLAJE RAM, 2d Dessaie of Sewurdhun.
      - 1, BAJEE RAO Paishwa, succeeded his father in his honours and posts.
        - BALLAJEE RAO NANAH, 2d Paishwa.
          - WISWASS RAO, killed at Paniput.
          - JUNARDHUN RAO, died young.
          - 3. MHADU RAO, Paishwa.
          - 4. NARRAIN RAO, succeeded MHADU RAO.
            - 5. SEWAI MHADU RAO NARRAIN.
        - A son, who died young.
        - RAGONAUT RAO.
          - Adopted IMRUT RAO.
          - 7. BAJEE RAO, Paishwa.
          - 6. CHIMNAGEE.
      - CHIMNAJEE APPAH, took Salsette and Basein in 1740.
        - SUDDABAH, killed at Paniput, had no son.

APPENDIX.

II.

DUTIES proposed to be levied by the Nayib of Massowah; referred to in p. 230.

FOUR dollars for a bale of tobacco of fifteen maunds.

One-fourth of a dollar for one Bengal bag of 166 lb. of rice.

One dollar and twenty-two komassie for nine frassel of pepper.

Three dollars for twelve Bombay maunds, (28 lb.) of cotton.

One-fourth of a dollar for one frassel of kalai (block tin).

One fourth of a dollar for one frassel of gessel (tutenac).

Three dollars for twenty frassel of red copper.

Two dollars for four guz (twenty-eight inches) of red or blue broad-cloth.

Eight dollars for one corge (twenty pieces) of fine piece goods.

Five dollars for one corge of blue cosses.

Two dollars and a half for one corge of coarse cloth Baftas.

One dollar and a quarter for one corge of chintz, coarse or fine.

One dollar and a half for eight guz of kincaub or silk.

Two dollars for eight guz of velvet.

No duty on iron or gunpowder.

III.

EXTRACTS from Captain Court's Report on his return from Massowah; referred to in p. 398.

ON the 20th of July, having left Mr. Salt, with a guard of sepoys under Mr. Crawford, at Arkeko, I reached the vessel about eleven o'clock; and as the land wind almost ceased to blow before we left Arkeko in the cutter, I suffered much from the intense heat which prevails during the interval of calm between the land and sea breeze. I had hardly been on board one hour, when a hard squall of hot wind off the land suddenly arose, in which we parted our cable. Enveloped in a cloud of dust, and suspecting from the appearance of the sky that we were about to encounter very severe weather, I thought it unsafe to let go another anchor, and at once determined to avail myself of the opportunity then afforded me, by the wind blowing from the north-westward, to run the vessel out of the harbour, and endeavour to get sea-room, before the gale should become too violent; and, in the event of the weather clearing up, it was my intention, as well with a view to intimidate the Nayib from raising any more obstacles to Mr. Salt's immediate departure, as to facilitate Mr. Crawford's return to the vessel with the guard of sepoys, to have tried to effect a passage into Arkeko Bay, and bring the Panther to an anchor abreast that town. The squall continued with great violence till half past four P. M.; and it was not till half past seven o'clock that we had accomplished the purpose abovementioned.

As soon as the vessel was anchored, I sent the cutter on shore well manned and armed, under charge of Mr. Denton, and was much pleased, about nine o'clock, to see her returning with Lieutenant Crawford and the sepoys, all safe. I had also the great additional gratification to learn from Lieutenant Crawford, that the appearance of the Panther standing into Arkeko Bay had produced, in the minds of the Nayib and his faithless and rapacious Ascari, the exact sensation and effect that I had hoped, and expected it would ; and that it was not until she hove in sight, that they ceased to importune Mr. Salt for more money upon new pretences, to which every fresh instant gave birth.

On the 21st, I quitted Arkeko Bay to proceed to the Island of Dohul, where we had been informed that provisions and fresh water might be obtained. As we passed Massowah, I hove the vessel to, and sent an officer on shore in the cutter with a message to Currum Chund, respecting the anchor we had left in the harbour, and at the same time desired him to inform the Nayib that I should be back in six days, when I hoped to receive, without delay, Mr. Salt's dispatches for Lord Valentia from his hands, as I had not the least doubt of their arriving from Dixan by that time. Having received a satisfactory answer from Currum Chund, I proceeded on to Dohul, and anchored the Panther in safety off the N. W. side of it at sunset. Being informed by the islanders that the proper anchorage was on the east side of the island, and the account I had received at Massowah, "that plenty of horned cattle, sheep, and goats, with abundance of good water, might be procured at this place," being confirmed, we weighed anchor, and worked round the south side to the proper anchorage, where we came to in three fathom at the distance of one and a quarter from the island. A spit of sand which runs off the south end of Dohul breaks the sea, and shelters the roads in some measure, in that direction, and a similar one to the northward protects it from the violence of the N. W. winds ; but it would be dangerous riding here when the wind blows hard from any point on the eastern-board.

On our first coming among them, we found the inhabitants of this island, who in number did not exceed thirty grown persons, inoffensive, mild, and hospitable ; and I was in hopes that my presents of rice, tobacco, and blue cloth, might have made them so much our friends, that they would have cheerfully supplied us with water, and such live stock as we wanted, at a reasonable price; that is to say, at the rates we had been accustomed to procure them, at Massowah. I was led, however, very soon, to entertain a different opinion: for the islanders, in consequence of injunctions, no doubt brought from the Nayib by a boat which arrived here shortly after the Panther, entirely changed their conduct towards us; and from being very forward and willing to render us every service in their power, became quite the reverse, and seemed extremely desirous to get rid of us as soon as possible. In addition to this vexatious circumstance, I had the mortification to find that, in consequence of the long drought universally complained of in the Red Sea, the Dohul wells, which are, I believe, in number about twenty, several of which however were dry, could not supply us nearly so expeditiously as I wished and expected, with the large quantity of water we required to replenish our stock; I therefore determined upon going to Dhalac, where I was certain that we could, in two or three days, procure as much as we wanted.

After purchasing a few young goats, which are here, as well as at Valentia Island, excellent, I left Dohul on the 26th of July P.M.; but owing to contrary winds and threatening weather did not reach Nockara Roads, until the next day about noon, at which time it blew a hard gale from the westward. At five P.M. the wind began to veer round to the southward, and the weather to wear altogether so threatening an aspect, that I was induced to strike the lower yards and topmasts. This and every other possible precaution being taken, and all our anchors down, saved us, under God's providence, from shipwreck. Since I have been at sea, I never have in any vessel rode out a harder gale of wind at anchor; nor was I ever in my life at anchor on a lee-shore with so awful a prospect of inevitable destruction, had an accident happened to one of our cables. The gale continued with unabated violence from four P. M. of the 27th, until ten A. M. of the 28th. During the whole of the night loud peals of thunder, vivid lightning, and a sea of fire, encreased the terrific horrors of our situation. Thanks be to God! we rode the storm out, which began to abate considerably about noon on the 28th; and in the evening Unus brought us off sixteen casks of water.

At five P. M. on the 30th, having replenished our stock of this article, we weighed and made sail for Massowah harbour, in which we anchored in safety a quarter before ten A. M. on the 29th, and were fortunate enough, with the assistance of a diver, procured us by Unus, to recover the bow anchor we had parted from, and left behind us on the 20th.

Having learned that a kafila was arrived from Dixan, I applied to the Nayib to know whether letters had not come by it for Lord Valentia; but received an answer that none had arrived. On the 31st, having gained intelligence from Unus that dispatches from Mr. Salt were certainly in the possession of the Nayib, I wrote to him by Unus to demand them, and to say that I would not wait any longer, but should proceed to Mocha, with or without them, and would there receive Lord Valentia's instructions how to act, in consequence of such wanton and unmerited perversity, but that I would leave Unus for forty-eight hours, in hopes that the Nayib would perceive the injustice of his conduct, and the unpleasant circumstances to which it must lead; and in consequence, be induced to send the letters by him.

By the assistance of a fair spirt of wind we got out of the harbour at eleven o'clock P. M.

On the 1st of August we found in the morning that we had been driven by the strong northerly currents in sight of Dohul. We beat against these currents and a strong S. E. wind for another twenty-four hours, and found ourselves in precisely the same situation on the following morning.

On the 2d, I had the pleasure of seeing Unus's dow leave the harbour of Massowah, and make directly for us. In a few hours he came on board, and delivered me letters from Mr. Salt, announcing his safe arrival at Dixan. For the six following days we beat against adverse winds and currents without being able to get round Hurroo point. At length we rounded it in the burst of a land gale from W. N. W. under a fore staysail, at midnight. We had afterwards a fair wind, and passed the Aroes at sun-set on the 10th.

At three o'clock on the 11th we were abreast of the town of Mocha in nineteen fathom. At five it became so black and threatening over the land, that although in six fathom, we could see neither shipping nor town. Having no land mark to guide us, we erroneously supposed ourselves to be to the north of the town; but on the weather clearing, discovered that we were ten miles to the south of it. Trifling as was the distance, it was six days before we were able to beat up against the strong northwester, which generally kept us under our close reefed top sails. On the 16th we anchored in Mocha roads.

(Signed) CHARLES COURT.

END OF VOL II.

VOYAGES AND TRAVELS
TO
INDIA, CEYLON
THE RED SEA
ABYSSINIA AND EGYPT

VOYAGES AND TRAVELS TO INDIA, CEYLON THE RED SEA ABYSSINIA AND EGYPT

IN THE YEARS
1802-1806

GEORGE VISCOUNT VALENTIA

IN FOUR VOLUMES
VOL. III

ABYSSINIA - RED SEA - EGYPT

ISBN : 978-93-5324-451-4 (Set)

ISBN : 978-93-5324-454-5 (HB)

First Published, London,1811

Published, 2020

Published by

Facsimile Publisher
12 Pragati Market
Ashok Vihar, Ph-2
Delhi-110052
E-mail: books@facsimilepublisher.com

Printed at: G. Print Process, Delhi.

Voyages and Travels to India, Ceylon The Red Sea Abyssinia and EGYPT

Author: George Viscount Valentia

VOYAGES AND TRAVELS

TO

INDIA, CEYLON, THE RED SEA, ABYSSINIA, AND EGYPT,

IN THE YEARS

1802, 1803, 1804, 1805, AND 1806.

BY

GEORGE, VISCOUNT VALENTIA.

IN FOUR VOLUMES.

VOL. III.

ABYSSINIA.—RED SEA.—EGYPT.

LONDON:

PRINTED FOR F., C., AND J. RIVINGTON,
ST. PAUL'S CHURCH YARD.

1811.

CONTENTS.

VOL. III.

7

CHAPTER I.

CHAPTER II.

CHAPTER III.

CHAPTER IV.

CHAPTER V.

CHAPTER VI.

CHAPTER VII.

CHAPTER XII.

APPENDIX.

CHAPTER I.

MR. SALT'S NARRATIVE CONTINUED.—*Departure from Dixan.—Journey thence to Abha.—Agowma. Chelicut.—Arrival at Antalow.—First Interview with the Ras.—Transactions at Antalow.*

"AUGUST 14, 1805. Although at day-light I urged our people to make all expedition, it was nine o'clock before the baggage was properly arranged, when we left Dixan on our way to Antalow. We had the satisfaction of finding our mules not inferior to those that brought us to Dixan.

"We passed the church to our right, and then proceeded over a rocky hill, at the foot of which were some small vallies, and beyond them a village called Hadawe. We had scarcely passed this latter place, when we were followed by some of its inhabitants, who much wished us to halt there; among these was one of the Baharnegash's sons, named Socinius, whose urgent anxiety to prevail upon us, evidently showed how much he was interested in our detention. We however pressed forward, passing over the plain of Zarai, which strongly reminded me of the vale of Evesham, in Worcestershire. The whole was in a high state of cultivation, and disposed in ridges for the convenience of irrigating the land. A little farther on, we passed a clear brook running down the middle of the valley, on the bank of which a party of travellers were resting themselves. We also saw here an Abou Gumba, and many Guinea fowls. Hence we began to wind round the side of the mountain, which makes a very conspicuous object in the view from Dixan; and soon came in sight of another village on our left, called Adishud, on a very lofty hill, that would form a good situation for a fort. Immediately in front of us, at about the distance of three miles, was the village of Adioolta, placed as conspicuously as the one before mentioned. A large Daroo tree stands in the middle of the plain, near which we were not a little surprized at meeting with a band of musicians, who immediately ran forward before us, blowing their trumpets and beating their drums, so as to make a most discordant concert. There being some appearance of rain, our guides conducted us towards Adioolta, where we were met by another Baharnegash, for so they call every head man of a town. We were not received by him with much civility, and he appeared very unwilling that we should enter his territory. In a short time however he relaxed, and at length shewed us to his house; but our treatment there was so unsatisfactory, that, when our baggage approached, we were glad to hasten away.

"The inhabitants of this place are all, nominally, Christians, and they acknowledge no authority except that of their head man. The village and its vicinity exhibited every appearance of neatness and plenty, and the valley below was well cropped, especially with Indian corn, which is usually more forward, in this climate, than any other grain. The people manufacture a particular kind of coarse cloth, from the wool and hair of their sheep and goats; they first spin the materials into small ropes, instead of threads, and these, when sewed together, make a covering like a quilt. The woman of the house retained great remains of beauty, and had two fine children in her arms, plump and healthy. We descended thence through the cultivated grounds nearly in a southerly direction, leaving on our right a lofty hill not unlike that of Riacotta, in the Baramaal country. A material alteration now began to take place in the vegetation; the kolqual became less frequent, and the whole face of the country was again covered with acacias, the verdure of which, and the freshness of the turf, composed a scene very like some of our forests in England. We passed another very large Daroo-tree, growing by the side of a brook, the wide spreading branches of which covered a space of at least three hundred feet in circumference. Our guides were very unwilling that we should take up our quarters under it for the night, lest we should be seriously incommoded by the expected overflowing of the brook; and indeed its roots, bared to a great extent, by former torrents, shewed that this apprehension was by no means without foundation. In consequence we proceeded two miles farther, to the village of Bakauko, where we halted, having been overtaken by the rain just before we reached it. Our lodging was a place that in England would scarcely have served for a cow-shed; but the civility of the people, who brought us goats, and plenty of milk and honey, made it more comfortable than a better place would have proved with less hospitality. The rain continued very heavy till evening.

" August 15.—That part of our baggage, which for want of a sufficient number of mules we were obliged to have conveyed by men, arrived in the morning under the care of our friend Guebra Michael. We were yesterday joined by a female Hadjee, or pilgrim, who had spent three years at Mecca, and was on her return to the distant country of the Galla. It was, I suppose, on account of the sanctity acquired by this long pilgrimage, that one of our chiefs, who was himself a Hadjee, treated her with much respect, and shared his coffee with her.

" The Baharnegash of Dixan arrived at nine o'clock to take his leave; he informed us that he should make haste to the presence of the Ras, where he expected to arrive in three days, and would send on for more mules for our accommodation. He told us that he dared not accompany us farther, having had a skirmish sometime back with a neighbouring tribe, in which many of the opposite party had fallen; he however, left his son Guebra Michael to proceed with us two days journey on our way. We paid, by the advice of our guides, six dollars to the people of the house where we lodged, and were by no means pleased to find that they were extremely dissatisfied with so ample a recompence. At half past ten we were on our way, and having passed on the left the village of Maroko, built on a hill of moderate height, we found ourselves in a plain interspersed with hillocks. Here Captain Rudland shot a goose, and an Abou Gamba; the former, through the idleness of our people, escaped; the latter we carried on to Asceriáh. The country was in a good state of cultivation, and many villages appeared on the hills around; Murgah was on our right, Mandoobah opposite to it on our left; and beyond, on a much loftier hill, was the Hadowé mentioned by Bruce.

" Soon after we made our way through a grove of wild olive trees, and afterwards along the edge of a tremendous precipice, looking directly down into a gulley, in which were small pools of water but no running stream. We then descended, and passed along the bed of the torrent for some distance; a shower of rain overtook us, but it was over before we had ascended the hill on which stands the village of Asceriáh. At this place we were received with great coolness by the inhabitants; they offered us no shelter but that which a tree afforded, and we were for some time apprehensive that this would be our only accommodation for the night. At length, however, an old man received us into his house, which was a better one, and more abounding in family conveniences, than any which we had seen before. I took here a view of the mountains, which are extremely wild in their forms; and a sketch of the Abou Gumba, of which Bruce has given a very correct representation.

" August 16.—We were awakened at a very early hour in the morning by Negada Moosa, who seemed anxious to hurry us away from this inhospitable place; I call it so, from the difficulty that we found in procuring even water for our consumption. One man only, superior to his neighbours in civility, brought us a small portion of milk. We soon left our baggage behind, but had not got far before we were overtaken by a party of men, one of whom, we were given to understand, was the chief of the place that we had quitted. He employed all his eloquence to prevail on us to return, which however we resisted, both on account of the inhospitable treatment we had experienced, and because we were well assured that his present importunity arose only from his fears of Ras Welletta Selassé, and not from a real desire to atone for his former neglect

"The mountain of Geshen was far on our left hand, when we made a rapid descent northward into the fine plain of Tushalloo, which is fully six miles in length, and about two in breadth. The village of Addagé, belonging to Kantiba Socinius, overlooks it from a rising ground on the right, as Nissom and Menju do on the left. It is interspersed with Tombo trees, which in appearance are not unlike the mulberry tree. To the north was pointed out to us the district of the Sewarré, and the villages of Adowmo and Diggé; opposite to the last is another called Ambullah. From Asceriáh we had been going nearly north-west, on account of the impassable mountains to the south; but we now turned off over a rising ground to the south, and, passing Bat'ha, soon reached Abha, the residence of the Baharnegash Subhart. We were very cordially received by the old man in a small house, built under the brow of a projecting rock, that completely sheltered it from the inclemencies of the weather. He was seated on a couch surrounded by his attendants, and almost enveloped in a long white mantle with a red border and fringe. He was small in person, with a face deeply marked with the furrows of age. We found here that much more attention was paid to form than at Dixan. The mode of salutation in use is to present the hand, and afterwards kiss the back of it twice; no person is permitted to go into the presence of the Baharnegash without uncovering to the waist, nor is he addressed by any one except in a whisper, with the mouth covered and applied close to his ear. Soon after we had been seated, he gave us plenty of hydromel, and seemed to think that we did not make sufficiently free, though some of our party were so complaisant, as to drink two brulhes* full; he also treated us with cakes covered with curds. He told me that he was originally much attached to Ras Michael Suhul, and supplied him with a large tribute in kind, but having had some disturbance with a neighbouring tribe, the Ras came with an army and burned down the whole of his town. It had been afterwards rebuilt by him, but was destroyed a second time, and for a similar reason, by Ras Welleta Selassé, about eight years ago: he farther mentioned, that he was at Gondar before the war broke out between Ras Michael Suhul and Waragna Fasil, and that his brother was present at the battle of Damot, fought between those parties. He was very urgent that we should spend the ensuing day with him, it being one of their fast days, promising, on our compliance, to see us safe on our way to the Ras. Guebra Eyut, a boy belonging to the Ras, having mentioned to our servants that the hope of obtaining a handsome present was the only reason for the Baharnegash's pressing our stay, and that he knew the Ras was most anxious for our arrival at Antalow, I sent for Hadjee Hamed and Negada Moosa, and after some conversation resolved to follow their advice, which was to take my departure the next morning; when I informed the Baharnegash of my intention, he remonstrated much against it, but with politeness, and promised to send his son to attend us.

" I walked up to the church in the evening,

* Venetian glass decanters holding about a pint.

which is partly excavated out of the side of the rock: the road to it is winding and steep, and so difficult of access, that I fear it has but few visitors; unless the inhabitants of the place are more devout than they appear to be. The view from it amply repaid us for our trouble, as we thereby gained a distinct prospect of the valley which we had passed in the morning, beyond which was a fine range of rugged rocks and mountains, rising behind each other at a great distance, until they were lost in the clouds. The opposite side of the hill was thickly covered with houses, rocks, and trees, and formed so very interesting and characteristic a scene, that I sat down on a rock to sketch it, but had not time enough, before the evening came on, to do it justice.

"Our fare this day was abundant, having been provided by this "nobleman," as Bruce terms one of his predecessors, with five sheep and plenty of maise, of a much superior quality to what we met with at Dixan. Maise is a liquor made of honey, fermented with barley, and strengthened with a bitter root called taddo; it is called hydromel by Bruce, and mead by Poncet: the latter has accurately described the process of making it. (Vide note page 218 in Lockman's translation, published at London 1743.) Mussulmauns as well as Christians seemed to enjoy this beverage, and some of the former found it necessary to sleep away the rapid effects of it on their senses.

"August 17.—Early in the morning the Baharnegash brought me a cow and some honey, hinting his expectation of my making him a present in return: this I evaded on the plea, that, as I was going to the Ras, I was not furnished with presents for any other person, but, that if he wished to be paid for what we had received, I must refer him to Hamed Chamie, to whom I had entrusted every arrangement of this nature. I was advised by the Ras's people to give him thirty dollars, being assured by them, at the same time, that this would be the last expence of the kind, there being no person between this place and Antalow, who would think of making any demand upon us. As the Baharnegash had really been very friendly, I ordered Hamed Chamie to give him twenty dollars, which, to my surprize, was received with great satisfaction. I now gave orders for the mules to be loaded, when the Baharnegash came up, with a very serious air, and informed me that he had intelligence of a large body of armed men, three thousand in number, who had assembled in order to intercept us, and that unless he were with us we should run great risk of being plundered; he again therefore begged that we would stay till the morrow. I told him, in return, that we were not easily alarmed, being well provided with fire-arms in case of molestation, and, if we were overpowered by numbers, the aggressors would be answerable with their lives to the Ras, who, I had no doubt, would take exemplary vengeance on them; more words, therefore, on the subject were useless, since I was determined to proceed immediately in spite of every obstacle. This put an end to the scheme which had been planned for our detention; in which I have every reason to believe that Negada Moosa, if not Hådjee Hamed, was concerned.

"At half past eight we left Abha, and waited on the first rising ground about half an hour till all our baggage came up. We were at first somewhat surprised at seeing great numbers of the villagers with goats, calves, and other cattle closely following, or passing by us, on the same road that we were travelling, but on turning round an angle of the mountain on our left the whole was explained; for we there found a large concourse of people assembled from all the neighbouring villages to barter the produce of their different hills. It being a new and interesting sight to us, we rode up and took a circuit round the market. Among other wares we observed in it iron, wrought and unwrought, for ploughshares and other purposes, cattle of all kinds, horses, skins, cotton, ghee, and butter; the latter in round balls, and as white as in England; also baskets of chillies, and of a red pod found on the neighbouring hills which the inhabitants eat when ripe. This market is held weekly. The women whom we saw here, were generally tall and well shaped, and many of them handsome. Notwithstanding the number of persons that had already assembled, which could not be less than three hundred, we afterwards met on our road as many straggling parties, with merchandise, as would probably double the throng.

"The plain through which we were travelling, was about two miles in breadth, and the road passed close to the abrupt descent of the mountains on the left, between various isolated rocks, among which was one in the form of a tower, of vast bulk and height. We passed on our left the village of Guragubbo, and on our right that of Muzembah. About three miles farther the soil became of a more sandy nature, which produced several species of Ixia.

"The Baharnegash soon after overtook us, and rode on before us, till we ascended an eminence at the bottom of a semicircular ridge of mountains, over which there is but one pass by which it is possible to ascend; here we waited for nearly an hour before all our mules arrived. In steepness and ruggedness this hill may be compared to Taranta, though its height is considerably inferior.

"When we had arrived nearly at the top of the pass, the Baharnegash led us out of the road, up a scarcely accessible ascent to a projecting rock, and it was not till we had toiled up with infinite difficulty, that we found our conductor had brought us thither for the idle purpose of gaining a shelter from the impending rain. With great labour we got our mules back again into the road, and began to descend the hill, which we found much more difficult than the ascent; soon afterwards we were overtaken by the rain, but after traversing two more hills of moderate size, we reached a miserable village, where we took shelter. As soon as the weather had become fair again we recommenced our march, and travelled about three miles farther, nearly in a S. E. direction, to the ruinous village of Recaito, where, after having experienced much difficulty in procuring a shed, we halted for the night. The thermometer was 68°: The distance from Abha to Recaito we computed to be from ten to twelve miles.

"August 18.—We procured a little supper last night, and eggs and milk this morning, in exchange for a few beads, but we found the damsels very keen in making bargains. The woman of the house was sufficiently civil, but the rest of the inhabitants appeared little disposed to accommodate us, and we discovered in the morning, that they had neglected to procure food for our attendants, so that we had to wait a considerable time till it was prepared.

"All the villages in this district bear strong marks of the ravages committed by the Ras's army, or some other military devastation, for the greater part of them are at present mere heaps of ruins, and, as the Baharnegash told me, the people have no inclination to rebuild them.

" In quitting Recaito we went first to the eastward, and afterwards proceeding due south, ascended a lofty and extremely steep pass, on the top of which ran a stream of water that oozed through its porous channel, and dripped on the rocks below. The whole side of the mountain was covered with Acacia-trees, among which grew the Serge, the Tabbib, and other sweet-scented plants and shrubs, besides many beautiful flowers of which I collected specimens. About half way up we turned again in an eastern direction, and on reaching the summit, found a level and extensive flat, which, though moist and swampy from numerous springs, appeared to be very capable of cultivation, and if it were properly drained, well fitted for corn.

" I collected here three species of bulbous plants, and a few specimens of iron ore, which lay scattered in great plenty on several of the hills that we passed. After resting an hour by the side of one of the springs, we proceeded, with all our baggage, along the edge of the flat to the village of Hadjaian; thence, after winding round to the southward, and crossing a small stream, the banks of which were shaded by the Laham, a tree much resembling the Mango in its growth, we ascended a hill, on the west of which stands the village of Shihah.

" The Baharnegash behaved with much politeness during the whole of this day's journey; he even dismounted, and offered me his own mule, which was far superior to that on which I rode; but he afterwards hinted to Captain Rudland, that a little more money would be acceptable. A tolerably good house was prepared for us; but we were much incommoded by smoke, being obliged to cook in our sleeping-room. It is, probably, this smoke which injures the sight of the inhabitants, for we observed that even the children were many of them nearly blind, and almost every woman advanced in years had lost one, and many of them both their eyes.

"We were roused about two o'clock in the morning by the Baharnegash, who called out most vociferously that an enemy was at hand. It was some time before we could get a light, during which our own party had armed, and was prepared for the expected attack. A rumbling noise or sound like that of a drum, or tom-tom, from the hill in our rear, confirmed us in the belief that some danger was at hand. A light being brought, we found the whole of the Baharnegash's attendants ready armed, with lighted matchlocks, spears, and shields; and a most "warlike" figure they made. Captain Rudland in the mean time had gone out to reconnoitre, and discovered that what had been mistaken for the beating of a drum, was nothing more than the noise made by an old woman in grinding her corn, which here, as well as in Arabia and India, is always done in the night. The alarm however continuing, we at length learned from Hamed Chamie, that two brothers, Agoos and Subagadis, with their army, were coming to take possession of the town, and that the whole country was in a state of uproar; we were informed at the same time, that the only danger to ourselves was the risk of being accidentally molested during the confusion of a nocturnal attack, for it was by no means their intention to do us any voluntary injury.

"In the mean time, Hadjee Hamed and Negada

Moosa prepared themselves to go out and meet them, should the news be true. Spies had been already sent, who returned one after another with intelligence, and we at last were informed that one of them had been detained on the road by the chiefs, who on hearing that we were in the town, declared their intention of deferring the attack till we should have passed on to the Ras. With some difficulty we prevailed on the Baharnegash to retire, and then putting some ghee in our lamp, we lay down with our fire-arms at hand, and slept till day-break. Hadjee Hamed, at his own request, slept at the door of our room during the remainder of the night.

"August 19.—We had another call to arms before our baggage was ready, upon which, we ascended, with the Baharnegash, a hill close by the house where we lodged, and which commanded a view of the country around. On this, as a strong post, the villagers had all assembled, to the number of thirty or forty, with their spears and shields, ready to defend it. Here and there we saw women and children driving in their cattle, and armed men on horseback on the look out, but no enemies made their appearance, except a few stragglers on the eminences at a distance. After some time we were finally told, that it was a false alarm, upon which we returned to our house, and prepared for our departure. As we were quitting the village, the Baharnegash and his son took leave of us, finding they could not get any more presents, and not choosing any longer to encounter the dangers and fatigue of the march.

"The alarm had not extended far, as we found the inhabitants of the next village very peaceably at work in their fields. We crossed a plain, through which ran a brook shaded with shrubs, and bordered with many kinds of plants of exquisite beauty; afterwards, descending a rugged steep, we entered a valley of rich pasture land, the grass of which was so plentifully mixed with white and red clover, yellow crowfoot, and dandelion, that it had the exact appearance of an English meadow in spring. The cattle feeding upon it were all in high condition. Captain Rudland shot a bird resembling the lapwing, and a little farther on, a couple of fine wild ducks. At the end of this valley was another steep pass, which brought us in sight of a plain surrounded with woody hills and towering rocks, very similar, in general character, to some of the finer valleys in Derbyshire. We halted at a village called Calaut, in the centre of the vale, intending to pass the night there; but, after having waited some time, and finding there was no house prepared, nor any probability of our procuring one, I ordered the tent to be pitched under the shade of a large Daroo tree, and left the village not very well pleased with the want of hospitality in its inhabitants. We afterwards accepted an invitation to the house of a Mussulmaun, named Hadjee Abdalla, in the lower town, who was a friend of Negada Moosa. This man treated us with much attention, prepared bread for us, and brought us milk, which, with the two wild ducks, made up our repast for the day. The thermometer was 70°.

" August 20.—In the morning we were given to understand that it was impossible to procure people for the conveyance of that part of our baggage which was not carried by the mules, the Chief of the village having absented himself, in order to evade the orders sent by the Ras for providing us with every thing necessary for our accommodation. We were obliged, therefore, to remain another day.

"In the course of the day, Tigra Mokan Welleta Samuel, Chief of the villages of Debra Muttai, came down from his hill with a present of a sheep and milk, and also engaged to supply us with people at an early hour on the following morning. He made an excuse for appearing in a squalid dress, by informing me that he was in mourning for his brother. His shirt was blackened with dirt, and was to be worn eighty days. In confirmation of this, Hadjee Hamed informed me that all the Christians in Abyssinia mourn in the same way, and also tear the skin off their temples, to shew their affection for the deceased.

"From this worthy man, who seemed more shrewd and sensible than any we had yet met with, I procured some information, which, when joined with what I had before obtained, pretty clearly explained the present state of this part of the country. This man's father, Woldo Kemellet, was chief of the district of Agowma, in extent three days march across, in which are the villages of Seraxo, Gullimuckidah, Akran, Duccakallah, Calaut, and many others. This territory, in the time of Michael Suhul, yielded to him, as Ras, much tribute in gold, matchlocks, and cattle; but after Ras Welleta Selassé came into power, Woldo Kemellet was forcibly driven out of his country by Shum Woldo, a celebrated warrior, the friend and favourite of the present Ras, who styled him brother, though there was no relationship by blood between them. Since this revolution, the district has only paid to the Ras annually two hundred skins of honey, two hundred sheep, fifty cows, and ten matchlocks, being a trifling tribute in comparison to what it before yielded. As a compensation to the family of Woldo, the Ras gave to Welleta Samuel the villages of Debra Muttai, with the surrounding land, to be held free of all tribute.

"It is now three years since a battle was fought between Shum Woldo and Baharnegash Yasous of Dixan, near Bakauko. Yasous came up, with all the dependents he could muster, to attack the former. Their forces, if such they could be called, were said to have amounted to five thousand men on each side. In the action Yasous was victorious, having killed one hundred and fifty of the opposite party, and carried off a band of musicians belonging to Shum Woldo.

"The district of Agowma has since fallen, by the death of Woldo, into the hands of his four sons, Thadoo, Guebra-Gurroo, Subagadis, and Aggoos, who for some time were in intimate alliance with each other, and conquered many of the villages around, but at length quarrelled about the distribution of their new acquisitions. The Ras favours Thadoo and Guebra-Gurroo, who have been for some time in his presence. The latter of the two is however considered as a cipher, being a man of weak capacity. In the mean time Subagadis and Aggoos are making use of the absence of their competitors to get all they can into their own possession; it is supposed however that Thadoo will soon arrive with assistance from the Ras to stop their farther progress, as he has already sent orders to the people of Shiha to make a vigorous defence till he comes to their succour.

"About ten in the morning Hadjee Abdallah was sent for by Aggoos, who, I was given to understaud, was the chief of Calaut; and shortly afterwards, having made proper enquiries, he did us the honour of a visit, attended by a large train of warriors, of whom a few were armed with matchlocks, and the rest with spears and shields. He appeared to be little more than twenty years of age, handsome in person, but fierce and rude in his manners; he briefly told us, that he was absent when we arrived, otherwise we should have met with a better reception, but that he had now brought us a couple of bullocks; he also mentioned, that on hearing we were travelling this way, he had deferred his intended attack on Shihah. He then rose up, and went away with as little ceremony as he came, and in the evening we received from him some milk and sixty-five cakes of teff bread two feet in diameter, as also twenty-five of the same kind from Welleta Samuel.

"August 21.—Though we rose at a very early hour this morning, it was eleven o'clock before all was ready for our departure: in the midst of our preparation we were joined by the young chief Aggoos: he contented himself with looking on in silence, till all our mules were loaded, and then by blows and threats, very speedily made his people take up the remainder of our baggage.

"Almost the whole of this part of the country consists of rocky hills and cultivated valleys, through which our road wound in a general direction from south-east to south-west. About six miles from Calaut, we passed Gullimuckida and Ersubhah on our right hand. We had scarcely gone two miles farther, when we were overtaken by the young warrior Aggoos, attended by two of his fighting men on horseback. He stopped to speak to Hadjee Hamed; but his impatient spirit could not brook travelling at the slow rate we were going; accordingly, in a few minutes, he galloped away, and we soon lost sight of him behind the hills in our front A messenger on horseback soon after met us to gain intelligence of our approach, and with him our friend Negada Moosa rode forward to get all things in readiness for our reception. The country was very rich in pasturage, and we saw vast herds of cattle feeding in the different valleys, also a few horses, of a small breed, but which were however capable of much work. We alarmed two jackalls on the plain grubbing up roots, but they fled so swiftly up the hills that Captain Rutland could not approach within gun-shot of them. About three o'clock we arrived at Genáter, the capital of the district of Agowma. It is a village, consisting chiefly of conical huts, overlooked by a high rock, steep on every side, and on the top of which is an area about one hundred feet in diameter, occupied partially by a citadel. Here we were met by Subagadis, the elder of the four sons of Shum Woldo. He uncovered himself with great humility on approaching, and saluted us by kissing our hands; he then led us into his state room, which was not unlike a hall in some of our old English mansions, being lofty, and supported by round posts in the centre. Here he treated us with an excellent fowl-curry, wheaten loaves cooked in steam, and plenty of maise; he also presented me with three bullocks, four pots and two skins of honey, as he expressed it, by the Ras's order. All this time his brother Aggoos had been standing behind him, not being allowed, as it should seem, to sit in his presence. We spent this day very pleasantly, being treated with great hospitality by the master of the mansion, who was in his manners by far the most polished Abyssinian we had yet seen. He had a mild expression in his countenance, his features were regular, his hair was short and curly, but not woolly, and his limbs, though small, were well formed. The thermometer was 66°.

"August 22.—In the morning I made a present of a looking-glass, some beads, and a few cloves, to the lady of the house, who was of a much lighter complexion than any we had before met with, and was distantly related to the Ras. These trifles were received with much satisfaction, and, for the first time, we found ourselves among people who were above begging. In the course of the day, Subagadis took an opportunity of speaking to me about the unfortunate dissensions in his family. The Ras, he said, had ordered his father's country to be equally divided between himself and his brother Thadoo; but the latter, dissatisfied with his share, had ever since been continually plundering all his villages, as well as many others belonging to the neighbouring chiefs. He observed, very properly, that a country thus divided could never prosper; and he hoped, as he was the elder brother, that I would use all my interest with the Ras, to have him reinstated in the whole of his father's possessions; begging, at the same time, that I would speak to the Ras as soon as possible on the subject, as the present was the month for the annual settlement of the provinces. He also wished me to represent to the Ras, that, although his order for supplying us with provision and other necessaries at the villages through which we passed, had been regularly transmitted to Thadoo's people, yet no preparations had been made. In answer to this, I told him, that I was only a stranger going to the Ras, and that therefore my interest could not be considerable; that it was not my business to meddle with state affairs; but that, as he had treated us with great hospitality, I would certainly do him all the service in my power. I then presented him with a piece of muslin, with which he was greatly pleased, saying, that I had been much more liberal than he had any reason to expect; and, taking me by the hand, declared that he should ever think of me as a friend. In return, I only begged of him, that if he should ever meet with Englishmen again, he would exercise towards them the same kindness that he had shewn to us.

"We were entertained in the morning by the sight of an Abyssinian banquet, at which, although new guests were continually relieving those who were satisfied, we counted ninety-five persons feeding at the same time in the hall. It might frighten many a man to go into the midst of such a throng cutting away at the raw meat with their long drawn knives, and handing it about in large pieces, from the higher to those of inferior rank. Sometimes, if it chanced to be a coarse piece, it was observed to go through six or seven gradations. At the farther end of the hall sat Subagadis and his wife, with her female attendants, behind a half drawn curtain. On our entering the hall we were invited to take a seat among them, with which we willingly complied. The lady, whom we could now more particularly attend to, was young and pretty, and both gentle and agreeable in her manners; she asked me for a pair of ear-rings (which I had before been erroneously given to understand the Abyssinian ladies did not wear); I sent accordingly for a pair of some that I had procured at Mocha, and presented them to her.

"During our stay, Captain Rudland shot two eagles, which I suppose to be the male and female. The people, having never before seen a bird killed when flying, were much delighted on the occasion,

We left Genáter about ten o'clock, travelling at a slow rate. On our way we passed two priests dressed in light scarlet garments; one of them carried in his hand a bell, the other a large and curiously ornamented key. The first eight miles lay in a southward direction, through a fine grazing country; then winding round the hills, we ascended a high pass, the top of which divides the district of Shum Woldo from that of Ayto Welleta Michael. We were desired to wait on this hill, as Ayto Welleta Michael, chief of the village of Takota, whom we were going to visit, was out on a warlike expedition against Sahána, a town belonging to Thadoo. In a few minutes we saw him coming down a hill to the east, with, I suppose, at least one thousand followers, horse and foot, thronging round their Chief in most unmilitary confusion, like the attendants of an Eastern prince on a visit of ceremony. A few were armed with matchlocks, and the rest with spears and shields. When they came abreast of us, they divided off into two parties, one of which consisted of Welleta Michael's own troops, and the other of his auxiliaries, led by Ayto Guebra, and the chiefs of some distant villages. Welleta Michael himself proceeded to Takota.

"Guebra Welleta Selassé, a messenger from Antalow, had met us on the hill with a grey mule belonging to the Ras, which he had sent for my own riding. This man we dispatched to the Chief of Takota, to inform him of our approach, but he returned with so unsatisfactory an answer, that it was judged prudent to proceed about four miles farther, to a village belonging to Ayto Guebra, where we at length procured a small though tolerably comfortable room for the Ras's mule and ourselves for the night.

August 23.—Last night we were presented by the Chief of the village with a bullock and two sheep, a part of one of which was made into a country curry, with bread and maise, for our supper. I was informed this morning, that the present dissensions between Thadoo and Ayto Welleta Michael, arose from the plundering dispositions of the people subject to the former, who had been constantly in the habit of coming openly in the day time, and carrying away the cattle belonging to the latter. In order to put a stop to this, Ayto Welleta Michael assembled all his friends and followers, and marched to the village of Sahána, where most of these depredators live, to demand satisfaction. Nothing however was settled yesterday, nor was any blood spilt on the occasion; and though it is supposed that matters will be accommodated (to enforce which Ayto Welleta Michael to day again marches out to Sahána), it is the opinion of my informant, that the cattle will not be returned, as the parties aggrieved stand much in awe of Thadoo, who is very powerful when his forces are collected.

" We left this place about nine A. M. attended by the Chief of the village, but had not travelled above two miles, before we were desired by our guides to halt at the bottom of a hill on one side of the plain of Ayaddah, on which are the twelve villages of Amba Manut. After a long consultation between Negada Moosa and Guebra Selassé on one side, and the Chiefs of the villages above who had come down to meet us, on the other, the former endeavoured to prevail on us to stop for the rest of the day. This I refused: upon which the Chiefs surrounded us, and with most earnest and humble supplications (placing at the same time stones upon their heads and necks), endeavoured to persuade us that their lives would not be safe if we did not comply. After many fruitless endeavours to get away quietly, by remonstrating with our two guides upon the absurdity of this detention, I was at last actually compelled to force my way through the throng, and gallop off to my companions, who had gone on a little way before; but all my endeavours to prevent so serious a loss of time were to little purpose; for, after going about two miles farther, we arrived at another village, when the rain came on so violently, that we were not sorry to take up our abode for the night, in a good house prepared for our reception.

"We were treated with much attention by the master of the mansion; but our food, &c. was all brought over from the village where we had been first pressed to stop.

"I had seen in coming in, a plant very like the Ensete of Bruce; on examination in the evening it proved to be a new species of Musa. It grows from thirty to forty feet high; the trunk or stem is bare (when the first leaves have withered away), about fifteen feet from the ground; here about twelve leaves branch out, incasing each other at their base, as in the plantain. The mid-rib of each leaf is bare for about two feet and a half before the spreading part of the leaf commences, and is at the back of a bright red colour. The leaf is about four feet across at the broadest part; about twenty feet long, and pointed at the end. The fruit springs from the centre or body of the plant, and is protected when young by four or five small, but strong leaves, which firmly embrace the whole cluster. The parts of the flower are very similar to the plantain, as in appearance is the fruit; but it differs decidedly from it in being filled with hard irregular-shaped seeds, each of the size of a hazelnut; the form of the plant may be learned from the drawing of the mountains of Adowé, where it again occurred.* The thermometer was 64°.

"August 24.—The lady of the house, who was sister-in-law to the wife of Subagadis, paid us a visit in the morning.; she was far inferior to the latter both in personal charms and in manners. I presented her with a looking-glass and some beads; but she was dissatisfied with them; nevertheless, on our going, she took them away. The Chiefs also of the villages that we had passed the day before paid us a morning visit, and presented us with a bullock and other articles. About nine we left the village, and pursued our journey, in a southward direction, over a more rocky country than we had lately passed through, and in consequence saw more of the kolquall. In the neighbourhood however of the villages, to the right, were many small patches of pasture ground. The hills beyond presented many strange and uncouth forms, and sheep of all shades, from white to black, were grazing on the sides of them. After a ride of about five miles, in the course of which we passed several small villages, each containing one principal house, surrounded with a stone wall, we mounted up a hill to a larger village, the residence of Ayto Guebra. We were welcomed by this chief, who is married to a niece of Ras Welleta Selassé, with much hospitality. Tecla Hammainout, the husband of his lady's sister, and some other friends, were also assembled to receive us. Few words passed at our introduction. Maise, curry, and immense piles of bread, being laid before us, we were given to understand, that to eat and drink

* This Musa is growing in the conservatory of Lord Valentia.

heartily, was the best compliment that we could pay them; and indeed they plied us so fast with the maise, and that of so good and strong a quality, that I found it absolutely necessary to rise and depart in a hurry, lest all our servants, to whom they had been as liberal as to ourselves, should be incapable of proceeding. On coming out of the banquetting room, we were ushered rather unexpectedly into the lady's apartment, who received us very cordially, and paid her compliments in a very easy and polite way. She was by no means handsome, yet there was something very pleasing in the expression of her face. I made an excuse for not being able to make her a present, as all the baggage was gone on. She received my apology with great good manners, saying at the same time, that her only wish, in trying to prevail upon us to stay, was to have the pleasure of our company; but as the end of this would have been only a general drinking-bout, we resisted even the entreaties of the lady, and taking leave of her, mounted our mules, and rode on some miles with good speed to the mansion of Debib, Chief of Negashé. It had been the intention of our guides, however, that we should have taken up our quarters at a village much nearer to the one we had last quitted, so that when we arrived, the Chief was unprepared for our reception, and had to get out his holiday clothes: he received us however, very kindly, though we were at first unable to enter into any conversation, having left our interpreter behind with the baggage. A second feast was soon prepared for us, and four hundred cakes of bread of the usual size were given to our people, together with bullocks, honey, ghee, &c.

"August 25.—The master of the house rode on

with us this morning, as had been the general custom since we left Abha. He sat his horse firmly and gracefully, like most of his countrymen of rank, who make by no means an unhandsome figure on horse-back, with their white dresses, and black sheep-skins thrown loosely across the left shoulder. They wear nothing on their heads, but consider it as a mark of dignity to cover the lower part of their face with the loose part of their dress; and are generally attended by eight or ten followers, with matchlocks and spears.

" About five miles on the road, after ascending and descending some steep mountains, we were taken to visit a church or convent cut out of the solid rock, called Abuhásubha. This place is situated on the side of a rock which commands a view of a large and beautiful plain, thinly set with daroo and wild date trees. In front of the excavation is a thatched and two storied entrance, built in a style much resembling that of the Portuguese. From this three doors lead into an oblong square room (A), the dimensions of which are about fifty feet by thirty, supported by two rows of columns, each consisting of four pillars and two pilasters; the former are about three feet in diameter, and from their plainness and proportions, resemble those of the Tuscan order. Beyond is a room (B), answering in some degree to the chancel of modern churches; it is divided from the larger excavation by two square pillars, and has a dome-shaped cieling about forty feet high, of very excellent workmanship. In this room are contained the baptismal font, and the various articles used in the ceremonies of the church, which are concealed from view by a curtain suspended between the two pillars at the entrance. On each side is a smaller room (C), communicating by a door and window with the larger excavation. The cieling in front of the centre room in the larger excavation, is hollowed out into a kind of dome about thirty feet high, curiously painted and carved; and in front of the side rooms it is also adorned in the same manner, but without the dome. The floor is flagged with square stones, and the walls are carved and ornamented with crosses, paintings, and incriptions in the Ethiopic character, which, I was informed, entirely consist of sentences taken from Scripture. The most conspicuous of the paintings are representations of Christ, the Apostles, and Saint George combating the dragon: the white horse of the latter is both well designed and executed. We were allowed by the priests to examine every part of this singular temple, which is damp, and full of bats and insects, particularly the side cells, in each of which is a tomb. One of the most curious circumstances in this excavation is, that water continually issues from one of the pillars, which deposits a ferruginous sediment, that seems not in any degree to have corroded the stone. On the outside are several tombs excavated in the sides of the rock, and only covered over by loose stones. The priests who attended us were all neatly dressed in white, with light turbans or rather wrappers round their heads. I gave them two dollars for their attentions to us, with which they were well satisfied.

"The rock out of which this temple is excavated is of a very hard consistence, so that much labour must have been bestowed on the work. We observed nothing from which we could form any opinion as to the period when it was undertaken. It is certainly more antient than the time of the residence of the Portuguese in Abyssinia, and is probably one of those that were formed at the command of the Emperor Lalibala, by workmen sent for, for that purpose, from Egypt.*

"Resuming our journey, we passed through a luxuriant copse, and observed growing on the rocky sides of the pathway, several beautiful species of Filices, of which I procured specimens. We then mounted successively many high and rugged hills, our road turning at times to every point of the compass, till after a most laborious and fatiguing day, we reached our halting place for the night, at the top of one of the loftiest hills. It was some time before we were joined by our attendants, with the baggage, who had gone by another route, in the course of which they had visited a mosque held extremely sacred by the Mussulmauns. We had a miserable hut to sleep in, where we were under the necessity of crowding all together. The man of the house, however, who was a servant of the Ras, treated us with great attention, and on bringing the maise, presented me with a neatly turned horn, the peculiar manufacture of Abyssinia, which was the more acceptable from the obliging manner in which it was given. Curry and other provisions were prepared, and a cow was offered for our acceptance. The thermometer was 68°. The length of our days journey we computed to be from fourteen to sixteen miles.

"August 26.—We were on the road at an early hour in the morning, and after travelling about five miles, met a Chief on the road, who told us that the Ras had appointed a village about two miles further on, for our resting place on the ensuing night; as thence we might easily reach An-

* Vide Ludolf, Lib. ii. ch. 5.

talow in the course of the following day. On our arrival, however, we found no preparations made for our reception; and, in consequence, much altercation passed between our guides and the Chief of the place, who, frightened by their violence, came to throw himself on the ground before my mule, with a stone on his neck. As I evidently saw that our stay was not wished for, and as it was of importance to lose as little time as possible, I determined to proceed.

"After travelling about six miles farther over a mountainous country, we came to the town of Derhah. This place, from the hill by which we approached it, appeared of far more consequence than any that we had before seen, being surrounded by a wall and wide fosse, and most of the houses being built of stone. There is no resident chief at Derhah, as it is under the immediate command of the Ras, who has appointed six head-men to rule over it. They paid me a visit, but seemed to think so much of supplying our wants, that I at last was obliged to tell them that we did not come as beggars into their country; and if the Ras had not issued orders concerning us, we would willingly pay for whatever they might supply. On this they departed. The people of the house were, however, very kind, and prepared for us bread, maise, and a curry of mutton.

"About seven in the evening we received a message from our friend Subagadis, informing us that he had arrived in the town, but had not been able to procure a house for the night; that he should, however, remain in the neighbourhood, and would be ready to accompany us at an early hour in the morning on our way to Antalow. Mr. Carter, at my desire, immediately went out to him, to offer such accommodation for the night as our small house would afford, which, after several refusals, on account of the inhabitants, of whose conduct he meant to complain to the Ras, he accepted. The supper, of which our guest partook very heartily, was served up in the true Abyssinian style. We were much pleased at this opportunity of shewing to him our gratitude for the hospitable treatment which we had experienced at Genater, the capital of his district of Agowma. The thermometer was 70°. Our journey was from twelve to fourteen miles.

" August 27.—About six o'clock we left Derhah, in company with Subagadis and his attendants, and travelled about ten miles over grazing plains and high rocky hills. The soil of the plains was of a black colour, extremely rich, and full twelve feet deep, as we ascertained by the broken banks of a stream which runs meandering through it; the hills also would admit of cultivation, if the large stones with which they are incumbered were removed; but this the inhabitants are too idle or ignorant to undertake, even on the flat land; so that it is with the greatest difficulty that they are able to plough it. After descending a steep pass, from which we had a full view of the hill of Antalow, we arrived at the village of Chelicut, where we were accommodated in a house belonging to the Ras, built on a beautiful spot close to the borders of a stream. We were at this place treated with more than usual ceremony and respect, and were informed that the Ras had ordered the greatest attention to be paid to our wishes. In the afternoon we were taken out to visit the church, attended by a multitude of priests, all handsomely cloathed in white. On entering the first gateway, they requested us to take off our shoes and hats, with which we immediately complied. I was somewhat surprized to see that the Mussulmauns were permitted to enter into the first circular avenue. A sufficiently accurate idea of the whole building may be formed, by imagining three concentric circular walls covered with a thatched roof, surmounted by a ball and cross. The spaces between the two outer walls were open avenues; the space included within the central one forms the body of the church. The walls were coated with whitish-red plaister, ornamented with gilding, and covered with representations of Noah and the Ark, Christ and the Virgin Mary, the Apostles, the martyrdom of the saints, many extravagant designs taken from the prophecies, and St. George fighting the dragon. This latter saint seems to be the national favourite, and every where makes a most conspicuous figure upon his white horse. The colouring of all these figures was very gaudy, but some of them, particularly one picture of the Virgin Mary, the face of which was covered with glass to preserve it, was executed in a style superior to the generality of eastern paintings. The Infant Christ was placed in one instance in the left hand of his mother, and in another in her right.

" In the outer circle of the church was suspended a very handsome glass chandelier, presented to the Ras by the Sheriffe of Mecca. From the church we were taken to the store-room, to view the rich vestments and furniture of the officiating priests, which were of great beauty. Among other articles were eleven mitres of pure silver inlaid with gold, two dresses of black velvet richly studded with silver, a large silver drum hooped with gold, besides a rich Venetian cloth very handsomely embroidered. The priests seemed to have much pleasure in shewing us their wealth, and afterwards conducted us to the Ras's garden, which, though in a very wild state, and overgrown with grass, was enriched with many valuable fruit trees, as oranges, citrons, pomegranates, and bananas, most of which, from their names being evidently derived from Arabic, I supposed to have been originally brought from Arabia.

"Chelicut is the residence of Azoro Mantwaub, one of the Ras's wives; she is a daughter of Ayto Ischias, and sister to the present king. She was extremely polite in her attentions to us, sent us many flattering messages, and provided our table with plenty of curry and maise. Notwithstanding the great attention paid to us, we had much difficulty in procuring provision and maise (though we at last accomplished it) for our friend Subagadis, who had not presumed to come near the Ras's house; nor did the villagers even dare to furnish him with a house, though the weather was very inclement, for fear of displeasing his brother Thadoo, who was said to be in great favour with the Ras. At night, however, some of those who favoured his party, gave him a wretched hovel to shelter him from the rain. The thermometer was 64°. The length of our day's journey was about eight miles.

"August 28.—Having prepared ourselves as well as circumstances would permit for going into the presence of the Ras, we left Chelicut at an early hour, and were joined by Subagadis on the opposite side of the brook which runs through the village. Between this place and Antalow is a lofty mountain, for the purpose of avoiding which, we continued to wind round the eastern and southern sides of it, for nearly ten miles, over hills which skirt its base. The small vallies which we passed, were wet and swampy with the last night's rain, which much impeded our progress. We passed a large village called Asgool, belonging to Ozoro Ambeah, another of the Ras's wives, the principal inhabitants of which came out to pay their compliments. At length, after our patience was nearly exhausted by mounting hill after hill, we came suddenly in sight of Antalow, distant from us about a mile. As we approached, our train increased very rapidly, and before we reached the Ras's residence, we had to pass through an assemblage of at least three thousand of the inhabitants.* They pressed so hard to get near us as we were going through the first gate, over which were sitting some of the officers of state, that it was with great difficulty, we could force a passage. We were not allowed to dismount from our mules till we had got into the entrance of the great hall, at the farther end of which was seated the Ras, on a couch with two large pillows upon it covered with rich satin. On each side of him, seated on the floor, which was carpetted, were all his principal chiefs, and among others, our friend Baharnegash Yasous. On being ushered with much bustle into his presence, according to the custom of the country, we bowed, and then kissed the back of his hand, and he in return kissed ours; he then pointed to a vacant couch on his right, covered with a beautiful skin, on which we were immediately seated. After this the usual compliments passed, the Ras on his part expressing his pleasure at seeing us, and we on our part making a proper return, with additional compliments from Lord Valentia at Mocha. We were then given to understand that nothing more was to be said at this visit. In a few minutes after Captain Rudland was taken away to inspect the apartments allotted

* The great number present was, as we afterwards found, partly owing to its being market-day.

us, and on his return we withdrew, attended by a minister of the Ras, through whom we were to communicate all our wishes.

"The hurry, with which our first interview was conducted, did not permit us to make many observations concerning the persons present, and our attention was of course principally directed to the Ras. He is remarkably small in person, and delicately formed, quick in his manner, notwithstanding his age, which was said to be seventy-two, with a shrewd expression in his countenance, and considerable dignity in his deportment. Though he did not move from his couch, on which he partly reclined, yet our reception was considered to be particularly gracious, as, by kissing our hands, in return, he placed us on an equality with himself. We had previously been required to uncover our heads and prostrate ourselves before him; but this we most positively refused.

"We were furnished in the course of the day with abundance of provisions, and were much pressed to eat and drink profusely, by way of doing honour to the house. In the evening we had several polite messages from the Ras, who sent for our fire-arms, and treated Pearce and Ibrahim who took them to him, with great attention, seating them on his couch, and giving them plenty of maise. He was highly delighted with the guns, and in return sent us a fishing net, acquainting us at the same time, that he seldom staid at home in the night, but took his pleasure in fishing and hunting. He sent us also a dish of stewed fish, which was thought very delicious by some of our party. We had a pretty good example of the Ras's watchfulness, for about twelve o'clock he sent us some clouted cream, and at four I was called up to receive the compliments of the morning.

"August 29.—At about ten in the morning we were invited to breakfast with the Ras, and were received with the same distinction as yesterday, being seated on a sofa, while his minister was placed close by on the carpet. We were very plentifully fed by the Ras himself with eggs, fowl in curry, and balls of a mixed composition of wild celery, curds and ghee, after which we were offered brinde; but on our expressing a wish to have it dressed, the meat was afterwards brought grilled, and cut into small pieces by one of the attendants, and handed to our mouths by the Ras, much in the same way as boys in England feed young magpies. It is scarcely possible to describe the scene that was going on in the mean time in the hall, where the people were squabbling and almost fighting, with their drawn knives, for the raw meat that was handed about, and the teff bread that lay heaped up around the table; there were, however, some masters of the ceremony who carried long white sticks, with which they frequently chastised those who were too hasty in seizing their portion.

"We afterwards spent the day very quietly, as the time for receiving the presents from Lord Valentia was deferred till the morrow. The thermometer was 68° in our room, and frequent storms of rain occurred during the day.

"August 30.—A copy of Lord Valentia's letter, which I had ordered to be written in case the original should not have safely arrived, was delivered to the Ras in the morning at four o'clock, by Hamed Chamie, who also, as far as I had authorized him. entered into an explanation of the nature of my mission from his Lordship. About six o'clock I was sent for, and found the Ras alone, in the hall; I then delivered to him, in the name of Lord Valentia, the presents sent by his Lordship, which consisted of two entire pieces of broadcloth, one blue and the other red; a handsome watch, a telescope, some pieces of kincaub and satin, a dress of gold tissue, a gold ring and broach, and several pieces of muslin. These presents gave great satisfaction, more particularly those articles which were new to him, namely, the watch, telescope, and trinkets; and the kincaub and gold dress he repeatedly ordered to be opened out before him. On stating, in the name of his Lordship, the impossibility of procuring at Mocha such presents as he would have wished to send, he stopt me at once, by expressing his entire satisfaction with what he had received; and assured me, that his only regret arose from the impossibility of communicating in our own language, the friendship he felt for us, who, strangers as we were, had come so far from our parents, our friends, and our country, to visit him, while those who were near to him, and ought to be his friends, thought only of making war upon him. He then asked me what were the wishes of Lord Valentia, and the objects for which I had come. In rêturn, I informed him that Lord Valentia's sole motive in sending me, was an anxious desire to promote an intercourse of friendship between two such powerful countries as England and Abyssinia, the inhabitants of which were moreover of the same religion; and that if the Ras was inclined to form such a connection, to represent to him how much it might conduce to the interest of his country. That Abyssinia having hitherto been accustomed to receive all her imports at the third or fourth hand, an immoderate duty had been paid at every separate transfer; whereas an intercourse with the English, who are uncontrouled masters of the sea, would enable the Ras to supply himself at once with whatever commodities he might want, and of a quality far superior to any that had hitherto found their way into his country: that, in all this, Lord Valentia was actuated by no motives of personal advantage, having only in view the mutual benefit of England and Abyssinia, to which a free interchange of each other's produce would materially contribute. His Lordship, I added, was now proceeding to England, and would gladly take charge of any communication which the Government of Abyssinia might choose to make on the subject to the British Government.

"After a silence of a few minutes, the Ras asked me, whether Massowah, or any other port in the neighbourhood, would be most convenient for English vessels to deliver their cargoes at. To this I replied, that I believed there was no harbour, but only anchorage at Beiloul, otherwise the vicinity of that place to his capital, would give it a decided advantage over Massowah. That there was indeed a convenient port at this latter place, and a tolerable supply of fresh water; but both the town and adjacent territory were at present under the command of Nayib Edris, who seemed inclined rather to thwart than promote the interests of Abyssinia, as the interception of my letter to the Ras, (for the conveyance of which I had been obliged to pay thirty dollars) doubtless in consequence of orders from the Nayib, would sufficiently prove; and that moreover, I had been forced to give him five hundred dollars for liberty to pass through his territory, and for the promise of mules, &c. for our accommodation, which latter agreement had been scandalously violated. The Ras expressed much displeasure at this conduct of the chief of Massowah, and said that the former Nayib, Hannes, had always been a good friend of his, and that the present Nayib had given no cause for dissatisfaction, until about five years ago, when he had been obliged to send thither a military force to bring him to reason, and that he then should have cut off all communication between Massowah and Abyssinia, if the Nayib had not appeased him by the most humble supplications. He farther added, that there was a place on the coast belonging to himself called Buré, not more than four days journey from Antalow, well supplied with water and cattle; the inhabitants of which had often solicited permission to open a trade with the ships that were constantly passing within sight of them. That the road between Buré and Antalow was very practicable for kafilas, excepting one day's journey, in which no water was to be procured; and that if this place should be deemed sufficiently convenient, he would immediately turn the trade into that channel. In order that I might satisfy myself on the subject, he offered to send for one of the chiefs of the place, from whom I might obtain any additional information that I chose; and when I represented to him that no verbal report would be so satisfactory, as sending one of the gentlemen who had accompanied me to make inquiries on the spot, he immediately assented to the proposal. He then said, that a hope was expressed in Lord Valentia's letter, that I might go to Gondar; but, though it was his anxious wish to comply with all our desires, it was at present impossible to secure the safety of our persons on the journey, he being on bad terms with Gusmatie Guxo, who had possession of Gondar. The Ras then entered into a detail of the circumstances out of which the present dispute between himself and his rival originated, and of this the following account, corrected in some particulars by Hadjee Hamed, who was well acquainted with the circumstances, is a correct abstract.

" The differences arose at a very early period. Ras Welleta Selassé placed Welleta Solomon on the throne, after the abdication of his father Tecla Hamainout; but the new sovereign was soon opposed by the contrary party; afterwards the Ras raised Tecla Georgis to the supreme command. This appointment, however, was not more agreeable to the opponents of the Ras, than the former had been, who compelled Tecla Georgis three several times to fly for protection to Tigré, which was more immediately under the controul of his patron. The presence of the Ras being required at his capital in Tigré, every exertion was made by the other party to raise Ayto Ischias, and afterwards his son Ayto Gualoo, members of another branch of the royal family, to the throne. At length, the Ras finding, as it should seem, his two favourites, Welleta Solomon and Tecla Georgis, unequal to maintain the royal authority, was induced to give his sanction to the establishment of the crown on the head of Ayto Gualoo; and in order to bring over the king to his interest, in opposition to that of Guxo, he married Ozoro Mantwaub, the sister of his present majesty. Gusmatie Guxo, in the mean time, after successfully increasing his power and re-establishing his influence over all Amhara and Begemder, took advantage of Ras Welleta Selassé's absence from the capital about three years ago, to send an arrogant message to the king, recommending to him his daughter as a wife, if he had any thought of remaining at Gondar. The king, whatever were his inclinations, was under the necessity of complying with the proposition, and accordingly married the lady.

"At this period, affairs seemed to wear a better face; both parties affected satisfaction at what had taken place, and all animosity was for a time suspended, the tie of kindred being now added to that of allegiance; but this calm was not of long duration. Two years had not elapsed, when, on the death of the late Abuna, Guxo broke violently into the house of the deceased, and plundered it of gold and valuables to the amount of five hundred wakeas of gold, which was considered not as the private property of the Abuna, but as belonging to his office of high priest, and was by custom to be expended in defraying the expences of bringing his successor from Egypt.

"Religion was too fair a pretence for war to be neglected by Ras Welleta Selassé, who thereupon raised his forces, and being joined by Ras Gabriel, governor of the provinces of Samen and Waldubba, commenced his march towards Gondar. Guxo, unprepared for so immediate an attack, sent a deputation of priests to restore the money, and thus conciliate the favour and prevent the approach of the offended Ras. In this they succeeded, the cause of war being done away by the restoration of the property; upon which the Ras having made an addition to the five hundred wakeas of gold, sent immediately a deputation for a successor to the deceased Abuna.

"Guxo's pride, however, had received too severe a mortification to acquiesce in what had taken place, and being moreover supported by two of the chief priests, Eustachias and Tecla Haimanout, who had taken upon them all the power of the Abuna, was supposed at this time to be preparing war against Welleta Selassé and his allies. In order still farther to strengthen his party, he is said to have formed a league with Siban son of Kolassé of Michaellis, who is at the head of the Edjow Galla, and is reported to be able to bring into the field thirty thousand cavalry, besides double that number of spearmen. This united force commenced its operations by an attack upon Ras Gabriel, in his province of Samen, and obliged him to fly to Ras Welleta Selassé for assistance. After gaining a promise from the latter, that he would join him without fail, as soon as it was possible to cross the Tacazza, he returned to defend his own province, and is at present besieged in the mountains of Geshen-hai.

"Ras Gabriel is said to have one thousand matchlocks in his army, with which he holds out against the united force of Amhara, Begemder, and the Galla. Ras Welleta Selassé, on the first news of Guxo's preparations, sent off a man of rank to enquire into the cause of them; but his messenger was seized, put in irons, and imprisoned, by order of Guxo, and in consequence of this, the breach is now irreparable. The king is obliged to be a quiet spectator of these contests for power between his rival relatives, and to submit to the unconstitutional hostilities of his father-in-law against his brother, who is invested with the legal authority in civil and military concerns. The Ras told me, however, that he would defer his march till we were safe back at Massowah, as during his absence the enemy would be anxious to get us into their power; for, hearing that we were come on some mysterious concern, they would be afraid that with other dowa (physic), we might have brought poison to extirpate the whole army. He concluded by saying, that after we had spent a few days with him, we might visit any part of Tigré, and that he should be extremely happy to shew us the whole of Abyssinia, if God pleased to give him success in the expected contest, were it possible for us to wait so long.

"I returned him my grateful thanks for the manner in which he had opened to me the situation of public affairs, stating at the same time, that I considered him the best judge of the possibility of our taking the projected journey to Gondar in safety, and after the full explanation which he had given, I could not think, however much I had it at heart, of pressing the subject any farther. I hoped, however, that he would be able to shew us Waldubba; in our journey to which place, I should have an opportunity of seeing the Jews' rock and the Tacazza. The Jews' rock our interpreter could not make out; but on mentioning it to the Ras, he instantly knew it, and told me that he was the first person who ever succeeded in an attack upon it. Ras Gabriel of Samen, with whom he some time past was at war, shut up Tecla Georgis upon it, whence he was released by Ras Welleta Selassé. There are a few Jews yet remaining at this place. The Ras assented to my proposal, and promised that I should visit Tecla Georgis at Waldubba, and Welleta Solomon at Axum; that though the former place was not indeed in his dominions, yet as it belonged to his friend Ras Gabriel, we might go thither in perfect safety. I then requested a copy in Arabic of the History of Abyssinia, from the reign of Joas to the present time; he told me in reply that the chronicles were kept at Axum, and that he would take care I should not be disappointed. On my shewing him the drawings in Bruce's volume, he said that he knew Yagoobe well; he came into Abyssinia after the battle of Fagitta, and afterwards went to the head of the Nile.

"Nothing more passed at this interview, except some trifling conversation, which being ended, we left the hall, and did not again see the Ras during the day. It being a public fast, we had provisions brought up to our private apartments. No person had been permitted to come near us, and our persons were kept quite secured from the gaze of the vulgar.

"We have had rain, thunder, and lightning, every afternoon since our arrival. The thermometer was 62°, and the weather very wet and cold.

CHAPTER II.

MR. SALT'S NARRATIVE CONTINUED. — *Continuation of Transactions at Antalow.—Departure of Mr. Salt on a Tour to Axum.—Arrival at Muculla.—Visit to the Church there.—Arrival at Kasunko.—Arrival at the House of Barrainbarras Toklu at Gullybudda.—Visit to Fit Aurari Yasous.—Arrival at Adowa.—Residence there.—Introduction to Fasilydas, son of Yasous, formerly King of Abyssinia. — Arrival at Axum.*

"AUGUST 31.—We had a message at an early hour in the morning, to enquire after our health, and an invitation to breakfast with the. Ras; nothing took place except a recurrence of the scene on Thursday, only that, as a favour, we were permitted to make a bow to our good friends Subagadis and Baharnegash Yasous, who were kept at a great distance by the Ras. All the dishes were extremely good; the Ras was in high spirits, and in great good humour, and at his earnest request, we this day, for the first time, ventured on some small pieces of brinde.

"September 1.—Our servants, not having been permitted to go beyond the walled inclosure, about twenty or thirty feet square in front of the building which we occupied, were much dissatisfied, and began to presage our detention in the country. In the morning, I complained to the Ras of this unreasonable strictness, and he said in reply, that it was only intended to prevent any harm happening to them. I notwithstanding requested, that he would allow them to go out when they pleased, and to take care of their own safety. I was going to proceed on other subjects, when his brother and several chiefs were admitted into the hall, which entirely put a stop to all business. Mules were brought in for our riding, of which Captain Rudland and myself availed ourselves to take a survey of the mountain of Antalow. We first skirted the western extremity, and then ascended the northern side by a steep path that had seldom before been attempted by mules. We found the summit covered with verdure, and pastured by numerous herds of cattle. On passing over to the southern brow, we had a complete view of the town of Antalow, the adjacent villages, and the high mountains that divide Tigré from the country of the Galla to the south.

"Antalow consists of upwards of one thousand houses, with conical thatched roofs, erected upon an uneven rising ground in the valley below. The house of the Ras is conspicuous from its size, from the different shape of the roof, and from a wall by which it is surrounded. With this exception, the rest of the place makes a most wretched appearance, and the country around is extremely uninteresting, there not being a tree to be seen in the whole extent, except a few small ones that surround the two churches in the vicinity of the town.

"The top of this hill was formerly used as a place of defence, and, on many of the ledges of the rocks, walls yet remain formed of loose stones, for the purpose of impeding the progress of assailants. The last time that the inhabitants fled to it, was in the time of Ras Michael Suhul, when they were attacked by the Galla, under a chief of the name of Waldo.

"On our return, we were obliged to dismount from our mules, the descent being steep and broken, and well calculated by nature for defence. The upper part of this hill is composed of loose calcareous stones, of a reddish sandy colour, lying in horizontal strata, bare, and perpendicular at the edges; lower down is found a bed of breccia resting upon a mass of hard black stone (probably basalt), of which the whole base of the mountain consists. At the bottom we passed two villages, and after crossing a few low ridges, reached Antalow, where we were received by some hundreds of the inhabitants who had assembled to view the strangers.

"On our arrival, we found the Ras at breakfast, and were invited to join him; the dishes were the same as usual, with the addition of boiled cow-heel. The Ras was in good humour, and asked many questions about our churches, our king, &c. An old woman was standing behind him, whom he very significantly introduced as a proper person for us to become acquainted with, as she had many young ladies under her care. He had often before joked with us on the same subject, but had never gone so far as on the present occasion. After taking our usual quantity of maise, the Ras shewing an inclination to sleep, we retired.

"In the evening we went into the hall, and found the Ras at chess in the midst of his chiefs. The chess men, which are coarsely made of ivory, are very large and clumsy; when they have occasion to take any one of their adversary's pieces, they strike it with great force and eagerness from its place. I observed that their game differs much from ours. Bishops jump over the heads of knights, and are only allowed to move three squares. The pawns move only one step forward at starting, and get no rank by reaching the end of the board; they play with much noise, every person around, even the slaves, having a voice in the game, and seizing the pieces at pleasure, to shew any advisable move. We observed, however, that they always managed with great ingenuity to let the Ras win every game.

"A repast was afterwards served up, at which many ladies were present, among these one, who, we were informed, was one of his brother's wives, sat on the same couch with the Ras; others were seated on the floor, and all seemed to do justice to the brinde and maise.

"We were much distressed in the evening at the loss of our interpreter, Hadjee Hamed, who withdrew himself, as he informed us, from dissatisfaction at the treatment he had experienced from some of the Ras's people, telling me, that he would, "Please God," return in the morning.

"September 2.—We did not see any thing of the Ras in the morning, our breakfast being brought to our own apartment, and from hearing less noise than usual in the large hall, we had every reason to suppose it was one of their fasts. The day passed over, and we heard nothing of Hadjee Hamed, although we sent repeated messengers after him. From this circumstance, and certain reports which our servants collected in the town, we were led to believe that there was something not very pleasant going on; but what it was, we were unfortunately not able to ascertain, being shut out from all communication, except with the Ras, to whom we sent our salaams in the evening, which were politely returned. The thermometer at noon, in our room, was 63°: much rain fell in the course of the evening.

"September 3.—Being determined to explain myself, as well as I could, through Ibrahim, who spoke imperfectly the language of the country, I sent early in the morning to the Ras, requesting to speak to him. He returned for answer, that he would see me on the morrow. I sent a second message, but with as little effect, as he excused himself on the plea of being much engaged in business. I then pressed him to send for Hadjee Hamed; upon which he returned back word, that our interpreter did not dare to come, being in fear of his life, which he said we had threatened to put an end to. This message gave us considerable uneasiness, as it appeared reasonable to suppose that so palpable a falsehood could only be invented by Hadjee Hamed, for the purpose of counteracting our interest with the Ras, which he might conceive detrimental to that of the Sheriffe of Mecca; or by the Ras, for the purpose of throwing on us the blame of his departure, which, on the contrary, was occasioned by the misconduct of his own impertinent slaves; and in either case it was likely to be the forerunner of much mischief to our views. The only circumstance that led us to impute it to Hadjee Hamed was, that we before had discovered that he endeavoured to lessen as much as possible the value of the presents which we gave to the Ras.

"The Ras sent in the course of the day a message of enquiry after our health, accompanied by a present of oranges, limes and dried plantains. Our food was as usual brought to our apartment; it consisted of a fowl in the morning, and a small mutton curry in the evening, which, though rather a scanty allowance, put us to no real inconvenience, as we had a plentiful supply of good bread and maise; in addition to which we this day received from the Ras, about noon, some of his own fine wheaten bread.

"I was engaged during the morning in penning some of my sketches, and Captain Rudland in teaching one of the Ras's principal men how to make a white-wash for the walls of the house, from a chalk stone that we found on the hill of Antalow.

"Mr. Carter got an observation at noon, by which he fixed the latitude of this place to be in 12° 48′ 30″. The latter part of the day was extremely gloomy with much rain, thunder and lightning; the thermometer at noon was 60°.

"September 4.—I repeated my message to the Ras by means of Ibrahim at an early hour in the morning, stating our wish to pay him a visit; which he politely put off till mid-day. Soon after, he sent a request to Captain Rudland that he would accompany his builder to the hill, in order to point out the stone that they made use of on the day before. I afterwards took this occasion to send Hamed Chamie to the Ras with the Mussulmaun builder, who spoke Arabic, to beg that another interpreter might be assigned me, and that Hadjee Hamed might be brought into his presence, that I might have an opportunity of shewing how falsely I had been accused. The latter request he evaded, by saying that Hadjee Hamed would not come any more, but that I might procure any other interpreter that I chose. Hamed Chamie then stated to him in the true Arabic style, that we were his strangers, that our lives and property were in his hands, and that he might do with them as he pleased; in return, he expressed himself in very friendly terms, and promised that all our wishes should be complied with. After our breakfast, consisting of half a fowl curried, the Ras sent us a large citron, with the usual salaams.

"Pearce went out into the market in the morning, and found it so crowded, that he could with difficulty ascertain the articles brought for barter; corn, butter, ghee, onions, skins, and cattle, seemed to be the staple commodities; the small currency, if it may be so called, consisted of wedges of rock salt, each weighing two or three pounds, and estimated at one thirtieth of a dollar.

"Weekly markets are held in many parts of the country, at a distance from all habitations; one we passed on our way from the residence of the amiable Ozoro Mantwaub, and another on our way to the mansion of Debib, chief of Negashé. In all these many hundred men were assembled, who therefore do not consider it infamous (as Bruce asserts) for them to attend a market.

"At twelve o'clock I sent Hamed Chamie to the Ras to solicit the promised audience, but hearing that he stood unnoticed in the hall, I determined at once to go without ceremony into the presence, attended by Captain Rudland; thinking it absolutely necessary to come to an immediate explanation concerning the absence of Hadjee Hamed, and other unpleasant circumstances which had reached our ears; more especially as all the persons with me had expressed great uneasiness about our situation, being in considerable alarm lest we should be detained in the country. We found the Ras engaged at chess with one of his chiefs; on seeing us he offered his hand, seating me by his side, and Captain Rudland next to me. Our patience however was nearly exhausted before the game was completed, not a single word during this time being spoken to us. Some of his people who had been waiting for a considerable time presented him cakes of bread, honey, a sheep, and fire-wood. He now dismissed the whole party, and after a few minutes conversation with a priest, who was to give us intelligence concerning the latter portion of the Abyssinian history, the room was cleared.

"I proceeded to express my regret at the conduct of Hádjee Hamed, whom I most solemnly declared I had always treated with the greatest attention, as being sent to me by the Ras; I stated also, that this man, on leaving me, had given an entirely different reason for his going away, and that I was fearful that he had been saying something prejudicial of us, and had altogether been acting an underhand part; in consequence of which I had been extremely anxious for a personal conference, wherein the whole might be explained. The Ras was gloomy for some time, and at last said that he did not as yet clearly understand the motive of our coming into his country. This I immediately ascribed to the fault of his interpreter; and then proceeded to enter fully into a repetition of what had passed on my laying the presents before him, and concluded with saying, that by his invitation we had come up to his presence through barbarous districts, where nothing but his name could have protected us, and had entrusted him with our lives and property, which were all at his disposal; and that now our only desire, during the remainder of our stay in his country, was to act in strict conformity to all his wishes; but that we expected to be treated as friends, and at least to have the full liberty to go out whenever we pleased, and to move about wherever we might choose in his territories, as above all things, confinement was particularly irksome to us. On this he began to relax a little; said that there had been a mistake made by Currum Chund in inviting us; but that, as we were here, it was all well; that it was his anxiety about our persons which made him wish we should have no communication with the inhabitants, who were little to be depended upon; and that he would rather lose two thousand of his own subjects than that any one of our people should come to harm.

"I made a proper return to this unexpected sally of friendship, and then proceeded to remark, that as I could not now depend upon any thing that Hadjee Hamed had interpreted, I could no longer be certain whether the mules were sent down by the Ras for our conveyance and accommodation; that, if they were, I begged to return him our most grateful acknowledgments; but, if they belonged to any other person, I should be obliged to him to permit me to make the owner of them a proper recompence. By this I hoped to alarm his pride, if he had any, and prevent any further complaints or demands on that account. He was, as I expected, hurt at the remark, and begged that I would not mention any thing of the kind again, as they were "bad words;" that my wishes, whatever they were, should be complied with; and that I had only to make them known to have them immediately carried into effect. I proceeded directly to urge Mr. Carter's going down to Buré, as an affair of the greatest importance. The Ras told me that he had sent two messengers thither for the chief of that place, who would certainly arrive by Saturday next, and that Mr. Carter might then return with him as I desired.

"Our journey to Axum and Adowa was the

next topic; the Ras said, that it would be my best plan to set out as soon as possible, since his army was, in a short time, to assemble from all quarters, and I might return to Antalow with the detachment from Adowa; he added, that as he could not trust our persons on the road between Adowa and Dixan (without stating some reason for it), he wished us to return to Massowah by the road which we came, as being perfectly secure.

"I entirely assented to these points, adding, that he was, no doubt, the best judge of what was practicable. After which, I informed him that I should wish to set out for Axum the day after the morrow, and that as he thought; from the state of the roads, that it would be better for me to go with as few attendants as possible, it was my intention to take with me only two servants, and during my absence I would leave Captain Rudland under his protection at Antalow, and Mr. Carter might at the same time execute the plan of paying a visit to Buré. He was perfectly satisfied with this arrangement, and said, that two mules should be in readiness for me, and men to carry what baggage I might want. I then returned to the subject of the Jews' rock, and expressed my anxiety to see it, as being desirous of giving my countrymen some idea of a place that, till he took it, had been always considered as impregnable, and which Ras Michael Suhul had not dared to attack when Ayto Tesfos, governor of Samen, had fled thither for refuge. He expressed much surprise at my knowledge of this circumstance; but was evidently highly pleased with the compliment, and promised to arrange the expedition for me on my return from Axum, as by that time the waters of the Tacazza would have subsided. He added, that there was not such another fortress in the whole country; that it was extremely high, and the water upon the top was often covered with a substance like glass, and as hard as stone, (by which he undoubtedly meant ice) and moreover that a plant was found there, which would kill any person treading upon it, if he happened to have the least sore upon his foot. He concluded by telling me that he would order Hadjee Hamed to come to me in the morning, who, notwithstanding what had passed, would be the best person to attend me to Axum and Adowa, as he was well acquainted with both those places. He then shook us cordially by the hand, and we returned to our apartment, to the great satisfaction of a number of his chiefs, who had been long waiting at the door for an audience. The happy turn which this conference had effected in our favour, was likewise very gratifying to our whole party.

"September 5.—We passed this day in our apartment, the Ras being assiduously engaged in deciding causes of considerable importance. He indeed gives up the greater part of every morning to hearing the complaints of his subjects, over whom he rules with most absolute sway, as their lives and property depend entirely upon his nod. The parties who appear before him are very vociferous, and, when provoked by their opponents, often employ such violent gesticulations, that one would suppose, that at times, even the presence of the Ras would scarcely withhold them from proceeding to blows.

"Baharnegash Yasous paid us a visit in the morning with permission from the Ras, and was treated by us with all the attention in our power. He was about to return to Dixan, not daring to stay any longer at Antalow without the consent of the Ras, of whom he stood greatly in awe. I made him a present of ten dollars for his expences on the road, informing him that I was afraid of parting with more, lest I should be unable to supply my own wants. He was very grateful for this trifle, and made many professions of friendship, the sincerity of which I had no reason to question. It is a remarkable circumstance, that two of our best friends, Yasous and Subagadis, were bitter enemies. We had some reason to fear that poor Yasous, during his stay at Antalow, had been but slenderly provided, even with food; for he sent to us several times for bread; a fact which indicates in how abject a state all ranks are kept by the present governor of Tigré. Hadjee Hamed paid us a short visit, and positively denied having told the Ras that he had been induced to absent himself for fear of his life.

"I sent to the Ras in the evening, to remind him of my intended journey to Axum. He informed me in return, that he had fixed Monday next for our departure, on which day he intended to accompany me as far as Mucculah, where a celebrated church stands, at which solemn prayers were to be put up for the success of the ensuing campaign. I told him that I had not before so understood him, but that it was the more agreeable to me, as I was anxious to see the chief from Buré before I left Antalow, which I should now probably have an opportunity of doing.

"I this day prepared a letter for Lord Valentia, to be sent by Mr. Carter, and finished some more of my sketches. Much rain fell, which made the air cold. The thermometer at noon was only 61°.

"September 6.—It being fast-day with the inhabitants, we received a citron and a quantity of wheaten bread from the Ras. I dispatched a message this morning, requesting that the priest might be sent for, from whom I was anxious to procure information concerning the history of this country. The Ras replied, that he was at present much engaged, but that he would send for the priest, and as soon as the hall was cleared, would give me an audience. After some time I took the liberty of sending in another message; but notwithstanding all my requests and remonstrances, I was unable to get a sight either of the Ras, or the priest, during the whole day.

"At five o'clock Hadjee Hamed again visited me, and after a preamble, in which he denied having before refused to accompany me to Axum, he at length told me, that he intended to quit my service, having hitherto received no compensation for his trouble. I told him, that it had always been my intention to make him a suitable present; but that with the English, there was also a great distinction between making presents, and paying. I begged, therefore, to know whether he had received any thing from the Ras. He replied, that he was indeed in the yearly pay of the Ras, and had attended upon us in consequence of his orders; but that at the same time, he had been informed that he would receive from us handsome presents. Upon this I said, that if I could procure any money upon a bill in my possession, drawn upon the Ras by Currum Chund, I would immediately give him what I had at first intended; but, that if I should be deceived in this expectation, it would be much more convenient if he would go with me to Adowa, where I probably might, by negotiating the bill, raise a fresh supply of money, as the stock that I had brought into the country was nearly exhausted. To this he replied, that the Ras had no money, nor should I be able to get any at Adowa, nobody in this country knowing any thing about bills of exchange. On which I answered, that if such were the case, it was the more necessary for me to be careful of the little I had left; and so ended our argument. This information proved extremely unpleasant, as our stock was then reduced to less than three hundred dollars. The conference, however, in some degree let me into their secrets, and I had no doubt but that Hadjee Hamed had been acting a double part throughout. There was rain in the middle of the day, and the air was cold, the thermometer being 60 and 61° in our room at mid-day.

"September 7.—The Ras again evaded seeing us till evening, on the plea of business, which I believe was the truth. At the time appointed I went down into the hall, and found him engaged in a conference with Subagadis. In the court-yard beyond, was Thadoo, who, after the departure of his brother, was also called into the Ras's presence. By this time it was so late that our meeting was again postponed till night, for which purpose I was ordered to keep awake. Captain Rudland, however, saw the Ras, and found him in his usual good humour. There was rain in the afternoon, but the evening was very fine. The thermometer was 62°.

"September 8.—At four in the morning I was called to attend the Ras: he was in the hall crouching by a large fire, with his brother Manassé; Hadjee Hamed and the builder were in waiting as interpreters. I proceeded to express my regret at not having seen him for some days, which he politely excused on the plea of business. After some desultory conversation about our intended journey, he once more put the question, "what are you come for?" adding, "I have much in my heart to say to you, if I could explain myself without speaking through so many mouths, and I judge from this, that you have much to say to me." I was proceeding to explain again the purport of our mission, when he stopped me, desiring that I would commit to writing what I might have to communicate; promising in that case, after giving it full consideration, to reply in a similar way, by which means he thought that we should more fully understand each other. Nothing could be more agreeable than this proposal, to which I immediately assented.

"Foreseeing the probability of wanting a supply of cash, I thought the present a favourable opportunity to present my letter of credit from Currum Chund; yet I was somewhat loth to do this after having understood the sense of it, (for I had in conference with Hadjee Hamed, examined its contents) as it appeared to me rather a petition for presents, than a proper letter of business. Not knowing, however, the way in which these matters were transacted between Currum Chund and the Ras, and there being no other sufficient cause for my keeping it back, I determined to deliver it. On opening the subject to the Ras, his first question was, "what did I want money for?" as it was his intention to supply us with every thing requisite till we should again arrive at Massowah. I then gave him to understand, that it was rather from the necessity of satisfying the demands of his own servants, than from any want of money for my own use. After my reply, he thus continued: "this is a town of cattle, bread and honey; why do you want money? there is none to be had here; and besides, Currum

Chund has with me neither money nor credit; and it appears to me that he has been playing tricks with you." He added; " however, it is of no consequence; we are friends; and every thing that you may want, you shall have, till you are safe at Massowah." After this I could not say more on the subject, except explaining, as well as I was able, the nature of money transactions among the English, and that the present letter was merely a matter of business. We then took leave.

" After this, being obliged to consult rather my ability than my inclination, I presented to Hadjee Hamed ten dollars, and as many pieces of blue cloth, and the same to Negada Moosa; both of whom received the donation with a very ill grace. I had an intimation from the Ras, that when I arrived at Dixan he was informed all our boxes were filled with gold. I took pretty good care to undeceive him on this head, and I should think that he has since been pretty well satisfied of the truth of my representation.

" September 9.—At four o'clock in the morning I was awakened by Pearce, who brought me word that the Ras was gone, and had left only three mules for our accommodation. As there was no person able to explain to me the arrangements made by the Ras for our expedition to Axum, I was for some time greatly at a loss what to do, especially as it had before been determined that Captain Rudland and Mr. Carter should go with the Ras, as far as he intended to accompany us on the way to Adowa; a plan which was now entirely frustrated. After much anxiety on the subject, I was at length in some measure relieved by the presence of Guebra Selassé, who had received orders to attend me on my journey. He said that the Ras was waiting for me at no great distance from Antalow, and that, as no directions had been given respecting our baggage, it would be my best way to lose no time in overtaking him, as I might then procure an order to have the baggage sent after me.

" Having parted with our friends, about seven o'clock, I set out on my journey, attended by Pearce and Andrew, mounted on mules, and Ibrahim, my interpreter of the country language, on foot; and in order to provide against accidents, I made Pearce conceal fifty dollars about his person; for at this time it was not very clear what were the intentions of the Ras.

" After passing a small brook in the valley, we began to ascend the north-eastern side of the hill of Antalow, the brow of which was steep, rugged, and bare. On our left, at the bottom, were lying large fragments of rock, that at some distant period had fallen from the summit. The ridges over which our road lay were partly cultivated, and by no means difficult of ascent. On the highest point over which we passed were the ruins of a village, and beyond, almost concealed by high trees of luxuriant growth, was a picturesque village called Haraqué. Our guide, Guebra Selassé, and a chief who was going by, both dismounted from their mules as they passed the church, a mark of respect which is generally paid by the Christians of this country. Our descent was rapid from one hill to another, the tops of all which were well clothed with plants of various kinds. On a rising ground to our right was a village of considerable extent called Lahaina, from which place our road, turning a little more to the west, led through a more cultivated country, thickly set with Acacia and brushwood and flowering shrubs; at the bottom of one of the hills was a brook, the banks of which were shaded by the kantuffa, which I here met with for the first time. It runs among other low trees, and being then in blossom, made by no means an unpicturesque appearance. After passing several more hills we came in sight of Mucculla, in the vicinity of which, on the top of a hill, is a large church, that forms a very conspicuous object across the plain. The land about the town is in a high state of cultivation; the soil consists of a rich black loam. We found the Ras at this place. He had just finished his morning's repast; but after receiving me very cordially, and having seated me on the couch beside him, he ordered some beef to be grilled, which, though brought to me nearly raw, I eat with great satisfaction, the journey having given me a very keen appetite. After drinking four brulhes of maize, (without which the Ras would not permit me to depart), I begged leave to retire, and was led to a small but comfortable hut in appearance, within the first wall surrounding the church. I recognized in my conductor, Debib, chief of Negashé, who was come up to attend the Ras.

" I computed our course this day to have been nine miles, in a direction nearly N. N. E. The stone, of which some of the uncultivated hills that we to day passed over is formed, lies in horizontal strata, and is divided by vertical fissures into square blocks, when exposed on the sides of the hill, which often gives it the appearance of ancient ruins.

" September 10.—After passing an uncomfortable night from the swarms of vermin with which the hut was infested, and a continual noise kept up by the priests, I arose and paid a visit to the church, where I understood the Ras had been in the course of the night. I was received with much attention by the priests, the greatest part of whom were engaged in singing, and jingling keys, one of which was in the right hand of each; they accompanied this with most violent gestures and grimaces, performing rather the part of antics on a stage, than of persons employed in devotion. After complying with the custom of the country in kissing the threshold of the door, I was admitted into the inner circle. The church, however, presents nothing particularly worthy of observation: it is ornamented with paintings, like those at Chelicut; and the only difference that I observed was, that on a cross was written I N R I. in Roman characters, the meaning of which the priests seemed perfectly to understand. I afterwards proceeded to the Ras's house, where I found a long table set out, and a great quantity of bread cakes piled up: I was seated on the couch beside him, and had the honour of being fed from his own hands. There were present the Ballambarras, or master of the bread department, the Baharnegash of Dixan, the Chief of Debib, who was in waiting, and many others of equal authority. There were four changes of guests at the table, and three large jars of maize were emptied, each of which contained at least half a hogshead. I was prevailed upon by the Ras to eat a small portion of brinde, and am satisfied that it is merely prejudice which deters us from this food. The priests of the neighbouring churches were fed first, and all did justice to the brinde and maize.

" The Ras pointed out to me two Falasha, or Jews, who came in during the feast, and afterwards politely sent them to the house where I lodged, that I might ask them what questions I pleased. I procured from them, however, but little information. They acknowledge no king, except the sovereign of the country, the line of Gideon being extinct. They told me that they were very numerous at Gondar, and in the provinces of Knara and Samen, and that their chief employment consisted in building and thatching houses. They have not any books of consequence except at Gondar, and those are of no great antiquity. They pretend to have entered the country in the time of Memileh.

"I was afterwards visited by Debib of Negashé, who came to solicit presents for his attention to us on the road. Captain Rudland had just arrived from Antalow, and was eating some mutton that had been provided by our guide; Debib joined him with much satisfaction in the consumption of the joint, during which I gained from him the following intelligence. He commanded a very considerable extent of country, containing at least thirty villages, for which he paid to the Ras one hundred and fifty wakeas of gold, twenty oxen, and as many skins of honey, besides one matchlock; but for this latter, if difficult to procure, he compromised for fifty pieces of cloth, valued at about one dollar each. He owned that his father had paid a tribute double the amount of this in the time of Ras Michael.

"I sent to the Ras in the evening, and mentioned Captain Rudland's arrival, saying, that we would pay our compliments to him whenever he might appoint. He fixed upon seven o'clock, but afterwards put it off till the morning. The thermometer was 64° in the evening. There fell a little rain in the afternoon.

"September 11.—On rising in the morning, we were much surprised to receive salaams from the

Ras, and information that he was gone; nor was it, till after much enquiry, that I could ascertain that he had gone on a hunting party, and would not be back until evening. It was not without much regret that I left Captain Rudland without an interpreter; but every preparation being made in Mucculiah for our departure, I was unwilling to lose any more time, and accordingly set out with my attendants for Adowa. The view of the village of Mucculiah from the bottom of the hill is extremely picturesque; but as we had a long journey before us, I was not able to spare time for a sketch. We first went over the plain of Jambela, in a N. N. W. direction. The whole of this plain, extending about eight miles in length, and from two to four in breadth, was in a high state of cultivation, or rather of preparation for it, as the inhabitants were busily employed in ploughing. It contains at least forty inhabited villages, beside several in ruins. Afterwards we turned off to the westward over a barren hill, where the road was much incommoded by loose stones and shrubby bushes and trees, which, as we advanced, were so closely set as to form a thick and shady covert. Before us was a house belonging to the Ras, in a small valley through which runs the river Gibbeh, from which the mansion takes its name. Our guide here desired us to halt, and produced for our refreshment some cold mutton, of which we made a very hearty meal. Pursuing our road, we passed along a narrow and rather deep valley, part of which had been lately cleared for cultivation; the rest was thickly set with brushwood, and afforded a fine cover for grouse, guinea fowls, and partridges, all of which were in great abundance; but we did not see a single deer, though the country appeared of a description highly favourable to these animals. This gully, as it may be called, is about five miles in length, and at the end of it we mounted a lofty hill, on which is the village of Hasemko, by the Chief of which we were received with much attention. Our course I reckoned to be about fifteen miles in a north-west direction. The thermometer on our arrival was 86°.

" September 12.—We left the village at an early hour, after making the lady of the mansion, who was a very agreeable and pretty woman, a trifling present; it having been intimated to me that she had been put to much inconvenience to make room for us yesterday evening.

" Our road lay over the hill to the south-west, the inhabitants, who seem ever desirous of turning the road from cultivated plains, having led it in this direction to a gap in the side of the hill made by the falling down of a great mass of rock. We now wound round the summit of the hill, chiefly in a western course, till we reached the village of Admára, about three miles distant, above which is a church dedicated to St. Mary Magdalen. We here inclined more to the north, passing a sloping plain, some part of which the inhabitants were ploughing for the first time, in spite of the stones and shrubs that impeded the progress of the bullocks, whose unnecessary toil we could not but pity, especially when we saw them lashed unmercifully by the drivers, who carry in the right hand a whip that leaves a mark wherever it strikes. We now came to the lower part of a mountainous ridge called Atbara, where we were joined by our guide, who had before gone off another way, and had appointed to meet us. I had just killed a small bird, much like the humming bird, and had with great difficulty dug up a few bulbs. The descent hence is extremely steep, and so much incommoded with loose stones, that we were obliged to dismount from our mules, and before we reached the bottom, had reason to exclaim that it was as bad as the descent of Taranta. About half way down a few houses and a church are built under the shelter of projecting rocks, in a very picturesque situation. We met a kafila on its way to Antalow preparing to go up the steep that we had just descended. After we had with much toil reached the bottom, it was not a little provoking to find that, on passing the brook, it became necessary to climb another ascent before we could get out of the valley. Afterwards, the vegetation began to vary considerably, the country being much more thickly set with trees, some of which were of a large size. The soil was poor, and of a sandy nature; and we passed one entire bed of loose sand nearly a mile in extent. Proceeding about three miles to the north, we halted by a running stream, and took our usual repast; and being soon after overtaken by rain, we pursued our journey with all expedition for another stage of about six miles, when we arrived, just as it grew dark, at the mansion of Barrambarras Toklu. We were received kindly by the master of the house, and treated most hospitably with a banquet of brinde and maize. In the course of it he introduced to us his wife, who is the sister of Subagadis, to whom I presented beads and a looking glass. Our host was the chief of the district of Tembla, and a man of consequence, having many soldiers with matchlocks in his service. He was in high spirits, was very jovial, and wished me to stay in the country, promising to give me his daughter in marriage. Much jocular conversation ensued, the maize was handed briskly around, and we all took our ful.

portion, about sixteen brulhes being drank by each person present, ladies as well as gentlemen.

"September 13. — At a very early hour in the morning we quitted the village of Gullybudda, where we had been so hospitably entertained, and which appeared to be a place of considerable extent and population. We travelled about three miles N. N. W. through a picturesque and tolerably well-wooded country; but the trees were of a small size, and scarcely timber. Birds of many different kinds were singing among the branches of all the lower trees, the extremities of which were hung with numerous nests. Our first halt was by the side of the river Warie, * which was running with great rapidity to the westward. Though at present a small stream, there were evident marks of its magnitude in the rainy season; for on both sides were seen sticks and weeds among the branches of the trees at least fifteen feet above the surface of its present bed, which had been lodged there by the floods. Our people soon made a fire, killed a sheep which had been presented to me the day before, and grilled a part of it for our breakfast. From this place our road turned more to the westward, over lofty and rugged hills, all of which, however, were for the most part cultivated. We passed the villages of Tsai: which, with their territory, form a free district under one of the Ras's nephews. It is however but a wretched domain, the soil being very sandy, and entirely occupied in many parts by kolquall; the surface is farther incumbered by rocks of slate in nearly vertical strata. After having journeyed about six miles north northwest from our last station, we made another halt

* Warie means merely a torrent.

at about two o'clock by the side of a stream, where we saw several birds, one of which I have no doubt was the black eagle of Bruce. His drawing of it appears to be very correct; but in its habits, this bird more resembles an hawk than an eagle, for it perches on the tops of trees, and on being driven from one, flies to another. We again resumed our march, passing over wild hills covered with brushwood, part of which was clearing for cultivation, till we gained the top of a hill about four miles and a half from our last halting place, where we were to be accommodated for the night. Fit Aurari Yasous, the master of the mansion, was absent; we were however ushered into the hall, and on his return were presented with a goat and other eatables. There being no maise for drink, we were obliged to put up with booza, which is made from the crumbs of all sorts of bread, and greatly resembles bad, sour, small beer with a toast in it. Our present host was advanced in years, very tall, fierce and ugly; he is said to behave very tyrannically towards his people, and we ourselves could bear testimony to the roughness of his manners.

"September 14.—We found our host much more civil and attentive in the morning than on the preceding evening, bread and hot milk being prepared for us at a very early hour; and he himself insisting on accompanying us to some distance from his house. Our road lay over a plain, skirting along the side of a lofty conical mountain, at the top of which is the church or convent of Abou Sama. On our right we saw a house formerly belonging to the Ras, and presented by him to Barrambarras Toklu. After travelling about three miles and a half, we arrived at the mansion of Bashaw Guebra Eyat, a man of much consequence in the country, who is able to bring into the field a large body of soldiers armed with matchlocks, a circumstance on which the importance of the Chiefs much depends. He was a middle-aged man of pleasing manners, and treated us with much hospitality. We proceeded, in about an hour, on our journey, winding round rugged hills covered with brushwood, and along the ledges of steep precipices, a fall from which, into the plain below, would have been certain death. The kol-quall abounds in this part of the country, which, though cultivated wherever circumstances would admit, is not very productive, on account of its dry and sandy nature. We met a poor woman, on the hill, who accosted me in a supplicatory tone, and begged that I would give her some physic for a child which she carried at her back, and who, according to her report, was afflicted with an evil spirit. I could only recommend her to the protection of God, assuring her that the nature of such dreadful maladies was far beyond my skill.

"The hills that we had been passing over consist almost entirely of a brown calcareous stone, being for the most part in perpendicular strata; hence, instead of flat tabular elevations, as is the case where the strata lie horizontally, the forms presented by these hills are generally inclining to pyramidal. The whole country is well watered, springs being found on almost every mountain.

"As we advanced, the country bore a better appearance; the plains were covered with richer soil, but for want of draining were much swamped from the springs above. We had advanced about nine miles, ascending and descending, when we mounted a ridge that brought us in sight of the church of Abba Garima, which, though not in the straight road to Adowa, I determined to visit. In order to reach this building, we had to cross a nearly circular valley, closed in on all sides with high but irregular hills. A stream of water runs through this valley, and wild date trees, at that time covered with fruit, were scattered over its surface. From having found this tree only in the neighbourhood of religious houses of unknown antiquity, I am led to conjecture that it was introduced by the Christian fathers who came hither from Egypt.

" The church of Abba Garima is said to have been built in the reign of Guebra Mascal, about the year 560; it is situated on a low projection of the circular ridge, by which the valley is bounded on the north-west, and is not very difficult of access. It is surrounded by oxy-cedars and daroo trees of luxuriant growth, and wild date trees of so great a height as to have the appearance of cocoa-nut trees.

" The road, winding to the church, is much incommoded with large and rugged masses of rocks, among the crevices of which runs a trickling stream; from the head of this path, thirty rough steps lead up to a wretched shed, forming the porch of the church. We passed through this into an open area walled round, in the center of which is the main building, of a square form, and divided by a passage that runs through it into two unequal compartments. It is built of solid masses of stone and timber, which have in some places been strengthened by bars of iron, and the but-ends of all the beams and planks have been rounded and left projecting, as ornaments. Within are some miserable paintings, of which one represents Abbou Garima, with a long white beard and mustachios, wearing a turban, and seated according to the Turkish fashion. He is attended by many others dressed like himself, among whom is one with mustachios only. Several priests were present, and were very attentive in shewing us the whole of the building. The only account that they could give of the place, was the fabulous one, that Abbou Garima, 1500 years ago, was brought from Secundria hither in one night by the angel Gabriel, and after residing here a long time, was carried away in as mysterious a manner, and has never since been heard of; in commemoration of whom this church was erected by Guebra Mascal, who then reigned in Abyssinia. This, according to the Abyssinian annals, would bring his coming down to 500 anno Domini instead of 300, as Guebra Mascal was the successor of Elesbaas, who was cotemporary with the Roman Emperor Justin.

"We were obliged to hasten away as speedily as possible, in order to reach Adowa before night; and after toiling over a road perpetually ascending and descending, sometimes swampy, sometimes rocky, and at all times much incumbered with loose stones, we at length came in sight of the town, enveloped in smoke. The market was just over, and the people, who were returning to their respective villages, were all curious enough to see the strangers; but they uniformly behaved with much respect and civility. We arrived by sunset at the end of our journey, and were immediately conducted to the Ras's house, and introduced to Nebrida Aram and Basha Abdallah, who were waiting to receive me. A nephew of Nebrida Aram soon after came in, accompanied by a great number of his people. The evening was spent with great conviviality; many chiefs of considerable rank were present, among whom was a nephew of Ras Michael, with whom I had much conversation about his uncle; nor shall I soon forget the astonishment excited in the whole company by my knowledge of the public transactions in Abyssinia during the last fifty years. Nebrida Aram appeared very old and infirm, having lost the use of his left arm; he is said to be very rich, and doubtless possessed much power, being left here in charge by the Ras, whose horses were still fastened up in the hall. An upper apartment was prepared for me, but I found it so cold that I returned into the hall. The old gentleman politely made an excuse for not giving up to me the whole of the hall; he ordered it, however, to be divided by a screen, and we all slept in this apartment, Nebrida Aram and his suite, the Ras's horses, myself, and servants.

"September 18.—I retired to the room prepared for me, that I might finish some rough drawings of plants. After breakfast the mules were brought, and I proceeded to examine whatever was interesting in the town and neighbourhood, accompanied by Pearce and Andrew, who fortunately had completely established their character as Christians, in consequence of which I was enabled to get over many difficulties which would otherwise have been insurmountable.

"We were first taken to the church of St. Mariam, and on our way saw a hyæna lying dead in the road, of the same species as the one Captain Rudland killed at Dixan, but much larger; it had been killed by spears.

"St. Mariam affords nothing worthy of remark; it is built exactly in the same style as the churches already described, but is inferior in every respect. We were attended by a crowd of the inhabitants, who pressed forward to get a sight of us, shouting and laughing, and the women making a clapping noise peculiar to themselves, all expressive of their pleasure and astonishment.

"We now proceeded westward out of the town, crossing the plain, and a stream called Assa, till we arrived at another called the Mai Gogua, which runs northward with great rapidity down the valley. After riding along the bank of this stream about three quarters of a mile, we crossed it, and ascended a hill immediately beyond, on which stand the remains of the convent of Fremona, as it was called by the Jesuits, by whom it was founded; but this name, if ever adopted by the inhabitants, is now wholly unknown. Within the walls, which are at present in ruins, stands the church of St. George, a poor and wretched edifice in the form of a parallelogram, with the internal walls painted in the usual style. The roof is an awkward and imperfect attempt at a dome. On the north side of the church is the appearance of a large tank or pool, and upon a small and higher eminence at the extremity of the northern brow of the hill, is a square building, with an open doorway on each side, in which is hung a large bell marked with Ethiopic characters. The outer wall, and all the inclosed buildings, are composed of small stones, laid very inartificially, and cemented with mud. Some parts of the wall are still thirty feet high, and at the angles are round abutments; yet it does not appear to have ever been a place of strength, though Bruce has thought proper to represent the buttresses as flanking towers, and the belfry as a citadel.

"On our way back we turned off to the church of St. Michael, which is placed on a rising ground on the east side of the valley. It is surrounded on all sides by trees, and is by much the most respectable in appearance of any at Adowa. We had by this time been joined by our attending crowd; and on my coming out of the church a woman fell at my feet, and implored me to heal her son, who was deaf and dumb; nor was it without great difficulty that I was able to get rid of her importunity, by representing to her that the performance of such a cure was a miracle, and only capable of being effected by the immediate power of God. I found in waiting a mule, belonging to the Ras, which Nebrida Aram had sent for my use; accordingly I mounted, and proceeded amidst the acclamations of an immense throng into the city.

"Adowa, situated on the eastern side of a valley, about a mile across, is a place of considerable extent, and has a striking appearance on account of the multitude of Wanza trees, which are thickly planted in the inclosures around the houses. I this day procured the flower and fruit, the latter of which is said by the inhabitants to be good eating when ripe; and I found Bruce's drawing of this tree, so far as it goes, correct.

"Adowa supplies great quantities of cloth, principally of a coarse quality, which circulates as money through the country, and is the principal currency in which the chiefs pay their annual tribute. Each piece is about sixteen cubits long, and one and three-quarters wide; its value is thirty pieces of salt, or one dollar. Some of the finer cloths are valued as high as twelve dollars for a dress, each dress being fifty cubits in length: these are worn only by the principal men of the country. The native Christian manufacturer will make only three dresses of the fine cloth in a year: the Mussulmauns will make more, but of an inferior quality, and therefore bearing a less price. I received from Nebrida Aram a bullock and two sheep, and another from his nephew; also two sheep and two jars of maise from the head men of the place, and one sheep from Basha Abdallah.

"September 16.—We did not leave Adowa until ten o'clock, having been detained by some difficulty about our baggage, occasioned by our having bought a few samples of fine and coarse cloths manufactured here, which we found it impossible to leave in safety at Adowa, as Nebrida Aram and Basha Abdallah were both going to Antalow to the muster of the troops before the Ras.

"On going down into the hall to pay my compliments to Nebrida Aram, I was unexpectedly introduced to one of the royal family, who was sitting with him on the couch. This was no less a person than Fasilydas, son of Yasous, who was placed on the throne by Ras Guxo. He gave me an extremely polite reception, and was very curious in examining every thing belonging to my dress. He asked me whether I intended to go to Gondar; and on my saying that I wished it, but was prevented by the unsettled state of public affairs, he asked me to go with him; which I was obliged to decline. I soon took my leave, as it was impossible for me to ask any questions, owing to my ignorance of his present situation in Tigré, and from knowing that my guide, who was present, was extremely suspicious of every thing that I said. After I had mounted my mule, the Prince came out with his slender retinue, and requested me to dismount, seeming extremely anxious to speak with me in private. On my complying, and going apart with my interpreter to hear what he had to communicate, Guebra Selassé called out most vociferously to him in an angry tone, which compelled us very reluctantly to part in silence. His complexion was extremely dark, but his features were good: he was living at this time under the protection of the Ras; by whom, under the guise of respect, he was kept in a state of honourable restraint.

"Our road from Adowa lay along the valley in nearly a westward direction: we crossed the Mai Gogua, and another stream, which I suppose may be the Riberani of Bruce; and after travelling about five miles, arrived at the extremity of the valley, marked by a peaked hill, green to the top, on which stands the church of Hannes; and immediately opposite, on a smaller rising ground, the church of Anna Mariam. Hither the Ras, as governor of Tigré, when residing at Adowa, used to come out to meet any message from the King. The direct road to Axum passes by the side of this hill; but our guide informing me there was a curious place called Calam Negus, in the neighbourhood, we turned off a little to the northward for the purpose of visiting it. On our way we met with a grandson of Ras Michael, mounted on a mule; he stopped to ask me for some medicine for a well known disorder said to be very prevalent here, which I was obliged to evade on the true plea of having left it at Antalow. Notwithstanding this application, from all the enquiries we made during my stay in the country, I am of opinion, that the venereal disease does not exist in Abyssinia: debility, and a bad sort of itch, common in the country, are generally mistaken for it. This last disease always yielded to an application of gunpowder and lemon juice. The descendant of Michael the Great was living on a scanty allowance drawn from the province which his grandfather ruled with such absolute power. He had twenty fields allowed him by the Ras Welleta Selassé, who also had the condescension to make him the same annual present as he bestows on his soldiers. This small possession was probably not far distant, for we soon after passed an old woman who was formerly an attendant on the old Ras. We continued journeying nearly due west, and passed over a hill, the top of which was one continued bed of iron ore. The next hill was covered with spar. Beyond this we crossed a plain fully six miles in extent, which brought us at length to the place of our destination. Its appearance promised but little; but on examination it proved, to our great satisfaction, to be of far more consequence than we had expected.

"It consists of two excavations formed in the hill, and cased and covered with large blocks of brown granite, one of which, serving as a cover to one of the cells, measured eleven feet and a quarter by eight and a quarter. An idea of the whole will be best obtained by inspecting the plan drawn on an accurate scale from a measurement made on the spot.* These caves are, with respect to each other, in a direction very nearly north and south; the workmanship is good, but rough; the stone having all the marks of the chissel. The first, (marked B, vide plan), our guides informed us was the road by which Calam Negus went to Ierusalem, and, "if any person should take a candle into it at night, he would distinctly see the whole of the way to that holy city." This personage I suppose to be Caleb Negas, a king who reigned in the country about the year 522, and who was cotemporary with the Emperor Justin: he was

* This is lost, but one is supplied from memory

celebrated for a successful incursion into Arabia against the Homerites, and on his return sent his crown to Jerusalem to be suspended in the temple.* We managed to find the entire extent of this cave, at which our guides were not a little astonished. The second cave, (marked C.) is very nearly closed up by earth that has fallen in; but as there was a glimpse of something like pillars, I determined not to be deterred by any trifling difficulties. Accordingly Pearce and myself crept down into it on our knees, and when we had once passed the entrance, found it to be much more curious than the first. The door way, leading into the outer cell, is extremely well fashioned; the capitals of the supporting pillars are formed with the butt ends of the cross stones projecting over the erect ones. Within are three plain tombs standing at right angles to the walls of the cell, in a direction nearly east and west, on a pavement raised about four inches from the floor. The cover of the center one is displaced, and lying partly broken on one of the others; the two side tombs are entire.

"The side cells of this excavation are of much greater depth than the middle one. We satisfactorily ascertained the whole extent of the place, by following the walls till they brought us again to the entrance, not being able to procure lights. The only living creatures that we perceived within, were bats. At a little distance were some large loose stones, ready squared for building; but to what purpose they had been applied it was impossible to ascertain. A ridiculous circumstance occurred on our being about to leave this place: I had left my whip in the first cave; all our Habesh attendants supposed it to be in the other, to which

* Ludolf. lib. 2, chap. 44.

they sent one of the boys to fetch it; in the mean time I myself descended into the first, and brought it up; nor was it possible to persuade them that Calam Negus had not brought it to me out of the other, which absurd story they often afterwards seriously repeated. These curious remains of antiquity lie nearly west of the hills above Adowa, which were at this time in sight, and about a mile from the skirts of Axum, to which we descended in a south-western direction.

CHAPTER III.

MR. SALT'S NARRATIVE CONTINUED.—*Account of Axum.—The Obelisk,—the Church,—the Priests,—the King's Chair.—An Ethiopic Inscription, and conjectural Explanation of it.—A Greek Inscription.—General State of the Ruins.—Observations on Mr. Bruce's Account of Axum.—Departure from Axum.—Arrival at Adowa.—Visit to Ozoro Tishai.—Return to Antalow.—Captain Rudland's Account of his Proceedings during Mr. Salt's Absence.*

"THE first impression on beholding Axum church, is its great resemblance to the Gothic seats of noblemen in England. As we came nearer, we passed the fallen ruins of a great number of obelisks, some of which present no appearance of having been ever decorated with sculpture, while others seem to have had much attention paid to them in this respect; at length, after passing a large reservoir of water on our left, we were much gratified with a view of an obelisk still erect, which had been hitherto concealed by a large Daroo tree, and is undoubtedly the one mentioned by Poncet, and afterwards described and drawn by Bruce. It is about eighty feet high, and formed out of a single block of granite, curiously carved, and in excellent proportion. My attention was for a long time rivetted on this beautiful and extraordinary monument, of which, however, the elevation published by the traveller last mentioned, can furnish no idea. It is difficult to conceive the method by which such a solid mass of granite was raised; and the astonishment excited at the magnitude of the work was more particularly striking, after passing through a country now reduced to so rude a state as Abyssinia. A little way below this only obelisk that has withstood the effects of time, and which appears so perfect that it might be supposed to have been lately erected, we came opposite to the church, which Bruce has most unjustly depreciated, since, when compared with all others in Tigré, it has no rival (except Chelicut) with respect to size, richness, or sanctity. The priests were very unwilling at first to admit us; but the name and authority of the Ras, at length brought them to a compliance. The only cause of their reluctance, as we afterwards discovered, arose from their not having prepared all their finery to enhance the dignity of our reception. The principal circumstance worthy of notice in the external appearance of the church, is its height, which cannot be less than forty feet. The colonnade in front is supported by four massive square pillars about five feet in diameter, composed of small stones, and covered with plaister. On requesting to see the inside of the building, the farther folding door was thrown open, and singing was heard in a distant apartment; some of the priests then came forward reciting prayers, and burning incense. All the books and rich dresses belonging to the church, were afterwards brought for my examination: the former are of a large size, and covered with gilding and figures in relief; the latter are so like those which we saw at Chelicut, as not to need a particular description.

"I learned from the books in this place, that

the first Christian church at Axum was built eleven hundred and forty years ago, at the same time as that of Abrahasubah, and was destroyed by Mohamed Gragné in the year 1526; the present church was built by Sultan Ayto Fasil, son of Ayto Socinios, in the year 1657.

"In the evening I had a visit from the chief priest, and others, who came with their books to try me in the Scripture. My knowledge, though not very great, was fortunately fully equal to enable me to answer or evade all their questions, so that I came off with great credit; and the High Priest kissed my hand in rapture at my intimate acquaintance with the sacred book. Before he left me, I took the opportunity of presenting to him, for the church, a piece of red satin stuff, as I found that no information was to be gained without some kind of bribery. The priests were all highly pleased with my offering, but begged that I would keep it till morning, and then deliver it in public at the church. The clerical establishment at this place seems to be on a far superior scale to any I have seen in Abyssinia, except Chelicut, which, from being the favourite church of the Ras, and close to the vicinity of his principal residence, is of course more particularly attended to, and enriched, during the continuance of his power. Axum is, however, looked up to with great deference, as having been for so long a period the seat of royalty; and the Chief Priest claims a very high precedence over all the churches to the eastward of the Tacazza. Even at present, on great occasions, as after a victory, the Ras thinks it necessary to pay his devotions at this place, to conciliate the priesthood, the influence of which still continues to be considerable.

"The dress of this order of men differs in some

degree from that of all the other ranks. They wear a close vest of white linen next the skin, which covers every part of their body to the knees, in addition to the large folding mantle and close drawers, which constitute the simple dress of the Abyssinians. They also wrap neatly round their heads a thin shawl of cotton, leaving the top of their heads exposed. This difference in dress gives great respectability to their appearance, and as far as I could learn, their conduct and manners are equally becoming.

"September 17.—I went to the church at a very early hour, and was received with great attention by the priests, and on my request was admitted into the inmost apartment. The whole body of the church, consisting of four apartments or rooms, was covered with handsome carpets. On my presenting the piece of satin, I was desired to kneel down with my face to the ground, in which position I continued about two minutes, during which time the High Priest recited a prayer over me. This ceremony being over, I was led up some square steps of granite to the top of the building, which is flatly roofed, covered with mortar and stucco, and surrounded with Gothic ornaments. We here measured the size of the church, and found it to be one hundred and eleven feet in length and fifty-one in breadth. The view hence gives a good idea of the situation of the obelisks and of the reservoir, I therefore took a sketch of it, which is given among my larger views.

"Hence I was conducted to see two walls lined with stone, which are at some little distance from the church, as also a small square inclosure surrounded by pillars; on a seat within which, the ancient kings used to be crowned (vide B in plan), as is shewn in the Vignette of this volume. In the inclosure behind the king's seat, other remains are scattered about in different directions; but on none of these, after a careful and repeated examination, was I able to perceive the least appearance of any inscription, excepting one, which is very short, in Ethiopic characters, of which the following is an exact copy.

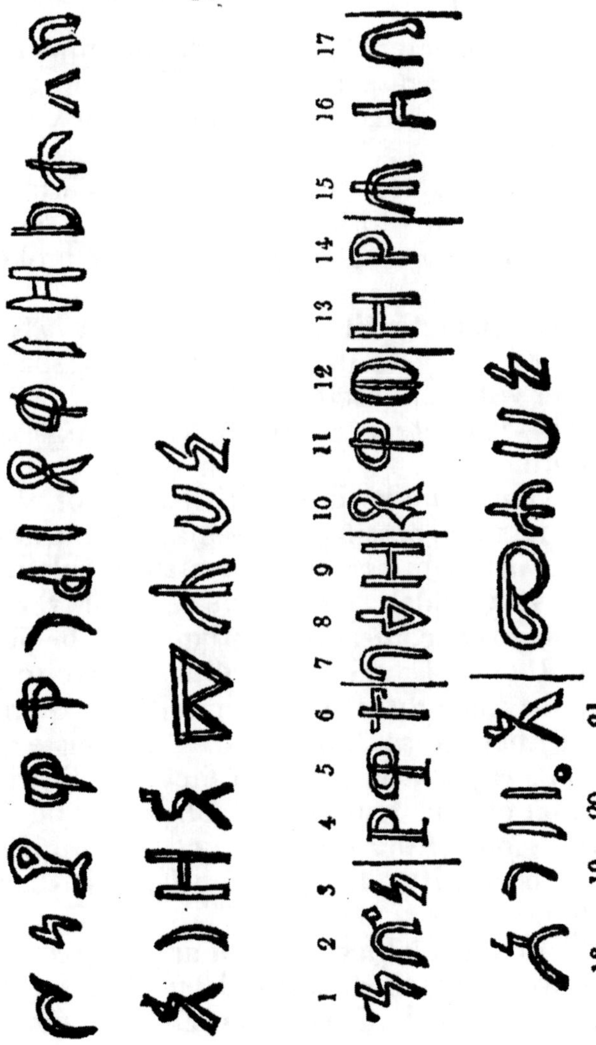

"In the two last lines I have given the Ethiopic inscription, as I think it ought to be restored.

"The character marked 1, does not exist in the original; but I can have little doubt of its having been there, as with the characters marked 2 and 3, it forms the word Aboona, or chief priest.

"The characters 4, 5, 6, I conjecture to be Dawit, or David.

"The characters 7, 8, 9, require much alteration to make sense of them. According to the form I have adopted, they would mean Gay-za, or removed.

"The characters 10, 11, are very clear; but a part of 12 seems to have been erased. As I have restored it, they would be Ja-ka-wa, or, broke them to pieces.

"The characters 13, 14, are Zy-ja, or here.

"The characters 15, 16, 17, are Ha-za-ba, or, he thought within himself.

"The characters 18, 19, 20, 21, are A-ga-zi-y, or, the Lord.

"I can make nothing satisfactory of the four last letters, and possibly there may be some error in them as in the former letters, for the whole inscription is very rudely cut. The sense of the latter part may be conjectured from the beginning: "The Aboona David removed and broke to pieces here; he thought within himself the Lord was pleased that he so should do." If this explanation be just, it accounts satisfactorily for the destruction of the temple and obelisks; but I feel too conscious of my ignorance of the original language, to give it to the public otherwise than as a conjecture.

"Those ruins which were in any degree worthy of notice, I sketched, assisted by Pearce. I also took a front view of the church. I was taken hence to an upright stone (vide R in ground plan) about half a mile from the church in a north-east direction, on which was said to be some ancient writing. As I approached it, my curiosity was so highly raised, that I could scarcely refrain from running with eagerness to the spot. The first side of it that I examined, disappointed me much, there being only some slight remains of unknown characters; I was however soon repaid by a view of the opposite side, as I found it covered with Greek characters, fairly and deeply cut in the stone, each letter being nearly two inches in length. For the preservation of this inscription in so perfect a state, it is greatly indebted to a fortunate inclination to the northward, which the nature of the ground has given to the stone, by which that side of it is entirely sheltered from the rain. This monument is about eight feet high, three and a half broad, and one thick. As it was getting late I returned to breakfast, and was afterwards detained some time with the priests, who brought me a book of Ras Welleta Selassé's wars. I then returned with Pearce to the inscription. My first care was to trace every letter with white chalk, and then to copy it on paper, correcting the whole by going over it a second time. We had been several hours thus engaged, and had not proceeded half through before the rain came on, and obliged us to desist. In the evening I wrote down the best account I could get from the books of Axum, of Ras Michael, and his rebellion in Tigré against the Emperor Yasous; his standing a siege on the mountain of Samayut; and his subsequent concession and pardon, to which the Emperor with difficulty acceded; all which confirm the historical account of the same transactions as related by Bruce.

"This day a circumstance occurred of trivial moment, but which I shall narrate, as it throws some light on the state of mental cultivation among those people. I was sitting alone where a fire of wood had been lighted, when a man of very wild demeanor, taking the opportunity of the absence of my servants, rushed in and began to remove the lighted branches. I in vain ordered him to desist, till at length, provoked by his insolence, and desirous of dismissing him at once, I threw at his head the drinking bottle which was standing before me on the table. The man was not touched, but immediately ran out in a great fright, making a most vociferous outcry, which immediately brought Guebra Selassé and others into the room. On being informed of what had passed, they searched for the bottle, and to their great surprise found that it had received no injury (doubtless on account of its lightness and globular figure). They turned it round and round with increasing astonishment; and from that time it was one of the anecdotes concerning me that they had most pleasure in repeating, declaring that such a man could never be in want of a weapon; a conclusion, which it may be supposed I was at no pains to controvert.

"September 18.—I rose at an early hour and hastened to the inscription. After I had completed and corrected with the greatest attention the copy of every letter that was in sight, we began to dig up the earth, in order to get at that part of it which was under ground. We fortunately cleared away nearly a foot and a half, without bringing the stone on our heads, and at last, to my great satisfaction, came, as I supposed, to the end of the inscription. This being done, I went to take a drawing of the obelisk still erect (vide L in ground plan). I found it to be extremely different from the representation given of it by Bruce; the ornaments, which he is pleased to call triglyphs and metopes, and guttæ, being most regularly, instead of irregularly disposed, as will be seen in my representation of it. I am now perfectly satisfied that all Bruce's pretended knowledge of drawing is not to be depended upon, the present instance affording a striking example both of his want of veracity and uncommon assurance, in giving, with a view to correct others, "as a geometrical elevation," so very false a sketch of this monument. The broad sides of it front north and south, of which only the south is sculptured. It is inferior in size to one that has fallen down, which also differs from this in the form of its ornaments, and in its having been carved on both sides, or else on the opposite side to the corresponding one of that which is now standing. It is a noble monument, but of its antiquity, who can judge? For Bruce's theory on the subject is, I fear, so ill supported by facts, as to deserve little credit.

"After finishing my sketch, I went to the top of the hill to the eastward (marked P in ground plan), in hopes of finding some more remains. There is the appearance of a double door-way excavated in the rock on the western side of this hill, and on the northern side are steps leading to the top, but on the summit itself there is not the least appearance of any work of ancient art. My labour however was not entirely fruitless, as hence I took bearings of all the principal objects, and thus compleated my idea of the situation of Axum.

"The town of Axum stands partly in and partly at the mouth of a nook (y y y in the ground plain) formed by two hills on the north-west end of an extensive valley (z z), the soil of which is very fertile, and interspersed with small pieces of spar and agates. North of the plain stands the church of Abba Lucanus on a lofty hill, the summit of which is covered with trees; to the north-east is the church Abba Pantaleon, built on the point of a bare and rugged rock called Mantillees; on the south-east are the towering hills of Adowa; and on the south-west the convent or church of Tecla Haimanont. The road from Adowa (T T in ground plan) lies directly west across the plain, and winds round the bottom of the hill that stands to the east of Axum, which hill is entirely composed of a brown coarse granite. Upon the first rising of this hill, and about two hundred yards north north-east from the stone with the inscription, stands a plain obelisk (S in ground plan) about twenty feet high, and in a line eastward are fourteen more that are fallen. The one that is now standing, I suppose to be that mentioned by Bruce on his entering Axum, as the high road from Adowa leads close under it; though by the way in which Bruce has described it, the reader would be led to look for it above the convent of Abboo or Abba Pantaleon, which is impossible, that place being on the very summit of an high eminence on the left hand side of the great road. After passing this obelisk on the right, there is a line of regular rock, in part resembling a rough wall, which is probably the same that Bruce has described as a wall of red marble surmounted by pedestals, (vide V in ground plan). We were not however able in any portion of it to trace the workmanship of art. It seemed to be a regular stratum of rock left by nature, as I have often before seen, forming the very base of the hill. It is of a loose, soft, chalky nature; but the influence of the air, and the mosses growing upon it, have formed a reddish coat on the surface. It is very irregular in its measurement, in some places being twelve feet high, and in others not two, and is from ten to five feet across. There is no appearance of pedestals upon it, but a little to the south are lying five pedestals or altars (C in ground plan) which are at present evidently removed from their proper situations.

"The chief modern building is the church, which stands at the northern extremity of the present town, and seems in part to occupy the situation of an ancient temple. It has in front of it two flights of steps (O in ground plan); the lower flight consists of twelve steps, one hundred and eighty feet in length, and the upper one of eight steps, thirty-six feet in length, with an interval of sixteen feet between the two flights: from the uppermost step to the church porch is thirty-eight feet. A row of broken pedestals still remaining before the church (C in ground plan), indicates the principal entrance.

"The situation of the monument called the King's seat, has been already described, and the only additional circumstances that I have to relate concerning it, are, that the seat itself, and the slab on which the feet naturally rest, are of granite, and not of free stone, as is in this instance alone, among so many ruins, so suspiciously described by Bruce; and they contain not the least trace of an inscription; and yet I cannot think that they have been much disturbed during the last thirty-five years; as they have not been applied to any purpose, and are rendered nearly inaccessible to the barefooted natives, by being surrounded on all sides with nettles of a large species, which sting more than any I have before felt. Nor can I believe that an inscription, which had stood for ages, would have totally vanished in so short a period, without leaving even a trace behind. I therefore conceive Bruce's inscription to be altogether fictitious. In the inner inclosure, on a paved way leading to the flight of steps before the church, is a broken stone, on which are figured two spears, the one barbed, and the other not, like those now in use.

" All the monuments around the church form a group, and are probably part of one great edifice; but it is impossible to make out what might have been the plan of this ancient building, because the houses of the modern town are crowded all round the south and western sides of the church. All the information that I could procure at Axum, concerning the history of the singular remains there, was from the attending priests, who informed me, on the authority of their books, that all their ancient monuments and obelisks, originally fifty-five in number, of which four were of the size now standing, were built by Ethiopus, the father of Abyssinia, about one thousand five hundred and forty-four years ago: and, which is probably entitled to more credit, that the great reservoir from which every house in the town was formerly supplied with water, was constructed during the reign of Isaac, King of Abyssinia, by the Aboona Samuel, who died at Axum three hundred and ninety-two years ago, and was buried under the Daroo tree still remaining near the church; and that in the year 1070, a female named Gadit, in great authority, came from Amhara, and from a superstitious motive, destroyed, as far as she was able, these remains of ancient art; threw down the obelisks, broke the altars, and laid the whole place in ruins; an account by no means improbable, as there is every appearance of many of the largest altars having been broken by great force, and removed from their places. The Ethiopic inscription makes it however doubtful, whether this were not done by the Aboona David.

"From my account of Axum, it will appear that Bruce's description of the "mountain of red marble;" of the "wall cut out of the same five feet high," with its "one hundred and thirty-three pedestals, on which stood colossal statues of the dog star, two of which only were remaining;" and of the road cut between the wall and the mountain, are statements contrary to the existing facts, or at least so extremely exaggerated, as to cast strong doubts upon his authority; and it appears to me, that nothing but the fallacious presumption that no one, after the difficulties which he had described with so much exaggeration, would dare to follow his steps, could have induced him to venture on such unsupported assertion, which the very next European who should travel that way would so certainly refute. His never having seen nor heard of the inscription that stands so near the road by which he passed, is somewhat singular. It is indeed partly concealed from sight by a small rising ground, and his attention might easily have been diverted by the obelisk on the right. Moreover, his account of the church, and his general remarks on the priests, give reason to suppose that he had no communication with them; yet these were probably the only persons capable of giving him any information on the subject. In this instance, his neglect of them was well repaid, by his being left in ignorance of the most valuable monument in the place.

" The lower class of the inhabitants of Axum seemed to be more rude to strangers, and less under authority, than any we observed during our excursion, so that it was not easy to prevent the occurrence of a serious dispute. Ibrahim, our boy, seized a much stronger fellow than himself, who was particularly troublesome, and having made fast his garment, brought him to the top of the church, at the time we were there, and delivered him over to our guides. After frightening the offender with the Ras's displeasure, we were induced to dismiss him unpunished, at the request of the High Priest. This custom of seizing the garment of an offender is very general; when any person is injured, his first attempt is to get hold of his adversary's apparel, which having fastened in a hand knot to his own, nothing can force him to quit till he gets into the presence of his superiors to whose decision he means to appeal; and it is singular, that those who may have stolen double the value of their garment, will not consent to part with it in order to escape, from the disgrace attached to such a proceeding.

" We observed here rather a rough mode of keeping children in order; one of Nebrida Aram's boys had large iron shackles on his legs, as a punishment for some truant tricks of which he had been guilty.

" A bullock was sent to me by the master of the house in which I lodged, who is a brother of Nebrida Aram, and bread and booza were supplied twice a day by a daughter of Ras Michael, styled Ambati Ozoro Tuckai. I had not however the pleasure of seeing her. Having staid one day longer than was expected at Axum, we found some difficulty in getting provisions. Our guide, who had great respect paid him wherever he went, from being in the immediate service of the Ras, laid this tax upon my friend the priest, who thought himself, however, amply compensated by a piece of muslin and a small cornelian cross, which I presented to him. This was indeed but a small return for the uniformly kind attention with which he had treated us. There fell much rain accompanied by lightning in the evening.

"September 19.—While our attendants were getting the mules ready for our departure, I set out with Pearce to the inscription, which I again copied with the utmost care and attention. The morning was particularly favourable for seeing every part distinctly, and I hoped, in which I was not disappointed, that when compared with the copy finished the day before, there would be found but little difference. At all events I felt satisfied that every possible care had been taken to avoid error; wherever a letter was doubtful, or wanting, I marked it as such, and wherever there was the appearance of a date, I copied it separately upon a large scale. I had again an opportunity to compare the copy with the inscription, and to add a few letters at the bottom, which had before escaped observation, when I visited Axum on my way to Massowah. I shall give a fac-simile of it when I come to that part of my work.

"Being joined by Guebra Selassé and our mules, we crossed the large plain for a distance of about five miles, and then descended by a rough road through a gully, along the banks of a stream, till we arrived at the foot of a hill on which stands the church of Hannes, where on the 16th ult. we had quitted the direct road, in order to visit Calam Negas.

"On crossing the plain to Adowa, we met a poor man who had been robbed of his corn, and much beaten. He had run after the offender and secured his garment, and now delivered him over to Guebra Selassé, who took his jambea, or knife, from him, and brought him on to Adowa. On our arrival there, we were informed that Nebrida Aram had just set out for Antalow, having waited till this day in expectation of my arrival from Axum. He was said to be accompanied by two hundred soldiers armed with matchlocks, and two thousand spearmen.

" Two sheep, three large jars of maize, bread, &c. were brought to me by the chief Mussulmaun. I had a long visit in the afternoon from an Ozoro, or princess, upwards of thirty, who was fair for an Abyssinian, and very fat. I had also a polite message from Ozoro Tishai, requesting that I would call upon her in the evening, as she was very anxious to see me. At the hour appointed for my visit, there came on one of the heaviest storms that I ever remember to have witnessed, attended with vivid lightning, and very loud thunder, which rattled over our heads like cannon. It did not last long, so that when it was over (as I understood the lady expected me), I set out. It was quite dark, and I had to pass through so many alleys and passages, that I could form no idea in what part of the town the house was situated. At length, however, we reached it, and I was introduced to the lady, who was expecting me, with a large party of her friends and attendants. She was seated at the upper end of the room, on a handsome couch placed in a recess, which was divided off by an undrawn curtain, with the lower part of her face covered. I made a drawing of the Ozoro, which, I can assure the reader, gives an accurate delineation of the costume of a lady of her rank, although it has no resemblance to the fancy figures given in the last edition of Bruce, as Abyssinian princesses. She gave me a most gracious reception; and as far as the absence of my interpreter (who was sick) would allow me to understand them, the visit was perfectly agreeable. What was wanting in conversation, was made up in laughing, joking, and drinking; for the lady most urgently plied us all with maize, taking at the same time an equal portion herself. She was not so great a beauty as Bruce's princess, being dark in complexion, though of very pleasant manners.

"September 20.—As I wished to procure a few articles for Lord Valentia at this place, being extremely doubtful whether we should get any at Antalow, I had determined to stay another day at Adowa. Judging from the rate at which we made our purchases, I should conclude every thing to be exceedingly dear in this place; but I rather suppose that we were buying through a dear channel, as our guide was the only person whom we could employ, and he no doubt made us pay handsomely for his trouble.

"Early in the morning I took a sketch of part of the city of Adowa, and the hills, from a small loft in front of the Ras's house. The view itself has not much to recommend it, but the effects of the morning sun were extremely fine, throwing into happy obscurity, the wretched mansions of which the whole capital consists.

"In the course of the day I received a message from Ozoro Tishai, requesting me again to visit her in the evening. As soon as it was dark I proceeded to her house. She received me with the same kind attention as on the evening before. Besides a plentiful supply of maize, which she was very urgent in pressing us to drink, she had prepared a supper, of which, for my own part, I was too unwell to partake. Pearce and Andrew, my servants, however, did it ample justice. The lady was this evening exceedingly curious, and asked many questions concerning our Sovereign, the nobleman who had sent me, our houses, churches, &c.; but all this was done with great politeness; and there was evidently a very striking distinction between the manners of this princess, and those of the generality of the women whom I had seen in Abyssinia. She told me that she had heard of Bruce, but had never seen him; that he was a great favourite both of Ozoro Esther and the Iteghé. She added, that she felt the same friendship for me that they did for him. On my taking leave, she presented me with a piece of cloth of the finest Adowa manufacture, and begged that I would not let any person wear it but myself. She was very reluctant to break up the party; and I was obliged at last to bring our visit to a termination, by making our interpreter, who had but a weak head, drink an additional quantity of maize, which soon incapacitated him for his office.

"September 21.—I left Adowa in the morning not without regret, as I considered its inhabitants to be much more civilized than those of any other part of Abyssinia that I have visited. We ascended the hill to the east, and continued in a route somewhat to the south of that by which we came; so that we did not pass within sight of Abba Garima. At the distance of about five miles, our road lay below the hill on which stands the village of Occabessa, then partly in ruins, but which was formerly the residence of old Ras Michael, after he had quitted the busy scene of politics. The church is named after his favourite Emperor, Tecla Haimanout. Hence we kept winding round many hills till we reached the village of Angara. Here the door was shut against us; so we proceeded to Dichora, where we procured a small house, and good accommodation for the night. The chief of the former village came in, and made his peace by bringing bread, booza, milk, and two goats, to which the man of the house made an addition of one, after having in vain pressed me very much to accept a dollar's worth of cloth in lieu of it.

"September 22.—After travelling about six miles, we came into our old track, near the spot where we met the poor woman with her blind deaf and dumb child. We passed below the mansion of Basha Guebra Eyut, who was gone to Antalow. In crossing along the plain at the bottom of Abbo Samuel, we saw several very small and beautiful birds, in their habits not unlike the linnet. I dismounted with my gun, and after waiting patiently for some time, at length got a shot at one in a bush, which I luckily killed, much to the astonishment of several chiefs, who, with their followers, had all stopt to observe me; after which, at their request, I allowed them to examine the gun, which excited the admiration of all. In the course of the day I killed five more birds of different kinds, two at one shot, which completely established my character as a sportsman, among my fellow travellers, many of whom were chiefs, on their way to the muster at Antalow. While we were halting by the side of the same stream where we had before refreshed ourselves, an old priest, named Allula Lucus, came to pay his respects to me, having been formerly, as he said, well acquainted with Yagoube at Gondar. On my questioning him, he told me that Bruce lived at Koscam, and made two attempts, the first of which failed, to visit the Nile. It was supposed that he went to stop the source of that river; and as they believed he could make gold, and turn any waters, they thought him capable of accomplishing this project; that he never went to war, but staid during those times in the house of the Aboona; that Yusuff, the Aboona's interpreter, whom I had before seen at Adowa, often interpreted for Bruce, as he understood well neither the language of Amhara nor of Tigré; but that he had also an interpreter of his own, named Michael; that he never had any command of cavalry, the Koccob horse, in particular, being at that time under one of the Sultan's servants, whose name he had forgotten; that a man named Kuara was Governor of Ras-el-feel under Netcho, in whose province of Tcherkin it was included; and the same Kuara held it afterwards under Ayto Corfu, who succeeded to the province on his father's death. Finally, that Bruce was a great favourite of Tecla Haimanout, with whom, however, he had once quarrelled, on account of the Sultan's taking off his hat or turban, which he indignantly resented.

"Barrambaras Tocklu having marched with his troops into Antalow, we were under the necessity of passing the night at a small shed, which was capable of keeping out neither wind nor water: the master, however, presented me with a sheep, and bread and booza for our bearers.

"September 23.—We set out with the earliest dawn of day, having a long and difficult march before us. Our road first lay across the plain, which is of very unequal ground, till we came to the bottom of the pass of Atbara, where the ascent became very steep, and much incommoded with the Kantuffa, which, like the bramble, tears any linen that comes in its way. On reaching the top we discovered an encampment of troops, amounting to nearly one thousand, scattered about in parties, the numbers of which varied according to the consequence of their respective chiefs. They were refreshing themselves after the fatigue of the ascent; and being invited to partake of their provision, we seated ourselves on the grass, covered over in the country style with an outspread cloth, supported by spears stuck in the ground, and regaled upon some fine wheat and peas bread. Our own people, meanwhile, were grilling some mutton, in doing which a serious quarrel took place, which was very near ending in bloodshed. The parties went so far as to draw their knives, but were prevented from doing mischief by the bystanders, who rushed upon them with their spears and shields, and seized all concerned in the affray. Guebra Selássé picked out one of the offenders, and put him in irons, to carry before the Ras. He was only fastened with a chain to a young boy; yet such is the influence of established custom, that no delinquent, in such cases, ever thinks of breaking away.

" The road hence was crowded with marching troops, asses carrying provender, and with caparisoned horses and mules in abundance; the last of which are invariably preferred to the horses for travelling. Among other chiefs was Shelika Welleta Raphael, of Beit Koccose, near Abba Garima, who behaved towards me with much civility. He first took Ibrahim behind him on his mule, which was a very fine one, and afterwards, seeing that my mule's paces were not good, dismounted, and insisted on my taking his, with which I the more willingly complied, as he had another mule ready for his own use.

"About four miles from Muchaie I returned this gentleman his mule, as he was going direct to Antalow by another road. After getting completely wet through with a heavy shower of rain, we reached Muchaie, where we remained for the night. Three travellers were introduced to me by the master of the village; and we were furnished with such abundance of provisions, that I was enabled to send them a large portion of bread, and also a goat to a friend of our guide.

"September 24.—We left the village of Muchaie at a very early hour, and in the first part of our road met with little worthy of notice. Having passed through the narrow valley described in our former journal, we arrived at the stream on the bank of which we stopped; here we bathed, and afterwards took some refreshment. I must observe that the Abyssinians, as far as I have seen, are very fond of bathing, whenever they have an opportunity of doing so in a running stream.

"We now passed close by the mansion of Gibbé, which was at this time deserted, and in ruins. We were told that formerly the Ras had a mansion at each stage from Antalow to Adowa, computing by the journies that these people make, which are about double the distance of those we have been able to perform; for, as they are accustomed to a mountainous country from their infancy, they disregard the ascent and descent of the steep passes that intersect every part of Abyssinia. I could not, until this day, conceive the reason of the Ras's having quitted Adowa, which appeared strange to me, as his buildings and other accommodations at that place are more numerous and larger, (though in the same style) than those at his residence at Antalow. I have been told, however, that a part of these buildings formerly belonged to one of his subjects, who not choosing quietly to resign his possession, was forcibly expelled, and killed by the Ras's people. From that time the place is said to have been haunted by the ghost of the deceased; and my informant added, that the Ras was one night beaten violently, and some of his attendants killed, by the ghost; upon which, he collected the rest in great alarm, left the place, and has never since returned to it, transferring his capital to the province of Enderte. In confirmation of their terrors on this subject, I have to remark, that when Pearce and Andrew attempted to go into the rooms in search of some curious owls that had taken up their abode there, the people were much alarmed, and did every thing in their power to prevent them: they however persisted, and went over the whole of the apartments without meeting with any supernatural being, or other molestation.

"The country from Gibbé to Muccullah has been before described; to which account I have only to add, that a rapid stream runs through the vale of Jambela, which we again crossed. A worthy priest, whom we met on the road travelling with his bible, offered me an excellent mule, on which he was himself riding, to carry me to Antalow. I declined, however, his friendly offer, as I found an English saddle much easier than those made use of in Abyssinia. On our arrival at Muccullah, we learned that the Ras had left orders to have every thing prepared for our reception, and among other articles of good cheer, plenty of maize was provided, which we had been without from the time that we left Adowa, having been obliged to rest satisfied with booza, the common drink of the country.

"September 25.—I went out at daybreak, and descended the northern side of the hill of MucculIah, which is extremely steep, in order to take a sketch of the church and town, a drawing of which is given in my larger views. The situation is beautiful, and may serve to give an idea of the churches and villages in Abyssinia, which, for the most part, are built on one common plan. We were completely fatigued on our return, with the difficulty of the ascent, which, however, the natives of the country, from habit, do not seem at all to regard.

"We returned hence to Antalow by the same road that we came. We now saw, on coming down one of the hills, the town of Chelicut, which we had before passed unobserved. The whole of the road was thronged with chiefs and their followers proceeding on their way to Antalow, who entirely took up my attention. All the great men were extremely curious in examining every thing belonging to me, and I was by this time so accustomed to their manners, that I always indulged them with the inspection of my gun and sword, which I even entrusted to their own hands. They were accompanied by a relation of Ras Michael, extremely wild both in his dress and manners, and much resembling the inhabitants of Suakin, having his hair dressed out in a most fantastic style, with a long wooden pin run through it. He was attended by a large band of musicians, several led horses, and many followers. At about three in the afternoon I arrived at Antalow, and found all my friends safe, and happy to see me again. Captain Rudland returned here yesterday, after having spent a fortnight with the Ras, during which time he was under the necessity of making himself understood by signs and nods, not having an interpreter, and the Ras not permitting him to send for one to Antalow. I found Mr. Carter rather unwell. Instead of having been to Buré, as my previous arrangements had given me reason to expect, he had, from some misconception of the natives, been almost entirely confined to the house, and scarcely permitted to have communication with any person; besides which, he complained of having been kept rather short of provisions; his whole daily allowance not having been more than part of a fowl and bread. This was however in some measure to be attributed to his own mismanagement, as he certainly might, though with some difficulty, have gone on the expedition to Buré, which I much regretted he had not done, as I conceived that he would have obtained some very valuable information. He had written to Captain Rudland; but this gentleman was so situated as not to be able to assist him, as will appear by the following journal of occurrences during my absence. Hamed Chamie and our Mussulmaun servants also complained much of their treatment during my absence, having had only three sheep allowed them in that time, though plentifully supplied with bread. I did not see the Ras in the evening, as I understood that he was much fatigued by having been present at the exercise of his troops.

"Captain Rudland's Journal.

"Monday, September 9.—Yesterday afternoon, as I happened to pass through the hall, I saw the Ras disengaged and alone; he called me to him, and repeated his wish that we should all of us accompany him on the morrow morning to Muccullah, at which place he was going to spend a few days; he also informed me that he should set out very early. I communicated this to Mr. Salt on my return to our apartment; and in consequence, before we went to sleep, we prepared ourselves for the journey, and for the Ras's expected summons; but to our surprize, at day-break the next morning, we found the Ras had already set out, and had left only three mules for our accommodation, which number had been previously engaged for Mr. Salt and his attendants, who were to set off at the same time on their journey to Adowa and Axum. Mr. Salt, with Pearce, Andrew, and Ibrahim, left me about seven o'clock.

"Tuesday, September 10.—At three o'clock this morning I was awakened by a messenger from the Ras, with a request that I would proceed immediately to join him at Mucculllah, acquainting me also that bearers were in readiness for the conveyance of Mr. Salt's baggage, who, on quitting Antalow yesterday, had been obliged to leave it behind. As soon as it was day-light, I was conducted to the house of the Ras's brother (Manassé), who had been left in command here during the absence of Ras Welleta Selassé; he gave me his own mules, and appointed an officer of rank to attend me as a guide. The road lay across the hill of Antalow, whence I had a view of Chelicut, and then passed over a brook that flows by the last mentioned place, and arrived about noon at Muccullah, having crossed no intermediate valley in my way thither.

"Wednesday, September 11. — I joined my friend Mr. Salt on my arrival yesterday at this place, whom I found occupying a priest's hut in a corner of the church-yard, as miserable in reality as its owner in appearance. This morning we were awakened at an early hour by a servant of the Ras, who informed us that his master had gone on a hunting party, but that he would return here in the afternoon. Mr. Salt proposed to set off on his journey towards Axum, and after having taken a little milk by way of a breakfast, left Mucculiah with his attendants about seven o'clock.

"Being now left by myself, without a single creature around me to whom I could speak a word in any language so as to be understood, I again lay down and slept, having had little or no rest during the night, owing to vermin of all kinds, with which the place swarmed. I imagine I did not awake till twelve or one o'clock, when Guebra Eyatt, a boy of the Ras, brought some maise and bread, and some heated ghee, which I could not eat. I confess that now, almost for the first time in my life, I found myself rather uncomfortable, being absolutely precluded from conversation with a single individual; nor was my situation likely to be improved on the return of the Ras, unless there should happen to be some one in the train capable of speaking a little broken Arabic.

"At four P. M. a messenger arrived from the Ras, who by signs and gestures led me to understand that dinner was ready, and my company was requested. I returned with this good man to the Ras, and found him sitting on his couch, with all his head people about him; he seated me by his side, and fed me very kindly with fish, fruit, bread, and vegetables. After I had eaten a sufficient quantity, I was obliged by nods, winks, and smiles, to inform the Ras of the circumstance, for fear of being choaked with kindness. The maise went round cheerfully, and the Ras and company were in the highest spirits and good humour.

"Thursday, September 12.—I passed a most wretched and uncomfortable night, among swarms of bugs, lice, and fleas. Milk was brought to me at the usual hour, and about ten I was invited to attend the Ras at breakfast. He received me with his accustomed attention, and seated me at his right hand, on the same couch with himself. His brother Manassé had arrived this morning from Antalow, so that there was a very large party; and brinde and maize were handed about to all very briskly. I eat none of the former, but drank too much of the latter, and returned at one o'clock to the "parsonage," where I remained uninterrupted during the remainder of the day.

"Friday, September 13.—The quantity of maize I was forced to drink yesterday affected my head, and the pain it occasioned prevented me from sleeping during the night. At four this morning I was roused by a message from the Ras, requesting that I would attend him on a hunting party. Unwell as I was, I got up, and found a mule in readiness for me; but the Ras was already gone. The attendants informed me by signs, that the place where he had turned off his dogs this morning was not far off; I therefore followed, and rode about four miles to the village of Droosa, a little beyond which I fell in with the Ras, and found his sport this day consisted in giving directions to his soldiers, who were employed in fixing large stones across a rivulet, both to serve as a bridge, and as a dam, to form a head of water for the sake hereafter of fishing, an amusement of which the Ras is exceedingly fond. He begged, when I had joined him, that I would mount a favourite horse, which is led before him whenever he goes on parties of this kind. This condescension I considered as it really was, an extraordinary favour, for no one beside himself ever mounts the back of this animal, except a Gallee eunuch, a great favourite of the Ras, who in the presence of his master is permitted sometimes to exercise him. This being a fast day with the Ras, I found myself rather in an awkward situation, having left Mucculiah without my usual draught of milk; but the Ras, ever thoughtful about what would conduce to my accommodation, was sensible that I should be as well pleased with a feast, and accordingly ordered the chief of the village in the vicinity of which we were, to prepare a fowl curry for me. I accompanied this good man to his house, and received the kindest attention from himself and his lady. A fine curry, with bread and maize, was speedily introduced, and the hostess was so polite as to insist on feeding me. My kind entertainers did not choose themselves to violate their fast day; but as the lady had placed next to me her beautiful daughter, about twelve or fourteen years of age, I gladly made the most grateful return that I was able, by dipping bread into the curry, and feeding her in the same way as I had been treated by the mother. There was a skin spread for me, on which, after I had eaten enough, I enjoyed a comfortable sleep. I afterwards rejoined the Ras, and at four P. M. we again reached Mucculiah, where a dinner was prepared of fish, fruit, bread, and vegetables. I returned to my detestable quarters about seven o'clock.

"Saturday, September 14.—Yesterday during dinner the chief from Buré was pointed out to me by the Ras: he had come hither in consequence of an order from the Ras, originating from a conversation already detailed between him and Mr. Salt, in which it was arranged that Mr. Carter should proceed to

Buré, under the protection of the chief, for the purpose of surveying that place. I this morning begged of the Ras, to permit me to return to Antalow, to acquaint Mr. Carter with the arrival of the Chief, that no time might be lost; but this was not consented to. I then proposed sending a note to him, to which I got no reply; however, all this I attributed to the effects of the maize; for we had taken our breakfasts, and the Ras and his chiefs appeared determined to make up for the abstinence of yesterday.

"I now complained to him of my filthy quarters, shewing him my skin; and by winks and gestures (for we now began to understand each other tolerably well) acquainted him that I could get no sleep. He immediately ordered the ladies' apartment to be prepared for me, near the large hall, which accordingly I occupied during the remainder of my stay here. When the Ras had refreshed himself with a four hour's sleep (an invariable custom with these people after eating), he sent a messenger to me in the upper room over the entrance door. As soon as I went down, he gave me a most cordial shake by the hand, and called in the Chief from Buré, and a Mussulmaun attendant, who could interpret what was said, in nearly as good Arabic as I speak myself. However, I contrived to get a person dispatched to Antalow, with my note to Mr. Carter, and an order from the Ras for him to be accommodated with mules, and to come here to morrow morning, this place lying in the direct road.

"Sunday, September 15.—I had a good night's rest in my fresh apartment, it being tolerably free from vermin, because the building, being a new one, they had not yet had time to accumulate. The Ras attended divine service at the church in the night or rather early in the morning: he returned thence at four o'clock; I arose at six, and found him in close conference with Ballambaras Guebra Amlaw, or the master of the household. I drank my milk, and afterwards took a walk; on my return I breakfasted with the Ras, who introduced me to a son of his late brother Subhartz, and to a daughter of Dehub, another of his brothers. The latter I presented with a small box and a looking-glass. We had a most excellent feast of cow heel, game, eggs, &c.; the maize went round cheerfully.

"I was much pleased this morning to observe the Ras's attention to our friend Baharnegash Yasous, whom, whenever an opportunity occurred, I mentioned to the Ras in the most favourable terms; and I firmly believe it was in consequence of my representations, that he was admitted into his presence at the eating hour with the first class. The meal being finished, the Ras, as usual, retired to sleep; I walked out with my gun, killed a brace of partridges, and was much pestered by the inhabitants: the evening I spent with the Ras, who was engaged over the chess board with Tokla Sangaltor. Their game differs more from ours than we at first supposed; the queen moves diagonally, and only one square at a time; the castles either have not the power of the same piece in the European games, or the players do not make use of them so frequently; nor do they seem to value a castle so much as a knight. We had supper at eight, at which time the Ras acquainted me that Mr. Carter would be here in the morning, and that he himself should leave this place for Chelicut the day after to-morrow, so as to arrive by the following day at Antalow.

"Monday, September 16.—I took my usual

walk this morning on the Antalow road, in hopes of meeting Mr. Carter; but was disappointed. I returned about nine, and at the dinner hour attended the Ras. I had not seen the only man who was able to communicate a word with me in imperfect Arabic since yesterday morning, but was given to understand by the usual gestures, that the chief from Buré was about to return, and that Mr. Carter was not coming here at all; and, as far as I was able to learn, the Ras meant to return to Chelicut on Wednesday or Thursday. I supposed the Buré chief to be in the interest of the Nayib, which, in some measure, accounts for the sudden turn that affairs had taken; but I resolved as soon as I could again make use of my tongue to the Ras, I would have it explained. We supped at eight; during the meal the Ras invited me to accompany him in the morning on a hunting and fishing party.

"Tuesday, September 17.—My attendant, Guebra Eyatt, awoke me at half past three this morning by the Ras's order, and informed me that he was waiting for me in the hall. I hurried on my kaftan, and running down, found him surrounded by fifty of his slaves by the side of a large fire. Our mules were also ready harnessed in the hall. We set out about four, descended the hill by the church, and had proceeded across the valley in an eastern direction about four miles before day break. We passed the village of Bellimackdam, the inhabitants of which joined the party. The Ras knowing that I was in the habit of taking a cup of fresh milk every morning (without saying a word to me, for we now understood each other tolerably well in the eating and drinking way,) ordered some to be brought. I took my usual draught; but the Ras, thinking that after a time I should be glad of some more, ordered (without my knowledge) that a pot of it should be carried along with us. Our fishing party went a different route, the Ras preferring the amusement of hunting this morning, which he in reality enjoys much. He has about fifty dogs of an inferior cast, not unlike the English lurcher, and at least five hundred men. These are disposed among the thickets of acacia, with which the small hills around are covered, in order to rouse the deer, hares, growse, partridges, and guinea fowl. As soon as one of these is put up (for the birds fly only to a very short distance), it is instantly pursued by the dogs and men who happen to be nearest. Upon this an universal shout and yell is set up, which so frightens the poor animal, that, together with the keenness of the dogs, it seldom happens that it escapes. We returned to Mucculiah at ten, with six brace of partridges and growse. I had an opportunity on our way back of shewing the Ras how the English gentlemen enjoy this kind of sport, and told him, that I myself could have killed more birds this morning than his fifty dogs and five hundred men. They have not an idea how the bird is brought down when on the wing. One of his chiefs asked me, with a very grave countenance, if it was done by a charm. I kept my shot concealed from them as much as possible; they always, therefore, examined the animal when killed for the bullet wound, not supposing that any thing but a single ball was made use of.

"On our entering the first gate to the hall, the knife was flourished over the cow's throat; for if the animal can be killed in the presence of the Ras, it is not only considered as the more respectful, but the brinde is the more delicious. In the present instance, the skin was only partly taken off, and a favourite slice of the flesh was brought immediately to table, the muscles of which continued to quiver till the whole was devoured.

"Two chiefs appeared at breakfast this morning in irons; they had been brought the day before yesterday to the presence of the Ras, under an accusation of murder; one of them had killed eight, and the other five men.

"The evening passed off with chess, and a supper as usual, during which a singing boy was introduced, who with his songs, and the strange gestures of his body, seemed to amuse the Ras, and greatly to delight the company. This boy could not be more than eight or nine years of age; he had a spear and shield adapted to his size, which he handled astonishingly well. His pert answers to the Ras made him laugh heartily. I fancy his songs were not of the most delicate nature. There was a lady in company belonging to one of the chiefs, but she did not seem to be much incommoded, for she smiled, and appeared as well amused as any one.

"We have had most delightful weather ever since I have been here, not unlike the month of May in England. I had an opportunity of observing in two instances this day, that it was not a general custom with these people to dismount from their horses or mules when they pass a church, &c.

"Wednesday, September 18.—I observed that this day is as strict a fast with the Abyssinians, as Friday. The Ras was engaged during the whole of the morning in deciding causes, and at six o'clock had a dinner of fish, ghee, fruit, and different kinds of bread. The fruit was sent by Ozoro Mantwaub from Chelicut, and consisted of citrons, plantains, lemons, and dried grapes. I walked out in the afternoon to the spring whence the water is brought that supplies the town, and a delightful one it is; it flows from a rock of soft stone, mixed with veins of iron ore, and I imagine discharges no less a quantity than half a hogshead in a minute.

"Thursday, September 19.—At midnight I was informed by my attendant that the Ras wished to see me. I hurried down half asleep, and found him with his Fit Aurari, and two other chiefs, round a small table by the fire side, with a supper prepared of fowl curry and grilled mutton. I was obliged to eat, although it went much against my appetite, and drank three bruhls of maize, and again retired to rest; but in the morning I felt myself not at all the better for it. I learned on enquiry, that it is usual for this meal to be served up in the night of every Wednesday and Friday, as soon after the hour of twelve as possible, as they get but little during the preceding twenty-four hours.

"Friday, September 20.—The Ras was in readiness at an early hour this morning to attend divine service, which was performed under a temporary building in the center of the valley to the east of the church, and about a mile distant. He sent to me to accompany him, and I of course complied. On entering this place, there were many priests assembled, who had formed themselves in a circle, chanting the psalms, with a drum or tom-tom in the center. The seat the Ras occupied was screened from the view of all without by a curtain, within which was placed a crown of gold, resembling those which we saw at Chelicut, some frankincense, dried grapes, and wheat; the former was burned, and the two latter were made use of instead of the bread and wine.

After the prayers were over, and the Ras had read a chapter in the Bible, we all went out on the middle of the plain. The Ras seated himself on the ground, and in an instant two or three of the dresses of his slaves were spread out, being fixed upon the ends of their spears so as to form a complete covering, which seemed to keep off the glare of the sun, which now began to be very oppressive. The chess board was introduced; and here the Ras continued to play till past four in the afternoon, when we returned to Mucculiah, where the usual Friday's repast was prepared.

"The good Ras was aware that I had had nothing to eat in the morning before we left the hall; accordingly, soon after we were seated on the plain, with much kindness and attention he ordered one of his chiefs to get another dress or two spread over a fowl curry that had been brought on purpose for me, and which my religion did not prevent me from eating; on the contrary, I devoured nearly the whole of it, and never relished any thing more in my life.

"I yesterday saw a funeral of the wife of one of the principal inhabitants of Mucculiah. Whether it be the custom on the death of a female for none but females to weep and scratch themselves, I have yet to ascertain by further enquiry; but certain it is, that none but women were seen to manifest their grief on this occasion, either by shedding tears, or scratching the skin from their temples, foreheads, and even noses, till they were as raw as brinde. All the beauty of Tigré was present in the valley this day; so, while the Ras was engaged with his game of chess, I slipt away once or twice to give the many charming girls, (whom curiosity had led as near as the sticks of the Ras's slaves would permit them to approach) a clearer view of me, they never having seen a white face before. On re-entering the building, I unexpectedly saw the Mucculłah princess Ozoro Endett, and three other ladies belonging to the chief men of the place; they appeared by no means alarmed at my presence, but rather otherwise, for they invited me to sit down, with which I accordingly complied. The Ozoro was covered with trinkets and chains of gold and silver; even her shoes, in the hands of her slave girls, were of silver studded with gold. These ladies were very free in examining my dress and skin; but nothing seemed to excite their surprize so much as my hair, which, until they touched it, they would not believe to be natural.

"I did not know how the Ras might relish my presence among them; therefore, after shaking the ladies by the hands, I withdrew. I imagine there could not have been less than 10,000 persons assembled together this day, of whom two thirds were females. When the Ras was about to return, a deputation of priests was sent to the building for the crown and other valuables; they were carried back by students, dressed in rich velvets of different colours, and Indian kincaubs; over each of them was carried a red satin umbrella. All the females joined this procession, and in the hand of every one of respectability was a large brass key, made in the same form as those in the hands of the priests. I retired to my apartment at six. The Ras invariably slept after eating.

"Saturday, September 20.—The Ras attended divine service at the church at four this morning, and continued there till seven; at eight, one of our servants arrived from Antalow, who brought me a note from Mr. Carter, acquainting me that they were distressed for provisions, the Ras's slaves at that place having given him a very scanty allowance since my departure. I instantly mentioned this circumstance to the Ras through his head feeder, Welled Michael, while at breakfast; and he immediately ordered a messenger to be called. This man being familiar with the Tigré language, and perhaps aware of the severity of the all-powerful Ras, replied to every question the latter put to him, "all was well, and no complaints." I could not (however vexed I felt) press the matter farther, although I was by this time on such terms with the Ras, that I felt not the slighest hesitation in expressing my satisfaction, or disapprobation, in a proper manner on any occasion. I wished that Mr. Carter had taught this man his lesson before he sent him to me.

"After dinner, when I had returned to my room, a Galla slave of the Ras's came and intruded himself into my apartment, and in a very impudent manner asked me for a cloth. This fellow I had often observed about the person of the Ras, and also the Ras's frequent familiarity in conversation with him. I told him repeatedly to go, as I had nothing for him; but to this he paid little attention. At last I insisted on his quitting the room, and took up a small stick I had at hand. He instantly put his hand upon his jambea, as if to make a kind of resistance. My sword was near me, but I did not choose to put myself on an equality with such a fellow, and therefore went down to the Ras, who by this time had retired to his cot, and when that is the case, it is treason of the highest order to disturb him. However I paid no attention to this, but pushed my way through twenty or thirty Galla slaves, pulled down the purdah, and in a violent pet muttered all the Tigré in my power, strengthened by very intelligible gestures. The Ras instantly understood me, sent for the rascal and ordered him an immediate drubbing, which was so severe, that I myself called out for mercy on him.

"Sunday, September 22.—I was unexpectedly awakened this morning at four o'clock to accompany the Ras to Chelicut. We left Muccullah half an hour afterwards. It was a delightful morning, and the first rays of the sun were extremely pleasant, as my fingers were aching with cold, a sensation I had not before felt for some years. Soon after sun rise the dogs were let loose; a great hue and cry ensued, several mules had their knees broken over the rugged ground, and much game was killed. I spied a fine spotted deer, at which I got an excellent shot, but my gun missed fire. I was extremely vexed at this disappointment, which, however, was not to be wondered at, as these people in my absence were perpetually examining the gun, and snapping the lock.

"We arrived at Chelicut about nine, and attended the funeral of one of the Ras's servants. I observed, as at the former, that women were the only persons seen to weep. I afterwards visited the church with the Ras, to look at some fresh paintings done by one of the priests; whence we attended a breakfast prepared by the charming Ozoro, which consisted of curds, milk, ghee, brinde, currys of different kinds, a variety of fruit, bread, wheat, peas roasted, and excellent maize, which was handed about cheerfully to all. An old female water-carrier, that constantly followed the Ras, was now introduced with the musical boy; but the tricks that were played with this poor child were as disgusting to behold, as they would be indecorous to relate.

"I fully expected that we should have left this place on the morrow, but the persuasive powers of the Ozoro prevailed upon the Ras to stay till the next day. Supper was served as usual, and the Ras was in high spirits. He introduced me to a sister of Tecla Georgis, the late king, who is now at Waldubba. The Ras was seated between this lady and myself on the same couch, I therefore could not get an opportunity of speaking to her.

"Monday, September 23.—I went out this morning with the Ras, as I imagined on a hunting excursion, the dogs and attendants having accompanied us; but found that, instead of hunting after birds, all his train was set to clear the weeds from the wheat and teff growing on each side of the stream that runs by Ozoro's mansion.

"This amiable Princess manages her fields so well, that she always gets three crops in a year, having trenches cut to let the water from the river upon the land, whenever it is requisite. I remained an hour, and then returned to the house. It is as customary for the Ras to go out on these parties with an empty stomach, as to go to sleep with a full one, both which habits are so different from what I had been used to, that I was sometimes made very uncomfortable from being obliged to adopt them.

"I rejoined the Ras about three in the afternoon, and returned with him at four to Ozoro's dinner, which was much the same as yesterday. Here I again met Ozoro Romai, sister to the late monarch Tecla Georgis. I had a fuller view of this lady now than when we met last; and while the Ras was engaged in conversation with his chief in front, I whispered a word to her through the head feeder. She had the remains of a fine person and a beautiful countenance, with a fair skin; from her appearance, I should have judged her to be no more than thirty or thirty-five years of age. I enquired after Ozoro Mantwaub, and asked the reason why she did not join the Ras in public; to which she replied, that it was not the Ras's pleasure, otherwise she would be very glad. This lady is very affable and free, and spoke to me always with her face unmuffled. She is very religious, and reads the Bible twice every day to her cousin Mantwaub. She asked me for some beads of the mock pearl kind, which I promised to send to her from Antalow, but immediately presented her with a cross, which pleased her so much, that she gave me her hand on the occasion.

"Tuesday, September 24. The Ras called me about five this morning, and we left Chelicut soon afterwards, proceeding by the same route as on our journey out from Dixan. The Ras amused himself with his dogs, while I pushed on in front, anxious to see Mr. Carter, and reached Antalow about nine. We were afterwards, on the Ras's arrival, invited to breakfast with him, and when the meal was over returned to our apartment.

"Wednesday, September 25. I amused myself in the early part of the morning by noting down in our journal, the remarks made by me during the fifteen days I was absent from Antalow with the Ras, and highly regret that I was so situated, from ignorance of the language, as not to have had the opportunity of a free communication with him and his chiefs, as I should have been able to have made my observations more fully.

"Troops had for several days past been assembling at this place from all quarters of the Ras's dominions, for the purpose of attending a review that was to take place, the next day. Numbers were exercising in presence of the Ras, within the court yard of his house. I joined him about ten o'clock; he had previously seated himself in the verandah of a detached building, with his two brothers and other principal chiefs, to view the troops. The number of people collected on this occasion was great, but most of them were lookers on; for I do not suppose more than six or eight hundred fighting men were present, of whom from forty to fifty were cavalry. The whole were armed with spears and shields, excepting now and then a matchlock. The horsemen galloped round a circle, flourishing their spears in a manner similar to the footmen, who were all in a cluster in the center. I was but little amused, for their actions and gestures were more like the antics of a lunatic, than military evolutions; and being desirous of concluding my journal before the return of Mr. Salt, whom I had every reason to expect in the course of the day, I withdrew about noon. Mr. Salt arrived at three. I was extremely glad to meet him. We had our curry in our apartment in the evening, and amused ourselves with the different adventures we had experienced during our separation.

CHAPTER IV.

Mr. Salt's Narrative continued.—*Account of the Review of the Troops of Tigré, &c. by the Ras.—Description of a Brinde Feast.—Arrival of Basha Abdallah at Antalow.—Political conferences with him and the Ras.—Determination of Nathaniel Pearce to remain with the Ras, who promises to provide for him.—Preparation for Mr. Salt's return to Massowah.—Character of the Ras Welletta Selassé.—His attachment to the English.—Some observations on the Manners and Dispositions of the Abyssinians.—Information respecting the Sources of the Nile, and present State of Gondar.—History of the Revolutions in Abyssinia since the time of Mr. Bruce.*

" SEPTEMBER 26.—This day being considered as the principal day of muster, I went with Captain Rudland after breakfast, to the Ras, but Mr. Carter was too unwell to accompany us. On this occasion, I clothed myself in an Abyssinian garment, and Captain Rudland in his British uniform. We found the Ras seated in a small verandah in front of a building, converted to the purpose from a butler's hall, which overlooked a walled inclosure about three hundred yards in circumference. Around him were seated many of his principal chiefs. He received us with his usual attention, seemed much gratified by our change of dress, and placed us immediately beside him on his couch.

"It is difficult to describe the scene that ensued. The outer part of the inclosure was lined with crowds of the inhabitants, and others had mounted the walls, which soon were completely covered with them. Opposite the Ras was a gateway, in a room over which sat a number of officers of state, appointed to regulate the review. Through this gateway the chiefs came in separately, one after the other, each with his respective followers. First entered the cavalry, with the chief at their head, galloping round the circus, and brandishing their spears with great agility. The dresses of these consisted for the most part of kincaubs, embroidered damask, flowered with gold, or black velvet studded with ornaments of silver, thrown as a scarf over their shoulders, and fastened with a gold clasp across the breast. Round their heads they wore bandages, formed of yellow, green, or red satin, tied behind, long, and streaming loosely as they rode. Some, instead of this ornament, had only fillets of skin round their heads, the hairs of which standing upwards, gave an additional wildness to their appearance. Some few had horns of gold, either perpendicular above their foreheads, or projecting forwards; and several, on the upper part of their arm, had a silver disk, of both which Bruce has given a representation. Others wore bracelets of silver, in the shape of a horse collar, round their right arms, equal in number to the enemies they had slain. The horses were richly caparisoned, and bore on their fronts the bloody garments of foes slaughtered by their riders. Each chief, after riding round the circus seven or eight times, presented himself directly before the Ras, in a menacing attitude, recited in pompous language the actions which he had performed, and concluded by throwing down before him the indubitable trophies of his valour, which had before been hanging above the bracelets on his right arm.* One chief brought only a knife, that he had taken from his opponent. The chiefs are not the only ones who thus present themselves before the Ras, for every ragged rascal, among the foot soldiers who enter in a throng after the horsemen, has the same privilege. Among these latter, horrible to relate, were some wretches, probably followers of the camp (for they were not soldiers), savage enough to produce unquestionable evidence that boys, not men, had been the victims of their fury. At this I expressed to the Ras my abhorrence so strongly, that, actuated by the same feelings, he refused them those marks of his approbation which he had invariably shewn to others. The inferior warriors were clad in skins, chiefly those of sheep, some of which were bordered with blue and red of different shades. Intermixed with the foot soldiers, who were mostly armed with spears and shields, the matchlock men came in most irregular order to the number of at least fifteen hundred, whose gestures were if possible, more ludicrous than those of the spearmen, imitating, as it appeared to me, men hunting wild beasts among the bushes; the conclusion of their frolic was firing their musquets as nearly as possible to the legs of their opponents, then drawing their knives, and making a blow to finish the murderous execution of their match-

* Ludolf, speaking of this custom, among the Galla, from whom the custom is probably derived, says, "Adhuc necesse est indicium cæsi hostis post pugnam afferre. Primo quidem capita ceu honestissimam corporis partem attulêrunt; at postquam de sexu imberbium dubitaretur, turpissimum viris amputavêre. Res dictu fœda numerant et cumulant exercitus coram. Hac ratione sciri non potest hostis an socius fuerit

locks. There were in this way many single mock fights between spearmen and musqueteers, but it was always managed that the latter should prove victorious. This extraordinary review was concluded by the marching in on one side of the Ras's band, mounted on mules, and beating the heavy drums, and on the other of men bearing the ornaments of the church walking in procession.

" This day greatly biassed our opinion in favour of the horsemanship of the Abyssinians: I think them in this repect fully equal to the Arabs, and, considering the stirrups that they use, which are merely small rings of iron into which they put the two larger toes, this is no slight praise. In the use of the spear they are particularly expert, and they have a peculiar method of vibrating it in the hand, which has a very warlike and classical appearance. In fine, they seem to be as complete horsemen as possible without discipline, of which indeed they are totally ignorant. If Ras Michael Suhul could bring 5000 matchlocks into the field, the strength of Tigré must have dwindled away since that time very considerably under the present Ras; which I believe to be the case, as he permits his tributes to be paid in cloth, instead of fire arms. It is also probable that he has no matchlocks in store, for on this very day, when a damaged one was brought him, he supplied its place by taking another out of the hands of one of his soldiers.

" It is necessary, in order to give a complete idea of the dependence of the chiefs upon the Ras, to state, that several of those who were the most elegantly dressed and attended by the most numerous followers, were men holding situations in the Ras's household, such as the chief of the maize, of the bread, and others.

"There were a few, however, very haughty and imperious in their manners, among whom the most remarkable was Fit Aurari Zogo, a man of very handsome person and expressive countenance. This warrior obliged at least two hundred persons, who were sitting between himself and the Ras, to move, before he would condescend to make his address, which he at last did in a very proud and dignified manner, turning his horse round and round, and at each time resuming what he had before said. After the soldiers there were also a great many unarmed elderly men, cultivators of the ground, who came and made their obeisance before the Ras. During this last ceremony he sat very unconcerned, taking little notice of any excepting two of the most conspicuous. During the review, the Ras was extremely attentive, and his notice of the chiefs was acutely distributed in proportion to their power. As we were going away, he stopped us all to witness a Galla dance and song, with which he was particularly amused. The review being concluded, the principal chiefs came up and joined the Ras; among whom I noticed a Galla Mussulmaun, who had twenty-nine rings of silver on his arm; and many of the other chiefs had from ten to twenty.

"From this exhibition we adjourned to the great hall, where every thing was prepared for a grand feast. A long table was placed in the middle of the hall, at the upper end of which, in a recess, the floor of which was raised about half a foot above the level of the room, was a couch, with two large pillows covered with striped satin, and behind this stood a lower couch covered with a handsome skin. The Ras led the way, leaning on two of his principal chiefs, and took his seat on the higher couch, inviting us at the same time to occupy the couch behind. The chiefs in the mean time ranged themselves on their haunches (for there were no benches) on each side of the table, and behind the Ras, crowding in two or three ranks towards the upper end of the room. The sides of the table were covered to the height of a foot by piles of teft bread in the form of round thin pancakes, about two feet and a half in diameter, and down the middle of the table was ranged a single row of dishes, consisting of hot curry made of fowl, mutton, ghee, and curds. A quantity of fine wheaten bread in large rolls, was prepared for the use of the Ras; these he broke, and first distributed to us, and afterwards to some of the chiefs by whom he was surrounded. This ceremony served as a signal to begin the feast; upon which several female slaves, placed at different parts of the table (having previously washed their hands in the presence of the Ras), dipped the teft bread into the curries and other dishes, and distributed it among the guests. A man, whose particular business it was, performed the same office for the Ras, who immediately handed a portion to us, and then to some of the chiefs, who, on receiving it, got up and bowed: balls also of curds, greens, and teft bread mixed together, were handed about.

"During this time the cattle were killing on the outside of the hall. This is done by laying the beast down on the ground, and with a jambea knife nearly separating the head from the body, pronouncing at the same time, "Bis m' Allah, Guebra Menfus Kedus," a style of invocation that seems to be borrowed from the followers of Mohammed. The skin is then stripped with all possible expedition from one side of the animal, and the entrails, lights, liver, and tripes, are taken out, which latter the attendants voraciously devour as their perquisite, sometimes even without paying much regard to the trouble of cleaning them. The flesh of the animal, of which the rump and heart are considered as prime delicacies, is cut into large pieces, and, while the fibres are yet quivering, is brought in to the guests, who, by this time, have consumed as much as they please of the curries and other dishes.

"The brinde, as this raw flesh is called, was in irregular pieces, but commonly adhering to a bone, by which the attendants carried it; it was then handed round to the chiefs, who, with their crooked knives, cut off a large steak, which they afterwards dissected very dexterously into strips, about half an inch in diameter, holding it at the same time between the two fore-fingers of the left hand.

"Having thus prepared their meat, they took it up with the left hand and put it into their mouths; such at least was the usual practice with the Ras and all the chiefs whom we had an opportunity of observing, on this and many other occasions. I mention these seemingly trifling particulars, to shew that Bruce is mistaken when he asserts, that, "no man in Abyssinia, of any fashion whatever, feeds himself, or touches his own meat;" indeed so far from this delicacy being observed, it is extremely common for the highest chiefs to help their neighbours round, and not unfrequently even their women, as we afterwards particularly observed at the table of Gusmati Ischias, who was one of the first fashion at Gondar when Bruce was there. If the piece happened not to please the person who cut it off, he handed it to a dependant behind him, from whom it sometimes passed to a seventh hand, if not approved.

"While the brinde was serving up, of which the quantity consumed is scarcely credible, the maize was distributed about very plentifully in brulhs, or Venetian glasses, horns being used only for booza. The first party being satisfied, retired from table, and was succeeded by another of inferior rank, by which the remains of the brinde were consumed. After these came a third, a fourth, and even a fifth party, who were obliged to content themselves with the coarse teft bread, and a single horn of booza, and were driven away by the master of the ceremonies before they had taken their fill. Near the conclusion of the feast, the Ras sent off from the table large quantities of teft bread, for the followers of those chiefs most in favour. The whole ended with a violent scramble for the last cakes, during which it seemed to be a point of etiquette to make as much uproar and confusion as possible. During the feast, there were a few boys permitted to remain, by favour, under the table, to pick up what fell from the guests; but if any one be discovered there who has not permission, he is beaten severely by blows given with the elbow. There were also one or two men with small crosses in their hands, which they held out, intimating thereby that they were at that time obliged to fast.

"There were present at this feast many chiefs that I knew, especially Nebrida Aram, Basha Tokla, Basha Guebra Eyut, Ballambaras Guebra Amlac, and Welleta Gabriel, all of whom were very polite in paying their compliments to us, and seemed to be very anxious to attract our notice. I afterwards gratified them highly by distributing some snuff and cherry-brandy among them, of which they are all exceedingly fond. Of the former the Ras partook; the latter he could not be induced to taste, though all his chiefs much commended it.

"September 27.—I was waited upon at an early hour by Basha Abdallah, who had come from Adowa at the Ras's desire, in a great measure for the purpose of settling the arrangements between us. I had not seen much of him at Adowa, but was given to understand that he was a man of considerable ability, and much in the confidence of the Ras, holding a place under him of great importance, and being considered as at the head of the Mussulmauns in Tigré. Through him all correspondence with the Court and the different chiefs of the country is carried on; and all interior arrangements of trade are entrusted to him. As, however, he was attended on this occasion by Hadjee Hamed, whom I knew to be particularly inimical to us, and completely in the interest of the Sheriffe of Mecca, I did not think it advisable to enter into any full discussion about the purpose of our coming, of which they still pretended ignorance, and therefore I merely repeated what I had before stated on the subject. I then turned the discourse to the necessity of our immediate return, as by the time we could reach Massowah, the ship would be waiting our arrival; at the same time I urged a wish, that we might go back by the way of Adowa, as my friends, Captain Rudland and Mr. Carter, were extremely anxious to visit that city. I concluded by saying, that if the Ras had any communication to make to Lord Valentia, or through him to our Government, I should hope his letters would be speedily prepared.

"Basha Abdallah, in return, said, that the Ras was extremely anxious about our safety and accommodation, and would be glad, he was sure, to comply with our wishes; that there had indeed been persons attempting to bias him against us, but that he was still, as much as ever, our friend. He particularly alluded on this occasion to Currum Chund the Banyan, who, he said, had written to the Ras since our arrival, bidding him beware of us as dangerous persons.

"I had at this time given up all intention of farther incursions into the country, which had been proposed in my former conversations with the Ras; and this I was compelled to, from the certainty that we should even now suffer some distress for want of money, our stock being already reduced extremely low; besides, the period when I expected the ship to be at Massowah was fast approaching. In the course of the day we received fruit and bread from the Ras, it being a fast.

"September 28. — Having heard nothing of Basha Abdallah in the morning, I took the opportunity of the Ras's being alone, after his mid-day's repose, and went down to him in the hall with Captain Rudland (Hamed Chamie and Ibrahim being out in the town); our communication with him at the first was of a trifling nature. We presented to him some small trinkets for his Ozoro, which gave him much pleasure; I also gave him an English guinea, which he said he would have fixed on the top of one of his knives. He then sent for some arrack made at Antalow, of which we drank a small quantity. He was very curious concerning the method of making this spirit, and expressed a wish that we would manufacture some for him from a quantity of dried plantains then in his possession. We represented the impossibility of this from want of proper apparatus, and also from our never having been engaged in any pursuit of the kind, this being in our country, as we informed him, the business of a distinct set of men, who sold it, when made, to the rest. Our interpreters now coming in, I requested some private conversation with the Ras, on which all the slaves were sent out of the room.

"I now urged to him my surprize at having heard nothing from Basha Abdallah, in answer to the communication which I had made through him. The Ras said, that he had had many strangers with him in the morning, which had prevented his sending us an answer sooner, but that he expected Basha Abdallah every minute, and if I pleased, would send to hasten his coming. I told him that I was sorry that it was not in my power to speak my sentiments to him at once without an interpreter; that the interest of Mussulmauns was so directly contrary to ours as Christians, that it was impossible for me to say through a Mussulmaun interpreter, the things which I wished to communicate; that all these people were in the interest of the Sheriffe of Mecca, who at present supplied his country with all its imports, at double the rate of what the English could do, if he were to cultivate their friendship: how, then, could I speak through men so interested? He seemed much struck by these words, and in some measure distressed, like a man, who sees some advantage before him, which he is afraid of grasping at. After a pause, he asked me if we were at war with the Sheriffe; I told him, no; but that, on the contrary, he had sued to us, only so far back as last year, for assistance (being conscious of our superior power) against the Wahabee, by whom he was surrounded. Many ejaculations of surprise burst from him on hearing this. He would not, however, permit me to proceed until the arrival of Basha Abdallah, who came in a few minutes after.

"The Ras now made him repeat the whole of what had passed in my room on the day before, which he seemed to do in so clear and manly a way, that I was at once satisfied of his being a very different person from the former interpreter, Hadjee Hamed. There were many parts of his discourse which excited the Ras's admiration, and he repeatedly turned to me with ejaculations of surprise.

"After listening attentively to the whole account, he replied, that he, as well as myself, had been much imposed upon; as, until this moment, he had never fully comprehended the motives of our visit; that he had repeatedly received letters from different quarters, advising him to be upon his guard against us; that his chiefs, also, had been constantly urging him to send us to a distance from his house, as they knew that we meditated his destruction; and that they had even advised him not to eat or drink in our presence, lest we should poison him. All this, nevertheless, had made no impression on his mind; he had found us very different in our conduct from what they had reported, and he felt much attached to us. "They have also been advising me," he added, "to send my soldiers to open your boxes, as they believed them to be full of gold, silver, and jewels; but how could I be guilty of an action like this? I should expect, if I had set such an example, in a short time to have my own house pulled down and plundered. No, I replied; and I asked them, how would these people have journeyed safe through different countries, if they had been unwise enough to carry treasures of this kind?" He went on to declare, that his heart was now entirely with us, and that if we wished it, he would swear to comply with all our wishes, and to protect us and every article belonging to us safely to Massowah. " Or stay with me," he continued, " as long as you please, and be your safety on my head." His mind being now at ease, he spoke with great pleasure upon the subject of future communication with the English; at the same time giving me to understand, that I should hear farther from him on this subject through Basha Abdallah.

" I then turned the conversation on our going away, which I proposed to be on the following Monday, expressing my desire to go by the way of Adowa. To this he gave no positive answer, saying, that he did not wish to trust our persons on the road between Adowa and Dixan, as the people there were not under his command. He also begged that I would defer our journey a few days longer than I proposed; to which I immediately assented.

" September 29.—The Ras in the morning sent us a bullock, and soon after one of his attendants came with three double pieces of cloth of the finest Adowa manufactory, as presents to me, Captain Rudland, and Mr. Carter; to which we returned suitable compliments. The day passed without any thing worthy of remark. I was engaged in penning my sketches of Axum, and Captain Rudland in copying our journal.

" September 30.—Our bullock, which was slaughtered yesterday, furnished all our followers with brinde, after we had selected a considerable quantity of the flesh to be cured for consumption on the journey.

" We were upon such familiar terms with the Ras, that we went in and out of his room whenever we chose, and we had, these two days, much more communication with the town. He also permitted several young men, educated to the priesthood, to attend upon us; and we found them, as well as all the Christians with whom we had any communication, very willing and apt to acquire information.

"I was engaged this day in painting a picture of the Virgin Mary and Christ for the Ras, at his particular request. In the evening I and Captain Rudland paid him a visit. We found him, as usual, on the carpet playing at chess, to which he devoted much of his time. His common adversary at this game, was a man apparently of no rank or consequence, paid for the purpose, and whose great skill appeared to consist in keeping the game alive; always permitting the Ras to be victorious, and to cheat as much as he thought proper. A lady came in during our stay, who brought a present to the Ras of two cows, and was in consequence very graciously received. The weather was fine.

"October 1.—The day passed in our usual occupations of drawing and writing. Having finished the picture for the Ras, I this evening presented it to him. It excited great admiration, particularly the workmanship of the chair, and eight little angels flying around, which I had finished highly on purpose to please him.

"Pearce had several times hinted to me his wish to stay in the country, having been invited by the Ras, who promised to provide for him, and take him under his immediate protection. I had hitherto declined any opinion on the subject, but rather advised him to the contrary, from a fear that he might be deceived in his expectations. I was, however, very unwilling absolutely to prevent his following the bent of his inclination, as the disappointment might afterwards remain in his breast a continual subject of discontent; his gratitude to Lord Valentia was unbounded, for having rescued him from Mocha, and formed the only tie that I had upon him. He had however declared, that he would make no engagement without having previously obtained my approbation. The Ras this evening asked him the question in my presence; when I took the opportunity of telling him, that I should leave him entirely to the guidance of his own wishes, as I did not conceive myself intitled to thwart him in any scheme of life that he might choose to adopt. In consequence of my advice, he had in the evening a personal conference with the Ras, who treated him with great attention. He questioned him much with regard to his capacity as a soldier, his ability in painting, and his knowledge of physic; to which Pearce very properly answered, that he was only slightly acquainted with the two latter arts, but would do his best for him; that as to the other, it had been the employment of his life. The next enquiry was, whether he could write and read English; in both of which he was a tolerably good proficient. This seemed greatly to please the Ras, who said, that he hoped shortly to see more Englishmen; and that he would, in the mean time, provide him with every help for studying the Abyssinian language, that he might be of service in explaining their mutual wishes. He farther added, that he need be under no apprehension, as all the chiefs would treat him as a brother; that he would keep him always near his own person, and provide for him accordingly; that he should, in the first place, attend him on the expedition to Gondar, which would commence as soon as we were safely on our journey, and afterwards he should have time to study the language, and make some drawings for the churches; which being done, he would have permission to go into any part of the kingdom that he pleased, with a special protection from him, the Ras; and that whenever he became tired of his situation, he should be provided with the means of returning to Massowah. To these terms Pearce assented, and in reply to the first part of the Ras's speech, told him, that being an Englishman, he never knew what fear was; with which the Ras was much gratified; and answered, that, though very old, his own feelings were the same.

"I was of opinion, that Pearce's determination to stay in the country might be of considerable importance, for the following reasons: he is quick in acquiring any language, which will very much facilitate any intercourse hereafter with the inhabitants. He writes well, and expresses himself with sufficient clearness on any subject, and possibly may be able to collect much interesting information; if engaged in the wars with the Galla, or if permitted to visit Gondar, or elsewhere, in which case, his knowledge of drawing, which is for an untaught person considerable, might be brought to good account. He is, so far as I have seen, well inclined, and a deserving man, and will not, I think, disgrace his country by cowardice or meanness.

"October 2.—I spent this morning in making preparations for our journey, writing instructions for Pearce, and finishing some sketches of plants. At about three, I went, with Captain Rudland, down to the Ras. We found him in the further yard, surrounded by a small party of his chiefs. He invited us to partake of their repast, as also Mr. Carter, whose company he sent to request.

We were, as usual, seated beside him, and were all much gratified with our entertainment. It being fast day, we were regaled with several dishes of fish, which were excellent, and with parched wheat and peas, the former unripe: these constitute a considerable part of the Ras's food on all fast days. There were present the two great rivals, Baharnegash Yasous, and Subagadis, seated on opposite sides of the table: but the latter was only in the second rank. It has generally been observed by us, that young men, even of the highest rank and consequence, are kept much in the back-ground when in presence of the Ras.

"Basha Abdallah was sent for by the Ras, that we might have some conversation with him; it was entirely of a light description, not worthy of being recorded. The late Aboona's interpreter came to pay his respects to me; he seemed to be in tolerable favour at court. On our taking leave, the Ras appointed a conference with us at an early hour on the morrow.

"October 3.—After taking coffee, about five we were informed that the Ras was ready to receive us. We entered upon the conversation, by presenting him with as many of our medicines as we thought we could spare, which, after enumerating their several uses, were put under the care of Pearce, who was then regularly engaged in his service. A singular request was made to us, with which, however, as we found him earnestly bent upon it, we complied. This was to swear, that whatever physic we left with him, should not poison him. This both Captain Rudland and I did, by laying hold of his hand, and declaring, "that in the presence of the God whom we both worshipped, we solemnly declared that the physic we then left with him, was for his benefit, and not to injure any one." Hamed Chamie afterwards swore by Mahomed as to the justness of his interpretation. This ceremony had a great effect upon the Ras; he seemed perfectly happy in consequence, and declared that he should ever esteem the English as his best friends. From this it would appear, that great respect is paid here to the solemnity of an oath.

"After this I began upon the subject of our journey, pressing him very strongly to permit us to return by the way of Adowa, as I was extremely anxious to have another examination of the ancient ruins at Axum. It was a long time before I could obtain this point, and I should never have been able to accomplish it, if the Ras had not had a request to make in return, with which he was extremely desirous I should comply. This was, that I would make him a present of a blunderbuss, with a spring bayonet, which I had with me, belonging to Lord Valentia. I at first refused, on the plea, that this was the only thing not in my power to give away: and on his urging it a second time, I begged to defer resigning it till I arrived at Massowah. This would not satisfy him. He said, he was sure that Lord Valentia would let him have it with pleasure, when he knew how anxiously he desired it. Finding that no refusal would be taken, I at length complied with the best grace in my power, telling him, that there was nothing in my possession belonging to Lord Valentia, which he so highly valued as this blunderbuss.

"He now expressed his intention of sending to Lord Valentia, a spear, a shield, and a knife, as specimens of the arms of the country; that he would send his own knife, and whatever spear and shield I might choose. Among several spears I selected one with two heads, as being more curious than the others. We then proceeded to settle about our mules for the road: three had been given me by Baharnegash Yasous; the Ras told me that he would also give me three, and lend me three others as far as Adowa, from which place I must trust to my friend Basha Abdallah. Bearers were also to be provided by the Ras as far as Adowa, where I was to hire others to Dixan. This inconvenience attending our road, was before mentioned by the Ras; but the advantage that I hoped to derive from it, was much more than equivalent. The Ras sent me in the afternoon the spear and shield.

"October 4.—I was engaged the whole of the morning in finishing some sketches, and making a few drawings of heads, and one of St. George and the Dragon, for Pearce's use. In the evening Captain Rudland and I went down to the Ras, and partook of his fast-day's repast. He expressed much pleasure on seeing us, and presented me the knife for Lord Valentia, which had been sent to have a new scabbard made for it. It is as handsome as the generality of those worn by the principal men in the country. It is however to be observed, that the Ras seems greatly to pride himself on the plainness of his dress and accoutrements. He gave me a brace of partridges, that were just brought in by his sportsmen; and a little after the large horns of the country being fortunately introduced, he presented a very large one to Captain Rudland, and another of a finer sort to me, which was at the top nearly seven inches in diameter. All these horns are said to be brought to Tigré from Gondar; but they are chiefly manufactured, or made into cups, in Gojam. The animal which produces them is called Gusht, or wild cow, which chiefly abounds in the province of Walkayt, but they are said to be domesticated in the province of Ras-el-Feel. The horns hang back on the neck of the animal, from the skin of which, shields also are made. This would lead to the supposition of its being a buffalo, were not the horns smooth, round, and very different from those of this last named animal. The use which the Abyssinians make of the entire horn, is to carry maize for them when on a journey.

"We learned this evening from Basha Abdallah, that, in consequence of intelligence of the death of Ozoro Tuckai, at Axum, having just reached him, it would not be in his power to leave Antalow at the time we had fixed upon, he therefore hoped that we would put off our journey till Thursday, the Ras also having letters to send, which would not be ready before. With this I, of course, complied.

"October 5.—I went down in the evening to the Ras, and finding him busily engaged with Basha Abdallah in private conference, I sat down with Captain Rudland to the chess-board; but we had not finished a game when the Ras came to us. He was in high spirits, and much pleased at finding us amusing ourselves. It was now communicated to us by Basha Abdallah, that he was desirous all our baggage should be got ready, that he might ascertain how many men would be required to carry it; he also hinted, that he wished me to mention to the Ras, my consent to stay until Thursday, in order to go with him; with which he was much gratified. I had afterwards private information from Basha Abdallah, that the Ras was highly pleased with the thought of an intercourse with England; and for this purpose he wished much that our vessels should come to

Buré, as he had found the chief of that place, who had been with him during my absence, extremely well inclined to our interests; that letters expressing these wishes would be expedited by Government, and that some of the finest cloths in the country were preparing as presents.

" October 6.—I was engaged in drawing the picture of a young Galla boy, kept at Antalow by the Ras, and thought to be the son of a chief of high rank; he was taken in war when an infant, and much respect was paid him, being allowed several attendants. I also made a drawing of Pearce in his Abyssinian dress. I paid a visit to the Ras in the evening, as usual, and found much company there, among others, Ozoro Romai, and Ozoro Esther; Basha Guebra Eyut, Barrambaras Toklu, Fit Aurari Zogo, the chief who distinguished himself so much on the day of the festival, and Ayto Selassé from Adowa. On our first entrance, we found a violent dispute going on between the latter and Barrambaras; both were pleading in strong terms their respective causes before the Ras, and confirming their assertions by giving their right hands, and swearing by one of their most sacred oaths, which is, " Welleta Selassé emot," or " May the Ras die if it be not true."—The Ras soon afterwards retired; and we had an opportunity of remarking in what a free and unreserved style the Abyssinians pass their time in private parties. Barrambaras was lying with his head in the lap of Ozoro Esther, whispering in her ear, and another chief was endeavouring to interpret between Captain Rudland and Ozoro Romai. There seemed indeed very little restraint among them; and I do not doubt that they carry their familiarity much farther, when perfectly at liberty in the houses of mutual friends. We waited till the return of the Ras, paid our compliments, and retired.

"October 7.—We were engaged as usual, in drawing and writing, and in the evening paid a visit to the Ras, who was at his old occupation, chess. He was in higher spirits than in general, and invited us to stay supper with him: many ladies of rank were present, but Ozoro Romai was distinguished above all, by being seated on the Ras's couch. I understood she was only the mistress of Tecla Georgis, who for a short time filled the throne: she was fair, and possessed some remains of beauty. The discourse was, as usual, perfectly unrestrained. The old Ras encouraged the freedom of conversation; he also offered Captain Rudland an Ozoro if he would stay in the country. On that gentleman's answering that he would return to him, "I fear," said the Ras, "that I shall be dead before that time." After supper, one of our Arab attendants, Seid, highly amused the Ras and his ladies, by the performance of some slight-of-hand tricks, with swords and staves, at which the Arabs are extremely expert. The Ras was indeed so much gratified, that he tried much to persuade him to stay in the country, making him many promises; to all of which he remained obdurate, saying, "where my master goes, I will go; if he does not stay, I will not, though I should receive a thousand dollars." The evening, upon the whole, was passed very pleasantly, with great glee and merriment.

"October 8.—Basha Abdallah came to me early in the morning, and accompanied Captain Rudland and myself to the Ras. Every thing was finally arranged for our journey, which was to commence on Thursday morning. Two of our mules having died, the Ras offered us two more as far as Adowa. Hadjib and Seid, our Arab servants, were sent for by the Ras to amuse him with their feats, and he again tried much to persuade them to stay in the country.

"The troops from the different districts remained encamped on the surrounding hills; the chiefs had small tents made of the common cloth of the country, and their followers occupied convenient sheds, formed with the branches of trees, covered with grass.

"In the evening we went to the Ras, and were again invited to sup with him. Many young ladies of rank were present, among whom I noticed Welleta Aram, a daughter of Belgaida Welleta Menassé, and the two fair daughters of Poolar, the chief cowkeeper to the Ras. The first of Nebrida Aram's daughters was also fair; the other, a daughter of the Ras's brother, was extremely dark, though possessing more regular features. The conversation this evening was of a more modest nature than usual; and, in their general behaviour, these girls appeared to be much more reserved and decorous than most of the women of rank we had hitherto met with. The evening was passed pleasantly, but the Ras was far from being in good spirits.

"October 9.—We had a visit this morning from our friend Baharnegash Yasous, who expressed great pleasure, both on account of the manner in which we had been received, and also at the idea of accompanying us on our return so far as Massowah. We learned that our friend Subagadis had been put in irons by the Ras, for some hasty words spoken to Belgaida Welleta Hannes, who enjoyed great consequence at the court. We had also a visit from the keeper of the Ras's cows, who was daily in the habit of bringing us milk in return for some physic that Captain Rudland gave him, to drive out, as he expressed it, "a devil in his inside;" which most fortunately succeeded. We were fully occupied with preparations for our departure. Guebra Welleta Selassé, at my request, obtained permission from the Ras to attend us to Massowah, and anticipated much delight from seeing the ship, the guns, the great men, &c. I used to call this fellow the Devil (at which he always laughed), for in cunning, deceitfulness, and perversity, I never have seen his equal; yet in travelling he was very useful to us, though difficult to manage. This man was originally a Mussulmaun, but has been converted to the Christian faith, and is now employed by the Ras as a messenger: for his pay he receives forty dollars and as many pieces of cloth per annum, and a mule; besides which, there is a piece of land assigned him, which yields forty gerbuttehs of grain, six of which sell on the spot for a dollar, and for only four, if carried to Adowa. This, with what he gets on his mission through the country, which we are told amounts to much more (especially when he is sent to settle any dispute about tribute), enables him to keep four servants; to three of whom he gives five pieces of cloth, and to the other, two, besides their food. We had repeated solicitations from many persons, and from some of considerable consequence, to take them with us to England; and, in fact, I believe that there are few who would not be very glad to go with us. The chiefs, it is true, fare well; but as for the lower class, I believe that they rarely get sufficient, even of the coarse teff bread of which their food almost entirely consists. The pay of the Ras's soldiers, beside their food, is only from thirteen to fifteen pieces of cloth in the year, and his head builder has but six wakeas of gold a year, and two gerbuttehs of corn per month. Money seems to be an extremely scarce article, from its being chiefly employed in the Massowah commerce; and the want of small currency for common use, is a most serious inconvenience throughout the country. The carriage of a dollar's worth of salt to any distance, would scarcely be repaid by the small sum which it produces; and that this is the case, can be only owing to the cheapness of labour and provisions. The price of maize is about one penny per quart. The value of a dollar at Antalow is equal to twenty-eight pieces of salt; but the greater part of the traffick is carried on by exchange. One piece of cloth (about a dollar) will buy five gerbuttehs of grain.

" Letters were delivered to me this morning by the Ras, from his Sovereign, for the King of England, which I was requested to convey safely to Lord Valentia. With them several complete dresses of the finest cloth, manufactured in the country, were sent as presents. These were delivered to me in great form. In the afternoon I went down with Captain Rudland to the Ras, and he invited us to partake of his fast-day's repast, consisting, as usual, of fish, Indian corn, and wheat grilled. He was kinder than ever in his attention to us, and gave me, on their being accidentally brought in, two rhinoceros's horns, and a partridge; the latter of which I sent to Mr. Carter. I, in return, as a parting gift, presented the Ras with a convex lens, having observed his great delight on seeing the effect of the sun's rays through it, which I had before repeatedly tried on gunpowder, and the cotton clothes of some of his attendants. We afterwards took our leave with great, and, I trust mutual regret, not knowing whether we should meet again before our departure, which we had fixed for an early hour in the morning.

"The kind attentions which we received from the Ras during our stay at Antalow, must ever make me remember him with respect and esteem; yet I do not consider him as a man of any great ability. He gained his power by cunning, rather than by strength of character; and though not remarkably brave, maintains himself in his high station by a dexterous management of parties. But to accomplish this, he sacrifices in a great degree the importance of his command; for to conciliate a chief, he will often remit a portion of his tribute. His power, notwithstanding, is very great, and the district immediately under his rule is very extended, comprehending the whole of that part of Abyssinia which is to the eastward of the Tacazza, and which includes the provinces of Siré, Tigré Enderta, of which Antalow is the capital, Upper and Lower Buré, and the whole of the Midré Bahar, or district bordering on the Sea.

"After the cruel administration of Michael Suhul, the mild government of the present Ras is most grateful to the Tigrians; and from the number of matchlocks in this district, it always has held, and is still likely to keep up a superiority over the more remote provinces of the empire. I had no means of judging of the population, except from the land being cultivated wherever it admitted of it, and from the number of the troops assembled at the review, which certainly exceeded ten thousand. More than double this number, I understood, could be assembled in time of war.

"During the rainy season, from May to October, the Ras resides at Antalow. I do not exactly know what induced him to make choice of this place in preference to Adowa, but it appears to me ill calculated for a capital, as water is only to be procured at a considerable distance from the dwelling houses, and there is not a single agreeable spot in the neighbourhood for a residence. It is also very difficult of access; but this objection which, in more secure states, would be a great inconvenience, is perhaps the very circumstance which gives a peculiar value to the situation, as it forms a barrier against the incursions of the Galla.

"A good deal of attention is paid to ceremony at Antalow. Most of those who come into the presence of the Ras uncover themselves to the waist; others expose only the breast, and afterwards replace their garments. Mussulmauns are permitted to appear before him with their heads covered, as also the priests, and some few of the Christian chiefs. All mechanics, or people employed in business, such as cooking, &c. wear a cloth about their heads. No one in public addresses the Ras without rising from the ground, and uncovering to the waist; but, after the first address, they are often permitted to speak sitting. This does not hold good, however, in their private parties, where they all are huddled together on the ground in a most happy equality. Equals salute each other by kissing whenever they meet, and repeat their compliments over and over again like their neighbours the Arabs. With all their freedom, they are scrupulous observers of the laws of good breeding established among themselves, and are particularly attentive to their friends, especially at meals, where they make it a point to feed each other. The Ras wears a small piece of the finest cloth upon his head, and has always six or seven slaves in attendance, one of whom brushes the flies away with a choury made of cow's tail; the business of another is to replace his garment, when it falls down from off his shoulders, unless the minister should be present, to whom this office then devolves. All ranks appeared to stand in great awe of his authority, expect a few favourite slaves, who seemed to be perfectly at their ease; among them were two blacks from Sennaar, who had the broad Negro features, and whose hair, the Ras once observed, was like black pepper.

" In the decision of causes, which ever party may be in the wrong, it generally turns to the advantage of the Ras, who decides the matter. The parties begin by denying each other's statement: one then proceeds to say, that if he is found in the wrong he will forfeit to the judge a quantity of salt, a mule, slaves or gold, or whatever the other may be willing to stake upon his veracity. The other having agreed to a fixed penalty, the cause is put off until farther evidence is brought, when the party in the wrong is convicted and punished, only by the loss of what he had voluntarily pledged himself to risk: they then kiss the ground three times and retire.

" I was informed that land descends by inheritance from father to son, and if there is no son, to the brother; but that all the children and relations have a claim to a maintenance. In default of kindred, people often make over their land to a friend to be sold; half the produce going to the poor, and half to the priests. The Ras never thinks of removing any chief, or of interfering with him, so long as the established tribute is paid. There are many of his relations, to whom he has granted land free of all rent, among whom are Barrambarras Toklu, and Basha Guebra Eyatt. I enquired, if there should be another Ras, whether they would be compelled to pay tribute? to which

I was answered, no! they will plead not having paid it to the former.

"Great men take as many wives as they please; but it is difficult to get rid of them, owing to their connections, who always resent any affront offered to the women. Shum Woldo, in particular, had forty wives, and left behind him upwards of one hundred children. Having divorced one of his wives, her father made strong remonstrances on the subject, and repeating this too often, the haughty Shum's temper was at last so much enraged, that he made an attempt in his anger to kill the old man, by firing a matchlock at him. Marriages are very easily made up; the parties go to any friend's house, and there enter into an engagement with each other, without the presence of a priest being necessary.

"So far from enjoying a free intercourse with the males, as is asserted by Mr. Bruce, it is certain that the married women are watched with some caution by their husbands, and even occasionally secluded from male society, as in the case of Ozoro Mantwaub. So alive is the Ras to the feelings of jealousy, that he has never acknowledged his only son, a child about three years old, in consequence of a suspicion of its mother's fidelity. Mr. Bruce has been equally incorrect in stating that bastards, or the offspring of a connection between the master and a domestic servant, can inherit the father's property. They are, in fact, considered as little better than menials, except that they are not obliged to work. They are savage in their treatment of children, yet respectful towards women, whom nevertheless they, in our opinion, treat with little regard to decency in their conversation; but the gross and disgusting scenes which Mr. Bruce describes as following a brinde feast, I firmly believe existed only in his own imagination. His account of the flesh cut out of living animals was repeatedly enquired into by our party; all to whom we spoke, denied its ever being done. Raw flesh had been observed by all travellers, before Mr. Bruce, as the common food of the Abyssinians, but Mr. Bruce makes no distinction between the two, or rather wishes to confound them together, that he may seem to have the countenance of Poncet and the Jesuits; but none of them ever mentioned the eating of flesh stripped from a living animal, though Mr. Bruce is bold enough to say that this was the ordinary banquet of citizens, and even of priests, throughout all the country. The feast given by the Ras on the grand review of his troops, at which we were present, was a most convincing proof to the contrary.

"Calves and lambs are not eaten; but I doubt if this be not done from the prudential motive of keeping up the stock of cattle, the consumption of which is enormous. Wild fowl is also a prohibited article, which seems to be the adoption of a Jewish custom. Hogs are not kept tame; but in opposition to the Jews, they seem to have no objection to them wild; a quarter was presented to Captain Rudland while residing with the Ras at Mucculłah. With Mussulmauns they will neither eat, drink, nor smoke, but have no objection to do so with strangers, when convinced that they are Christians. They are least particular with respect to drinking, as I have repeatedly seen them drink out of the same cup. The Mussulmauns will eat of the bread and fish from the Ras's table, and even in his presence. The higher orders are extremely regular in attending to the established fast days, which take up one third of the year, but this does not hold good with the lower class, who devour rather than eat, whatever they can get, at all times. They are charitable in assisting the distressed; our servants often saved bread to give to beggars, which at the time that we returned from Adowa, were very numerous, sitting by the highway. Even to dogs they are humane, though they dislike them, permitting them to have free access to their houses.

" We had several strong instances of their honesty to us, which might however have been caused by fear; for we witnessed many instances of their roguery, in attempting to convey away articles belonging to the houses we stopped at. They are also exceedingly suspicious of each other; which pretty strongly proves that the lower classes are addicted to pilfering. All are eager for presents, which they frequently rather demand than request.

" When I found that I must give up all hopes of penetrating beyond the Tacazza, I took every occasion to make enquiries of such persons as were likely to give me any intelligence respecting the Nile. Their accounts generally agreed with each other, but it appeared to me that they spoke from what they had heard, and not from personal knowledge. Its situation near the village of Geesh; the marshiness of the plain, the elevation of the spot whence it flows above the surrounding country, its circuit from Gojam, its course being distinguishable through the lake Dembea, were points familiar to them all; but they differed considerably as to the number of fountains from which it springs, some speaking of three, others of four, and one person of five; but this, they said, depended on the seasons; for if much rain fell, the accumulation of water would force open fresh passages. Hadjee Hamed had been half way there when sent by the Iteghé to recover Mr. Bruce's lost property when he first attempted to visit the sources of the Nile; but he confessed that he had no curiosity to go on; and like all the others whom I had spoken to on the subject, appeared to attach some degree of mystery to Yagoub's anxiety, about what appeared to them all so uninteresting.

" Both Christians and Mussulmauns spoke in high terms of the magnificence of Gondar, and the splendour of the court when the King and Ras were together; but as the scale of their ideas was extremely different from our own, it was difficult to estimate rightly their assertions. From their flattering account of Adowa, I was completely deceived until I reached that place; and I should suspect, that a visit to Gondar would be productive of the same disappointment. The town has neither wall nor fortification. The principal building is the palace, to which are attached four churches, one at each corner. In the rest of the town it is said there are no less than forty-two. For the comparative splendour of these buildings they are indebted to the Portugueze, who erected them during the continuance of their power, and have left them as models for the artizans of the present time. The want of wood, and the difficulty of procuring stone, have rendered the little science which still glimmers in the country almost useless, for they are ignorant of the art of making brick. A few Greek artizans are generally to be found in the country, but they are little better than the native workmen. The roofing of the houses and the neatness of the thatching are most to be admired, but this is entirely done by the Falasha, or Jews.

" The Royal family are no longer confined to the mountains of Wechné, or Way-gne; this custom having been abolished some years ago. They are now living dependent on the chiefs of the different provinces.

"The charming Ozoro Esther is dead, but a daughter of her's is living at Gondar. Tecla Mariam, her companion, the beautiful daughter of the secretary of that name, Ayto Aylo, Ayto Confu, and most of the other friends of Mr. Bruce, are also no more; but the families of the two last are living at the capital in considerable splendour.

"The manufactures of Abyssinia are but of trifling importance. They have the cotton plant in many parts, particularly around Adowa; but they are unacquainted with the method of separating the cotton from the seed, and therefore import it from India, in a state fit for working up into their dresses. Coarse carpets are made in Samen, and at Gondar, from the wool and hair of the sheep and goats, which are dyed red, and light blue; the former from a tree called Haddie, the latter from a plant resembling Indigofera. They also procure a yellow dye from the Mocmoco, and a black from an earth: they have no dark blue.

"Knives are made at Adowa, spears and razors at Antalow; the iron they procure from Sennaar and Walkayt, a district about six days journey from Adowa, and also from Berbera, between which place and Gondar a considerable trade is carried on; the Abyssinians carrying with them ivory, slaves, and horses, and bringing back iron, cotton, and India goods: the latter make their way to Ras-el-Feel, where the kafila from Sennaar halts and makes its purchases. The profit the Abyssinians receive is supposed to be one hundred per cent. on these articles, which have before been loaded to at least an equal amount either at Mocha or Aden. Kafilas travel between Darfur, Funge, and Gondar;

but I was not able to obtain any accurate information of the different articles in which they trade.

"The revolutions in Abyssinia have been still more frequent since the departure of Mr. Bruce, whose history is in general accurate. The following short sketch may be found not uninteresting: it was received from Ligantur Metcha, a priest of some rank, having married Ozoro Brelhé, daughter of Sultan Hannes, and who was sent to me by the Ras, as being well acquainted with the recent changes in Abyssinia.

"Yasous the Second reigned twenty-five years, which agrees exactly with Bruce's account.

"Joas succeeded him, and reigned fourteen years. The character of this prince, the events of his reign, and his assassination by Ras Michael Suhul, as related by Bruce, were all confirmed by the testimony of my informant. To Joas succeeded Hannes, who after a reign of only five months died of disease, and not of poison, as stated by Bruce.

"Tecla Haimanout, son of Hannes, a remarkably fair and handsome man, succeeded to the throne. He was greatly attached to Ras Michael Suhul, who, during his reign, was often in a state of open hostility with Fasil of Gojam, whom he beat at the battle of Fagitta; a short time after which, as Ligantur Metcha remembered, Bruce came into the country. A powerful party was formed against Ras Michael, and Gusho was made Ras; upon which the old warrior retired to his province of Tigré, to the government of which Kefla Yasous never was considered as having a title. After reigning eight years, Tecla Haimanout was driven from his throne by Wordo Wossan (Powussen), and soon after died in retirement at Waldubba, leaving one son, Welleta Solomon. It is singular that the dethronement of this king should have happened through Powussen, in exact conformity with the remarkable prediction recorded by Bruce in his account of the black eagle.

" Upon this vacancy, Ayto Solomon, in no way related to his predecessor, succeeded to the throne. This king was a son of Ayto Edayut, and was supported by the forces of Begemder and Gojam, headed by Powussen and Ras Ayto. The reign of this prince continued only two years, and upon his death Tecla Georgis, brother of Tecla Haimanout, was raised to the sovereign authority by Confu Adam and Ras Ayto, who then commanded the provinces of Gojam, Maitsha, the Agows, and Damot. In the second year of this reign died Ras Michael Suhul, at Adowa, in the eighty-eighth year of his age (A. D. 1780) and was succeeded in the government of Tigré by Welleta Gabriel, his son. Tecla Georgis having reigned only five years, was dethroned, and after wandering about the country for several years, at length retired to the mountain of Waldubba, where he still continues. To him succeeded Yasous the Third, who was raised to the supreme power by Ras Ayto. The new king died of the small-pox, after reigning four years, and was succeeded by Beda Marian, through the united interests of Ras Ayto and Degashie Welleta Gabriel, Governor of Tigré, the latter of whom soon after died at the age of thirty-two, being slain in battle by Ras Ally, of Begemder.

" After a reign of two years Yasous was dethroned by Ras Ally, Governor of Begemder, supported by the Edjow Galla; upon which he retired to Samen, and still lives there under the protection of Ras Gabriel, governor of that province. His successor was Ayto Ischias, son of the last Sultan Yasous, who after having enjoyed the sovereignty for six years, was dethroned by the Ras Merrid, son of Ayto of Gojam, and obliged to fly from his capital; but (since the accession of his son) he has returned, and is now alive at Gondar. Ras Welleta Selassé, in conjunction with Merrid, raised Ayto Solomon, son of Tecla Haimanout, to the throne; he was not, however, able long to hold the situation, though supported by Tigré, for after two years he was dethroned, and fled for protection to Ras Welleta Selassé, and is now living at Axum.

"The province of Begemder now gained the superiority, and Ras Iserat of that province placed Ayto Iunus on the throne; he had reigned however only three months, when Guxo, chief of the Edjow Galla, and son of Guanguê mentioned by Bruce, removed him, and placed Ayto Edimo, brother of Tecla Georgis, on the throne. Iunus fled to Lasta, and now lives under the protection of the governor of that province. Ayto Edimo lived but two years afterwards, and was succeeded by Ayto Gualoo, the present King, who likewise was set on the throne by Guxo, the latter having ever since maintained considerable power at Gondar.

"The preceding narrative is probably true, as it agrees with the circumstances of the country; and the period of the several reigns, taken together, exactly coincides with the time that has elapsed since the days of Joas the First.

"Welleta Gabriel commanded in Tigré eight years, after which Guebra Mascal was appointed by Tecla Georgis; but the latter had scarcely taken possession of his province, when he was attacked by Welleta Selassé, then commanding in Enderta, who seized his person, and after keeping him some time in confinement, gave him a village, where he died a few months ago.

"Welleta Selassé has ever since commanded

in Tigré, and was made Ras about seven years ago, at the accession of Ayto Edeneo, whom he was principally instrumental in raising to the throne.

" He has during his command in Tigré been engaged in several contests; an account of some of these I give, as extracted at Axum, from the chronicles of this period.

" Fourteen years ago the present Ras marched through the province of Tigré, which was in a state of rebellion, almost to the borders of Samhar: it was at the time of harvest, and he destroyed the whole country before him; he cut off the heads of all the chiefs in rebellion, and the inferior subjects he sold as slaves. After his return, he gave his niece in marriage to Fit Aurari Zogo, on which there were great rejoicings: he afterwards paid a visit to Axum, to make his peace with God, attended by a great assemblage of warriors. He then carried the war into the province of Sire, where a general alarm spread among the inhabitants; and not even the strongest holds were able to resist his power, for he carried destruction before him wherever he went; never was there such a hero known since the time of Fogara Yasous.

" After this he crossed the Tacazza, went into Samen, made an alliance with Ras Gabriel, and staid three days feasting in his capital. Being joined by Ras Gabriel, he attacked the provinces of Walkayt, Gojam, and Begemder, then governed by Ras Ayto and Aguldon Welled Gabriel, brother of Ras Israel. He dispossessed the chiefs of their power, and obliged them to fly from their provinces: they sought assistance from Hamed, then Nayib of Massowah, who refused it on the plea, that " he was as much afraid of the Ras as they were." On this they went to the Ras, humbled themselves with stones on their necks, and consented to pay any tribute that he might demand. The Ras restored them to their commands; they afterwards drank out of the same cup, and were as brothers.

" Tusfarten, Baharnegash of the country lying between the Nayib's and Tigré, terrified at what was passing, came in with immense tribute, which he had long before neglected to pay. From this time presents were interchanged between Ras Gabriel of Samen and Ras Welletta Selassé, which it would seem were always in favour of the latter, for the former soon grew tired of the intercourse, and sent to Welletta Selassé acquainting him that he might as well be subject to him, as be obliged to make presents equal to an annual tribute. On this Welletta Selassé collected his forces, crossed the Tacazza, and marched against Gabriel, who had shut himself up in the strong hold of Ambahai. There was but one pass known by which this hill was accessible; yet after a long siege the Ras overcame every difficulty, and got possession of the hill, which, to his great astonishment, he found deserted, Ras Gabriel having fled with all his people by a secret pass. The conqueror in his anger laid the whole place in ruins. Gabriel then sued for peace, and the Ras again put Amba-hai under his command, after having obliged the inhabitants to go over to Axum, and swear allegiance to his person. Before matters were settled, Gabriel had come towards Adowa with a stone on his neck, but was met on the road by Nebrida Aram, who brought him the good intelligence of the Ras's forgiveness. Presents of great value, consisting of a red tent, gold, muskets, &c. were made by Ras Gabriel on this occasion; and for some time afterwards he never saw any of the Ras's people without treating them with great marks of respect and honour. These transactions happened in the year 1795; but the chiefs have been at war three times since. Every pacification, however, has been concluded in favour of Welleta Selassé, and they are at present on the best terms of friendship.

CHAPTER V.

MR. SALT'S NARRATIVE CONTINUED.—*Departure from Antalow.—Arrival at Axum.—Greek Inscription—Observations on it, and the Inscription preserved by Cosmas Indicopleustes.—Departure from Axum.—Journey to Adowa.—Difficulties in arranging the Journey to Massowah.—Visit to Gusmatie Ischias, Son of Ras Michael.—Conversation with him respecting Bruce.—Other Communications on the same subject.—Account of the Serawé.—Arrival at Dixan.*

"OCTOBER 10.—WE were much astonished at not hearing any thing of the mules or baggage till nearly eight o'clock, when at last Guebra Selassé came, and there began to be something like the appearance of preparation; many difficulties were however started about the quantity of the baggage, and the number of mules required, and it was twelve before every thing could be arranged satisfactorily.

"We then went to the Ras, and paid him our compliments for all his kind attention to us; when I took this last opportunity of again recommending Pearce to his protection, as his own guest, and our countryman. This he most feelingly promised. Our parting was an unpleasant moment to us all: the Ras, himself, was much affected, and could not speak at the time he took us by the hands.

" As our road lay over the ground which we had twice passed before, there remained nothing particular to be observed; the vegetation was getting brown, the corn fast ripening, and the soil was in part turned to a fine dust, which indicated approaching heat.

" We travelled only a short distance, and stopped at the village of Fiana, commanded by Ayto Guebra, who had been sent forward by the Ras from Antalow to prepare accommodations for us. We were soon overtaken by our guide, Guebra Selassé, who had the charge of our cattle, which formed a considerable drove; the Ras having given us nine bullocks and ten sheep, that we might be secure of provisions on the road.

" October 11.—We were detained some time in the morning by the loss of one of our mules, which had strayed away in the night, and while waiting, we took for breakfast some bread, milk, and boiled mutton, the remainder of a sheep that was presented us by the master of the village, the evening before. After passing the brook at the bottom of the hill, we turned off to the left, out of the road by which we had before gone to Mucculah, and ascending a hill, we came into the plain of Jambela, by almost imperceptible descents, and halted by the side of a clear pool of water, under a momunna* tree, which, though scarcely in leaf, afforded a most excellent shelter. A little before us was the village of Debre, which we afterwards passed on the right, and about two miles beyond came to Neguida, where we were to rest for the night. In the course of the day we saw a profusion of the white jasmine in flower, the blossoms of which differed in the number of

* A large species of Mimosa.

segments of the corolla, which varied from four to six. Though part of the corn was gathered, and the greater part of the remainder nearly ripe, yet there were but few of the inhabitants ploughing, or rather, as Captain Rudland said, disturbing the stones; for the ground was here at least in three parts out of four covered with them. Soon after our arrival we were joined by our baggage: the master of the house presented us with a bullock, and brought a small quantity of maize, and two hundred and fifty cakes of bread. Our party was at this time so large, that I was obliged to make a considerable addition to this allowance to my attendants, for their immediate consumption. The bullock might indeed have been enough; but as the greater part of my bearers were Christians, they would not eat what the Mussulmauns killed, nor would the rest, who were Mussulmauns, eat what the Christians had killed, which often put me to great inconvenience in providing for them both. I had, in all, about thirty in number, besides my own party. The master of the house was named Ayto Rossie; his son was the handsomest and fairest man whom we had seen in the country; he married a daughter of Fit Aurari Yasous.

"October 12.—We left Neguida soon after sun rise, and passing through a country in great part covered with brushwood, came at length by a long though gradual descent, into a vale, through which runs the stream of Gibbé, on the banks of which, we halted about a mile and a half below the Ras's deserted mansion. Our road then lay over a hill to the east of the narrow valley, which brought us in a direct line to the church of St. Michael, on the top of the hill where I before parted from Shelika Welleta Raphael. Here we found a copious spring of water flowing from the summit through a small aqueduct, constructed with little art by the inhabitants. This spot is on all sides surrounded with trees and shrubs, so as to form altogether a beautiful retreat. Hence we travelled partly over the old road to Atbara, a wretched village belonging to Basha Toclu Shum, of the district of Giralta. This chief had sent no orders from Antalow that we should be supplied with provision, we therefore got only two goats and one hundred loaves of bread, and were obliged to kill for our people one of our own bullocks.

" October 13.—We left the Basha's residence with much satisfaction, being happy to quit so inhospitable a village. We passed over the same ground as before, and descended the pass of Atbara. We had just before observed to the right some ruined houses, or rather caves, dug out in the perpendicular side of a high projecting rock, near the bottom of the ascent: we saw a few monkeys of the same species as those brought about the streets of Mocha; and two Abba Gumbas, seated in state on the branch of a wide spreading tree.

" Vegetation seems to be remarkably quick in its progress here; for several trees, which were just blooming when we passed before, were now covered with seed nearly ripe. On entering the plain, we turned off immediately to the left, and proceeded almost a mile to the village of Maquarea, built partly on some huge masses of rock that have fallen from the mountains above, and partly under the ledges of the mountain itself. There are a few large Daroo trees immediately below, and a spring of water issuing from under one of them. The houses are all very small, and it appears upon the whole a wretched place, though built in a wild and romantic situation. It is in the district of Tembra, now under Barrambaras Tokla, who, it may be observed, is no relation to the Shum of Giralta.

"We obtained from this village two hundred cakes of bread and two goats. In the evening I received a message from Basha Abdallah, informing me of his arrival in the neighbourhood, and that he should be glad to proceed on with us tomorrow. I sent back a proper answer, and a present of a cow.

October 14.—We left the village of Maquarea at an early hour, by which our opportunities of shooting were greatly increased, as the birds always retire to the trees for shelter soon after sunrise. Having passed through the valley of Guillibuddah, we arrived at the river, on the bank of which we had before halted. There we found Basha Abdallah, who received us with much attention, and provided us with some hot bread and maize. Afterwards we passed over a ridge of high ground into the district of Tsai, and turning a little to the left of our old path, proceeded to the mansion of Ayto Ischias, the chief of the district. To the east of this place, and about nine miles distant, is the strong hill of Amba Harimat. On this hill Deghaie Welleta Gabriel killed, a few years ago, with his own hand, Deghaie Welleta Raphael, grandson of Belletana Gueta Toclu, of Adowa, who had occupied it as an impregnable post. Here also Debid of Negashe, Deghaie Toclu, Shum of the district of Giralta, and Ayto Rossie, resisted all the power of Welleta Selassé, after he had subdued the rest of the province (seventeen years ago,) so long and successfully, that he was compelled at last to grant them their own terms. To the north are the villages of Nebitot and

Toorbo, given by the Ras to Gusmatie Guebra Michael, after he had driven him from his command of the province of Tigré. He is said to have died here, much regretted, about a year ago.

" The master of the mansion being absent, we received a cow from his lady, who in the course of the day sent a message to Captain Rudland, requesting his company.

" October 15.—We set out at an early hour, and passed over a wild country, thickly covered with brushwood, till, after descending a steep pass, we entered the plain where, in my former journey, we had seen the black eagle. We took some refreshment by the side of the brook, and then wandered about in search of birds, but met with none that were new to us, excepting a kingfisher, or a bird much resembling it.

" Hence we turned off rather more to the west than we had formerly done, leaving Ounah Samuel on our right, as also the mansion of Basha Guebra Eyut, and proceeded to the valley of Damo, in which was situated the house of a son of Gusmatie Ischias, and grandson of Ras Michael, to whom we had already been introduced by the Ras at Antalow. We found the master of the place particularly agreeable, and willing to accommodate us in every respect; he spoke with pride of his grandfather, yet owned that he did not regard the lives of his subjects. He was accompanied by his cousin, the son of Deghaie Gabriel, whom I before saw at Adowa, who was now humbled at the farther end of the room; and, after we had taken our repast, was happy to make with his body a footstool for his cousin. Gusmatie Ischias's two wives were also present, one old, and the other young, fair, and handsome. Hamed Chamie declared, at first sight, that she would bring in Arabia one hundred and fifty dollars. There were other ladies present, particularly the young and beautiful wife of Nebrid Aram: they were all in high spirits, and by their agreeable conversation made the evening pass away very pleasantly.

"October 16.—We parted from our kind host at an early hour, and proceeded on our journey. It is remarkable that the Ras permits this chief's father to keep the title of Gusmatie, or Governor, of Tigré, of which all his family are not a little proud.

"The road this day brought us into our old path near the village of Occabessa, whence we again turned off westward over the mountain of Adowa; for it seldom if ever happens, as far as I have observed, that the Abyssinians travel twice over the same road, each person following the path that appears to him most convenient; all being alike good, or rather, properly speaking, bad.

"On our arrival at Adowa, we found the house in which I had before slept so filled with fleas, that no person would venture to stay in it; in consequence, we were under the necessity of adjourning to one of the haunted apartments. Provisions were soon after sent us by Basha Abdallah, who himself paid us a visit in person; as also did several of the principal men of the place. The remainder of the day we passed in a jovial way, leaving all our business for the morrow.

"October 17.—We went at an early hour in the morning, according to promise, to visit Basha Abdallah, much against the wish of our guide, who did not approve, in the least, of any Arabic conversation. The Basha treated us with great attention, having a curry and maize in readiness for us; and we gained, during our visit, much interesting intelligence, there being present an old man, at that time in the service of Yannes, who went hence with Bruce to Gondar, and several other persons well acquainted with the transactions of the last thirty-five years. They agreed in telling us, that Bruce passed four months at Adowa; that he did not speak the language of Tigré, but afterwards made himself in part acquainted with the Amharic; that he was two years at Gondar, and visited the source of the Nile, and was robbed of his books and instruments; that two of the battles of Serbraxos were fought some time (two years) before he came into the country, and that a third engagement took place afterwards at the same spot, at which, however, Bruce was not present, as he never went out to war, and at the particular time alluded to, was actually at Gondar: that the king gave him a house, but no land, command, or employ, during his stay in the country; that he was a good horseman, and used to shoot from his saddle; that he had two interpreters, Michael, and Georgis, of whom one spoke Greek, and the other wrote Arabic; and that when he was at Adowa, he resided in the house of Yannes, who sent fifteen mules for him down to Dixan.

" I was also confirmed in a fact, that I had lately heard, but had hesitated to commit to paper, from a doubt of its truth:—After Ras Michael Suhul's disgrace at Gondar, Kefla Yasous was appointed to the province of Tigré, of which he took possession accordingly. Soon afterwards Ras Michael gained his liberty, marched directly into the province, where his party was still very strong, and with little resistance reinstated himself in his command. Kefla Yasous falling into his hands, he first made him pay five hundred wakeas of gold; and not satisfied with this, caused both his eyes to be plucked out, and his hands and feet to be cut off, and in this condition exposed him in the court yard of the house at Adowa to the sun by day, and the rain and cold by night; no one was permitted, on pain of death, to give him a mouthful of water: and yet in this horrible state he remained for a space of nearly two days before he died.

" Gusmatie Ischias was bold enough to object to this act of cruelty in his grandfather; and this protest has since, perhaps, been the means of saving himself and the residue of his family. It is said that the present Ras was appointed to the government, as a compensation for the death of his father.

" It is singular, that though we passed three months in the country, we never heard the subject hinted at before we last left Antalow by any person whatever; nor could we ever learn what had become of the Ras's father. After our return from the Basha's we had a visit from the Negeda Ras's, or head-men of the town, who brought us a sheep, curry, bread, maize, boosa, and a pumpkin.

" After leaving orders with Hamed Chamie to buy mules for us, and hire more for our baggage, &c. we determined to proceed to Axum on the morrow, which, however, I could not finally arrange without having a dispute with our guide. The evening passed very pleasantly, as we were at a place where we could procure, for money, whatever the country produced.

" October 18.—We left Adowa about eight o'clock, and proceeded to Axum by the same road that we had travelled on our former return thence; the path lies through the plain, and is much incommoded with stones, as are also the cultivated lands around, the inhabitants never troubling themselves, as I have before mentioned, about removing any such incumbrances. On our arrival opposite the eastern hill of Axum we dismounted from our mules, for the purpose of examining more closely into the nature of the stone composing this hill, and also the better to survey the ancient remains in its vicinity.

"After taking a view of the obelisk that is still standing, of which a drawing has been given, we proceeded again to the church, re-examined all the pedestals, the square inclosure, and the slab, on which we found no trace of an inscription, except the short Ethiopic one before mentioned; and we were all of us satisfied that there never had been any other. The stone of the slab is of the same grey granite as all the other remains. We were then conducted to the mansion in which we had before taken up our residence. I now made many enquiries after another stone with writing upon it, telling them that I was well informed there was a second, like the one which I had before copied. All the people present assured me that there was no other, except some boys, who said they would go and show me one. As I was determined to procure every possible information on the subject, I went out, accompanied by Captain Rudland, to a spot about three furlongs south-west of the obelisk: here we found large stones of granite regularly cut, piled two and two, and placed at regular distances (as in the plate of the ruins of Axum marked A), which evidently appear to have formed part of the foundation of some ancient edifice. About two hundred yards south of this, in an inclosure of one of the houses, we were shewn the entrance, as it appeared to me, of some subterraneous building completely filled up; at least the upper stones are now on a level with the earth. These stones are very regularly laid (as may be seen in the drawing of them marked B, in the plate above referred to), and kept at exact intervals from each other by loose stones, at least so they appear externally; three hundred yards from these are others not so regularly laid (as C of the same plate); but on none of these did we meet with even the least appearance of any inscription, and were glad to return to our habitation, having kept fast hitherto during the day. I also made very strict enquiries among the priests on this subject, but wholly without success; all of them agreeing that they never heard of any other inscription than that which I had already copied. While our meal was preparing, we went down to the church-yard, where I took a sketch of all those pedestals and altars remaining which I had not before drawn, and corrected my former observations; in which, however, I was glad to find that I had little alteration to make.

" We again searched more accurately for Bruce's inscription; but nothing like it was to be found. After dinner we proceeded to the obelisks, measuring and examining all of them, beginning with the westernmost one. There are seven large ones, as we now discovered, all ornamented nearly in the same manner as the one now standing; the smallest is thirty-six feet long, but the dimensions of the largest considerably exceed the erect one. Behind these is another small fallen one, which has almost completely buried itself, on which a shield is sculptured. It was dark by the time we returned.

" October 19.—We proceeded at day break to the inscription, and examined it letter by letter, Captain Rudland having one of my copies in his hand, and Mr. Carter another, which they corrected as I read it over. We found at the bottom of the stone several more letters than we had at first been able to trace, but not an entire line; and it now appeared that we had the whole of the inscription.

"For the purpose of elucidating the contents of this inscription, a copy of it is given, etched by myself, in which I have endeavoured, as far as was practicable, to give the precise form of each of the letters, several of which, from the effects of time, were dubious. Many errors of course occurred; but these have proceeded almost entirely from the similarity of some of the Greek characters, used in the inscription, to each other, as alpha (A) and (Λ) lambda, epsilon (E) and (Σ) sigma, gamma (Γ) and rho (P), kappa (K) and beta (B), delta (Δ) and lambda (Λ), omicron (O) and (Θ) theta. All these difficulties I have been fortunate enough, by attention to the subject, and the assistance of several friends, to clear up; and at present, Dr. Vincent, who most kindly has given me every assistance in his power, considers the whole inscription, with the exception of one passage, as perfect.

"For the following copy of the inscription in modern Greek characters together with the notes, I am indebted to Dr. Vincent.

1 Αειζανας Βασιλευς Αξωμειτων και
2 Ομηριτων και τȣ Ραειδαν και Αιθι-
3 οπων και Σαβαειτων και τȣ Σιλεη
4 και τȣ Τιαμω και Βȣγαειτων και τȣ
5 Καιȣ βασιλευς βασιλεων υιος Θεȣ
6 ανικητȣ Αρεως Ατακτησαντων
7 κατα καιρον τȣ εθνȣς των Βȣγαει-
8 των απεϛειλαμεν* τȣς ημετερους
9 αδελφȣς Σαιαζανα και τον Αδηφαν
10 τȣτȣς πολεμησαι και παραδεδω-

κοτων αυτων υποταξαντες αυτȣς
ηγαγον προς ημας, μετα και των θρεμ-
ματων αυτων βοωντε. * * * * και προ-
βατων * * * * και κτηνων νωτοφορων
θρεψαντες αυτȣς βοεσιντε[b] και επισιτ-
μω αννων [c] ποτιζοντες αυτȣς ζυτωτε[d]
και οινω και υδρευμασιν παντα[e] εις χορ-
τασιαν· οιτινες ησαν τον αριθμον βασιλισ
κοι εξ συν τω οχλω αυτων τον αριθμον * * * *[f]
ννωνευομενοι[g] καθ εκαστην ημεραν αρ-
τȣς σιτινȣς * * * * και οινον. † επι μηνας.
Αχρεισ[h] ȣ αγαγȣσιν αυτȣς προς ημας
τȣς[i] ουν δωρησάμενοι αυτοις παντα τα επ
ιτηδεα, και αμφιεσαντες μετοικησαν κ
κατεςησαμεν εις τινα τοπον της ημετερας χω-
ρας καλȣμενον Ματμαχ. εκελευσαμεν αυ-
τȣς παλιν αννωνευεσθαι παρασχομενοι
τοις εξ ασιν[k] βασιλεισκοις[l] * * * βοας * * υπερδε
ευχαριστιας τȣ εμε γεννησαντος ανικητȣ Αρεως
ανεθηκα αυτω ανδριαντα χρυσȣν ενα και αργυ
ραιον ενα και χαλκȣς* επ' αγαθω.[m]

Where this mark * occurs the reader will refer to the original.

[a] απεςιλομεν without the ε.

[b] βοεσιντε to be Greek should be βȣσιν.

[c] Αννωνα is found in Meursius, but no verb from it; it seems here contracted.

[d] ζυτωτε should be ζυθω, bouza.

[e] παντα agrees with nothing; suppose we say παντα, the whole body, εις χορτασιαν, till they had abundance; χορτασια signifies a supply of all sorts of provisions, but constantly with the idea of superabundance.

[f] These and the other numerals are inexplicable.

[g] ννωνευομενοι; does νε in the preceding line belong

† This reading was suggested by the Dean of Litchfield.

to this word? I could almost think, that the engraver took the sound from the mouth of a Greek; if so, it might be read *ευ αννωνευομενοι*,* *supplying them well;* but I had below interpreted *αννωνευεσθαι*, passively; both probably are deponent.

[h] Αχρησυ may be the name of a place, or of a month.

[i] *τως*; the first letter is imperfect in the inscription; by the context *εκων*, *wherefore,* would be the proper sense, but the sigma seems perfect. *τως* with *αυτοις* is redundant.

[k] *ασιν* is the only word I cannot make out, and the only one in which I suspect the copy of the inscription.

[l] I read this *βασιλεισκοις*, the diminutive, in contemptuous opposition to *βασιλευς*, *βασιλεων*. *ει* is by the ear for *ι*.

[m] *επ' αγαθω*, for the success already obtained, and in hopes of future protection. Our vulgarism, *for good luck sake,* is, I believe, precise.

The following is as correct a translation of the inscription, as I have been able to make, with the assistance of Dr. Vincent and other friends.

(We) Aeizanas sovereign of the Axomites and
Homerites and Rhaeidan and the Æthi-
opians and Sabaeites and of Silee
and of Tiamo and the Bougaeitæ and To
Kaens king of kings son of God
the invincible Mars,—when the nation of the Bougaeitæ
upon a particular occasion were in a state of insurrection

* *ε* is turned into *δ* in *αμφιασαντες* infra.

(We) sent our brothers
Saiazana and Adéphas
to conduct the war against them, and upon
their surrender, [my brothers] after subduing them
brought them to me, with their children and with their
oxen to the number of..... and their sheep
to the amount of..... and beasts bearing burthens on their backs
They maintained them with oxen
they supplied them with bread, they furnished
with beer and wine and water in abundance
The number of prisoners was six of royal rank
with the multitude that followed them to the amount of.....
the whole had prepared for them every day of wheaten bread
and wine for a very month*
until the time that they brought the whole body to me
whom after supplying with all necessaries
and clothing, we compelled to
change their abode, and established them in my
own kingdom at a place called Mataia
here we ordered them to be again supplied
with bread, and furnished their six chiefs with.... oxen
In gratitude to him who begat me
I erected to him one statue of gold
and one of silver and three of brass, for good luck.

The commencement of the inscription completely baffled the researches of the Archbishop of Mount Sinai, and several other learned persons to

* Or they brought them to me in the month Achreisus; but such month is not known. Vincent.

whom it was shewn, till at length I was fortunate enough to meet in Ludolf (vide his Commentaries, pages 59 and 232) with the Greek names of an Abyssinian king, and his brother "Aizana et Sazanus" which at once cleared away the difficulty, and led me to the true reading, which undoubtedly ought to run thus: Αειζανα ϐασιλευς Αξωμιτων, &c. Aeizanas King of the Axomites. It will be seen, that in copying from the stone, I mistook the ϐ for K, and the Λ for A.

This discovery gives a particular value to the inscription, as it fixes, within a few years, the period when this monument was erected; for Aizana was king of Abyssinia, or rather of the Axomites, in the reign of the Roman Emperor Constantius; and there is a letter still extant in St. Athanasius (vide St. Athan. Apol. pages 693-6, Paris 1627*) from that emperor to Aizana, at the time that he was reigning conjointly with his brother Saizana, who, it is to be observed in the ninth line of my inscription, is mentioned only as his brother and general. There is a slight variation in the spelling of both names, from that which is used by Athanasius, Aeizana being there Aizana, and Saiazana, Saizana; but this is so trifling, as to signify little, particularly as ε is found redundant in other places in my inscription, as in αχξεις for αχεις, and ϐασιλεισκοις for ϐασιλισκοις. The letter of Constantius was written in the year of our Lord 356, and the purport of it was to disgrace Frumentius, who had been appointed Bishop of Axum, and those sent out by Athanasius in the year 327.

If it were established as a fact, that the king himself, as well as the people, had at this time been converted, it would fix the date of the Axum inscription to about the year 327; for it could

* This letter is given in Appendix.

not have been much before, because when Frumentius left Axum for the purpose of being appointed, the king, we have reason to think, was scarcely out of his minority; and it could not be after, as had the king been a Christian, he would not have been styled Son of Mars. But this circumstance of the king's conversion is by no means clearly made out; for though Baronius* says, that Aizana and Sazana were "tunc Christianos," he had no authority for the assertion, except the single circumstance of the emperor's having addressed them as such, which is no proof of the fact; and, certainly, the very existence of this inscription, leads to great doubt on the question, as it is scarcely possible that on the king's conversion he would have permitted such a monument to remain. Besides that, if the Adulitic inscription were allowed to be erected by this king in his twenty-seventh year, which it appears to me there is good reason to suppose, it would be at once decisive against it. Therefore, though I venture to fix 330 to be about the period, it is impossible, I think, to ascertain the precise date.

The word αξωμιτων is conformable to what we find these people were, with little variation, styled by Greek and Latin authors,† and it is curious, that in their ancient books they called themselves Axumians, which circumstance I had from the priests at Axum.

After the first line, the inscription proceeds to enumerate Aizana's titles, και των Ομηριτων,‡ and of the Homerites. This is the first actual information that we have of the Abyssinians having, at so early a period, conquered any part of Arabia (και

* Vide Bar. Eccle. Annales ad annum 356, n. 23.

† Vide Nonnosus, Procopius, and the Periplûs.

‡ We have Ομηριτω in the Periplûs.

του Ραειδαν)*, and of Raeidan. This was a district in Arabia, as appears from an obscure verse, extracted out of the poet Amriolkerius's works; it is quoted in a book called "Historia imperii vetutissimi Joctanidarum in Arabia felice (published 1786 at Harderwick) of which the following Latin translation is there given.

Et Hainaha cujus opes occiderunt
In Raidana, quum advenisset Occasus
Is potentem reddidit incolam, et viam emunivit
Ad Raidanam præcelsus gloria in accessus.

The Arabic word used is ويدان

Και Αιθιοπων και Σαβαειτων και Σιλεα.

And of the Æthiopians, and the Sabeans, and of Zeyla.

Σαβαειτων is a peculiar spelling, and is only to be found in the Periplûs, where Σαβαειτε occurs, which had been considered as a corrupt reading. Σιλεα, I have no doubt, is Zeyla, which is an ancient (as well as modern) Arabic name of a port on the Abyssinian coast, as appears in the Historia Joctanidarum before quoted, page 141, "Ad eum (" regnum Jemanæ) transfretarunt Habassii e regionibus Natza et Zeilaa," (وزيلع) que litorales sunt Habassiæ." This was about the fifth century. The same Zeila is in all modern charts.

Και του Τιαμω και Βουγαειτων

And of Tiamo; this I conceive to be the Tehama of Arabia; or, it may be the same place as the one mentioned by Cosmas in Tigré. The Bougaeites, I consider to be the Bogenses of Edrisi; I conceive the *g*, to have been pronounced soft like *j*; hence to be the same as the modern Beja tribe near Suakin. Τοκαεω is the only name for which I have no conjecture to offer. The title of βασιλευς

* Another instance of ε redundant.

βασιλεων which follows, is most exactly conformable to Negus Negashi, or King of Kings, which the Abyssinians assume to this day.

" The υιος θεῳ ανικητῳ Αρεως, which winds up the title, in imitation of the Greek Kings, is extremely curious, and, as well as the concluding dedication, will be hereafter referred to.

" Considering that this monument has been erected one thousand five hundred years, the circumstance of its being found in so very perfect a state, is somewhat remarkable; and it strongly proves the want of research and inattention among the Fathers who visited this country in the fifteenth century, or the extreme inaccuracy respecting matters of this nature, as the following account of it, given by Father Tellez, will sufficiently prove.* " Non procul abhinc erectum est saxum tribus cubitis latum, insculptum literis partim Græcis partim Latinis, sed temporis injuriâ ferè exesis. Hoc indicium est, omnes istas structuras esse artificum Europæorum à temporibus Justini, et aliorum Imperatorum Orientalium, qui (teste Procopio) magnam cum Regibus Æthiopiæ amicitiam coluerunt. Quamvis tunc temporis mixtura fuerit linguarum Græcæ et Latinæ, quia milites unius et alterius idiomatis in iisdem castris militabant." " Verùm imaginari mihi non possum mixtam scripturam in illis saxis reperiri, multo minus rationem istius rei valere puto. Oculatiores inspectores (aut nimium fallor) aliquando reperient scripturam merè Græcam, atque in ea literas A. B. E. Z. I. K. M. N. O. P. C. T. X. quas Latini cum Græcis communes habent, quamvis non in omnibus æqualis sint pronunciationis;" so that by this it appears, that they must either have been totally

* Ludolf. p. 251.

ignorant of its contents, or they must have purposely perverted the sense, in consequence of its interfering so decidedly with their account of the history of the country, since, by this monument, all claim of the Abyssinian monarchs to a descent from Solomon, and the conversion of the Abyssinians to Judaism, is taken away, as it was not likely a monarch so descended, would style himself Son of the God, the invincible Mars, or erect statues to him on the high road so near to the capital.

"Tellez's assertion, which is referred to Ptolemy, I conceive to have been taken from some knowledge of the Adulitic inscription, and a wish to confirm it.

"The same reason seems to have induced Bruce to invent his inscription at Axum, which, however, he executed in so unsatisfactory a way, as led Dr. Vincent* to remark, even before any one after Bruce had visited Axum, "how much more authentic would a fac simile of the inscription have been, than the restoration! in which, by an error of the author, or the press, EVERΓETOΥ is read for EΥERΓETOΥ."

"The subject of the inscription itself is not very interesting, as it is merely a record of a successful expedition against a tribe called the Bougaeites, whom I suppose, as I have said before, to be the Bogenses of Edrisi, in whose country were the mountains of Alahabi, famous for their goldmines. Dr. Vincent (from the letter Γ being dubious in the fourth line of the copy), conjectures them to be the inhabitants of Buré, which opinion I had also entertained, until I met with the account of the Bogenses above referred to. Still,

* Second vol. p. 112.

though the general tenor of the subject is not so interesting as might have been expected, yet there are several very curious particulars interspersed in this record; such as the hospitality with which the King treated the enemies whom he had subdued, and the attention which he paid in providing them with meat, bread, wine, and beer; which is in exact conformity to the mode of treating strangers, so long kept up and still practised in the country, as may be seen in every page of Poncet's journal, as well as my own. But the parts which are most valuable in this inscription, are the beginning and the end, which establish the fact of Axum having been the capital of a people called the Axomites; and gives great credibility to numerous accounts handed down by several authors of that people, and of different embassies sent to them by the Romans; all of which had before been very dubious, from the want of any known fact or monument existing in Abyssinia in confirmation.

" It proves the existence of a king called Aeizana, King of the Axomites, who had a brother called Saiazana; which in the most decided way, establishes the authenticity of a letter addressed by the Emperor Constantius to these brothers, under the title of Τυραννιδες Αξόμιτων.* Now, on this letter, the fact of the introduction of Christianity at that period into Abyssinia in a great measure rests. It farther establishes, that the empire of Abyssinia was even at this early period very powerful, and that their king had already, at least, assumed the sovereignty over a great part of Arabia, which makes the duration of their power in that

* Ludolf, p. 125.

country, and consequently in the Red Sea, much longer than had ever been before suspected.

"By being found so far in the interior, we may deduce from it, that the Greek language had become very familiar in the country; and herein it confirms the account given in the Periplûs of the learning of Zoskales. This inscription contains, moreover, the first intimation which we have of the Abyssinians having adopted the Gods of Greece, and as I have before partly stated, sets aside the descent from the Queen of Saba, and the conversion of the nation to Judaism, as also up to the period of its erection, the authenticity of those chronicles, called the Chronicles of Axum, so far at least as they refer to the religion of the country.

"The knowledge of this inscription, also throws a new light on another, equally curious and important, which according to the account of Cosmas Indicopleustes, was found by him at Adulis, and has greatly excited the attention of many learned men, and particularly of Dr. Vincent, who has written a treatise on the subject. It is not without great hesitation, that I venture to differ from so learned and able a writer, but I feel it a duty to submit to the public, the ideas which have arisen in my mind, from a mature consideration of the inscription discovered by me, and from my local knowledge of the places mentioned.

"Cosmas lived during the reign of the Emperor Justin, and as a trader visited Adulis: during his stay, he undertook to decipher an inscription existing there in Greek characters in compliance with the wishes of Elesbaas (or Caleb Negus), King of Abyssinia, who was then on the point of undertaking an expedition into Arabia, and who had probably been told at Axum, that the contents referred to conquests made by one of his predecessors. One part of this inscription was cut out on a basanite tablet, which, after enumerating the titles of Ptolemy, (Euérgetes), proceeds to give an account of his victories in Asia; and the other part was engraved on a chair of white marble, containing a long account of his victories in Abyssinia, connected, as Cosmas supposes, with the first, though he does not even positively assert it, simply saying ὡς ἐξ ἀκολυθίας καὶ εἰς τὸν δίφρον ἐγέγραπτο οὕτως.

The general objections which are to be made to this inscription merely relate to it when regarded as a whole, in which light alone it has hitherto been considered; first, that Ptolemy Euergetes actually reigned only twenty-five* years, though in the latter part of the inscription on the chair it is said to have been erected by a king in the twenty-seventh year of his reign; secondly, that the first part, or the part on the tablet, is written in the third person throughout; and that the second part (on the chair) is written entirely in the first person; thirdly, that the language is also extremely dissimilar in the second parts, different words being employed to express the same meaning, as, where ϛρατεύμα and ϛράτεύματα are used on the basanite, δυνάμεις and δυνάμεων are made use of on the chair; where χωρας is in one εθνος is invariably in the other, and where κυριευσας is in the first υπεταξα is found in the second. Fourthly, that in the first, Ptolemy styles himself son of Ptolemy, descended from Hercules on his father's side, and Dionysius (Bacchus), sons of Jupiter, on his mother's, while, in the second, he styles himself son of Mars. Fifthly, that Agatharcides, Strabo, Pliny, nay, all

* Vide Playfair's Chronology.

writers between the time of Ptolemy and the Emperor Justin, make no mention of any such conquests of Ptolemy in Abyssinia, or the Red Sea; yet, it is impossible to suppose that Agatharcides, who gives an account of that very coast, should have been in total ignorance of Adulis; (a place that must have been so well known, had that part of the inscription referred to Ptolemy), and that he who collected his information from the libraries of the Ptolemies only fifty years afterwards, should have been unacquainted with events of such great importance, and about which he was collecting information for the instruction of a prince descended from Ptolemy himself.

"To these objections may be added, that, in summing up the victories at the end of the second part, there is not the slightest allusion to those mentioned in the first; for on the basanite are recited conquests in Syria, Bactria, Persia, &c.; whereas on the chair, the extent of the conquests is carried no farther eastward than the coast of the Red Sea.

"Though some of these objections have been before started, they have none of them hitherto been satisfactorily answered; and against the inscription, as a whole, they appear to me absolutely unanswerable. There is a way, however, in which these difficulties may all be solved; and that is, by considering the two parts as distinct inscriptions; for all these obscurities attached to them, it must be observed, proceed solely from their having been taken as one inscription; for which, too, there is no other authority than the single circumstance of their having been found near to each other; for, as to the supposition of Cosmas, it is easily accounted for, from the great difficulty he must have had in fixing upon any person to whom to attribute the second part; besides, that Cosmas (as must appear to any one who looks into his work), was a weak, simple, and credulous man, whose assertion, even if he had said so, would have had no weight whatsoever. Farther, it is to be particularly noted, that the tablet, on which is found the first inscription, is not only unconnected in every way with the chair, but the chair is never once mentioned on the tablet, nor the tablet referred to on the chair. The shape, too, of the tablet is so different, that it could never have been meant to form a part of the chair; and they were apparently the workmanship of different periods; the pillars, constituting a part of the chair, being evidently of the lower Roman empire. These reasons added to what has been before mentioned, of their being composed of different materials, are quite sufficient, I think, to prove beyond all doubt, that they were two distinct inscriptions. I shall therefore call the one on the basanite the first, and the other on the chair, the second Adulite inscription.

"I consider the first to be a record inscription of the victories of Ptolemy in Asia, confirming accounts alluded to by several authors; but, being in the third person, I conceive it may have been brought to Adulis, in conformity with the King's orders, by some of the trading vessels, without Ptolemy having ever visited the coast himself; or it may have been engraved and brought there at a subsequent period. As to the second inscription, I consider it to have been erected by an Abyssinian king, to commemorate the victories of a long reign; and my principal reasons for this are as follow:

"First, its extraordinary conformity with the inscription which I found at Axum; both are in the first person; both speak in the same lofty tone of trifling exploits, and make use of the same peculiar words in expressing the King's gratitude ευχαριϛαι; a word not common before the time of the Christian era, and in both the same words are also made use of, as υποταξα, επολεμησα, εθνη, &c. in contradistinction to the basanite inscription, in which, as before observed, other words are generally employed. Secondly, the names used are Abyssinian, and some of them identically the same; and they are so little altered in turning them into Greek, as to be easily traced; which wo[illegible] scarcely have been the case under a Ptolemy. Thirdly, the language is bad in both, the singular person being repeatedly made to agree with a plural verb; and masculine and feminine nouns are used for the same thing, as τȣ βασιλεωȣ, and της βασιλειας, which is not very Ptolemaic. Fourthly, the writer of the inscription on the chair styles himself in the conclusion, as Aizana does in the Axum inscription, son of Mars; the one dedicating a statute "in honour of the invincible Mars, who begot me;" τȣ εμε γεννησαντος ανικητȣ Αρεως; and the other dedicating a chair in honour of Mars, Αρεως ος με και ἐγεννησε, a conformity that is extremely remarkable. Fifthly, that the whole account can be traced with facility, as relating to an Abyssinian king, which is by no means the case, nay, is attended with insuperable difficulties, if considered as referring to Ptolemy.

"Before I enter on the following statement, I must make one preliminary observation, that the omission of Axum in the inscription is strongly in my favour, since a king of Abyssinia would be likely enough to omit all mention of his capital, as is the case in the Axum inscription; whereas if Ptolemy had been there, which he must have been to make the conquests described, he would not have failed to record something concerning it, as it would have been the most important part of his victory. But, it may be objected, that Axum was not then in existence, and that it may have been built by Ptolemy! Still more extraordinary would it appear that such thing should be here recorded, and that no knowledge of such a circumstance should have ever reached Egypt, or be known to Agatharcides, Strabo, or Pliny. Taking the inscription, therefore, before me, as it stands in Fabricius and Montfaucon, and considering the exploits recorded as the conquests of a King of Abysinnia who set out from Axum, I proceed to show how the whole may be traced on the accompanying map corrected from Ludolf, supposing that these conquests were made at different times, for which a reign of twenty-seven years would have given ample time.

" The first place taken is Gaza, which we find under the name of Adegada, or Gaza; (Ade simply meaning a town or district,) a place of great consequence lying in the way to Adulis, where the trade was even then, in all probability, carried on, and was afterwards one of the strong places of defence held by the Jesuits. The next place conquered is Agame, which was formerly a very large district, and is even now of considerable importance, forming one of the principal districts under the viceroy of Tigré. Returning hence, on account perhaps of some insurrections near home, he reduces the province of Sigue or Siré (as Dr. Vincent says.) He next proceeds upon a southern expedition, conquers Awa or AVA, which is Ade-Awa, or Adawi, a considerable district bordering on Axum; thence direct to Tziama, or Tzama, which is in Ludolf's map; and thence to Gambela, or Jambela, a rich and fine district in the province of Enderta, of which Mucculļah, its principal town was once the capital. After these he subdued Zingabene and Angabe, or the province of Bugné, inhabited by blacks (or Galla), and Angabet, or Andabet in Begemder. Unable to penetrate farther, he returns by the river Tacazza, and conquers Tlama or Tmas (unknown), and Ath-Agaws, or the Agaws; Lasta, or Lasine, being left untouched, whose strength might have offered an opposition too powerful to be overcome.

"Another season finds him undertaking a more extensive conquest, and one better planned; two armies (we will suppose) are marched, one to take possession of Laeta, and to follow up his last year's conquests, and the other across the Tacazza, or Mill. He there subdues Halaat or Salait, Sembre or Samen; then proceeding down the Tacazza, conquers Shawa, or Zaa, Gabala, or Aba Gale, Atalmo, or Lamalmo, and then falls in with the other army, after its conquest of Lasta; and they together subdue the whole kingdom of Bega, or Bega Midra,* Midra being only terra, or regio, a district, as in Midra Bahre, Regio Maris, as in Ludolf's map. The south being now quiet, a fourth expedition is planned to the north, of which our account is very short, perhaps from the greater part of this country being previously in their possession; for it is to be remarked, that it was from this point that their power in Africa † arose; the Tangaite on the borders of Egypt are subdued; and here we meet with this remarkable expression, which could never have been used by an Egyptian monarch, "and then I made them open a foot road from the places of my dominion into Egypt." απο των της εμης βασιλειας τοπων μεχρις

* Vide Ludolf, p. 123.

† Vincent, p. 99.

Αιγυπτυ; a road, which was kept up until the time of Justinian, in 506, as we learn from Procopius, who says, Ab Auxomide ad Elephantidem urbem Romani imperii limitaneam in Egypto, tantum est viæ quantum diebus triginta vir expeditus conficiat. After this he turns again to the south-east (would Ptolemy have done so, would he not rather have gone on to Egypt?), conquers the Aletine and Annine, or wild tribes on the mountains, and subdues the Sesea or Shiho (as I suspect), the Rausa (or modern Rusamo perhaps), a nation of the Frankincense country, and afterwards the Solaute, or shepherd tribes, to whom he gave the care of the sea coast, of which (if they are, as I think, the Somaulé) they have ever since been in possession. After these an expedition is undertaken against Arabia: and it is here that we find the origin of that power which the Abyssinian kings afterwards so long possessed over a great part of that country. For this purpose a land and sea army were prepared, precisely as was done afterwards by Elesbaas.* Now it is to be here remarked, that it was not likely that Ptolemy should attack Arabia from Adulis, neither would his army, after the conquest of Arabia, have returned to Adulis, when it could so much better have gone directly to Egypt. Having now returned from Arabia, what can be more completely convincing than what follows? Having thus (by my generals) conquered all the nations surrounding my territory, "παντα τα εθνα τα ομοϱουντα τη εμηγη," from the east so far as the frankincense country, from Ethiopia on the west to Sasus [nearly opposite Aden, which can only apply to a king of Abyssinia], having settled all this my world at peace, I descended to Adulis,

* Vide Baronius.

[mark, descended; whence? from Axum, than which nothing can be more probable after the return of his army from Arabia; but how could this be said by Ptolemy?] to sacrifice to Jupiter, Mars, and Neptune, for those that navigate [not Bacchus or Hercules, whom Ptolemy would surely have mentioned], and having collected here all my forces, I consecrated this chair to my father Mars in the twenty-seventh year of my reign." The conformity of this last with my inscription; the extraordinary circumstance of their both taking Mars for their father, is to me perfectly convincing, not only that this was erected by an Abyssinian Prince, but that the date of the period when it was erected was at no great distance from the time of the Axum inscription, and that it was perhaps erected by the same king; for it is a most remarkable fact, that Aeizanas reigned just twenty-seven years, according to Bruce's history.

"It is extremely to be regretted, that we have not the beginning of this inscription; but it is not surprizing that it should be obliterated in the course of three hundred or four hundred years, which period we may fairly compute between the time of its erection, and the age of Cosmas; or even if it remained, it may have confounded our decipherers, who were far from being learned, or it may have stood in the way of their opinion that the whole referred to Ptolemy. May it not have been passed over, or, (but that Cosmas's character appears too plain and honest to have committed such an act), suppressed, for the purpose of attributing to one of his own sovereigns the honour of having conquered this remote country? for it is to be remembered, that Cosmas was a Greek (a nation whose veracity is not to be relied on), and of course more interested about a Ptolemy than about a king of Abyssinia. Sufficient for Ptolemy be the credit which is given to him in the first part, and which, by these conjectures, if admitted, is divested of all the difficulties that hitherto have attended it; cleared of all obscurity, it will then stand a most valuable document authenticating what had been before recorded; while the latter part confirms, and accounts for the great power of the Abyssinians in Arabia, and their consequence in the general scale of politics for several centuries, which, from the present very low state of that nation, has hitherto appeared somewhat doubtful; though it be asserted by several cotemporary writers, as Procopius, Nonnosus, &c. and confirmed by many of the Byzantine historians. At all events, I think it is clearly demonstrated that there were two inscriptions. The second point does not admit of equal proof, but the evidence I have adduced is, I trust, sufficient to render it an object worthy the consideration of those better qualified than I am, to decide upon the question.

"We returned to breakfast, and then set out on our way, determining once more to visit Calam Negus, which I conceive to be the catacombs belonging to the ancient city. We took lights with us, and went down into both the excavations. I have nothing, however, to add concerning them. Hence we travelled straight to Adowa by the old road.

"I received a message in the evening from the Ras, by a soldier in his service, enquiring after our health, &c. This man declared that the Ras expected five mules back; but this being contrary to what the Ras himself told me, I sent to Basha Abdallah, to declare, that if such were the case, I should not accept one from him, as I preferred to walk, rather than be thus imposed upon.

"October 20.—We were engaged during the day in making preparations for our journey. In the morning Basha Abdallah paid us a visit, and brought us four mules that were offered for sale, from which I chose two. Thirty dollars was the sum at first demanded, but I bought them for twenty each, to be paid at Massowah. We also engaged forty bearers for two dollars per man, to be paid at the same place. In this Basha Abdallah much assisted us; but no money was to be procured; a circumstance which, I had reason to fear, would subject us to most serious inconvenience before we could reach Massowah. It was settled this morning on my strong remonstrances, that only four mules should be returned to the Ras, accompanied with a letter from me, explaining to the Ras my sentiments on the subject, stating that I was willing, if it were his wish, to send all the mules back, except the one given me by Baharnegash Yasous. The letter was written and ready to be dispatched, when I was informed that, unless I made a present to the messenger (who was a brother of our guide's), he would not take it, but would go back with five mules. Being much incensed at this attempt to impose on me, I tore the letter in pieces, and desired all the Ras's servants to depart, and take the whole of his mules with them, declaring, that if five mules went, not one of the servants should stay with me. Before night they came to make their peace, expressed their sorrow for what had passed, and requested that another letter might be written. I referred them to Hamed Chamie, saying, that I should not trouble him to write another, unless they could prevail on him from themselves to do so.

"October 21. — Guebra Selassé brought me another letter written by Hamed Chamie, which was dispatched. I was engaged the whole of the day in making out a fair copy of the inscription at Axum, and in conversing with some of the inhabitants, and Captain Rudland was employed in writing the journal. Mr. Carter lost his Habesh cloth this morning, it being stolen, while he was a few minutes absent, from the place where he had slept.

"October 22.—This being the day appointed for our departure, we were all in readiness at an early hour, but had to wait a considerable time for Basha Abdallah, who had promised to pay us a visit before our departure. He came about eight o'clock, and proved a most welcome visitor, bringing us a packet from Lord Valentia, dated Mocha, 20th of August, which had found its way from Aith through Buré, and by way of Antalow; it was accompanied by a note from Pearce, giving us a very satisfactory account of his present situation. We were at this time so situated, that it was not in my power to have any further communication with the Ras, on the principal subjects of his Lordship's letter; all that I could do, therefore, was to write to Pearce, desiring that the man who was waiting at Antalow, might be sent back immediately to Aith, with intelligence (should the ship be waiting there) of our being far advanced on our way to Massowah. I had afterwards some conversation with Basha Abdallah concerning the Nayib and Currum Chund, and he was, I believe, as well convinced of their rascality as myself. He told me, that, in consequence of this, the Baharnegash had orders to provide us with a guard, and to see us safely to Massowah. An additional mule was brought us, which completed the number wanted; its price was the same as that of the others. A new difficulty, which I had expected, now arose; all our Christian bearers refused to stir, till they had received part of their pay; a demand which, though by no means unreasonable, I was under the necessity of refusing, as our remaining stock of cash was too small to allow me to part with any, not having above five and twenty dollars left; no money being procurable here at any rate, for I had offered twenty per cent. for it in the morning, but in vain. The mules being ready, I pointed out to Hamed Chamie the most valuable part of our baggage, that it might be conveyed by the Mussulmauns, who remained faithful to us, and left orders with him to stay here till evening, to endeavour to procure carriers for the remainder, and if not, to join us at the first stage. Having thus finally arranged every thing by eleven o'clock, we quitted Adowa, after taking leave of our friend Basha Abdallah, whose ability and integrity had much attached us to him, and whose kindness had rendered us all his debtors. We directed our course to the north of Abba Garima, over a moderately high range of hills, and afterwards along a beautiful valley, through which a stream of fine water runs, which the inhabitants had carefully led off, in the Indian method, into the corn fields. We then ascended a steep hill on the right to the village of Mumsai, commanded by Ayto Guebra Amlac, expecting the arrival of our attendants, but in vain; and, consequently, we were obliged to be satisfied with such fare as we could pick up, beans, Indian corn, and a wild fowl. I shot this day a black and white hawk, with a red dusky tail, the eye large, and of a dark brown colour. This bird is remarkable for the height to which it soars. We passed on the road in the course of our day's march, Ozoro Tishai and her attendants, on their way to pay a visit to Ayto

Ischias. This lady sent me a small quantity of maize in the evening.

"October 23.—We waited with some impatience for the remainder of our baggage, which did not come up till mid-day, during which we amused ourselves with shooting small birds to add to our collection. The Hillets chiefly abound in this valley, flying about among the loose grass and rushes; they are very often seen in pursuit of some small birds much resembling the reed sparrow; yet they are ill calculated for swiftness of flight, as their tails appear to be too heavy for their bodies; they are small birds with remarkably long fan tails, of which there are four or five species or varieties; one is black; another is black with bright spots of red on the pinion of the wing; another with bright yellow spots; and a fourth is spotted black and white. We killed three this morning, and we had procured two before. In the most perfect specimens we found twelve feathers in the tail, in pairs of unequal length. I discovered some of their nests, built in the rushes; they are very small, and covered over, as appears to be the case with almost all birds nests in this country. The Derhomais are also numerous here; they are fond of roosting among the steady branches of trees, and make a hoarse croaking noise much like the raven.

"We found, on Hamed Chamie's arrival, that our leaving Adowa had been of great service in forwarding our baggage; as immediately afterwards, Guebra Selassé, and the Basha, by promises, threats, and blows, soon compelled the Christians who had engaged themselves in our service to bring on every thing belonging to us. We stayed at Mumsai till about three o'clock, when the master of the house came, and made us a present of a bullock and two goats, with a view, no doubt, to get rid of us, for we were advised by our guide to set off immediately after for another village. Our road lay up the valley of Mumsai, which is every where in a good state of cultivation, part being laid out in gardens, chiefly, as it appears, for the cultivation of the capsicum. This is no doubt the stream and vale of Ribierani of Bruce, but neither the name, nor anecdote connected with it, is any longer known to the inhabitants in the neighbourhood. At the upper end of the valley we ascended a steep and rocky hill, leaving the mountain of Samayut, the refuge of Ras Michael, when in arms against his sovereign Yasous, on our right. Our guide now took us to a village on a high hill to the left, called Asshashen. The villagers here were not much pleased with our arrival, and soon after came in a body, armed with sticks, shields, and spears, as it appeared, to drive us away; one more impudent than the rest, came close to me, as we were sitting on a couch in front of one of the houses, and shook his weapon at me. I did not choose to bear this, and therefore drew my hanger, and declared that I would cut him down if he came a step nearer. On this a general disturbance took place; all our people seized their arms; while, on the other side, the men stood threatening us, and the women on the tops of the houses were ready with stones in their hands to assault us. Abyssinians generally talk more than they act, so that the whole ended on their side, in a violent wrangling, squabbling, and noise. As soon as it was over I left the place, and went down into the valley, where we spread our tent on the ground, for the purpose of taking up our abode for the night; but soon after, a deputation of the head men came down, making many apologies for what had passed, promising to supply whatever we might want, and to put the offender in irons, and to send him to the Ras. In order to accommodate our people, I consented to return to the village, where we occupied a house belonging to the elder Gusmatie Ischias, who holds the command of the district. As our guide wished to stay here another day, to settle concerning the punishment of the man who had insulted us, I ordered a couple of bullocks to be killed, one for the Christians, the other for the Mussulmauns, and to be cut up in strips for our subsistence on the road. A trick of our guide's at this village may serve to give some idea of his cunning. Soon after our arrival here, my English bridle was missing, upon which our guide made a prodigious outcry, threatening, in severe terms, the anger of the Ras; and by these means extorted from the head men of the village an additional bullock, two sheep, and several other articles, of which our people were in want; and then drew forth the bridle from a corner of the room where he had himself hidden it, and laughed to their faces at the dexterity with which he had outwitted them.

" October 24.—I took a view this morning of the mountains of Samayut and Assor, from the top of one of the houses of the village. The head men of the village presented us with a cow and a sheep, and about three in the afternoon we received a message from Ozoro Tishai, at the village of Gunduftch, requesting our company in the evening. This message was accompanied with a horn full of maize, and a small quantity of green wheat for parching.

" It was accordingly arranged, that Hamed Chamie and the Mussulmauns with our baggage, should go forward to another village, while we ourselves proceeded about sunset to Gunduftch. This village is situated on the north-east side of a small, beautiful, and fertile valley, divided only by a moderately sized hill from the plain of Samayut. It is built on the first ascent of a steep mountain, the summit of which is terminated by pyramidal masses of bare rock. It is interspersed with cedars and wanzah trees, and makes a very picturesque appearance from the valley below.

"We were received with much attention by the chief, Gusmatie Ischias (a son of Ras Michael by Ozoro Galadait) who is much advanced in years, as also by Ozoro Tishai, who was there on a visit. We spent the evening in the true Gondar style, the conversation being extremely free. After drinking each a glass of arrack, the maize was handed briskly about; something like a supper was in the mean time introduced, consisting of one fowl curry, with which the ladies crammed themselves so speedily as to leave our party only a few bones, some half, and some entirely, picked; which, with some duck balls (as one of our attendants aptly termed them) made up of coarse flour, ghee, and hot water, and a quantity of sour teff cakes, of which there is generally a profusion, constituted the whole of the supper. Beans and green wheat were afterwards introduced, which we begged leave to make over to our mules. In the early part of the evening I managed to get a few questions concerning Bruce, answered by the old gentleman, who said that he was well acquainted with Gondar. He stated that Bruce was a great favourite with the King, who gave him an excellent house to live in, and provided him with food, but that he never gave him any land, nor command; that he was much with the Iteghé and

Ozoro Esther; and but little with the Ras; that he never went out to war during his stay in the country, but kept much in the house, and was very curious after plants, stones, &c.: he added, that at that time he himself commanded Ras-el-Feel, and that he was at the hunting-match at Teberkin, at the time Bruce was there on his way to Sennaar.

"I had every reason to be convinced of the authenticity of this relation, from its agreement with the accounts which had been given me, by the many persons to whom, at different times, and in different places, I had applied for information respecting Bruce.

"Hadjee Hamed, the person I have before mentioned as being sent by the Ras to see us safely to Antalow, a man of about fifty-one years of age, remembered Bruce very well, and said that it was thirty-five years since he came into the country; that he continued in the country between one and two years, and was well received by the King, Tecla Haiminout, who used to give him money, and daily send him provisions, but that he held no government nor land under him. Ras Michael gave him a house at Koscam, but never employed him in any of the offices of state: he was a favourite of the Iteghé, and of Ozoro Esther: he went to the Nile, and was robbed on his way thither by the son of Absa Bega, at Koringa, and he (Hadjee Hamed) was the person sent by government to recover his property. He declared positively that Bruce never had any country given him, not even at the head of the Nile; nor was any command conferred on him, either by the King or the Ras; nor was he in any of the battles between Welleta Fasil and Ras Michael; and during the battle of Serbraxos, especially, he was residing in the house of the Aboona Joseph. He generally lived at Koscam with the Iteghé, by whom, as well as by the King, the Ras, and Ozoro Esther, he was much respected: it was by the interest of the Iteghé, in particular, that he recovered that part of his property, of which he was robbed in his way to the head of the Nile. He did not understand well Amharic or Tigré, and did not speak much more Arabic than I do, but had with him an interpreter named Michael: he generally avoided going much into company.

"Yusuph, interpreter to the late Aboona, paid me a visit on the 26th of September. He had accompanied the Aboona hither from Alexandria thirty-five years ago, and is related to Marcus, the present Greek Patriarch. He said that he knew Bruce well, and sent three of his own people to attend him to Sennaar; that he heard of his having got safely there, but had never learned what became of him afterwards. He spoke of him with much regret, and appeared sorry to hear of his death. He and every one with whom I have conversed confirmed the character of Ras Michael, as given by Bruce. He said that the late Aboona held that station thirty-three years; but that he remembered Abba Sulama, whom, he said, Ras Michael hung with Negardus, and some others: he added, that every thing went on well during the reign of Tecla Haiminout, he himself, in particular, being well provided for, and possessing plenty of every thing; but that divisions afterwards occurred, and continual changes of kings; and that when the Aboona died he was left destitute, and had since been obliged to sell his matchlocks, of which he had ten, his swords, and all he was worth: he wished much I would carry him with me to Egypt.

"A Greek named Georgis, who had resided

some time at Gondar, was a more intelligent man than those I usually met with; he had travelled over India, and spoke Indostanee; he also wrote Arabic, and brought me two books, of the Old and New Testament, in Arabic and Latin, printed at Rome in the year 1671, in each of which was written "pertinet ad Missionar. de Prop. Fid. anno 1746." These he shewed with pride, and said he had bought at Adowa. As he could have no motive for deceiving me, I put the usual questions to him about Bruce, and his answers fully confirmed the accounts I had before received.

"Ligantur Metcha, another priest whose name I am unacquainted with, Negada Moosa, and the Ras's principal builder, also remembered Bruce, and concurred in declaring that he never received any place, government, or land, from the King. They also affirmed, that he never was commander of any troops, particularly the Koccob horse, at the head of which corps was an intimate friend of the priest's, at the time that Bruce was in the country.

"In the different conversations I had with the Ras, I endeavoured to turn the subject on the arrival of Bruce in the country. He spoke of him extremely slightly, and evaded any question concerning him as much as possible. All that I could get out of him was, that he came into the country immediately after the battle of Fagitta, when he himself was appointed to the provinces of Begemder and Amhara; that Bruce went to the head of the Nile, and was not present in any engagement, nor held any public situation while in Abyssinia; and they never could learn why he came into the country.

"These testimonies, together with the accounts

(already inserted in the journal) given by Ayto Ischias, by the priest whom I met on my return from Axum, and by the servant of Yunus at Adowa, compose a mass of evidence sufficient, in my opinion, to throw great doubt on the authenticity of the account given by Bruce of many of the transactions in which he represents himself concerned, during his residence in Abyssinia.

"Gusmatie Ischias was the only person, excepting the priests, whom we saw dressed in an under garment, or as they call it, "comise;" but all persons about the King, we were told, dress in this way. He informed me that he had left Gondar twenty years, before which, he entirely resided there, and at Ras-el-Feel. His sister Akalasa held great power in Tigré, and greatly influenced the Ras in the early part of his administration.

"October 25.—We took leave of the Gusmatie at an early hour, and proceeded on our road, passing to the westward of the mountain of Gunduftch, and across the plain of Yeehah, which is uncultivated, except a few spots near a village on our right. We then left the mountains of Yeehah on our left; these, like the mountains of Adowa, terminate in vast masses of bare rock, the strata of which are nearly vertical. The view of Samayut, in my larger views, will serve to give a tolerable idea of their forms, as they are all more or less inclined to the two figures there represented.

"We stopped for a short time under a Momunna tree, by the side of a spring of water strongly chalybeate; we then proceeded over some rocky ground scantily covered with poor soil, in an eastward direction, about six miles and an half, till we came to the river Angueah. This stream is seldom more than twenty feet broad;

and though in some parts its depth is seven or eight feet, in others it is not so many inches. There are few shrubs and no trees on its banks; and we observed the largest fish that we had met with in Abyssinia, apparently a species of mullet, some of which were at least a foot long. We staid here to bathe, and were soon after joined by Hamed Chamie and all our train. They passed the night at a neighbouring village, where they were well treated, being presented with a sheep, bread, and booza. From the Angueah we proceeded by so circuitous a route over some high hills, that it was scarcely possible to make out our track. We had not, however, travelled more than two miles before we reached Dogai. This village is under the command of Lecka Moqua Ayto Selassé, whom I had met with at Adowa. He was at this time at Antalow.

"October 26.—The old man of the house, who appeared to be wretchedly poor, paid us much attention, and waited upon us with so much good will, that on our departure I made him a present of two dollars, and was only sorry that the great reduction of our money would not allow me to spare more: he was, however, exceedingly grateful for this trifle. About seven we descended from the village of Dogai, and after travelling nearly four miles, came to a spot where two streams, one from the east, and the other from the south, join their waters and run northward, dividing the districts of Gella and Techo. A little before the junction, we observed some deep beautiful basons in the rocks (where the water was remarkably pure) forming most convenient places for bathing. We accordingly took the opportunity of refreshing ourselves in the stream. We afterwards travelled eastward for some time in a line with one of these rivulets, crossing and recrossing it twenty or thirty times. We met with a species of kingfisher, which Captain Rudland shot.

"Quitting the stream, we travelled about four miles farther over irregular hills, till we came to the village of Awaledo, leaving the village of Zonquib about five miles on our left. The inhabitants of the former place were very unwilling to accommodate us; but finding that their remonstrances could not induce us to depart (for we had spread our tent and were preparing to take up our lodging), they thought proper to afford us a house, and after much wrangling, brought us three cakes of bread, and prepared others for our bearers. The master of the house where we lodged informed me, that this district was under the divided command of Barrambaras Guebra Amlac, and Belletina Gueta Welleta Georgis, sons of Ayto Rossai. In the time of Ras Michael it was ruled by Ayto Gueta Tucklai. All kafilas passing through, pay the following rates of tribute at a village called Bet Negus (or the king's house) by the side of the river Mai Kolqual. For each man bearing a load, two handfuls of pepper; and for each loaded ass, two pieces of blue cloth. If the Shum knows of a kafila passing, he takes a piece of Surat cloth, or a brulhé, and in return presents the owners with a sheep. When the caravan arrives at Antalow, the Ras takes five or six brulhés, Surat cloth, or other articles in proportion. Each of the two chiefs of the district above mentioned annually pays to the Ras one thousand pieces of Adowa cloth, and the collector of the taxes, Ayto Confu, pays two matchlocks. The old man added, that in King Yasous's time, the chief of this district paid only three hundred pieces of cloth; Ras

Michael raised it to three thousand; but on the accession of the present governor he reduced it to two thousand.

"October 27.—We received a sheep from the villagers, and at an early hour resumed our journey. The whole of this district is surrounded with high and rocky hills, the summits of which are bare, and composed of regular and horizontal strata. We had to pass over one of the lowest ridges, near which are the ruins of a considerable village; at the top we saw the black eagle of Bruce, but could not get a shot at it, but Captain Rudland killed an Ashkoko. Hence we descended to a small pool of water in the midst of some fine Daroo and Lahaam trees. After descending a steep hill a little farther on, we proceeded through a valley thinly set with brushwood; and leaving the villages of Nurtha and Mai Kolqual on our left, passed over a rugged point of the mountain, into a small and uncultivated plain. The next three miles were over rugged hills, partly covered with kolqual, after which we continued our road between the two towns of Bellassa and Gella (Kella of Bruce); the former being immediately on our right, the latter about three miles and an half on our left. At the distance of about one mile east of Bellassé we came to the village of Negote, where we stopped for the night. It is surrounded with very steep hills, with scarcely any interval of plain ground between them; the water running only through narrow gullies. The sides of these hills are formed by walls into ridges for the purpose of cultivation, but the scanty soil that is upon them is poor and unproductive, and the whole country around has a very barren appearance. The principal grain that is cultivated here is the Leoghé, of which Bruce has, by mistake, given a drawing instead of the Teff. This district of Bellassé is under Bashaw Guebra Eyut, and free of tribute. There is a toll established here for the kafilas, both as they go up and return, which, like all the others, is very irregular. It is at present in the hands of Ayto Isghé and Tecla Hamainout, who in consequence annually pays four matchlocks to the Ras. A horn of civet pays a quarter of a dollar, a slave the same, and loaded asses half a dollar each; sometimes a piece of Surat cloth and a handful of pepper. The toll for men carrying burthens is the same as at Gella. There are said to be three of these Guebras, tolls, or bars, (as they may be most properly termed) between Dixan and Adowa, namely at Lughoe, Bellassé, and Gella; and at Adowa is a fourth. Nearly north of Negote, and about six miles distant, is the mountain of Tucklee, which appears a post of considerable strength. It stands in the district of a chief in rebellion against the Ras, called Negale Hatzé, to whom it has three times afforded a secure retreat against the troops of Basha Guebra Eyut, who has been as often sent against him by the orders of the Ras. The first symptom of his rebellious disposition was a refusal to go up to the presence, about four years ago, on receiving a command, to that effect, from the Ras; on which Basha Guebra Eyut, in consequence of holding a district closely bordering on his country, was ordered to march against him. The force of Hatzé was unable to stand a contest in the open field; after a skirmish, in the plain, he fled for refuge to the hill. The expedition ended, as usual, in burning the villages, and massacreing all the helpless inhabitants. It seems the chief did not consider himself altogether safe in this strong hold, for he compounded with the

Basha, and agreed to submit, and pay a fine of five thousand head of cattle; merely however to gain time, for on the Ras's sending his people to receive the cattle, he caused them to be way-laid and attacked. This brought on a second visit, about two years ago, from Basha Guebra Eyut, which ended in seizing ten of Negale Hatzé's soldiers, whom the Basha carried before the Ras. The chief still refused to trust himself in the presence, which last year brought on a third attack, which ended as unsatisfactorily as the others. The spirit of the rebel remains unsubdued, and he continues to defy all the power of Tigrè. He has a body of three thousand spearmen under him, but no matchlocks. We received a goat from the head man of the village of Negote, and bread for our bearers, and we killed our two remaining cows.

October 28.—We left the village of Negote at day break and descended about two miles in a north-easterly direction to the plain of Bellassé, through which runs a clear but shallow stream. Captain Rudland here shot a hooper and a species of lapwing, remarkable for a strong spine on the pinion of each wing.* For three miles we passed over flat and poor ground; after which we came, by a slight descent, to another stream called Nuzeránch. About three hundred yards before we reached it, I was fortunate enough to get a shot at the black eagle of Bruce, which was perched on the top of a high bush. I wounded it in the head: but it still had strength to rise into the air, where it flew in a circle six times round,

* It is common in Egypt, and, as a German naturalist very gravely informed me (who was collecting for the Emperor) is the bird which feeds in the mouth of the crocodile.

and then fell. I was much delighted with this addition to our collection, which was now growing pretty considerable. Bruce's drawing we found to be very correct.

"We stopped by the side of Nuzeránch for nearly two hours, baked some bread, made an excellent repast, and afterwards bathed in the stream. As the mode of our baking bread is somewhat curious, and may hereafter be useful to travellers, I shall here describe it. Our flour, (which was generally the unsifted produce of barley, ground between two stones,) was first made up with a little water into dough. It was then flattened out, and a stone (of the hardest consistence we could find) which had been in the mean time heated red hot, was put into the center of the dough which was afterwards completely closed over the stone into the form of a round ball. It was then put upon the clearest part of the fire, and in a few minutes produced us excellent cakes; at least what we at that time considered as such. This mode of baking bread is in common use with travellers in Abyssinia. From Nuzeránch the country is flat, barren, and covered with brushwood. Hence we passed between too hills with rocky summits, like castles, and about four miles farther fell into our old track to the south of that hill where we first saw an Abyssinian market. After proceeding about two miles and a half we reached Abha. Baharnegash Subhart was absent,* but we were furnished with bread by Baharnegash Yasous, who here overtook us. He informed us, that as soon as the Ras had received Lord Valentia's letter, he ordered him to accompany us as far as Massowah.

* We afterwards discovered that his absence was merely a trick, to prevent supplying our retinue with food.

"October 29.—We left the Baharnegash's village at an early hour, and after evading all demands for money, passed into the Serawé plain; but instead of turning off eastward, we kept more to the northward, for a considerable way along the edge of a gully through which flows a torrent in the rainy season; and after a march of about four miles and a half we arrived at the wells of Haddadin, formed in the bed of the torrent. A number of shepherds, spear in hand, were busily engaged in watering their cattle, and it was with difficulty we got a scanty supply for our mules. The cattle were all of them in health, and most of them were fat. I was told that they belonged to a hundred different owners, some of whom had brought them several days march, no water being procurable on the eastern side of the country. These shepherds were Mussulmauns, and of the tribes below the mountains: most of them spoke a little Arabic. The wells at this place must bring in a very considerable income to the owner of the land, as a tribute is paid for all the cattle watered here, the rate of which is regulated by the dryness of the season. Hence we proceeded to a village above the wells, called Barraddo, the residence of Kantiba Socinius, the chief of this district, who was a man of good person, and had all the appearance of a warrior. He received us with much attention, and treated us with a quantity of Maize. We were put into a shed, part of which was occupied by a family of the Hazorta tribe, which was come up to assist in getting in the harvest. In the evening I had an opportunity of observing the manner of living among these people, and of gaining additional information concerning them. Their evening's meal consisted solely of coarse cakes of bread, which were made from the grain collected that day in the field. The old woman first sifted away a portion of the husks; the grain was then ground by her and a young girl, and afterwards mixed up into a thick batter, which was spread out with the hand on a broken dish placed over a brisk fire; the old woman and the girl in the mean time being busily engaged in watching its progress. An old man, who seemed to be the head of the family, was sitting at his ease smoaking a country hookah: a boy of about sixteen was lolling on a seat in a recess at the farther end of the room, and two children, a cow, and a few goats, formed so excellent a group, that I could not resist the pleasure of drawing it. The family had scarcely patience enough to wait till the first cake was baked; and no sooner was it taken from the fire, than it was most eagerly devoured, and, that nothing might be lost, the old woman picked out of the ashes every crumb that had dropped. They seemed however to be perfectly happy over this frugal repast, which was concluded with a hearty draught of water.

" Having to rise at dawn of day, we went to bed soon after dark, but at about ten o'clock we were awakened by our host, who brought us, for ourselves and bearers, three hundred cakes of bread, about six gallons of milk, and a jar of honey; he had before presented us with a fine cow, and had made many excuses for a deficiency of maize.

" October 30.—I was given to understand that a present was expected, our host having heard of the money given to Baharnegash Subhart, with whom he was then at variance; he, however, was extremely civil in bringing forward the subject; and as I was anxious to leave friends in the country (most of the chiefs on the borders being nearly independent of the Ras), I thought it right at once, to present him with a Spanish doubloon, which Captain Rudland chanced to have in his possession. With this he was much pleased, and we parted excellent friends.

"Our road this day, after passing up the valley eastward, which may be said to constitute a nook of the Serawé plain, lay over wild and uncultivated hills, covered with acacia and brushwood. After about six miles riding we came to a gully, at the bottom of which we were happy to find a slow trickling stream, occasionally expanding into pools, in the deep holes, made by the torrent, which must, from the nature of the ground, be very violent in the rainy season. We breakfasted here and bathed; after which, resuming our journey, we came in a short time upon our old track, near the spot where Captain Rudland killed the Abou Gumba: hence a ride of a mile brought us to the village of Bakauko, where we immediately procured our old house, and experienced a very attentive reception from its master. Two of our bearers fell sick and returned to Adowa.

"In the course of the day, and during our last night's stay at the village we gained some additional information about the Serawé, who are all Christians, and are considered as being properly under the governor of Tigré, but whose power they have for a long time defied.

"After the Ras's return from his expedition to Hamazen, he dispatched Fit Aurari Zogo against the Serawé: in his attack he is said to have been victorious, and to have killed one hundred and fifty people. It was in consequence of this that the Ras gave him his niece in marriage.

"It is now only a year since a chief of the Serawé, named Aguldum, was in arms against the Ras. A family feud was the first occasion of the Ras's interference. Ayto Aylo, Aguldum's brother, who held with him a divided command, is said to have been very licentious in his conduct, and to have carried, from his brother's villages, many of the beauties, to satisfy his amorous inclinations. This was resented by Aguldum; a quarrel was the consequence; and Ayto Aylo being the weaker, fled to the Ras for protection. The fugitive found the Ras already well inclined to support him against his brother, owing to the following circumstance. Some of Aguldum's soldiers, who had deserted from him a short time before, had entered into the service of the Ras; but being soon after dissatisfied with their new master, they abused him, by saying that he was inferior in every respect to their former chief, to whom they determined to return, an intention they accordingly put in execution. These two inducements concurring, the Ras marched out in person against Aguldum, who, on his approach, fled across the Mareb. The Ras marched on, burning and destroying every thing in the country before him, but soon met with a check from Aguldum, who making a secret march, attacked him, while reposing in full security, during the night, and cut off many of his people. The steps of the assailants were traced in the morning to the village of Gella Garoo, which the Ras entered and destroyed, but not before Aguldum had escaped to a place of greater security. The Ras returned to Antalow, but sent strict orders to Baharnegash Subhart, and all the chiefs in the neighbourhood, to give no shelter to Aguldum in their dominions, and to collect their troops, and pursue him with all diligence.

"The chief of Gella Garoo, getting information of his place of retreat, attacked him in the night, and speared him as he was sleeping in his wife's arms: he had strength enough, however, to rise, but was cut down by their knives before he could make his escape over the walls: his wife, after being ravished, was slain also, and one of his sons fell in the attack.

"The Ras, at first, disbelieving the information, thought proper to send some of his people, among whom, was Guebra Selassé, to ascertain the fact. They found every thing as had been stated, and in consequence seized his property for the Ras, consisting of four horses, one mule, and twenty cows; also his spear, shield, knife, and sheep-skin, which latter the Ras gave to Guebra Selassé as a reward. We saw Ayto Aylo at Antalow with the Ras, and I was informed that the Serawé were then upon the best terms with the Ras: they were commanded by Welleta Ayto Backral and Ayto Aylo.

"October 31.—We distributed our spears this morning among our bearers, by which they still managed to carry the whole of our baggage. I found a man at Bakauko, who left Massowah eight days ago, and learned from him, that the ship was not then there. We left the village of Bakauko at an early hour, and travelled over our old road to the plain of Zarai, where, on the eastern end, we found some running water, near a fine Daroo tree, of which there are several in the vale. This rivulet, however, does not extend across the plain, being dried up before it gets through the valley. There is another stream which comes from the northward, running more to the west, that still carries a considerable stream. We stopped here to take our breakfast, after which we continued our journey, ascending the hill on which is situated the village of Adehadid. On the way we met a servant of Baharnegash Yasous, who informed us that his master had made arrangements for our staying there for the day, and proceeding to Dixan in the morning: accordingly we took possession of two sheds prepared for our reception. For my own part, however, conceiving it pleasanter to be in the valley by the side of the stream, than in a miserable hut at the top of a barren hill, I returned, accompanied by Mr. Carter, to the vale of Zarai, and took with me all the mules, for the sake of the excellent pasturage which I had observed there, the hill itself affording nothing except kolqual and acacia.

"November 1.—We left Adehadid at daylight, and travelled over a country entirely parched up, not a blade of green being visible, except a few Justitias, and great quantities of acacia and kolqual. There is scarcely any plain ground between the hills that form the ascent to Dixan, which we again reached by an early hour.

CHAPTER VI.

Mr. Salt's Narrative continued.—*Favourable reception at Dixan.—Account of the different Grains cultivated in Abyssinia.—Journey from Dixan to the Passes of Taranta.—Conversations with Shum Ummar, a chief of the Hazorta.—Some Account of that Tribe.—Arrival at Arkeko.—Reception on board the Panther.—Dissertation on the History of Abyssinia.—Character of the Inhabitants.*

" ON our arrival at Dixan, we were received with many demonstrations of joy by the inhabitants, and their chief, Baharnegash Yasous, and very soon after, our former plague, his brother, at the head of the chief men of the place, brought us two hundred cakes of bread, and a bullock, as a present from the town. This alteration of conduct was indeed remarkable, but may be easily accounted for, by the impression our favourable reception at Antalow had made on the Baharnegash, and the gratitude which I believe he really felt for our having used our influence with the Ras so powerfully in his favour, that, soon after our departure, he had obtained the regular investment of his office as Baharnegash, which he had in vain applied for ever since the death of his father. We also derived some benefit from the information relative to the history of Abyssinia, which we had acquired from Bruce and Poncet, and which was to the natives a source of perpetual astonishment.

Bruce's drawings of Gondar, and its vicinity, which we shewed to the Baharnegash, tended to raise us, in his opinion, almost beyond the level of mortality. We killed two bullocks for our party, one of which we bought at the village of Adehadid, for four dollars, which, with the five dollars that we had been obliged to send forward to purchase flour, ghee, and others articles, completely exhausted our stock, and we should have been now absolutely pennyless, had we not been able to procure a loan of three dollars from our guide Guebra Selassé. I went out with Mr. Carter in search of plants and seeds, and procured a few of both, and also a quantity of black drawing chalk, which abounds here. We had at noon a recurrence of the scene at Adowa, concerning the mules; Guebra Selassé insisting on sending back one more to the Ras. As we had not received any answer to our letter from Adowa, I remained fixed to the old point, and declared that he might take back the Ras's three, but not the one presented to me by the Baharnegash. The dispute ended by his telling me that he would take the three; to which I again replied, that he might do so if he pleased, and broke off the discourse by declaring that I would not hear another word on the subject. Our hero, nevertheless, thought proper, in a short time to change his tone, and sent to Hamed Chamie once more to accommodate matters. I afterwards procured from him ten dollars more as a loan, to secure him farther in our interests, of which I gave five to our bearers, that they might lay in a stock of provisions for the remainder of our journey. I also settled with the Baharnegash, who was present at the before mentioned dispute, to leave Dixan on Sunday, for it was impossible for me to wait for news of the ship's arrival at

Massowah, having too many mouths to supply, our party then consisting, altogether, of nearly sixty persons.

"The Hazorta chief Ummar paid us a visit in the morning, when I took the opportunity of giving him some snuff, and a piece of blue cloth, expressing the pleasure I should have in seeing him below Taranta. He told me that he was going down to meet a kafila, and escort it hither, but that, whatever were my wishes, he should be happy to comply with them; enquiring at the same time, if I should want any cattle, bearers, or camels, below Taranta. I answered, that I was fully provided with bearers, but should require eight or ten sheep, which he promised to have in readiness. He was well satisfied, and promised to be a useful man to us.

"November 2.—We had an application from the Baharnegash in the morning, to visit a spot which formerly yielded a constant supply of water, but which, by some chance, has since ceased to run. In compliance with his wishes, I and Mr. Carter set out on our mules. The place, which was at least three miles from Dixan, bore evident marks of there being water beneath the surface, as the grass was much greener, than on the land around: about two hundred yards beyond was a gully, in which we found several fine natural basons formed in the rocks, and full of water, but these reservoirs, though they are never dry, did not satisfy the old man, and he begged that I would look in my books and see if it was not possible to make the water issue out from above. I told him that it was impossible to do so, since the water had once found its way into the valley. But my declaration had no effect, so firmly convinced are the Abyssinians, that Europeans possess some magic power of accomplishing works of this nature. We had another visit in the afternoon from the Baharnegash, who anxiously requested me to put off our departure till Monday. To this plan I made many objections; but the old man pressed so urgently for it, that it was at last arranged that we ourselves should go on before, and that the Baharnegash should join us early on Monday morning at Hallai. We were engaged in making the necessary preparations for our journey. The thermometer was 70° at 4 P. M. in the cave.

"The weather had been invariably fine since we left Antalow; the sun at times, being extremely hot, but the nights cold. During the whole of our journey from Adowa we saw the inhabitants gathering in their corn, treading out the barley with oxen, and beating out the teff with sticks. It was my wish, in compliance with the instructions I had received from Lord Valentia, to have procured specimens of the different grains cultivated in Abyssinia, but the disappointments I had experienced in money concerns at Antalow, had left me so totally destitute, that I was obliged to depart without them. The following is the best account I could collect of their mode of cultivation.

"Wheat (of which there are two varieties cultivated in Habesh) sells from four to six gerbuttehs for the firk of cloth, or dollar. This is made into large loaves, which are either baked or prepared by steam, and is eaten only by the first class; indeed it is rarely seen but at the Ras's table, and is called Gogo. Teff constitutes the chief food of all ranks, and being considered of equal goodness with wheat, generally fetches the same price; it is made into the thin cakes of a large size called Engara. It varies extremely in quality and colour, from pure white to black. Neug, a small grain, not unlike the Raggy of India, is held next in esteem; it sells for as much as the two grains before mentioned (and often, from being scarce, fetches double the price); it is mixed with teff or barley, and is a dry and harsh grain.

" A species of flax is extensively cultivated in the neighbourhood of Dixan: it is not in great esteem for bread, but is much eaten when parched, by the lower classes. There is also a species of vetch in much request which is chiefly eaten in the morning, either mixed up with the ghee and curds into balls, or eaten with teff: it is always seen at table on fast days, at which time are also introduced green wheat and parched Indian corn and beans.

" Of barley (called Ambasha) there are two kinds, one of which is of a black colour. There is a great quantity cultivated, but it is less prized than any other grain, and fetches not more than half the price. This partly proceeds, I imagine, from the difficulty of cleaning and preparing it; for when properly purified and mixed with wheat it makes one of the best kinds of bread used in the country, and is made in the form of cakes about a foot in diameter, and three quarters of an inch thick: it is however dry and harsh, and is the only corn given to horses and mules. Indian corn or maize is much cultivated between Gella and Dixan, but I never saw it made into bread.

" It is scarcely possible to ascertain the actual price of any kind of corn, from the circumstance of its being only exchanged as an article of barter, and not having any fixed price as in other countries; besides, almost every man cultivates just enough for the consumption of his own family, and therefore seldom goes to market either to buy or sell it.

" A gerbutteh of grain is said to make from

eleven to fifteen of the large cakes, or engara; two of which are considered as sufficient for the provision of one man per day: this, reckoning six gerbuttehs to the dollar, will make the keep of a servant amount to somewhat about two-pence per diem; but I consider this to be about double the actual cost, as the servants are rarely more than half fed, not to mention many other circumstances all turning in the master's favour.

" Their implements of husbandry are extremely rude, the plough being shaped, to the purpose, out of the root and branch of a tree; sometimes indeed a ploughshare of iron is added. Two oxen are invariably yoked to the plough, and it is guided by men alone; in all the other parts of agriculture, the women take an equal if not a greater share. The luxuriance of the soil, which in the low lands will admit of two crops annually, produces a great number of weeds; and the clearing of these is one of the most irksome of their toils. For this they often turn up the ground a second time, and pick out most carefully every root; but as this is not sufficient, when the corn is about half ripe, they collect together men, women and children, forming a line along the field, and with singing, and much merriment, pluck forth all the weeds from the corn. The labour of reaping is entirely thrown on the females. On passing any field where the women were at work, they uniformly greeted us with the sharp and shrill cry, which is undoubtedly the Ziraleet, described by Dr. Russell as being used by the women of Syria during the harvest, who also quotes from Pietro della Valle a most accurate description of it, that it is "a sharp and loud cry of joy," made in concert, by a quick and somewhat tremulous application of the tongue to the " palate, producing the sound heli li li li li li li li."

"November 3.—We set out from Dixan at a tolerably early hour, and travelled a little to the southward of the road by which we came to that village. The ascent was gradual from hill to hill. We passed two villages on the left, and one on the right, and then arrived at Hallai, situated on an elevated plain, well cultivated, and the hills around thickly covered with oxy-cedar. Here we took possession of a shed that was assigned us, and afterwards walked to the southward in search of plants and birds. Of the former we found a few new species, but did not see any birds except thrushes. About a quarter of a mile from the village of Hallai is a fine spring of water, which runs successively into several natural basons in the gully below. It issues out of the side of a rock, and affords a plentiful supply of water throughout the year. We felt here a very perceptible difference in the atmosphere, the air being cold, and in some degree moist, as if rain had fallen. The country around also was not so much parched as below. I bought four sheep for two dollars, two of which I ordered to be killed. The thermometer was 75°; our distance from Dixan was six miles and a half.

"The master of this village, who is dignified with the title of Baharnegash, or Kantiba, brought us some soar (a grain) and milk in the evening, as also eighty cakes of bread for ourselves and bearers. I presented a looking glass and beads to his wife in return, and one dollar to the old man, with which he was well satisfied.

"November 4.—We left Hallai at day light, after having threshed two or three of the villagers who attempted to stop our baggage, for what reason I know not. We soon came to the descent of Taranta, for Hallai is situated on one of the heights of this mountain, which we walked down with much ease to ourselves and mules. This pass is at present incommoded with large and loose stones, but is capable of great improvement, if it were in the hands of industrious people. There is a yellow flowering shrub that was in great profusion on its side: the kolqual was also in flower. We halted at our old station at the foot of the pass, where we found several large kafilas on their way up to Abyssinia, loaded chiefly with cotton. They had been here three days, and expected to remain five or six days longer; Ummar, the Shum of the Hazorta in this district, had the charge of seeing them safe to Dixan.

" This chief soon paid us a visit, and from him I gleaned the following information.—That there are three thousand fighting men in their tribe, under five different chiefs: First, Shum Moosa, who commands in the district of Assahcurry, to the south of Taranta; second, Shum Ally, who commands at Assalatha; third, Shum Hussien, at Dallieth; fourth, Shum Hamed, at Assubah; and himself, Shum Ummar, at Dufferkydah, in the neighourhood of this place, who also commands the passes of Taranta. All these chiefs, whose territories extend from near Dixan to the sea, live in strict amity with each other, and acknowledge Shum Abdallah Welled-el-Zangarah as supreme. He resides at Zulla, by the sea side, somewhere near to the island of Valentia, where water is procurable throughout the year; that is, there are wells, which though generally exhausted in the evening, are, like those at Arkeko, full again by the morning. To this place they all go down in the rains with their cattle, and remain there four or five months, till the force of the waters is abated. On their return, they bring with them a considerable quantity of salt, which they exchange for grain in Habesh, and the districts of Baharnegash Yasous and Subhart. This salt is procured from a mountain two days journey from Zulla. They cultivate a little grain themselves, but subsist chiefly on the flesh and milk of their cattle. Subboolah is the name of a species of fig tree, which they lop for their cattle when grass is scarce. There is a powerful tribe to the south, called Bussamoo, with whom they are at war, and another tribe to the north called Tecroor; all of them speak the same language, which he called Dancalli. They trade with the Dancalli tribe, but are afraid of them. When they go to Massowah, they give two or three cows to the Nayib; and whatever is stolen from Habesh is taken to Massowah, where they receive, in lieu of stolen property, Surat cloth, spear heads, and other articles from the Nayib, who monopolizes this scandalous traffick, and punishes any one who attempts to participate in it.

" My informant farther told me, that the Shiho tribe at Hamhammo was two hundred strong; that it spoke the language of the Hazorta; and was commanded by Shum Hamed, who lives at the village of Daghah. It has little communication with the latter, but if at any time the tribe molests the kafilas, it is always resented by the Hazorta. Near Hamazen, and subject to it, are two Christian tribes, Saharteh and Woggurta. There is plenty of water all the year round at the foot of Taranta.

" I presented to this chief two pieces of cloth, two looking glasses, four knives, and a pair of scissars, some snuff, and a sash that I wore round my waist, to which he seemed to have a fancy. He was much delighted with these trifles, and professed that he should always regard the English as friends.

"In the afternoon we had a messenger from Dixan, informing us that the Baharnegash would not leave the place till the morrow. We did not consider our present situation as a very pleasant one, there being too many of the Nayib's people at hand, as also a considerable number of the Hazorta, all of whom are alike in the habit of plundering; I therefore ordered the mules to be prepared, and determined to go on to Assubah.

"The moment our intention was made known, a hundred difficulties were started, and it seemed at once as if every soul in the neighbourhood was concerned in our detention. The Hazorta fled to their arms, and took possession of the pass, threatening us if we dared to proceed; the Mussulmauns in the kafilas, Shum Ummar, and two of the Nayib's Ascaries (old acquaintance) advised us not to move, as night was coming on, for we should certainly be attacked, and all cut off by the Bedowee. They assured us, moreover, that there was no water on the road, and no food for our mules. Guebra Selassé declared that he would not stir, and our bearers to a man refused to proceed. Hamed Chamie came to me in great alarm, entreating that we would stay, as he was sure some harm would ensue. If we had now given up our purpose, it would have had so much the appearance of fear, that even from a regard to prudence we determined to persist. We laughed at Hamed Chamie's fears, desired the Nayib's people only to give their advice when it was asked, brought Guebra Selassé over, by telling him that he was no soldier; and partly by taunts, and partly by promises of reward, prevailed upon a great number of our bearers to take up their loads. Mr. Carter, incensed at some detention he met with from Shum Ummar, dismounted from his mule, and marched forward on foot by the Hazorta, who seemed chiefly to have an eye on our baggage.

"I was now informed by Shum Ummar, that the chief who headed the party which stood ready to oppose our passage, had lately been made desperate by the death of some relation, and that he wished to make up for his loss by obliging us to pay tribute. Shum Ummar accordingly went to him with a goat in his hand to appease him, and we advanced. A violent scuffle now ensued: one party of the Hazorta attempting to attack us, and the other, headed by our friend Shum Ummar, forcibly preventing them. The latter succeeded, and we at length marched unmolested through the pass. After advancing about three hundred yards, our only remaining cow was missed; on which our bearers, all at once grown courageous, laid down their loads, seized their arms, and determined to attempt a rescue. It proved on farther enquiry that the animal was with the advanced parties. Those of our bearers that had strayed behind, in a little time joined us with Guebra Selassé, who had remained to secure the rest of our baggage. We were shortly after overtaken by our friend Shum Ummar, who came to take his leave; he told us that he had got a bruise in the scuffle, but that all was now well. On his going away I gave him a dollar, with which he was well satisfied. It was nearly dark before our arrival at Assubah, where we pitched our tent for the night, baked some bread, which constituted the whole of our meal, and retired to rest. It is to be remarked, that we found a fine clear running stream all the way from Taranta, which completely refuted the assertions of the Mussulmauns respecting the scarcity of water.

"November 5.—Before day-light we struck our tent, and commenced our march, having bought another cow with the last four dollars that we could muster among our people. We found the stream increasing as we advanced, and could scarcely recognize Tubbo as we passed it, the late torrents having in every part altered the appearance of its bed, leaving every where strong marks of their ravages. Trees in many parts had been thrown down by their force, large masses of stone removed, and the whole of the bed from Taranta, was strewn with pieces of kolqual brought down from the mountain.

"At this time there was scarcely a blade of grass to be seen on the banks of the stream, yet there were young oxycedars springing up in abundance, and the trees still continued in flower. I procured seeds from two trees much resembling the Wanzah, and saw a great quantity of large monkeys on the hills, as also a few very small ones, that seemed to run from the former. About eleven o'clock we arrived at Sadoon, where we halted during the heat of the day, employing our time in bathing, and taking our morning repast. We proceeded about four, on our march, notwithstanding the remonstrances of a deputation from a kafila that was going down with us, which came to me, accompanied by Guebra Selassé, to advise me by no means to proceed, as the next stage was a dangerous one, and the halting place unsafe. In reply, I recommended them, if they thought so, by no means to proceed; at the same time I promised to Guebra Selassé a dollar for every five of the natives whom he might see together at one time on the road. We met at least two hundred bullocks and asses in the afternoon, going with salt to the upper country, attended by a few straggling Hazorta. At about five o'clock we halted under a Momunna tree, on the spot where we had before rested on our journey from Hamhammo. Having pitched our tent, we ordered the two remaining cows to be killed, and grass to be cut, from the hills around, for our mules. Our bearers were all very watchful during the night, and we heard them at all hours exercising their slings, for the purpose of keeping off the Shiho, who inhabit the hills around. In the course of the night an old man and child came to us for food, being allured by the smell of meat.

" November 6.—We struck our tent and set off at day-break, but had not advanced two miles, when we saw with surprize one of our people ahead throw down his load at the mouth of a gully on the left, and seizing his spear, shout aloud; making at the same time all the gestures usual with them on going into battle. Captain Rudland supposed that the Shiho were coming down to attack us; for my part, I thought that it was a sort of war challenge, calling upon the Shiho by way of bravado; we were however both mistaken, for on looking towards the gap, whom should we see but our friend Baharnegash Yasous on foot, with four or five followers. He had left Dixan only two days before, and had come across the hills by a near road to meet us. Thus reinforced, our bearers went on with spirit, and soon brought our baggage to a spot a little to the northward of Hamhammo, where the stream was still running, though we had often lost it on the road. Here we rested, took our breakfast, and again sent out the bearers for provender for our mules. After remaining a few hours we recommenced our journey, and, at the distance of about a mile, passed an encampment very much like the one before mentioned in my former journal. The Hazorta were busily engaged in cutting down the branches of the acacia for their goats, of which they seem to have a good stock. We bartered a little flour for some milk, and our people also exchanged some skins for different articles.

"We saw soon after the ruins of another encampment that had been deserted. Hence we continued along the bed of the torrent for about a mile farther. The stream indeed, properly speaking, ceased at Hamhammo, but there were a few holes, where water was still found in the bed so far as this place. Here, however, the water came entirely to an end, being lost in a bed of sand, that spreads over a plain of considerable extent to the eastward. With some difficulty we ascertained our right track, in which we proceeded in an easterly direction. A hill to the right was pointed out to us as Asalitha, the residence of one of the chiefs of the Hazorta; beyond are the hills inhabited by the Russimous, who are said to have been beaten and plundered by the chief Shum Waldo.

"After travelling for a few miles over a barren and wild country, thick set with acacia, we passed the Shiho encampment where we before slept, and thence went on to Weah. We found no stream here, but plenty of water in the hollows under the rocks. We did not pitch our tent, intending to go on in the middle of the night. Here we saw several hyænas and jackals, and were so much incommoded by musketoes and ants, that it was impossible to sleep. Our bearers also seemed little inclined to repose, but amused themselves in dancing, singing, and performing their war antics till nearly eleven o'clock. Soon afterwards they proposed, as it was a light night, to proceed on our journey, for the purpose of avoiding the heat of the ensuing day, there being no water between this place and the vicinity of Arkeko. We were glad to comply with this proposal, and accordingly mounted our mules, and rode on to a spot near Shillokee, where we halted, and slept from one o'clock till a little past four; we then set out for Arkeko, under no small anxiety, lest the report which we had heard on the road of the absence of the ship, should prove true; in which case, from our former experience of the hostile disposition of the Dola, we anticipated no small trouble and personal hazard. In order to keep up the spirits of our attendants, I had ventured to express myself perfectly certain, that the ship would make her appearance as soon as we reached the coast; and by a most fortunate coincidence, as the day broke, we were gratified by the sight of a vessel in the offing, which we were soon convinced was no other than the Panther. The effect which this had on the whole party is scarcely to be conceived; the old Baharnegash, in particular, kissed my hand with profound respect, saying, You know every thing.

"We reached Arkeko about half past seven, went to our old house, and were there informed that the Nayib was at Massowah. Mr. Carter soon after walked out, and had stones thrown at him by several of the inhabitants; those of us also who remained in the court yard were welcomed by a few of the same compliments. Not knowing how far this might proceed, I sent for the Nayib's son, loaded in his presence all our muskets, and declared I would shoot the next person so offending; which fortunately prevented a recurrence of the outrage.

"In the course of the morning we walked round the beach close by where the Panther was lying, and after discharging all the fire arms that we possessed, as a signal of our approach, we were happy to see the old cutter come off, which soon carried us on board, to the mutual and heartfelt joy of ourselves and friends."

End of Mr. Salt's Journal.

The investigation of the earliest accounts of Abyssinia, having led Mr. Salt to form opinions on its history, different from those hitherto entertained, he, at my particular request, drew up the following dissertation, which I consider as forming a very valuable addition to the knowledge we have acquired by his residence in that country.

"Abyssinia is a corruption of the Arabic word Habesh, signifying 'convena.' This name has been invariably used by the Arabians, though adopted in modern times only by the Abyssinians, who prefer that of their different provinces, as Amharians, Tigrians, or the more general one of Cashtam (Christians), of which they are extremely proud, and which generally was the first word they addressed to us on our entering the country, accompanying it by laying hold of a blue silk string round their necks, which is with them the indisputable proof of their being entitled to the appellation. In their books they are styled Ethiopians, sons of Ethiopia, Agazi, and Axomians; by a similar name to which (Axomites) they were alone designated among the Romans. Many authors, particularly Ludolf,* a writer who has entered very deeply into their history, have supposed them to have passed over from Arabia; but to this there are many objections, for I do not recollect any

* Vide his Comment. 58, 59.

instance of a nation having sent back settlers to its mother country; yet we have an account in Procopius, of a band of the Axomites, on invading Arabia, having been so pleased with it, that they gave up their own country, and continued there.* It appears more probable from the general tenor of their history, that they were refugees from Egypt, who conquered, and mingled with, the aborigines of the country; else, from what source could they derive their veneration for the Nile, of the consequence of which, in Abyssinia, they could form no idea? Whence their style of building, so totally different from any in Arabia? Or their written character, which is as essentially different from that of the antient Cufic? The Greek or Ethiopic being written from left to right, the Cufic from right to left; the former having each character distinct and square in its form, and the latter chiefly consisting of curves running wildly into each other. Even the very form of their government, which always appears to have been monarchical, points out Egypt, rather than Arabia, for their origin.

" But as this is a point of considerable importance, it may not be uninteresting to enter a little deeper into the discussion.

" In the earliest records of history, we find the Ethiopians represented as a very numerous and powerful people; their importance, however, progressively declined, as Egypt advanced in consequence; for as the population of that country increased, it naturally extended its conquests in the direction of the Nile, compelling the Ethiopians to retire towards the south. Meroe seems to have been the point at which their progress was

* Vide Procopius de Bello Persico, Lib. I. c. xix. Paris, MDCLXII.

stopped; yet, beyond this, bands from Egypt afterwards emigrated and settled themselves among the Ethiopians; of one of these flights we have an account in Herodotus, who mentions that it consisted of two hundred and forty thousand in number; that they were called, as a nation, Asmack, or Askham; that they fled from Psammiticus six hundred and thirty years before the time of that historian, and went as far beyond Meroe as that place is from Elephantine. These people are considered by Dr. Vincent to be the same as those described by Strabo, under the name of Sebritoe, or Sembritoe (Advenæ), who inhabited all the country above Meroe, and extended across the mountains nearly to the Red Sea. They are also described, more accurately perhaps, by Pliny under the names of Semberritoe and Asachie, on the mountains. These I consider, with Dr. Vincent, to be no other than the Axomites, or, as they term themselves in their most antient books, Agazi.

"The Abyssinians, in their modern books, lay claim to great antiquity, as being descended from Ham.* They also boast that one of their queens, named Maguedâ, was the Queen of the South, who visited Solomon, by whom she had a son named Menilech, from whom their present kings are lineally descended. The only thing like evidence on this subject, depends on the authenticity of a series of chronicles, said to have been kept regularly by the priests at the ancient city of Axum. The authority of these has, however, been with reason disputed, as it is scarcely possible that they should have been preserved, considering the wars in which the country has conti-

* Mendez and Bruce's History.

nually been engaged. Besides, the evidence of the Axum inscription seems decisive against them, as a king certainly would not call himself son of Mars, who prided himself on his descent from Solomon. It seems, on the whole, probable, that this idea was borrowed from their dependents, the Homerites, and was assumed long after the introduction of Christianity.

"Whatever their religion may have been in early times, they do not appear to have been exclusively attached to it, since, when the Romans succeeded to the trade of the Red Sea, they found the Axomites, as they were then called, ready to receive, together with their merchandize, the worship of their gods. This is proved by the inscription I found at Axum, where the sovereign of the country styles himself son of the God, the invincible Mars; even if we do not refer to the second Adulitic, which, if allowed to have been erected by an Abyssinian king, would be still more satisfactory.

"It is only about one or two centuries after the commencement of the Christian æra, that the Abyssinian history begins to emerge from obscurity. A very close commercial connection was then formed with the country by the traders from Egypt, as appears in the Periplûs; and the Greek language became so common that it was used by the king of Abyssinia to commemorate his exploits, even so far in the interior as Axum, which also most strongly corroborates the knowledge of Greek attributed by the Periplûs to Zoskalis.

"This connection with Egypt seems to have added greatly to their power and consequence in the Red Sea: for in the first information we have of them, we find them confined to the western coast, and the trade chiefly in the hands of Arabians: but in a few centuries afterwards, we perceive they became masters of the greater part of the Arabian coast, and appointed viceroys over the Homerites, who, after conquering the Sabeans, had in their turn become subject to the King of Axum.* To effect this, however, required a long period of time; and might never have taken place, had not a peculiar series of external and favourable circumstances, concurred to farther their progress.

"After the Phœnicians had ceased to be a maritime power, Egypt had occupied the Red Sea with her fleets, and had engrossed all the valuable productions of India and the east of Africa: but she was content to hold this monopoly in conjunction with the Arabians, who, from time immemorial, had been joint possessors of the trade. When the dynasty of the Ptolemies had been overthrown, and Egypt had become a province of the Roman empire, the Romans succeeded of course to this trade: but the genius of that people was ill-formed for commerce; and the very nature of their government was such, as to render their power of short duration in this part of the world; for so long only could they hope to hold it, as they followed the line marked out to them by their predecessors. On the contrary, instead of adding strength to the union that ought to have subsisted between them and the Arabians, their desire of conquest led them to take possession of their sea ports, and even to send an army into the heart of their country.† In this expedition, however, they

* Procop. Caput xix. Baronius, Lib. vii. art. 22. A. D. 522. Nicephorus Call. Lib. xvii. Cap. 32. Paris MDCXXX.

† See both Strabo's and Pliny's account of C. Gallus's expedition.

effected nothing of consequence, but were harrassed, baffled, and driven back with disgrace. The remoteness, too, of their seat of government, was in itself alone sufficient to prevent a long continuance even of their influence here; for the viceroys of Egypt were more likely to think of enriching themselves, than of benefiting the Egyptian traders: besides that the empire itself was hastening fast to its end. These circumstances, added to the supineness and indolence of the Arabians, made an opening for the neighbouring powers, too advantageous to be long neglected; and accordingly we find, that it was shortly afterwards laid hold of, and by a nation which, until the Christian æra, had been known only by vague report.

"These were the very Egyptian tribes, which, mingling with the ancient inhabitants of the country, had extended their conquests eastward, and had established their power at Axum, under a feudal sovereignty; a government which, more than all others, is likely to attach the neighbouring tribes to its interest, since it does not require any change in their general system of policy, to enable them to become an integral part of the state. From Axum, their conquests soon extended to the Red Sea; and here, finding friends in the inhabitants of the city of Adulis (which had also been built by refugees from Egypt), they together formed a very powerful nation, which was enabled to assume a consequence in the Red Sea, that the then possessors of the trade were unequal to oppose. Of these facts we have information also in the Adulitic and Axum inscriptions, and in the Periplûs, written, I conceive, after the time of Pliny, who, except Strabo, was the first to notice this rising nation; the latter writer having only remarked, in his account of the Ethiopians, that "as yet none of the Ethiopians had interfered with the commerce of the Red Sea." From the date of the Adulitic inscription, their power became supreme in this part of the world; and they formed a maritime barrier between the Romans and the Persians, which induced the former to conciliate them by repeated embassies, and annual presents, the magnificence of which strongly points out the consequence that they held in the scale of eastern politics,* which consequence continued, in some degree, until a considerable time after the rise of the Arabians under Mahomet.

"As idolatry declined among the Romans, by the same channel that the worship of Mars had been introduced, the true religion of Christ found its way into Abyssinia, and at length was happily established as the religion of the country, about the year 330, in the reign of Abreha, or, as he was called by the Romans, Aeizana, (who had at this time taken his brother Abybeha, or Saeizana, to share in the empire). The persons to whom the introduction of Christianity is attributed, are Frumentius and Ædesius,† according to the account given by Rufinus, who declares that he had it from Ædesius himself, who also returned from Abyssinia, and was made Bishop of Tyre: but he spoke of it as in India, which occasioned much confusion; yet it is most clearly made out to refer to the Axomites, by St. Athanasius, and Constantius's letter to Aeizana and Sazana; and that the former reigned at Axum, is clearly established by the Axum inscription.

* Nicephorus, p. 719, ch. cxviii.

† Vide Fred. Spanheim Historia Christiana, Secul. iv. cap. iv. viii. and Socrates, lib. l. cap. xix.

"Frumentius and Ædesius, two young men, Christians, but unordained, in company with one Meropius, a Tyrian, were shipwrecked on the coast, where, being captured by the barbarians, Meropius was killed; but the young men were taken before the King of Axum, and accepted into his service. Afterwards, on the king's death, they rose to great honours, even to the administration of the government, by the appointment of the Queen, during the minority of her son.

"By their influence, the foundation was laid for the conversion of the Abyssinians; and for the purpose of promoting it, Frumentius returned to Egypt, and was there appointed Bishop of Axum* by Athanasius, in which capacity he returned to Abyssinia. On the disgrace of St. Athanasius, Frumentius was attacked by the Arian party, as appears by a letter from the Emperor Constantius to the Kings Aiezana and Sazana, now extant in St. Athan. Apol. (vide B) requiring that they would send Frumentius to Alexandria. An embassy also was sent about this time for the same purpose into Arabia and Abyssinia,† as appears in Philostorges, an Arian writer; and it is not improbable, that by this embassy was sent the letter of Constantius above referred to. The chief of this embassy was Theophilus, an Arian bishop. The account of his mission is valuable, and appears to me not to have been before sufficiently noticed.

"He was an Indian, who in Constantine's reign was sent as a hostage from the Divæi‡; and be-

* St. Athan. Arch. Alexand. ad Imp. Constantium Apol. Paris, MDCXXVII. p. 693.

† Philostor. Ecc. Hist. Lib. iii. and Nic. Call. Cap. XVIII.

‡ Inhabitants of islands in the eastern seas. Vide Vincent, 495.

ing a man of great learning and knowledge, was afterwards raised to the episcopal dignity. In this mission he is said to have carried out two hundred Capadocian horses, besides other presents, to the eastern princes. He built three churches, one at Tapharon in Arabia, another at the Roman emporium at Aden,* and another on the island of Ormuz. He then passed over to Diabé, and to many other parts of India; crossing from Arabia, he went over to the Æthiopians called Axomites, who lived on the left side, to those sailing up the Red Sea, and who were so called from their metropolis, Axum. Having there settled every thing to his satisfaction, he returned to the Roman territory. Besides his extensive learning, he is recorded to have understood medicine (hunc enim divina virtute morbos curare fama celebris erat). His success in Abyssinia, however, though asserted in general terms, can scarcely be allowed, when we consider the high favour in which Frumentius was held; for if we may believe the Abyssinian annals, which here are perfectly consistent with the Byzantine writers, both he and the other missionaries with him, were, on his return, received with open arms by the chiefs, treated with high honour and respect, and by the common people almost venerated as divine agents. No nation, indeed, ever received the Christian religion with more willingness than the Abyssinians, so that a great part of them were in a short time baptized to the faith; lands were set apart for the priesthood; churches were erected, and others afterwards excavated out of the solid rocks, by workmen sent for out of Egypt, by the orders of the Abyssinian emperors, and which

* This circumstance tends to make the Periplûs of later date than this period, as Aden was then evidently not destroyed.

they to this day retain. One of these I saw at Abhahasuba, which is undoubtedly of great antiquity, and resembles much the architecture of Egypt. With the rites of Christianity, however, they either incorporated many ceremonies which they had borrowed from the Jews, or, which is perhaps as likely, they received Christianity mixed with many Jewish rites, which had not, in the early periods of the church in Egypt, been so decidedly separated from it. Over this church, from its first foundation, the supremacy of the Patriarch of Alexandria seems to have been acknowledged, for the Emperor Justin writes to Asterius, Bishop of Alexandria, to incite the King of the Axomites against Dupaan*; and it was wisely determined that the chief priest, or Aboona, should be a stranger appointed by him; thus securing to so remote a country, on the death of each Aboona, a renewed supply of learning and Christian knowledge, superior at least to what was likely to be found there. In subsequent periods, from time to time, many holy men went over from Egypt, who were invariably received with reverence by the inhabitants, particularly nine or ten of great sanctity, between the years 470 and 480, whose memory is still highly respected in the province of Tigré, where as many churches were built and called after their names.

"The faith which they received with enthusiasm, they maintained with firmness; for so early as the time of Justin, about the year 525, when it appears that they were absolute masters of the Red Sea, we have a well authenticated account of a formidable army having been sent over to assist the Christians in Arabia by Caleb Negus, or Elis-

* Vide Baronius, lib. vii. A. D. 522.

baas, which proved successful. It was to this prince that Nonnosus was sent as embassador by Justin, part of whose account is still extant in Photius,* and the Adulitic inscription was also copied at this time by Cosmas.

" This, and the succeeding reign of Guebra Maskal, or Hellestheus, who was cotemporary with Justinian, and to whom the latter sent Julianus† as embassador, for the purpose of awing the Persians, and gaining a monopoly of the Indian trade, particularly silk, form the brightest period of the Abyssinian monarchy, as clearly ascertained in history; but I think we may presume, that it was also powerful at the time of the second Adulitic inscription being erected: to ascertain the date of this, is therefore of the greatest importance. But even computing from the time of the Axum inscription, when Aeizana was styled King of the Homerites and of the Sabæans, it will give us a space of upwards of two centuries for the duration of the superiority of Abyssinia over Arabia, and consequently of its command of the Red Sea, although the Arabian authors allow the Abyssinians to have absolutely ruled by their viceroys over Arabia Felix for no more than seventy-two years.‡ Soon after Hellestheus, or in the latter part of his reign, their power began to decline in Arabia, owing to the desertion of their own troops, who became independent settlers§ there, and to the increasing power of the Persians, who were gaining in this part a decided superiority, and who succeeded at last in driving them from the country, though they molested the coast afterwards by

* Biblioth. N. 3, p m. 2, &c. † Procopius, C. xix. page 60.

‡ Historia Joctanidarum, page 135, 151, and 41.

§ These may be what are often called the Abyssinians in Arabia, which afterwards, confused even Ludolf.

frequent invasions, and kept up their influence in the Red Sea even to a later period than the time of Mahomet; for we find in Abulfeda,* that the King of Abyssinia gave protection to all the refugees who then fled from Arabia, among whom were some of the first families in that country, particularly Gafar, the son of Abu Taleb, in defiance of all the solicitations made to him to give them up. Afterwards, when the Mahomedan dynasty became all-powerful in this quarter of the world, though all their Arabian possessions were taken from them, their commerce and their consequence annihilated, their country invaded, and even their capital itself endangered, yet the Abyssinians remained firm; and alone, of all the nations of the East, successfully continued to defend their faith against the ferocious attacks of the surrounding Mahomedan states. Yet the struggle in which they were engaged was severe indeed; and it is almost certain that they would ultimately, and even shortly, have sunk under it, had not, almost at this last extremity, the Portuguese arrived, after the discovery of the passage round the Cape of Good Hope, to their assistance. This happened in the year of our Lord 1541, when Claudius sat on the throne, who, as well as his father David, to whom he had just succeeded, had been for some years engaged in a defensive war against Mahomet Gragné, King of Adel, one of the most blood-thirsty savages history has recorded. The accession of European troops, as might be expected, soon changed the face of affairs; and after many desperate battles, in which the Portuguese were chiefly engaged, under their brave commander, Diego de Gama, who in enterprize, though

* Abulfeda Muslemiis, Vol. I.

not in success, almost equalled his brother, the Moors were driven back, their king killed, and their armies nearly annihilated; while all hope of resources from the other coast were cut off by the Portuguese fleet, which then rode triumphantly in the Red Sea.

"It has been usual with many to condemn altogether these crusading expeditions; yet, in this instance, the effects resulting from it were in a high degree beneficial to the empire of Abyssinia, which was, in fact, completely saved, by the mode of warfare then introduced, and by the progress in civilization which the natives made under the tuition of the Portuguese, and to which alone is to be attributed the superiority which they have to this day retained above all the nations around them. This superiority has, however, been kept up only by a continual struggle, which gradually has tended to weaken their power, and render their situation every day more and more precarious, so as to make it likely that they may not, without assistance, be able much longer to stand out against the superior numbers of the Galla.

"Much, however, as we may admire the effects resulting from this expedition of the Portuguese, we cannot but condemn the bigotry with which their priests attempted to force the Roman Catholic religion on the Abyssinians, which succeeded only for a short time, merely from the weakness of one of their kings. For they were not content with infringing upon their ancient rites and ceremonies; with altering their fasts, and denying them a participation in the holy supper; with burning their altars, and consecrating new ones; but they were absurd enough, which more particularly incensed the people, to treat them all as pagans or idolaters, by insisting on their re-baptism and the re-ordination of their priests; thus unnecessarily heaping, as their king complains in one of his letters, baptism on baptism, and priesthood on priesthood. To this their Patriarch added the folly, not to give it a worse term, of daring to excommunicate the legitimate sovereign of the country. Such repeated acts of aggression at length brought on them the merited punishment, and the exhausted patience of the Abyssinians gave way to a bitter rancour, which burst forth in the destruction of part of the priests; in the expulsion of the rest; and finally, in the exclusion of all strangers from the country. Yet the gratitude still felt for the services, which, as soldiers, the Portuguese had rendered them, induced the Abyssinians to treat all, but the priests, with kind and continued attention, which cannot be more strongly shewn, than by an extract from a letter, written by Basilides,* when he expelled the fathers from the country.

" ' Lo, our messengers have faithfully delivered to us many things that you said, and various reasons that you urged, when they declared to you our command that you should return to your own country. First, you say, " we did not come of our own accord, but were sent in consequence of repeated letters written to invite us." What! do you still pretend ignorance of the numerous causes, though so clearly laid before you in our former letter, for which we have obliged you to migrate to your own country? why seek you that we should again repeat them? Recollect you not the late fierce disputes between you and the people of Abyssinia, nay, which have always existed, from the contempt in which they have held your rites,

* Ludolf's Commentaries, page 537.

your ceremonies, and your religion; and which have been carried to such a length, that, had not God protected you on high, and the favour of our emperor below, would have prevented your staying, I will not say twenty-two years, but even half a year, in the country. It is needless to describe how many men for this cause have been sacrificed, or how many labours and troubles the late emperor suffered in your cause, since all this must be fresh in your memory. But, in truth, the Emperor finding that this change of religion could by no means stand, himself, as he had first introduced, so he again changed it; returning to the fundamental doctrines of his fathers, which is the rock of the Alexandrian faith; and this he confirmed by his public edicts, so that it may not again be altered from generation to generation. What belongs to the faithful account of those brave Portuguese, whom you have wished to recall to our memory, who, in defence of religion, came into Ethiopia in the time of the Emperor Claudius, we perfectly know that they came for a good cause, and that in the very year they entered the country, peace flowed in like a river, and one people no longer rose against the other. For they did not teach the doctrine of persecution, or assemble together for the purpose of destroying the ancient religion handed down by the fathers and Apostles, nor did they force any one to observe other rites than those which were in public use, but rather fought in the defence of them, to free their country from the hands of a plunderer and a robber, commanding an army too truly Mahommedan. These men are worthy of every praise, and they received their reward from our kings, so that they planted their vines, and tilled their lands in a country, where they had received nothing, not even a foot of land, as an inheritance. And whatsoever they have left, it remains to their children who to this day live among us, upon the bread granted by us, and bequeathed to them by their fathers; nor is there any one who can say to them, What do you here? or, what business have you in this country? since all know that they came for the public good.'

"From these facts it will appear, that although partial heresies and gradual corruptions may have crept into the Abyssinian church, which was the natural consequence of their peculiar and isolated situation, yet they can justly claim the honour, not only of having resisted the open and formidable attacks of the Mahomedans, but likewise the more insidious attacks of the Romish church; as also, in its earlier period, of having resisted the Arian schism, and like the Coptic Greeks, to whom their church is nearly allied, may still consider themselves as adhering to the faith which they first received. At the present moment, however, the nation, with its religion, is fast verging to ruin; the Galla and Mussulmaun tribes around are daily becoming more powerful; and there is reason to fear that, in a short time, the very name of Christ may be lost among them. Some events have lately occurred likely to hasten their fall; namely, the death of their late Aboona Marcus, and the failure of their endeavours to procure another from Egypt. By this, the last tie which bound them to the mother country is cut asunder; divisions among the priests have already ensued; the consequence of which is, that their most holy rites are likely to become objects of derision, from the slovenly manner in which they are performed, and the sacred character of the priesthood to fall into contempt, from the dubious authority by which the priests are now ordained to its duties. To this may be added, that the little learning they have among them will soon be exhausted, being cut off entirely from the source that supplied it.

"It appears to me, that these circumstances call for the serious consideration of all Christians; for when so much trouble is taken, and so much expence incurred, in endeavouring to convert infidels to the faith, might it not be of equal, or more consequence, to give relief to a nation, already professing, generally, the same faith with ourselves, who at so very early a period received the Christian religion, cherished and defended it against its open and secret enemies, and who still maintain it; not pure indeed, but as their established faith; and to prove that they are a people not unworthy of our care, let us refer to what the Jesuits have said of them, at a time indeed when they were friends, but which, as Ludolf well observes, they never afterwards contradicted. In a letter from Fremona they write thus: 'Let it be particularly noted, that although the Abyssinians have fallen into many and great errors concerning the faith, yet excepting these, it is certain that they still preserve that excellent disposition, and good natural inclination to all virtue and piety, which, from of old, they have possessed; and that even now, according to what the Fathers have seen, much fewer sins are found among them, than in many other Christian countries in Europe, where our holy faith remains as yet uncorrupted.'* Again: 'They give with much willingness alms to the poor, and treat strangers with hospitality.

"The Patriarch Alphonso Mendez also thus

* Ludolf's Com. 194. Ex Epistolis de annis 1607-8.

speaks of them, and his authority is of great weight, considering that he retained these opinions after his expulsion from the country: 'They are wonderfully affected towards divine matters; and have, from the time of the Apostles, amid the darkness of the Gentiles and Mahomedans, kept alive a spark of faith and of the Christian name. Above all things they are inclined to reading and knowledge. As to what belongs to their disposition, I can generally say, that the more noble and cultivated among them do not yield to Europeans, and that those of the lower order far excel our common people; so that there is scarcely one among them who can be called stupid and foolish,' &c.

"Poncet, whose fidelity as a traveller must ever rank him high, (p. 242) bears witness to their piety, attention to the duties of their religion, and their singular moderation with regard to others differing from them in point of doctrine. In addition to these, my own observations tend fully to corroborate what I have here quoted. I believe them in general to be possessed of most excellent inclinations, with great quickness of understanding, and an anxious desire of improvement; and I am fully persuaded that there is no part of the world where European influence might be exerted with more beneficial effects than in Abyssinia."

HENRY SALT.

CHAPTER VII.

Observations upon the probable result of Mr. Salt's Visit to Abyssinia.—Views of Bonaparté respecting the Red Sea.—Means of obviating them.—Present State of Abyssinia.—Advantages which she may derive from a Connection with England.—Exports from Abyssinia.—Probable increase of Trade with the Interior of Africa.—Accounts from Pearce since Mr. Salt's departure.—Death of Mr. Carter.—Proceedings in England, and Mr. Salt's departure for Abyssinia.—Observations on Mr. Bruce's Map of Abyssinia and Chart of the Red Sea.

THE direct communication between Abyssinia and other Christian nations may be considered as again opened, by the visit of Mr. Salt to Tigré, after having been closed since the year 1558, when Soolimaun Basha conquered Massowah, Dhalac, and Suakin, and deprived the Abyssinians of all access to the Red Sea. In the course of the two succeeding centuries, the power of the Turks declined more rapidly than that of their Christian opponents; and the want of provision from the more fertile table land, induced the possessors of the ports in the Tehama, to permit a trade to be carried on through their country, though they loaded it with the most oppressive duties.

Within the last fifty years the Turkish power has been little felt, even at Jiddah, and at Massowah not at all. The Nayib, unable by himself, to resist his more powerful neighbours, prudently yielded to the stream, and used some degree of moderation in his demands of duty on the goods imported into his harbour. Still the gate of Habesh was considered by him as his; and he probably entertained a hope, that he might one day have it again in his power, to raise the duties to an height, that would liberate him from his pecuniary embarrassments. Abyssinia itself was torn by intestine broils, and Arabia was more violently convulsed by the civil and religious hostilities of the Wahabee, against the followers of Mohammed. That, under such circumstances, the Nayib should behold with alarm the arrival of a powerful nation in his seas, is not surprising. He must have been immediately conscious that he was at their mercy; and he must have suspected that they would be attached to his opponents, who professed the same religion, and whose country produced those articles of trade, of which his own was totally destitute. The Banians also, who saw plainly that a direct trade, between the British and Abyssinians, would put an end to their vast profits collected both at Mocha and Massowah, added to the alarms of the Nayib, by the invention of a thousand idle tales, and probably used even bribery to excite his brothers and his Ascari, to force him into those measures of perverseness and hostility, which were, I am convinced, contrary to the natural bent of his inclination.

These palliative circumstances would induce me to wish, that the Nayib should be considered as a friendly power by the British, if any permanent arrangement should take place between them and the Abyssinians. The Island of Valentia might, with little difficulty, be procured from him, as it only yields him a revenue of a few dollars; and all disputes respecting duties would be at an end, as the goods might pass direct to Zulla, the village mentioned by Mr. Salt, as situated on the sea shore, in the territory of the Hazorta, and which is the same I before alluded to, as being at the bottom of Annesley Bay. This amicable arrangement might prevent the immediate ruin of Massowah as an independent state; but, as its power is merely artificial, and depends only on the troops it is able to maintain, by the revenues arising from trade, its gradual decay is inevitable, and it will soon either become a barren sand, or sink again into the empire of Abyssinia.

Independently of those occasions on which they were guided by their intolerant zeal, the Portuguese have generally acted in Asia, in a manner that other nations might copy with advantage; and I trust that Great Britain, which has succeeded to their power in India, will also follow their example in cultivating a connexion with Abyssinia. The crescent of Mohammed no longer, indeed, forebodes danger to Christianity, but the equally terrible eagles of regenerated France threaten universal destruction to ancient establishments; and it is apparent, that their formidable master has more particularly formed his plans against the eastern Empire of England. It was for the furtherance of this object that Egypt was conquered; and it is a continuation of the same policy, which has brought Seid Mohammed Akil to the Red Sea, to cultivate the friendship of the Arab powers. Abyssinia is of infinitely more importance than these; but fortunately, France knew not that Abyssinia was accessible. She conceived that, by securing the Island of Camaran, with its excellent harbour, its fresh water, fuel, and provisions, she could form an establishment which would command the passage of the Red Sea; and that, by entering into alliance with the Wahabee, whose offers had been slighted by the Bombay government, and with the Imaum of Sana, who hated the British name, she should render a continuance in the Red Sea impracticable to any fleet except her own, by cutting off all the necessary supplies. These expectations are completely annihilated by the discovery of Dhalac, Valentia, and the other islands, and by the connection with Abyssinia, whence the whole British navy might be supplied with provisions. It is a source of infinite gratification to me, that the conduct of Mr. Salt, Captain Rudland, and Mr. Carter, was such, during their visit to the Ras, as not only to conciliate his esteem, but to leave a favourable impression of the national character throughout the country. It is therefore completely in our power to form that connexion with Abyssinia, which will for ever shut out the French; but if we should neglect the opportunity, they will profit by our folly, as they have done in Arabia; and the discoveries made on the eastern shore of Africa, instead of becoming a national benefit to the English, will only tend to increase the already too preponderating power of her implacable adversary.

The advantages that Abyssinia will obtain, by a direct communication with European nations, are incalculable. At present, she is suffering under all those evils that attend an inefficient government. Her king is invariably in the power of one ambitious subject or another; and receiving no revenue but from the nearly independent governors of his different provinces, he is incapable of securing a sufficient force to sustain himself, or of preventing them from wasting the resources of the country in mutual hostility. The consequence is, that the Abyssinian of Tigré fights against the Abyssinian of Begemder; and the Galla, taking advantage of their enmity, is gradually incroaching upon both. The Governors of the different provinces are obliged to diminish the revenue by grants to their followers, who, conscious that they have no legal right to the sovereignty they assume, would otherwise desert them, and seek for a more munificent master. The result of these measures has been shown in Mr. Salt's account of Tigré, the revenue of which seems to have been reduced to about one half of what it was in the time of Ras Michael Suhul.

Still the power of Tigré preponderates; and the Ras Welleta Selassê is vested with the constitutional, but immoderate, power of prime minister. This is fortunate, as through that province alone can any communication be carried on, at present, with Gondar. An alliance with the British would supply him with arms, ammunition, and revenue, and thereby enable him to liberate his sovereign from the oppression in which he is now held, and to place in his hands the sceptre of the finest part of Africa. Abyssinia under one master would resume her ancient consequence; her people would cultivate their fields in tranquillity; and her eternal enemies, the Galla, would soon be driven, by the possessors of fire arms, into their own country. Nor would they, in all probability, long remain unsubdued. It is only difficult to fix in imagination the boundaries of the Abyssinian empire. By an alliance with Great Britain, the Christian sovereign of these realms would be rendered independent of his refractory chiefs, and those repeated insurrections and revolutions, in which the people invariably suffer equally with the monarch, would at once be at an end. He would have time to learn from his allies the arts of peace; and the amiable character of the Abyssinian, which Mr. Salt has drawn from his own experience, and the accounts of former writers, gives a fair promise, that a little labour would produce incalculably good effects. I cannot but flatter myself that Christianity, in its more pure forms, if offered to their acceptance with caution and moderation, would meet with a favourable reception; at any rate, the improvements in arts and sciences, which follow trade, would ameliorate the national character, and assist in bringing back their own religion to a degree of purity, which it has long lost. This would be greatly furthered, if the English were to use their influence with the Archbishop of Alexandria, to send out as Aboona, a man of education and talent. Hitherto no man, who had any expectation of rising in his native country, would accept an office which was, in fact, a perpetual banishment, to live among a barbarous people, with whose language he was unacquainted, and who were surrounded by Mussulmauns, cutting off all communication with other Christians, and gradually incroaching on their territories. An Aboona, going out under British protection, would have far other ideas; and the fairer side of the picture would tempt an ambitious man to accept an office which would give him the supreme control over a numerous clergy, among a people highly reverencing his sacred character, in a healthy, fertile, and pleasant country, where, in affluence and rank, the sovereign alone could be considered as his superior.

The restoring of tranquillity to the provinces, and a legal trade to the united empire, would also have the very important effect of putting an end to the exportation of slaves, which here is not only liable to the same objections as on the western coast of Africa, but to the still greater one, that the slaves exported are Christians, and that they are carried into Arabia, where they inevitably lose, not only their liberty, but their religion.

England has felt it an imperious duty, to step forward and liberate the unfortunate Negroes from slavery; and I trust the similarly hard fate of many thousands of Christians, requires only to be known, to call equally for her active exertions in their favour; especially as those exertions will, in every point of view, be beneficial to herself.

The trade, that is at present carried on by Abyssinia with Arabia is of considerable importance. From Jidda, she receives many articles of European manufacture, embroidered velvets, arms, glass ware, silks, and satins; from Mocha, India goods of every quality, from fine muslins and kincaubs to the coarse Surat cloths, which are used as articles of apparel in a great part of Africa. On these, as I have before observed, when speaking of the fair of Berbera, the Banians demand what profit they please; the Imaum has a duty of ten per cent. on the export and import, and the Nayib another to the same amount. To the consumer, therefore, the article comes above one hundred per cent. dearer than it would do, were the importation direct: yet the value of the goods imported at Massowah is estimated at four hundred thousand dollars per annum, exclusively of raw cotton, which is purchased by the Abyssinians for their dresses, from an ignorance of the way of cleaning it, although the plant grows in their own country. Of this article there is, at present, so great a scarcity, that Hadjee Hassan declared to me, three ship loads would find a ready market. It is worth half a dollar per rottol, though the usual price is only fifty dollars per bahar. No merchant of Massowah has a capital sufficiently large to enable him to purchase a cargo, nor even a large proportion of a cargo; but experience has given rise to a confidence in the honour of the dealers, which justifies the captain of a ship in trusting his property in their hands. Hadjee Hassan or Currum Chund would receive the cargo, and consider themselves responsible for the whole; they would dispose of it in smaller quantities to people whom they knew worthy of credit, who would depart with it into the interior, and would, in about three months, return with the value in gold and other articles. A large ship belonging to the Nawaub of Surat arrived a few years ago, and actually disposed of her cargo in the above manner, but the captain was obliged to pay five hundred dollars for anchorage, and Hadjee Hassan is of opinion, that the Nayib, in defiance of his engagements, would insist on receiving the same from any British merchant vessel which should trade in his country. Till a regular arrangement shall have been made with Abyssinia, it is an object hardly worth dispute.

The only articles of value which Abyssinia produces, are gold and ivory: but of these the quantity is sufficient to pay for the manufactures at present imported; and the former would increase, as the trade should extend to the eastward into those countries, where it is produced in the greatest abundance. A considerable caravan arrives at Massowah in February, which brings down slaves, mules, cattle, honey, zibet, ivory, rhinoceros horns, and a few trifling articles. The balance of trade is in favour of Abyssinia, so that several thousand dollars find their way there, but are hardly considered as a current coin. Two hundred wakeas of gold were brought down by the last caravan; and Currum Chund informed me, that, at a month's notice, he could procure two thousand, to pay for goods that were desirable. The wakea, or ounce of gold, costs at Massowah eleven dollars and three quarters, which, at two shillings and six-pence the dollar, is two pounds twelve shillings and tenpence halfpenny. One pound of this gold contains as follows:

	oz.	dwt.	gr.
Pure gold	9	6	6
Fine silver	2	10	0
Copper -	0	3	18
	12	0	0

An ounce of this gold is worth *2l.* 18*s.* 4*d.* if pure gold be worth *4l.* which gives a profit of *5s.* $5\frac{1}{2}$*d.* per ounce. The following estimate will shew the value of the ivory trade.

		£	s.	d.
1000 frassel of $32\frac{1}{2}$lbs. each, at $22\frac{1}{2}$ dollars per frassel, at 4*s.* 6*d.* -	dollars	22,500		
		£5062	10	0
Agent's commission on the purchase, 5 per cent. - - - - - -		253	2	6
Shipping, and delivery on board, 1 per cent. - - - - -		50	12	6
Cost on board		£5366	5	0
Freight on $14\frac{1}{2}$ tons, at *10l.* per ton, being an article that might be stowed among the interstices of the cargo - - - - -		145	0	0
Insurance on *5900l.* at 6 per cent. not being subject to average -		354	0	0
Policy duty $\frac{1}{4}$ per cent. - - -		14	15	0

	£	s.	d.
Interest on 5366*l.* first cost, for nine months, at the rate of 5 per cent. per annum - - - - -	201	4	6
Cost in London	£6081	4	6
Landing charges 1 per cent - -	60	16	3
Duty on 32,500lbs. viz. 290cwt. 0qr. 20lb. at 2*l.* 7*s.* per cwt. 27½ per cent. and 8*l.* 6*s.* 8*d.* per cent.	926	5	6
Cost in the warehouse	£7068	6	3

This quantity would produce 8125*l.* at the average price of 28*l.* per cwt. or about 15*l.* per cent. profit if for home consumption; but if for exportation, there is a drawback of 1*l.* 4*s.* 5*d.* per cwt. On the larger teeth the profit would be greater.

Basha Abdallah, in his letter to me, which was delivered by Mr. Salt, strongly expresses his wish of becoming better acquainted with the English, and hopes that, if any farther intercourse should take place, he may be mentioned as a person desirous of being employed by them. His conduct to Mr. Salt and his companions was so liberal, and so free from those prejudices which usually narrow the mind of a Mussulmaun, that I feel it a duty to make public these expressions of his regard. Indeed it must be the interest of every trader to Abyssinia, to attach to his interest a man, who has more property and more power in that country, than any other of his religion, and whose agent, Hadjee Hassan, is the most respectable merchant in Massowah.

Should a national arrangement ever take place, and Valentia become, as I am convinced it then would, the great emporium of trade with Eastern Africa, many buildings must be erected in that island, that the barter trade may be conducted under the superintendance of proper officers, and the goods warehoused till they shall be wanted. It would then be unnecessary to send them up into the interior on credit; the native merchant would bring his gold and ivory to the spot, and take in exchange, the manufactures of Europe and India: a traffic which the want of specie renders necessary. That the consumption of Abyssinia would increase greatly, even in the first instance, by the reduction of price, and the temptation of many novel and useful articles, which the ingenuity of our merchants would soon discover, appears to me certain; but I look forward to still greater advantages, from the facility which that country will afford of supplying Kordofan, Darfur, and the other neighbouring states, with every article, at a much lower price than they have hitherto obtained them, either from Egypt, by the way of the caravan, direct to Sennaar, or by the more circuitous rout of Mecca, Jidda, and Suakin, or from India, by Mocha, and the fair of Berbera.

Cobbé, the capital of Darfur, is at a distance of nine hundred miles from Siout in Egypt, whence the caravans enter the desert. It is only necessary to read the interesting travels of my friend Mr. Browne to perceive the many, and almost insurmountable difficulties, under which the merchants labour, who pass from one country to the other. On the other hand, Cobbé is only distant from Gondar between five and six hundred miles, and the greater part of the road is through a fertile country, instead of the inhospitable deserts of the interior of Africa. Even in the present disturbed state of Abyssinia, caravans still make their way to Darfur unattacked, and find a safer passage than among the predatory tribes of wandering Arabs.

It is so difficult to turn a trade from its ancient channel into a new course, that I should be less confident of the success of my speculation, were it not that the circumstances of the present times are particularly favourable. Egypt, whence all supplies were formerly received, is divided into two kingdoms, the upper half under the Beys, and the lower under the Turkish Pacha, without any commercial communication being permitted between them. The Mamelukés are consequently themselves distressed for all European articles, and have none to spare for the supply of Cobbé or Sennaar. The pilgrimage to Mecca having been also put an end to by the conquests of the Wahabee, the great concourse of merchants, who, in fact, only made religion a cloak for their commercial speculations, has ceased to visit Arabia, and my friend Emir Mohammed of Suakin, has been obliged to obtain from Mocha, those supplies, which he formerly drew from Jidda. But the difficulties of a longer voyage within the prevalence of the violent monsoons, add greatly to the expence, which was before considerable, from the necessity of passing over a dreary desert for nearly six hundred miles, in order to reach Sennaar; so that there can be little doubt, that the European and Indian goods might find their way through Abyssinia to the same place, incumbered with much less charge for carriage, as well as for prime cost. The old sources of trade being completely annihilated, it is evident that new ones must be sought. Great Britain, as producing every suitable article within her own dominions, and being mistress of the sea, has certainly the power to succeed to Egypt, in the advantage of supplying the interior of Africa; but I feel it a duty again to repeat, that if she do not, the French will; for I know from undoubted authority, that the attention of the Government of the Isle of France has been already called to my discoveries.

In order that the reader's attention may not be called back to Abyssinia, which I am now about to leave, I think it right in this place to lay before them the information which I have received since my return to England.

On the arrival of Captain Court at Mocha, he found a letter lying there from Pearce, dated on the 28th of February 1806, giving an account of his continuing in good health, and rapidly advancing in acquiring the language. He was in high favour with the Ras, who had placed him immediately under the protection of Ozoro Tishai, with whom he lived, and who treated him with the utmost kindness, assuring him that she would, at any time that he might wish, send him to her friends at Gondar; whither she intended to retire herself, if any thing should happen to the Ras. The divisions still continued between the provinces; but the Ras had made a truce with the Galla, and had assembled all his forces to march to Gondar, and liberate the King from the controul of Guxo, who is supposed to be a Mussulmaun. The governors of several provinces had joined the Ras on this occasion, and the clergy universally supported him. This letter Devajé attempted to suppress; but fortunately it had been delivered to him in the presence of another person, who gave notice of it to Captain Court. This was evidently the result of those suspicions with which the inhabitants of Mocha, and particularly the Banians, beheld my attempts to cultivate an intercourse with Abyssinia, which they justly considered as likely to annihilate their monopoly.

It was with the deepest regret that I learned, by the same letter, the untimely end of Mr. Carter. Mr. Pringle having departed from Mocha, in consequence of orders from the government of India, who had considered any connection with Arabia as useless and expensive, Mr. Carter proceeded to Aden, where he was induced, by an American Captain, Orme, who commanded the ship Essex, to accept the situation of supercargo in her, and go up to Loheia to procure a cargo of coffee. Seid Mohammed Akil having procured permission to fortify the island of Camaran, had rapidly advanced in his settlement, but kept his ship with him. Off the island he fell in with the Essex, and, professing great regard for the Americans, offered his services, not only to show them the way to Loheia, but also to send on board some of his slaves, to assist the small crew of the Essex in working her up to that place. In an unfortunate hour the offer was accepted; and the same night the twenty Caffres murdered the Captain, Mr. Carter, and every white man on board, and threw their bodies into the sea. In the morning the Seid came on board, took out the treasure, amounting, as it is said, to one hundred and twenty thousand dollars, and then scuttled the ship. Poor Carter's body was washed on shore, where it was found, and recognised by Hyder, who was my servant during my first voyage in the Red Sea. He mentioned it to Captain Court; in consequence of which the Dola threatened his life; and so alarmed him, that he escaped on board the Panther with a determination to leave his wife and children, his parents and country, and depart for India. This was not what the Dola wished: he therefore applied to Devajé, who offered himself as security, that Hyder should not be injured either in his person or property. This was considered as satisfactory by the lad; but Captain Court thought it advisible to state, in the strongest terms, to the Dola, that he considered Hyder as entitled to the protection of the British Government, and that they would certainly resent any injury offered to him, for having reported the cruel fate of a British subject. Seid Mahommed Akil, I fear, still exists unpunished; and as a retreat is ever open to him in Arabia, there are but little hopes of his meeting with the fate he merits. The Mornington and Ternate were sent from Bombay to seize him, and to drive him and his allies the French from Camaran; but he had timely intelligence of their destination, and quitted the island, leaving but little vestige of his having been there.

It was some counterbalance to this unfortunate intelligence, that very favourable accounts were received from Massowah by Emir Mohammed, who met Captain Court at Mocha. The Nayib, roused at length, by the repeated insults he received from his brothers, applied to Jidda for assistance, and, having obtained some troops, attacked and conquered the Dola of Arkeko, reducing his turbulent followers to subjection. The Sirdar of the Ascari was sent to Jidda, and the Nayib requested Emir Mohammed to assure me, through Devajé, that he was a real friend of the English; that he never had sanctioned the demands of his brothers; and that he had seen, with unfeigned regret, the hostilities which had taken place, and of which I shall give an account in the following chapter. He expressed a hope that every thing would be forgotten, and that the English would trust to his friendship, now that he had recovered the power of protecting them. This intelligence, I own, gave me the greatest satisfaction, as I ever felt a regard for the

Nayib, in defiance of the disapprobation, which the timidity of his conduct could not but frequently excite.

On my arrival in England, I felt it my duty to wait on the Court of Directors of the East India Company, and to lay a memorial before them, stating my ideas on the trade of the Red Sea, on the advantages which might be derived from it, and the establishment which would be necessary to carry it on. It seems probable that they differed from me in opinion on all these points, for America has been permitted to carry on the trade uninterruptedly, to the exclusion of the British. The President and Board of Trade listened, however, with considerable attention to the application of Messrs. Jacob, who, being convinced by the statement which I have laid before the public, were anxious to send a vessel direct to the Red Sea. I have understood that the Chairman of the India Company, on being applied to, to know whether they intended to put any part of my plan into execution, declared they did not, believing it to be chimerical, and founded on no real knowledge of trade. Such being their opinion and intentions, they could not reasonably object to granting a license to Mr. Jacob, to trade direct to Abyssinia, who accordingly obtained one, though fettered with many restrictions. He laid in a cargo according to my recommendation; and I feel confident, that the result of his voyage will be a conviction in every impartial mind, that my statements have been correct, and that the India Company have for many years neglected the most profitable trade within their charter.

The letter which Mr. Salt brought down for the King of Great Britain from the Emperor of Abyssinia, had been delivered by me to Lord Spencer, when Secretary of State for the Home Department, and by him laid before his Majesty, together with the present of fine Habesh cloth. On its being definitively settled that Mr. Jacob's ship should go to the Red Sea, I stated all these circumstances to Mr. Canning, the Secretary of State for Foreign Affairs, and represented the advantages which, I thought, would result from conciliating the King of Abyssinia, and thereby excluding the French from obtaining any influence in that part of Africa. I also took the liberty of suggesting, that as his Majesty had been pleased to receive the letter, and accept the presents of the Emperor, it was but decorous, that some notice should be taken of them, when an English vessel was going direct to his ports.

Insignificant as the Abyssinian monarch might appear, the haughty sovereigns of Spain had corresponded with them at different times, and had treated them as equals, by giving them the title of Brother. James the First of England had written to his contemporary; and his letter, on this occasion, furnished a precedent for his Majesty's. The wishes of Ayto Galoo, the King, were, that a person should be sent to him who understood raising water, a medical man, and a carpenter. It was, unfortunately, not possible to comply with these requests by a merchant vessel; but I was directed by Mr. Canning, to prepare such presents as I thought would be acceptable, and would, at the same time, serve as specimens of our finer manufactures.

It being considered decorous that his Majesty's letter should be delivered by a gentleman sent for that purpose, I pointed out Mr. Salt, as by far the most eligible person, from his having been already in the country, from his amiable manners, and respectable character. He was accordingly appointed; and I made all possible haste in preparing the presents, which consisted of arms after the fashion of the country, but ornamented with gold and jewels; satins, cut glass, painted glass, jewelry, and fine British muslins, in the whole amounting to about fourteen hundred pounds; a sum inconsiderable in England, but which, when laid out in the above articles, has procured an assortment of novelties, that will surpass all which the court of Abyssinia has beheld since the time of Yasous the Great, and will certainly impress the present monarch with a favourable idea of the power and riches of his new ally.

A more useful and highly important part of the presents was, two pieces of curricle artillery, with the harness complete, one hundred and fifty rounds of ball, and a quantity of powder. If these should reach Antalow in safety, the Ras will be able to march from one end of Habesh to the other without meeting an enemy, as may be easily supposed, for a cannon has not been seen there since the time of the Portuguese; and the sound alone would terrify a race of people, who have never heard a louder explosion than that of a matchlock. That the connection with England may tend to tranquillize Abyssinia, and restore it to its former independence, is the wish nearest my heart, and that such a result is now likely to take place seems extremely probable. The communication being once opened, I trust that it will never be closed by the baneful spirit of monopoly, and that the interests of individuals will not be permitted to interfere with the truly British objects of greatly increasing our foreign trade, and at the same time benefiting, in every point of view, an amiable, oppressed, and, what ought to have still greater weight, a Christian country. Mr. Salt departed for Abyssinia the end of February 1809.

I have annexed to my Chart of the Red Sea, a map of that part of Abyssinia, through which Mr. Salt travelled, as laid down by himself, chiefly from the daily observations of the bearings of his journey. I have also felt it my duty to mark the track of Mr. Bruce, as given by himself. The very great difference between the two, requires that I should state to the public some circumstances, which may enable them to judge of the credit safely to be given to the observations of Mr. Salt. Fortunately for him, Taranta, which lies close to Dixan, is visible from Massowah. The bearings of it were frequently taken by Captain Court, and perfectly confirmed the important fact, that it lay nearly due south from that place. This being so, it is impossible that Dixan should be where Mr. Bruce has placed it; indeed his own journal is as irreconcileable with his map, as Mr. Salt's. He states, in his fifth Book, Chapter III. that on leaving Arkeko, he took his road southward; that it continued in that direction till he had passed Shillokeeb, when he turned westward through the mountains, and reached Hamhama. Unfortunately, he does not afterwards state his bearings, but reached Zila, at the foot of the mountain, where he finds a rivulet, and declares that he had constantly ascended since he left Arkeko.

According to the map it would nevertheless appear, that he had constantly, from his leaving Arkeko, moved to the eastward, till he reached Zila, on the sea shore, when he had again turned to the west. I need not observe, that his having constantly ascended during a journey of fifty miles, is incompatible with Zila's being on the sea shore, and having a current of fresh water running near it; nor can his own description of the neighbourhood be reconciled with a maritime position. Mr. Bruce's journal, and his own chart, differ also in a very unaccountable manner; Dixan is given by him, at the end of the chapter above mentioned, as lying in latitude 14° 57′ 55″ north, and longitude 40° 7′ 30″ east of Greenwich; but in the chart it is laid down in latitude 15° 9′ north, and longitude 39° 52′ east. It would be difficult to account for this contradiction, but it is unnecessary, both positions being due S. E. of Massowah, and therefore equally erroneous; for in that direction Ras Gedam rises to a height, that precludes the possibility of Taranta, or even a much more lofty mountain, being seen at a distance of sixty miles; but to the westward of Gedam, a valley runs all the way to the foot of Taranta, along which this object may be seen from Massowah, in, as I have before stated, a southerly direction.

The real situation of Dixan is, I conceive, sufficiently ascertained to be where Mr. Salt has placed it, which I am the more anxious to put beyond controversy, as it is impossible to have equal evidence of the authenticity of the other parts of his map, and which also widely differ from Bruce, particularly in the distance between Adowa and Fremona. If, however, in the track from Massowah to Dixan Mr. Salt is proved to be accurate, I conceive that he is fairly intitled to credit, and that credit may be still more strongly corroborated by the positive evidence of gross errors in those by whom he is contradicted. In addition to the facts above stated respecting Zila, as laid down by Mr. Bruce on the sea shore, the account of Fremona, as given by him, will enable any person to judge of the credit due to his geographical observations.

In the map, Fremona is laid down as distant thirty miles from Adowa, yet he himself visited it from that place, as he says, on the 10th of January; which seems to imply, that it was not so far off, as to require a journey to reach it, and he describes it as situated "in the middle of a large plain, on the opposite side of which stands Adowa," which, if the distance be correct in the map would make the plain extend for sixty miles in each situation! although in the beginning of the same chapter he observes, that "Adowa is situated on the declivity of a hill, on the west side of a small plain, surrounded every where by mountains." In these two descriptions we again discover contradictions, which I believe no advocate of Mr. Bruce will attempt to reconcile; but till it is done, I conceive I have a right to claim, that his assertions shall not be adduced as throwing any doubt on the accuracy of Mr. Salt's observations. Antalow, the limit of Mr. Salt's journey, is placed in 12° 45′, from several observations made by Mr. Carter, which was confirmed by the daily distances, and by a computation of the journeys made by the Jesuits from the Red Sea, whose route was at right angles with Mr. Salt's, but which perfectly accorded with it.

As it is possible that the accuracy of Mr. Bruce's latitudes in the Red Sea may be adduced as a ground for giving a greater degree of credit to him than to Mr. Salt, I think it right to add a copy of those latitudes; in another line the latitudes as given by Mr. Niebuhr; and in a third, the real positions that have been since ascertained.

	Mr. Bruce.	Niebuhr.	The True.
	° ′ ″	° ′	° ′ ″
1 Jibbel Zumrud	25 3 0 N	—	23 48
2 Macowar	24 2 0	—	20 38
3 Ras Mahommed.	27 54	27 54	
4 Yambo	24 3 35	24 5	
5 Djar	23 36	23 36	
6 El Horma	23 30 30		
7 Rabac	22 46	22 45	
8 Jidda	21 28	21 28	
9 Konfodah	19 7	19 7	
10 Ras Heli	18 36	18 36	
11 Kotumbal	17 57	17 57	
12 Djezan	16 45	16 45	
13 Duime	16 12 5		
14 Camaran	15 39	—	{15° 30′ N. extrem. 15 18 S. extrem.
15 Bab-el-Mandeb	12 39 26	12 38	12 39
16 Crab Island	13 2 45		
17 Loheia	15 40 52	15 42	15 42
18 Ras Asab	13 5		
19 Fusht	15 59 43		
20 Jibbel Tier	15 38	—	15 35
21 The Bank	15 28 15		
22 Racka Garbia	15 31 30		
23 Dobelew	15 42 22	—	15 42
24 Ras Shouke	15 27 30		15 33
25 Ras Antalow	15 54 30	—	15 50
26 Massowah	15 35 5	—	15 35 30

To any person accustomed to nautical observations, it must appear most singular, that seven of the above latitudes should agree precisely with those given by Mr. Niebuhr, though the one was travelling by land, and the other by sea. Even with the excellent instruments which are now used, it frequently occurs that, in the same vessel, in calculations made on the same data, the result differs by a mile; how astonishing, then, must it appear, that with different instruments, and certainly more imperfect ones, the result should here be the same. It is equally extraordinary that Mr. Bruce, in a coasting voyage, should invariably find it convenient to ascertain the latitude of those places only in Arabia, which Mr. Niebuhr had before given to the public, in a work which Mr. Bruce refers to in speaking of Mocha, while he passes over many others of equal, if not greater importance. Rabac differs from Mr. Niebuhr's latitude only one mile; Yambo only a little more; Duime is not mentioned by him, nor El Horma; but the former Mr. Bruce owns he passed in the night, and does not even pretend to have made any observation to ascertain it; and the latter he describes as being close to Muftura, which is laid down by Niebuhr in 23° 5′ N.

Could any doubt remain after this, that Mr. Bruce had copied the latitudes in Arabia from Mr. Niebuhr, it would be removed by the publication of the original observations of the former gentleman, in the second edition of his travels, in which the situation of not one of these places appears to have to been even attempted to be ascertained, except Yambo, Jidda, and Loheia.

Of the remaining observations, those respecting Jibbel Zumrud, Macowar, and Camaran, are completely false; of the island eastward of Dhalac we have no opportunity of judging; and of those below Loheia it appears probable he was not the author, nor indeed is it probable that he actually made the voyage he has described to the Straits of Bab-el-Mandeb. This has been placed in so strong a light, by the anonymous author whom I have before mentioned, that I shall give his observations nearly in his own words.*

" On the 27th of July, 1769, Mr. Bruce, according to his travels, sailed from Loheia in the Red Sea, upon a voyage of observation to the Straits of Babel-el-Mandeb, from which he returned

* Monthly Magazine, December, 1807, p. 549.

to Loheia on the 6th of August. On the 5th of August, however, the very day preceding his return, two observations taken at Loheia appear in his journals, (vol. vii. p. 356,) in which there is no notice whatever of three observations taken during the voyage, and inserted in his travels (vol. ii. p. 208, 217). Mr. Bruce, in a letter given in the appendix to the second edition of his travels, says, "We left Jidda the beginning of July. The beginning of August we arrived at Loheia. Here we waited till the end of September, when we embarked on board a small boat from Massoua. In this second voyage across the Red Sea," (vol. i. p. 279,) yet this would have been the third, had he really performed an intermediate voyage from Loheia to the Straits of Babel-el-Mandeb. The editor justly observes, that "Mr. Bruce does not mention here his southern excursion;" (ibid) but takes no notice of the equally striking fact that Luigi Balugani is also silent, who was employed to keep the journals from their leaving Cossier; and the first is, "Viagio di Cossair, à Jimbo, ed à Gidda; 2° Viagio di Gedda â Locheia; 3° Viagio di Locheia â Massoua," &c. containing the routes and distances measured by time; but not the least intimation is given of the pretended voyage to the Straits of Bab-el-Mandel (vol. i. p. 364)."

He adds in a note, "the voyage to the Straits was probably taken from a ship's journal, obtained through the same channel, and adapted by Mr. Bruce to his own adventures. As a proof of this, the observations are made with a Hadley's sextant or ship's quadrant, as it is called, an instrument which Mr. Bruce did not possess, but which would have been far more useful and portable than the large and unwieldy French quadrant which he carried to Abyssinia. That quadrant is fit only for a very able astronomer; Mr. Blunt, the optician, who had this instrument to repair, informs me that it was so incorrect in its formation, that a good observation could not be taken with it; but Bruce was enraged, when told by Herschel, that Hadley's sextant would have served every purpose much better. His fictitious voyage, to the Straits of Bab-el-Mandeb, was probably suggested by Irwin's voyage up the Red Sea, published in 1780."

Facts stated by an anonymous author, certainly ought to be received with caution; but no name is requisite to give weight to his arguments, particularly if they be equally conclusive with those I have just quoted, and which I think, prove incontrovertibly that Mr. Bruce never was below Loheia.

The chart of the Red Sea by Monsieur De La Rochette, was re-published by Mr. Faden 1781, with many additions by Colonel Capper. This, though far superior to the chart of Monsieur D'Apres de Manevillette, had many errors, by all of which Mr. Bruce was misled in his fictitious voyage. He reaches the Island of Rasab at five in the morning, passes Camaran at six, at twelve passes a low round island, and at one is off Cape Israel. This, according to Faden's chart, is perfectly correct, but unfortunately Camaran is nearer to Loheia than Rasab: and instead of its being a six hour's voyage from Camaran to Cape Israel, they are not above three miles asunder. The anchoring on a shoal, which lies immediately east of the north fort of Mocha, where no shoal actually is; his description of Perim, as five miles long and two miles broad, when in fact it is only three miles long and not one broad; his assertion, that the narrow Straits of Bab-el-Mandeb are two leagues wide, when in fact they are not one; his calling the islands in the great Straits low, when in fact they are lofty rocks; and his account of the chain of hills along the African shore, when the hills are single, and at a great distance from each other, are errors which a person who had visited the spot, could never have fallen into. Crab Island had been named and placed in the chart of 1780, by De La Rochette; from its position, it is probably designed for one of the small islands near Ras Firmah; but is given of a much greater size than it really is.

It is a consolation to my feelings as an Englishman, that this voyage is so evidently a fiction; and the real friends of Mr. Bruce ought also to rejoice, that the opprobrium is removed from his character, of having wantonly attempted to murder the innocent Samaulies, at Assab Bay, and having probably succeeded in his attempt.

No one, I trust, will assert, that the idea of his being on the very spot where the crew of the Elgin were murdered, and the more improbable conjecture of his being in company with the very people who had committed the murder, could be any justification of the firing on thirty men, who quietly kept at a distance, according to his orders, while some of their party placed themselves, with unlimited confidence, in his power, answered his questions, and endeavoured to supply his wants. I cannot, in his own story, find the least grounds for his suspicions or alarm; and even if the tale itself be a romance, the feelings which he professes must have been his own. This is too strongly exemplified by many of his former adventures; first at Thebes,* where he declares that "he was resolved upon revenge;" and accordingly not only fired his own gun where the voices were heard, but also "took his servant's blunderbuss, and dis-

* Dhalac, Vol. I. p. 135.

charged it where he heard a howl" (4to. Vol. i. p. 199). Secondly, when he applied to Ibrahim, Sheik, of the Ababdé, and received a promise from him that "Hassan should not die in his bed." And, thirdly, at Traitor's Island, when he hesitated whether he should not shoot the unfortunate Arabian, who did not understand his language, and fear to trust himself with a stranger, who was better armed than himself.

It is greatly to be lamented, that a man of Mr Bruce's talents should have given way to a vanity, which has caused his book to partake more of romance than reality. The difficulties which opposed his progress must have been sufficiently great to have obtained for him the just praise of perseverance and courage; and the country through which he travelled, afforded novelty that must have excited the interest of every reader; yet as it is, he has so mixed truth with falsehood, that it is impossible to separate them; and the deceptions which have been exposed, where any traveller has followed him, give but too much reason to fear, that the same would be the result, were a person of veracity to visit Ras-el-Feel, or Sennaar.

The translation which he has given of the chronicles of Axum, is interesting, and I believe faithful: but the account of the descent from Solomon is now proved to be false, by the inscription at Axum; the theories of the victories of Ptolemy fall before the same evidence; and his worship of the Dog-star at this capital of Abyssinia, vanishes, with the proofs adduced by him of the many remains of their pedestals and statues.

If Mr. Bruce be proved incorrect by the discoveries of Mr. Salt, and the ascertaining that the reliques of ancient magnificence at Axum have no resemblance to Egyptian architecture, it is satisfactory to find, that the authenticity of the author of the Periplûs is confirmed in an equal degree, by the proof that, so late as the reign of Aeizanas, a king, who spoke Greek, remained on the throne of Zoskales, and ruled over the same country.

It is also satisfactory to know, that the Christians of Abyssinia, however they may have fallen from the purity of the religion they profess, are not the monsters of cruelty and depravity which Mr. Bruce describes them, and that their country is not so inaccessible to Europeans as he represents, I fear, for the purpose of preventing others from following his steps, conscious, as he must have been, that his own exposure would be the inevitable consequence of an impartial person's comparing his romantic account, with the real habits, manners, and condition of the Abyssinians.

CHAPTER VIII.

Departure from Massowah.—Danger of the Panther during a heavy gale from the North.—Narrow escape from Shipwreck, with the loss of all the Anchors, on Lightning Shoal.—Return to Massowah.—Disputes with the Ascari.—Hostilities with the Inhabitants of Arkeko.—Voyage to Jidda.—Transactions there.

NOVEMBER 14, 1805.—With the land breeze we left Massowah; but it was five before we reached Dohool, in consequence of light airs and calms. We went to the east side of the island, where we were obliged to anchor at the distance of a mile from the shore on a hard sand, there being only a few feet water when closer in. We let go in a quarter less than three, and wore out only half a cable, yet the vessel struck in two and a half: this was owing to the swell, for we did not draw so much. After hauling off, we put out our stream anchor ahead, and lay very comfortably all night.

The next day Captain Court and Mr. Salt went on shore: they found the island in a wretched state for want of rain: the sheep and cattle were half starved, but there was plenty of water in a natural tank. This the people willingly let us have, but it was with the greatest difficulty they could be made to bring down their sheep and sell them; always starting some new objection, that the owner was not there, or that they did not know how to sell them. The truth seemed to be, that they had formerly received instructions from the Nayib, when Captain Court was last there, not to supply him, and they did not know whether they ought now to let us have them. By inquiries we learned that their subjection to the Nayib was merely nominal; they pay him nothing, but when they visit Massowah, they take a present of sheep or goats. He appoints one of themselves to an office something like Dola, who is changed annually. We weighed at three, and stood round the south end of the island.

November 19.—Till yesterday morning the winds, though hanging to the N. of E. enabled us to make tolerable way. The sky then began to darken, and the wind to freshen. We were running along by a new chain of islands off Port Mornington, which we named Duncan's islands, in compliment to the benevolent Governor of Bombay. Between these we understood were several passages out into the open channel.

We were within fifteen miles of the track of the Panther in 1795, when the wind freshened so much from the northward, as to oblige us to lie to, in hopes of keeping our own till morning. We had on our former voyage run along at a small distance from the main land, and thought all was clear between that and the islands. We drifted gradually to the S. W. keeping the lead going. It lightened very violently, and about eleven, by a very vivid flash, Captain Court discovered we were drifting on a shoal, and at the same time the soundings were fourteen fathom. We instantly let go the small bower—veered out two-thirds of a cable, and let go the best bower under foot. We now thought ourselves safe, and Captain Court congratulated me on the Panther's riding so well at anchor as to leave us nothing to fear, though it blew very fresh, and a very heavy sea was rolling in. However, before one, we parted from the small bower; we instantly veered out the whole of the best bower cable, and dropped the sheet anchor with a new cable, and veered out thirty fathom. At three our alarms were greatly increased by the best bower's parting. Our only hopes now were that the sheet anchor, the whole cable of which we veered out, would hold till morning; our little stream anchor could otherwise be of no use. The swell and wind were greatly increased, so as to render rest impossible; nor could our dead lights protect the cabin from the sea, which worked in by the violent pitching of the vessel. Morning at length came, but not to bring us comfort. We discovered that we were in a kind of bay, formed by two reefs, and a sandy island at the bottom. It was so hazy that we could not distinguish whether or no there might be a small passage on either side of it. The sea broke so as to render it difficult at a distance to distinguish it from breakers. There was every reason to fear that no passage existed, as the ground under us was extremely foul. Should our anchor part, it was, as the wind then blew, impossible to weather either point of the reef; we could therefore only trust to Providence. I own, that the dread of such another night as the last; the certainty that if the cable did part in the night, nothing could save us all from destruction; the little hopes that it could hold in foul ground with an increasing swell and an undiminished gale, made me almost wish that ere night our anxiety might be ended. There was then a hope, though a faint one, that our lives might be saved, though the vessel were lost, by at once laying her ashore on the island which we then supposed to be one of Wellesley's islands. At a quarter past twelve the expected event took place. Captain Court was cool and collected. He said to me, taking my hand, alas! poor Panther! nothing can save you—we must now be all broken together, and do the best we can for each other. He accordingly determined to run for the island. The men, both white and black, were active and steady.

The sails were set most expeditiously, and we all looked with an anxious heart to our approaching danger. We attempted first to weather the western reef; but finding that impossible, wore round for the sandy island. At that moment Captain Court perceived the wind had changed a point, and instantly determined to try and weather the eastern reef, which before the change was impossible.

In a heavy gale, which carried us gunwale under water, we had the felicity of passing the point of the reef, on which the sea broke tremendously, at the distance of only two cables length. Our first sensations were those of joy for our escape, and gratitude to that almighty Being, who had so wonderfully preserved us, in the moment of otherwise certain destruction, by the change of wind. When, however, we became a little calm, other and very painful feelings obtruded themselves. We had lost four anchors and cables; we had only a spare one left in the hold without a stock. To venture to Jidda in such a situation was impossible—to run into Port Mornington without an anchor was equally so. Our first idea was to return to Massowah, and send a dow to Mocha to communicate our distress, and try to procure relief.

Our fresh provisions were nearly out, and our salt store was so small as to render the using them a very serious business. We therefore put before the wind—as we advanced, and found it did not diminish, we had hopes it might, as on a former occasion, carry us all the way to Mocha—we therefore determined to make a trial.

We called the whole crew aft, and returning them our thanks for their excellent behaviour, I gave them a present of one hundred dollars from myself, and Captain Court the same sum in the name of the Company.

We saw poor Unus Barilla when we lay to, but never afterwards. We could not but be extremely alarmed for his safety, though we greatly hoped he bore away for the south, in which case he had nothing to fear. We found by the observation at twelve, that this shoal, which we called Lightning shoal, from its having been seen in a vivid flash, is ten miles north of Port Mornington, and lies detached. There was a pilot's mark on one end of it.

As we reached Massowah the wind died away. We did not wish to lose time in going in, so only lay to, and in the morning fired three guns as a signal for Unus, in case he should be there. As we saw nothing of him, we were more alarmed for his safety.

November 25.—As we advanced southward, we found the wind came round against us, so that we only reached the latitude of Amphila on the 24th. —At night it came on to blow so heavy a gale from the S. E. with a violent swell, that we were obliged to lay to. On consultation between Captain Court, Lieutenant Hardy, and myself, on the deck, about eleven, it was deemed advisable to recur to our first intention, and bear away for Massowah;

but instead of entering that narrow harbour, to anchor in Arkeko bay, where there is an excellent mud bottom. We decided on this from the idea that it was improbable we could make Mocha against the heavy gales, which we now found blew between us and that place, and that we were losing time in not communicating our distress by a dow, in case we should be ultimately driven back. Yesterday morning, as we passed Valentia, we perceived Mr. Pringle's boat coming out to us: we bore up, and soon joined her. We found that Devajé had supposed her return to be contrary to Mr. Pringle's orders, and had therefore directed Abdulcauder again to set off for Massowah, where he had arrived eight days ago; that he had no money, and had applied to Currum Chund, who refused to advance him a dollar; that the Nayib had then ordered him to quit Massowah harbour, or he would put him in prison. We anchored in eleven fathom, mud, with our only anchor, about eight o'clock.

November 26.—I sent Andrew on shore in the jolly boat; Mr. Crawfurd had orders to permit no other man to land. I directed him to see Hadje Hassan, to tell him, and the Nayib, if at Massowah, that I was come to enquire for Unus, and to beg to know if he had heard any thing of him; also to desire Hadje Hassan to procure us fresh provisions and water, and to come on board himself. In the evening they returned. The Nayib was at Arkeko, so that Hadje Hassan could not come, but said he had sent to the Nayib for permission, and would be off in the morning with fresh provision. Some people had pelted Mr. Crawfurd, and one of the custom-house people had asked him what business the boat had there, and ordered him never to come again. He brought off the naqueda of a dow belonging to Hodeida, who offered to carry letters for us to that place, and accompany Mr. Pringle's long boat. We agreed for thirty dollars, and that he should send his brother thence with the letters by land, who should receive twenty dollars on his reaching Mocha. We gave Abdulcauder money to buy provisions for Mr. Pringle's people; and as the Nayib's conduct was so hostile, to keep peace, if possible. I did not again send our boat on shore with Andrew, but ordered him into the long boat, in which there were none but natives.

Andrew and the boat returned early in the morning, with the information that none of them had been permitted to land, and that the naqueda of the dow had been seized for coming to us without permission. Andrew was given to understand, that the Sirdar of the Ascari had heard of our distress, and that he flattered himself with the hope, that by cutting off all supplies of fresh provisions and water, and by preventing any person from carrying our letters to Mocha, he should oblige us to surrender to him the large property which the Panther was supposed to contain.

I immediately consulted with Captain Court on the measures which it would be proper to pursue. The imprisoning of the Hodeida naqueda, and the seizing his boat, were evidently acts of open hostility, as the man was in our immediate service, and, consequently, under our protection. It was therefore determined that we should endeavour to liberate him, by securing one of the market boats, which passed daily from Arkeko to Massowah; for this purpose the cutter and long boat were manned with Europeans, and armed.

The boats appeared about two on their return, when Mr. Denton gave chase in the cutter, having received positive orders from Captain Court not to fire on them, unless hostilities were commenced by them, and on no account to land, either on the island or main. On perceiving the cutter approach, the natives made for the nearest shore, when Mr. Denton, finding he could not overtake them, inconsiderately fired two guns over their heads to bring them to; which they could not understand as a signal, but considered as an act of hostility. The first boat reached the shore, and the men escaped; but a second boat was behind and might have been secured; unfortunately, however, Mr. Denton, unmindful of his orders, and hurried on by the heat of youth, landed and followed the crew who had fled towards Arkeko.

We could easily distinguish from the ship, that the Ascari were running out from Arkeko, and that our people were advancing to meet them. Extremely alarmed for their safety, lest they should be overpowered by numbers, we immediately sent off Mr. Crawfurd in the long-boat, armed with wall pieces, to support them. A firing soon began between the parties on shore; when, in hopes to alarm the enemy, we fired several shot towards them, which reached the shore, but not the town, having hoisted the signal for the boats to return. This was at length obeyed, and we were rejoiced to find that not one man had been wounded belonging to the Panther, nor have I reason to suppose that much mischief was done to the subjects of the Nayib, for the boat's crew, in their impatience to land, had leaped into the water, and spoiled their cartridges, consequently, had they been pursued, many must have been cut off.

I was extremely mortified at this failure of our attempt to secure a hostage for our naqueda, and a medium of communication with the Nayib, who might possibly be ignorant of the conduct of his people at Massowah. I was also vexed at the apparent inferiority of our party, who might be considered as retiring defeated, which would diminish greatly that awe which the idea of the power of our fire arms had inspired. I was unwilling to leave them, even for a day, under this impression; but it was thought advisable to run to Valentia, and secure a supply of fresh provisions, before the inhabitants of that place could hear of hostilities, and then to return and prevent all communication between Massowah and Arkeko, till the Ascari, and their Sirdar, were brought to their senses, and delivered up to us our naqueda, and liberated his dow.

November 28.—We began to get up our anchor at three in the morning, but the land wind was so stiff, that it was daylight before we were under sail; and I was even, at one time, afraid that we should have lost our solitary anchor. The day was remarkably calm till evening, when a strong breeze set in from the eastward, and obliged us to give up all hopes of weathering the northern point of Valentia, and reaching the anchorage off the village, where alone we could procure provisions.

Captain Court wished much to push on to Port Mornington, where fresh provisions were equally procurable, and if the favourable breeze should continue, to run every hazard of being reduced to short allowance, and try to reach Jidda. The chance of this banished from our minds all ideas of resentment, and we trusted, that when their hopes of our being obliged to surrender were removed from the minds of the Ascari by our departure, all motives for detaining the naqueda and his dow would be at an end, and he would of course obtain his liberty. As Mr. Pringle's boatmen could, without our aid, procure nothing, and as they were too ignorant to navigate the boat to Mocha with European sails, we determined to take them in tow to Jidda, and send them thence in a larger vessel. It was dark when we once again bore away for Port Mornington, leaving our enemies at Massowah to make what conjectures they pleased on our sudden disappearance.

The wind came round on the 29th to the southward which determined us to lose no time at Port Mornington, but take advantage of so favourable a wind. We lay to last night, and early this morning bore away for the straits, leaving Lightning Shoal to the eastward, and making directly for Tella Tella. We kept the lead constantly going, and found, in general, a good mud bottom, with plenty of water; but occasionally, very sudden overfalls. To the eastward were several islands, forming a continuation of Duncan's Islands, between which and Tella we passed into the open sea, through a channel about seven miles wide. The ascertaining of this passage was a satisfactory conclusion of our discoveries, as it was alone necessary to prove the great value of Port Mornington. It is now certain, that that noble harbour is accessible from the main sea, and that no danger awaits the navigation, except near Lightning Shoal, which, when once known is easily avoided.

It would have given me great satisfaction to have surveyed the coast from Macouar to Cosseir, which, I believe, has been totally neglected since the time of Don Juan de Castro. If the ruins of Berenice Pancrysos actually exists in Foul Bay, a visit to them would be particularly interesting; and in the harbour mentioned by the Portuguese admiral, as lying between 24° and 26° north, the port of Myos Hormos may probably be looked for with success by some future navigator. The crazy state of the Panther limited our ambition to arriving in safety at Suez. The coast above mentioned is of little importance to navigators, and the headlands are already laid down with sufficient accuracy.

After quitting the straits on the 1st of December, we were tormented by strong gales from the N. E. and N. W. On the night of the 3d, after a heavy fall of rain for two hours, it blew so fresh as to oblige us to lie under our bare poles, while the swell was so great as to preclude the possibility of keeping in our cots. The morning of the 4th brought with it but little consolation, for the gale continued; and the idea of the northerly winds prevailing at this season, excited a well grounded alarm as to our future voyage. It moderated towards evening, and only left a very heavy swell. On the 5th, at night, it was less; and on the 6th, it was calm, which gave us some chance of a fair wind. We were not forty miles from Jidda, and therefore hoped that a moderate breeze might take us there in the course of the next day. High land was visible to the eastward, in the morning.

At length we reached the harbour of Jidda, after having been repeatedly baffled by adverse winds and currents. On the 7th it continued calm till night, when the squalis recommenced with rain, and obliged us to go under double reefed topsails. It blew, however, from the south, and in the morning of the 8th gratified us with a sight of Jidda. The current, which ran at the rate of fifteen miles in twenty-four hours, towards the W. by N. had taken us to the north of the entrance about three miles; and this short distance we were unable to make in the course of the day, as it blew very fresh. We ran in close to the reef, and fired signal guns, but no pilot came off. In the night we had again very heavy squalls with rain, which obliged us to take in all our sails. The wind came round to the northward in time to bring us off Jidda on the morning of the 9th. On repeating our signals, a pilot came off, and by one o'clock we were safely at anchor. I do not know that my mind was ever relieved from so great a load as on this occasion. It seemed as if we were ever to be baffled when near a port where assistance could be procured. Our situation was such as to have excited real anxiety. We had no rice nor fresh provisions, and of salt meat or water, not a sufficient quantity to last us a month. I instantly sent Mr. Crawfurd on shore with the letters I received from Seid Dond, to the Vizier, and to Ibrahim Jelani. I desired him to state our wants, and to say that, if agreeable, I would pay a visit to the Vizier on the morrow. He returned in the evening with a very civil answer, that the Vizier would be happy to see me at ten o'clock, and that I might depend on being received with every compliment due to my rank. Jelani said he would do his best to serve us; but that at present every thing was very scarce at Jidda, as the Wahabee were in great force all round the town.

We were delighted to perceive that Unus's little dow was here in perfect safety; he came on board, and informed us that he had been obliged, in the gale, to throw his anchors overboard but had escaped into Port Mornington, whence he sailed for this place.

December 10.—At ten I left the Panther attended by Captain Court, Captain Rudland, and Mr. Salt. The landing-place was in front of the

Vizier's residence. Several of his officers were in waiting to receive me, very handsomely dressed in scarlet English broad cloth, lined with yellow satin. A double line of soldiers reached to the door, and extended to the hall of audience. At the foot of the stairs I was met by the Vizier's secretary, who made his compliments, and preceded me. The whole of the troops made a very respectable appearance. The palace is pleasantly situated close to the sea, which here forms an inlet, and is nearly surrounded by the walls. The audience chamber had two large windows opposite to each other, about twelve feet long by four wide, and raised a foot from the ground: in both of these were seats covered with carpets, and rich cushions. On the southern were seated three Arabs, who rose up on my entrance, and made their salaams, which I returned. An old fashioned large elbow chair was placed for me opposite to the centre of the window: it was covered with very rich cushions. Plain English chairs were placed for the other gentlemen. Soon afterwards the Vizier, who was a stupid looking eunuch, entered, with his train borne, and seated himself in one corner of the window. The usual compliments having passed, he lamented our misfortunes, and assured us of every possible assistance from him in retrieving them; but regretted he could do but little, from the scarcity which prevailed. I requested his permission to employ Ibrahim Jelani, and consult with him on the subject. He said he would immediately send to him, and I might go there on my departure from him. Coffee was presented to us, but none of the Mussulmauns took any, as it was Ramadan. He asked respecting the business at Massowah, which he had heard of from the Samaulies of Abdulcauder's boat. I found great difficulty in explaining this, and indeed every thing else, as Andrew's Arabic was of a low cast, and the Vizier spoke the best. He, however, at length understood it, and expressed great resentment at the Nayib's conduct to a friend of the Sheriffe, and the Sultaun of Roum. He said he should write very severely to him, and would make him give a strict account. Rose-water sherbet was presented, which was excellent, with embroidered napkins to wipe our mouths. He expressed a wish that I would write to the Sheriffe now that I was here. I said I had no secretary for Arabic, nor did I understand it. He replied that his secretary should write any thing I pleased. I said, I would wait on him in a more private way, and would talk the subject over with him; at length it was settled I should return from Jelani's. Rose water was now given, and our faces perfumed; after which we took our leave. He did not quit his seat. We were preceded by the same people in scarlet cloaks, who kept off the crowd. The common people were very civil; and as we passed through the bazar, the elder tradesmen made their salaams. Ibrahim Jelani met me at the door, and conducted me to the place of honour at the corner of the court, seating himself next me. The gentlemen were on chairs facing us. I began by telling him, that I understood he had ever been the friend of the English, and that therefore I should open all our wants to him, and consult with him without reserve. He assured me of his extreme anxiety to render us every service in his power. He promised some rice, hoped he could procure two anchors, and as for water, he said there was plenty that was tolerable, and he would let us have ten casks of good. Sheep were not to be bought, goats were eight and nine dollars a piece, and a bullock thirty or forty. Fish, however, he said, might be had in sufficient quantity, through the medium of the Emir Bahar, to supply our ship's crew. This was a great object to us. He offered us the use of his house during our stay; we therefore settled to remain a few hours with him on the morrow, and arrange every thing. I now asked him whether any presents would expedite our supplies. He said, yes; one hundred dollars to the slaves of the Vizier. This could only be an excuse for the master; we therefore agreed to give it, and requested him to advance the money, which he instantly did. I then enquired what I ought to give to the different people. He directed thirty dollars to the Ascari, ten to the gunner, five to the Derwan, and five to the chief man who walked before me. I now spoke of the attempt of the French to seize Camaran, and Seid Akil's assisting them. He said they only waited for his arrival here to seize his ship: that he had here twenty-five thousand dollars and a house. He said the Vizier knew of the business. As he understood Andrew's Arabic, I explained to him the whole Massowah transaction, and requested him to tell it fully to the Vizier. He said he would go with us and do so. We had coffee and sherbet, but he, also, took none. No one was at the Vizier's but his secretary. We had a long conversation on many subjects. He wished much for powder from us, but I positively assured him we had none to spare. The Massowah transaction roused his wrath, and he absolutely squeaked with indignation, declaring he would seize all the dows that arrived thence till they accounted for their misconduct; and this I have no doubt he will do, happy in any pretence to plunder their property. My letter was written and signed: heaven knows the contents, nor did I much care what they were. I was told it contained an account of my arrival, compliments, the transactions at Massowah, and at Camaran, a wish to receive any commands of his for India or Egypt, and a request of assistance for the ship. I promised to stay eight days for an answer, if, in the mean time, they would regularly supply us with fresh provisions or fish, which they undertook to do. They wished to know if I thought any arms or ammunition might be procured in India; I said I thought there might, and offered my best services in making the application, which were willingly accepted. The Vizier and Jelani both urged very strongly that we should leave them four of our men, who understood the use of great guns. He declared that they should not be tempted to change their religion, and that they should be allowed a house, and be made as comfortable as the place would admit. I assured him we had none to spare, and that even if we had, it was contrary to our laws to dispose of any Englishman who belonged to a ship of war, or to any other, without his own consent, and, that I was sure none of my men wished to leave me. I gave strict injunctions to my servant and Andrew, on my return, not to mention this to any one, as I was by no means so confident as I pretended to be. I promised to send an officer with my seal to put it to the Sheriffe's letter; which I did when we reached the ship at five o'clock, heartily tired with the day's work, though every thing had been most satisfactorily conducted, and we had reason to hope a relief from most of our distresses.

December 11.—I went on shore about ten, landed at the Vizier's quay, and proceeded directly to Jelani. He was waiting to receive me at the door. We more fully detailed our wants. He promised twenty-five bags of rice, which was half the quantity we wanted, and said he would try for the rest. He seemed to speak more hesitatingly on the subject of our supplies; complained of the great scarcity, and told us at once no fire wood was to be had. At length it turned out that we ought to make a present to the Vizier. I was vexed, but Captain Court and I agreed there was no remedy. Our distresses were such, as to make our obtaining supplies not a matter of convenience, but of necessity. We therefore determined to comply with a good grace. Of my originally large stock of Asiatic articles, I had nothing left but a few shawls, which I knew I should want in Egypt; I therefore requested Jelani to procure the proper articles, which he said ought to be to the amount of three hundred dollars; he immediately produced from his stores some pieces of kincaub and muslin, which would not have cost one hundred and fifty rupees in Bombay, but which were here considered as worth the former sum. These were immediately sent to the Vizier, and every thing was again well. We had heard that there was camel's flesh in the bazar: but that the Vizier should be spoken to, that he might order us a regular supply of forty pounds a day. Though wood was not to be purchased, yet it might be fetched by water in two days: Unus should have a person to attend, and shew him the place. The fishermen should be ordered to stop at the ship as they returned, and offer us what they had. He however informed us, that, in consequence of the siege, a large fish, was, on shore, worth a dollar. He gave us two water melons and some radishes. declaring that there were no other people on earth to whom he would have parted with them He showed us all his sabres, some of which were very fine: they were all Persian, but some had been lengthened in Egypt at both ends, so as to give the Mameluke point, which cuts both ways. One was watered in straight lines instead of curves: this he valued at one thousand dollars, and declared that the Capitan Pacha himself had not so fine a one. He had also a large stock of guns and pistols.

He sent for his little daughter to us; she was extremely fair; and he took off her cap, that we might see her hair was quite brown. He himself is tolerably fair, short and fat, with a black beard. His grandfather was the first Mussulmaun of the family. He told us that his family were Mograbis, inhabitants of Barbary, opposite to Gibraltar, which they still call Jibbel Tier. Several of his relations were there, and one uncle who was as white as any of us. The room we were received in was flagged, and open at top.—The house was three stories high: at the first floor a curtain was placed, which could be drawn horizontally across. It was open, and permitted us to see the range of latticed windows handsomely carved, which we soon perceived belonged to his Zenana. Several ladies were looking through the holes, but at length they lifted up the window. I was playing at chess with Jelani, whose back was towards them, and only ventured to look up, when I perceived his eyes and those of his attendants were fixed on the board. When my eyes met their's they smiled, and turned their heads a little on one side, but did not attempt to move. They were as fair as Europeans, had black hair, eyes, and eyebrows. Their lips were of a most beautiful vermillion: some were so young, that I think they must have been his daughters. Fatima is by one of his wives, who is fair, and was probably one of those we saw. He has a son by a slave, who is very black, but none by his wives. At the opposite end of the room, from which we entered, was a raised room of smaller dimensions, separated partly by a rail; to this was an ascent of two steps. It was covered with a carpet, and had cushions on three sides: on the right, by the rail, was his seat, upon which his box and writing materials were placed: at the end of this room was a store room, where he kept his money, swords, and other valuables. We were seated as on the first day, in the open room, which had a range of benches on the right and left, covered with green cloth and cushions. I was seated in the left corner from the entrance, on a cloth with a gold border, as a mark of distinction.

The houses in Jidda are far superior to those at Mocha. They are built of large blocks of very fine madrapore. The doorways are handsomely arched, and covered with fret work ornaments, carved in the stone, not put on in plaister: the zig zag, so prevalent in the Saxon arch, was the most common. The windows are numerous and large. I could not but be struck with the resemblance which exists between these arches, and those in our cathedrals; some were pointed like the Gothic, including three semicircular windows; others, particularly those which were over the doors, were flat like the Saxon, and retired one within another, till the inner one was sufficiently small to receive the door, which is never large. Jidda is a new town; but these excellent houses are probably formed after the model of the more ancient habitations of Mecca. If so, the architecture we call Gothic, existed in Arabia, long before it was known in Europe. The streets are very narrow, which is an advantage in a tropical country, as they are consequently shaded during most part of the day. The palace is very pleasantly situated on the water's edge. The upper story, which we did not enter, seems to contain some excellent rooms, particularly one which terminates a wing running to the west. It is open by balconies to that point, and to the north and south. The custom-house faces the sea, and is a handsome, lofty building. The ground rises from the sea, and gives the town a much better appearance than Mocha, though it is not so long. The sea also washes its walls at both ends, and is close to the houses in the middle; this adds greatly to the effect. The bazar was well filled, though it was Ramadan, with plenty of wheat, pulse, dates, figs, raisins, and bread. The latter was in small cakes, but very good. Jelani gave us some of a finer sort, but it was a little perfumed with carraway seed. Mr. Salt asked for a hookah, and got an excellent one. Captain Court went to see the anchors they proposed for us, but both turned out to be miserable dow grapnels. We had seen one in the water near shore, but could not learn to whom it belonged. They at one time said it was the Vizier's, but that he would not part with it, unless we gave him powder in exchange; this we positively refused. A cable they undertook to make for us. We staid till nearly four. He began then to despair, and gave us a hint to be gone, by producing rose water. We departed, but without our interpreter Andrew, who was gone with the washerman.

I again spoke to Jelani about Seid Akil's ships. He had changed his note. He said he did not believe they were French ships, or that the French had any thing to do with them. He told me the

Pacha of Jidda was coming down in a dow, and was expected soon. We looked at the anchor as we came back to the ship, and found it was a tolerable stream anchor.

December 12.—Captain Court went on shore to see what was to be got: he secured one very good grapnel of three hundred weight. They asked why I did not come, and were told that I was unwell. We got our camel's flesh, which was good, and plenty of excellent fish, though dear. Yesterday evening two dows came in from Cosseir with sheep and grain. We bought fifteen of the former for six dollars each, and were offered the same number at the same price in the morning; but on sending for them we learned they had been all sent on shore. The selling them to us was a trick of the naqueda's. Jelani was very urgent to buy some pistols. The Captain told him there were none on board except common ones—that I indeed had one pair, but those I wanted for my own protection. He begged at least he might be permitted to see them. The Vizier sent to request the Doctor would visit some of his slaves, who had been wounded by the Wahabee.

December 13.—All the party, except myself and Captain Rudland, went on shore. Mr. Macgie had a great many patients, but the slaves were not to be seen, though he went to the palace twice, because the Vizier was asleep. A great many questions were asked about me: why I had been to India, as I was neither an admiral, a general, nor a governor? and what was to be the consequence now I was on my return home? To all this they got very unsatisfactory replies; curiosity they knew nothing about; and it would have been very difficult to persuade them that pleasure brought me so far from home.

In the morning the Emir Bahar came off with an answer from the Sheriffe to my letter. Andrew being on shore, we had no one to translate it; he therefore left it, and said he would come again the next day.

December 15.—The Emir Bahar came off according to his promise, and read the Sheriffe's letter, which Andrew contrived to explain tolerably well. It contained the usual Asiatic compliments, and expressed his satisfaction, that his Vizier had received me in a manner becoming my rank, which he would have done himself had he been at Jidda. He regretted that he had not the power to punish the Nayib, for Massowah was not his port, but belonged to the Sultaun of Roum. He assured me of his being "all as one with the English," and that he would write to Sheriffe Hamood of Abou Arish, not to permit the French to have a settlement on Camaran. I presented the Emir Bahar with a piece of embroidered muslin for a turban, and gave his servant five dollars.

I went afterwards on shore, with Mr. Salt and Captain Rudland, to Jelani's where I again met the Emir Bahar. I complained that we had only received ten casks of water, but was informed that sixteen more were gone off. I next spoke about rice, but could only obtain an equivocal answer, and at length Jelani plainly confessed, that the present we had made to that officer, was not considered by him as sufficiently handsome. We were at his mercy, and I was therefore obliged to promise an addition of a piece of kincaub, if he continued his exertions in our favour. Every thing was now right; twenty-five more bags of rice, a quantity of dol, a boat load of fuel, without sending for it, and as much water as possible was now promised. I tried hard to obtain two large pigs, which I had seen at the Vizier's gate, as being very improper inhabitants of so holy a town, but in vain, for they said the smell of them did their horses good.

I now produced my pair of pistols, which Jelani had requested to see; they were plain, but double-barreled, with gold touch-holes and pans. He instantly besought me to let him have them, saying they were of no value to me; that there was no danger in passing the desart to Cairo; and that there I could get others. He finished by saying, that, as he should probably never see another Lord here, I ought to give them to him. I was sorry to part with them only because they were of service to defend myself, having before determined to give him a present of more value; but it was in vain I pleaded my journey, against so conclusive an argument as his last, and was obliged at length to submit. The present being ready for the Vizier, my servant staid to present it at four. The Vizier gave him forty dollars. Jelani asked much if there were no other pistols nor guns on board to be bought, but my servant assured him there were not.

December 17.—I went on shore with Mr. Macgie, who was going to see some of the Vizier's slaves, having received a very civil message from that minister, expressing his regret at his not having been awakened on the former occasion; that he had punished his people for their neglect, and ordered the Doctor's immediate admission if he would call again. I went to Jelani, who was not up, though it was past twelve. Mr. Macgie joined me in about an hour, and gave a melancholy account of his patients, who amounted to above one hundred. A few of these had been wounded by the Wahabee, but the greater number were suffering under dreadful ulcers, which they never wash, nor the rags that are over them, but leave them there for months: he urged the necessity of cleanliness, and a frequent change of plaisters, which he taught them how to make and spread. Jelani had formerly procured from us some flints and powder; he now begged some more of the former, which we promised. I spoke again about water, as they did not send off above fifteen casks a day, and yesterday none. He sent to Emir Bahar, who came immediately, and explained, that he could not let us have more than from fifteen to twenty casks of good water per day, as it came from the country; that yesterday the Vizier had taken the water, as he did not know we wanted so much. This is probably true, for when the British fleet was here, the water they procured was very bad, and ours is excellent, which could only be owing to the quantity then required being greater than the actual supply; they therefore took it from the brackish wells. He informed me that a boat was come in with fire wood, and that he would order the whole along side for us to-morrow morning. The camel's flesh went down very well, and we had a plentiful supply of very fine fish. The market yielded dried figs and nuts, we also procured a supply of excellent Egyptian dol. Jelani gave us fine bread; and we bought enough for our men of a coarser sort.

December 19.—In the morning, to our great surprise, the Emir Bahar came on board; it turned out that his only business was to request some flints for the Vizier. I gave him fifty, which were two thirds of what I had left. We had got all our rice, and had we been worth another anchor, should have been once again in a very comfortable situation. The winds were steady to the north, but Ramadan moon ending the next night, a change seemed approaching. In the morning it blew from the east. It changed at noon to N. E. We rode by an anchor made of two guns and our chain, perfectly safe.

December 23.—On the 22d in the evening the new moon was visible, and was saluted by all the guns of the town. We received an invitation from Jelani to feast with him at ten, on the 24th, which we accepted. The Wahabee had kept the town in an alarm every night, and on the 22d sent in an old woman to give them notice they should be there at night. We were again applied to for assistance, and it was proposed, by Jelani, that Captain Court and his crew should head the garrison, march out at night with the guns, and beat up the Wahabee's quarters. This, however, did not meet with our approbation, and we only generally said, we should be happy to do any thing in our power. Neither side seemed fond of fighting. On my asking Jelani what were the numbers of the Wahabee: he replied, "what is the use of talking of numbers; the whole country is Wahabee to Suez." The Wahabee, on the 22d, got possession of the wells, but the next day they were free. The water came but slowly, and during these holidays the people will not work, so that we got none at all. Our cable was making, but not likely to be ready before the end of the month. The weather was very fine and the winds more moderate.

December 24.—Three guns were fired about nine, which, we afterwards learned, were a salute to the Vizier on his leaving the palace to visit Jelani. We went on shore soon afterwards. We found Jelani seated in his inner square, which was much more richly furnished than during Ramadan, the cushions being of satin. When I entered, the commander of the forces was seated in my usual place in the corner; Jelani next to him: I sat on his right, and chairs were placed for the other gentlemen. As soon as the chief departed, Jelani made me take his place. A great number of people came in to congratulate him on the Ede, to each of whom on their entrance was presented sherbet, with an embroidered napkin to wipe their mouths. When he thought any person had staid long enough, the rose water and perfume gave the hint for his departure, which he always took. The people of consequence had hookahs presented to them; Jelani, who was in high good humour, gave me a short account of each as he entered. I was very much amused by the difference of their dresses, which were all very rich in their kind. They varied most in their turbans, but no colour seemed particularly to point out the rank or descent: several were in green who could have no pretensions to a descent from Mohammed, and among them were Jelani's slaves. We saw many Bedowee, and a Moulah from Medina. The under dresses were rich satins or kincaubs; the kelauts, of English broad cloth, or a stuff like camelin: Jelani himself had an under one of silk lined with ermine, and over that, another of black fox skins. All the slaves had new dresses. Jelani told us we ought to pay our compliments to the Vizier, but as the crowd would be very great, we, by his advice, put it off till the morrow. He made an excuse on going out himself to pay some visits, and requested we would consider his house as our own. Tea was served to us in English tea things, it was execrable, and they had brought no milk; we did not drink any, at which they were greatly astonished, supposing it was our favourite beverage. Jelani returned by one o'clock, when an English table was brought, and chairs placed round it. Two

Mussulmauns, besides himself, sat down to table with us. We had bread placed before us all; knives and forks only for our party. The first dish was a soup made of milk, meat, and some kind of acid, which was excellent. They took it out with small horn spoons, and handed it immediately to their mouths; we had ours in small basons. Next came very rich forced-meat balls; then water melons in slices; then meat again, stewed; then pastry, and so alternately sweets and meat to the number of fifteen or sixteen dishes. Only one dish was put on the table at a time, which was so rapidly removed that we were not half an hour at table. We finished with pomegranates, bananas, and sherbet with raisins in it; after which each person turned round and washed his hands over a bason, into which water was poured by a slave who held a white napkin. The dishes were so excellent that I never made a better dinner. We had coffee and rose water when we took our leave. I learned from him that the Arab's first meal is soon after day break, and consists of milk, rice, fruit, sweetmeats, bread, and coffee. We partook of the second; and the third, consisting also of meat and pastry, is after sun set.

The people in general were in new and handsome clothes in the bazar and streets. The coffee houses were now opened and filled: all shops, except those that sold eatables, were shut; in short, every thing wore an air of festivity in despite of the Wahabee.

December 25.—As soon as we had breakfasted we went on shore to pay our compliments to the Vizier. We waited some little time at the door. The Emir Bahar came up, and after salaams, went in. He soon returned, and conducted us to a large open court, at one end of which was an apartment carpeted and elevated, like Jelanis: on each side were long benches covered with crimson satin and rich kincaub cushions. Close to the elevated apartment on the right entrance was the seat of honour, large enough to hold two. It had a covering of wood, and was ornamented with beautiful silk carpeting and cushions. I was seated here, and soon afterwards, the Vizier entered, followed only by his slaves, one of whom bore his train. The Emir Bahar stood the whole time, as did a line of slaves opposite to us. The Vizier wore the dress in which I had before seen him, but all the rest had new and handsome clothes. After the usual compliments had past, he complained of cold, and asked if it was more severe in my country. He seemed in good humour. The conversation soon turned on the sick people, and Mr. Macgie was obliged again to direct what was to be done. He found they had left off his plaister, because the sore appeared to enlarge; and they had by no means obeyed him in the article of cleanliness. Through the medium of the Emir Bahar, who understood Andrew's Arabic better than the Vizier, we again explained every thing, and urged the necessity of cleanliness. He declared that we should be obeyed, but requested permission to send some one on board the ship to learn to make salve, which was willingly complied with. On our entry we had coffee, and afterwards sherbet. These we took without any fear; though our poor friend Unus had come off to request we would not, as we should certainly be poisoned. Unus never having been here before, had not till now heard of the Sheriffe's frequent crimes of this sort. We relied on the fear of our arms, not on his humanity, and therefore laughed at all our friend's warnings. The wind was light, and inclined to be southerly; and the heat, in the sun, so violent as to produce a head-ache. We however all enjoyed our Christmas dinner together, and drank to our friends in England.

December 28.—Yesterday morning a ship was in sight from the mast head. As she fired guns, and had a signal flying for a pilot, we sent one off towards evening, but it was too late for her to come in. This morning we had the pleasure to see her safely at anchor alongside of us. She proved my old friend the Olive, commanded by Captain Loane, who was at Mocha with Captain Sparks, and was loaded with rice and sugar. We had the satisfaction of receiving by him English newspapers down to February, and Bengal news of only two months old: and first heard of Lord Wellesley's departure, and Lord Cornwallis's arrival, and death on the 5th of October last. He brought me a letter from Mr. Maxfield, informing me of his arrival at Bengal, of his having been favourably received by the Marquis, and his expectations that he should be employed to complete the survey of the Red Sea. I had also a short letter from Mr. Graham, who, however, thought there was little chance of its reaching me in Asia. We now learned that the government of Bombay had been most kindly attentive to all our wants, and had actually forwarded every kind of stores to Mocha by the Prince, Captain Young, which was taken up for this purpose only. Mr. Young arrived on the 15th of November at Mocha, and received my letter, and Mr. Pringle's ordering him to follow us to Massowah, but with which he did not choose to comply. Had he done so, he would have met us there after our misfortune on the 18th, would have liberated us from our difficulties, and have enabled us to settle with the Nayib. Captain Loane informed me that Mr. Pringle was recalled, and meant to return in the Prince to Bombay. Unfortunately he had detained every article, and even our letters, under the idea that before this we had reached Suez. Captain Loane supplied our wants so far as lay in his power, by letting us have twelve dozen of wine, some butter, pickles, geese, and biscuit. He also parted with a small stream anchor, which he had over and above his complement. Jelani's uncle and some merchants came on board the Panther in the morning, to request I would introduce them to the British Captain, which I promised to do. They took coffee and sweetmeats. The Emir Bahar was of the party, and a Mussulmaun priest from Constantinople, who laughed at Mr. Salt's drawings, and was persuaded by the rest to have his picture drawn. They were delighted, as the likeness appeared on the paper.

December 29.—By my recommendation, Captain Loane determined to employ Jelani as his broker. On going on shore to introduce him, we met the Emir Bahar and Emir Bazar, who told us that the first visit should be to the Vizier. We accordingly went there, and found him civil and conversable, and afterwards proceeded to Jelani, who promised to do his best to dispose of the cargo.

The Emir Bahar procured me some slaves, who could dive, and procure the Yusser, a species of kerotophyte, which abounds in the harbour of Jidda, and has a most singular effect under water, from its gently waving motion when agitated by the tide. It is of a deep black colour; and although the stem at the base, where it adheres to the madrapore, is not thicker than a quill, yet its slender branches extend to a length of above four feet. It is covered with a brown, glutinous substance, which is evidently composed of millions of animalculæ, proceeding from the small pores in the Yusser, which become visible when they are removed. On being taken up it is flexible, but when dry it becomes very brittle. The divers went down in fourteen fathom, and procured some beautiful specimens of madrapore, which form the shoals of the harbour: One species my divers were very anxious I should touch with my tongue; suspecting a trick, I made them to do it, and soon found by their grimaces, that it stung severely. I was informed that Yusser is found at Yambo of a white colour. I have seen specimens of both kinds nearly an inch in diameter at the base. It is formed into beads by the Arabians, and takes a polish.

December 30.—Captain Court went on shore to settle the accounts. The prices charged were most enormous: for rice ten dollars a bag; for dol the same, though in the bazar it was only eight. The boat load of fire wood was eighty dollars; and about seventy-five butts of water five hundred dollars. The grapnel and the cable supplied by Jelani himself were more reasonable; and some excuse must be made for the distress of a siege, and the real scarcity which existed of some of the articles. The Emir Bahar got his additional present of seventy-five dollars, and we were obliged to give a similar one to the Emir Bazar, as he had sent us two goats and two sheep, which he yesterday took care to inform me were his private gift, and did not belong to the butcher. The camel's flesh was nearly a dollar a pound. The Emir Bahar asked me if I would give him a letter of recommendation to any English that came there: I said I would.

December 31.—By appointment I went on shore, to take my leave of the Vizier. He received me without ceremony, made many excuses for not having been able to supply our wants better, and wished us a good voyage. We had coffee and sherbet, as usual. I spoke of Captain Loane as a friend whom I wished him to serve. He assured me that he would render him every assistance in his power, and that the duties should be moderate, as an inducement to him to come again. Our next visit was to Jelani, whose conduct had been uniformly kind and liberal during our stay. He now very handsomely agreed to take Captain Court's bills on Mocha, for the whole amount of our expences, without charging any interest or exchange.

I gave him letters of recommendation to the Governor-General of India, and the Governor of Bombay, and also left with him a certificate of the liberal treatment we had received from him. I asked him if he wished them to be delivered in private, but he preferred receiving them in the presence of the crowd of merchants, who were assembled to consult about the purchase of Captain Loane's cargo. I parted from him with expressions of regard, and returned to the Panther under the usual salute.

A dow caught fire in the evening and was burnt to the water's edge, in defiance of the active exertions of the Emir Bahar and his people. One unfortunate man was blown in two, by the bursting of a powder tub, and a second had his legs and thighs dreadfully shattered; in this state he was sent off to Mr. Macgie, by the Vizier, with a request that he would do any thing for him that he could, and even, if necessary, cut off his legs: a very extraordinary permission from a Mussulmaun, as, in general, the idea of amputation is abhorred, and its being done by a Christian would be considered as an aggravation of the injury. His case was however hopeless, and therefore Mr. Macgie declined interfering.

CHAPTER IX.

Observations on Jidda.—Its ancient and present state.—Condition of the Slaves.—Decline of the Family of Mohammed.—Account of the Harbour of Jidda, its Trade, and number of vessels employed between it and Egypt.—Departure from Jidda.—Voyage to Suez.—Transactions there.—Arrival of Schech Chedid and the Caravan from Cairo.—Anecdotes of him.—Present state of Suez and its Trade.—Observations on the Passage of the Children of Israel through the Red Sea.

JIDDA owes its celebrity from being the nearest sea port to Mecca, whence it is distant about forty miles. This holy city, being surrounded by a country unproductive in every article necessary for the support of man, has invariably depended on Africa for the supplies that its numerous regular inhabitants, and its still more numerous religious visitants, required. Egypt, fertile in grain, being in the possession of the Turks, the Sultaun used the influence which, in consequence of this circumstance, he thus obtained, to secure to himself a share of the profits of the extensive trade of Jidda. He therefore, regularly appointed a Pacha, who lived in the citadel of Jidda with a Turkish guard, and divided the receipts of the customhouse with the Sheriffe.

While the power of the Sublime Porte continued undiminished, its minister was treated with great respect, for any insult would have been punished by the powerful force which annually accompanied the caravan of pilgrims from Syria; but when Egypt was torn by internal convulsions, when the Pachas of Asia threw off in a great degree, the control of the Porte; and when the Wahabee power arose, and cut off the communication between Constantinople and Mecca, the Sheriffe became disinclined to give half his receipts to a person, whom he no longer feared, but considered as an useless incumbrance. Disputes naturally ensued, which at length ended in open hostilities; and Ghalib, the present sovereign, actually attacked the Pacha in the citadel, nearly destroyed it, and got rid of him by the more secret means of poison. At present no representative of the Protector of the Holy Places, (for so the Sultaun is considered throughout his dominions,) is to be found in Arabia.

Although Ghalib has thus succeeded in securing to himself the revenues of Jidda, he has in reality only contributed to his own more rapid destruction. The Wahabee have taken advantage of the absence of the Turkish troops, whom, from their superiority to their own undisciplined bands, they were unable to oppose, to conquer the holy city, and to besiege Jidda itself. Yambo being free, many supplies are procured from it, and from the islands which lie near it; but unless supported by a Turkish power, Ghalib must at length resign Mecca, Medina, Yambo, and Jidda, to the Wahabee: and indeed it may be doubted, whether it be an object to him to retain them under their present circumstances, when the expence so greatly exceeds the revenue.

Without the walls of these towns, the Sheriffe cannot be considered as having a subject. Every

Arab, who falls within the control of Suud, adopts his religion, and receives permission to plunder those who have not done the same; no victory, therefore, could restore the country to the Sheriffe, who could only retain that proportion which his troops might cover. From the lands, therefore, all revenue is at an end; and the profits of the great fair annually held at Mecca, by the pilgrims who assembled there, much more from mercantile than religious motives, no longer flow into his coffers. The trade of Jidda still yields a small income, not equal, probably, to the expence of defending the place.

Thus situated, Ghalib, when besieged by Suud in Jidda, had determined to fly with his ill gotten treasures to India, and had, for that purpose, deposited them all on board his ships in the harbour. On the retreat of Suud, he carried back a large proportion of them to Mecca, which probably he would now find it difficult to remove; and even his own escape to Jidda, where a considerable sum still remains, under the care of the Vizier, is an attempt of danger, now that the Wahabee cover the country between the two places. In this distress, it would seem that he looks anxiously for the arrival of a new Pacha from Egypt, as the only hope of safety; though he must naturally dread, that the murder of two Pachas may call down the vengeance of their successor. Jelani informed me, that the new Pacha was supposed to have with him two thousand men. A much smaller force would protect Jidda and Mecca, but a much larger would be insufficient to recover the country. I suspect, however, that the Wahabee are much less considered on this occasion than the Sheriffe, and that it is against him, in the first instance, that hostilities will be directed. If the holy places can only be preserved by the Turks, they will naturally be inclined to secure them for themselves, instead of participating in the power of a man, who has already proved himself a secret enemy; and whose repeated murders, and insatiable avarice, have done more to undermine the power of the followers of the Prophet, than all the external attacks of the Wahabee.

The Arab character seems to have declined rapidly in Hedjas; for in 1763, when Niebuhr was at Jidda, a Sheriffe was always Vizier there, because, as he says, no descendant of Mohammed could, in so holy a country, be judged by one of an inferior race. At that time, also, the sovereign of the country, Moosnud, was active, able, victorious, and so rigid an administrator of justice, that it is said a camel might go safely from one end of Hedjas to the other. During the nineteen years that his son has ruled, how totally has every thing been changed? The proud Arabs of Beni Koreish, the descendants of the Prophet, to whom the earth was given, are shut up in four wretched towns, whence they behold their country devastated without the means of saving it; and instead of receiving that respect, which for twelve centuries they have claimed throughout Asia, they are obliged to submit to the mandates of an Abyssinian slave, who has no real merit except valour, but who is recommended to his master by a willingness to commit every crime.

The martial spirit of the Arabians seems to have subsided together with their religious zeal. The larger proportion of their soldiers, and many of their officers, are slaves, purchased from Africa, who fight bravely for their masters, though, from their number, they might at any time render themselves free, now that arms are put into their hands.

A slave in Arabia is by no means an object of compassion; and, were it not that the loss of liberty embitters every enjoyment, he would be in a better situation than in his native country. He is considered as a part of the family of his master, he lives well, is comfortably lodged, and splendidly cloathed. The Mussulmaun law limits his punishment, and enables him to quit his master if he should dislike his situation; for, at the request of a slave, the Cadi will order him to be publicly sold. He may even look up to the highest offices in the state; and his slavery can hardly be felt as a severe degradation, in a country where the despotism of the Sovereign reduces every person to the same level of insignificance and implicit obedience.

The soldiers of the Vizier are in number about one thousand, who are all richly cloathed, and their matchlocks and jambeas highly ornamented with silver. If this be so in the time of the present Sheriffe, is it possible to believe that it was otherwise in the time of his more splendid and more powerful father? Yet Mr. Bruce calls the Vizier's soldiers a parcel of naked blackguards, in his account of his proceedings at Jidda, to which I gave but little credit, knowing that a very different story is told by Captain Thornhill, who, with the other merchants, was obliged to purchase secretly a valuable present for the Vizier, to put an end to the disputes between him and Mr. Bruce respecting the duties on his baggage, which the latter refused to pay.

The Wahabee, who are chiefly cavalry, never wait for the Vizier's infantry, but retire on their approach, and after fatiguing them by a fruitless chase, follow them again to the walls, whence they are obliged to retrace their steps. They seem to choose the night for their attacks, and to place their hopes of success on either setting fire to the town, or starving it into a surrender. The horses feel the blockade most severely, and are the pictures of famine. The Vizier has procured a few from Cosseir, and says, that he expects shortly one hundred and fifty, which, if they arrive, will mount his most active slaves, and enable him to keep the enemy at a distance, till a want of fresh food renders them incapable of service.

The harbour of Jidda is formed by innumerable reefs of madrapore, which extend to about four miles from the shore, leaving many narrow channels between, in which there is a good bottom at from six to twelve fathom, and where the sea is as smooth as glass, when it blows the heaviest gale. The entrance is of course difficult, but the rocks are visible when the sun is behind the vessel, and the native pilots unerringly steer in safety by the eye alone. Even large ships can enter; but for dows it is a most excellent harbour, and the number that even now frequent it, is very great. Sir Home Popham has given an excellent plan of the harbour, which differs but little from those of his predecessors.

An idea has been entertained in England by many able men, that Bonaparte, even with the possession of Egypt, would find it impracticable to reach India, from the want of vessels to convey his troops. My residence at Jidda has fully convinced me that this idea is erroneous; and Jelani gave me some information on the subject, which I think conclusive. He assured me, that the trade of Cossier, Suez, Jidda, and Yambo, would at any time supply a sufficiency of vessels to convey ten thousand men; and added, as a proof, that there were at that moment forty dows, either at Suez, or on their way thither, to bring down the Pacha and his followers, which would carry from fifty to one hundred and fifty men each. There would be no necessity for large supplies of water or provisions; for the wind being favourable during nine months of the year, they might then run down with such rapidity to Loheia, as to find every night a place where these articles would be procurable. Thence to Mocha, if the wind should be adverse, they might go by land; and at the latter place vessels, under American colours, might be assembled, sufficient for their conveyance to India, without exciting a suspicion in the British, who would consider them as coming for the usual supplies of coffee and gums.

The danger will certainly lessen every year, with the decay of the Arabian trade; and will be nearly annihilated, if Abyssinia and Sennaar should be supplied directly from Europe and India, and the British obtain permission from the government in Egypt, to send their Indian manufactures to Suez. Hitherto this has not been permitted, in consequence of the influence of the Sheriffe of Mecca, at Constantinople, who obtained an order, that all vessels bound for Egypt should stop at Jidda, and pay a duty there. To confirm this arrangement, the Sheriffe obliged the merchants to unship their goods, and remove them to other dows, so that the vessels, which navigated the lower part of the gulf, were different from those which navigated the upper; and the seamen were so ignorant of that part of the sea in which they were unaccustomed to sail, that they dared not venture into it, however willing they might be to escape the payment of duties at Jidda.

Many of the richest merchants have already retired from a place where trade is every day declining, and where their lives are perpetually in danger. Jelani would, I believe, be rejoiced to follow their example, but the Vizier has no intention of permitting so rich a prey to escape, and therefore watches him so closely, that a removal of his family is impracticable, and he would not wish to leave them behind. He may make terms with the Wahabee, and thereby secure his property, in case of their success; but this must be done secretly, or he would share the fate of his father, who perished by poison.

The English formerly carried on a considerable trade with Jidda, but it gradually declined, in consequence of the extortions of the Sheriffe and his servants, under the name of presents, and, for many years before the expedition into the Red Sea, not a vessel had arrived, except the Surprise, Captain Gilmore, which the Vizier immediately plundered, but which Admiral Blanket as quickly obliged him to restore. From that time, till the arrival of the Olive, the English flag had not been seen in Jidda. The Sheriffe has had time to meditate on his folly, and Jelani assured me that he was at last inclined to be reasonable in his demands.

There was at Jidda only one renegado, a Frenchman of some abilities, whom we found of use in assisting Andrew to interpret for us. The Vizier treated him with great contempt, observing to us, that he was only a common seaman; but the lower orders had a respect for him as a physician, and he added a trifle to his allowance by his medical practice. I enquired of him after the English renegadoes who had quitted Mocha; he coolly replied, that they were gone to the devil different ways; that two had been killed in battle, one had been blown to pieces by the bursting of a gun, some had deserted to the Wahabee; and Thomas, whom I had known at Mocha, had gone up with the Sheriffe to Mecca, and had not since been heard of.

It would certainly be the interest of any merchant who may hereafter visit Jidda to employ Jelani, although Hammed Nasser is the British agent, on account of the great weight which his large property gives him among the other merchants, and the real respectability of his character. The duties proposed by the Vizier amount to about eight per cent. and the presents to himself, the Emir Bahar, and their servants, to about four more; but I am by no means sure that a merchant could depend upon having no other demands made on him, when he was once in the harbour, whence it would be almost impossible for him to escape without a native pilot.

We took leave of Captain Loane, who went on shore to try once more to dispose of his cargo. They had hitherto offered him only three dollars per bag for his rice, though they charged us ten. He asked six and a half, and was determined, if they would not give that, to quit the harbour.*

With the morning breeze from the land, we quitted the harbour by the northern passage, when, dismissing our pilot, we proceeded on our way, till

* Captain Loane did not sell his rice, quarrelled with the Vizier, who would not give him a pilot, ran aground in attempting to leave the harbour, but got off, to be captured by a French privateer in the Indian seas.

we saw the breakers off Charles's river. We were then much surprised and gratified at discovering a vessel to the westward, which, on approaching, we were convinced was not Said Doud's ship, nor his grab, we therefore hoped it might be the Prince, with our stores. We fired several guns, and made signals, but without obtaining any answer, or inducing her to alter her course, or wait for our coming up. We continued the chase all night.

At five in the morning we came up with the strange vessel, and discovered, to our disappointment, that she was the Soolimaun, Captain Wilder, an Arab ship loaded with rice, but sailing under English colours. During the day we had light land and sea breezes from the southward.

January 5.—Yesterday evening the favourable wind, which had carried us into lat. 23° N. left us, and a stiff breeze set in from the northward, accompanied by a heavy swell, which greatly damped our expectation of a favourable passage. We were obliged to double reef our topsails, and strike our topgallant yards. Unus did not like the appearance of the weather, and disappeared; probably he returned to Jidda.

January 6.—In defiance of the foul wind, a strong current to the N. W. enabled us to make some way. In the morning the Arabian shore was in sight, near Yambo. It forms that part of the great chain of Raduan, which is called Lamlam, and is the land mark to the dows which are bound to Yambo.

January 8.—We had a slight southerly wind, and a current to the N. W. which carried us seventeen miles in the twenty-four hours. At night the breeze gradually freshened till it blew a gale from the S. W. and obliged us to clew up, and furl our square sails. We afterwards lay to under the fore staysail and mizen. The swell was great, and so short, that sleeping was impossible till after twelve, when it moderated sufficiently for us to set our double-reefed topsails and courses.

January 9.—We were on the look out for a reef laid down by Sir Home Popham, in lat. 26° N. but could not discover it, though we sailed over the very spot where it should be. The night was hazy, but in the morning the Arabian shore was in sight, distant four or five leagues. We stood towards a remarkable cape, that rose abruptly to a great height, and off which we discovered breakers, and a shoal. As this was laid down in no chart, and was an important headland, I named it Cape Barry, after my friend Colonel Maxwell Barry. It lies in 26° 32′ N. At twelve, on sounding, we found only twenty-six fathom, rock. We instantly tacked, and were shortly in good soundings, from twenty to twenty-four fathom, mud. Our friendly current was succeeded by one to the S. E. We again looked out for the reef, near the northern extremity of which we were obliged to pass, but with the same want of success as before.

On the 9th, at night we experienced as heavy a gale from the N. W. as on the 8th, which obliged us to take in every sail, and lie to for some hours. At sun rise Cape Barry was in sight, forming a conspicuous headland at the distance of eleven leagues. As the weather was cloudy, we were not able to take an observation.

January 11.—We had variable winds during the whole of the night, inclining to the northward, and on the 11th, in the morning, we had the heartfelt satisfaction of beholding the long sought for land of Egypt, at a distance of about eight leagues.

We ran in for it, and at twelve were only four leagues off in lat. 25° 40′ N.

January 13.—On the 12th, the northerly breeze continued, and obliged us to work along shore, and prevented us from making more than sixteen miles. During the last twenty-four hours we had a favourable wind from the S. and afterwards from the W. with which we reached latitude 26° 36′ having passed within the islands called the Brothers. At twelve we were close to the shore, off which is a shoal, that is well laid down in Sir Home Popham's chart. The mountains are here higher than to the southward. Mr. Bruce describes them as beautiful from the green and red marbles that compose them; but though I have seen them from latitude 25°, I have not been able to discover any other appearance than the dull tint which stone generally acquires when long exposed to the decomposing powers of the atmosphere. At any rate, I could not perceive the least grounds for the supposition that they were sufficiently red to have originally given a name to the sea, from their colour. Calms continued to baffle us, and when a breeze sprang up it came from the northward.

January 15.—On the 14th, we had only light airs or calms, which brought us by twelve to 26° 45′ N. On the 14th, at night, we had no alteration for the better; but the scene was changed, by our being the next morning close over on the Arabian shore, within sight of the islands of Tiran and Shaduan, and nearly opposite to Ras Mohammed. Before night the wind freshened to a gale from the N. W. We stood in close to the Jaffateen islands.

January 21.—From the 15th, to the 21st, the gale

continued from the N. W., blowing through the narrow straits between Shaduan and Ras Mohammed, with a violence equal to any thing I have experienced. We were generally obliged to lie to under our fore and mizen stay-sails; but whenever it moderated a little, we were glad to carry our courses, to avoid being driven to the southward. In this we succeeded, so that on the fifth day we were within a mile of the same position, in which we were on the first. The sea had been so rough as to deprive us of all rest at night, and all comfort in the day. The dead lights rendered our little cabin gloomy, and the water which washed in, in defiance of them, made it as damp as the deck. We stretched across from shore to shore, and had therefore several good opportunities of ascertaining the real position of Tiran: it is in latitude 27° 43′ N. longitude 34° 27′ 50″ E. It rises to a point in the centre, and has a small island at each end, which, at a little distance, appears as if attached to it. It is laid down by Sir Home Popham too far within the Gulf of Akaba.

The Jaffateen islands were an object which excited my interest, even in defiance of my annoyances, from their being considered, by some authors, as the three islands that lie off the Myos Hormos of the ancients. We ran as near them as we dared, and discovered that there were four of different sizes; the largest lies in latitude 27° 11′, longitude 33° 46′ E. Their number precludes them from the honour of being Myos Hormos; and I think the claim of the Two Brothers must be considered as inadmissible for the same reason; otherwise there is evidently an opening in the mountains behind them, through which a communication might have taken place with Egypt. A little to the northward are the Sefadja Hills, a rugged and lofty pile visible from a great distance. Shaduan is well laid down by Sir Home Popham. It has a single, horizontal, white stripe, that runs along its western side. It is valuable as a bold and lofty mark of the entrance into the narrow straits of Jubal.

Mr. Niebuhr does not seem to have laid down Ras Mohammed with his usual accuracy; instead of 27° 54′ N, the southern Cape, which is high land, and divides the sea of Suez from the sea of Akaba, is in 27° 44′ N. I cannot account for this difference any other way, than by supposing that Mr. Niebuhr might consider the south-westermost point of land, which is opposite to Jubal, and forms the straits, as Ras Mohammed.

Had we not considered ourselves as certain of a fair wind at this season of the year, we should have hired a pilot from Jidda, who would have taken us into some harbour during these heavy gales; but ignorant as we were of the coast, and badly furnished with anchors, it would have been madness to attempt to enter even the sea of Akaba, which looked free from all danger, and is perfectly protected by the mountains of the peninsula from the north west wind which tormented us.

January 22.—The wind on the 22d in the morning was variable and moderate: about twelve it came round to the S. W., when we made directly for Shaduan, and by midnight were ten miles to the north of it, when Captain Court lay to, as he did not think it prudent to enter the narrow straits of Jubal in the night.

January 23.—At day light we found we had drifted close to Ras Mohammed, when we bore away for Jubal with a fine breeze from the southward, which continued to freshen. We passed the high land of Zeyte, which can only be called so comparatively, from the low land near it. It is bluff to the sea, and is of a red colour, beautifully veined with purple. At one we were opposite to a mountain, called Agrib in our charts, though its real name is Ghareb. It forms a remarkable point on the African shore, from its being the last high land with a pointed and ragged summit: to the northward all the hills had either round or flat tops. At two we were off Tor, but felt too anxious to profit by our southerly wind to think of entering it. The celebrated mountains of Sinai and Horeb reared their pointed tops over a range of hills, which extend from Ras Mohammed to Ras Jehan. They were lofty, but their effect was diminished by those in front. It blew very fresh towards night, and we passed Ras Jehan on the Arabian shore in a gale of wind, accompanied by rain, and then considered ourselves as almost in safety, for here the sea narrows considerably, and the vessels during the expedition had frequently a great difficulty in weathering this cape, which is lofty and bold.

January 24.—We had reason to rejoice at our good fortune on the 23d, for in the night the wind came round to the northward, and blew so fresh, that had we been on the other side of Ras Jehan, it would have been impossible to weather it. The swell was but trifling from the narrowness of the sea, and the little depth of water. After we had entered the sea of Suez we constantly had soundings. The change in the climate was very sudden; and the cold rendered the cabin quite uncomfortable. At day light we were close in with Hummaum Faroun, or Pharaoh's Bath, so called on account of some warm springs which break out there. It is a very high, bluff point, in latitude, 29° 7′ N.; but the point is in 29° 10, off which

Captain Court anchored in 1795. During the day it was hazy, but cleared up towards the evening, and for the first time we were enabled to discover land all around us. To the north of Hummaum Faroun the hills were low and flat; on the opposite shore was a high and long bluff land, called Abou Daraja. It was red, veined with purple, as were the others, which we had seen since passing Shaduan. The wind moderated at sunset, when we had the pleasure of seeing Attaké, the last mountain on the Egyptian shore, and close to Suez.

January 25.—The light airs from the north still prevailed, but the smoothness of the sea, in a bason not twelve miles wide, permitted us to make but little way. The day was beautiful, and a clear sky enabled us to see the African mountains to great advantage; yet our impatience to reach Suez, which seemed at length almost within our grasp, precluded the possibility of our enjoying the scene. At twelve we were in latitude 29° 29′, and an opposing tide left us no hope of reaching the shore before the following morning.

January 26.—With the assistance of the tide we reached the anchoring ground of Suez by four o'clock; but not being aware of a spit of sand, which separates the narrow gut, that runs up to the town, from the sea, we went too far to the north, so that when we sent the boat on shore, she had half a mile to pull to the southward, before she could keep a direct course. A boat soon came off from the Dola, who commanded in the absence of the Aga, with a present of eggs, loaves, and a live sheep. We heard that Captain Bartou was at Suez, and therefore wrote to request he would immediately come off to us; with which he complied. We learned from him, that there was no

Pacha there for Jidda, but that four hundred of his troops had sailed for the latter place, in five dows, a few days ago. The Capitan Pacha was said to be still at Alexandria, whither Major Missett had been obliged to retire from the disturbances at Cairo. Mohammed Ali, the celebrated Albanian chief, was then Pacha, but was pressed by the Beys, who were said to be near the Pyramids. Money was so difficult to procure, that he had seized the whole caravan of coffee, which had last left Suez, and confiscated it for his own use: an act of violence, which will prevent any more from being sent from this place for some time to come. Captain Bartou arrived on the 27th of December, and instantly forwarded all the letters with which I had intrusted him, but as yet, no answers had been received to them, or to the letters he wrote to his owners.

Captain Bartou had stopped at Jidda, where he was promised freight, but was disappointed by the Vizier, who had sent for the merchants, and told them that, as there were many dows in the harbour unemployed belonging to true believers, he could not approve of their giving a preference to a Feringi; and, in short, declared that he would put the first in prison who did so. Captain Bartou had no communication with Jelani, but received great assistance from the renegado. Having a native pilot on board, he put into the creek called Charles's River, which he describes as an excellent harbour, capable of containing many vessels. The outer part is sheltered from every wind except the west; the inner is perfectly landlocked. He then went to Yambo, in hopes of procuring fresh provisions and water. He found there a most respectable man in the office of Vizier, who afforded him every assistance at a reasonable price. Sheep were only two dollars each, and every thing else in proportion. The harbour he describes as good, and the people, as civil. There can be little doubt that it is a place preferable to Jidda. He procured during his stay some very fine shells, and other marine productions. On arriving at Shaduan, he experienced the same unfavourable weather that we did, and it continued for fifteen days. His pilot took him to a good anchorage among the Tiran Islands. There is clear ground all round them. The islands Sanafir, Barkara, Abou Schuscha, and Joboa, which are laid down by Niebuhr, were visited by him, and are, he says, small, low, and sandy.

January 27.—The Dola sent off, early in the morning, the chief officer of the Ascari to invite me on shore, and to say that, if I pleased, a house should be prepared for my residence. Soon after breakfast I quitted the ship, and proceeded to visit the Dola. His house was not very good, but he gave me a very cordial reception. He was a venerable old man, with a large, white beard. He laughed, and talked freely, without any of the dignity of a Turk. He was seated in the window on a carpet, with several other respectable men near him. I had a chair placed for me; and cushions were provided for the other gentlemen. After coffee, pipes were offered, and accepted by every one except myself. I then entered on business by stating, through Captain Bartou, that it was my wish to depart for Cairo as soon as possible, and that therefore I begged his permission to hire camels for the journey, and make an arrangement with the Arabs for my protection. He replied, that I might command every assistance in his power, but that he considered himself as responsible for my safety, and consequently, could not venture to let me go without receiving the Pacha's instruction as to a guard; he therefore requested that I would write to the British Agent, to make every arrangement at Cairo, and that he would send the letter by a messenger, which he should, according to his orders, immediately dispatch to the Pacha on the subject of my journey, having already sent to notify my arrival; that the caravan from Tor was expected in four days, by which time I should receive an answer from Cairo, and be at liberty to act as I might think advisable. This was so reasonable, that I immediately complied.

I next stated to him, that I was no merchant, and had nothing with me that was merchandise, except one bale of coffee, for which I was willing to pay duty; but that I hoped he would permit my trunks, and boxes of shells, to pass unopened. He appealed to Captain Bartou if they had even opened his trunks; how much less, then, would they do so by me; and as for the coffee, if I had ten bales, they should not think of charging any duty on them. I expressed myself very much pleased and obliged, and it was determined that I should hire a warehouse, and send my boxes on shore, as I packed them.

I was now presented to the custom master, who was a fat laughing Christian named Michael, who offered me his services, but turned me over, for a supply of provisions, to a namesake of inferior rank, who was agent for the vessels consigned to Signor Carlo Rosetti. He informed me that supplies were very uncertain; that even the water was brought in by the Arabs daily, and that we should not be able to procure any of that for the ship, without giving these plunderers a present of ninety-two dollars, an extortion to which we were obliged to submit. He said, that when our arrival should be known, some sheep would probably be brought down, and that he would try and procure us a few bullocks; but that they were worth fifteen dollars per hundred weight. Eggs and fish alone were in abundance, and cheap. My servant had forgotten to bring the present intended for the Dola, I was therefore obliged to apologise to him on my taking leave, but he with his usual good humour assured me it was of no consequence. I took Michael with me on board Captain Bartou's vessel, where I wrote to Mr. Aziz, the British Resident at Cairo; and inclosed him letters for Major Missett, and my friends in England. We were an hour and a half in reaching the vessel, in consequence of being obliged to go round the shoal. The weather was very cool, the thermometer being at 54° in the morning.

February 1.—I sent several of my trunks to Michael's, and my servant with a piece of muslin richly worked with gold for the Dola, which the old man was pleased to say, was not of sufficient value for him to accept, though it cost at Mocha fifteen dollars. Nothing can be a greater insult among the Mussulmauns than to return a present: I however, said nothing, and determined to take no notice of his conduct till I should have heard from Cairo.

February 2.—Early in the morning Captain Bartou came off to the ship, with answers to my letters. Mr. Aziz had made the necessary arrangement for my passing the Desert, and had procured a supply of stores for the Panther, which would be sent off by the first caravan. He informed me that Mohammed Ali Pacha had issued his orders for my being treated with every mark of respect at Suez, and that my baggage should be passed free; I was therefore under no obligation to the Dola for his civility. Major Missett very kindly congratulated me on my arrival, and forwarded the agreeable news of Lord Nelson's victory at Trafalgar.

February 4.—I yesterday sent off another express to Mr. Aziz, to represent the distress of the Panther for spirits and wine, and to desire him to procure either one or the other. The wind had blown from the north-west or east, ever since our arrival, and, occasionally, in strong puffs: to-day it came round to the southward. Captain Bartou informed me, that it had continued in that point for twenty days successively since his arrival.

February 7.—Seeing a caravan approach on the Cairo road, I thought it might be the one we expected, and therefore set off to meet it. It consisted, however, only of pilgrims, in number about six hundred, who were on their way from the coast of Barbary to Mecca. A little white man addressed Captain Bartou in Lingua Franca, and offered him one thousand dollars for the freight of his vessel to Jidda; an offer which he could not accept, as he had neither provisions nor men, and both must have been procured from Cairo. Had he been ready for sea, he might have made a good speculation, not by accepting his little friend's bargain, but by taking each pilgrim at from five to ten dollars per head; for so short a passage he could have stowed from four to five hundred.

On the beach between Attaké and the town, we procured some very fine specimens of bivalve shells, and on the spit of sand, a variety of marine productions. I also greatly increased my collection of sea weed, with which the Red Sea abounds more than any other. Yet Mr. Bruce asserts, in his Dissertation on the origin of the Hebrew name

Yam Suph, that he never saw a weed of any sort in it; and adds, "indeed, upon the slightest consideration, it will occur to any one, that a narrow gulf, under the immediate influence of monsoons, blowing from contrary points six months each year, would have too much agitation to produce such vegetables, seldom found but in stagnant waters, and seldomer, if ever, found in salt ones."!!! The ignorance displayed in the comment, is equal to the falsity of the original assertion. My friend, Mr. Dawson Turner, in his beautiful work on the Fuci, has given drawings of many of the specimens which I brought home, and Forskal confirms the fact of their being the production of the Red Sea.

February 9.—Early in the morning I received a letter from Mr. Aziz, informing me that brandy was to be procured, but that he feared wine was not. He notified to me that the caravan had actually set off, under the escort of an Arab chief, Nasr Chedid, who, by the orders of Mohammed Ali Pacha, had undertaken to conduct me in safety to Cairo. I determined to go immediately on shore, and superintend the necessary arrangements for my journey, in which Captain Court was so obliging as to permit Mr. Macgie to accompany me, to bring back my dispatches, and those of Major Missett, which would not be ready for some little time. It was four o'clock in the evening when my party quitted the vessel, attended by Captain Court. It was really not without some regret that I did so. She had proved a safe conveyance to me in many perilous moments, and the recollection of these, and the idea of the different scenes I was going to enter on, excited strong emotions in my mind. I should very soon have to bid adieu to Captain Court, whom I could not but love and esteem, and to the other officers, whose conduct had been certainly meritorious, and, towards me, uniformly kind and attentive. It was a painful moment to us all; and I believe no one was rejoiced when my flag, after flying for thirteen months, was hawled down, the moment the last gun was fired.

We found that the caravan was arrived, consisting of fifteen hundred camels, three hundred armed Arabs, and about thirty Turks, with two officers, who came to guard the mahmal, or sacred covering for the Kaaba of Mecca. Mr. Thomaso, a native of Surat, who had been a Christian, and was employed in the house of Mr. Rosetti, arrived to act as interpreter or dragoman. He brought a letter from Mr. Rosetti, congratulating me on my arrival, saying, that he had received letters from his friend Mr. Tiretta, of Bengal, requesting him to pay me every attention; that he had, therefore, sent "his Thomaso," and should feel highly flattered if I would accept the hospitality of his house at Cairo. I also received a packet of the Courier de L'Europe down to August, which afforded many details of which we were before ignorant. In the evening the Schech visited me. He was a handsome looking man, of about thirty, fat, with very black hair and beard. He seemed good-humoured, and was, I understood, a great lover of brandy. Captain Court staid with us till bed time, and then went on board. Michael's house was a wretched residence: the walls were broken in many parts; and as the numerous windows had only wooden fretwork in them, we found it very cold at night. My couch and curtains sheltered me, but the other gentlemen suffered severely. Schech Chedid was on ill terms with the Tor Arabs, and till their disputes were settled, it would by no means have been wise to attempt to leave the town. All was, for the present, adjusted on the 11th, and were to depart on the morrow, with a kafila chiefly of coffee, worth at least one hundred thousand pounds. It was owing to this dispute that the Schech brought so many of his people. One of his men shot a pilgrim through the head. The Schech immediately arrested him, and declared if the man died he should be punished; but as they sailed in the dow yesterday, the fellow is to-day at liberty. Schech Chedid dined with us every day, and drank abundance of brandy, but not satisfied with that, after our dinner, generally retired to Mr. Thomaso's room, and added to it a few glasses of gin. I one day sent a dram to the door for his chief follower: he saw it, and said, laughing, "Aye, I know he drinks, but he must not do it before me." This was a mark of respect due from an inferior to a superior, not to violate the law in his presence. Chedid would not scruple to drink in the presence of his servants, nor the followers in the presence of their inferiors.

Chedid is very pleasant and gay in his conversation; talks of their being all robbers, and says these are good times for him—that he stays close to Cairo, and seizes many things—if they are enquired after, he pleads ignorance, and lays the offence on Elfi Bey, who is in great force in the Ac Faiume. At the same time he has the highest principle of Arab honour, and told me an anecdote of his family, which was confirmed by Thomaso. Osman Bey, greatly alarmed at the arrival from England of Elfi Bey, who, since the death of Murad Bey, had been his rival, determined to cut him off, and for that purpose sent down two boats with troops to intercept him as he was coming up the Nile. A violent gale of wind, accompanied by a cloud of sand, came on; Elfi sheltered himself behind a point of land, on which was a village. The boats with the troops of Osman Bey passed without seeing him; but he perceived them, and having some suspicion, immediately landed, and quitting his baggage, with five or six followers escaped into the Desert. These soon left him, as the way was long and difficult. At length, after a tedious march of ten hours on foot, he arrived at the tent of Nasr Chedid in the Desert, with whom he was on ill terms, and claimed protection. Nasr was himself absent with Osman Bey, whom he had joined with all his people at his camp before Cairo, where he waited the event of the attack on Elfi. Chedid's wife received and concealed him. Some of Osman's people came there, and asked if she had seen Elfi. She said, yes; and that he had passed by a way she pointed out to them. As soon as they were gone, she told Elfi, and bringing him one of her husband's favourite horses, and a dromedary, she desired him to escape to Upper Egypt, but to avoid the road which she had directed the troops of Osman to take. Elfi hesitated, and told her he was unwilling to endanger her husband's safety, who was in the power of Osman. She replied, it was no matter; her husband's honour required that she should assist him in escaping; and that were he there, he would do the same himself, and that he would make her suffer if any thing happened to him. Soon afterwards on being told the way that Elfi had escaped, Osman sent for Chedid, and accused him of having assisted his enemy. He replied, "You know, Osman Bey, I have been three days here with you, how then is it possible that I could do so?" "Well then," said Osman, "It was your wife that did so." "It was," replied Chedid.

" Elfi demanded protection from her, and she only did her duty—had she done otherwise, I would have cut her head off with this sabre, though you know Elfi was never a friend of mine." He declared to me that he certainly would have done so, as she would have dishonoured his name. He frequently spoke of his family; told us, laughing, he had four wives who beat him, and that he wished we would give him something to make him strong. He had one son and two daughters. I told him I would visit him. He said nothing would make him so happy; that he would give me plenty to eat, a horse to ride, and a tent to sleep in; but that he had nothing to drink but water. He said he was called the English Schech—that he loved the English, and only wished that they had the country, instead of the Turks, who were all rascals. The Mamelukes were bad enough, but not so bad as they. He urged me frequently to tell him why we had not kept it, and when we meant to return. He assured me, that all the Arab tribes were most anxious for us, but that they would be glad even to have the French, in preference to their present masters. An assertion which I firmly believe, for the common people were certainly in a much better situation under the French government; for the impositions were then less, and grain cheaper, as all export was stopped by the activity of the British cruizers.

He was extremely anxious that the King of England should hear of his name and of his attachment to the English, and urged me much to mention him, and let the world know that he was the most powerful Arab in the Desert, and had a greater number of horse and people on foot. His camels are his chief profit, but he also receives money from the caravans for permitting them to pass the Desert. The Maugrabin pilgrims paid him from one to two zequins each for protection, though they came alone, besides the hire of the camels which they had from him.

I met the Dola in the morning in the street, who was very happy to see me, and assured me that he did not know I was on shore, or he would have waited on me to pay his compliments. He also informed me, that the Turkish commander of the escort wished to wait on me. I replied civilly, and just as we sat down to dinner they came. The Turk was a respectable man, named Emir Effendi, belonging to the secretary's office of Mahommed Ali. He said he came to ask my permission to accompany my caravan; which, of course, I granted. The old Dola hoped I was perfectly satisfied, and regretted that his duty here prevented him from attending me to Cairo. I was amused with the change in his conduct, but answered civilly; however, in the evening, I sent Michael to insist on paying him for the sheep and eggs which he sent on board the Panther. He pleaded that they always sent a present to a vessel on her arrival, and that his only motive for refusing to accept mine in return was, that they would have believed at Cairo he had received one of great value, and that he did not like to accept one worth only five dollars. As this contemptuous depreciation only aggravated the offence, I replied it was very well—I should take care to represent the whole business at Cairo. He instantly sent his chief officer to conjure me not to do so, as the consequence would be his total ruin, and to make every kind of apology. I had too much regard for the old man, who had, in every other respect, treated me with the greatest civility, to intend to put my threat into execution, and therefore assured him that every thing unpleasant should be forgotten.

Michael very wisely refused to make any charge for the use of his house and warehouse, or for his trouble, which he well knew would reduce me to the necessity of making him a present. As he had been very useful and attentive, I gave him a shawl for himself, and the piece of muslin for his wife, which the Dola had refused. I also gave twenty dollars to his servants. All the officers that could leave the ship, dined with me after I came on shore, to partake of the good things which the caravan brought from Cairo. The greatest luxuries were the oranges, vegetables, and fresh butter, which Mr. Aziz had sent over; but Mr. Pringle having left Mocha, we considered a cargo, which he had ordered by Captain Bartou, as fair plunder; and this consisted of figs, raisins, Sardinias, fish roes, and pickled mullets. The arrival of the caravan made it impossible to procure any thing in the market but fish and eggs.

Suez was formerly a place of considerable splendour, each Bey having a house there, in which his factor resided. The buildings are many of them large, but are, at present, little more than a heap of ruins, chiefly owing to the wanton injuries of the French, who thus revenged themselves on the Beys for retiring into Upper Egypt, and not permitting themselves to be subdued. The fortifications never were of any strength, and were merely mean to keep off a sudden attack of the Arabs. It would be useless to fortify a place which has no water within its walls, and which must, consequently, be ever at the mercy of that power, which can keep possession of the country around, unless it should be thought of sufficient consequence to keep a large garrison, and to supply it regularly with provisions from Cairo, which the occupiers of Egypt must always be able to do. The French seem to have intended to remain; for they erected a battery of one gun on a hillock which commands the town. Suez has suffered as much by the stagnation of trade, which followed the occupation of Egypt by the French, as by their hostility, for no one will reside in so wretched a place, who is not tempted by his interest. An Arab house, which is flat roofed, soon falls into decay, if its preservation be not carefully attended to. At present the place seems rising again into consequence.

The chief trade of Suez has ever been in coffee, as the whole quantity which was consumed in the Turkish empire, came through that port and Cosseir. The tumults in Egypt, which ended by the Beys occupying the upper provinces, divided the country, and no communication is permitted between the different parts of it; consequently, no coffee is sent to Cosseir, except for the use of the Beys, and the residue finds its way to Suez, where, however, it is liable, not only to the exactions of the Pacha, but even to seizure. The owners of four cargoes, now in the harbour, are unwilling to land them, without having payment insured; and as the purchaser is equally unwilling to run any hazard, a stagnation of trade has taken place; but I understand that the Pacha has most faithfully promised to receive the duty only, and that sooner than take back their coffee, they are determined to trust him; and, accordingly, the whole is to go with my caravan.

The disadvantages under which Suez has ever laboured, have been considerable from its situation; at the extremity of a narrow sea, down which the wind blows with irresistible force for at least nine months in the year. It was in early times some counterbalance to this, that a navigable canal extended from it to the most fertile province of Egypt, whence grain must always have been exported for the supply of Arabia. But even the advantages which water carriage has over land, could not preserve to Suez the great trade of the Red Sea. The Ptolemies, many of whom seem to have been admirable judges of what was for the benefit of the country they ruled over, found it more advisable to establish a new emporium at Berenice, although it was necessary to convey the goods from that place upwards of two hundred miles over land, before they could be embarked on the Nile at Coptos, the modern Koust.

Were Egypt to be once again tranquil, and under the control of one master, and even were the ancient canal to be cleansed, I still doubt whether Suez would become a place of great trade, for the improvement of the science of navigation has not yet extended to the discovery of any means, by which a vessel could resist the force of the northerly winds, which blow in the upper part of the Gulf; but as it is only at the island of Shaduan that they become so violent, Cosseir is always attainable; and the diminution of the distance by land, from two hundred miles, to about one hundred and twenty, would fully repay the additional sea voyage of one hundred and forty miles, and would probably lead to a transfer of the trade from Berenice to that place. The road is indeed not very good for ships, but it is protected from the N. W. which is the most prevailing wind, and, when it begins to blow from the east, a vessel might run to any of the numerous harbours which were entered by Don Juan de Castro These have not since been examined; but if one of them should be the Myos Hormos of the Periplûs, it must have a means of communication with the plain of Egypt, and be by far preferable to Cosseir. Had I had the voyage of Don Juan de Castro with me, I would have visited Shakara and Shawna, in defiance of the deficiencies under which the Panther laboured.

Every traveller who has visited the upper part of the Red Sea, must naturally have turned his thoughts to the miraculous passage of the Children of Israel through it, and the destruction of the host of Pharaoh. Pococke, Niebuhr, Pere Sicard, and Bruce, have all given to the public their opinions as to the spot, where this event actually took place. I perfectly agree with the last named gentleman, that to seek for natural causes to explain a miracle, is perfectly absurd; and that it was as easy for the Almighty to carry his people through the widest and deepest part of the sea, as through the narrowest and most shoaly. But as the division of the water is the only thing that is represented by Moses as being miraculous, we must look to the position of the mountains on its western side, to discover in what spot it was possible for the children of Israel to approach the Red Sea.

A chain of hills extends from the high land of Zeyte nearly to Abou Daraja, between which and Attaké is the first valley, by which six hundred thousand men, their children, and cattle, could reach the sea from Egypt. Sicard and others have believed this to be the line of their march, but I am inclined to the conjecture of Niebuhr, that Attaké was the southern boundary of their journey.

To place this in a clearer light, it will be necessary to ascertain, whence the Children of Israel began their journey, and to consider the account given of their movements by Moses. The ancient metropolis of Lower Egypt was On, or Heliopolis, and there it is probable the Pharaohs resided in the time of Joseph. Joseph placed his brethren in a part of the country named Goshen, but which is afterwards called Ramesses. In the 46th ch. of Genesis, it is said that Joseph went up to meet Israel his father to Goshen; which is translated in the Septuagint καθ' Ηρώων πολιν, εις γῆν 'Ραμεσσῆ. Monsieur Du Bois Aymé, in a paper read before the Institute of Egypt, very justly observes, that, as this translation was made by the Seventy only fifty years after the Macedonians had established themselves, the Egyptian names must have been still known, and consequently that we are perfectly safe in believing Heroopolis to have been situated in the land of Ramesses, or Goshen.

To fix the position of Heroopolis is rather difficult, in consequence of the apparently contradictory assertions of ancient authors. Moses, in the text above referred to, clearly shews that it was on the direct road from Canaan to Heliopolis, while Strabo speaks of it as being near to Arsinoe, and at the top of the gulf called Heroopolitan. To reconcile these assertions in any degree, the Arabian Gulf must have formerly extended much farther north than it does now, or a considerable latitude must be allowed to the expression of Strabo.

The French engineers discovered, when in possession of Suez, that at a little distance to the north of that place are marshes which extend for above twenty-five miles, and are actually lower than the sea, though they are not overflowed, in consequence of a large bar of sand which has accumulated between them; nothing therefore can be more probable, than that, in times so far back as the departure of the Israelites, the sea itself extended to these marshes; and that since, the same gradual incroachments of sand from the Desert, which have formed the Tehama in Lower Arabia, have annihilated the sea in a place where it was so much narrower. The contradictions may be still farther removed by the supposition, that Strabo considered himself as justified in describing a place as being on the Gulf, which was actually situated on the canal that united it with the Nile, and which, from being of the greatest consequence in the province, gave its name to it.

Were we, however, inclined to give every weight to the description of Strabo, his evidence would be set aside by the higher authority of Moses, who proves that Goshen was in the way to Canaan; and by the short account of Ptolemy, who declares that Heroopolis was on the confines of Arabia, and that the canal of Trajan ran through it (p. 120). The course of this canal has been traced by the French engineers, from longitude 31° 52′ to 32° 20′ running in nearly an east and west direction, in about 30° 32′ north latitude.

It is therefore within this line only, that we can look for it; and I am inclined to admit the opinion of Monsieur Aymé as well founded, that the ruins he discovered at Aboukechied, indicate the spot where Heroopolis stood, and where, consequently, the Children of Israel actually resided, extending themselves over a country that sustained their numerous flocks and herds, to the borders of that part of Egypt where grain was cultivated, but in which they would not be permitted to sojourn, in consequence of their destroying the sacred animals. I cannot, therefore, for a moment believe, that Heliopolis was within their bounds, or that they ever went either to the south or west of it; though it appears, indeed, from the account of the sacred historian, that they were near to this capital of Pharaoh; but Moses is spoken of as having gone out to his brethren, which would seem to imply that they were at some little distance.

Taking, therefore, any part of the country between Aboukechied and Heliopolis, as being the province of Ramesses, whence the Children of Israel departed, how improbable does it appear, that they should proceed into the low land of Egypt, to the very banks of the holy river, to round Mokattem, and enter the valley, which, beginning there, extends to the Red Sea; and this at a time when they were thrust out from the land of the Egyptians, who did not believe themselves safe, till they had got rid of them.

In the 13th chap. verse 17th of Exodus, it is declared that "God led them not through the way of the land of the Philistines, although that was near" (verse 18th), "but about through the way of the wilderness of the Red Sea." Now, both these observations are perfectly true, if they set off from the vicinity of Heroopolis, which was actually on the way of Canaan, but would be false, if they began their journey from opposite Memphis, whence it would be much nearer to reach the Red Sea than the land of the Philistines.

By the supposition that the Children of Israel resided nearer to the Desert, we get rid of the difficulty of their having to march sixty miles in only three stages, which is the distance from the Nile to the Red Sea, and which seems almost impossible, incumbered as they were, with children, cattle, baggage, and kneading troughs, even supposing that their three marches were in a direct line east, which appears to have been by no means the case; for they were directed, after the second day's march, when they quitted Etham on the edge of the wilderness, "to turn," and encamp before Pihaheroth, between Migdol and the sea.

Confiding in the promises of Moses, confirmed as they were by the miracles which he had wrought, it is probable that the Israelites had prepared for their departure, and were all assembled at some one place, waiting impatiently for the result of his last interview with Pharaoh. The spot chosen must have been where they could either move towards Canaan, or the Red Sea; and it must have been at such a distance only from the Desert, that they could, although incumbered, reach the confines of it in two marches, and the Red Sea in three.

If the Red Sea terminated then, as it does now, at Suez, it appears to me impossible to fix on any spot that unites these requisite points; but if it extended then over the marshes, surveyed and laid down by Monsieur Aymé, the difficulty would be removed, and the vicinity of the modern Balbeis, on the banks of Trajan's canal, would accord with the description of the sacred historian, for it is in the direct road from Heliopolis to Canaan, and not above thirty-five miles from the sea.

As the great weight of my argument depends on the fact, that, from the present appearance of the country, there is every reason to believe that the Red Sea did actually extend, in former times, twenty-five miles north of Suez, I think it may be right to observe, that the Savant, from whom I have derived my information, is not a person who, being zealous for the cause of religion, might have falsified a little to get rid of a difficulty, but that, on the contrary, he feels it necessary to justify himself from the suspicion of believing in the miracles of Moses, in whose book he declares that the transactions are doubtful, and the philosophy absurd. We may surely admit the evidence of such a witness, when it tends to confirm the authenticity of religious history.

It is evident that Pharaoh could have no expectation of the Children of Israel's return, when he had so frequently experienced their refusals to depart without their cattle, and their children; and he must have been confirmed in this idea, by their carrying with them the bones of Joseph. But the terror of the last dreadful visitation probably hung over him, and prevented his pursuing them, while they continued their proper route, and seemed under the guidance of their Almighty Leader; but when they turned aside, and were actually entangled in the land, and shut in by the wilderness, he had reason to hope that he might again recover so valuable a body of slaves. This is the reason assigned by Scripture for his pursuit; and I cannot, therefore, agree with Mr. Bruce, that he was influenced by resentment at the Israelites' carrying away the jewels. In fact, the idea is absurd, that he should feel tranquil while they were carrying off the spoils of the Egyptians to a country, whence he could never hope to bring them back, and that his anger should be roused when they were once more, apparently, in his power.

The sufferings of Egypt, in consequence of the residence of the Children of Israel, were only temporary; but there is good reason to suppose that the benefits were permanent. By the policy of Joseph, the whole of the land of Egypt became the property of the sovereign, and the people and their children his slaves; an event which, however unpropitious it might be in any other country, was necessary there, where every harvest depended on the Nile, and where the equal distribution of its waters could alone produce a general cultivation. When the lands of Egypt were private property, would it be possible to induce individuals to sacrifice their possessions, that they might be turned into canals for the public benefit? or, when the canals were constructed, would it be possible to prevent the inhabitants of the upper provinces from drawing off more water than was requisite for their own use, and thereby injuring the cultivators lower down? But when the whole belonged to one man, the necessary canals would be constructed, the distribution of water would be guided by prudence, each district would receive its necessary proportion, and the collateral branches would then, as they are now, only be opened when the height of the river justified such a measure for the public benefit. It is evident that no canals were constructed before the time of Joseph, for Herodotus even attributes these mighty works to Sesostris, who did not reign till three hundred and ninety years afterwards.

CHAPTER X.

Departure from Suez.—Passage across the Desert.—Arrival at Cairo.—Visit to the Pacha.—Visit to the Citadel—to the Pyramids.—Observations on them.—Taher Pacha.—Visit of leave to the Pacha.

EARLY in the morning, February 13, the Schech sent the camels for our baggage, and soon afterwards arrived himself with those that were intended for our accommodation. I travelled in a Takterouane, which is more like a box than a palanquin, and being only five feet long, is very uncomfortable. It is slung between two camels, by large shafts which pass underneath it; between these the camels march. We had ten Mohaffas, in which the other gentlemen went; these are a kind of little couch, two of which are slung sideways on the opposite sides of a camel, with an awning spread between to keep off the sun; we had also fourteen camels for our baggage and water. To avoid the necessity of dressing food in the Desert, we provided plenty of cold meat, bread, fruit, butter, and cheese. We were obliged also to provide coffee, bread, and rice for the soldiers of Chedid, and the men who attended on the camels. It was half after ten when we took leave of our estimable friend Captain Court, and the other companions of our voyage, and mounted our camels. I found the motion by no means pleasant, but had reason to suspect, from the violent movements of the gentlemen in the Mohaffas, that they were still more incommoded. Nor was I mistaken, for, on meeting at the wells where the rest of the caravan had halted, they were loud in their complaints, and agreed in opinion, that a camel afforded the most uneasy conveyance they had ever experienced. We reached the wells by twelve, a distance of about four miles, and immediately pitched our tents.

Our station was in the front of the line, close to the Schech's tent: our baggage was around us. The Turks were nearer the sea: their chief, Emir Effendi, sent in the evening to Chedid, to say that he had heard we were likely to be attacked on the morrow, and therefore wished to arrange with him the order of march. It was determined that a part of the escort, with the Turks, should go in front, a part in the middle of the caravan, and a few in the rear. The robbers of the Desert are not supposed to exceed in number five hundred, and are consequently little to be feared by Chedid, who is himself as brave as a lion, and can depend upon his followers. It was, however, wise to take every precaution, as the appearance of preparation might often prevent an attack; for the Arabs, like other banditti, never fight, except when they conceive themselves so superior as to be sure of success.

Chedid dined with us, and expressed great approbation of the cherry-brandy, which he drank most freely, though, the tent door being open, his people could distinguish that he did so. He was in great good humour, laughed, and told several stories of himself, which were interpreted by Mr. Thomaso. He at length began to praise my tent, which was lined with green cloth, so highly, declaring that it was superior to any he had for his wives, that I was induced to promise it to him on my arrival at Cairo, after which I could have no occasion for it.

February 14.—At half after five we took a dish of coffee, and mounted, and did not halt till a quarter before six in the evening. I think our camels never went less than three miles an hour, and therefore suppose we travelled over about thirty-three miles of a road, which winds considerably among the smaller hills. At nine we passed a building on our right, which was formerly used as a fort by the Turks, when they were more powerful, to protect the caravans from the robbers; at present it is nearly in ruins. Soon afterwards the road became more stony, and we quitted the plain of Suez, and had small hills on our right and left. This was considered as the most dangerous spot; our escort was therefore on the alert. The Turks marched in front, displaying two flags; the first, belonging to the mahmal, was white, with a yellow border, and in the centre the two-bladed sword in yellow: the other, belonging to the Sultaun, which was half green, half red, the former uppermost. Chedid was with them as Commander in Chief, and always preceded the caravan to the top of the ascents, where he waited till they came up, and then went on as before. None of the party could this day procure the loan of a horse, except my servant, who made interest with a young Arab to let him have his, with sabre and musket, on promising to fight if we were attacked. A more complete coxcomb than this youth I never beheld. He had a very small musical instrument, something like a guitar, but with only four strings, on which he played with his fingers for several hours, while he continued to march on foot by the side of my Takterouane. At night he produced a little box containing a glass, a comb, and a toothpick, took off his turban, combed his hair, picked his teeth, and contemplated himself in the glass, with all the airs of a finished petit maitre.

I collected during the march several very beautiful specimens of Egyptian pebble, with which the whole road was covered, to the great annoyance of the camels. The only vegetable productions which I saw, were a few stunted Mimosas, an Artemisia, which is probably the Absinthium of Bruce, an Echium with a purple blossom, and an elegant but leafless Spartium, with a purple and white blossom. Chedid dined with us; but he complained of the effects of the cherry-brandy, and would take neither wine nor spirits. The Emir fired a gun at night, as he had done in the morning, before he moved from his station.

February 15.—At six precisely the gun of the Emir warned us to mount. Our camels were evidently fatigued, and we did not reach our halting place till five, though it was not above twenty-two miles. The road was more winding than yesterday. From the time that we quitted the wells, till half after four this day, we had been gradually ascending; at that hour we reached the highest point, and beheld a descent before us, which led to the fertile plain of Egypt, dark with verdure, through which the Nile was winding its course. The whole was a beautiful scene, and appeared still more so, from the contrast formed by the arid foreground of the Desert.

The day had been by no means sultry, and as all danger was supposed to be over, every person who wished it, procured a horse. My friend the Emir sent to offer me one of his, but I declined accepting it. Chedid had parted with us early in the day, and gone on to his own residence, which was distant a few miles. He left a message for me, with his chief officer, requesting that I would not pitch my own tent, but occupy his, as it was intended we should set off again at midnight, he having heard that the robbers meant to follow, and attack us in the morning. I complied, though assured by Mr. Thomaso, that the whole was a trick to get us into Cairo as early as possible, for this was to me as desirable an object as to them. Our two barrels of water had not been opened, nor should we now want them, I therefore told the Arabs that they might have them. A violent dispute arose about the division; and even my friend the Emir sent to request that I would give him some of it.

February 16.—It was three o'clock before the caravan departed: at eight we reached an opening in the hills, down which we rapidly descended, and at the bottom were met by Mr. Aziz, the acting Resident for the British during the absence of Major Missett. We here parted from the rest of the caravan, and passing by some magnificent Mussulmaun tombs, kept along the walls of Cairo, till we reached an ancient and lofty gate, called Bab-el-Fituch, which we entered, with all our baggage, orders having been issued for that purpose by the Pacha. We soon arrived at the European quarter, and took up our residence in the British factory. We had scarcely time to dress ourselves, before the Reverend Fathers, and the Principal of the Franciscans of Jerusalem, paid me a visit, to congratulate me on my arrival; and immediately afterwards came the Franciscans of the Propaganda, with their Principal. Mr. Macardle, of

Rosetti's house, and the other European gentlemen resident here, also came to pay their compliments. We dined at home quietly; and went to bed early, highly pleased to find ourselves in an excellent house, and in civilized society. His Highness Mohammed Ali Pacha sent in the evening to congratulate me on my arrival, and to learn privately on what day I meant to visit him.

February 17.—His Highness's Interpreter came again in the morning. He made an offer, in his master's name, of every assistance I might want to visit the town and neighbourhood, and expressed his regret that the situation of the country was such as to render it uncomfortable to strangers. He sent the Interpreter to consult with Mr. Aziz, as to the proper etiquette in receiving me, assuring me, that it was his wish to pay me every possible attention; that he was attached to my countrymen; and that it was even his interest, having been recently raised to so high an office, to cultivate the friendship of those nations which were friends of the Porte; that immediately on hearing of my arrival at Suez, he had issued his orders to his servants there, to treat me with every respect, which he trusted had been complied with; and that if any thing should hereafter be neglected which ought to be done, he hoped I would attribute it to his being a rough soldier, little accustomed to the formalities of peace.

I expressed my great obligations to his Highness, and assured him that I felt too sensibly his past kindness, to doubt his future attentions. It was settled that I should visit him to-morrow, and the whole etiquette was arranged with Mr. Aziz.

I received a visit from the Reverend Fathers of the Greek Convent, situated in the Greek quarter, which is dependent on the Patriarch of Alexandria.

In the morning I returned Mr. Macardle's visit, and accepted an invitation from him to be present in the evening at an Egyptian dance. I went, but was not much amused. The dancers were veiled, not from modesty, but to conceal their ugliness. They sung somewhat in the manner of the Indian nautch girls, but never raised their voice to an artificial pitch. The dances were infinitely too indecent, even for description. Mrs. Macardle, a pretty Greek, and a great number of ladies, were there; none of them seemed the least discomposed; but, on the contrary, laughed excessively: yet unquestionably this was by no means the effect of vice, but solely of habit, which had rendered the scene so familiar, that they did not perceive its impropriety, and even, when asked, danced themselves in as indecent a manner. In the intervals of the performances, the dancing girls went round, demanding money from each person.

In so turbulent a city as Cairo, every house is wisely constructed for defence, and, consequently, has no windows, or only a few of small dimensions, towards the street; they are generally built round a court, and contain a small garden within their walls. The house of Mr. Rosetti, in which Mr. Macardle resides, is very large, with lofty rooms, and well furnished; a part of the end of the state apartment is raised from the floor, and covered with rich carpet, around which are couches composed of cushions, in the Eastern style, which is called a Divan. The whole room is covered either with a mat or a carpet, and in the middle are chairs and tables: the windows are large and glazed.

The female Greeks born in Egypt are pretty, fair, and well made, when young, but child-birth destroys their figures by relaxation, and their bosoms become large and flaccid. Their head dress is Asiatic, and richly adorned with gold, pearls, and diamonds; their robes are of the same style, and consist of satins and velvets, faced or lined with fur. Unfortunately, in the same proportion in which the outside is adorned, the inside is neglected. The mind of a female Greek is a total blank, or worse.

The gentlemen of Mr. Rosetti's house are chiefly Italians, sensible, and well informed. Of the French nation there are very few. A kind of Agent goes occasionally to the Pacha, but he cannot be received in any public character, as Buonaparté is not recognised as Emperor by the Porte. The evenings are generally spent at Mr. Macardle's, where the different gentlemen resort, and play at cards.

February 18.—At three o'clock we went, by appointment, to visit the Pacha, who does not reside in the citadel, but in a large house in the Osbeckia. His Highness had sent five horses, most magnificently caparisoned, for me and my suite, and a party of his Chaous, with silver sticks, to attend us and keep off the crowd. The apartment, into which we were shewn, was crowded with soldiers, and was remarkable neither for its size nor richness. As soon as we were seated, he entered by a side door. I arose, and paid my compliments in the European fashion, while Mr. Aziz, as a native subject of the Porte, kissed the hem of his garment, and continued standing during the audience. He is a little man, of an intelligent countenance, with a reddish brown beard of moderate dimensions, but of which he seemed to be proud, as he was continually stroking it. He seated himself close to me on a Divan, and began the conversation with the usual train of compliments on my arrival, addressing me by the title of General. I thanked him for all his kindness; and, as I had been previously requested by Chedid, mentioned how well he had behaved in the Desert, and at Suez. His Highness gravely answered, that if he had behaved otherwise, his head should have answered for it. He expressed a great regard for the English, saying that he had been much with their officers, when they were in Egypt, and that he had uniformly been kindly treated; that it was therefore his inclination to do every thing in his power for them all, and particularly for a person of my consequence. It was also his duty, since he knew that we were the steadiest friends of the Porte. We conversed on the reports which had circulated of Buonaparté having taken Vienna: he said he could hardly believe it, though every thing was possible in such wars as these. He told me that the French Agent had been to notify it to him, and to inform him, that it was now the great Emperor's intention to reconquer the Crimea from Russia, and restore it to the Porte: that he had answered, "the Porte does not want the Crimea; she has already so widely extended an empire, that she cannot manage the whole of it; she only wants friends." I told his Highness, that if Buonaparté got the Crimea, he would restore it to the Porte as he did Egypt. He replied, he knew that very well; and if France should be victorious, he was very much afraid they should have to fight again for this country, and that the Turkish troops were not capable of resisting the French; that they were not now what they were formerly. I observed, that they had fought bravely, and resisted successfully, the Emperor Joseph in the last war. He replied, "aye, yet they were then much divided among themselves." He offered me every assistance in his power to visit the Pyramids, and desired I would not scruple to apply to him for every thing I wanted. Coffee was served on our entry; the cup out of which he drank was set with diamonds; our cups were of gold embossed. When sherbet was served, we took the hint to retire. He said, he hoped to see me again, and should any thing particular occur, he would send to me. His Highness was plainly dressed, and wore no jewels of any kind.

February 19.—In the morning I returned the visit of the reverend Fathers of St. Francis. The Jerusalem Convent is a very good building, and sufficiently strong to keep out the natives in a time of tumult. The church is handsome, and has some tolerable pictures, but they are spoiled by having gold crowns introduced over the heads of the saints. A very reverend Father, with a silver beard, who had lived fifty years in the convent, but who was still lively and intelligent, shewed me, with great satisfaction, the figure of St. George, his patron saint. He was extremely delighted when I told him that my name was George, and advised me to recommend myself to that saint, night and morning. They all seemed gay and contented. The Superior was a man of sense and information. These are the Capuchins whom Bruce mentions, as he always does the clergy, with disapprobation. They have a good organ, and a library tolerably filled. It has been formed by an accumulation of the private collections of such Fathers as have died in the convent:

they who remove, always take their property with them. This is the most ancient establishment of the Franciscans, and has a noble friend in the house of Rosetti. In the sacristy they shewed me the splendid habiliments, in which the Cardinal de Rohan formerly celebrated high mass, and which were given to them by Mr. Macardle. They are entirely supported by charitable contributions.

I next visited the Franciscan Fathers of the Propaganda, whom Mr. Bruce accuses of having instigated the assassination of Monsieur de Roule. He gives a minute detail of a transaction, which passed seventy years before he was in the country, but does not quote his authorities. This, at least, he should have done, when accusing a reverend body of so horrid a crime. They had heard of his accusation; and it was probably a feeling of resentment that induced them to repay the obligation, by charging him with having destroyed Luigi Balugani, the Italian youth who accompanied him into Abyssinia, in order to take the credit to himself of the drawings that he brought home. It was impossible to convince them of the injustice of their charge, though they did not attempt to produce any other evidence, than that Balugani could draw, and Mr. Bruce could not. These Franciscans are very poor; they formerly received a miserable pittance of sixty dollars each from the Propaganda at Rome, which is no longer paid. They subsist only on charity; and as they have fewer friends than the Capuchins, live very indifferently. Their convent is small, their church decent, but poorly furnished. The Superior was a Pole, an intelligent man, who spoke Italian, and a little French.

As the weather was fine, I took a walk in Mr.

Rosetti's garden, which is large, and would be very pleasant, were it not that the Albanians intrude whenever they please, take what they like, and even cut the trees with their sabres. On my return home, I received a deputation from the Greek Archbishop of Mount Sinai, excusing himself for not having visited me. He was so afraid of being insulted, that, although he had been here a year, he had never ventured to quit his convent. Having been assured that he was a very pleasant and intelligent man, I returned an answer, that I would do myself the pleasure of visiting him.

Schech Chedid, and Mohammed Ali Pacha, were by no means friends, in consequence of the former refusing to pay any tribute, and occasionally interrupting trade. I found that, when Mr. Aziz suggested to his Highness the eligibility of sending this most powerful chief to escort me across the Desert, it was difficult to induce him to enter the town; but at length he was prevailed upon to do so, on receiving the Pacha's passport, and security for his personal safety. He came in again this day, and settled with Mr. Aziz for my journey. In addition to the tent, I presented him with a shawl for himself, and a very rich piece of gold tissue for his wife, with which he declared himself more pleased than if I had given him ten times the amount in dollars. By the custom of the country, a Chief escorting a caravan was entitled formerly to four dresses; Mr. Rosetti reduced the number to two, which were also given to him. He charged eight dollars for the hire of each camel. Though only two were employed in carrying the Takterouane, yet the price was thirty-two dollars, in consequence of an idea that it is injurious to the animal. The whole expence of passing the Desert was upwards of six hundred dollars.

February 20.—In consequence of a notification to his Highness, that we wished this day to visit the Citadel, he sent early in the morning seven richly caparisoned horses for our use, an officer of the troops to conduct us, and two Chaous Bashi to keep off the crowd. We set off, accompanied by Mr. Aziz, Mr. Macardle, and many European gentlemen; and by the assistance of the Pacha's servants, who rode on asses, and did not spare their whips, made our way through the narrow streets, which were, as usual, crowded, till we reached a kind of open place before the gate of the new Citadel, opposite to which is a very noble mosque. We mounted a steep hill, paved with large flag stones, surrounded by ruins of houses lately destroyed in the disputes between the Turks and Albanians, till we reached the walls of the new Citadel, which are lofty and strong. On entering, we went directly to the hall of audience, where we expected to find the Pacha's son, but he had gone to visit his father. We were, however, received by an officer of the garrison, who presented us with pipes and coffee, in a room which was formerly the zenana of the Pacha when he lived in the citadel, and looked directly over the walls towards Old Cairo and the Pyramids. In the middle was a fountain; but in other respects, it had nothing but its size, and its consequent coolness in summer, to recommend it. The officer attended us himself to the mint, where they coin gold zequins, half zequins, and quarter zequins; also in silver, piastres and parahs. As these are much adulterated, the profit of coining is very great to government, bringing in from one thousand to twelve hundred purses: it was more in the time of the Beys. The machinery for striking the coin, is similar to that used in Europe before the inventions of Mr. Bolton, but of inferior merit. Instead of using rollers to flatten the metal, they beat it out with hammers.

We next visited Joseph's well, which has been too frequently described to require an account of it here. It is an astonishing work, for it required no common mind to sink an oblong pit of twenty-four feet by eighteen, to the depth of one hundred and forty-six feet through the solid rock, and then, not baffled by the difficulty and want of success, to persevere in sinking another, still through the solid rock, to the depth of one hundred and thirty feet, where the rock ended, and the water was found. The size of this second is only fifteen by nine, according to Norden, which is sufficient for every purpose of utility. It was probably thought unnecessary to make it larger, as it is not visible from the top, and not forming one single piece, could not be considered as ornamental.

I do not see any reason to doubt the tradition reported by Mr. Niebuhr that this, as well as the other noble works which are attributed to Joseph, were constructed by the celebrated Saladin, whose real name was Yusuff, and in whose time the citadel was constructed, though others attribute it to his minister. We next visited the Divan, which has nothing to recommend it, but its great size, being one hundred and forty-nine feet long, eighty-six broad, and between thirty and thirty-five high; formerly indeed it was splendidly ornamented, but now it is rapidly falling to decay. The French used it as an hospital, for which it is admirably adapted. The view hence, and from every part of the ramparts, which are themselves lofty, and are elevated on a rock, is most beautiful.

It extends over the ruins of Old Cairo, the villages of Boulac and Gheza, with the great Pyramids, the Pyramids of Sacara, and the Nile, to enrich the prospect. At that time the extensive plains of light-green wheat formed a singular contrast with the arid desert, and the barren rock of Mokattem. This last commands the citadel, which would otherwise be a place of great military importance, as the whole city of Cairo lies at its mercy. The French engineers wished to remove it, but Buonaparté would not consent to a measure that did not originate in himself. It would be a work of great labour, but certainly not impracticable. The new and old citadel cover a great extent of ground: they were formerly separated, but the French opened a communication between the two. All the splendid remains of antiquity are in the new citadel, where is also a very handsome place d'armes. The houses are chiefly in ruins. In the old citadel are a great many houses in better condition, but no noble public building. The walls have a parapet, and towers at equal distances, of two or three stories high, built of solid stone, with vaulted roofs; in each of which are cannon. After quitting the Divan, we visited the hall of Joseph, a noble apartment, but in ruins; four enormous pillars of red granite sustained the roof, which is now gone. They are each of one piece. The capitals are Egyptian, and seem to have been removed from some more ancient building. The walk along the ramparts on this side is as beautiful as on the other: the view from it commands the town of Cairo, with its numerous minarets, and public buildings: beyond lies the Nile, the island of Rhoda covered with large sycamore trees, the verdant plain, and the Pyramids. The line of forts erected on the different hillocks from the citadel to the Nile, are seen to a considerable distance on the left: the aqueduct of old Cairo extends to the same distance on the left, and the noble mosque which I have before mentioned forms a bold foreground to the view. On this side of the fort many cannon and mortars are mounted. The Turks considered the citadel more as a place to overawe the town, than to protect it from foreign enemies. When first built, the use of gunpowder was unknown, and it was equally valuable in both points of view, as it was too far from el Mokattem to be injured from it by any thing except artillery. We next passed to a very noble room, supported by numerous pillars of granite, each a single piece: all of these, except four, were Egyptian; the others had Corinthian capitals. The roof had fallen in, but at a great height a cornice of wood four feet broad still remained, ornamented with inscriptions from the Koran. Mr. Salt's drawings will give a better idea of these than any description. I believe all the pillars to have belonged to some more ancient building. Opposite to this room is another, which overlooked the city: it had been intirely covered with mosaic, of which a considerable part remained, though the buildings themselves had fallen to ruins, and were now filled with rubbish, instead of being occupied by the manufacturers, who used here to embroider the rich covering of the Caaba at Mecca. It is indeed a melancholy circumstance, that the many splendid remains of the ancient Sultauns, which the citadel contains, should be so rapidly disappearing. The outer walls may continue to defend the garrison within, and the massive columns of Egyptian architecture may survive the destruction of the apartments they were meant to adorn; but civil broils will destroy every other vestige, that could point out the citadel of Cairo as the former abode of monarchs. Near this is the mortar battery, whence Hurshid Pacha bombarded the town during the late disturbances. We visited a round tower, somewhat resembling the castle of Saint Angelo at Rome: it consists of three stories, with one chief apartment on each. The stair case is excellent. Cannon are mounted on the tower. The whole is of stone with vaulted roofs, and is probably as old as the foundation of the citadel. We rode through the old citadel, but returned into town by that gate of the new by which we entered.

With my own party and Mr. Macardle, I visited the Greek Archbishop of Mount Sinai. He is a handsome young man, of considerable talents, an excellent scholar, and liberal in his sentiments. He was educated at St. Petersburg, and spoke French fluently. The convent is small, but extremely neat. He informed me that it was founded in the third century. He had a good library of books, among which was Norden, and several other writers on Egypt. He had not got Niebuhr; I therefore requested his acceptance of my copy, which I could easily replace in Europe. He informed me that there were forty monks of the order of St. Catharine, here and at Mount Sinai; that they had convents at Jerusalem, in Asia Minor, and in Russia; the whole number of fathers amounting to about two hundred. He said that he wished to get out of this place, but that the Arabs demanded one hundred thousand piastres every time the doors of a convent were opened to admit a new archbishop, and that they were not at that moment in a situation to pay such a sum. This is the only occasion on which the gates are ever opened. All visitors ascend to a window by a basket, as in the other convents among the Arabs. I observed, that he would be nearly as much a prisoner at Mount Sinai as here; he replied, that there he should have a fine climate, and an excellent and large garden to walk in, which is surrounded by a high wall, and is separated from the convent, but communicates by a subterraneous passage. He would also have the consolation of being in a most holy place, for St Catharine's of Mount Sinai is as much venerated in the Greek church, as Jerusalem is in the Catholic; pilgrimages are made to it, and the good fathers dispersed over Europe and Asia, make large collections from the faithful, which are remitted to Mount Sinai, and enable the archbishop to sustain the expence of his entry, and of nearly feeding all the Arabs around, who, on this account, willingly convoy the provisions from Egypt, without which the reverend monks could not exist in the desert. He informed me that one tower exists that was built by Helena; but that the rest of the convent was erected by Justinian. I enquired respecting manuscripts; he said he was informed that there were some, but of what kind he could not yet say, as he had never been there.

He presented us with sherbet, coffee, and liqueurs. Every thing was neat, and had an air of affluence. The library, which they used as a council chamber, was filled with an infinity of small pictures of different saints, most of which had crowns of real gold, and some had the whole drapery in the same strange way. There was a small picture of a beautiful St. Catherine, without any of this meretricious ornament. Monseigneur attended me to the door, and declared he was determined to venture out, for the first time, to have the pleasure of paying his compliments to me.

February 21.—The scenery from the Citadel had excited in me so great a degree of admiration, that I determined Mr. Salt should take a set of views from it, which would answer as a Panorama. Early in the morning he therefore set off, with one of the Chaous Bashi to protect him, and Mr. Thomaso to interpret for him. He continued there several hours, and met with no molestation.—The Archbishop of Mount Sinai sent me a present of apples, pomegranates, and almonds, from St. Catharine's, also a large flask of Cyprus wine, which he assured me was ten years old.

February 22.—It was impossible to persuade Mohammed Ali that my objects were not political, and as the English had ever been on friendly terms with the Beys, and latterly their protectors against the Porte, he was extremely jealous of my having any communication with them. The most distant hint of visiting Upper Egypt, therefore, excited alarm, and I was obliged to abandon the idea altogether.

The Archbishop of Mount Sinai fulfilled his promise, and this day paid me a visit, accompanied by two of his clergy. They were much interested by the Axum inscription, which he requested me to lend him, that he might endeavour to translate it. One of his attendants read a great part of it with facility. Mr. Salt again went to the Citadel, and sketched a proportion of the view, in defiance of a high wind, which raised clouds of dust among the ruins.

February 23.—I went to the mass of the Franciscans of Jerusalem. As it was Lent, the organ did not play. The voices were fine. Afterwards we accompanied the Superior to the Refectory, where, according to their constant custom, coffee, liqueurs and gingerbread were served round. The custom of taking liqueurs is very general.

February 24.—Signor Filippo Agnelli, who is employed by the Emperor of Germany to preserve animals, and collect other curiosities in this country, arrived to-day from Damietta at Mr. Macardle's, and immediately waited on me. As I knew that his Imperial Majesty was much attached to natural history, I gave Signor Agnelli a very large collection of shells, which I had found in the Red Sea, and every duplicate in my possession, either from India, Arabia, or Abyssinia, to be presented, in my name, to his master. The skins of the Abyssinian birds, which Mr. Salt had brought from Tigré, being infested with vermin, I was fearful that they would never reach England in a state to be described: anxious to preserve them for the public, as many specimens were perfectly new, I thought it of little consequence whether they were in my own cabinet or another's, and therefore gave the whole, amounting to one hundred specimens, to Signor Agnelli, who promised that he would immediately begin to put them in order. He was extremely delighted, as with all his assiduity, he had been able in three years to make no very large collection. At Suez, in particular, during a residence of three months, he had obtained fewer shells than I had done in fifteen days. Alone, and without servants, it is impossible to accomplish much, for the Arabs will do nothing that gives them trouble, even for money.

It rained very heavily last night. The houses are ill adapted for wet weather. Mr. Macgie was driven from his bed, and my room was deluged with rain. The thermometer was at 55°.

February 25.—We had hitherto intended to visit the Pyramids on the 27th, but at present were afraid of a disappointment. Elfi Bey has appeared in the neighbourhood, and his advanced guard is said to be within an hour's march of Gheza, and he himself within four. He has a force of ten thousand men, and may mean to march into Lower Egypt and spread devastation, as he did once before. If so, we may be able in a day or two to go thither; if not, it will be impossible, although we have nothing to fear from him, who is attached to the English, and ever speaks with gratitude and delight of his reception in England. Yet, mixed as his army is with Arabs and Albanians, it might be dangerous to fall in with them; besides, Mohammed Ali would have fair grounds of suspicion that I had some political intention in meeting him. That he has already taken the alarm at Elfi's approach, was hinted to me to day by Malum Gali, the Coptic receiver general of the revenue of Egypt, here called the Bas Kateb, a respectable and able young man. He excused himself from not having called before, by assuring me that he had not heard of my arrival, which is very possible, as he is occupied from morning till night. He said, laughing, that he felt himself quite comfortable at escaping for a few minutes from incessant persecution; but at that very moment a fellow, who had chased him to the British House, entered with a paper, on which he laughed, and took his leave. I have no doubt that he was sent by the Pacha to give me the hint not to see Elfi. After all the attentions I had received from his Highness, I would, on no account, do any thing that might be disagreeable to him; besides, were he to have any suspicions, in such critical times as these, all the Europeans might suffer for it. A private individual might do much, which I cannot, from the consequence they have been pleased, unfortunately in some respects for me, to attach to my title, which has been increased by my having a Company's cruiser to bring me to Suez. Malum Gali has promised to give me information of Elfi's motions.

I paid a visit to Signor Filippo, who shewed me his whole collection. The fishes are most beautifully preserved; those of the Nile are very curious, and some of an enormous size. I was surprised to see among them a species of the same genus as that which blows itself up, and is covered with spines. I thought it was peculiar to the sea. He was so kind as to give me several specimens, and to offer to teach any of my people how to preserve them, and the birds. He has been several years in the Emperor's service, and told me that he once preserved for his Majesty a favourite negro, whom he has seated on the back of a camel.

February 26.—If Elfi were at the Pyramids, it seems he has marched on; for his Highness sent this evening to inform me, that his horses were ready for to-morrow, and that he had ordered the Governor of Gheza to attend me with all his troops, and to answer with his head for my safety. I deferred our journey till Sunday, as Saturday is the great festival of Beiram, and it would have been rather hard to take the good Governor away from his people on such an occasion.

February 28.—Mr. Salt went again to the Citadel, but was soon obliged to return, as they began to celebrate the festival of Beiram, by firing musquetry with balls; an amusement by no means safe for the by-standers. I went to see his Highness pass to the mosque, which he did in very great state. Some of his Chaous Bashi were most magnificently dressed. His two sons preceded him: the eldest is a fine boy; the second is less handsome, but is said to be intelligent. Some young Mamelukes attended him, whose complexions were fairer than any Europeans, and if they were not painted, the vermillion tint of their cheeks was superior to any thing I ever saw in nature. His Highness was plainly dressed, and, as at my interview, incessantly stroked his beard.

March 1.—The French Agent notified to his Highness that he had official intelligence from Constantinople of the peace being signed between France and Austria, and of a very great victory obtained over the Russians by Buonaparté. He, at the same time, requested the Pacha to lend him some cannon to fire a salute on the occasion. The Pacha replied that he did not believe his story, and that if he did, he would not let him have the cannon.

March 2.—The disturbances in Egypt during the last three years, had rendered a visit to the Pyramids too dangerous for individuals to venture, and I, consequently, had numerous applications from the Europeans who happened to be in Cairo, to permit them to attend me, with which, of course, I complied. The Pacha supplied my party with horses, and sent two Chaous Bashi to take care of us, as usual. About eleven we quitted the city, and passing among the innumerable hillocks, composed of broken pottery, decayed bricks, and sand, which rise to a great height between New and Old Cairo, at length reached the convent of St. George, which is within the walls of the Citadel of the latter. It consists of a lofty round tower, divided into many apartments, and some square buildings, both of great antiquity.

As the air is salubrious, and the vicinity to the

river and the groves of the island of Rhoda, renders the scene more pleasing than the narrow streets of the city, it was formerly the custom for many respectable families to reside here during the summer months, the good fathers supplying them with provisions, and by the presents they received in return, adding somewhat to their own scanty pittance. The heavy contributions which Mohammed Ali was obliged to levy on that part of the country, which is under his control, in order to satisfy the rapacity of the Albanian banditti, who raised him to power, have ruined numbers, and have reduced the monks of St. George to so wretched a state, that they have been obliged to abandon this large convent, and retire to one smaller within the city. They however came out in order to receive me, as I wished to sleep at their house, that I might have the whole day before us to reach the Pyramids. The church is neat and clean, and, as it is dedicated to the Patron saint of the English, a corner is reserved for the sepulture of such of that nation as die here. The pictures are in the worst style of modern Greek art.

Our party did not consist of less than forty, who, after resting, determined to take a walk, and look at the Mekias. This building has ever been a greater object of curiosity than it seems to merit, though the pillar in the centre is very handsome. This is divided into numerous compartments, as is shewn in the drawing of Norden, and affords the means of ascertaining the rise of the Nile, with which the bason that surrounds it has a communication. Every traveller either has visited it, or wishes to have it supposed that he did so. Pococke's drawings are always so bad, that the sins of omission and commission, which cover his view of the Mekias, do not lead me to doubt of his having seen it. But that Mr Bruce should have preferred his naked and erroneous view to the perfect drawing of Norden, if he had ever himself seen it, I cannot believe; yet so he has done; for the drawing given in his work is an exact copy from that of Pococke. Mr. Bruce, as usual, talks of the difficulty of his attempt to see it, and this certainly was the case at all times to a native Christian, but never to a Frank, except during the time of the rise of the river, when, from political reasons, all access would be denied.

We wandered for some time among the ruins of a palace which stood around the Mekias, and had several flights of steps descending to the river. A mosque had formerly been its chief ornament, the roof being supported by Corinthian pillars of Italian marble. But even this holy edifice had not been spared during the civil wars between the Beys and Albanians, and the artillery of both parties had equally contributed to its destruction when they occupied the opposite sides of the river, and were constantly firing at each other.

Our next visit was to a Jewish synagogue, which had nothing remarkable in it, but its filth; and we afterwards examined a Coptic church, which was not only more cleanly, but was an object of curiosity, from its being believed to contain the cell, in which the Virgin Mary resided during her abode in Egypt. It is a vault under the body of the church, containing an ovenlike aperture, where the infant Jesus was supposed to have slept. Many of our attendants took the opportunity of so free an access, to chip off small bits of wood from the beams which supported the roof, to wear as amulets about their persons.

We returned to the convent and found an excellent dinner provided, and plenty of good wine sent from the Residency. I invited all the gentlemen to partake with me. This was the day fixed on by the French Agent to celebrate the victories of his master. He had invited the Pacha's interpreter to be of the party, but his Highness ordered him, "to go and dine with the General" (as he always called me), "and accompany him to the Pyramids." I was very glad to see him join our party, as it added a consequence to us, and greatly increased our security by the certainty which every one felt, that if any thing should be wrong, he would report it to his master.

March 3.—We were all up by five, and immediately passed the river to Gheza, but, when there, discovered that the Governor, who had been ordered to attend us with all his garrison, had gone out, in the night, to a neighbouring village, in consequence of the appearance of a Bey, and some Mamelukes of Elfi in its vicinity. Our friend the interpreter went to him, and soon returned with assurances, that the Governor had certain information of the enemy being one thousand strong, that he believed they were come down solely to attack us, and that therefore he had felt it his duty to communicate to his Highness this unexpected circumstance, and must wait for his commands before he could venture to move. He very politely added, that as he hoped to be able to make them retire in the course of the day, I might not like to return to Old Cairo, in which case his house was very much at my service. I declined his invitation, and preferred lounging during the day in the groves and gardens of Rhoda, while the Interpreter went to the Pacha. He joined us again at dinner, and brought a message from his Highness, expressing his extreme regret at what had happened, assuring me that he would send over troops sufficient to protect me, and that his houshold cavalry, and the French Mamelukes should attend me as a body guard to the Pyramids.

March 4.—We sent over our horses yesterday evening to avoid delay, and were up early: but our impatience was useless. It was ten before a Mameluke appeared, and then the guards were not arrived. At length, to my great surprise, I was informed, that Taher Pacha, Mohammed Ali's nephew, was arrived, and sitting on the bank of the river. I immediately went to pay my compliments to him, when he received me very civilly, and offered me a share of the carpet on which he was sitting, which I accepted. He told me his uncle had sent him over to Gheza to make arrangements for my visit to the Pyramids, that he was taking over many men, that more were passing by Boulac, and that he expected, in the course of the evening, every thing would be settled, in which case he would send to me. He now began to joke with the Mameluke boys around him, and obliged one to own himself a French lad, and speak in his native language to us. He was an odd-looking, little animal in his Mussulmaun dress, and carried his master's snuff box. The conversation then turned on Jidda, and he told me he was going there when Egypt was quiet. I warned him against the Sheriffe; he replied, he knew him well, and would take care of him.

I should myself much doubt if Taher Pacha will ever go to Jidda. His uncle was appointed originally, but when the revolution gave him Egypt, he appointed this young man in his stead, but has hitherto kept him here. The Porte can hardly choose to give an office of such high respectability to so young a man, and the relation of a person whom they already fear. I have been told that, in general, the Pachalic of Jidda has been considered as an honourable banishment for life, as the Sultaun himself is obliged to rise to receive the minister of so holy a place on his return, to avoid which, as being derogatory to the dignity of the sovereign, he is never recalled.

I heard an anecdote of the present Sultaun Selim, which, if true, does him the highest honour. On his accession, the Pacha of Jidda was his tutor, for whom he had the greatest regard. He determined to recall him, but the Divan remonstrated, representing the indecorum of his getting up to receive him. "What," said he, "shall I be ashamed to get up to my second father? No, let him be sent for immediately." He accordingly arrived, and Selim not only rose, but advanced to the door to receive him, and, after embracing, placed him by his side.

When all his troops were over, Taher Pacha got up himself, and, smacking his open hand against mine, took his leave with great good humour. He is young and rather handsome, has the appearance of being good-tempered, but did not seem to possess much ability. He sent in the evening to say, that every thing was settled, and that I might come over in the morning.

March 5.—Our party passed the river as soon as it was light, but Mussulmauns are not to be hurried, and it was some time before the governor of the town joined us with a large body of cavalry, and a piece of curricle artillery. We crossed the plain direct for the Pyramids, while Taher Pacha kept between us and some villages to the north, where the Mamelukes and Arabs were said to be. He had with him full two thousand infantry, and another piece of curricle artillery, a force more than sufficient for our protection. I cannot say that I was struck with that astonishment, which many have expressed on approaching these vast masses. The idea of a Pyramid is easily conceived, and consequently surprise cannot enter the feelings of a person when he first beholds them. When, however, reason points out the prodigious labour, with which they must have been erected, and the incomprehensible motives, which could have led to such vast exertions, astonishment gradually increases, and the mind is lost in conjecture and admiration.

On reaching the entrance into the great Pyramid, we were joined by many Arabs, residing in the neighbouring vaults, who offered their services in assisting us among the ruins, and clearing the passage that led to what is usually called the Sepulchral chamber, from the sand that had accumulated in it. This was rapidly executed, and the flambeaux being lighted, the party entered. The different passages and chambers have been so often visited and described, that it is impossible for any new discovery to be made by a modern traveller. The French have ascertained the actual dimensions, and it is curious, that Diodorus should have been proved to be correct, who has stated the base to be seven hundred feet, and the elevation six hundred. The British army had leisure to visit it frequently, and the officers have added their testimony to that of their predecessors, that the great pyramid is built of a stone found in the vicinity, and of which the rock itself on which it is erected, is composed. If ever this, or the others, were covered with marble or granite, not a vestige now remains to prove the fact; but it is probable that they were at least intended to be thus adorned, from the passages being of the finest white marble, and the chambers of the red granite of Upper Egypt.

If it were dubious in the time of Herodotus, by whom, or for what purpose, the pyramids were constructed, it is scarcely possible that modern ingenuity should clear away the deeper gloom with which the course of ages has covered the mystery; yet every person, who has written on the subject, has embraced some decided opinion, and many have laboured hard to prove, what must ever remain doubtful. Among these, Monsieur Maillet is the most remarkable, who has described the process of closing the great pyramid, as accurately as if he had been present when it was done. I am myself inclined to believe that it never was intended to be shut up, nor that any pains were taken to conceal the approaches to the great chamber; for if such were the case, nothing could be more absurd, than to line the passages, from the entrance to the extremity, with a highly polished white marble, which would have served as a guide to any depredator, and would have precluded the possibility of erring either to the right or left; whereas, if the passage had been formed of the same materials as the rest of the building, nearly a moiety of it might have been destroyed before its contents could have been discovered. If, on the contrary, the pyramid were intended to be open for the celebration of any of the sacred mysteries, the lining of polished marble to the passage, and the splendid coating of granite, which adorns the chambers, would be at once accounted for, and the sarcophagus might have been destined to contain the supposed body of Osiris during the annual lamentations for his loss.

The usual account of Cheops having finished it

for his own interment, seems hardly reconcileable with the account of Herodotus, of his being buried in an island surrounded by the Nile, which might be *under*, but could not be *in* the pyramid, from its being elevated one hundred feet above the level of the plain. The ridiculous account of the Arab historians, of the body of a king having been discovered adorned with jewels, when Sultaun Almamoun opened the pyramid, is unworthy of consideration, for it appears that the passage was open in the time of Strabo and Pliny, who mention the oblique descent, and the well of eighty-six cubits. The conjecture of Pococke seems worthy of more attention, who believes that the whole point of the high land, which protrudes due east into the plain of the Nile, was intended to be covered with an uniform pile, of which the existing pyramids were to form a part, and that others were to be erected, to correspond with the great pyramid and the third. The second pyramid would then be in the centre, with the sphinx in front of it. The regularity of the excavations which surround this building on two sides, leaving an opening to the east, and the fact that the causeways extend in the same direction, seem to prove, that this was intended as the front of the pile, and thereby confirm the conjecture of our learned countryman.

Mr. Bruce, who certainly visited the pyramids, has given us only one observation, and that is totally contrary to the truth, viz. "that large fragments of the rock are visible in the roof of the great chamber, where the sarcophagus stands, and also in the top of the roof of the gallery, as you go up into that chamber." I have before stated that the pyramid itself is built of a stone found on the spot, but that the gallery is lined with white marble, and the chambers with the finest granite.

Among the renegado French, who escorted me, was a man, who said he had accompanied Buonaparté on his visit to the pyramids, and assured me that that General had sent down a man into the well, with a cord fastened to him, but that, after he had descended some distance, they found it impossible to get him out, probably from some curve in the passage. It is to be regretted that the experiment failed, for the description of Herodotus gives sufficient grounds for believing that we are hitherto unacquainted with many of the mysteries of this gloomy building.

Taher Pacha sent so frequently to hasten my departure, that, at length, we were obliged, however unwillingly, to comply. He immediately prepared to attack the Mamelukes, who were lurking in the date groves; but his Albanians thought it safest to proceed so slowly, that the enemy had sufficient time to retire before they were within reach. Taher Pacha told them plainly, that they were only fit to extort money from the peaceable natives, but that they would never be induced to seize it from an armed enemy. Our cavalry attended us across the plain to Gheza, a distance of only six miles, but rendered very fatiguing by the cultivation of the ground, over which we were obliged to move, and by the heat of the sun passing through an unclouded sky. We were all heartily fatigued when we reached Cairo, after having been in motion for twelve hours.

March 6th.—I received a letter from Captain Court, informing me that they were in the greatest distress for water and provisions. At my request, Mr. Macardle very kindly sent off his

Archbishop of Mount Sinai, to take my leave of servant to Schech Chedid, desiring him instantly to forward to Suez, forty sheep and three bullocks.

I went this day to visit his Highness the Pacha, to take my leave. I mentioned to him the distress of the Panther for water. He instantly ordered a letter to be written to the Governor on the subject: it was sealed in my presence, and delivered to me to be forwarded. I observed that he watched the Secretary very closely the whole time the seal was in his hand. He presented me a sabre with his own hand, requesting I would keep it for his sake. His attendants gave one to Mr. Macgie, Mr. Salt, Captain Rudland, and my servant. Shortly afterwards, I was presented with a rich pelisse of sable, worth here about two thousand piastres. He made a great many professions of regard, and apologies for any neglect that might have taken place. On asking if he had any commands for England, he requested me to procure him a good pair of pistols, which I, of course, promised. He pointed out his two sons to me, who were standing on my right hand. On my taking leave, he rose up and spoke to me—a most pointed compliment, and contrary to his religion, as well as his dignity.

March 7.—We hired a boat which had been taken by the Pacha to carry up the troops, but which, at our request, he immediately discharged. I sent his Highness a diamond ring, more than equal in value to his presents. He requested me, through the interpreter, to procure him a gun, as well as a pair of pistols, and promised that he would not be behind hand in making a suitable return.

March 9.—I called, in the morning, on the

him, and to request that, on his arrival at his monastery, he would examine the manuscripts, and let me hear from him if there were any thing that was valuable; which he promised to do. He certainly had not weaned himself from the vanities of this world, for he shewed us, with evident complacency, his mitre, and a brilliant cross, which had been given him by the Emperor Alexander. The poverty of his convent, I suspected to be an excuse for the delay at Cairo, while the real cause was a lurking hope, that he might be able to obtain some preferment in Europe, and thereby avoid a perpetual seclusion on Mount Sinai. We determined to quit Cairo on the morrow, and therefore sent our baggage to Boulac, and hired a small boat for the cook and provisions.

The rank which the Pacha had been pleased to bestow upon me, of General, and the consequence which he annexed to my arrival, were so far fortunate as they enabled me to see the pyramids, and every thing that was interesting in Cairo, but the expence which it brought on me was very great. The journey to the pyramids cost me above four hundred dollars, and the visits to the Pacha three hundred more, in presents to his servants. The Bedowee Arabs brought in many Egyptian antiquities, which I purchased under the guidance of my friend Signor Filippo, before whose arrival I had, as is usual, been most completely imposed upon. My stay had been rendered very comfortable by the unremitting attentions of Mr. Macardle, a countryman by extraction, though born in Italy, and whose long residence in Egypt enabled him to be particularly useful to a stranger. My worthy friend Mr. Macgie, who had attended me with the utmost anxiety, during repeated indispositions, was now obliged to return to the ship. Chedid undertook to provide him with a Tackterouane, and to protect him to Suez, with the different articles which he had purchased for the officers and crew of the Panther.

CHAPTER XI.

Departure from Grand Cairo.—Arrival at Rosetta.—Conference with Carlo Rosetti.—Voyage to Alexandria.—Visit to the Governor.—Journey along the Coast to Rosetta.—Preparations for a Tour in the Delta.—Berimbal.—Voyage on the Lake Bourlos.—Boltine.—Arrival at Damietta.—Account of Antiquities found there.—Observations on Mr. Savary's Account of ancient Damietta.—Descriptions of the Lake Menzale, and the Ruins of Thouna.—Visit to Matarieh.—Account of the Schech.—Return to Damietta.—Voyage to Mansoura.—Journey to Timai in the Desert.—Description of the Ruins.—Journey from Mansoura to Bahbeite.—Remains of the Temple of Isis.—Journey across the Delta by Mahallet-el-Keber to Foua.—Dispute with the Albanians, and its consequences.—Arrival at Rosetta.—Observations on the Delta.—Return to Alexandria.

MARCH 10.—About ten we mounted the Pacha's horses for the last time. Mr. Macardle and Mr. Aziz attended us. We passed by the Osbeckia, a large square covered with grain, but which the French had planted, and laid out in a very beautiful style. Every tree was however cut down by the Turks as soon as they were gone. Here was the palace of Elfi Bey, the best in the town, and where Buonaparté lived: it was set on fire by the Arnauts when they bombarded Mohammed Pacha, who had fortified it, and the outer wall alone remains. Boulac is completely in ruins. It joined Cairo in its revolt against the French, though an open town, and was taken by storm in about a quarter of an hour. It was given up for three days to the plunder of the troops, who set it on fire in several places. Mr. Rosetti had here an excellent house and garden; the latter was destroyed by the French, the former by the Turks. He has now a small house pleasantly situated on the river, with excellent warehouses. We here took our farewell breakfast, and about two embarked, taking Mr. Thomaso with us to secure supplies. The wind was tolerably fair, but our Rais, or Captain, had not all his people on board, and therefore crossed from side to side. At length they came, and we set off in earnest. I was in a canja, the boat described by Mr. Bruce, and looked about for his main yard two hundred feet long; ours was but one hundred; though I understood few were larger, and those only a very little. I looked also in vain for his little stick, with which a single man was to move so prodigious a weight as a yard of one hundred feet, with a proportionable sail annexed. Alas! the present race has lost this valuable discovery, which, not even Mr. Bruce's elegant drawing and section could preserve, and it is now necessary to employ seven or eight men to dip the yard, and change it from one side to the other. Our cabin was comfortable, though low, and we were furnished with excellent provision through the care of Mr. Thomaso. The Rais went on till about two, when he stopped for day-light to pass a place considered as dangerous, in consequence of piles driven into the river to turn a part of the stream into the Damietta branch, which was nearly dry. This work succeeded, but occasioned the loss of several vessels.

The river winds so considerably, that every half hour the wind must be adverse, let it come from what point it will. It blew fresh towards the middle of the day, and drove us against a bank, where we were obliged to track. We reached Menuf about twelve, March 11, but our cook-boat did not make its appearance till three. During our stay I received a very polite message from the Kacheef, saying that he should be happy to see me, or would pay me a visit. I went to him. He was a sensible Turk, who made very civil speeches. He wished to know if I wanted any thing. He expressed a regret that, as he had not many sheep, he had been able to send me only two, but had a bullock at my service if I wished for it. This I declined, and soon took my leave. I found the sheep had arrived, with a cargo of bread, and some coffee. A present was requisite in return. I sent him a muslin embroidered shawl, and, in consequence of a hint, given to my servant, two bottles of brandy. He was highly pleased with both, declared the latter excellent, and gave my Arab servant twenty-five piastres. My cook-boat had leaked; the Kacheef offered me another; but as the leak was stopped, I did not like to lose time. We were in motion about five, and sailed all night with a fair wind.

March 12.—The wind continued fair and fresh all day. We passed rapidly through a country generally in a high state of cultivation, and crowded with villages, but which afforded no variety of scene. We landed occasionally when the windings of the river made the wind adverse, and tracking necessary. We entered the villages without the smallest fear, and uniformly met with a civil reception from the inhabitants, who seemed to be wretchedly lodged, and to have no visible property. We did not stop to view Rahmanie, celebrated by the engagement between the French and English, but hastened on to Rosetta, where we arrived at ten, and were most hospitably received by Mr. Petrucci, the British Vice Consul.

March 13.—In the morning Mr. Rosetti, who acts as Consul General for the Emperors of Russia and Germany, paid me a visit. He is now very old, having acted a considerable part in the revolutions which have taken place from the time of Ali Bey till the arrival of the French. His figure is dignified, and his faculties still unimpaired. He has several monopolies for the government, and still carries on a more extensive trade than any other person. After the usual compliments, and my having returned him thanks for the invaluable assistance he had afforded me by sending Mr. Thomaso to Suez, and permitting him to accompany me to Rosetta, he inquired of me if I had known Mr. Bruce, which immediately led to a conversation respecting that traveller. He said, that he had known him well, while on his way to the Red Sea; that he had accompanied him in his canja to Cairo, and had been constantly with him during his residence there; that he had therefore begun to read his book as soon as he had received it, but had never finished it, from finding so many mis-statements respecting Ali Bey, all the adventures with whom were, to his knowledge, romances. "You may know," said he, "that Bruce never saw Ali Bey, by the description he gives of the diamonds in his turban: every one will inform you, that no Mameluke ever wore any jewels there; it is contrary to their custom." Rosetti was in Italy when Bruce returned, and saw him, as he says, at Venice. He and another gentleman were shewn the drawings made in Egypt and Abyssinia; but the latter observed that they were in the Italian manner, which so extremely offended Bruce, that he refused to exhibit any more. I expressed to him my regret that he had not himself given us an account of Ali Bey, and the revolutions which had since taken place, a task which no one was so competent to execute. He replied, that he had once begun a work of that sort, but that his partner had committed it to the flames in a time of tumult, fearful that his enemies might seize it, and use it as an instrument to injure him with the Beys. He said he was now too old to begin it again; but at my request promised that he would mark in Savary, Volney, and the other authors who had written on Egypt, what was true, and what was false.

March 14.—I had the pleasure in the morning of hearing from my friend Captain Court, that the Pacha's letter had a very beneficial effect on the Dola of Suez, who expressed the greatest anxiety to comply with his Highness's orders; in consequence of which they received a daily supply of water, but the quality was so indifferent, that the scurvy began to appear among the sepoys; and he feared, if the vessel were detained much longer for Major Missett's dispatches, that many would suffer severely. I hoped that the supply of forty sheep and three bullocks, which I learned from Mr. Macardle had actually been sent off by Chedid, would counteract the ill effects of the brackish water. After having been so fortunate as not to lose a single man, during a continuance of thirteen months in the Red Sea, out of nearly ninety persons, it would have been painful to see them perish, when about to return to the comforts of India.

March 22.—On the 20th all our baggage was embarked on board a jerm, to sail for Alexandria, but we had scarcely quitted the shore when the wind came round to the westward, and blew so heavy a gale, that it was impossible to pass the Bogaz, or shoal at the mouth of the river; and even if that could have been done, no jerm would have ventured out with a foul wind, for there is no place in which shelter could be found between it and Alexandria. We yesterday went down to the mouth in Mr. Petrucci's boat, and found a very heavy surf beating on the shore, and shoals, though the wind had moderated. The fishermen were actively employed in the shallow water, and caught, while we were there, a great number of very fine mullet. The Mediterranean afforded me no interesting marine productions on my first visit, and the arid sand of the sea shore was equally unproductive of vegetable curiosities.

March 23.—The swell having gone down, in consequence of the wind's coming round to the south, we sailed from Rosetta at half after five in the morning, accompanied by an intelligent young Italian, of the name of Cravazza, in the employment of Mr. Petrucci. An officer is constantly appointed to attend at the mouth of the river, to point out the course to the vessels passing. He is called the Captain of the Bogaz, and was at his station, anchored in the shallowest part, to pay his compliments, and ask for a present, which was given him.

The wind was very fresh, but so far favourable that we could lay our course. After passing Aboukir it became more foul, but by a single tack we were enabled to reach the new harbour of Alexandria. As soon as the British flag was seen from the shore, the Major dispatched his interpreter, Mr. François, to receive us. On the beach I was met by Major Missett, and the other members of the mission. The Consuls of the different European powers, not at war with Great Britain, sent their dragomans to attend me, and the Governor sent forty of his Chaous. I proceeded to the house of Mr. Briggs, the British Consul, where I found myself most excellently lodged.

The reception I met with in Egypt was most uncommonly flattering, and I felt the more pleased with it, as I found that it extremely mortified the French Agents. Mr. Drovetti, their Consul, could not contain his vexation. He exclaimed, "how very ridiculous to make such an uproar about a private individual!" but he well knew that, although in fact his observation were just, yet that I was on this occasion a public pageant, as no one believed that I had come without political motives; an idea which Major Missett encouraged, to counteract the intrigues of the French, whose agents had for some time unblushingly asserted, that England considered Egypt as of no consequence, and did not wish to keep up any connection with it. I received a message from the Governor of Alexandria, stating, that he was rejoiced to hear of my safe arrival, and that he would have paid his compliments in person, if he had not been particularly engaged. This was a Turkish compliment, and a very high one to a Christian; although untrue, for he was, in fact, perfectly at leisure; but he justly considered himself as entitled to the first visit.

March 24.—The different Consuls paid me a visit, and were received with due civility. A very respectable native, who acted as Surbaje, or chief magistrate of Alexandria, during the time the English were there, was also introduced to me. He had quitted Egypt with them, and retired to Malta, where he was astonished and gratified by a reception as friendly as if his assistance had still been required. He received from them a pension of ten shillings per day, on which he lived very comfortably, having a few villages of his own. He openly professed his attachment to the English, and refused to hold his former office under the Turks. He was nevertheless on very good terms with the present Governor, and highly respected by the Arabs, and inhabitants of the town. In the morning I visited the Governor, who had drawn out a considerable detachment of the Turkish soldiers, disciplined after the European manner, who presented arms in a very good style; he himself, at the head of his houshold, received me at the outward door, and condueted me to the audience room, where I partook of the usual refreshments, sweetmeats, coffee and sherbet, after which he again escorted me to the street, when I was saluted by the Turkish frigates in the Old Harbour. Mr. Drovetti, the French Agent, wrote to me in the evening, expressing his regret that political circumstances put it out of his power to wait on me.

On the 25th I returned the visits of the Consuls; on the 26th the Governor returned my visit, and on the 29th accepted an invitation to dine with Major Missett, on condition that we would dine with him the day following. He showed us the whole of the house, which is new and elegant, particularly the hall of audience and the room over it, where we dined, which has a beautiful view of the Old

Harbour. These rooms are richly ornamented with arabesque paintings and coloured glass, and are of a size well adapted to a sultry climate. The whole was built by a former Governor, who commanded when the French stormed the place, and who was beheaded by them. Emim Effendi, the Aga, was a Candiot, and belonged to the navy, having commanded a frigate before his elevation to the government. He had with him an adopted brother, Dervish Effendi, who with the Surbaje formed our Mussulmaun society. The dinner was excellent, particularly the pastry and confectionary. The whole was served in the European style, and wine was freely drank by the whole party. Arab music was played during the dinner, and afterwards, the Aga and his brother amused us greatly by singing several Greek and Turkish love songs. The whole passed off with great good humour, and it was a late hour before we took our leave.

April 13.—Our friend the Surbaje considered it as a compliment that we should dine with him, we therefore did so. His house was plain and neat, and his table well served, but not so splendidly as the Governor's. He informed me that he had no family, and only one wife, which he said was the custom of his family. Emim Aga and Dervish Effendi were of the party. Mr. Briggs gave a ball this day to the European inhabitants of respectability, at which several very pretty Italian girls were present: twelve couple danced English and Piedmontese dances, to a band composed of several violins, played on by gentlemen, and a large English harpsichord brought out by Elfi Bey, and which had been purchased, from his plunderers, for two hundred piastres.

April 19.—No vessel had arrived in which it was possible for us to sail, nor could we hear of any that was expected. Major Missett therefore had the goodness to write to Sir Alexander Ball, at Malta, representing my situation, and the ineligibility of my running the risk of falling into the hands of the French, with all my papers, and suggesting that an armed vessel should be sent for me. As however it would be full six weeks before we could receive an answer, I determined to visit Damietta, and the lakes that separate the Delta from the sea shore. Mr. Briggs, Captain Vincenzo Taberna, and his brother, accompanied us. In the morning I sent off our baggage and servants, by a jerm, to Rosetta, where we were to make our arrangements for the journey, by the advice and with the assistance of Messrs. Rosetti and Petrucci, who were in the mean time to engage our Arab attendants. The Major gave a party at the gardens to the Governor and the Surbaje, who afterwards took a farewell dinner with us.

April 20.—After an early breakfast we departed by the Rosetta gate, where we found Emim Aga seated, watching for our arrival to take leave, and wish us a good journey. He had lent us two tents, and had even extended his politeness so far as to offer to send a Turkish frigate with me and my party to Damietta. This I declined, as I did not consider the coast as a very safe one for unskilful seamen. We passed by the Canopic gate, which is distinguishable from the hillocks of rubbish on each side. Thence the great road still remains open, passing between two lines of detached buildings, some of which are small, and being all broken open, shew evidently that they were tombs, the most perfect having a cavity within, of the size of a body, lined, like the cells of the catacombs, with a very hard red plaister.

It was nine when we reached a small fort, occupied by the disciplined troops of the garrison of Alexandria, to guard the narrow pass between the lakes of Mareotis and Aboukir, from the incursions of Elfi Bey and his Arab allies. The English cut away the neck of land on which the Alexandrian canal passed, in order to deprive the French of fresh water, and to re-form the Lake Mareotis, which would prevent the town from receiving any fresh supplies from the Arabs. The Turks found it necessary to re-construct the embankment, that the water might again come to the town, and the celebrated Capitan Pacha, Hassan, employed a Swedish engineer in the work, who has certainly done it well; but it is to be regretted that, instead of re-constructing a solid mound by sinking caissoons filled with stones, he had not carried the canal across the breach on arches, leaving a free passage underneath for the sea. By these means the strength of Alexandria would have been greatly increased as a military position, and its salubrity would have been promoted, by the passing of the hot winds over a large expanse of water. As it is, the lake is gradually drying up, and will soon become a salt marsh.

A boat was here waiting for us, in which we embarked, and with a fair breeze passed across the lake of Aboukir in two hours, to the narrow channel which opens into the sea; though there was little swell, yet the water was so shallow that we struck in getting over the bar, and our men were obliged to get out and push us on. The same pleasant breeze carried us through the Bay of Aboukir in an hour and a half, to the Lake of Edco, which we had no difficulty in entering, as the passage is wide and sufficiently deep when the swell is not great. A little before three we reached Edco, where we were cordially received by the Schech, who is much attached to the English, and to the Beys. He is a powerful Arab, and his town is of importance, from commanding the narrow passage along which the only road goes from Rosetta to Alexandria. It is his duty to allow no one to pass without permission from government; yet he was then suffering for having done so. A party of Osmanlis was going by at night, of whose approach he had no notice from government, and consequently fired on it. Mohammed Ali made the Governor of Rosetta send for him, promising that he should be permitted to return, but when there, he was detained in prison. Several hundreds of his people came into the town, and by force liberated him, on which the before-mentioned Albanian chief went against him, and he was obliged to compromise the business by paying twenty-five purses for having done his duty. He received us most kindly, presented his children to us, and gave us fowls, roast pigeons, and mutton. His village is prettily situated on a hill close to the lake. Mr. Petrucci had sent two horses for us; we procured the rest, and some asses for the servants, from the Schech. The first part of the road was over moveable sands, and very heavy; the date trees were frequently covered nearly to the top; the latter part was much harder, except close to Rosetta, where the date trees and sand began again. We reached Mr. Petrucci's before it was dark.

April 21.—The morning was occupied in receiving the visits of the different gentlemen of the place, and in preparing for our journey. Mr. Petrucci having dismissed Paulino his secretary for staying at Alexandria, at Major Missett's request, I invited him to join our party, which he was happy to do. The boat, with the rest of our baggage, arrived safely, after having been aground on the Bogaz, and nearly lost by a sudden squall from the S. E. which brought so much sand that they could not see the way. It blew a kamsim all day, but the heat was not nearly equal to the hot winds of India: we could walk out without great inconvenience. Mohammed Ali had withdrawn all the soldiers, and not more than twenty remained in the town. The Albanian chief went off to day: he demanded large presents from the Europeans. Mr. Rosetti, who had some objects of trade to carry, gave him shawls and watches; the Vice Consul of the Seven Isles was bullied into a similar compliance; but Mr. Petrucci stood out, and positively refused to give him any thing. On going away, he sent to say, he would make him repent it. We hired asses ourselves for the whole way to Damietta, at twenty piastres each.

April 22.—We sent on our servants and baggage in the morning for Berimbal. In the evening we went up the Nile, in Mr. Petrucci's canja, to the same place. We landed at Mr. Rosetti's country-house, to whom we paid our compliments, and then adjourned to our tents, where we learned that the Schech of the village had sent us bread and milk as a present, and had waited on us himself, promising to supply us with camels for the morrow.

April 23.—We were up at five; but only two camels were ready, and we required five. The Schech paid us a visit, and brought the others. The Commandant, who was a young Mameluke that left the service of his brethren for that of the Kiahia of Mohammed Ali, stopped, and sat for some time with us, as he was proceeding to Rosetta, to bring all the boats to the eastern bank of the river, that the Mamelukes might not pass over. At eight we set off, Mr. Rosetti accompanying us to the marsh by the Lake Bourlos, which we reached in half an hour. At the time of the rising of the Nile, the lake reaches this spot, but we were an hour in passing the place where the water then was; our course was east, a little north. We here found several fishing boats, but to our great astonishment none had been hired for us, nor did we owe their being there to any thing but chance. We hired four to carry us and our baggage to Bourlos, for six Venetians. The wind was favourable when we left Berimbal, but when we embarked at twelve it was quite calm. The boats were built for fishing, decked at each end, but at the stern sloping to a level with the water, for the facility of drawing in the nets. The lake, though salt, is only three or four feet deep, with a muddy bottom. The men, as it was calm, pushed us along with poles. We had ordered the Rais to keep together, but one boat went away to the south, and, in defiance of our signals for her to join us, continued her course till she reached the shore, and took in four fellows. A fine breeze sprung up, with which we made tolerable way, but at four we were not a quarter of the way to Bourlos, and therefore determined to stop at a little island ahead. We reached it at five, and took a hearty dinner of cold mutton and pork, and our example was followed by our boatmen, in defiance of their religion. I prepared my couch as a tent; the other gentlemen procured a small tent about ten, and slept under it.

April 24.—We proceeded at eight, but the breeze being very fresh and unfavorable, we were obliged to tack frequently among the islands. Our Rais wished us much to stop at another island, where there was fresh water, but we positively refused, and obliged him to go on, though he pleaded that there was not water enough close to Bourlos, and that we could only go over the bank when the wind was fair and strong. At two we were off the spot he represented: it was indeed very shallow, and we were glad to send some of our party into a small fishing boat, to lighten our own, when the breeze blew very fresh, and we got safely over. The shoals near Bourlos obliged us to go a considerable round, before we could reach the channel by which the sea enters the lake. The current here, in consequence of the N. E. wind, was so strong that we were obliged to track. It was dark when we reached the town, which is close to the Bogaz. The Schech came down to us, and invited us to his house, where we took coffee, and inquired about our way. We now found, to our infinite vexation, that instead of being able to procure every thing we might want here, as Mr. Petrucci had represented, (to whom we had left the arranging of our route), that three camels only were to be had, and that those were at Boltine, distant two hours march, where the Schech el Belled, and the Caimakan lived, and that there we must go for them. In short, we found that we had no business to come to Bourlos at all. Our other boats were not come up, so we desired the Schech to get us a dinner; he also offered us his house to sleep in. We sent off letters to Boltine, and determined to follow by water in the morning. Our tents came about eight.

April 25.—We were up early, and made a breakfast on coffee with cakes and eggs, sent from the Schech. We took a cordial leave of the old man, (who boasted he had a firmaun from the mighty Sultaun Selim himself), wishing never again to see a place which has nothing to recommend it, except a sight of the gambols of thousands of porpoises, that seem to take a particular delight in the rapidity of the current at the entrance, and the shallow, muddy waters of the lake. The French have built a tower on the opposite bank, which commands the passage. The wind was N. W. and the current came in so rapidly, that the lake evidently rose. We reached Boltine in about an hour. It was impossible to go close to the shore, but by means of camels and mens' shoulders we got there dry. The Schech el Belled met us, and made his compliments. We found that the three camels were all that were to be had, and the number of asses was uncertain. The Caimakan paid me a visit, and invited me to drink coffee at his house, which is a kind of caravanserai for travellers: this I accepted. He was a pleasant middle-aged man, who had been in Italy, and over all the Turkish dominions. He assured us it was impossible to procure any more camels even in three days, and expressed his astonishment at our taking so disagreeable a journey, as hence direct to Damietta, a twenty-one hours march, over a barren desert, where not even water could be procured. We then enquired if we could make our way any farther over the lake. He advised us to go to a place on the opposite side of the lake, within eight hours sail, where we could procure every thing we wanted, and should have a succession of villages to the Nile, on which we might embark for Damietta. He said he had been this way seven or eight times. We thanked him for his counsel, and determined to follow it. He expressed his regret at not having any thing in this place to offer us, for even water they were obliged to fetch from a distance. Date trees are in abundance, as, in their season, are melons and water-melons, the best in Egypt; but at that time none could be procured. We invited him to share our dinner, which he accepted. On returning to our tent, and telling the Schech el Belled our intentions of going by water, he started many objections. We suspected he was only interested to let us his camels and asses; we therefore sent to the Caimakan to request he would pay us a visit at the tent. He came, and soon obliged the Schech to acknowledge that the road was safe, and that there would be probably water enough, as the lake was rising. Orders were therefore issued for the boats to be hired. We took a walk in the town, which is tolerably large and populous. The people were all extremely civil. The more respectable inhabitants came up to make their compliments and shake hands. We found a broken stone with some singular hieroglyphics. The Caimakan dined with us; he drank wine; but on the Schech el Belled's coming in, removed the glass, and placed water before him in a silver cup.

April 26.—We were up by break of day, but it was some time before we could hear of the Schech; at length he appeared, and told us that he had not been able to find the Rais of the boats. in short, nothing had been done respecting our voyage. We asked for our bread, which he had been ordered to prepare for our breakfast: he coolly answered by desiring us not to be in a hurry, it would be ready in time. Irritated at his impertinence, Vincenzo gave him a hearty blow or two with his pipe, and sent him away for it. We now found nothing was to be done without the Caimakan, who came immediately on our sending for him. After much conversation between him and the different boat people, he seemed to hesitate with respect to the eligibility of our going by water; the lake had rather fallen in the night instead of rising, and the opposite shore in this case was supposed not to have any water for two miles from the town. The intermediate space was mud, from three to four feet deep, over which we could not walk.

Convinced by their reasoning, we gave up our favourite plan. Three camels were ready, but the asses were to be sought for. At eleven, nine only were found, and we were told there were no more. Our baggage required twenty; we therefore asked if we could hire a boat to carry part of our things by water. The Caimakan said, yes, but it was some time before he could induce the Schech to find a Rais, and when he came, he said he had never been at Damietta—an impudent lie! as their chief trade is with that place and Rosetta. At length he owned he had, but asked fifty dollars for his jerm. Violently irritated at this, the Caimakan gave the whole party a good flogging, not excepting the Schech, which immediately reduced the price to twenty piastres. The business was now settled. We only kept our tents, a single change of linen, our beds, the cantines, and wine sufficient for three days; all the rest of our baggage we sent to the boat, under the care of Mr. Briggs's servant, and Fowler. I gave our friend the Caimakan a gun, in return for two sheep he had sent us: to the Schech I gave nothing. We set off by five, after many disputes, to go due north to a village close to the sea, whence they procure all their water, Boltine affording none. We reached it in two hours and a half. Our camels did not arrive till an hour afterwards. I was mounted on a horse of Mr. Airut, the English Vice Consul at Damietta; the rest were on asses. The village is a small collection of huts formed of date leaves. Most of the males were gone to the cultivated part of the Delta, to assist in carrying in the harvest; for this purpose they had taken their camels, which was the cause of our distress, as Bourlos and Boltine, at other seasons, could produce sixty or seventy.

April 27.—At a little after five we were up, and having procured six large jars of water, set off at six. We went on at a brisk pace along the sea shore till nine o'clock, when we halted. The camels did not arrive till eleven. The country was a perfect desert on our right hand. We pitched our tent, and waited till the heat of the day was over. At three we sent off the tent, and followed at half after four. At half after seven we stopped on the banks of an inlet of the sea, which in the time of the rising of the Nile is the vent of a canal. This is probably one of the Pseudostoma, mentioned by Ptolemy, as lying between the Sebennitic and Phatmetic mouths of the Nile; but as it is the only one of which we could discover a trace during our journey, it is impossible to ascertain whether it be that of Pineptimi, or Diolcos; but, according to D'Anville, it would be the latter. This geographer has not laid down the country we were passing, with his usual accuracy; there does not exist a vestige of an inland narrow lake running parallel to the sea shore, nor is there any village, nor any ruins where he places Lashom.

Fearing we might want water, we had sent on an express to Damietta, ordering some to be sent to meet us: we found it waiting our arrival, to our great satisfaction, for ours was all gone. It blew very fresh in the night from the west.

April 28.—We observed the water had risen considerably, and were all obliged to pass on the camels. It was six when we mounted. At half after eight we were met by the Schech of Salanie, the district opposite Damietta, and soon afterwards saw the town, and quitted the sea side to make direct for it. Near the Nile we were met by Signor Giorgio's brother, Signor Gabriel Airut, the Russian Consul. Under some trees, on the banks, carpets were spread, upon which we partook of coffee and sherbet. The Governor, Achmed Aga, had sent his boat for me. As we approached the vessels, they hoisted their colours, and fired a gun each. I went directly to the house of the brothers Airuts, where I received the visits of the Vice Consuls, and among others of the French, who being also Swedish, came in the latter capacity. I found a letter from Mr. Filippo Agnelli, recommending me to apply to a reverend Catholic priest, of the name of Padre Basilio, for any information I might want respecting Damietta. I sent for him, and he came immediately. I found him very intelligent. We walked with him in the evening to see the remains of an ancient obelisk mentioned by Andreossi, as forming the door-sill of the barracks. It is of granite, but nearly worn away. We next went to two pedestals, placed near the door of a merchant: the one had a Latin inscription, which Mr. Salt copied; it consisted of only two lines, in capital letters, and was as follows:

LICINIAE LF SECUNDAE
DOMITI CATULLI.

the other had one of Greek, which was partly

concealed by a step, and turned topsy-turvy. We obtained permission from the owner to have it removed, that it also might be copied. He informed us that they were not found in Egypt, but brought in a vessel from Syria.

On determining to visit the Delta, we had written to Mohammed Ali Pacha, requesting a firmaun to the Governor of Damietta: one arrived yesterday, making him answerable, with his head, for our safety, directing him to afford us every assistance in his power, and to shew us every attention. We all went to the Hummaum in the afternoon, and were well cleansed from the dust of the Desert. Our baggage arrived at one; but we could hear no news of the boat and servants.

April 29.—I applied in the morning to the Governor, for the use of his boat to carry me to Lesbé, at the mouth of the Nile, which was immediately granted. This village was destroyed by the French, who began to erect on its site a fort which would have been strong, but which they had not time to finish. It has a lofty brick wall, but no ditch nor glacis; within, three excellent barracks were finished; but the ruins of the ancient houses were not removed. I examined the whole of the place to see if I could discover any of the ruins mentioned by Savary, as existing in his time, and which he conceived to be the remains of the ancient Damietta, which was first besieged and taken by the Crusaders, and afterwards by St. Louis; but without the least success; not a vestige of a wall was visible, nor were there any heaps of pottery, nor any mixture of lime and brick with the soil; but where the canals were cut, the black mud of the Nile alone appeared. The mosque he mentions, could not be the one left when the Sultaun of Egypt destroyed the town, as it is of modern date. Certainly, if Savary has faithfully translated the quotations he has given from Macrizi and Abulfeda, there can be no doubt that the ancient Damietta was destroyed, to prevent its being taken by the Christians, and a new town of the same name was built higher up the river; yet it is difficult to comprehend what advantage would arise from removing it only a few miles, to the site of the present town, or indeed for its removal at all, since the walls and fortifications alone were of importance, and their complete destruction would have precluded the possibility of its again becoming an asylum to a vanquished enemy.

The present town is not five miles from the mouth of the river, and I cannot but think it probable, that the ancient Damietta was at nearly the same distance; for the Crusaders found a great chain extended across the river from two towers, which were probably at some short distance from the sea, and after breaking that, found a space beyond sufficient to encamp their whole army, and surround themselves with a ditch and pallisade, although the Sultaun had erected a bridge to prevent their approach, and was encamped between them and Damietta. Lesbé is distant only a mile from the sea, and it is impossible to suppose that within that distance the whole of the armies, the bridge and the towers, with the chain, could have been crowded. I am therefore inclined to doubt the fact, as given by the Arabian historians, as well as the fidelity of Mr. Savary's translation.

Below Lesbé the Governor has established a village, where he obliges all the fishermen to live, and which seems in a very thriving state. I here observed a round tower of ancient masonry, which forms one extremity of a building, that extends to the river, and to which, I think it probable, that the great chain above mentioned was fastened. Every other building between Damietta and the sea has the appearance of being modern.

The Bogaz is not quite so bad as at Rosetta, for it admits vessels of much larger burthen than the jerms, which take advantage of the fine weather, to enter the river, and anchor close to the town, where there is never less than fourteen feet water. As we returned we were much struck with the picturesque appearance of the houses, which not only cover the banks of the river, but have generally stages extended over it, on which vines are planted, and seats disposed under their shade.

The Kiaia of the Governor called to pay his master's compliments, and excuse himself for not having been yesterday, by saying that he had fallen from his horse and hurt himself. As we knew it was only an excuse, we offered gravely the assistance of Vincenzo's brother, who was a surgeon, which he as gravely declined. I accepted the excuse, and said I would visit his master on the morrow. We again walked in the evening to the merchant's door, where the pedestal had been removed, and copied the Greek inscription, which was as follows:

Η ΒΟΥΛΗ ΚΑΙ Ο ΔΗΜΟΣ
ΛΟΥΚΙΟΝ ΠΟΠΙΛΛΙΟΝ ΒΑΛΒΟΝ
ΠΡΕΣΒΕΥΤΗΝ ΤΙΒΕΡΙΟΥ
ΚΛΑΥΔΙΟΥ ΚΑΙΣΑΡΟΣ
ΣΕΒΑΣΤΟΥ ΓΕΡΜΑΝΙΚΟΥ
ΤΟΝ ΠΑΤΡΩΝΑ ΤΗΣ ΠΟΛΕΟΣ.

April 30.—In the morning I visited the Governor. He received me at the custom-house, met me near the entrance, and conducted me to a very neat little apartment, which opened into a garden, where pinks and roses were in full bloom. He gave me the seat of honour, and paid the usual compliments. General Andreossi had mentioned a column in a mosque which has a Greek inscription on it. I requested permission to enter the mosque and copy it, which he granted, and ordered one of his people to attend me. Vincenzo recognised in him an old friend, who had saved his life at Tripoli, when they were both in the service of Ali Pacha. He is a brave soldier, but haughty and uninformed. Damietta, which formerly was the paradise of Egypt, where the gardens abounded with groves of oranges, and every fruit, where the finest rice was raised in the greatest profusion, is now totally changed, in consequence of the stream of the Nile having taken to the canal of Menouf, instead of passing to Damietta. The gardens have vanished, the rice fields are sown with wheat, and the inhabitants want even fresh water. Achmed Aga has constructed a large vessel to supply in some degree this latter defect, by bringing, in vast cisterns, water from above Fareskour, between which place and Mansoura the river has still sufficient force to repel the waters of the sea, driven up the channel by the strong northerly winds, which prevail for the greater part of the year. It is singular that Citoyen Girard, in a paper read before the Institute of Egypt, mentions this as having been then remedied by the Canal of Menouf being closed by a mound; yet I came down the canal of Menouf, and the evil is now as great as ever: at Damietta the water is quite salt. This plan of Achmet Aga shews some intelligence, as does the construction of the village of fishermen so near the Bogaz, purposely, as he says, that they may be at hand in case any vessel should be in distress, or wrecked on the shore. I returned the visits of the Vice Consuls, and then went, accompanied by the Chaous Bashi of the Governor, to the mosque. Mr. Salt entered alone, after the mats were removed. We gave two piastres to the attendant, and no objections were started. Many went in to pray, and saluted me as they passed; while I continued seated on the door sill. One man from Jidda murmured something, but he was soon silenced by the people. The inscription is to me quite unintelligible; it is certainly not entirely in Greek nor any other characters, but seems to be cabalistic. I have given a copy of it in one of the plates. We next walked to a mosque nearly ruined, at Menshie, a suburb nearer the sea. We found there an Arab inscription, which places its erection on the 1117th year of the Hejira. There were several very beautiful marble columns, but much injured. Near it was a marabout, the dome of which was supported by four jasper columns, the polish of which was as perfect as on the day they were finished; one alone had a small piece broken out of it; a fifth column of the same materials, and in as good a state, was at the entrance. We returned about five, having passed the whole length of the town, which is about two miles.

May 1.—Major Missett having informed me he did not wish to detain the Panther any longer, I was all day employed in preparing my dispatches, intending on the morrow to go to the Lake Menzalé, which was but little known till the arrival of the French in Egypt, when General Andreossi was directed by Buonaparté to make a survey of it. This was published in the first vol. of the Mémoires sur l'Egypte, with a memorial, giving a very interesting account of the lake itself, the inhabitants of its shores, and the ruins in its vicinity.

May 2.—In the morning we sent off the baggage, and soon afterwards followed ourselves on horses and mules, to the borders of the Lake Menzalé. Signor Gabriello and the Padre accompanied us. We had four vessels waiting for us; two very good and large; the other two, small fishing-boats. We embarked near the tomb of Schech Chaffa, with a very fair and stiff breeze. In half an hour we fell in with a chain of islands, which are totally omitted by General Andreossi in his otherwise excellent chart of the lake. After two hours sail we passed between two islands, through a channel not above thirty yards wide, on the north bank of which was the tomb of Schech Elsebi, which are accurately laid down in the General's chart. The wind continued fair, but the men said that it had driven the water from this to the eastern extremity of the lake, so that it would be impossible to reach Menzalé; we therefore determined to proceed directly to the island of Schech Abdallah, on which are situated the ruins of the town of Thouna. We arrived there by five, but found not a vestige of a building. The whole of the island is covered with bricks almost reduced to powder, mixed with small bits of glass and mica. There could never have been any building of great importance here, or very great pains must have been taken to destroy it. I should rather suspect, from its situation in the middle of a lake abounding with several kinds of very good fish, that it was an extensive fishing-town. We encamped for the night close to the Schech's tomb, having sent off to Menzalé to announce our arrival, and our desire to see the Schech.

May 3.—We had determined originally to visit the ruins of the island of Tennis, but having learnt that there were no remains of antiquity except heaps of powdered bricks, as at Thouna, and knowing from Sebastiani's account that the French had searched there, as they had done here, without success, we altered our intention, and ordered the baggage on board to proceed to Matarieh. In the Schech's tomb the French have carved several names, among which we observed that of Nouet.

We reached Matarieh by ten, and were received by the Schech of the Lake and of Menzalé, the son of Hassan Toubar, by name Ali. The father died in the time of the French, who, at the request of Ali, appointed his uncle Chelabi, Schech. They may be considered as equally Schechs at this moment, and are both here. This Hassan Toubar was, according to General Andreossi, whose account is confirmed by Messrs. Airuts, one of the most powerful individuals in the country, having a vast profit from the trade of the Lake, which he farmed from the Beys, and being able to protect himself from the usual oppressions, by the natural strength of his islands, which could not be approached by an enemy, all the boats on the lake being his own, and also by the friendship of the Arabs, whose chiefs he constantly bribed with liberal presents. His family were originally of Menzalé, and were said to have held the sovereignty, by their prudent management, for five generations. Our wish was to visit the ruins of Tanis, situated at Sann, on the banks of the Kaliz el Moez, where, according to the French accounts, several obelisks still remained standing. We consulted him on the subject. He informed us, that in the time of the rise of the Nile, it would be very easy for him to conduct us thither by water; but that at present it was out of his power, as the vicinity was much infested by the wandering Arabs. He said that one or two might make their way, by his sending to one of the tribes, and receiving hostages from them for the safety of the travellers; but that this would require time, and would, after all, be doubtful. The distance was said to be six hours march on horseback. As by his account, and that of General Andreossi, there was but little to be seen, we determined to give up the pursuit.

The Schech sent me six sheep, some rice, ghee, and bread, as a present. The town is but small; the houses chiefly mud, though a few are brick. The people are nearly naked, but robust, and healthy: the children are more numerous than I have seen in any part of Egypt. The inhabitants of the two islands amount to about eleven hundred males, besides females and children, the whole district of Menzalé is said by General Andreossi to contain eight thousand souls. At present there are six hundred boats employed in the fishery, particularly of the mullet, whose roe is cured and exported in great abundance under the name of botargo. In the time of the Mamelukes there were three times that number. Opposite Matarieh is another town on an island of equal size, the Schech el Belled of which came to pay his compliments. On my mentioning the name of Hassan Toubar, the old Schech immediately addressed himself to Signor Gabriello, and said, " How does he know any thing of Hassan Toubar? where could he hear of him? He also knew of Schech Abdallah, and ordered the people to go there; when did he learn this?" On its being explained to me, I told him the English knew well his brother, and all that belonged to him, which was unintentionally an odd sort of a compliment, as Hassan Toubar was very much attached to the French. The natives were uniformly civil to us; as we walked along the streets they always made their salaams. The women were veiled, but chatted freely. I observed several green turbans.

May 4.—We were up by three, and at half after four set sail. The wind was fair till ten. We reached the shore by two, where we found the horses and asses waiting for us by the orders of Signor Gabriello.

May 5.—We hired two boats to take us to Mansoura. Achmed Aga, the governor, sent to express his regret that I had not applied to him for what I wanted, to offer his canja, and to say that he would get me as many more boats as I wished. I told his Kiaia I did not want his canja, or I should certainly have applied for it. Vincenzo gave him a hint, as from himself, that he was surprised the governor had not paid me a visit; he said, it had been his intention, but that I had never staid long enough at Damietta. He departed, but returned again, pressing me to take the canja. I did not see him, but still declined the canja; soon afterwards the governor arrived: I met him at the door of the room, and handed him to a seat. He pressed me so strongly to take the canja, that I was obliged to comply. He offered letters to the Cacheefs of Mansoura and Semenoud, which I accepted.

After an early dinner we went on board. The wind was fresh and favourable; we therefore made one of the jerms take us in tow. We passed Fareskour too early to stop there: a place rendered famous by the captivity of St. Louis, and his whole army, but which now offers nothing interesting to the traveller. At sunset the wind fell, so that we made little way; we therefore stopped at Berishie, a village from which the inhabitants had chiefly fled, in consequence of some dispute with their neighbours of Fareskour. The village has a wall of mud, and gates to defend it from the wandering Arabs. A quantity of flax was on the shore, in the middle of which we pitched our tents.

May 6.—We got milk in abundance from the few villagers who remained, and set sail early. We stopped at Caffre Toura to take our breakfast, where a Schech resided, a friend of Messrs. Airuts. He was a Sheriffe, and a good looking man. The peasantry were working hard to raise water for their rice fields, as the river is here fresh. I saw some very fine cattle. The Schech presented us with bread, which was all we wanted. He spoke in melancholy terms of the oppression under which the country laboured; that scarcely a week passed without a contribution; and that at present their means of payment were totally exhausted. We got at night to Baramoun, where the Caimakan Mohammed Aga Blefié waited on me. He was formerly a Mameluke of Osman Bey Hassan. He spoke in a still more desponding way of the situation of the country, and the extortions exercised by the Albanians and the government. He said the inhabitants had nothing left; that all their cattle had been sold; that those who then worked night and day to raise water, belonged to Basilio Tacha, to whom the crops were mortgaged. He seemed completely heart-broken at being the instrument of these extortions, and prayed most earnestly that the merciful God would send the English to restore peace and plenty.

I was pleased to find our nation thus wished for,

in a part of the country where they had never been, but where their character could only have been learned from the other inhabitants of Egypt. He still begged me to mention any thing I wanted, as, in spite of their distress, he would find it for me. I declined every thing except milk and bread, articles which I ever made it a rule to pay for, and watched very closely that no extortions were practised in my name, by our numerous followers. Among these was the Chaous Bashi of the Governor of Damietta, who always wished to be taking what he chose, and to pay for nothing. He gave this day a good sample of Turkish manners. Our boat was in tow of the jerms, and the wind being very fresh, it was once or twice dashed against us; the Chaous struck the son of the Rais who was at the helm, with a stick, and not satisfied with that, drew his pistol, and was with some difficulty prevented from shooting him.

May 7.—At an early hour we set off, having secured three small boats, that, in case the river became shallow, we might take our baggage out of the jerms and put it into them. It was well we did so, for about five miles above Baramoun, the river ceased to be navigable for large vessels, and even the canja passed only by the men going into the water and pushing her along. Mansoura is very beautifully situated on rather a higher bank than usual of the Nile. It has several gardens in front of the houses, and some large sycamore trees adjacent. Its numerous mosques give it an extensive appearance. We landed about two, and pitched our tents immediately in an open garden, close to the river. The Intendant, Malum Yusuff, a Copt, immediately paid us a visit: from him we learned that the Cacheef was absent; we therefore sent the Governor of Damietta's letter to his

Kiaia. The Chaous had another private one for him, mentioning the very strong orders he had himself received from Mohammed Ali, and advising him to pay me every possible attention. We went to take coffee at the Intendant's, having ordered one of the hot baths to be prepared for us. We now learned that Timai was four hours distant, and had every hope given us that we should be well recompensed there for our past disappointments. He gave me two Egyptian figures in earth.

A very respectable old man of the name of Hassan Belgahie, who was formerly Governor of the town, and therefore still preserved the title of Surbaje, paid us a visit. We found it was his garden in which we were encamped. He asked many questions about me; who I was, and what I did here. Vincenzo told him that Mohammed Ali considered me as a very powerful man of England; but that as for my business in Egypt, it was a secret with which he was unacquainted, but that he supposed it was of great consequence. The old man was very civil, but soon left us to say his prayers. The Kiaia of the Cacheef soon afterwards paid us a visit. The Intendant came next, so that we had a full tent. It was now in a moment settled that every thing should be ready for our departure in the morning. Vincenzo recognised, in a person who attended the Kiaia, an old acquaintance who had been formerly in the service of Ali Pacha. He was also Caimakan of a village close to the ruins of Timai, and undertook to accompany us. Indeed I found them all extremely anxious to oblige and serve me.

May 8.—Early in the morning we went to see a piece of granite, on which were cut some hieroglyphics, but they were too much worn to be of value. As we went out, we were joined by the Kiaia, who took us to see a hot bath, where the water had a yellowish tinge, but had no particular taste. On our way we were shewn the upper part of a statue of Isis, which had been brought from Timai by the French, who had embarked it on the river, but it had fallen into the water. The bust was sufficiently entire to make it interesting. We had it carried to our tent, and determined to send it by water to Damietta. Mr. Salt drew it for fear of accidents. Our friend the Surbaje sent us a breakfast of excellent cakes and bread. I learned that an express was sent off by the Kiaia to his master with the letters.

It was necessary to hire a Schech of an Arab tribe to accompany us to Timai, which was settled by the Intendant. We could procure only three camels, the rest being employed in carrying the wheat. We all procured horses, but bridles and saddles were rare. We set off about two, accompanied by the Intendant, the Caimakan, and the owner of the village. The Schech Foud Abou Koura of Metel Hamour, accompanied us with about twenty horsemen. We halted at the first village till our camels passed us. They reached another unaccompanied, when the inhabitants thought it a good opportunity to plunder, and sallied forth. We just then came in sight, when our Schech and his people set off full gallop, and obliged the rascals to take refuge in the village, all of which have walls to protect them from the wandering Arabs. Their corn was all piled on the outside, in the open air. We reached Timai about six. The village Schech paid his compliments, and they permitted us to pitch our tents close to the mosque, and the tomb of Schech Abdallah, from whom this place take its name. We sat down, fourteen, to a cold dinner, spread on the ground; the Schech el Arab declined dining with us, but sent for a bottle of wine. All the Mussulmauns took their share of this prohibited liquor. The villages are built on sandy hillocks, though the plain is composed of the mud of the Nile. The strata of those hillocks which were open for pits were regular and horizontal; I conceive therefore that they are natural.

May 9.—Timai is the Thmuis of Ptolemy, and was situated in the Mendesian Nome, where, according to Herodotus, the god Pan was worshipped, and out of respect to him goats, particularly males, were held in great veneration, and one was more honoured than all the rest, and his death lamented by the whole Nome. Timai has been described by no traveller, and was visited for a short period only, by General Vernier, to collect the tribute from the Schechs in the vicinity. We arose early in the morning, and visited the ruins nearest to us, which are called Medinet Timai, or the Capital. We found a place where the soil had been a little thrown up, and appeared of the black colour of the Ibis mummies; on examining, there actually appeared some vases which contained mummy composition and bones. We procured several of different sizes; they seemed to have contained the bodies of the sacred goats. The ruins consist chiefly of heaps of broken bricks and pottery, with here and there a broken granite column, but the whole in such confusion, that neither the walls of the town nor the foundation of a building could be distinguished.

After breakfast we visited Gussur Timai, or the Palace of Timai, as it is called by the Arabs, which is situated on a hill, at the distance of about half a mile from the other. We were here compensated for all our trouble, by the discovery of a vast shrine of polished, red, Thebaic granite, which still continues standing, and of which the accompanying engraving will give the best idea.

The shrine itself is of a single piece, of the following dimensions:

	Feet.	Inches.
Height - -	23	4
Breadth in front -	12	8
Depth on the outside	11	3
Breadth of the chamber	8	8
Depth of the chamber	9	2

It stands on a pedestal of the same substance, five feet high, and that again on two layers, that amount to six feet three inches; so that the whole elevation is thirty-four feet seven inches. The polish on many parts continues perfect, but in others has been injured by time, or external injury. A large crack runs down it behind, and there is another on each side, which resembles much the effect of lightning. The front has been ornamented with hieroglyphics, chiefly at the top, but on the sides more scantily. The smooth surface reflected so strongly the rays of the sun, and the heat was so great from the surrounding banks keeping off the air, that it was impossible to draw the ornaments with accuracy. The top is not flat, but elevated to a point in the centre, as we found when we viewed it from a distance. It is hardly to be doubted, that a statue of a deity was originally placed in the cavity; I should suppose of Pan, for the height seems too great for the ram only. The shrine was placed facing the N. E. in the centre of one side of an irregular square, forty-three paces wide by thirty-six; at present marked only by very high mounds of earth, and some remains of a wall; it had apparently a shrine of a similar construction on each side of it. On a block of Thebaic granite, which had formed a part of one of these, was a figure of a ram with four horns; two which were visible were long and twisted, diverging horizontally from the top of the forehead: a third was shorter, a little curved, perfectly smooth, and lying close to the face; the fourth was concealed.

There were no other ruins within this square; but in a second, at the northern corner, were several very large blocks of granite, and the same in a third. The second and third square were both forty-three feet wide; but the former was seventy eight, and the latter forty paces long. At a small distance in front of these, and near to the canal, were three hillocks in a line, on which were probably some buildings, but at present not a vestige of them remains.

In walking without the squares, we discovered at least twenty troughs of granite, roughly excavated, chiefly of an oval form, and which, from their being under five feet long, could not be intended for sarcophagi. Not a fragment of a column could be found about the place; but we were shewn a piece of a statue about three feet wide across the breast, but so damaged, that it was impossible to conjecture for what it was originally intended.

A Kamsin, or hot wind, set in, and drove us to our tents, but in the evening we ventured out, and at one extremity of Medinet Timai discovered the ruins of a temple, the columns of which had been thrown down and broken; they were of granite, together with their capitals and bases. A little boy carried us to a spot, where we saw the lower part of a statue in basalt, of very fine workmanship; this I bought from him for a dollar, and hired an ass from the Schech of the town to carry it to Mansoura. Whoever discovers an antique, has a right to dispose of it; they say it is God's property, and he gives it to whom he pleases.

The Arabs brought me a few antiques, which were generally of little value, but which I bought for a few paras. The Schech gave me a little figure in lapis lazuli, of a ram with four heads, but it had not the long, horizontal horns.

May 10.—I wished to have dedicated this day to an examination of the ruins; but the Schech urged us to continue no longer in the country, as, from the present disturbed state of Cairo, the Bedowee were become more bold, and might, possibly, think it worth their while to collect a large party, and attack us. His arguments were conclusive, and we therefore gave orders for our departure; but in the mean time took a ride to Gussur Timai, whence we were soon driven by millions of sand flies, which attacked us without mercy.

I think that tradition has judiciously appropriated the two Timai's, for one has all the appearance of having been the residence of the priests and chief only, and the other of the common people. The Arabs have made many researches among the ruins of both, and have, at different times, found some valuable articles, which they sold for an insignificant price at Mansoura, whence they made their way to Damietta and Cairo, where the Europeans were always willing to purchase them. In the vicinity of the present Timai, a deserted village at some distance from the ruins, a pit was by accident broken into, in which were two hundred figures of Isis, from four to nine inches long, of a baked earth, coloured blue, and varnished a little on the outside, with hieroglyphics on the lower part. One alone was a foot long, which I purchased for about a shilling.

On our way back we made a bend to the south, to visit a village, near which are the remains of an ancient temple and town. The large blocks of granite that lie prostrate on the ground are uniformly broken. I cannot but suspect that the conquerors of this country found treasure concealed in some of the stones of the ancient edifices, and that the expectation of finding more, led to the laborious destruction of these massive temples, which seem to have been constructed to bid defiance to time itself. I observed a few blocks of a very singular shape, having the external form of a bell, but no cavity within, and being five or six feet in diameter at the base. They could not have formed a part of any building, nor can I conceive any use to which they could be put. I think Timai is ten miles from Mansoura, in a due east direction.

The Schech would make no charge for his men; I therefore gave him a double-barrelled gun for himself, and one thousand paras for his relation, who was next in command.

We reached Mansoura by two, and again took up our residence in the Surbaje's garden. After having indulged ourselves at the Hummaum, which the Kiaia had ordered to be cleared of all other visitors for our accommodation, we walked to the canal that runs to the east of the town, beyond which, on the plain, St. Louis and his army were encamped, till driven, by famine and disease, to attempt their retreat to Damietta. Nobody can doubt the courage nor religious zeal of St. Louis; but it is impossible to allow him those necessary qualifications for a General—prudence and judgment. The misfortunes of the first Crusaders ought to have warned him not to attempt to penetrate into Egypt during the inundation of the Nile, when every canal became a defensible post. Later invaders have wisely chosen to remove the attack to Alexandria, where the natural strength of the position, and the excellent harbour, offer every advantage for repressing the attacks of the inhabitants, and receiving supplies from the sea.

In the evening we received an express from Major Missett, informing us that a vessel of one thousand tons burthen had arrived from Malta, and meant to return thither shortly, and suggesting the eligibility of my taking my passage in her, as it was doubtful whether Sir Alexander Ball might have an armed vessel disengaged, to send for me. We therefore determined to hasten our journey, and visit such places only in the Delta as lay directly in our way. By the paper sent us, we heard of Sir John Duckworth's victory, and of the capture of the Cape, for which good news we fired three small guns; on which the Kiaia sent to congratulate us, and ordered a salute of seven to be fired from the town.

We took leave of our worthy friend the Padre Basilio, who returned to Damietta, having in charge the antiquities I had procured during our tour. Messrs. Airuts still accompanied us. We were up early, but it was two hours before the asses arrived which we had hired for the party, and which were to go with us into the Delta, lest we should not be able to procure any there. Our baggage and servants went in four boats. We breakfasted at Goraka, on the banks of the river, near which are some heaps of rubbish, that seem to indicate the site of an ancient town, but no granite was visible among them. The Schech waited on us, and was very civil, providing us with all we required, which was bread and milk. He amused me much by asking Vincenzo if I were the Sultaun who had landed at Suez, and on whose arrival at Cairo they had fired one hundred and sixty pieces of cannon. It was clear that a story did not lose more in Egypt by travelling than in other countries.

We here quitted the river to visit the ruins of Bahbeit, or the beautiful house, which D'Anville has considered, and I think with justice, as the Isidis Oppidum of Pliny. It is difficult to conjecture how, without the assistance of gunpowder, the vast masses of granite of which the ruins consist, could have been thrown into the form in which they now meet the eye of the astonished traveller. Blocks, ten feet long and five feet broad and wide, are piled on each other, in such a way as frequently to leave openings sufficiently large for a person to pass underneath, and view the beautiful sculpture with which one face of each is covered. The Arabs have removed the sand in the centre, by which means it is apparent that there is as much of the building underground, as there is above; and in several places the massive foundation still remains. Without any very great expense, the ground plan might be ascertained, by employing the Arabs to clear away the rubbish; but this can never be executed in safety while Egypt is under its present savage masters. Three different kinds of granite have been used in this beautiful temple: the first is a very fine grained red, mixed with black and a little white; the second is black, and of an inferior quality; the third is the common Thebaic red, with much white and a little black. On each of these the subject is different, and the style of carving dissimilar.

On the first are representations of the goddess Isis, seated, and a person offering gifts to her, with a border of written hieroglyphics about a foot broad, inclosing each pair of figures in a compartment. The head dress of Isis is not exactly the same in any two places, nor are the offerings similar, nor made by the same persons. Below these, but separated from them by a line of five pointed stars touching each other, is a range of smaller figures, bearing tables with three legs, on which are placed three vases and other ornaments. I could find no remains of the door way, except the vast block which covered it, and which had on it the globe, with the two serpents and the wings, as usually found in the temples of Upper Egypt. Nothing could be more admirably executed than the basso relievo of this part of the temple, which probably formed the front, or the wings; the polish remained perfect on the faces: the designs were good, but the figures were invariably ill drawn.

On the second, or black granite, which I conjecture to have covered the outer walls, are a number of figures, some seated, but the greater part standing, with their hands extended, among which we found one with the hawk's head, having in his hand the cross, with a circular handle, which has given rise among the learned to many fanciful conjectures. These are of inferior execution to the first, and instead of being raised, are sunk into the granite, and have only a little relief, but not so much as to bring the figure to the level of the surface in which they are cut.

The third kind has certainly been employed for the body of the temple itself, the roof is also composed of it, and is covered with the five pointed stars. The pillars, of which we could only discover the remains of three, are likewise of the same material: the capitals are formed of four gigantic heads of Isis, and the shafts are covered with hieroglyphics. The blocks of this granite, except those intended for the roof, are smaller than the others, and are only ornamented with hieroglyphics cut into them without any relief. Several of these are very singular, but the goose with the globe, and the serpent with the cap on his head, are the most frequent. At one extremity of the ruin is a great lion of the same granite, but so buried in the earth that we could not judge of its execution.

Pococke visited these splendid ruins, and speaks of them with a just degree of admiration. Savary, as usual, runs into a strain of panegyric, which is absurd. The features in the basso relievos are certainly beautiful, but the figures are out of all proportion, and display a total ignorance of anatomy. Since their times the devastations of the natives have continued, and many a valuable record of the ancient splendor of the Delta has been destroyed to form a millstone, or the sill of a door. The French also removed a few, but there are still remaining a sufficient quantity to gratify the curiosity of a traveller. I hope and trust that the day will arrive, when some of the most perfect will be conveyed to a country where they will be free from injury, and their merit be justly appreciated.

As it was impossible for Mr. Salt to finish drawing, during the evening, all the remains that were visible, he and Captain Vincenzo staid behind while we proceeded to Semenoud, where we were very civilly received by the Schech, who came to make the excuses of the Cacheef, for his not being able to wait upon us, in consequence of severe indisposition.

May 13.—It was very sultry in the morning, till the air was cooled by a violent thunder storm. Mr. Briggs and I went, as usual, to the Hummaum, which we invariably found refreshed and cooled us, and took off the sensation of soreness, which exercise in such a climate is apt to produce. The inhabitants were extremely civil; the better order complained heavily of the oppressions under which they laboured, and declared that the French did not use them half so ill. The poorer people brought me a few trifling antiques to purchase, and among others a small brass statue of Isis, as she is represented at Bahbeit, with large horns, and the moon placed between them; composing altogether a head dress which a mortal would be unable to sustain. Captain Vincenzo and Mr. Salt returned to dinner, having finished the drawings, and purchased for me a dovetail of metal, evidently intended to fasten two stones together. My friend, Mr. Davy, informs me that it is pure copper. On account of its singularity I have given a drawing of it, with the hieroglyphics that are still visible.

We were informed in the evening, that Mohammed Ali had ordered a fresh contribution of grain to be levied on the Delta, in consequence of the alarm excited by the appearance of Elfi and his troops in the vicinity of Menouf. His Highness seemed to suspect that it was the intention of his antagonist to occupy the Delta, and attempt to starve Cairo, and therefore wished to guard against it, by accumulating stores beforehand. We had an intimation of Elfi's plan before we left Alexandria, in consequence of which I wrote to him, and requested he would send me a passport. By the return of the messenger he sent me a very civil answer, conjuring me, on my return to Europe, to make known to my government the wretched situation of Egypt. He inclosed the passport, or rather letter, which was as follows:

"To all my dear and beloved children the Beys, to my children the Cacheefs, to all my Mamelukes, to all my Albanians and Turkish soldiers, to all the Schechs of the Arabs, and to all the Arab tribes. Health to you all! I notify to you, that our beloved and respected friend, Lord Valenzia, a chief of the English court, is going from Alexandria to Damietta. I will that none of you offer him any impediment, but that you let him pass with all his party, rendering to him all the honours which are due to his rank. Remember, he is a chief of the English court, our best and most dear friend, which is the reason of my issuing this order. Whoever disobeys it shall receive the merited punishment.

"Dated the 10th of the month Suffar, in the year of Hejira 1221."

From the disposition shewn in this order, to make use of me as an evidence to the Arabs of Elfi's friendly connection with England, I should have been by no means sorry to have met this Chief, as I should have been perfectly sure of a civil reception, and should have enjoyed the novelty of a Mameluke camp.

May 14.—We were up by day break, but our camels and servants were not ready till it became so hot, as to render our march to Mahallet-el-Kebeer very unpleasant. In the time of the Beys, one of their body resided in this place, which is the capital of the Garbie, or lower division of the Delta. It is a large town, containing some good houses, and is surrounded by extensive gardens; but like every other place we had visited, is going rapidly to decay. Mohammed Ali gave the district to his eldest son, whose deputy, the acting Governor, was formerly a Mameluke. I had sent on my interpreter to notify to him my approach, and to request he would have camels and asses ready for me to continue my journey: at first he seemed to care little about the business, but on being spoken to in stronger terms, became very civil, sent a man to point out a pleasant spot in the gardens for our encampment, and immediately on our arrival, came to pay his compliments in person. Vincenzo recognised in him an old acquaintance, and we were the best of friends in a few minutes.

We were greatly disturbed at learning that the camels of this place had all been sent to the army with grain, and we were therefore obliged, however unwillingly, to compel the servant of the Cacheef of Semenoud, to drive on those belonging to his master. We purchased six asses, and procured the rest that were necessary. The Governor not only sent us bread and sheep, but ordered one of his Mamelukes, and a Chaous, to attend us across the Delta, and provide for us during the journey.

The heat was great, but we wished to go on to a village at the distance of three hours march, where we had an order from our friend the Governor to procure the camels we wanted; but when every thing was ready, the men employed to load our camels were missing, having been taken away by the servant of the Cacheef of Semenoud. We were obliged to employ others in their stead, who were so awkward, that it was six when we began our march, and then we were forced to stop several times before we were out of town, from the baggage falling off. The night was dark, and the road so bad from the large fissures in the ground, that we determined to stop at the first village; but we took the precaution of sending the baggage-camels in advance, that we might not be taken for a party of plundering Arabs, and be fired upon. We at length reached a miserable assemblage of mud huts, the backs of which were outwards, and formed a kind of wall. The harvest was lying around, among the heaps of which we pitched our tents.

May 15.—Early in the morning the Schech brought us hot bread, with sweet and sour milk, and humbly requested to know if I insisted on his paying one thousand paras also, which he said my interpreter had demanded. I assured him that nothing could be more contrary to my orders than such a demand; that I was rejoiced he had applied to me, and that I would punish the servant who made it, by dismissing him from my service; which I did. When a great man formerly travelled in Egypt, it was always the custom of the country for the Schechs to present money to his people. When the British were here, the dragomans of the army attempted to continue the practice, as they had done to an enormous extent under the French; but it was instantly checked by severely flogging them at the head of the corps. My interpreter thought he might be guilty of a similar imposition, though I positively prohibited it, but I fear he had previously succeeded in other places. In three hours we reached the village, where we had orders for the camels and asses. As there was not a tree near it, we went into a room built over the gateway. Here, as the wind was very fresh, we were nearly smothered with dust. The Schech had been wounded by some Osmanlis for their amusement; he could not therefore wait on us, but his brother did, and gave us the camels and asses, with which our people immediately set out for Calim. This village had been attacked a few nights before, by the inhabitants of another, in hopes of carrying off their sheep and cattle; but they had been repulsed, with the loss of two killed and one taken prisoner, who had been sent to Mahallet-el-Kebeer. Soon after three we were on our way, and by seven reached Calim, and encamped under some trees, where the air was cool, and pleasanter than in the town. We were received very civilly by the Schech, a respectable man, whose father had been a Mameluke, and had married the daughter of the former Schech. Formerly the town must have been handsome, but now it is greatly decayed. We had passed a village, which our guides said had been a French village. This town, the Schech informed me, had formerly a fortification, which had been built before the Mussulmauns came into the country, but of which there was not now a vestige. The country we had passed through, is very rich, but a great part of it lies waste. Wheat formed the chief crop; many fields were sown with clover or hemp, and in some places the people were watering the ground for rice We saw only one field of oats, and a few plantations of cotton; cucumbers, water melons, and gourds, are raised near every village. The people seemed extremely industrious, in defiance of the oppressions under which they laboured.

May 16.—We took coffee and cakes with the

Schech, under the gateway of his house. He told us his brother had been shot by some Osmanlis at the gates of Cairo, as he was riding out, without his having ever spoken to them, merely to shew their skill. He complained of the total ruin that was falling on the country, and asked me why the English did not come and liberate it? A question I could not answer. He would not give us camels on to Foua, but changed our asses, which were bad. One of our camels, after being loaded, was seized with the cramp, and could not move. We again applied to the Schech el Belled, who still objected; we therefore gave orders to take one that was employed in the harvest. We marched three hours to a village, where we waited for the baggage, which came up in an hour and a half. We breakfasted on milk and some bad bread, which were brought us by the Schech, who was a Sheriffe. At one we were again on our way, as the heat of the sun was tempered by a fine breeze. We rested for an hour under the shade of a tree, to give our asses some clover and water, and reached Foua in the evening, after having marched seven hours in the heat of the day. The country was similar to that we had passed yesterday, but more rice was grown, in consequence of the vicinity of the Nile. We encamped on the banks, under the shade of a sycamore. I sent to the Commandant to notify my arrival, who immediately called on me. He was also Schech el Belled, the proprietor of several villages near, and an old friend of Vincenzo's. He offered every assistance in procuring a jerm for our baggage, and his own canja for ourselves, which were accepted.

May 17.—We went at eight to the Hummaum, which was the worst we had met with, and then waited on the Commandant, who took us to his garden, on an island which is well planted, but from which, he said, the soldiers had taken every thing. He had no soldiers he could depend on, being himself an object of plunder for the Albanians, who continually came hither from the army, which was at no great distance, under Taher Pacha, and was supplied hence with provisions; and he owned he could not receive us in his house, from the confusion that reigned. After an excellent meat breakfast, and coffee, we departed. Some of the party went into the town to view the ovens in which chickens are hatched, but the heat was so great, that Mr. Salt and I returned to the tents in the Commandant's canja. On the way we saw a jerm just arrived from Cairo. I called to know who was in her, when Dr. Raffaelli and his son appeared, and were rejoiced to see me, as they had fallen into the hands of a rascally Rais, who had taken on board twenty-eight pilgrims from Mecca, after the Doctor had paid for the whole vessel, and had been already delayed six days on the way. I immediately returned to the Commandant with my friends, and told the Rais to attend to make his defence. He was clearly to blame, and was told that, had he not been a person belonging to the Custom-house, he would have been flogged; that as it was, he must immediately go down to the place where my boats lay, and sail in the morning with me. I then returned to the tents with my friends, and soon afterwards the jerm arrived.

While I was writing my journal, a little dancing girl about nine years old, with two men to play on the usual instruments, came to the tent door. The child danced for some time, and several of the soldiers sat on a bank facing the large opening left for air. I conversed familiarly with them through my servants, and, as the weather was hot, gave several of them oranges. Soon after, a difference arose between my people, and some of those who crowded round the tent, whom they wished to drive away. I blamed my people, and told the men they were heartily welcome to stay. One soldier, however, who was drunk, became very riotous, and declared that Christians had no business, to have a girl in their tents dancing, and that he would take her out by force. Many of his companions opposed him, and strongly took our part, but he tried, in defiance of them, to force his way into the tent and draw his pistols, but was prevented. Two Albanians, in particular, took up our cause, and at length the fellow, baffled in his object, went in a rage towards the town. I sent also to the Governor to state our situation, and request his presence to send off these people, and in the mean time gave a turban to the man who behaved best, to secure him in our interest. He now conjured me to send the child away, as he said her life would not be safe if the soldiers got her, as she would be punished for being the cause of the dispute. I suspected that he wanted to give her to his companions in the boat, and told him so. He assured me I was mistaken; and said, if I would let her go, he himself would be answerable for her safety, as he would fire at the first man who attempted to follow her. I did as he desired, and she got off into the country without being seen by any of the boat people.

Soon afterwards, my head Frosh returned from the Governor to say he would send his people. I saw some soldiers coming, and thought they had been his, till they were close, when I too late discovered the rascal who had run away. They rushed towards the tent, and not seeing the child there, seized the Frosh, and said he must go to the Governor. They began instantly to beat him, and cut at him with their sabres, without accusing him of any thing, or listening to a word we could say. The confusion became general; several took our parts, but we were without arms, and unprepared. We seized our sabres and pistols, but as no person appeared from the Governor, and we knew not what number of drunken Albanians might come down against us, we thought it best to proceed to the town. A shot was fired after my servant, who was the last, and another at the Captain's servant, who was in a soldier's dress: fortunately neither took effect. We found the Governor seated at his door. He begged us to wait till the people returned. I told him, that after what had passed, I knew not if I were in safety, even near him. He declared to God I was, and begged me to wait. The fellows now approached with our poor wounded Frosh, and some shots were fired in the streets. We knew the Governor's want of power, and told him we would retire into his house, where we could not be shot unawares, and could, for some time, defend ourselves; which we did. The soldier had the impudence to deny having fired at any one, and said they took the Arab for one of the people who had offended us, and meant to oblige us by punishing him. This lie it was useless to refute. The Governor had no power, and we were at the mercy of a drunken banditti, any one of whom might with his pistol put an end to any of us with impunity. The fact was, that the men were enraged with our poor Frosh from his having been our messenger to the Governor, where they had been, and had told him that a girl was in the Christian's tent, and that if he did not instantly send to take her out, they would do it without him. He told them to take care what they were about, as we were people of great consequence, and it would be a very serious business, but that he would send for her. They however set off instantly. Fortunately the girl was gone, or she would have perished before we had time to arm in her defence, which we should certainly have done for our Frosh, had we not been so completely deceived by supposing them to be the Governor's people. When, in the dispute, Vincenzo told them that we were friends of Mohammed Ali and Taher Pacha, one of them answered, "I despise the beards of both of them;" literally, "I am on the beards, what care I for them? I will be master here."

Our first care on reaching the house was to examine the wounds of our poor servant, which were not dangerous, his turban having protected his head from the blows of their sabres. The Governor soon joined us, and earnestly requested that we would go to a small house without the town, whither he would follow us as soon as possible. We immediately complied, and he soon followed us. He was evidently alarmed, and anxious to get us away, saying that he would conduct us himself to our tents by a circuitous route, without going through the town, and that it would be advisable for us to embark in his boat, and proceed to Rosetta in the night. We thought it our duty to comply with every wish of his, in order that, in the discussion that was likely to follow, nothing might be attributed to our proceedings. On arriving there we found that nothing had been stolen. The two soldiers who had joined the Hadje in the attack on the Frosh, were in the boat with him, which had not sailed. We however were now prepared. We took our arms and little cannon, sent our baggage, and that of Mr. Raffaelli, in the jerm, and went ourselves in the canja. We embarked by six, and the Governor went with us to a village of his a few miles lower down. The pilgrim's jerm set off before us, but as the wind was contrary, we soon passed her, and received no insult, which indeed we were now well prepared to resent. We rowed all night, and at four in the morning reached Rosetta.

May 18.—As soon as I arrived, I communicated the transactions at Foua to Mr. Petrucci, and through him to the Governor, whom I called upon to secure the delinquents on the arrival of the boat, that they might be sent to the Pacha to answer for their conduct. The Governor promised that this should be done, and soon afterwards sent to say that the chief criminal had quitted the jerm above the town, but that the other two were well known, and should abide his Highness's pleasure. The poor Frosh was his own servant; I had therefore no reason to doubt his wish to punish the people who had so wantonly injured him.

After having passed through the Delta; after having examined its whole line of sea coast, and viewed both the great mouths of the Nile, I confess that I cannot discover a single argument in favour of the idea, that this fertile district has been formed by the mud of the river. For if, in ancient times, this had actually been the case, how happens it that, in these days, the same cause does not produce the same effect? Yet it is evident that the volume of water brought down is as great as ever, by its covering the whole plain of Egypt; and many of the ancient canals being closed, the quantity discharged into the sea at Rosetta and Damietta is still greater than formerly. Instead, however, of the land continuing to extend to the northward, and a mound of black loam being deposited at the mouths of the river, the bar, which at all times renders the entrance shallow, and which after a gale from the north becomes so considerable as to be impassible till the stream has formed a new passage, consists of an arid sand alone, uncovered by any more fertile deposition.

It cannot be argued that, in early times, the sea shore may have been sand, though higher up, and that it has been covered by the mud of the Nile; for throughout the Delta the same rich soil is discoverable in the deepest pits, without any strata of sand between, while the whole sea coast is now like other flat coasts, unoccupied by rocks, a sand so mixed with marine salt, as scarcely to produce any vegetation.

The present sea shore of the Delta has, to me, so little the appearance of having been formed since the deluge, that I must have better authority than Mr. Savary, or the traditions of the Egyptian priests, for believing that it was so. The former is a wild romancer, whose descriptions I have already been obliged to controvert at Damietta, and to whom I can give no additional credit, when he asserts, that the narrow strip of land below Lesbé has been the gift of the Nile since the days of St. Louis; an assertion completely disproved, by its being of the same arid sand as the rest of the sea coast, and not of the rich soil of the Delta; and it is only necessary to look at the map of Egypt to be convinced, that unless the Lake Menzalé had been united to the sea, it is impossible but that the land must then have extended as far as it now does, for it is scarcely of a sufficient width to keep their waters asunder. To the traditions of the Egyptian priests, I am inclined to give as little credit. They were celebrated for their anxiety to exalt their country, by giving it a remote antiquity; and what fable could be better adapted for the purpose than this? Slow and imperceptible as was the increase of the land at that time, how many ages must have confessedly passed away, before eighty miles of sea could have been filled up by the depositions of the river!

May 19.—The wind was so strong from the north, as to prevent our sailing for Alexandria, but we went down, in the evening, to a country house which belonged to Mr. Petrucci, and is opposite Fort St. Julien. Gardens in Egypt are by no means beautiful objects, although Savary is in raptures with them. The trees, as in India, are necessarily watered by little canals cut to them; the grass is not allowed to grow at their roots, and the trees are planted in regular rows, and as close together as possible. Mr. Petrucci has endeavoured to cultivate potatoes, but without success; with artichokes, and many other European vegetables, he has been more fortunate. I was much pleased to find that the Musa, and several other plants from Abyssinia, of which I had sown the seeds, were already above the ground. Egypt would undoubtedly bring to perfection most of the Indian fruits, if the seed could be procured fresh; but the captains of the vessels which come to Suez from Bombay, are not likely to bring with them so unprofitable an article. I suggested to Mr. Petrucci the writing to India on the subject, and having them sent to Mocha, whence they might come in his own vessels. I also recommended to him to procure the different grapes of Yemen.

May 20.—The wind was still northerly, so that it was five before we reached the Bogaz, though we sailed at three. The sea was smooth, and towards mid-day the wind lulled. We arrived at Alexandria in good time, and were met on the beach by Major Missett and his suite, with the Chaous of Emim Aga.

CHAPTER XII.

Observations on Alexandria, and the Ruins now remaining.—The Site of the Palace of the Ptolemies.—Conjectures respecting the Serapeum.—Dioclesian's Pillar.—Strictures on Sebastiani's Account of his Visit to Egypt.—Observations on the State of the Country.—Departure from Alexandria.—Description of the Bay of Finica in Caramania.—Arrival at Malta.—Quarantine.—Government.—Departure for Gibraltar.—Transactions there.—Voyage to England.—Arrival at Spithead.

OUR first business, on our arrival, was to visit the vessel that had arrived from Malta, which we found to be sufficiently large to accommodate our party, and stow my baggage, after having received all the articles she could procure at Alexandria; I therefore immediately agreed with the Captain for my passage, and prepared for departure.

On the 23d of May, at the request of Emim Aga, I accompanied him in his barge on board the Turkish frigate, which he commanded as Commodore. His boatmen were very well dressed, and as we rowed by her in the Old Harbour, each merchantman hoisted her colours, and saluted with three guns. The frigate, on our appearing on deck, fired thirteen guns by the order of Emim Aga, who shewed us over the whole ship, which was old and ill constructed, so much so, indeed, that there was a difference of six inches in her height between decks, on one side and the other. The same military compliments were paid on our visiting a corvette, which was kept in excellent order, having her brass guns highly polished, and her decks as clean as a room in a house. We were here presented with oranges, and some very fine apples from Rhodes, by the Captain, who was a Greek. I requested the Governor to go on board our vessel, the Queen, which he did, and was received with the same military honours that he had paid to me.

The just complaint made by Professor White, at the conclusion of his Ægyptiaca, of the want of evidence respecting the real situation of the ruins which surround the pillar, which has been usually called Pompey's, and the reproach which he has cast on the Institute of Egypt, for having so ill employed their leisure, and having added so little to our knowledge of that country; determined me to avoid a like censure, by using my utmost exertions to elucidate the geography of this ancient capital of the Ptolemies. Mr. Salt immediately commenced a survey, the result of which is given to the public in the accompanying map, which not only shews the present situation of the city, but, I trust, will enable us to ascertain the position of most of the great edifices mentioned by the ancient geographers.

The re-formation of the Lake Mareotis, by the English, has thrown great light on the extent of the city on the southern side, as it was known from the account of Strabo, that it was bounded by it, and had a port on it, which was even richer and more frequented than that toward the sea. The chain of hillocks, which is covered by the

French lines, limits the extent of the ancient city towards the east. The sea still marks the northern boundary, except where the accumulation of sand on the Heptastadium has formed an isthmus instead of a causeway; but the division between the town and the Necropolis, towards the west, it is now hardly possible to discover, though I am inclined to place it near to the spot where the Calish enters the sea. Strabo states that the length of the city was thirty stadia, and the breadth about seven or eight, giving a circumference of eighty stadia, or eight miles, which very well agrees with the plan of the ruins, supposing the tower at the extremity of the Calish to have been the boundary of the city on the shore of the Old Harbour, or the Eunostus. The assertion of Pliny, that it is fifteen miles round, is totally impossible within the bounds of the sea and lake; but the form which he has described, as having been given to it by Dinochares, is probably more correct, though some latitude must be allowed to the expression of its resembling a Macedonian mantle. It probably ran nearly in a straight line along the sea shore, from the spot in the Eunostus where the Calish enters, to the French lines, where the angular extremities might be supposed to end. The regularity of this line would be alone interrupted by the projection of the little Pharos, for the isthmus on which the new town stands, was not then in existence. The curve at the corners, which Pliny mentions, is more difficult to ascertain, as Strabo mentions that the length towards the lake was thirty stadia, or the same as that towards the sea, while the sides were seven or eight. It can at any rate have been but small, and probably included the Serapeum; and after running along in the direction of the Calish, turned up rapidly towards the sea, leaving on the outside, the S. E. heaps of ruins, which were covered with fortifications by the French.

The city is described by Strabo as having been laid out in regular streets, passable for horses and carriages, two of which were particularly large, and crossed each other at right angles. Of the actual position of one of these, which extended from the gate of Canopus to the port Eunostus, there can be no doubt, for the vacant space still remains, and is easily to be traced in the map, from the letter F to G; and it appears probable, that the street which crossed it extended from C to H. When, under the Mussulmaun government, Alexandria had gradually fallen from its former splendour, and one half of the city had ceased to be inhabited, it was thought advisable to lessen its extent. The old walls were destroyed, and the new ones were erected within. On this occasion, it is but reasonable to suppose, that as the streets continued in the same line, the new gates would be placed where they ran, unaltered except by a curtailment of their length, and if so, it is only from C to H, that the street we are enquiring for could have been; for at B alone, within the whole extent of the southern wall, is there any gate; and another exists in a direct line with it at C, which probably opened on the Heptastadium.

The following is the account which Strabo has left us of the Palace.* "At the entrance of the great harbour is an island, and on it the Pharos; on the other side are rocks, and the promontory of Lochias; on this is a royal palace. To those entering, on the left are other royal buildings,

* Book xvii. p. 1127. Oxford, 1807.

communicating with that on the promontory before mentioned, having various banquetting rooms and gardens. Contiguous to these is a private and inclosed port, accessible to the sovereign only. There is also the island Antirrhodus, near the artificial port, having a royal palace and a harbour. It has its name from a supposed resemblance to the island of Rhodes." He also adds in another place, "that the public buildings, which are very splendid, and the royal palaces, occupy a fourth, or even a third part of the city. Every succeeding prince was desirous of making some ornamental addition to the religious edifices, as well as to improve and adorn his own particular residence, as the poet says,

Some from one and some from another.

All these structures communicated with one another, as well as with the harbour and with the buildings beyond the harbour. One part of the royal edifices is the Museum, which has a walk, benches, and a spacious apartment, in which those persons who study there, take their repasts. Another part of the royal edifices is that called "Soma," which is inclosed, and contains the tombs of the kings and of Alexander."

The ruins, at present remaining, along the shore of the greater, or, as it is now called, the new harbour, are sufficient to prove the accuracy of this description of Strabo. The land which gradually rises from Cleopatra's Needles to the spot, marked by the letter D, may be considered as the promontory of Lochias, on which the first royal palace was naturally built, as it was by far the most conspicuous and elevated station within the walls. Hence to the level ground at No. 1, the whole surface is covered with masses of brick mixed with small pieces of differently coloured marbles, porphyrys and jaspers cut into figures, which evidently shew that they were formerly used in the rich mosaics of the royal apartments.

The slight projection of No. 4, probably marks the spot opposite to which the small island of Antirrhodus formerly existed, as there can be little doubt, from the shape of the ruins at No. 5, that there was the private port appropriated to the use of the sovereign alone. The recesses for the reception of the galleys are still sufficiently distinguishable. The ruin No. 4 is the most considerable on the shore of the harbour; it extends above one hundred feet into the sea, and beneath the water the foundations are visible still farther. The lower story was built on arches of stone, but the second story, of which a part remains, was of brick. Pipes of burnt clay are inclosed in beds of a mortar, harder than the bricks, which lead to a supposition that the royal baths were here constructed; nor would it be easy to account in any other way for the smallness of many of the rooms, the dimensions of which can still be ascertained. No. 7 marks the foundation of a round tower, and No. 16 and 18 of two small square buildings, whose use it is impossible to conjecture. Beyond the Pharos, are very extensive ruins of buildings, to which, probably, Strabo alludes as being beyond the harbour, although they were connected with the palace.

From the account above quoted, it is evident that the palace, with its numerous additions, and public buildings, must have covered a very large space of ground; and I am inclined to believe, that it was only bounded on the south by the great street, and on the east by another, which I conceive to have extended from D to E on the west. I should hardly suppose it descended the high land connected with the promontory of Lochias. Strabo, who goes on gradually along the shore of the harbour, says, after having spoken of the palace of Antirrhodus, "Beyond this is a theatre, then the Posidium running out in a kind of elbow, from what is called the Emporium. Here is a temple of Neptune. Here also are seen the Cæsarium, the Emporium, and the Apostases." The theatre may be considered as within the royal quarter, as may also the Posidium, which took its name from the Temple of Neptune, and which seems to be pointed out by the bend in the shore at No. 1, as having been in that spot; but if the Emporium were a public mart, as its name designates, it must be believed to have been beyond the bounds of the palace.

That I am correct in the position I have given to the Posidium, is still more conclusively proved, by the Cæsarium being next mentioned, which was undoubtedly so named from the Temple of Cæsar, which stood in it, and before which, according to Pliny,* were two obelisks, a fact which precludes the possibility of our going to the west of Cleopatra's Needles for the site of the Cæsarium.

It was from the Posidium that Antony carried out a mole into the harbour, at the extremity of which he erected a palace, which he named Timonium, and to which, when deserted by his friends after the battle of Actium, he retired with a determination to spend the remainder of his life in solitude. The mole and palace are no longer distinguishable, but the harbour is in this part considerably filled by heaps of stones, among which

* Lib. xxxvi. cap. 9.

some blocks of marble, and broken pieces of columns, are visible at low water.

From the manner in which Strabo mentions the Emporium, it was probably west of the Cæsarium; the temple of Cæsar may therefore have possibly formed a part of the palace; but if so, I conceive it must there have ended, and the public part of the city begun; for beyond it, to the Heptastadium, we only hear of the Apostases and the naval arsenals.

I have before observed, that the Heptastadium itself most probably commenced at the extremity of the street which ran from near the pillar of Dioclesian, by the present gate to an ancient square tower near the letter C, which the French have included within the lines that defend the new town of Alexandria. From that spot, therefore, the port of Eunostus must have commenced, although, now, the sand has much narrowed its limits. Of the buildings on its banks Strabo gives no account, but mentions the small artificial harbour called Kibotus, whence a navigable canal extended to the Lake Mareotis. This appears to have been the same as the modern Calish, and at once points out its position, which is still more confirmed by the line of the great street ending at that very place, and by the numerous heaps of ruins which are discoverable there, though under the water. The tower at G has every appearance of having belonged to the original walls, and I am inclined to think, that the town extended no farther on the banks of the port, from the expression used by Strabo, that "without the canal, was, a small part of the city." Beyond was the Necropolis, and still farther at a distance of thirty stadia, or three miles, was Nicopolis, which, at the time of Strabo, had drawn from Alexandria many of its inhabitants who attended the amphitheatre, the stadium, and the celebration of the five years' games.

The ruins at 9, 10, 11, and 12 are by no means considerable, nor would it be easy to conjecture for what purpose they were intended. Some of the spaces were too small for a human body, even of an infant, but others were evidently intended for sepulchres, and were lined with a very hard plaister, of a red colour. The ruin at No. 10, was a single room, one hundred and five feet long, divided in the centre by a row of square pillars, and had been originally arched; it had no connection with the water, but extended farther inland than we could trace the foundations.

According to Strabo, Alexandria was in breadth seven or eight stadia, which will preclude the idea of its not having contained the vast piles of ruin around Dioclesian's pillar, as any line drawn from the sea to the Calish within them, must greatly exceed that distance, nor could, in that case, the figure of a mantle, rounded at the corners, be preserved. In defiance therefore of the weight which Professor White gives to the assertion of Macrobius, "that no town of Egypt had received within its walls a temple of Saturn or Serapis," I must believe that the original wall of Alexandria began near the tower at G, and extended in a gradual sweep, till it joined the Calish at the hills near A, which is kept along till it again bent up towards the Canopic gate at F, leaving without it the Hippodrome, which, Strabo says, with other buildings, extended from it to the Canopic canal. Of these very considerable remains are distinguishable on the map; and an open line by the letter B, parallel to the great street, seems to mark the street also mentioned by Strabo, as going from the Necropolis to the Canopic gate.

The real position of the Panium, with its lofty, conic form, and spiral staircase, or the Gymnasium celebrated for its porticos, I cannot venture to conjecture. The very foundations of the greater part of the ruins are now concealed by heaps of broken brick and mortar, which are only removed by the natives for the sake of procuring the fragments of marble columns, which they burn to lime, without any regard to their beauty or rarity.

Of the splendid buildings which once decorated the great street, a few columns only remain; two, near the gate of Rosetta, were of granite, with white marble capitals and pediments. At K was a very large brick building, which had formerly a colonnade in front, of yellow marble, with white capitals and pediments, one of which was uncovered by the native workmen while we were making the survey, and at S, three massive columns of red granite, with pediments and capitals of the same, have resisted the ravages of time, and of the still more destructive caprice of the present masters of the country. The hills of rubbish undoubtedly conceal many fine remains of ancient art, and every day a few are brought to light. I observed a very beautiful sarcophagus of red granite, highly polished, lying level with the surface, near to the spot where the two great streets crossed each other. It was Grecian, ornamented with festoons of flowers, and perfect; I therefore sought out the owners, and purchased it from them for one thousand paras, although without any hopes of being able to carry it with me to England, but trusting that, on some future occasion, I might be more fortunate. The Turks and Arabs have no attachment to any of the splendid objects which still adorn their country, and excite the admiration of strangers. The French, had they been able to gratify their national vanity by carrying off, as they wished, the column of Dioclesian, would not have excited a single regret in the breast of any inhabitant of Alexandria; and they observed, with similar apathy, the preparations made by the English army, to remove the obelisk of Cleopatra to their native country, where it would have remained a perpetual monument of their victories. Knowing, as I well do, the indifference of the natives on this occasion, I cannot but regret that the plan was not carried into effect. Had they prided themselves on the possession of such a monument, the affair would have been different, and the reproaches cast against the French for their universal system of rapine, would have justly deterred the English army from doing any thing which could lead to a comparison between them.

Strabo only says of the Serapeum, that it was included within the canal that united the Kibotus and the Lake; but Professor White has, perfectly to my satisfaction, proved from the Grecian and Arabic authors, that the second library of Alexandria, which was founded by Ptolemy Philadelphus, was called the Serapean, and formed a part of that edifice; that this library, when destroyed by the orders of the Calif Omar, was near to the column of the pillars, and that this column of the pillars was no other than the column formerly designated Pompey's, but now known to have been erected in honour of Dioclesian.

The extent of the ruins justifies us in believing the accounts which Rufinus and Ammianus Marcellinus have given of the splendor of the Serapeum. The elevation on which the pillar stands is not natural, but raised on arches, now filled with earth and rubbish, but altogether so hard, that I laboured in vain, with Arab workmen, and their imperfect instruments, to penetrate to any depth. Here might well have been the one hundred steps which led to the temple of the deity, and in front of which, in all probability, the column reared its head in unrivalled splendor, long before it was dedicated to a Roman emperor by a servile governor of Egypt. The temple was destroyed by Theodosius in the year 389, but the palaces and other buildings which were contiguous, still remained in the time of Edrisi, who, in 1153, speaks of a palace situated in the southern part of Alexandria, which was of an oblong square shape, having sixteen pillars at each end, and sixty-seven on the sides, the columns of which were still remaining, and at a northern angle, one of much greater magnitude than the others, which had a capital and pediments. This noble building, for whatever purpose it may have been destined, whether for the residence of the priests, or for the reception of the second library of Alexandria, augmented by the gifts of Antony to Cleopatra, at present can only be traced by the foundations or rather the rubbish of bricks and pottery which covers them. Yet it may be no very hazardous conjecture to fix the site of it in the open space that is marked No. 2, 3, in the plan of the ruins. It is indeed possible that here may have been the temple of Serapis, and the palace may have been close to the column, but the descriptions of the Greek and Arabic authors are so vague, that it is impossible to do more than conjecture on the subject.

The column of Dioclesian has been described by every author; but the French, while in possession of Alexandria, at length ascertained its dimensions; to the English, however, they left the honour of decyphering the inscription, and of proving beyond controversy, that Dioclesian was the emperor to whom it was dedicated, and whose statue, on its summit, must have formed a most conspicuous object from every part of the country, and served as a still better land-mark than the pillar alone, which, nevertheless, is now a most useful guide to navigators approaching the low, sandy shore of Egypt. For several days Mr. Salt occupied himself in copying the inscription, giving the true shape to every letter, and marking its relative position to the others. This was done with less difficulty than we expected, for by applying chalk to all the rough indents, and then wiping over the whole lightly with a wet spunge, the white remained on the letters, but was washed from the polished surface, and the smaller hollows formed in the granite, by the wind from the sea. It is a most mortifying circumstance, that after having completed the work, I should not be able to present it to the public; but the paper is mislaid, nor can all my researches discover it. I can therefore only state, that in the last line the name of the exarch of Egypt was not Pompeius, for that the third letter of his name was undoubtedly a sigma. I cannot but express my astonishment that so many learned men, who have visited Egypt, should have failed in making out the inscription. Pococke alone attempted to give any part of it, and was right in the two first letters of the name of Dioclesian, and the three first in the name of the dedicator. From the position of the pillar with respect to the sun, the inscription is sufficiently distinct for four hours each day, and the name of the Emperor is more perfect than any other.

The Circus, marked 6, 7, 8, is in length above seven hundred paces, the upper circular division is cut out of the solid rock, and has in the centre an elevation with a hole at one end. This was filled with sand, but I employed men to clear it out in hopes of finding some subterraneous chambers; but after descending gradually to the depth of about twenty feet, in a passage cut out of the solid rock, sufficiently spacious for a person to pass freely along it, I had the mortification to find my farther progress opposed by the natural barrier of rock. We examined the end, the top, bottom, and sides, with the greatest care, and were at length convinced that we had reached the extremity of the passage, and could only wonder, for what purpose it had been intended. The hill marked 9, seems to be in part a natural elevation, and may have given rise to Rhacotis being called a promontory. It is of nearly the same height as the spot on which Dioclesian's pillar actually stands.

Modern Alexandria is by no means an ill built town, and its situation is extremely pleasant between the two harbours. The trade is still considerable with the Levant, and hardly a day passed during our stay, without the arrival of a Greek vessel. The New Harbour is indeed nearly useless; and instead of the largest ships being able, as in the time of Strabo, to approach the steps, and unload close to the wharfs, it is only in a small part of the harbour, near to the causeway of the Pharos, that the little vessels of the Turkish empire can find a shelter from the northerly winds, in from two to five fathom water. The climate is by no means unpleasant, as the heat is tempered in summer by the strong gales, which almost constantly blow from the north, and carry with them the thick black clouds that, after breaking on the mountains of the interior of Africa, return in the floods of the Nile to fertilize the plains of Egypt. It is only a knowledge of this that can reconcile its inhabitants to seeing them constantly pass over their heads without once falling in a refreshing shower.

The consuls of the European powers live together in tolerable amity, except when a war between their masters reduces them to the necessity of not visiting in public. The British and French Consuls General are indeed the leaders, and the rivalry between their countries rages with full force at Alexandria. Major Missett is a man admirably adapted for his situation. He is well acquainted with the chiefs who rule over the different parts of this once flourishing, but now distracted, country, knows their wants and wishes, and by a firm, but conciliatory, system of conduct, has baffled all the projects of the French, who still look back on Egypt with the steady determination of seizing on the first opportunity of re-conquering it. For this they have employed their emissaries in instigating the Beys against each other, and the Pacha against them all, and have thereby prevented tranquillity from being restored, which would, they justly think, preclude the possibility of their return.

At the convention of El Arish, they prepared to leave a force in the country, by reporting that numbers had deserted into Upper Egypt: General Dongelet with the 22d and 85th demi-brigades had, in fact, retired thither without any intention of departing, and a whole train of artillery was buried in the sands of the Faiume, to be employed on a future occasion. The victorious army of Abercrombie secured a faithful evacuation of the country, but though their troops were driven away, their arts and intrigues remained. Sebastiani was first sent there, and the report he made of his success is so curious, that I have inserted it in the Appendix; but as it is nearly one tissue of falsehood, I have thought it right also to give a true account of his adventures, and I request the reader will compare them together.

Towards the latter end of October, 1802, the French frigate La Corneille, in company with a brig, entered the old port of Alexandria, and shortly afterwards Major General Stuart, the commander in chief of the British forces, received a letter from Sebastiani, expressing a wish to have an interview with him, in order to deliver a message from the First Consul. The General returned no written answer, but sent Major Missett, his secretary, to congratulate Colonel Sebastiani on his arrival, and to know at what time it would be convenient to him to land, as, in compliment to him, the quarantine regulations should not be enforced. The hour having been fixed, Major Missett, with an escort of dragoons, waited at the landing place for the Colonel, whom he conducted to head quarters. The customary honours were paid to him at every post near which he passed. The message from the First Consul to the British commander in chief was a demand that, in compliance with the treaty of Amiens, he should evacuate Alexandria: to which General Stuart replied, that he had no orders to that effect from his government. Sebastiani then observed, that the General ought to consider the consequences of its being refused, as he must be aware of the inferiority of the British force in Egypt, and the consequently precarious safety of the troops in Alexandria, several of the forts being in the hands of the Turks. Justly irritated at so indecorous a behaviour, General Stuart abruptly put an end to the conversation, by declaring that were his force reduced to fifteen men, he would keep Alexandria, till ordered by his Government to evacuate Egypt. That day Colonel Sebastiani dined with Major General Stuart, and the conversation having naturally fallen on the antiquities of Egypt, the General observed, that the inscription on Pompey's pillar had lately been made out by some British officers; on which Sebastiani requested that Joubert, who acted as his interpreter, might have a copy of it. This was complied with, and some months afterwards, a paragraph appeared in the French papers, stating that Joubert had brought from Egypt an inscription which would determine at what period Pompey's pillar had been erected; but no notice was taken of the manner in which Joubert had obtained the inscription.

During his stay at Alexandria, Sebastiani received the most marked attentions from General Stuart: he was every day supplied with saddle-horses, and permitted to visit every spot within, as well as without the garrison, unattended by any British officer—a liberty of which he proved himself unworthy, by meanly holding private conversations with different soldiers of the foreign brigade, exhorting them to desert.

Soon after his arrival, Colonel Sebastiani had his audience of the Governor-General of Alexandria. General Stuart directed his interpreter, Mr. Reggio, to mix with the crowd, and learn what passed. Fortunately, Mr. Joubert was so little qualified for the office of interpreter, that he could not translate the first compliments. The Governor, distressed, called out aloud, "Is there no one here who speaks Franks?" Reggio immediately stepped forward, and acted as interpreter to the French agent, who began by assuring the Governor of the First Consul's high regard for his nation, that he was extremely afflicted that the English continued in Egypt contrary to its desire, but begged him to rest assured that the French would soon oblige them to retreat. Sebastiani was perfectly satisfied with his interpreter. It was only when speaking of Reggio to the French at Cairo that he discovered the trick that had been played him.

Sebastiani had brought with him a large collection of the First Consul's portraits, which he sent to the different Arab Schechs in the neighbourhood of Alexandria, with the same message to each, "that the First Consul continued to have the most affectionate remembrance of the poor Schechs of Egypt, and particularly of the person to whom he sent." The Schechs, who detested the French, and cared nothing for the present (a most ridiculous one certainly, and the sending of which shews a strange ignorance of their manners and prejudices), in general, returned no answer. One, however, replied, that it was impossible that the First Consul could have sent such a message to him, or have any recollection of him, for he had retired into the desert the moment the French arrived, and had not returned till the English landed.

At Cairo, Sebastiani never visited a single Schech, nor did one visit him. Schech Abdallah Scherkowie, of the great mosque, never was attached to the French, nor were any of his brethren, except Schech Soolimaun-el-Faiume. Sebastiani sent to this man to say he would pay him a visit; but the Schech, terrified lest the government should consider him as a friend of the French, sent to

Mr. Rosetti to conjure him to induce the Colonel to keep away. So much for "the enthusiasm excited among the Schechs by the view of the portrait of the First Consul!" The account of the insult offered to him at Cairo, is equally false and ridiculous. Sebastiani was riding through the streets, with a Chaous of the Pacha before him, when he was met by Mustapha Aga, Akil, or Agent of the Porte in Egypt (procureur de la Porte). This man reproached the Chaous for being such a wretch as to ride before a Frenchman, who had brought so many evils on his country; not, as Sebastiani says, for marching before a Christian; and made his people beat the Chaous. Sebastiani instantly returned to the house of Mr. Rosetti, who was absent at Boulac, and sent, in the most pressing terms, to desire him to come to town. Rosetti, on his arrival, found Sebastiani pale as death, and excessively alarmed. He told Rosetti how he had been insulted, and said that he suspected it was a plan of the English to have him assassinated. He was therefore determined to depart instantly, and that he had sent to the Pacha to inform him of what had happened, but to declare that he did not wish any steps to be taken on the occasion. Rosetti blamed him for this, and said it was a business that ought not to be passed over: that Mustapha was a friend of his, and he would settle the business. Sebastiani still hesitated, and said that he feared the consequences. At length it was left to Rosetti, who saw the Pacha and Mustapha: it was agreed that the latter should make an apology to the Colonel, who was to receive him graciously. Sebastiani on this became valiant: he wished to resent the affront on Mustapha's appearance, but Rosetti insisted on his keeping the terms agreed on, and they parted excellent friends. Nothing more passed.

Sebastiani never saw the Pacha, except in the presence of Mr. Rosetti. He never made any offer to him of mediation with the Beys; nor did the Pacha shew him his powers, nor enter into any political conversation with him. The usual compliments passed; but when Sebastiani said that it was his wish to visit the Beys in Upper Egypt, Mohammed Pacha most positively refused his consent, declaring that, in the present situation of affairs, it was a thing he could on no account permit; and insisting that he should pledge his word of honour to him, that, during his stay in Egypt, he would have no communication with them by letter, nor otherwise. With this Sebastiani complied; but on his return home he informed Rosetti that he had the First Consul's orders to offer the Mamelukes his protection, and that, therefore, as he could not go, he must write to them on the subject, and desired Rosetti to get it done. Rosetti, astonished, asked him if he had forgotten his honour so recently pledged: and finding that his argument had no effect, declined having any thing to do with a business which might end in the destruction of them both, should the letter be intercepted. This alarmed the Colonel, and the business was dropped for the present. When, however, Sebastiani arrived at Damietta, knowing that he should be safe before any thing could happen, he did write to the Beys, and sent the letter to Madame Murad Bey, who being afraid to meddle with the business, sent it to Mr. Rosetti, in whose possession it now is.

The assertion, that there was an attempt to excite the Albanians against him, is equally devoid of truth. There certainly was a report current, that the French were seen off Syria, and were coming to Egypt; but it was invented by the French themselves, and, Rosetti believes, by the orders of Sebastiani. This report was, at least, spread by him at Alexandria, where he officially notified to the Christians who waited on him, that they would not much longer be under the oppressive government of the Turks, for the French would soon be in Egypt. No letter was received from Rosetta on the subject; no person was summoned before him, nor was any communication made to the Pacha on the occasion.

General Stuart did indeed write to the Pacha, warning him not to credit the assertions of Sebastiani, that the English had hostile designs against Egypt, and apprizing him of the real designs of France as exemplified by Buonaparté's proclamation. It was his duty so to do, as the representative of the British nation in Egypt, and consequently, the guardian of its interests and character: nor could any thing, except the habit of contemplating crimes, have led to an idea that this was "an attempt to instigate assassination." Had General Stuart been the dupe of Sebastiani, he would not have been thus accused, nor have been reported to the First Consul as a man of mediocre talents. It was wounded vanity, and bitter disappointment, which instigated both assertions; assertions which General Stuart has, I think with propriety, considered as unworthy of reply, for no one who knows him, even by the report of his whole conduct in Egypt, can believe him capable of the one, or deserving of the other.

In May, 1803, the French establishment in Egypt was organized under Mr. Lesseps, who succeeded in creating a mortal enmity between Osman Bey and Elfi Bey, by exciting the former to assassinate the latter, on his return from England, under an idea that he was come with a sufficient European force to place him at the head of the government. On finding afterwards that Osman Bey was inclined to throw himself upon the protection of the English, he bribed Mohammed Ali and Achmed Bey, two Albanian chiefs, to revolt from the Beys, and to drive them from Cairo. This scheme proved successful, and Egypt became, as the French government wished, divided under three masters. A detail of all the events which led to this, and of the different intrigues by which the revolutions were accomplished, would occupy a much greater space than my limits will allow. The result has been, that one of the finest countries on the globe is sinking under the severest oppression.

Mohammed Ali Pacha rules over lower Egypt from a little above Cairo to the sea, including the Delta, Damietta, and Rosetta; he is, decidedly, a man of talent, but is necessarily the slave of the undisciplined freebooters whom he ostensibly commands, and is obliged to plunder the defenceless natives, to gratify their rapacity; for his revenue is by no means equal to his expenditure, even with all the additions which requisitions from the Arabs, and exactions from the merchants, can bring into his coffers. The trade that was formerly carried on, through Egypt, with the interior of Africa, is now at an end, and even the commerce with Jidda is greatly diminished from the dread of the immoderate extortion under which the merchant labours.

Upper Egypt is in possession of the Beys, nominally under the command of Ibrahim Bey, to whom the title of Schech el Belled belongs, but really under the influence of Osman Bey Bardessi, who is a man of talent, and the representative of the famous Murad Bey. As the government of the Beys was ever much more mild than that of the Turks, this province does not suffer so much from oppression as from the deprivation of every article which they were accustomed to receive from Lower Egypt, all trade with which has been cut off by Mohammed Ali.

Elfi Bey has possession of the Faiume, a fertile province, over which he tyrannises, and has extended his incursions to Damanour, which he might easily take, were he not afraid of sacrificing his Mamelukes in the assault, and thereby of comparatively diminishing his consequence with the other Beys. Many Albanians have deserted to him, and he has a very large Arab force, which he has influenced by the assurance that he is closely connected with England, and expects a large army from that country, to place him at the head of the government. Were Damanour to fall, Alexandria would be at his mercy, as he commands all the supplies of provision which come in from the desert. He, at one time, stopped every thing at the Peninsula, and obliged Emim Aga to consent secretly to his sending his officers into the town, to purchase cloth and other articles, for which he was in the greatest distress.

Excepting from the alarm excited by the plans of Elfi, Alexandria is in perfect tranquillity. The garrison consists of the Turkish soldiers, disciplined after the European manner, who are, in general, reasonable men. The export of such articles as Lower Egypt produces, still keeps the town and harbour alive, and a Christian can walk about the town, without fear or danger of insult. It is here alone that the Grand Signor can be said to reign.

How long the present system can be carried on, it is difficult to conjecture; poverty has already reduced thousands to the necessity of emigrating into the desert, and of sacrificing every remnant of property for the chance of saving life itself. The Copts are earnestly looking forward in the hope of England's assistance, to liberate them from as dreadful an oppression as the children of Israel groaned under, in the same country; and even the Mussulmauns, of high rank, join them in their wishes, in defiance of the arts employed by Bonaparté, during his command in the country, to persuade them that he was the favourer of their religion, and the instrument of destiny, to liberate them from all their oppressions.*

Schech Soolimaun el Faiume, a descendant of Mohammed, a priest of one of the mosques of Cairo, and who, before the arrival of the French, had a revenue of above one hundred thousand pounds sterling per annum, arrived at Alexandria in the end of May, and requested I would call on him, which I immediately did. He represented to me, in the strongest terms, the sufferings of Egypt, and conjured me, by those feelings of compassion, which the view of oppression must have excited in my breast, to state what I had seen on my return to England. His feelings so far overcame his prejudices, that he obliged me to dine with him; and on taking leave he embraced me, and with tears in his eyes, again besought me to recommend him and his unfortunate country to the protection of the English.

The most powerful Schechs of the Desert, the chief of whom is Chedid, are closely attached to

* As a proof of this, I have given in the Appendix, two interesting extracts from the Courier de l'Egypte.

the English nation, and avow their destestation of the French, but, at the same time, they declare that, if we will not protect them, so unsupportable is the yoke of the Albanians, that they will submit to any European power to ged rid of it. The Beys have frequently offered, either to hold the country subject to Great Britain; or, if we will assist them in driving away the Albanians, and placing them at the head of the government, that they will grant us such immunities and privileges as will, by placing the whole trade of the country in our hands, repay any expense we may incur. No answer has as yet been given, and the Consul General is obliged to act according to his own judgment, without having received a single instruction from home, by which he might regulate his conduct.

It is painful indeed to add, that the popularity of the English name has since vanished in Egypt, from the result of our late fatal expedition to that country; that, instead of the tranquillity which Alexandria then enjoyed, it is now a prey to the extortions of the Albanians; and that our friends the Arabs, instead of wishing for our reappearance, are lamenting over the loss of their habitations levelled with the ground, of their wives and parents massacred in cold blood, and of their children sold to perpetual bondage. Deep, undoubtedly, were the curses with which we were followed from that shore, on which we were received with acclamations, and indelible is the disgrace which has fallen upon us for having abandoned our friends to ruin and destruction: yet the whole business has been passed over in England with indifference, and no inquiry has been instituted to ascertain to whom the blame of failure ought to attach, and on whom ought to alight the deep obloquy of having sullied the British arms, and disgraced the national character.

On the 4th of June we celebrated the King's birth-day with the greatest festivity, and with all the splendour that Alexandria could afford. A royal salute was fired at sun rise, at noon, and at sunset, from brass patereroes in front of Mr. Briggs' house. The British flag was hoisted, and the populace were liberally regaled with coffee and sherbet, in the street before the door of the Consul General, while paras were thrown in profusion from the windows.

On the 5th I paid a farewell visit to Emim Aga, and in return for the numerous attentions I had received from him, requested his acceptance of a pair of richly ornamented pistols. I heard, in the evening, of the death of Signor Filippo Agnelli, at Rosetta. He was a very worthy man, and particularly skilful in preserving specimens of fish and birds. The composition he used was a mixture, in equal proportions, of white and yellow arsenic, and allum. He died of a fever brought on by imprudently bathing in cold water, after having fatigued and heated himself by dissecting an ostrich. I greatly regretted that the entire collection of Abyssinian birds would probably, by his sudden death, be lost to the public, as there was little hope that they could reach Vienna in a state to be preserved. I, however, wrote to Mr. Rosetti, as Consul General of the Emperor of Germany, requesting that he would lose no time in forwarding them, and the other things which I had entrusted to the care of Signor Filippo, to be presented in my name to his Imperial Majesty.

June 11.—In consequence of intelligence received by Major Missett, of a war being probable between Russia and the Porte, in which England would be involved, we were impatieut to depart, and only waited till the northerly winds enabled us to do so. Our friend, the Surbaje, meant to accompany us, as his declarations "that no man who had once been in the English service, would ever quit it," might call down on him the resentment of the Turkish government, should hostilities actually take place. In the morning, for the first time, we found that the climate of Alexandria could be oppressive; a sultry air came over the desert from the S. E. and warned us to depart. We took an early dinner with our amiable and able friend, the Major, and were afterwards accompanied by him, and the other Europeans, to the Old Port, where Emim Aga was waiting to take his leave. In the course of the night every one got on board, and at three we sailed with a moderate breeze.

June 22.—Our fair wind continued only two days, when it came round to the west; and, as the Queen was a very bad sailer, uncoppered, and her masts too small, we made four points of lee-way and were even rejoiced in the evening, at finding we had made good a northerly course, by coming in sight of the mountains of Caramania, instead of Cyprus. Our stock of water was so short, that we determined to put into some place for a supply; this was chiefly owing to the number of passengers which the Captain had taken on board, consisting, besides my party, of Turks, horses, ostriches, antelopes, monkeys, jerboas, and parrots. These, with the live stock, consumed a great quantity of water, and rendered the ship very uncomfortable, though the Captain was a good creature, and would have kept them in better order if he could.

June 23.—Though we stood in for the land, during the night, we were in the morning twenty miles from it. A Neapolitan cook, whom I had hired at Alexandria, was alone acquainted with the coast, and asserted, so positively, that the bay of Finica was to leeward, that the Captain, believing him, stood away for it, and got safely to an anchor by three o'clock in seven fathom. The bay is a good one, and was much frequented by the Russians during their last war with the Porte, in consequence of the facility with which water could be procured from a small stream, running into the sea, with a rapid and deep current. It is distinguishable at a great distance, in consequence of the lofty hills which rise above it, the centre one having a sugar loaf point, rising out of a gradual swell. This marks the centre of the bay, and had still snow on its summit. To the eastward are some lofty, rocky islands, apparently two, which separate it from the gulf of Satalia: these lie more south of Cape Cheledoni than Heather has placed them in his chart of the Mediterranean. According to our observation, he has also laid down the bay twelve miles too far north, and the anchoring ground too near the islands, from which, in fact, it is distant about twelve miles. We sent on shore my servant and a Turk to visit a village, at a small distance, beautifully embosomed in trees, and to report what could be procured. They procured only a tunny fish and some unripe pears, but many promises were made for the morrow.

June 24.—We began early in the morning to take in water, which was done by floating the casks over the bar at the entrance of the river, and there filling them. The wind became south, for the first time, the moment it was of no use, and considerably alarmed us lest we should be imprisoned in the bay; for the Queen made four points, at least, of lee-way, so that to work out would be impossible. In the evening, however, we were relieved from our fears, by a regular land wind.

I was unwell, and therefore staid on board; but the rest of the party set off, after breakfast, for another village at the distance of four miles. On their return they reported that they had found the natives extremely civil, but averse to their seeing or speaking with their women; that their dress was Grecian and picturesque, their houses, small and wretched; that the head man received them into his house, which consisted of one room only, and procured for them fowls, at twenty five paras each, goats at four or five dollars, and a buffalo and calf for ten dollars: honey, butter, eggs, clouted cream, apples, and apricots, were in abundance and reasonable; the harvest was not got in, and no grain was to be procured.

June 25.—Early in the morning a man came on board, who informed us that he belonged to a town, within sight to the eastward, whence grain and every article we wanted, could be procured. Mr. Salt and the whole party determined to go with him there, and accordingly set off, but found the distance so great that they abandoned the journey, and reached the vessel about midnight. They met several parties of armed men, but received no molestation.

I landed myself towards evening, and visited the ruins of a Turkish fort that extend for a considerable distance, on a hill which forms the western side of the bay. Above it, I discovered the remains of a small temple, about twenty feet square, built of stones very neatly worked, but without any ornament that I could discover. The door faced the sea, and in front of it was the pediment of a single column; the others might have been carried away to be employed in the erection of the fort. The side of the hill was covered with tombs which had been broken open in search of treasure. The inscriptions were in Greek characters, but most of them totally illegible. The scene must have been very beautiful when the small temple was uninjured, and the sarcophagi were probably shaded by lofty trees; at present the brow is nearly naked, except where a few stunted shrubs find nourishment in the crevices of the rock.

We next visited the vale below, where the soil was a black loam, on which the myrtle and oleander grew in the greatest luxuriance, but instead of the rich fields of grain which might be produced, were the country in tranquillity and properly protected, so far as I went inland, I could perceive nothing but a coarse grass, except on the banks of the stream, where rushes grew.

July 29.—On the evening of the 26th of June we quitted the Bay of Finica, and kept close to the shore, to have the benefit of the land breeze. We passed Rhodes on the 2d instant, and Scarpanto on the 4th, between which and Gozo, we found the passage to be much wider than is laid down in Heather's chart, and the latter a much larger island. On the 5th we sailed along Candia in a smooth sea, being protected by it from the N. W. wind which prevailed. The snow still lay on the summits of the mountains, whence squalls came down occasionally, with considerable violence. On the 7th we lost sight of Candia, and the Captain persevered in running south, although we made but little westing, and there was every appearance of a gale of wind setting in from the northward. On the 10th the gale came on, when we were in sight of Derna head, and obliged us to bear away N. E.; but for two days, in consequence of her sailing so ill, the Queen made only one mile of northing. When the gale abated, we got again in sight of Candia and of Gozo, distinguishable from the higher land behind it, by the difference of colour, which is of a reddish cast, while the mountains are of a deep blue, nearly approaching to black. After escaping from the narrow part of the Mediterranean, between Cape Derna and Candia, we found ourselves in a different climate: heretofore we had, invariably, winds from the north to west, but never, for above ten minutes at a time, did they come from the eastward. In fact, as regular a monsoon blows in the Levant during the summer months as in any part of the ocean. A gale of wind was generally foretold, as in the Red Sea, by a heavy swell and by some small black clouds, which rising visibly in the horizon, passed rapidly over the vessel. It always came from the north, and gradually veering to west, in about twenty-four hours subsided into a calm, when the swell became extremely disagreeable. On reaching the more open sea, the wind was more moderate, and the sky appeared dappled with many light coloured clouds, which were more stationary, and brought no wind with them. The weather became extremely pleasant, and on the 26th, for the first time, the wind came round to the eastward, and by ten o'clock this morning conveyed us to the port of Malta. Soon afterwards a boat was sent along side, empty, attached by a cord to another, in which were four men. We entered the former with our baggage, and were towed by the latter to the Quarantini, where we took up our abode in several very lofty stone apartments, with large windows looking over the harbour. The whole building is of the same materials, and surrounds a quadrangle; it is built on the solid rock, with a flight of steps down to the water, and is kept exceedingly clean. The lower story is used to receive goods that are unclean.

August 11.—In consequence of its being known that no plague had existed in Egypt for three years, it was only for the sake of form that we were obliged to perform quarantine. Had a King's ship arrived under similar circumstances, she would have been immediately allowed pratique, or free access to the town, but this indulgence is under no circumstances granted to a merchantman. The Board of Health met, and sentenced us to confinement in the Lazaretto, for twenty days; but, in consideration of our clean bills of health, and long voyage, gave us two days of grace, and left it to the discretion of the captain of the Lazaretto to give us two more, if we all continued well. Our imprisonment was by no means a punishment, after having so long been confined to a merchantman; the Governor, and many other gentlemen, paid us visits in the presence of an officer, whose duty it was to take care that they did not touch us, nor any article belonging to us, that could communicate infection. With books and newspapers we were plentifully supplied, and the luxuries of ice and fruit, to which we had long been strangers, assisted in consoling us for the want of permission to visit the town. This morning Sir Alexander Ball sent to inform me, that as the fleet would shortly sail for England, and as he understood that Captain Rudland wished to go in it, he would procure pratique for us in a few hours. This he did, and we immediately hastened to the Palace to return him thanks, and then took possession of some excellent apartments belonging to Mr. Roviere, who obligingly lent them to me during my stay at Malta.

June 18.—Sir Alexander Ball exerted himself to shew me every thing that was interesting in the island. I attended him to the races, where the horses were ridden by boys without saddles and bridles, but the crowd was great, and the spectacle altogether gay and interesting. I also visited with him Citta Vecchia, in the middle of the island, which has a handsome cathedral, shining with gold and painting, but without a picture of any merit; and afterwards, a hunting seat of the Grand Master's, now used as a prison for the French officers. It is in a castellated form, and commands an extensive view of the island, broken into undulations, but ugly and unpleasing to the sight, from the want of timber. Near the castle is a deep glen, which formerly was covered by a forest, but the French destroyed it, and a few ancient orange trees alone remain in the garden. The soil is a rich red clay, which would well pay the cultivation.

The knights of Malta, when sovereigns of the island, were as willing to keep it dependent on other countries for its supplies, as they were for their revenues; they consequently discouraged agriculture, and even looked with a jealous eye on the commercial attempts of their subjects, whom they were willing to feed well, that they might increase in numbers, but whom they by no means wished to become affluent. Malta produced a supply of grain for three months only, the residue was imported, and the Order had always sufficient for the consumption of a year, in their granaries.

Since the expulsion of the French, by the exertions of the natives, assisted by a British force, every thing has been greatly changed. Barbary being now in friendship with the inhabitants, affords abundant supplies; and the impossibility of a Turkish siege, or of the policy of foreign states inducing an attempt to starve the island, precludes the necessity of great magazines. From Sicily small vessels arrive daily with the produce of that island; but the most valuable article procured from it, is snow from mount Etna, which not only is a luxury to the rich, but an invaluable medicine in the hospitals. The Maltese, under the protection of the British flag, are rapidly rising in prosperity, by the success of their commercial speculations, and every inch of their little island will soon be cultivated like a garden. Sir Alexander Ball has wisely established a botanic garden, and actively exerts himself to procure every article which he thinks will flourish, and add to the comfort or luxury of the inhabitants. He, at the same time, conciliates the minds of the higher orders, by those attentions, which the suavity of his manners renders still more irresistible; and he attaches to his government the lower orders, by a proper attention to their innocent prejudices.

The French name is held in universal detestation on account of the severities they exercised, after the island was blockaded. On one occasion they made a sortie from Citta Vittorioso, and surprised the inhabitants of a neighbouring village, in the market place. They immediately put to death, men, women, and children; but a few who escaped, gave notice to the surrounding villagers, who intercepted them in their retreat, and put them all to the sword. After this, the indignation was so great throughout the island, that Sir Alexander Ball was obliged to offer a reward for every Frenchman brought in alive, to prevent their being put to death.

Towards the land, La Valetta is perfectly impregnable, and justifies the observation of Bonaparté, when he entered it, "that it was fortunate there was some one within to open the gates for him." In the hands of the masters of the sea, it is an invaluable possesion. Its harbours afford protection from every wind, and its dockyards furnish supplies for a fleet, at a smaller expense than they can frequently be procured in England; while its fresh provisions, fruit and vegetables, insure health to the seamen. As a naval station it protects the trade of the Levant, and renders the secret approach of a hostile squadron towards any part of the Turkish dominions, nearly impracticable; and so long as Great Britain preserves it, the gigantic plans of Bonaparté in the Mediterranean can never be carried into effect, nor can he impress, on the Barbary powers, that idea of his importance, which is necessary to induce them to abandon all connection with us. As trade increases, the island will become a depot for the woollens, cottons, and hardware of England, which will be thence carried away, to all the surrounding coasts, by the vessels of the inhabitants. This will greatly increase the revenue, and soon render Malta a profit instead of an expense; even at present the necessary civil expenses are but small, and but little, if at all, exceeding the revenue. Malta requires only four thousand men for a garrison, but that number has generally been exceeded, not for the use of the place, but as a valuable and healthy depot, whence they could be removed to any place where their services are required. This cannot be considered as part of the expense of Malta.

I was very much struck with the magnificent

church of St John, which still preserves the monuments of the illustrious Masters of the Order. The silver rail of the altar, and the lamps, have, indeed, disappeared, the invincible Bonaparté having carried them with him to Egypt. The pavement is nearly covered by a beautiful mosaic, composed of the arms of the different knights who lie underneath. The revenues of the church are still continued to it, and its splendour must remain stationary, a monument of the power of the Order, and of its having passed away for ever.

The library is a handsome building, and has a very valuable collection of books. It was accumulated from the private libraries of the different knights who died on the island, to whom the Order was heir. It also received, as presents, most of the splendid works which were published by the Catholic sovereigns of Europe. It contains about eight thousand volumes, and is chiefly deficient in English literature. It would be politic, as well as liberal, to appropriate a moderate annual income to remove this deficiency. The Maltese should not be permitted to discover, in any one respect, an inferiority in their present sovereign to their last. The splendor of their capital should be, by every means, increased, and not diminished. The present arrangements for the use of the books is inconvenient, access to them being allowed only from nine to twelve, during summer. There is a small collection of medals annexed to the library, and some antiques of value, which are the more interesting, from having been found on the island. These, as well as the furniture of the palace, and every other article of value, would, probably have been carried to Paris, had it not been for the closeness of the blockade, which precluded all retreat, till the capitulation put an end to the power of plundering.

The Maltese are frugal, temperate, and industrious. They proved themselves brave soldiers, during the blockade of La Valetta, when about three thousand of them were under the command of Sir Alexander Ball. They are as good seamen as any in the Mediterranean, and are rapidly improving by their connection with the English. During the voyage, I found them lively and good humoured, and was frequently entertained by the different games which occupied their time in moderate weather: they did not often quarrel, and when they did their shirts suffered more than their bodies. Their attachment to their religion is bigotted, and, consequently, their reverence for their priests. It was by plundering their churches, that the French roused them to resistance, after they had quietly submitted to the yoke which the treachery of their Grand Master had brought upon them. If this should prove a warning to Great Britain, she runs no risk of losing the island. The priests, indeed, are, doubtless, some of them attached to the French, and would wish a Catholic to possess the island; but, in general, they are satisfied with the respect with which their religion is treated, and would hesitate to accept a nominally religious despotism, when united with civil slavery, which they have too much reason to believe would be the case, were they again to become the subjects of Bonaparté.

August 24.—A fleet of transports having arrived from Sicily, where they had landed troops, and being about to return, nearly empty, to England, Sir Alexander Ball procured for me the cabin of the Diana, Captain Lamb, and an order for the conveyance of all my baggage. She was said to be the best sailer among them, and the Captain was a very civil, worthy man. My preparations were soon made, and this day we all embarked, after having parted with regret from Sir Alexander, who had, by his uniformly kind attentions, added greatly to the satisfaction I experienced at again finding myself in a civilized country. The fleet was convoyed by Captain Mowbray in the Active frigate. It was an additional pleasure to me to discover, that he was brother to my friend, Captain Mowbray, whom I had known at Ceylon, as aid-de-camp to Mr. North.

September 17.—After a pleasant passage, we on this day reached Gibraltar, having on our way seen Sicily, Sardinia, several of the capes of Africa, and, at length, the coast of Spain, along which we ran from near Carthagena. On the 1st we had a stiff gale from N. W. but in general, the weather was fine, and the Diana sailed so well that we had the pleasure of being always near to the Active, and frequently went on board her, while both vessels lay to for the rest of the convoy to come up. On the last day we had a fine breeze from the eastward, which lasted us till we got round Europa Point late in the evening, when it died away.

September 26.—Early in the morning, after my arrival, I landed, and went to pay my compliments to General Drummond, the acting Lieutenant Governor, who very politely offered me the use of the Convent, which is the official residence of the Governor, an offer which I willingly accepted, for Gibraltar is too crowded to afford much accommodation for strangers. I was considerably indisposed, and unable to visit many of the work, but, occassionally, rode with the General to view the different spots which have been cultivated by the garrison. The extent of ground, laid out in gardens, excited my surprise, and the beauty of several of the country-houses well repaid the labour of getting at them. The most beautiful belongs to the Navy Commissioner, Captain Middleton; it is situated on the southern part of the rock, and is embosomed in a grove of large trees.

The intercourse between the Spaniards and the garrison is permitted, in consequence of the advantages which both receive from it. The Spanish officers obtain permission, daily, to come into the town, to purchase articles which are contraband, particularly tobacco, of which the King of Spain has a monopoly, and which, in consequence, sells at ten shillings a pound. The Governor of Andalusia himself, sometimes comes in to pay his compliments to the General, when he always requests permission to take a walk in the town unattended, confessing that he and his party want to make some purchases. Even a relation of the Prince of Peace condescended to come in, on the same errand, a few days before I arrived. The trade between Algeziras and the garrison is carried on with the connivance of both parties, and the boats from the former arrive every morning with fruit, vegetables, and fresh meat; they are supposed to carry back money, but, in reality, their cargo consists of British manufactures and colonial produce. It is said that Bonaparté has taken offence at this amicable arrangement, and the Spaniards have hinted, that if the present negotiations do not terminate in a peace, they shall be obliged to put an end to it.

A perpetual war exists in the bay, between the Spanish gun-boats and the English ships of war; not that the former wish for fighting, but they are perpetually attacking the merchant vessels, and Barbary boats, which are, of course, protected, but frequently the current carries them across to the Spanish coast, where they become a sure prey to the enemy's small craft, or to the batteries which line the shore. Some gun boats had even the impudence to attempt to cut a merchant vessel out of the harbour, while I was there. The garrison consists of six thousand men, who would be healthy, were it not for the cheapness of wine, which leads to a perpetual state of intoxication. By the regulations of government, spirits are scarcely procurable for money. The Spanish army is said to be in the greatest distress, for want of pay, but they bear it admirably.

In consequence of the wind coming round to the east, I was obliged to hurry on board the Diana, which soon afterwards set sail, with the rest of the fleet, under convoy of the Athenienne. We passed the Straits before it was dark, with a stiff gale from the eastward, and as we kept close to Africa, had an opportunity of admiring its beautiful hills, covered, in part, with woods, beyond which were lofty mountains.

September 27.—By day break we were up with Lord Collingwood's fleet, off Cadiz. The Neptune, Captain Fremantle, was appointed to convoy us to England; and the Captain was so obliging, on my stating to him that I was severely indisposed, as to give me a passage in his ship, where I experienced every kindness from him, and every medical assistance from Mr. Nagle, the surgeon.

On the 24th of October, after a tedious passage,

with frequent gales towards the latter end, we came to an anchor at St. Helen's, but, notwithstanding our impatience, we were not permitted to land till the 26th, when I went on shore at Portsmouth, after having been absent from England, four years and four months.

APPENDIX.

APPENDIX.

No. I.

REPORT *made to the French Consul by Col. Sebastiani, extracted from the Moniteur of the* 30*th of Jan*. 1803.

ON the 2d of October I set out from Tripoli, and on the 16th arrived at Alexandria: the same day I waited upon General Stuart, commandant of the English forces by land and sea. I communicated to him the order of the Minister for Foreign Affairs, which enjoined me to proceed to Alexandria, and if the English still occupied that place, to demand a speedy evacuation, and the execution of the treaty of Amiens. General Stuart then told me, that the evacuation of the place would shortly be effected; but seeing that I insisted, and that I desired an answer less vague, he declared to me, that he had no orders from his Court to quit Alexandria, and that he even believed he should pass the winter there. General Stuart is a man of *mediocre* talents: he has for his aid-de-camp a French emigrant, called the Chevalier de Sades, a man of talent, and an enemy of France, who has much influence over the General. I went the same day to see Khourchid-Ahmid, the Pacha of Alexandria, and the Capitan Bey, commander of the forces of the Ottoman Porte. After the customary compliments, and some language agreeable to the Sublime Porte, I announced to them, that the agents of French commerce would assemble in Egypt. This communication gave them the greatest pleasure, and they did not conceal that they saw with grief the stay of the English in the country. I told them, that their stay could not be much longer, and that the general peace

4

left no doubt of their approaching departure. On the 17th I visited the Cheik El-Messiry. The same day I also visited the Cheik Ibrahim Mufti. On the 18th I visited the Coupure du Khalidj, which has formed the lake Mareotis. The current of the waters of the lake Madie is still very strong, and if the Porte does not make haste to re-establish this important canal, the overflows which take place on the little tongue of land that separates the two lakes, will render the opening so considerable, that it will be impossible to travel. I do not think that the Swedish engineer sent by the Porte to direct these labours, has the necessary talents. The formation of the lake Mareotis appears to have contributed to the salubrity of the air. The city has no other water than what it draws from the wells of Marabouf. This little fort I found guarded by an English and Turkish garrison, in order to protect the inhabitants who came to draw water. I employed the day of the 19th in perambulating the town, and receiving different individuals who came to visit me. On the 20th, I set out for Cairo, escorted by two Turkish officers, and six French soldiers, whom I had taken on board the frigate, but contrary winds obliged me to return to the port. The next day I was at Aboukir, where I passed the night. I profited by this opportunity to visit the fort, which is in a very ruined state. On the 22d I arrived at Rosetta, after having visited the fort Julien; I saw the same day Osman, Aga and Duvanny of the town, as well as all the Christians who reside there. The 23d I was at Faone, where I visited the commandant of the place, the Cadi, and the Cheiks; I received from the latter, and from all those whom I entertained, protestations of attachment to the First Consul. I passed the next day at Ralimanie, where I visited the Cheik Muhammed Abou-Aly; the fort of the town is almost entirely destroyed. I visited on the 25th, at Menouf, the Cheik Abdin, whom the First Consul had appointed Cadi. The other Cheiks of that town who came to visit me, held the same language as those of Faone. I said to them, 'The First Consul loves your country much, he speaks of it often; he interests himself in your happiness; he did not forget you, and recommended you to the Porte. He has made peace with Europe, and this country will feel the interest which he takes, and the recollection which he has preserved of the poor Cheiks of Egypt.'—Muhammed Kachef-Zourba Matzellem, who commanded at Menouf on my journey through that town, has been beheaded in consequence of being accused of communications with the Mamelouks. The two forts of Menouf are destroyed. I arrived the same day at Boulak. I sent immediately Citizen Joubert to inform the Pacha of Cairo of my arrival. The next morning, the 26th, the Pacha sent three hundred cavalry and two hundred infantry, commanded by the principal officers of his household, to accompany me to him, amidst a great many discharges of artillery. Having arrived at the Pacha's, I said to him, 'Peace has been concluded between the French Republic and the Sublime Porte: the ancient relations of amity and commerce have been re-established, and I am charged by the Great Consul Bonaparté, to assure you of his benevolence, and to announce to you the arrival of commissaries of the French commerce in Egypt.' The Pacha answered me, 'the benevolence with which the First Consul has honoured me, penetrates me with gratitude, and his commercial agents shall meet here the most friendly reception.' I proceeded then to the house which the Pacha had prepared for me. I received the same day the visits of all the principal men of the country, and of the Copt Intendants. On the 27th I again repaired to the Pacha, with whom I had a long conference. I spoke to him in these words: 'the First Consul takes in you, and in the country you govern, a very lively interest, and desires to contribute to your happiness; he has charged me therefore to offer you his mediation, in order to make peace between you and the Beys.'

The Pacha thanked me warmly and sincerely for the interest which the First Consul took in his behalf, but he protested to me that he had the most positive orders from his Court to make a war of extermination upon the Beys, and not to enter into any arrangement with them. I observed, that the unfortunate circumstances which had happened to the Ottoman troops (they had been beaten five times successively by the Mamelouks), rendered their position very critical, and that obstinacy exposed them to the loss of the province. He then communicated to me the order of the Porte, and I saw beyond a doubt that it was not possible for him to enter into any accommodation. I informed him that I intended to visit the different Cheiks of Cairo, and also Madame Murad Bey, and to inspect the environs and fortifications of the city. He ordered immediately that the guard which he had sent should accompany me wherever I wished to go, informing me, that he would use every means in his power to render my stay at Cairo agreeable.—The same day I commenced my visits, beginning with the Cheik Abdallah-el-Sherkowi, of the great mosque. As I was expected by him, he had assembled a considerable number of Cheiks. The conversation turned upon the interest which the First Consul took in Egypt, on his power, his glory, and on his esteem and benevolence for the learned Cheiks of Cairo. Their answers expressed their attachment to his person. He must have been a witness like myself to the enthusiasm excited at the view of the portrait of the First Consul, to form an idea of the exaltation of their sentiments. I have given it to all the principal Cheiks of Cairo, and of the towns where I have travelled.—On the 28th I invited the Cheik Omar El-Berky, Prince of the Shiriss; he was ill, and I saw only his son.—The Cheik Suleiman El-Faiume received me with much friendship, and assured me of his boundless admiration for the First Consul.—The Citizens Joubert and Beye have certified to me that the inhabitants of Cairo never testified so much attachment to France as on my arrival.—When we pass along the streets, every body salutes us. Their astrologers make predictions every day as to what concerns the First Consul.—On the 29th I went to visit Madame Murad Bey: her Intendant had already prayed that I would grant her an interview. I informed her, that the First Consul had charged me to interpose my mediation, in order to make their peace with the Sublime Porte; but that the Pacha had ordered that no negociation should be entered into.—I employed that day and the following in visiting the citadel, the Isle of Roda Gize, Boulak, and all the other little forts which surround the city. The Turkish soldiers murmured to see me visit their forts, but I feigned not to hear them, and continued my course and my observations.

On the 29th, in returning to Fort Dupuy, a soldier menaced me with his attagan; but as the inhabitants of the city testified highly their indignation against him, I did not stop at his menaces, and continued my route. A moment afterwards Mustapha Oukil, one of the chiefs of the city, passed before me on horseback. In passing, he reproached my guides with marching before a Christian, and above all, before a Frenchman, and menaced them with the bastinado after my departure. I could not be silent under such an insult; and upon my return I sent Citizen Joubert to the Pacha, to make my complaint, and demand a prompt redress. I declared to him that I expected this man would come publicly to me to ask my pardon, place himself at my disposal, and implore my pity. He found that Mustapha was greatly protected by the Pacha, and wanted to arrange it otherwise; but I persisted by declaring formally to the Pacha, that if this reparation was not made in the manner in which I demanded it, I should instantly depart, and immediately write to Paris and Constantinople to state my complaint. This declaration produced all the effect which I expected; and Mustapha, alarmed, came on the following day to me, conducted by Rosetti, and he publicly asked my pardon, and put himself at mydisposal. I told him that my first intention had been to cut off his head, and that I only gave him his life at the solicitations of the Pacha and M. Rosetti; but if in future he should ever insult the French, or those in their suite, his destruction would be inevitable. This affair, which was instantly spread throughout the whole city, produced the best effect.—The same day an attempt was made to excite the Albanese against me. Two letters from Rosetta, written by English protegées, declared that there had been seen upon the coasts of Natolia a French fleet of three hundred sail; that we were marching against Constantinople, and that my visit to Egypt had no other object but to deceive them, and blind them to their danger. I made the merchant come to me who had received the letter; I made him give it me—I instantly sent it to the Pacha himself, telling him that this absurd news was spread to occasion disorders, and to endeavour to alter the good understanding which existed between France and the Sublime Porte; and I guaranteed the falsehood of it with my head. The Pacha had discovered the snare, and did not fall into it. He even communicated to me a letter from General Stuart, which he had just received, and to which was joined an order of the day, of the First Consul, when he commanded the army of Egypt; this order of the day was dated in August 1799, and recalled to the recollection of the Egyptians, that Constantinople was tributary to Arabia, and that the time was now come to restore Cairo to its supremacy, and to destroy the Eastern Empire of the Ottomans. General Stuart begged the Pacha to consider the spirit of that order, and to judge from it of our attachment, and of our peace with the Turks. I was indignant to find that a soldier of one of the most polite nations of Europe should degrade himself so far as to instigate assassination by means of such an insinuation. The Pacha treated me with the greatest politeness, and the English at Cairo were witnesses of the attachment of that city to the French.

I received a deputation from the monks of Mount Sinai, whom I recommended to the Pacha: I wrote to their Superior, to assure them of the friendship and protection of the First Consul. The monks of the Propaganda at Cairo, whom I placed under the national protection which they enjoyed before the war, celebrated a Te Deum for the prosperity of the First Consul. I assisted at this ceremony, at which all the Christians at Cairo were present. The evening before my departure (the 2d of November) I had another interview with the Pacha, and recommended all the Christians of Cairo to his protection, as well as the Turks who, during the residence of the French in Egypt, were connected with them. He not only promised to respect them, but even to treat them with bounty. On the 3d, I set out in a conveyance of the Pacha's, in order to repair to Damietta. The Pacha ordered me to be escorted to Boulak, with the same honours that I received on the day of my arrival. I had written to Captain Gourdain, to repair to Damietta with the frigate, in order to convey me to Syria. On the 5th I stopped a short time at Simenoud, and afterwards at Mansoura, where I saw the Commandant of the city, and the Cheik Esseid Muhammed-el-Chenaoni, who came to see me, as well as all the other Cheiks. I spoke to them in the same manner as to the other Cheiks of Egypt, and received the same promises of attachment. The tower of Mansoura is destroyed. The same day I arrived at Damietta. The next day I went to Ahmed-Pacha-Behil, a creature of the Grand Vizier's; he returned my visit the same day. He conducted himself perfectly well to me during my stay in that city.

On the 7th I went to visit the fort of Lesbé, and the towers of Bogaz. They have not continued the works of that fort, which is in a bad state: those of Bogaz are in a good condition. There is a garrison of two hundred men in the fort and in the towers. On the 8th I received the visit of Hassan Toubar: his influence over the inhabitants of Menzalé is still the same. On the 9th I went to Seminie, where I saw the Cheik Ibrahim-el-Behlout, he who behaved so well to the French under the orders of General Vial, when they were taken and imprisoned. The First Consul had exempted his village from all contributions. I saw all the Cheiks at Damietta, particularly Ali Khasaki, whom the First Consul had invested with a pelisse: he is possessed of great credit, and is much attached to the French. There are at Damietta two Christians, who are men of merit, and may be very useful to us: they are M. Bazile and Don Bazile. They are possessed of good information, have very considerable fortunes, and are very highly respected. In Egypt, chiefs, merchants, people, all like to talk of the First Consul—all offer up prayers for his happiness. All the news which concerns him spreads from Alexandria or Damietta to the pyramids and the grand cataracts with astonishing rapidity. On the 14th the frigate arrived at Bogaz from Damietta: I immediately set out for Acre, at which place I arrived on the 19th.

No. II.

EXTRACT *from Le Courier de L'Egypte, No.* 21. 25 *Frimaire,* 7 *Année de la République.*

ON dit, parmi les Musulmans du Caire, qu'un saint personnage a été informé par une révélation d'une conférence qui a eu lieu entre Mahomet et le Destin. Le crédit qu'a obtenu le récit de cette révélation nous détermine à le consigner dans cette feuille.

Lorsque Mahomet vit la flotte Français approcher les côtes de l'Egypt, il alla chez le Destin et lui dit: *ô Destin, tu es ingrat, je t'ai fait souverain arbitre du monde, et tu veux livrer aux Français la plus belle des contrées soumises à ma loi. Le Destin lui répondit: ô Mahomet, le decret est porté; il faut qu'il s'accomplisse; les Français arriveront sur la terre d'Egypte, et en feront la conquête, je n'ai plus le pouvoir de l'empêcher: mais écoute, et console toi, j'ai décidé, que ces conquérants se feront Mahométans.* Mahomet, pleinement rassuré par cette réponse, se retira très-satisfait.

Il se trouve dans la ville du Caire huit devins de réputation. Les habitans du pays les consultent souvent et reçoivent leurs réponses avec une foi entière; on a remarqué depuis quelque temps que toutes leurs prédictions sont favorables aux Français.

No. III.

Extract *from Le Courier de l'Egypte. No.* 23. 9 *Nivose,* 7 *Année de la République.*

Proclamation du Général Bonaparté aux Habitans du Caire.

Des hommes pervers avoient égaré une partie d'entre vous ; ils ont péri. Dieu m'a ordonné d'être miséricordieux pour le peuple. J'ai été clément et miséricordieux envers vous.

J'ai été fâché contre vous de votre révolte, je vous ai privé pendant deux mois de votre divan ; mais aujourd'hui je vous le restitue : votre bonne conduite a effacé la tache de votre révolte.

Schérifs, Ulemas, Orateurs des Mosquees, faites bien connaître au peuple que ceux qui de gaité de cœur se déclareroient mes ennemis, n'auront de refuge ni dans ce monde ni dans l'autre. Y-auroit-il un homme assez aveugle pour ne pas voir que le Destin lui-même dirige toutes mes operations? Y-auroit-il quelqu'un assez incrédule pour revoquer en doute que tout dans ce vaste univers est soumis à l'empire du Destin?

Faites connaître au peuple, que depuis que le monde est monde, il étoit écrit qu'après avoir détruit les ennemis de l'Islamisme, fait abattre les Croix, je viendrais du fond de l'Occident remplir la tâche qui m'a été imposée. Faites voir au peuple que dans le saint livre du Koran, dans plus de vingt passages, ce qui arrive a été prévu, et ce qui arrivera est également expliqué.

Que ceux donc que la crainte seule de mes armes empêche de nous maudire, changent ; car en faisant au ciel des vœux contre nous, ils sollicitent leur condamnation ; que les vrais croyans fassent des vœux pour la prospérité de nos armes.

Je pourrais demander compte à chacun de vous des sentimens les plus secrets de son cœur ; car je sais tout, même ce que vous n'avez dit à personne ; mais un jour viendra que tout le monde verra avec évidence que je suis conduit par des ordres supérieurs, et que tous les efforts humains ne peuvent rien contre moi: heureux ceux qui de bonne foi sont les premiers à se mettre avec moi!

THE END.